ALSO BY DORIS KEARNS GOODWIN

Leadership:
In Turbulent Times

The Bully Pulpit:
Theodore Roosevelt, William Howard Taft,
and the Golden Age of Journalism

Team of Rivals:
The Political Genius of Abraham Lincoln

Wait Till Next Year:
A Memoir

No Ordinary Time:
Franklin and Eleanor Roosevelt:
The Home Front in World War II

The Fitzgeralds and the Kennedys

Lyndon Johnson and the American Dream

An Unfinished Love Story

A PERSONAL HISTORY OF THE 1960s

Doris Kearns Goodwin

Simon & Schuster

NEW YORK LONDON TORONTO

SYDNEY NEW DELHI

100 YEARS
SIMON & SCHUSTER

1230 Avenue of the Americas
New York, NY 10020

First Simon & Schuster hardcover edition April 2024

SIMON & SCHUSTER and colophon are registered trademarks of Simon & Schuster, LLC

Simon & Schuster: Celebrating 100 Years of Publishing in 2024

For information about special discounts for bulk purchases, please contact Simon & Schuster Special Sales at 1-866-506-1949 or business@simonandschuster.com.

The Simon & Schuster Speakers Bureau can bring authors to your live event. For more information or to book an event, contact the Simon & Schuster Speakers Bureau at 1-866-248-3049 or visit our website at www.simonspeakers.com.

Letter by Jacqueline Kennedy used with permission.

Interior design by Paul Dippolito

Beth Laski, Photo Editor

Manufactured in the United States of America

1   3   5   7   9   10   8   6   4   2

Library of Congress Cataloging-in-Publication Data is available.

ISBN 978-1-9821-0866-3
ISBN 978-1-9821-0868-7 (ebook)

To
Michael Rothschild

Short Story Writer ~ Sculptor
Print-Maker ~ Orchardist
Farmer

Dick's Best Friend
and
Mine

Contents

Introduction   *1*

CHAPTER 1   Coming of Age   *11*

CHAPTER 2   "A Sort of Dead End"   *38*

CHAPTER 3   Aboard the "Caroline"   *58*

CHAPTER 4   A Pandora's Box of Cigars   *83*

CHAPTER 5   The Supreme Generalist   *111*

CHAPTER 6   Kaleidoscope   *137*

CHAPTER 7   Thirteen LBJs   *168*

CHAPTER 8   "And We Shall Overcome"   *205*

CHAPTER 9   The Never-Ending Resignation   *235*

CHAPTER 10   Friendship, Loyalty, and Duty   *260*

CHAPTER 11   Crosswinds of Fate   *310*

CHAPTER 12   Endings and Beginnings   *359*

CHAPTER 13   Our Talisman   *383*

Epilogue   *401*

Acknowledgments   *407*

Bibliography   *411*

Abbreviations Used in Notes   *415*

Notes   *417*

Photo Credits   *451*

Index   *455*

Introduction

THERE WAS A BUZZ OF EXCITEMENT WHEN I ARRIVED AT MY Harvard office at 78 Mt. Auburn Street one June morning in 1972. Richard "Dick" Goodwin had just taken an office on the third floor of our old yellow building to finish a book project. We all knew who he was: He had worked in John Kennedy's White House in his twenties, served as Lyndon Johnson's chief speechwriter during the heyday of the Great Society, and been in California with Robert Kennedy when he died. An acquaintance who knew him said he was the most brilliant, interesting man she had ever met but that he was sometimes brash, mercurial, and arrogant—in short, he cut a scintillating and unpredictable figure.

I had just settled in my office at the top of the stairs when in Dick wandered, plopping down on one of the chairs reserved for my tutees. His appearance intrigued me: curly, disheveled black hair, with thick, unruly eyebrows, and a pockmarked face. Several large cigars stuck out of the pocket of his casual shirt. He introduced himself and asked if I was a graduate student. "No, I am an assistant professor," I countered. "I teach a lecture course on the American presidency. I conduct seminars and tutorials."

"I know, I know!" he laughed, holding up his hands to stop me. "I'm teasing you. You worked for Lyndon after I left."

So began a conversation about LBJ, the Sixties, writing, literature, philosophy, science, astronomy, sex, evolution, gossip, the Red Sox, and everything else under the sun—a conversation that would continue for the next forty-six years of our lives. We had missed being together in the White House by three years. I had become a member of Johnson's White House staff in 1968; Dick had left in the fall of 1965, already concerned that the escalating war in Vietnam was sucking energy from the Great Society.

Away from Washington, Dick told me, his misgivings about the shriveling funds and focus on domestic policy were supplanted by increasingly strong qualms about the war itself. When he made his first public statement against the war, he was assailed by criticism from the administration's foreign policy establishment. National Security Adviser McGeorge Bundy told him that, as a former member of the White House team, he didn't leave in the right way. He should have left silently, keeping his dissent to himself. And from Ambassador Averell Harriman had come the curious accusation that he was biting the hand that fed him.

"What did you say to that?" I asked. Dick's eyes flashed at the memory of his response. "I told him Lyndon didn't feed me. I fed myself." I wasn't sure if his tone displayed ironic humor or harbored a real contempt.

We talked for five hours straight. He had an edgy nonconformist streak, as well as a distinct gravity, a world-weariness, a sharp wit, yet in his eyes and gestures a kindness.

He suggested we continue our conversation over dinner that night at a restaurant on Beacon Hill in Boston. We had just settled at our table and chosen a bottle of wine when he leaned toward me. "Tell me," he began. "Where did you get your ambition? What were your parents like? How many times have you been in love?" What struck me was the intensity and eagerness of his inquiry. Given his prompts, I was off and running.

I told him I had grown up in the 1950s in Rockville Centre, a suburb of New York, where the neighbors on our block formed an extended family. With almost a dozen kids the same age as me, we ran in and out of each other's houses all day. Our street was our playground. I told him stories about my parents and my sisters, my love of history and the Brooklyn Dodgers, the joy I had always found in school.

Dick interrupted me several times but only to ask further questions about my mother, who had died when I was fifteen, and my father, who had died only a month before. Finally, I took a deep breath. I realized how artfully he had turned the tables. I was usually the one asking questions when I met people.

After we finished dinner, he told me about growing up in Brookline, Massachusetts, and attending Tufts College and Harvard Law School. His account was far more condensed than mine. He had recently returned to Cambridge from rural Maine, where he had moved not long after Robert Kennedy's death. His six-year-old son, Richard Jr. (called Richard), was ready for first grade, and he wanted him to be schooled in the Boston area. He spoke very little about his wife, Sandra. A gifted writer, she had studied at Vassar and the Sorbonne but had struggled with mental illness and been hospitalized for long periods of time. They had been separated for some years.

Clearly, there was far more to the story, but he abruptly changed the subject: "What about the Red Sox?"—the baseball team he adored despite a lifelong expectation they would fail, the team that had also become mine after the Brooklyn Dodgers abandoned me and I had made my home in Massachusetts.

When he dropped me off at my house, he cupped my face. "Well, Doris Kearns," he said, "a friendship has begun." He hugged me and said good night. With Dick's office in the same building as mine, we did indeed become good friends, the deepest friendship of my life.

———•——

Half a year later, Sandra had left the hospital and taken her life. In the months that followed I spent as much time as possible trying to help Dick and Richard hold their hectic life together. I came over in the mornings to take Richard to school. Dick and I juggled our days and nights, my teaching with his writing, my writing with Richard's care, school, and friends. We improvised as best we could during this chaotic, unstable time of great stress and sorrow, teamwork and fun. Before long, I came to the realization that I had fallen in love with Dick and I knew that he loved and trusted me.

But the turmoil and upheaval of Dick's life made it impossible for him to make a long-term commitment, which he knew I wanted. He worried about his son, his work, and his finances. Most importantly, he feared the consequences for the three of us if our relationship didn't work out. Until he pulled himself together, he said, it would be better for him to get his bearings, and to focus on Richard.

I understood, but nonetheless, I was devastated. My love for Dick had become a full-blown obsession. Before we had met, I had felt fulfilled by teaching, colleagues, family, and friends. I had been hard at work on my first book—the portrait of Lyndon Johnson that would enable my professional and academic advancement. My self-sufficient life had suddenly begun to unravel.

Indeed, I was so filled with confusion, passion, and anxiety that for the first time I sought support from a psychiatrist, Dr. Grete Bibring, who had trained under Sigmund Freud. I wondered if my obsession with Dick was simply because he was unavailable, or because my father had recently died? I had always had confidence in my ability to make things work. I'd been born with an irrepressible and optimistic temperament, which I liked to think I had inherited from my father. But that confidence had begun to waver. Dr. Bibring allowed me to understand that I had genuinely fallen in love with Dick but that if I wanted a lasting relationship to develop, I would have to wait, to accept his decision to stay apart for the time being.

Dick and Richard soon moved to Washington, where Dick had become political editor at *Rolling Stone* magazine. In their absence, I worked hard to put my life back together without them—until, a year or so later, when I ran into Dick on a street in Cambridge. He had come to the city for a meeting. On the spot, he invited me to dinner that night, and we resumed our long-interrupted conversation. The next day, he called and asked me to return with him to Washington and stay with him for the rest of our lives.

On December 14, 1975, a little more than three years after our first meeting, we were married. The wedding ceremony was held in the great meeting room of the two-hundred-year-old colonial house Dick and I had rented when we had moved in together earlier that fall. I walked down the aisle to *Man of La Mancha*'s "The Impossible Dream." Dick's best man was fiction writer Michael Rothschild, down from the mountains of western Maine. An Irish tenor sang "Jerusalem," the wedding hymn based on a poem by William Blake, one of Dick's favorite poets. Richard, now nine years old, and a group of his friends cut our four-tier wedding cake with a sword.

The Boston Globe's front-page story described the guest list as "A Great Society Reunion," combining "New Yorkian style, Washington power, and Boston brains; but most of all it was fun and friends." Senator Edward Kennedy, Boston mayor Kevin White, Arthur Schlesinger Jr., William vanden Heuvel, and several LBJ cabinet members were there, along with Norman Mailer, journalist Jon Bradshaw and his girlfriend, Anna Wintour, *Rolling Stone*'s Hunter Thompson (who left the tub running in Concord's Colonial Inn, flooding two floors), and a circle of my Harvard colleagues.

———•••———

Where would we make our permanent home? I longed for the bustle of big-city life, while Dick sought the tranquility of the country. Our debate was finally resolved when we struck a perfect compromise in Concord, Massachusetts, a town of eighteen thousand residents twenty miles west of Boston—close enough for easy access to the city, but still a country community with a long, winding river, wooded areas, walking trails, plentiful farms, and a classic main street. We were both drawn to the town's historical richness: the footprint of the antislavery movement, the circle of mid-nineteenth-century writers who had once dwelled within walking distance of one another—Ralph Waldo Emerson, Henry David Thoreau, Nathaniel Hawthorne, Louisa May Alcott—and whose homes were still standing. Dick revered Emerson's essays and poetry, particularly admired Hawthorne's tales (as much as he despised his politics), and was fond of Thoreau's writings on civil disobedience and *The Maine Woods*.

Furthermore, Concord was the seedbed of our country's formative days during the American Revolution. Dick was a boisterous patriot from the top of his head to his toes—a lover of fireworks, parades, and songs. In the years to come, he would drag visitors to the North Bridge and in his deep theatrical voice recite "The Shot Heard Round the World," Emerson's stanza carved below Daniel Chester French's Minute Man statue. I confess whenever I heard Dick's booming recitation of Emerson's words, I couldn't help but associate "The Shot Heard Round the World" with Bobby Thomson's ninth-inning home run off Brooklyn's Ralph Branca to win the 1951 pennant for the despised New York Giants, extinguishing the hopes of my beloved Dodgers.

Our marriage brought the joys, pressures, and exhaustion of an instant family. I had long wanted to have children and now, within two years, our family had grown to five. Richard was ten when I gave birth to Michael. Fifteen months later, Joe was born. During these early years of marriage and family, I was moving toward the decision to stop teaching and try my hand at becoming a full-time writer. Chance had given me the opportunity to write my first book on LBJ and its positive reception led to a contract for a second book. I didn't think then (though I might think differently today) that I would be able to teach with the intensity and absorption I demanded of myself, research and write books, and still spend the time I wanted with my young family. I barely made a dent on my to-do lists and could only dream of what seemed that mythical place—a "room of one's own."

I had confidence in my teaching and lecturing, but found defining myself solely and simply as a writer of biography and history unsettling. Dick strongly encouraged me. "You are a natural storyteller," he assured me again and again. "Write like you talk, only not quite so fast," he needled.

Dick's worry that I would write too fast proved way off the mark. Despite my rapid mode of speaking, it turned out I was an agonizingly slow writer. My second book on the Kennedys took eight years to complete, even though I was no longer teaching. At a Harvard party one afternoon, I overheard one student ask another, "Whatever happened to Doris Kearns anyway? Did she die?" What happened, I wanted to shout, is that I have three young boys!

Two writers under one roof offered unique problems and pleasures. Even though we eventually created our own writing rooms, working in the same house meant small separation between work and family. When Michael and Joe were toddlers, we hired a nanny to allow me greater time to write, but whenever the boys wandered into my study wanting to talk or play, I found it impossible to turn them away. I found a solution to my dilemma by creating a workspace in the stately Reference Room of the Concord Public Library. There, writing in longhand on a beautiful oak table, surrounded by sculptures and busts of the great Concord authors and a painting of Abraham Lincoln, I could focus for three or more hours each morning until one of the librarians would come to tell me that my husband had called to announce that lunch was ready.

My love of libraries had begun when I was still in middle school. One of my treasured memories was the privilege of walking to our town library each week, with my mother's adult card in my hand, along with the list of books she wanted for that week. The rheumatic fever she had suffered as a child had left her with a damaged heart, keeping her housebound. Although she had only an eighth-grade education, she read books in every spare moment. Through books she could travel to places she could never go. And what a joy it was for me to turn left into the adult room instead of right into the children's room. I felt older, taller, wiser.

Once all three boys were in school, I settled back into my study at home. Proximity allowed Dick and I to engage in one another's books and articles. We would often exchange pages in the late morning and then go over them at lunch. If we had reached obstacles in our writing or thinking, we would always put our heads together, and more often than not, work things out.

Book after book of my career as a historian, the practical knowledge Dick had gained during his years in the political cauldron of the Sixties filtered into and enriched my own comprehension of the pressures, limitations, and actual parameters of political choice and action. Though his full-time role in public service had come to an end many years earlier, the issues that had motivated Dick's political career sustained him for the rest of his life as he continued to write books, articles, and columns, searching out the passions and achievements that had animated change in the Sixties.

***

For the first half of our married life, we lived on Main Street in Concord. The library, bookstore, coffee shops, restaurants, playing fields, and schools were all within walking distance. Dick was the coach of Richard's Little League team. I was the team's scorekeeper, having learned to keep score from my father when I was six years old so I could record the plays of Brooklyn Dodger games on summer afternoons while he was at work. When he came home, I would recount for him every play, inning by inning of the game that he had missed. He never told me then that official box scores were published in the newspapers the following day. Without my scoring, I imagined, he would never have known the details of the games he missed.

Many weekends, we took the kids to Red Sox games. Seated at Fenway Park with my children, I could sometimes shut my eyes and remember myself as a young girl, sitting with my father at Ebbets Field, watching Jackie Robinson, Pee Wee Reese, Duke Snider, and Gil Hodges. There was an enchantment in such moments, for when I opened my eyes, I felt an invisible loyalty and love linking my sons to the grandfather whose face they never had a chance to see but whose heart and soul they had come to know through the stories I told.

When the boys were in high school, our lives were filled with wrestling matches, lacrosse games, school plays, guitar lessons, baseball card auctions, *Star Trek*, and comic book conventions. Our house became the nucleus of activity for dozens of our children's friends. We turned a garage into a big playroom with a pool table, pinball machine, air hockey game, and a giant TV screen. Many afternoons our boys came home from school to find a half dozen friends lounging on our couches, waiting for the action to begin.

***

The only problem with our choice of the Main Street house was that there was no extra space to accommodate the more than three hundred boxes of memorabilia Dick had accumulated over the years. He had saved everything—handwritten letters, mementos, and remnants of his life from his college and law school days through his years in the White House and beyond; there were reams of White House memos, his diaries, myriad drafts of speeches annotated by presidents and would-be presidents, clippings, newspaper editorials, old magazines, scrapbooks, photographs—a mass that would prove to contain a unique and comprehensive archive of the Sixties. What was inscrutable to me at the time was that Dick had such intensely conflicted feelings about the contents these boxes held. They represented a time that he recalled with both elation and a crushing sense of loss.

We hastily selected diaries, some drafts of important speeches Dick had worked on, personal letters, and memos between Dick and Presidents Kennedy and Johnson. The vast remainder we put into storage. But even that cursory overview was sufficient to recognize that his jumble of boxes was significant, not only to Dick, but to history.

When all our boys were off to college, graduate school, and the pursuit of career, Dick and I moved from Main Street down Monument Street past the Old Manse where Emerson wrote *Nature* and Hawthorne prepared his *Mosses*, past the North Bridge of the revolutionary battlefield, to the rambling old house where we lived the last twenty years of our lives together. The Monument Street house had a basement and a post-and-beam barn attached to the house which we converted into a gym. Between the cellar and barn, we finally had enough room to accommodate the train of cardboard boxes and plastic containers that had followed Dick through his life.

After decades in storage, the boxes and various containers arrived on a truck and were lugged down to the cellar until they encroached on the furnace and threatened to climb the cellar stairs. And when there was no more space, the remainder were sent off to the barn, to be stacked along the walls of the gym. Still, Dick resisted the idea of starting the process of excavating the files. He was not ready to go back. For him, the end of the Sixties had cast a dark curtain on the entire decade. Scar tissue remained. He was determined only to look ahead.

———•———

One summer morning, seven months after he had turned eighty, Dick came down the stairs for breakfast, clumps of shaving cream on his earlobes, singing "the corn is as high as a elephant's eye" from *Oklahoma!*

"Why so chipper?" I asked.

"I had a flash," he said, looking over the headlines of the three papers I had laid out for him on the breakfast table. Putting them aside, he started writing down numbers. "Three times eight is twenty-four. Three times eighty, two forty."

"Is that your revelation?" I asked.

"Look, my eighty-year lifespan occupies more than a third of our republic's history. That means that our democracy is merely three 'Goodwins' long."

I tried to suppress a smile.

"Doris, one Goodwin ago, when I was born, we were in the midst of the Great Depression. Pearl Harbor happened on December 7, 1941, my tenth birthday. It ruined my whole party! If we go back two Goodwins we find Concord Village roiled in furor over the Fugitive Slave Act. A third Goodwin will bring us back to the point that if we went out our front door, took a left, and walked down the road, we might just see those embattled farmers and witness the commencement of the Revolutionary War."

He glanced at the newspapers and went to his study on the far side of the house. An hour later, he was at my door to read aloud a paragraph he had just written:

"Three spans of one long life traverse the whole of our short national history. One thing that a look backward over the vicissitudes of our country's story suggests is that massive and sweeping change will come. And it can come swiftly. Whether or not it is healing and inclusive change depends on us. As ever, such change will generally percolate from the ground up, as in the days of the American Revolution, the antislavery movement, the progressive movement, the Civil Rights Movement, the women's movement, the gay rights movement, the environmental movement. From the long view of my life, I see how history turns and veers. The end of our country has loomed many times before. America is not as fragile as it seems."

I had been wrong to consider Dick's concept of one "Goodwin" to measure an eight-decade span of American history as simply whimsical. The light of optimism in his eye was in earnest. During the first half of the Sixties, a great window of opportunity had been opened. It had long been his dream, he told me, that such a window might open again.

So it was not out of the blue when he turned to me and said: "It's now or never!" The time had come to unpack, collate, and examine his treasure trove, box by box, file by file. We hired our friend Deb Colby to work as his research assistant, and together, they began the slow process of rummaging through the boxes and arranging them in chronological order.

Once that preliminary process had been completed, Dick was hopeful that there might be something of a book in all the material he had uncovered. He wanted me to go back to the very first box with him and work our way to the end.

"I need your help," he said simply. "Jog my memory, ask me questions, see what we can learn from this, find out what we can do with this."

"You've got it!" I exclaimed.

"I'm an old guy after all. If I have any wisdom to dispense, I'd better start dispensing."

That afternoon I joined him in his study, and we started on the first group of boxes that covered the Fifties and the early Sixties. We made a deal to try and spend time on this project every weekend to see what might come of it.

Our last great adventure together was about to begin.

CHAPTER ONE

Coming of Age

Dick and George Cuomo, his best friend from
Tufts College, circa 1951.

I HAD OFTEN ASKED DICK WHAT HE WAS LIKE AS A YOUNG MAN. To such questions, he would invariably roll his eyes and shrug. "How would I know what I was like as a young man? I was too busy being him."

When we first met, he was forty years old; I was twenty-nine. "If I had met you when you were in your twenties," I badgered, "would I have fallen for you?"

As a historian, I have daydreamed about meeting the presidents I studied when they were coming of age, that formative stage when choices were made that would define their future paths. After years of mining every accessible trace that their lives had left behind, poring over diaries and letters and considering the recollections of those who knew them, it was empathy and imagination that ultimately helped me develop an intuitive understanding, a feeling for what they were like when they were young.

There was Theodore Roosevelt, an undergraduate at Harvard—his quarters smelling of formaldehyde, skins, and feathers from his taxidermy projects scattered everywhere—eccentric, condescending, yet rippling with such uncommon energy that he seemed ready to dance a solo jig. And Franklin Roosevelt, not yet stricken by polio, playing tennis, golfing, swimming, leaping across a brook "like some amazing stag." Or gangly Lyndon Johnson, his curly black hair slicked back, at once magnetic and overbearing, yet spending half his first month's salary to nurture impoverished Mexican children during his first teaching stint in Cotulla, Texas. And who would not dream of lingering in the general store of New Salem, Illinois, in order to observe the odd and arresting clerk, young Abraham Lincoln, spinning stories to engage and buttonhole whoever stopped by.

It amused me to reflect that I had spent more time with Abraham Lincoln, Theodore Roosevelt, Franklin Roosevelt, and Lyndon Johnson than with any other man in my life besides my husband. After living upward of a decade immersing myself in each of these figures, I came to feel a powerful, sustained, and complex affinity for them. I had often publicly joked that these men were "my guys." Given the emotional and intellectual investment I had in them, I realized my designation was hardly in jest.

There was one undeniable difference, however, between burrowing through the presidential archives of "my guys" while engaged in long historical investigations, and my present research: these archives belonged to MY GUY, my husband of four decades, seated across the room. And while my old guy was initially of little help in my quest to bring the young Dick to life, I was thrilled when, early in our venture, I found a typed page of a journal Dick had begun when he was a twenty-year-old student at Tufts College. Finally, I thought, I will meet Dick coming of age:

September 20, 1952. Starting a journal is akin to beginning a new and intimate friendship. You must start slowly at first, a little cautious about confiding your ideas and thoughts, and you need assurance. Assurance that the paper, like the friend will be receptive to whatever you have to offer. For, there are few hurts as deep as a lack of understanding, where you have expected understanding. The difference, of course, is that in a friendship you must have confidence in others, in a journal confidence in yourself.

I am now torn by many conflicting desires and ideas. Activities are piling up on me. Personal affairs, which are pressing, are deteriorating under negligence. At the same time I am becoming farther and farther behind in studies and am carrying such a heavy load. I do not know if my customary last minute sprint will suffice. I will adopt a new resolve. Every time I have a new idea I will lie down for half an hour. I may not get much done but will certainly get a lot of rest.

No sooner had I finished reading this entry aloud to Dick than he began to criticize the prose style of his fledgling self. "Such an earnest young man," he said. "Already, he feels posterity looking over his shoulder."

"He's twenty!" I countered, "and already direct, emotional, filled with self-mockery and humor." I thought this opening entry was promising, and couldn't wait to keep reading. With this single page, however, Dick's diary came to an abrupt halt, not to be resumed until more than a decade later in the days immediately after John Kennedy's assassination.

Dick's aborted journal brought to mind the memory of a diary I had started and stopped on a February day my sophomore year in high school. *I am fifteen years old and my mother is dead.* That was all it said. And that said everything. Feeling inadequate to the task of capturing my feelings on paper, I had simply closed the cover and never wrote in it again.

My hunt to summon the twenty-something Dick continued. In the same box that contained the start of his diary, I found a packet of nearly fifty letters Dick had written to his closest college friend, George Cuomo, who later became an English professor and novelist. George had saved all their correspondence, later sending the letters back to Dick as a keepsake of their long and deep friendship.

These letters turned out to be an invaluable surrogate for Dick's short-lived journal, for their intimate friendship allowed Dick to speak freely without the worry of misunderstanding. His first letter set the tone.

June, 1953.

. . . You are the only person whom I dare write so ornately or so descriptively to, knowing that your understanding eyes will dilute my language and restore things to their proper perspective . . .

I don't know what you felt about graduation [George had graduated the year before Dick] but when I had time to think it over I felt a little lost. A little! —hell, I didn't know what to do with myself. It was damn sad.

I have definitely decided on Harvard Law. The monetary angle was too great to be ignored. They offered me $800 to start and $400 more in the middle of the year if I am passing. Tuition at the place is only $600 and the rest will cover a great proportion of my room and board.

Finances had become a source of family anxiety after his father lost his engineering job during the Depression. For reasons I'd never been able to fathom, he had never afterward been able to rebuild a steady career. The family lived in a small, rented apartment on Thatcher Street in Brookline. That summer before law school, Dick held down two jobs. During the mornings and afternoons, he was a Fuller Brush Man, selling brushes, mops, and household cleaning products door-to-door. In the early evening, he headed to Revere Beach, where he worked as a fry cook at Rudolph's on the boardwalk until 1 or 2 a.m. I laughed when I read about his nights as a fry cook since he had hardly cooked anything for the rest of his life! "Sweltering," he said, "working in that torrid zone above the fryolator, dropping clams, French fries, and onion rings into the boiling oil. I would have traded places with most occupants of Dante's Circle of Hell."

July, 1953. Beside the two jobs I am holding down I have got myself right in the middle of a big town fight for rent control. I am doing all the research for a citizens committee, which is leading the fight to continue rent control in Brookline. This work has entailed chasing all over Boston, seeing many people and even a personal telephone conversation with Senator Kennedy in Washington. I have a mass of papers and statistics on my dresser. On top of this we have almost endless meetings all over Boston. Of course, this is the type of thing I can enjoy doing and I'm meeting a hell of a lot of people.

That's it for my political life. My brush business has really taken a beating from the whole affair and so I have been putting in more time at the beach to salvage myself financially. This of course has irreparably destroyed my social life.

What drew a twenty-one-year-old—just graduated from college, short of time, short of money, and bemoaning an impoverished social life—to leap headlong into the fray of his town's rent control skirmish?

"Easy," he said, when I posed the question to him. "I loved being in the middle of the fight. The effort didn't take away energy, it gave me energy. Both sides—the renters and the property owners—were extremely passionate and well organized. I gave a speech at the big town meeting called to decide the question. The vote was close but we won. Rent control was extended. And when my speech made the front pages of the Boston papers, my social life picked up!"

Dick's letters to George during the fall and spring of 1953 presented a scathing yet humorous glimpse into the pressurized bubble that was his first year at Harvard Law School.

October 1953. A number of students have gone over to watch Harvard take on little Ohio University and most of the rest of them are listening to the World

Series so for the first time since I started I can do something besides study without the uncomfortable feeling that everybody is getting ahead of me. I'm not quite sure how I feel about the whole thing.

You spend your days going to classes and studying, your nights talking about the law or studying and your meals are periods of relaxation studded with constant reference to the law. This damned place is so self-contained that aside from an occasional Saturday night date you could live here for weeks without going as far as Harvard Square.

During the midterm practice exams in January, the pressure escalated. Dick caustically told George: *Last year only seven people in the school cracked up completely during exam time and had to be hospitalized. The Deans are confidently optimistic that they can keep the total as low this year. But there are doubts.*

As winter turned to spring and final exams came into sight, he confessed:

I never thought it possible to work so damned hard and learn so damned little. But finals are only seven weeks away and in the space of the last two weeks alone the tension has become incredibly more tense. "Incredibly" is a big word but it seems incredible that 500 guys should hate themselves for every hour they are not studying (including time spent sleeping or eating) thinking each hour might mean a percentage point in their grade, which might mean a difference of 40 places in your standing which might mean your future and so on in a continual horribly overblown, distorted, out of perspective view of the whole damn thing. But no matter how you realized how silly it all is it's hard as hell not to be caught up in the atmosphere.

"The weird thing," Dick told me after I had read him the passage, "was that the more difficult and challenging the work became, the more fascinating the whole study of law became for me. I started to take real pleasure in the intricacy of law."

Three months later, he learned that all his efforts and anxiety paid off.

July 1954. P.S. This letter has been sitting around my dresser since Saturday for want of a stamp. However it is a good thing. I have news. Just received my marks this morning. Straight A average. Pardon my bragging here but I'm in a state of intense euphoria and may be suffering from mild shock.

"After discovering I was at the top of my class," Dick told me, "I understood that so long as I kept up my grades, the doors to the most distinguished law firms would be opened even to a Jewish kid from Brookline."

Returning early to school that August to begin work on the *Law Review*,

Dick made a decision that had always puzzled me. He was in the library stacks verifying footnotes for an article to be published in the *Law Review*'s upcoming issue when his life took a radical swerve. At the very moment he was on the verge of clutching the golden key, set on the path to wealth and security, he bolted. Feeling claustrophobic, he fled the library, got into his battered Chevrolet convertible, drove to the Brookline Town Hall, waived his draft deferment, and enlisted in the army.

"Why?" I wondered, "I knew you took off from Harvard, but I never fully understood the reason why."

"It had nothing to do with reason," he answered. "I was strolling through the musty halls of the Law Library. I felt I had been going to school forever. It was hardly a choice. I had to escape."

"Do you think it had to do with panic, pressure, fear of failure?"

"Exactly the opposite. It was fear of success that frightened me, as if a roadmap had unrolled before me that was my future foretold."

If escape and adventure were what Dick sought in joining the army, little could he have guessed at the strange array of tasks he would be assigned, and the broad cross section of fellow Americans he would encounter there.

Fort Dix, New Jersey, November 1954. The other day our platoon sergeant walked through the door, saw me standing there, asked if I went to college, and when I said yes he shoved a first aid kit in my hand and informed me I was the platoon medic. I had my first major case the other day when a boy tripped on the stairs and fell through a window severely gashing his wrist. Everyone yelled "medic" and old Dr. Goodwin who used to go white when he cut himself shaving threw some large compresses over the wound, applied a tourniquet, using a handkerchief and a bayonet, and got the lieutenant's car to take the kid to the hospital where I was commended by the doctor who took 25 stitches in the kid's arm. I then had to go outside where I fought down a few waves of nausea and dizziness and returned to the company.

About thirty % of the platoon are college graduates, the rest include a couple of Puerto Ricans, a logger from Maine, a couple of truckdrivers, some who just finished or failed to finish high school or reform school. What is more amazing even than the diversity of background is the quickness with which the army has managed to make all of us think and act alike. In the mind of everyone from the PhD to the kid from reform school are much the same thoughts. We are tired together, and worry about cleaning our weapons together, and feel a common fear while waiting in line for shots, and hate together, with a fierce hatred for the sergeant who is making us run over soft, sucking sand.

During any free time he was able to muster, Dick retreated to the base library, where he found his own serviceable nook to smoke a cigar, relax, read, and study. He devoured one book after another, covering a broad range of subjects: poetry, history, science, cybernetics, fiction, drama, mathematics, philosophy, psychology. It was a habit that would mark every day of our lives together, for whenever and wherever Dick settled, he would soon enough be nestled in piles of books, magazines, newspapers, and catalogues.

January 1955. I recently read Mann's Buddenbrooks. I found it a fascinating if somewhat ponderous and slow moving affair full of half-hidden symbolism and a lot different from his later works but a hell of a good first novel. I also have begun one of those projects which one only dares attempt in the army. And that is reading Gibbon's Decline and Fall. I have read 50 pages and have only about 2500 to go. But then I have at least 17 more months to do it.

After basic training, Dick was assigned for eight weeks to an ordnance supply school and then to an advanced school in Parts Identification. It seemed an unlikely assignment. *It is a pretty technical school and one about as far away from my interests and abilities as the army could have managed. I will be taught to pick up an anonymous piece of metal and by a rapid glance determine whether it belongs to (truck, or gun, or binoculars etc.) and then to what specific item on that classification. And if you think I can pick up a carburetor brush and tell you whether it belongs to a 2½ ton truck or a jeep you have gone crazy. Why I can't tell a piston from a carburetor.*

I laughed as I read this letter; having been married to Dick for forty years, I knew well that he showed even less technical capability than cooking skill. Yet somehow, this placement proved fortuitous. Dick was sent to the Braconne Ordnance Depot in Angoulême, France—considered the most informal and friendly post in Europe.

———•◦•———

In the same box that held Dick's correspondence with George, we found an even larger sheaf of nearly one hundred letters and postcards, bound together with a ribbon, that Dick had written to his parents during his time abroad. Excited about this discovery, I looked forward to exploring it afresh early the next morning.

At 5:30, my customary time for waking up, I headed downstairs to my study. During those hours before dawn, when the house was quiet and my husband asleep upstairs, I found the best hours for work. I had all that was necessary to begin my writing ritual: a bathrobe, the old blue leather couch, a rug I had once hauled home from Morocco, a low chestnut table stacked with my research, and, with luck, several hours of undisturbed focus. With my back against a pillow on one side, a fireplace facing me on the opposite wall, and a throw blanket nearby, I had created a very homey study.

That morning, rising out of his old letters, I encountered an innocent, high-bouncing, consistently happy character I had never known. I had seen Dick in many joyful moods over the decades, but I would never characterize his basic disposition as happy.

The young man I met in these letters was convinced he lived under a lucky star. Indeed, it turned out that good fortune had landed Dick in a very different job than Parts Identification. The week before Dick arrived, an inspecting officer from headquarters had blasted the post's troop commander for their completely inadequate educational program. When Dick heard that the fur was beginning to fly, he asked to be reassigned to Troop Information and Education, where he managed to get himself designated "Professor Goodwin," and was given a free hand to create classes and a testing room for the troops. He gave lectures on public speaking, American government, business law, and leadership. He held discussions on current events.

A few months later, the inspector returned. Overwhelmingly pleased with the transformed and inventive new curriculum, the inspector gave the troop commander a special commendation. The commander, in turn, rewarded Dick with an uncommonly generous share of three-day passes and furloughs, affording a kid who had never traveled beyond the East Coast, the opportunity to explore European places he had previously only been able to read and dream about.

His ritual Sunday letters to his parents revealed a relentless enthusiasm, a wellspring of happiness, that drew me like a magnet.

Good morning. Another Sunday and your soldier son greets the sunny skies with a heart full of good cheer.

I walk around with a smile on my lips and a cheery greeting for everyone I see. At times I am positively exuberant.

Eureka, Joy unbounded. Whoopie!

Your wandering son is again on the move.

He traveled from one country to another as casually as he had moved from Brookline to Cambridge. He spent weekends on Paris's Left Bank, exploring Hemingway's shadows. He frequented the theater districts of London, where he saw Olivier in *Richard III*. He read "Tintern Abbey" as he sat on the banks of the Wye. He wandered through the house where Goethe had lived and worked. His mind, illuminated by the fireworks of such literary and historical sites, was often overwhelmed: *Forgive me*, he wrote George, after a two-week vacation, *I am in the midst of so many literary associations that it has been too great a strain for a lawyer's mind.*

The education he had so abruptly abandoned at Law School—consuming, and leisure-less—had given way to an explosive and emotional period of growth, an entirely different kind of education.

The commander of the depot took Dick under his wing. He was chosen to attend a Discussion Leaders School held in the picturesque seaport town of La Rochelle, France. The instructor at the school told him he was the best student he had ever had. When he returned, he was made a member of the depot's public speaking team, tasked with delivering a variety of speeches for the benefit of visiting dignitaries.

He even had a chance to act as a full-fledged lawyer when he and another first-year law student, Lawrence Kellam, were tapped to defend five GIs in actual court-martial cases. Their success in securing acquittals for four of their clients led to a sensationalized front-page story in a local paper, which Dick proudly sent back to his family in Massachusetts. The article suggested that the law firm of Goodwin and Kellam would be the envy of client-hungry firms in any American city since GIs were "practically waiting in line" to bring their troubles to these "legal supermen." The newspaper report failed to mention that neither Goodwin nor Kellam had a law degree.

He was not merely reading some romantic bildungsroman by Thomas Mann, he was living one.

I am having the most wonderful, exciting time of all my life, he told his parents, *I can almost feel my own growth and developing maturity. My travels have been an immense experience and when I think back to my thoughts and actions before I entered the Army, it is like looking at a different person. The sun is shining, the forest is in bloom and my heart is light. PS Please do something about the Red Sox. It's very embarrassing.*

I heard Dick stirring upstairs. My three-hour morning session had flown swiftly past. I hurriedly picked up *The Boston Globe, The New York Times,* and *The Wall Street Journal* from our front driveway, and set up his breakfast just in time to hear him bellow "Doris! Doris!" as he often did to announce his descent. I felt like I had just awakened from a dream, having finally made the acquaintance of my future husband as a twenty-five-year-old.

Over breakfast that morning, I read aloud from another long letter young Dick had written, this time describing a week's vacation in Geneva, Switzerland, chosen to coincide with the Big Four summit of leaders of the U.S., Britain, France, and the Soviet Union. Anticipating how electric the atmosphere would be with correspondents from all over the globe, Dick had persuaded three of his army buddies to go along.

July 1955. Week in Switzerland, one of best I have spent in my young life.

From behind a fence we watched the arrival of the delegations. Suddenly there was a shout behind us and we turned to see an open convertible. Bulganin and Khrushchev were arriving and had foregone the closely guarded approach to go out of their way to ride through the crowd of onlookers.

Then an open convertible full of FBI men sitting solemnly and following a closed Cadillac sedan from which flew the US flag and then another convertible full of Secret Service. The entourage entered the gate, six men jumped from the still moving convertible and jumped on the running board of the closed car where they completely shielded the occupants from view—Ike had arrived. The dictators had come in like South Boston politicians though the leader of Democracy had arrived with all the panoply of a medieval king.

But the crowd cheered Eisenhower where they only gasped at the Russians. I talked with many people in Switzerland and France and there is no doubt that most of them also "like Ike" and they liked him ever more after the conference. Democrat or not, I still got a tremendous thrill out of seeing MY President arrive to the cheers of foreign people and the Stars and Stripes flying from the cars.

After our glimpse of high level politics we left Geneva. Coming through the San Bernardino pass we rounded a turn past a waterfall and there was a small hotel in the middle of nowhere, and we stopped for a beer. In the downstairs room there were two very attractive Swiss girls and the woman who ran the place was delighted to see Americans and insisted we stay the night. We changed into good clothes and came down and played the part of rich American tourists, buying drinks for everyone. The Swiss girls joined us. They spoke excellent English and were witty, intelligent, vivacious.

This was a night only Steinbeck could do justice to. Beer and song flowed forth in equally herculean proportions. At 2 AM we rumbled out into the quiet mountain night. Hands over each other's shoulder we walked up the road singing, overcome with the feeling of good fellowship. I have often wondered of the feelings of the drivers of cars edging themselves through the narrow, dark roads high up in the mountains whose headlights suddenly illuminated four men, in sport coats and ties, arm in arm, singing Dixie at the top of our out of tune lungs.

The next morning we had breakfast and talking to the girls found they were driving to St. Moritz. So we got into our cars and went off to St. Moritz. That evening we all went to dinner at the Chesa Veglia. A world famous restaurant. They brought a large inverted wine decanter shaped like an inverted teardrop and when you pushed your glass under it the wine flowed into the glass. And so here we were, four American boys and two Swiss girls. Marvelous food being served us and the music and surroundings and the deep red of the wine and the blond hair and laughter of our companions. It was one of those supreme moments of my life. At the risk of sounding maudlin I was close to tears at the table.

My own eyes welled with tears as I finished reading this. "I am," I exclaimed, "totally smitten with this guy."

To my surprise, Dick did not seem to share my enthusiasm. "Well, I'm glad you like him so much," he said with a look of almost sadness behind his wild brows and thick lashes. "I rather envy him myself."

"Envy? But it *is* you!"

"No, it's not. And it's not simply that I'm much, much older now. He's got something I've lost along the way."

———•—•———

A new note was sounded in Dick's correspondence with George when he reached Fort Dix, awaiting his discharge. His travels and army experience had given him a new perspective on America.

June, 1956. The return to America has been an exciting one. For the first few days I seemed to view it almost as another of the foreign countries through which I have sped in the last 15 months. The unbelievable lights and sounds of music everywhere and commercials and all the other paraphernalia of American life were strange and disconcerting to one who hasn't heard a radio program or seen a TV show for 15 months. With all this it's a great country and alive and the people are tough.

I enjoyed Europe very much, in fact at first was a little overcome; but this is home and I'm very glad of it. It's really true that people are freer here and a poor kid can get somewhere and education is open to all or nearly all. Sure these things are filled with qualifications, but <u>in other places, there is not even the belief that they are true, not even the hope that they may be</u>.

I have need now to pursue my own White Whale. It will be difficult as I have many interests and praise has come too easily. I know I may be highly successful. I don't think that would be enough.

This last passage seemed to me to hold a kernel of what would become Dick's self-appointed mission: to do whatever work he could to close the gap between our national ideals and the reality of our daily lives. The story of his public life, as I have come to see it, is the story of a young man's love affair with America—not the geographic bounds of the country, but the constellation of democratic ideals that lay behind its founding. His belief in the credo set forth by Abraham Lincoln—the right of any man to rise to the level of his industry and talents—would inform every speech he drafted, every article he wrote, every cause he pursued. It would lend a coherence to the zigzagging vagaries of his public life.

The America that Dick returned to after nearly two years of service was not the same country he had left behind. The Supreme Court's decision in *Brown v. Board of Education*, ordering the desegregation of public schools, had sparked a nascent civil rights movement. In December of 1955, while Dick was teaching courses on American government at his army post, Rosa Parks refused to give up her seat to a white man on a Montgomery, Alabama, bus. A few days later, a young local pastor, Martin Luther King Jr., led a protest that evolved into a year-long boycott that eventually ended segregated seating on Montgomery buses. A movement that would change the face of the country was beginning to gain strength.

In late August of 1956, Dick returned to Harvard, reenergized to once again begin his second year of law school. No sooner had his classes and work on the *Law Review* begun, than he became deeply involved in a civil rights issue at Jackson College, Tufts's sister school. The local chapter of Sigma Kappa had been ousted from their national sorority after they pledged two Black freshman girls. The evasive letter revoking their national affiliation simply said that the ejection was "for the good of the sorority as a whole."

When Dick learned of the ouster, he contacted his state representative, Sumner Kaplan, and drafted a press release calling for a joint House-Senate committee to investigate discriminatory practices on college campuses and determine whether any state action could be taken. While Jackson's Sigma Kappa sorority was not a state-supported institution, there was a Sigma Kappa sorority at the University of Massachusetts. The creation of the joint committee made headlines throughout the state. Dick was appointed committee counsel, responsible for gathering evidence, interviewing witnesses, and holding public hearings. The fire that this appointment ignited in Dick radiates through his entire account of the matter to George.

There will be no pay, but the satisfaction will be enormous. I have even had my picture in the paper congratulating the President of the Senate for his firm stand on the matter. The inside plan is now to widen the investigation to include a study of all discriminatory practices on College campuses. There are many interesting legal points especially as fraternities and sororities partake of the tax exempt status of a University.

Sigma Kappa's national officials refused to appear, warning that they would hold the committee responsible for any unwanted publicity. Answering for the committee, Dick said: "We accept that responsibility. We have given them adequate opportunity to be heard." Jackson's dean, Katherine Jeffers, told the committee that the administration wholly supported the local chapter's decision to take in two Black pledges. The committee report concluded that the national office of Sigma Kappa had "engaged in discriminatory action which cannot be condoned," adding that the actions of the local chapter and the support of the administration "should be an example to all." In response to the committee's report, the Massachusetts legislature passed a resolution chastising private schools for allowing national organizations to dictate who their sororities could choose as pledges.

While Dick's original hope for mandatory legislative action to end discrimination on the campus of the University of Massachusetts proved premature, the hearings spurred a dialogue on the issue of racial discrimination on college campuses. An editorial in *The New York Times* praised the strong stance Jackson had taken, suggesting that if integration were to be achieved in colleges and universities, "college students—the future parents, teachers, businessmen and politicians of the nation—must take the lead."

How was it possible, I wondered, that during the many thousands of hours Dick and I had swapping tales over the years, he had never told me of his reckoning with campus discrimination? And then his story prompted my own somewhat vague memories of a similar experience at Colby College in 1960, when I joined Tri Delta, a southern-based sorority.

To help sharpen hazy memories, I called my former roommate and sorority sister, Marcia Phillips. Happily, she had saved a box of Colby memorabilia, which she kindly sent to me. In the box, I found material about Tri Delta, including a small yellow pamphlet, *Manners for Milady*. "What you do, how you act, what you say reflects not only on you but on Tri Deltas everywhere," one passage read, insisting that baggy sweatshirts and letterman sweaters only be worn in the privacy of your dorm rooms. "Clothes make the woman. Be sure a stranger can say, 'There's a well-groomed girl. She's a Tri Delta.'"

Though I had long thought of myself as "a Sixties girl," imbued with the rising spirit of liberation, the *Milady* precepts make it clear that vestiges of an earlier time survived. We were told that a young lady should "eat with only one hand above the table unless cutting meat or buttering bread. The hand not in use should be left in your lap. Butter bread one bite at a time. There should be no conversation between the waiters and the diners. When you are finished eating, leave your knife, fork, and spoon on an empty plate at the 10-4 position. Enter and leave a chair from the right." And how bizarre it seemed to be given advice on how to smoke gracefully, how to lift the cigarette to your lips and light it in one motion.

More to the point, when I served as rush chairman of Tri Delta, we took in our chapter's first Jewish pledge, Barbara Gordon, from Newton, Massachusetts. Two years later, we took in our first Black pledge, Judy Turner, from Brooklyn. We did not consider the invitation a test case. We liked her and wanted her to be in our sorority. The rules required a recommendation from an alum, which was readily secured. This step, we later learned, was regularly used to prevent local sororities from pledging sisters who would not be mutually acceptable to all the members of the national organization.

Looking back more than half a century later, Marcia Phillips remembers that two women from Tri Delta headquarters, dressed in beautifully tailored suits, flew to Maine to meet with us. While claiming that the sorority had no discriminatory clauses, they nonetheless issued a private warning: Our actions might result in the loss of our national charter. No further step was taken at that time. It was clear to us that the national officials were fearful of negative publicity that might result.

In the eight-year span between Dick's serious scuffle with Sigma Kappa and my tussle with Tri Delta, public sentiment against discrimination was slowly but surely growing. President Dwight Eisenhower had sent federal troops to protect nine students from a local mob which was attempting to block their entrance to Little Rock Central High. Three years later, a sit-in movement had begun when four Black students refused to leave a segregated lunch counter in a Woolworth's in Greensboro, North Carolina. The following year, Black and white Freedom Riders took bus trips through states in the South to protest segregated bus terminals and restrooms. And just before the start of my senior year in college, Martin Luther King delivered his "I Have a Dream" speech at the Lincoln Memorial to a quarter of a million people.

Although these fights Dick and I had encountered were but skirmishes, they told a story, with accelerating momentum, of a new future being born.

———

During Dick's second year in law school, as he wrote George, he witnessed, with commingled wonder and dread, the feeding frenzy that encircled third-year colleagues on the *Law Review*.

November 1956. Being on the Review makes you the choice target for firms throughout the country. The bidding this year has really been fantastic. The third year students are being treated as if they were outstanding high school athletes. They are being flown to San Francisco and Milwaukee and Tulsa as well as to New York and Washington, just so they can look over the firms and decide if they would like to work for them when they graduate.

I have accepted a summer job in Washington. I will be working for a firm called Covington and Burling in which [former secretary of state] Dean Acheson is a senior partner. It is one of the finest firms in the country. They give you summer housing in the mansions owned by the senior partners, which are vacant during the summer because the owners are cavorting in Europe or elsewhere.

Right now I don't think I want to practice in one of those high powered law firms. They are almost like legal factories, although on a very lavish scale. But I am anxious to see what it is like.

"That promised affluence cast a hypnotic spell," Dick told me. "I had been anxious about money all my life, but the price of conformity seemed oppressive. I didn't want to become The Man in the Gray Flannel Suit. There was a real tug-of-war going on inside me."

"Hard to imagine you ever becoming a good company man," I said.

"What I *didn't* want had become clearer to me than what I *did* want," Dick acknowledged.

By the spring of that second year, Dick's prospects had immeasurably broadened when he was elected president of the *Law Review*.

"The election itself was a fascinating process, running for three days—until 7 a.m. Sunday morning—without a final choice," Dick told me.

"It sounds like they were electing a new pope with puffs of black and white smoke," I said teasingly.

"It *was* a big deal. I remember Justice Felix Frankfurter telling me of a moment when he was a first-year law student. He overheard a student whisper reverentially of a young man passing in the corridor: 'That's the president of the *Law Review*.' Silly as it sounds, the justice had remembered that moment all his life." One way or another, Dick knew that his selection would impact the trajectory of his future career.

March 1957. This election opens all doors to me. Next year I can work for any law firm in the country of sufficient size to do hiring, or I can clerk for a Justice of the Supreme Court or I can take a $3000 stipend and go traveling around the world by the virtue of a Sheldon fellowship. And so my problem, which would not seem burdensome to some but is to me, is to make the right choice.

The burden of making the right choice still lingered in my mind when I happened upon a box containing staff papers of the *Harvard Law Review*, and a long rectangular photograph of the assembled members of 1957–58. There, holding the president's baton, sat Dick, front row center of three tiers of formally posed young white men. On closer inspection, on the far-left and far-right flanks of the sixty male staffers, I spotted the only two women. The small woman on the far right, wearing a distinctive white collar and dark jacket, was Ruth Bader Ginsburg.

I had known that the future legendary Supreme Court justice had been on the *Law Review* with Dick. I knew from Dick that work on the *Law Review* was nearly a full-time job—in addition to classes and exams. Dick had told me that Ginsburg had somehow managed to balance this academic and *Law Review* load along with a husband and a baby. Seeing this photograph, however, brought her challenging situation home to me for the first time. I took the photo into Dick's study and placed it on his lapboard so we could inspect it together.

"So many men," I said, "and only two women."

"Is that an accusation?" Dick asked.

"Not against you, personally, of course," I said. "But it is maddening nonetheless. Look, there is Ruth Bader Ginsburg, right up there at the top of the class with all of you; and yet, while you were bemoaning the burden of choice to George, it is well known that she was not offered a single job with any law firm!"

The photo of the assembled *Law Review* members so whetted my interest that it spurred a search for a better understanding of what the Law School was like for women in 1957. I discovered that there were only ten women in Dick's class of five hundred. While meeting with these ten women, the dean of the Law School famously asked: "Why are you here occupying a seat that could be held by a man?" Harvard provided no housing for women. There was no women's bathroom in Langdell Library. The women were relegated to using the janitor's bathroom in the basement. Certain university libraries were restricted to men only. How remarkable that this extraordinary woman, Ruth Bader Ginsburg, before whom so many doors had been closed at the start of her career, had then spent a lifetime opening doors for others.

We hung the group photo on the wall of Dick's study, where I passed it every day. Then one afternoon, I became intrigued by the other young woman who stood to the far left—one Nancy Boxley. She now lived in California, where I was heading for a lecture in several weeks. We arranged to have lunch together. In her eighties, she still cut a striking figure: stylish, elegant, with a sharp wit and a memory to match. In response to my question as to what impact the *Law Review* had on her life, she quipped, "It helped me fulfill my mother's dream. I married a Jewish surgeon."

She explained that like Ginsburg, she had two marks against her when she interviewed for a job: She was female and she was Jewish. But unlike Ginsburg, she was not yet married and did not have a child. She landed a job at Simpson Thacher & Bartlett in New York, where, at a party, she met her Jewish surgeon. She worked at the law firm for several years until she became pregnant with her first child, at which point one of the partners told her they were letting her go. "Not that we are embarrassed by your circumstance," he assured her, cradling both his arms before his midriff to suggest pregnancy, "but we fear a client might be." When she and her husband later moved to California, she had resumed her legal career. That earlier conversation, however, remained etched in her memory—as did her visit to a first-year contracts course while attending a Harvard Law reunion three decades after her graduation. Much to her satisfaction, she told me, the professor, an attractive young female, wore boots, a short dress, and was pregnant!

———•·•———

November 1957. The elfin good fortune which seems to dog the path of my career continues. I have been selected as a law clerk to Justice Frankfurter. There is no doubt that Frankfurter has the finest mind on the bench. He is also a warm man of wide culture and interests. He is known for taking a strong personal interest in his clerks and always discusses his opinions and ideas with them. His law clerks form a sort of an informal group and have a yearly dinner in Washington. It is very exciting to become part of that tradition.

"There was something magical about the Justice," Dick fondly recalled to me. "He was small and delicate, an elfin-like creature himself, who managed to simply materialize in a room and then just as suddenly vanish."

Dick always referred to Frankfurter as "the Justice," as if he personified that abstraction. "I remember the initial bit of advice the Justice gave to me when we first met at Harvard after my selection as his clerk—'Relax this summer. Take a vacation. I'll see you in September.'

"'I don't need one,' I insisted. 'I'd like to come down right after graduation.'

"'Young man,' he said, 'there's something I want you to remember for the rest of your career, the laws of physiology are inexorable.'"

Dick smiled at the recollection. "I think the Justice was afraid I'd burn out."

Nonetheless, Dick decided to forgo the restorative lures of summer. Rather than wait for his clerkship to begin in September, he arrived early, in time to attend a special session of the court called to deal with the Arkansas state legislature's attempt to delay the desegregation of public schools, as mandated by *Brown v. Board of Education*. The legislature claimed to be acting on the grounds that the present chaos required a two-and-a-half-year postponement of the court's ruling. In *Cooper v. Aaron*, the Supreme Court unanimously held that public opposition could not undermine the ruling in *Brown v. Board*. Arkansas must proceed to desegregate its schools "with all deliberate speed." This landmark ruling was the first case Dick heard argued before the Supreme Court.

What stood out most vividly in Dick's memory of his clerkship year were the stories he heard as he drove the Justice to and from work each day. Dick was spellbound by anecdotes about the great men the Justice had known: Franklin Roosevelt, Oliver Wendell Holmes, Louis Brandeis. He freely discussed a wide range of subjects, from the latest news stories to the comparative merits of two English chancellors in the eighteenth century, to the personalities of his fellow justices. Chief Justice Earl Warren, despite his beaming smile and warm handshake, struck Frankfurter as cold and distant; Justice John Marshall Harlan, one of the best men on the bench in his view, he saw as a majestic figure of sound and independent views; Justice Hugo Black, he considered the formidable intellectual leader of the liberal wing.

"When the Justice put an opinion before me," Dick said, "it was never to persuade me and certainly he wasn't seeking my agreement. He presented his opinion like a knife, and expected me to provide the steel to hone it."

"That doesn't sound awfully pleasant," I said.

"Nor was it supposed to be," laughed Dick. "His Socratic method was to draw me out, to challenge me, to encourage critical thought. He was a great and a crafty teacher. Maybe the best I ever had.

"Regularly, he cautioned and instructed me about the role of the court. And regularly, he throttled my activist approach to court decisions. He was constantly worried that if the justices imposed their own social or political views, the authority of the court itself would be chipped away. His institutional conservatism left a permanent mark on me.

"'Our job is to enforce the law, including the Constitution,' the Justice repeatedly said. 'We have nothing to do with your abstract notions of justice or liberty. Only with what the law provides. Trample the law for your own ends, Dick, and the time will come when you'll be trampled under someone else's ends.'"

During Dick's clerkship with Frankfurter, offers from big law firms kept rolling in. Despite the promise of pot-o'-gold ambitions and the lure of a larger salary than his father had made in the previous decade, Dick decided that practicing law in a big firm was not for him. Instead, he chose to stay in government service, to accept an offer from the House Subcommittee on Legislative Oversight, which had jurisdiction over all administrative agencies, including the Federal Communications Commission, which regulated the gargantuan, if still infant, power of television. It was a decision that would land Dick in the bullseye of a national scandal.

"Would you want to marry Charles Van Doren?" I remember posing that question to a group of my girlfriends in 1957, my freshman year in high school. To be sure, Charlie wasn't in the league of Elvis or James Dean, but he was an intellectual hero, a television rock star, and the biggest winner featured on *Twenty-One*—the most popular of a series of TV quiz shows, which had captured American families during the Fifties. My family was one of them. Wednesday nights would find me with my mother and father on our closed-in porch watching *Twenty-One* on our tiny, ten-inch screen. Few events—heavyweight championship fights, presidential elections, the seventh game of the World Series—so arrested tens of millions of American families as the reign of the quiz shows in the Fifties.

Every Wednesday night for fourteen consecutive weeks, there was Charlie—an English instructor at Columbia, with all-American good looks, the scion of a famous literary family. His father was the renowned Shakespeare scholar Mark Van Doren; his mother, Dorothy, a novelist; his uncle Carl, a Pulitzer Prize–winning biographer; Carl's wife, Irita, the book review editor of the *New York Herald Tribune*.

There was Charlie, his forehead furrowed, his expression a study in concentration as he stood in an isolation booth, straining to recall one arcane fact after another—the whole drama playing out beneath the logo GERITOL, a promised cure for tired blood ("twice the iron in a pound of calves' liver").

And Charlie was rich! After winning the largest amount on record, $129,000, NBC had given him a $50,000-a-year post as a cultural correspondent on the *Today* show. For that astronomical sum, he appeared once a week to read a poem, discuss a new book, talk about history or science.

But by 1959, rumors had begun to swirl about that the contestants on both NBC's *Twenty-One* and CBS's *The $64,000 Question* had been provided with both questions and answers ahead of time, that the shows were a hoax. In New York, a grand jury was convened.

That's where things stood when Dick commenced work on the congressional Subcommittee on Legislative Oversight. By the time Dick and I began sorting through the archive, I was well acquainted with Dick's involvement with the congressional investigation; after all, we had been able to build our pool and install a hot tub with the money Dick had received from the option on a chapter of his 1998 memoir that led to the production of *Quiz Show*, an Academy Award–nominated film directed by Robert Redford.

I hadn't realized, however, that Dick had initiated the federal investigation that ultimately unearthed the quiz show scandal. This became clear to me for the first time when I happened upon a nine-page memo Dick had written to the chief counsel of the committee, Robert Lishman, on July 24, 1959—only ten days after he had started his new job. In the memo, he told Lishman he had just learned that the judge (who later would be removed from the bench for corruption) had impounded the final report of the nine-month investigation of the New York grand jury—a highly unusual action. The entire matter was buried under a seal of secrecy. "If there was nothing wrong," Dick noted, "why keep it a secret?"

Dick's memo presented a series of legal, political, and moral arguments for opening a congressional investigation, which, he suggested, could begin with the immediate demand to release the grand jury minutes:

The prime attraction of course was the spectacle of the unknown genius whose wizardry and intellect baffled and attracted the nation. The winners on these shows became national folk heroes, and their daily activities were followed on the front pages of the nation's newspapers.

In the atmosphere of innuendo, half-truth and complete secrecy which now surrounds the true nature of these television quiz shows, certainly the American people who took on faith the representations that they were watching true contests of skill, are entitled to the truth. Moreover, it is highly important that such practices when discovered, be brought to public attention, for by so doing we help to ensure that similar fraudulent schemes will not be undertaken in the future.

On July 31, a week later, committee chairman Oren Harris issued a press release announcing a federal investigation. In all essential points and in the language used to express those points, the press release followed Dick's memo. The great attraction of the television quiz shows, the chairman explained, *"was the spectacle of the unknown genius whose wizardry and intellect baffled the nation."* If an investigation of these shows proves that contestants were coached and given answers, then "the American people have been defrauded on a large scale."

"Well, you certainly had a nose for trouble," I told Dick, "and an instinct for the center of action."

"Truth is," he replied, "I didn't have a clue when I began where this would lead. Armed with a pocketful of blank subpoenas, I went to New York to demand the release of the grand jury records. I wasn't even a member of the New York bar. I had taken the Massachusetts bar exam a few weeks earlier, but had not yet received the results. Yet I figured my impersonation of a full-fledged lawyer was less consequential than the fraud that had been perpetrated upon the American public if the quiz shows were rigged."

In the late summer and early fall of 1959, after Dick succeeded in securing the grand jury records, he began interviewing dozens of contestants, producers, sponsors, and network executives. The testimony of the producers and the contestants chronicled exactly how the deception was carried out. The producers not only provided contestants with the questions and answers ahead of time, they rigorously coached them on how to create the appearance of tension by biting their lips, mopping their brows, and drawing out their answers. And the producers decided—depending on the audience reaction, ratings, and advertising sales—who would win or lose, and at what juncture.

The most powerful evidence that the entire production was a concocted drama, an orchestrated entertainment rather than a contest of prowess and incredible recall, was provided by Herbert Stempel, the first big winner on *Twenty-One*. Surveys had increasingly revealed that viewers found Stempel awkward and his personality unappealing. The producers therefore contrived that the time had come for him to be "defeated." Short and stocky and born to a poor Jewish family, Stempel was convinced that anti-Semitism had hastened his demise. To make things worse, he had taken the fall to the graceful, gentile figure of Charles Van Doren. He had developed such an intense hatred toward the Ivy League Van Doren that he was more than willing, indeed eager, to admit his own role in the fraud if he could scuttle his privileged nemesis.

Van Doren was one of the last to insist that his performance was not a sham. Whatever might be true for others, he repeatedly told Dick, he had never seen the questions ahead of time. He had not been coached in any way. He was so persuasive that, for a moment, Dick began to question his own conviction that Van Doren was lying.

We found notes Dick had written after interviewing Van Doren:

I am torn and somewhat thrown off track by my feelings toward the two main characters in this national drama. On the one hand, I identify with Stempel. He is, like myself, of poor Jewish background with no family connections. I know he is telling me the truth but I am deeply troubled by his obsession with

destroying Van Doren. On the other hand, I like Van Doren. I want to believe
him. He has studied and loves literature. I see him as a mentor at a distance. I do
not want to believe that one of his family would take part in this scam.

I have plenty of evidence without implicating him. We are just emerging from
the McCarthy era. I have no desire to expose for exposure's sake. The contestants
are just being used. The real culprits are the big money makers—the producers,
the sponsors, the networks. They are my targets. They masterminded the effort.
They are the crystallized materialism of the fifties.

So I will tell Van Doren we will not call him to testify at the public hearings,
but once they begin, he must say nothing for if he chooses to defend himself pub-
licly the committee will be forced to bring him in.

No sooner had the public hearings begun, than Stempel implicated Van
Doren. Immediately, the NBC executives told Van Doren that unless he
issued a public denial, the *Today* show would be forced to sever ties with
him. To save his position at NBC, Van Doren issued a fatal public statement
professing his innocence. The committee chair now had no choice. He
instructed Dick to issue a subpoena and serve it on Van Doren in New York.

Still conflicted, Dick sought the counsel of his mentor, Justice Frankfurter. "We don't need his evidence," Dick explained to the Justice. "If only
he had kept quiet," Dick said. "To the public, Van Doren *is* the quiz shows,"
Frankfurter responded. "It would be like playing *Hamlet* without Hamlet.
You're not pursuing an innocent victim but a willing participant. The fact
others may have done worse doesn't make him guiltless."

Faced with the congressional subpoena, Van Doren decided that a full
admission of guilt was all that was left for him. He would admit that he had
lied to the grand jury. He would confess that he had willingly participated
in what he knew was a rigged show, a massive fraud perpetrated on the public. The night before he was set to testify, Van Doren and his father, Mark,
who until then had refused to believe that his son would be part of such a
hoax, went to Dick's house to review the next day's proceeding. Afterward,
Van Doren wrote Dick a strangely poignant, yet literary note of thanks:

What an extraordinary evening it was. I will of course never forget it.
Hunters used to say that the stag loved the hunter who killed it . . . thus
the tears which were tears of gratitude and affection. Something like that does
happen. I know. And Raskolnikov felt the same.
I should have taken your advice.

You must never, in any way feel any regret for your part in this. Perhaps it is nonsense to say that, but I thought it might be just possible that you would.

On November 2, 1959, the House Caucus Room was jam-packed with members of Congress and their staffs. More than a hundred reporters and photographers layered the walls. Dick remembered that a silence settled over the room when Van Doren took the stand. "I would give almost anything I have to reverse the course of my life in the last three years," he began. "I was involved, deeply involved, in a deception."

"He looked unbearably wretched," Dick told me. "His eyes were blood-shot and he appeared so shaken, I could hardly look at him. I was thumbing through documents when I caught sight of Stempel entering the room. Eager to get as close as possible to the action in front, Stempel literally crawled on his hands and knees so that he could look Van Doren in the face as he gave the testimony that would ruin his life."

Within hours, NBC announced that Van Doren had been fired and Columbia University released a statement that he had "resigned." The young instructor's promising academic career was over. Never again would he risk becoming a public figure. And Van Doren had been right: Dick confessed that a twinge of regret had always lingered, stirred by the very name "Van Doren."

After the hearings had concluded, Dick wrote an article for *Life* magazine, his first nationally published piece, telling the story of the quiz show investigation. And for the first time, serious public attacks were leveled at him—accusations that he had secured a "fat fee" from *Life* magazine for work that he had completed while being paid by the government with taxpayer dollars.

A syndicated columnist maintained that "any information he had on how they [the contestants] were deceived and how the dupers and the duped were brought to justice, should have been given—free—to his ultimate employers: The Public." His supposed unethical behavior, the columnist suggested, should be taken up in the courts and in Congress. A *Washington Post* editorial echoed this charge a few days later, again condemning the young investigator for profiting from public service.

"It still makes me angry," Dick said to me nearly sixty years after these events had taken place. "I hadn't divulged a thing that wasn't part of the public record. The committee counsel had approved the article before I submitted it. And I hadn't received a fat fee! I wanted to challenge the bastard to a duel on the banks of the Potomac, but first I went to Justice Frankfurter for solace and advice. He chuckled and found my duel idea rash and imprudent.

"'Some pains are like stomach infections which stay for months,' the Justice told me. 'Others are like toothaches which you can't even remember after you leave the dentist. This kind of thing is like the toothache.'"

In the end, Dick's mother, Belle, had the last word:

We are so proud of your magazine article. Life never had so great and wonderful an article. Our popularity has soared up—kind of nice to receive so many phone calls about you. And I love your picture cigars and all. I saw you on the movie tone news. Boy did we get a charge out of that. We are lucky to have a son who is tops, i.e., blessed.

If Belle saw her son as tops and blessed then, I only wish she had lived to see Robert Redford's 1994 movie *Quiz Show*. I remember sitting down with Dick and Redford after a glittering premiere in Rockefeller Center. When the three of us were alone, Redford asked Dick, "Well? What did you think? Did you like it?"

"What's not to like," Dick roared with laughter. "I'm the moral center of the story. I'm portrayed by a young good-looking guy. And I get to sum it all up with the last line, 'I thought we were going to get television. The truth is, television is going to get us.'"

Yet when Dick reflected on the movie, it wasn't with the feeling of accomplishment or triumph. "I never got to the root of it," he told me. "I never got to the real culprits, the big moneymakers—the sponsors, and the networks. The contestants were pawns, willingly exploited by the temptations of money, fame, even rationalizations of the good they were doing. No one showed much appetite for getting to the bottom of things—certainly not the congressmen. It was their deference to the sponsors and the network chieftains that disillusioned me most. Not only did they not pursue questioning, they treated the chief perpetrators as if they were fellow victims of the fraud."

The quiz show scandal proved to be a sentinel moment at the end of the Fifties, one that epitomized, in near allegorical fashion, the force fields that defined that decade: the hunger for material success, the instant celebrity granted by the new medium of television, the power of advertising, and the widespread perception that we were adrift, that we were losing ground.

Sputnik circled the earth, proclaiming our backsliding across the heavens. President Eisenhower, who had previously declared that the dazzling intelligence revealed by the quiz show contestants was our best answer to Sputnik, now had to concede that he was "astounded" and "almost dismayed" by the revelations of fraud. A general feeling pervaded the country that America was mired in a slough, that we needed a jolt to somehow get us moving again.

———•·•———

While still flying around the country interviewing contestants, Dick unknowingly became a contestant of sorts in a job search being conducted by Senator John F. Kennedy's aide, Theodore Sorensen. For some years, Sorensen had been toiling behind the scenes for the junior senator from Massachusetts on an unannounced presidential bid. Out of the blue, Sorensen called to ask Dick if he would like to try his hand at writing a speech. He did not mention that Dick was one of a dozen candidates—among them several published authors—auditioning for the post of junior speechwriter, who would work under Sorensen himself.

"At the time," Dick said, "I simply thought I was helping out on a speech."

All that Dick remembered of that initial call was the formula that Sorensen succinctly conveyed to him for a Kennedy speech. It was to be made of three "interchangeable parts" that could be snapped together as needed, like some version of Legos: first a tribute to the grandeur of the Democratic Party; second, a brief exploration of the "soup du jour"—foreign policy, arms control, health care—and third, an invocation of American greatness and our responsibility to make a great country even greater. "Sorensen," Dick recalled, "delivered the formula in a straightforward fashion, without irony. The important thing was that interchangeable parts would enable the senator to deliver two or three speeches from the same core speech, to fit the occasion without simple repetition. 'Why don't you take a crack at it,' Sorensen urged, and the call was over."

It was with great surprise that we discovered, folded in a manila envelope, Dick's long-forgotten maiden speechwriting venture.

It began with a quote attributed to an unnamed American playwright: "On the wreckage of all dead civilizations should be inscribed, 'They did not dare.'" Beneath this bombastic opening, however, was an exhortation that touched a nerve, a summons that would come to characterize a core theme of the campaign to come—a challenge to shake off the lethargy that seemed to have settled upon the country:

It has been charged that we have become too prosperous and contented, that we have lost the iron drive of the pioneer, and lack the daring to bring this new vision to the world, Dick asserted in this trial run. *And often, sitting in Washington, watching the paralysis of imagination and leadership which grips our administration, it has been hard not to listen to the doubters.*

But I do not believe them. I have crossed this great nation from end to end. And seen the people at work in farms, in factories, in offices and in homes. I have felt in these people the enduring strength of our land.

"You know," I said to Dick, "in a funny way, you've got your finger on something. Beneath the brass, I hear the summons to a new spirit of imagination, youth, and leadership."

"No great claims for this sample," Dick said, handing the sheaf of pages back to me, "except that it worked. It got me the job!"

A job and an opportunity that would forever transform his life. For if the quiz show investigations had drawn Dick into the center of action, that center would not compare to where his new job would lead him. "A human being lives out not only his personal life as an individual," remarked Thomas Mann in *The Magic Mountain*, "but also, consciously or subconsciously, the lives of his epoch and his contemporaries." The contours of an epoch may stunt or stir ambition. And an immense tailwind of social and cultural change was already beginning to drive the generation coming of age at the dawn of the Sixties.

CHAPTER TWO

"A Sort of Dead End"

*Six-year-old Ellen Anich presents a bouquet
of roses to Senator Kennedy in Ashland,
Wisconsin. March 17, 1960.*

I BEGAN TO FEEL A SENSE OF FOREBODING AS OUR TIME-TRAVELING
adventure reached the threshold of the Sixties. Some thirty archival boxes
covering Kennedy's campaign were stacked in more or less chronological
order in Dick's study, their precise contents neglected for many decades.
Both of us looked back upon these years with a decided bias. And our
biases were not in harmony.

During his twenties, Dick had the chance to join the small, select group
surrounding John Kennedy, who would become the youthful face of leadership for a new generation. Into his old age, Dick had retained a loyalty to
John Kennedy, as well as an enchanted memory of his introduction to the
often brutal world of politics.

In my twenties, the chance to work in Lyndon Johnson's White House
and accompany him to his ranch to assist on his memoirs had left a perma-

nent imprint on my life. During these early years, I developed an empathy for and loyalty to Lyndon Johnson that has lasted all my life.

A fault line between the Johnson and Kennedy camps had opened with the blowback following Kennedy's choice of LBJ as his running mate. This rift had deepened in the wake of Kennedy's assassination, and erupted with seismic force when Robert Kennedy chose to challenge LBJ for the presidential nomination in 1968.

Tremors from this division ran through our marriage, at times provoking tension as I repeatedly insisted that the great majority of Kennedy's domestic promises and pledges found realization only under Johnson, while Dick repeatedly countered that Kennedy's inspirational leadership had set a tone and spirit that defined the decade. "Had Kennedy lived," Dick would say, "the war in Vietnam—" Straightaway, he stopped himself: "Who knows?"

Our squabbles over the relative merits and demerits of the two administrations had such lasting power over us because they were neither academic debates nor historical assessments. Beneath all such arguments dwelled a clash of loyalties both of us had established before we met.

Thus, with Dick in his eighties and me in my seventies, we resolved to start from scratch as we opened the boxes, to scrape away these fixed opinions, the defensiveness and prejudices that had accumulated over the years, to see what firsthand evidence we could unearth.

"Let's set some ground rules," I said. "Let's start with our first impressions of John Kennedy and see how they changed over time."

"A clean slate," Dick exclaimed, and reached out his hand to shake mine. As we shook hands, we both burst out laughing.

AUGUST 1956

I never met John Fitzgerald Kennedy in person. I first encountered him on our black-and-white ten-inch television screen. As it turned out, television was the most winning way to be introduced to his charms. I was thirteen years old. It was a Friday afternoon in the middle of August 1956. I was in my bedroom reading when my mother called me downstairs so I could witness a grand moment that was about to take place. I was happy to hear an unusual animation in her voice. She told me that in a wholly unexpected move, the Democratic presidential nominee, Adlai Stevenson, had thrown the selection of his running mate to the floor of the convention—and that it looked like her choice, the handsome young Catholic senator from Massachusetts, was on the verge of winning.

From the small screen came the sounds of whooping and hollering, the confusion and din from a crowd numbering in the thousands, as if some tremendous sporting event were taking place. Before long, I was curled up on the sofa alongside my mother's chair, trying to keep score on a big piece of poster board. The magic number to win, the commentators kept repeating, was 686½. The rules of this game were far more peculiar than those of my accustomed, orderly universe of scoring baseball games with my father which progressed play-by-play, out-by-out, inning-by-inning. Here, numbers rose and fell as states waved their standards in the air, howling for recognition to announce their tallied votes, which somehow shifted from one candidate to another in the space of fifteen or twenty minutes.

At the time, I knew almost nothing about conventions. My parents were not especially active in politics. At the dinner table, politics was discussed no more than money or sex. All I knew was that my mother rarely showed the sense of vitality and elation that was apparent that afternoon of the Democratic convention. Rheumatic fever as a child had left her with a damaged heart. Angina attacks had begun in her thirties. Three summers earlier, a major heart attack had taken a permanent toll on her body. But on this day, her eyes were bright and her voice was strong.

She explained to me that even though the senator from Tennessee, Estes Kefauver—I'd never heard the name Estes before (to say nothing of Kefauver), and it struck me as funny—had led after the first ballot, Kennedy, showing a surprising momentum, had come in second, ahead of Senators Hubert Humphrey and Albert Gore Sr. And sure enough, on the second ballot, my mother's young Irish prince jumped into the lead—and she jumped to her feet and cheered.

Midway through the second ballot, after New York delivered big for Kennedy, I had my first glimpse of a long figure with big ears. It was Lyndon Johnson. He grasped the microphone and shouted that Texas would cast its entire vote total for John Fitzgerald Kennedy. Banners waved. Shouts for Kennedy filled the air. Ahead of Kefauver now, Kennedy was within 20½ votes of victory. Tension mounted in the amphitheater and in our family room.

What happened next made no sense to me. Senator Gore of Tennessee requested that his name be withdrawn in favor of Kefauver. All of a sudden, the incoming tide for Kennedy abruptly stopped. Then the tide ebbed as one state after another snatched their votes away from Kennedy and delivered them to Kefauver. It seemed ridiculous, as if my Brooklyn Dodgers had scored two runs in one inning, before both were suddenly taken away the next inning and given to the Yankees. Soon, Kefauver was safely beyond the magical 686½, my disappointed mother was close to tears, and I was angry at what seemed an utterly mystifying affair.

That was when the defeated candidate stepped to the rostrum. My mother and I both fell silent. He didn't look like anybody else up on the speaker stand, so slender, so young, with his full head of hair. His face looked weary. I could tell he was sad. But he maintained an earnest and graceful control in accepting defeat. He thanked his supporters from all over the country. He praised Stevenson for his "good judgment" in letting the convention select the vice presidential nominee, and, finally, asked the delegates to nominate Kefauver by acclamation. As Kefauver made his way into the convention hall to the strains of the "Tennessee Waltz" and the roar of the crowd, the television camera switched instead to a close-up view of Kennedy collecting himself in the aftermath of defeat, standing tall and clapping for Kefauver. Indeed, there was something in the vulnerability he displayed, his magnanimous demeanor, that transformed my mother's sorrow into pride, and suspended my own anger and bewilderment in favor of a newly minted curiosity.

More than six decades after watching Kennedy's concession speech with my mother, I replayed that day's proceedings on YouTube. In the years since, I had become familiar with the ebb and flow of delegate tallies. I had come to understand that when Senator Gore withdrew and the midwestern and Rocky Mountain states held firm for Kefauver, Kennedy had likely reached the limit of his support; once that situation became clear, a bandwagon effect in favor of Kefauver had set in. No one wanted to be on the wrong side after the finish line had been crossed.

In the decades afterward, I had studied and written about both JFK and LBJ. I knew that in contrast to Kennedy's praise of Stevenson's "good judgment" in allowing the convention to select the nominee, LBJ considered the decision "the goddamndest stupidest move a politician could make." As I watched a video of the convention online, I listened carefully to the words Johnson used when he delivered the state of Texas for Kennedy: "Texas proudly casts its fifty-six votes for the fighting sailor who wears the scars of battle, the fearless senator, John Fitzgerald Kennedy." I could not help but smile, for these flattering words were in stark contrast to the image

LBJ had painted of the junior senator for me one day at the ranch, calling him "a young whippersnapper, malaria ridden and yellah," who "never said a word of importance in the Senate" and "never did a thing." Such feelings mattered little, I now understood. For the Texas delegation, anyone was preferable to the outspoken liberal Kefauver. And Johnson believed that Kennedy had the best shot at beating Kefauver. Furthermore, in a political era marked by the rise of television, Johnson acknowledged that "Kennedy looked awfully good on the goddamn television screen."

My mother and I were alone in our house that summer afternoon, but the impression Kennedy made on the two of us was shared in all parts of the country by millions of people. It was this realization that struck me most forcibly during my recent rewatch of the convention: the power of television to ignite a personality in a single moment, transforming a young senator into a national figure, conveying an impression of vitality, excitement, and promise that would linger and grow in the years ahead.

MARCH 1958

Curiously, the romantic aura surrounding John Kennedy that both my mother and I had felt via television in 1956 was nowhere in evidence in March of 1958 when Dick first encountered the young senator in the flesh. A kind of introductory interview had been arranged by Sumner Kaplan, the state representative from Brookline who had championed Dick's first forays into politics during the rent control struggle and the fight to prevent discrimination in local fraternities and sororities. Sumner would become a lifelong friend and mentor to Dick.

Dick only had a vague memory of a chilly spring day and trudging up three flights of stairs to a cramped, shabby apartment at 122 Bowdoin Street in Boston. This tiny apartment—across from the State House and next to the Bellevue Hotel where local politicians gathered—had been Kennedy's official Boston residence since his first run for Congress twelve years earlier. An outer room was crowded with local politicians and lobbyists. After twenty minutes, Kennedy's aide, Frank Morrissey, showed Sumner and Dick into an adjacent room, where Kennedy greeted Sumner warmly and shook Dick's hand.

"I understand you're going to work for Frankfurter," Kennedy said, and then with a shrug and faint smile, added, "He's not my greatest fan."

"Kennedy remained standing," Dick told me, "and so, of course, did we. Then, with a skill that did not signal dismissal though indeed that's exactly what it was, Kennedy waved to a small group of men Morrissey was bringing into the room. Almost simultaneously, Morrissey reached for Sumner's arm to escort us to the door. But before we left, Kennedy took my hand a second time and, meeting my eyes, said simply, 'I'll be looking for people in January once I finish my reelection campaign. Come and see me.' We weren't in there very long."

Dick's description reminded me of Theodore Roosevelt's rapid-fire meetings with visitors when he was governor. It was said that his stately desk might well have been removed altogether for he was always standing, receiving and dismissing record numbers of visitors so adroitly that each person somehow felt he had truly and personally engaged with him.

A few days after the Bowdoin Street encounter, Dick wrote George Cuomo:

I recently had an interesting meeting with Senator Kennedy when he was in Boston. He intimated strongly that he would like to have me come to work for him next January after he finishes running for re-election for the Senate.

However, even if he wants me to work—and this is not at all certain—I am not sure. Work for him, no matter how interesting, is bound to be a sort of dead end for one so young.

"A dead end? So you thought, at twenty-six, you'd be stuck in some sort of Senate cubicle forever?" I asked.

"I'm not sure what I thought. Only that there was nothing intoxicating about the senator or his confining quarters. The size and impression of the place should have no bearing on the size of its occupant—but of course it does."

JANUARY 1959

After the dust of the Senate reelection campaign had settled, Dick followed up on Kennedy's invitation. Kennedy had been reelected by a historic, whopping 73 percent of the vote. This second meeting took place not in the cramped Bowdoin Street apartment above a cobbler's shop, but in the grand and formal setting of the Old Senate Office Building. The senator's office, Room 362, was across the hall from the Senate office of Vice President Richard Nixon.

"I don't know," Dick told me, "whether it was the regal Old Senate Office Building, Kennedy's resounding reelection to the Senate, or the crackling electricity generated by his impending presidential bid, but the atmosphere that day was charged."

After passing the hive of activity surrounding the secretarial desks—clacking typewriters, ringing phones, competing voices—Dick was guided into the relative tranquility of Kennedy's inner office. This time, Kennedy rose from behind his desk to shake hands and ushered Dick to a leather chair opposite the desk. This was not simply a Teddy Roosevelt meet-and-greet.

"He seemed different, more impressive," Dick recalled. "He asked me all kinds of questions about my experience at Harvard Law School, about my work on the court, reiterating that Justice Frankfurter was not one of his supporters."

Dick wisely chose not to enter into a conversation about the Justice. He knew that Frankfurter despised Kennedy's father, Joe, believing him an anti-Semitic Nazi appeaser during the early days of World War II. Frankfurter considered young Kennedy a lightweight.

"The conversation lasted twenty minutes or so. It was genial. He was sizing me up. His curiosity felt genuine. I didn't feel uncomfortable. I doubt I had grown much in size since the first meeting, but I felt certain that he had. The strongest impression he made was of a powerful, disciplined ambition."

"Were you projecting all this on him, imagining him as president," I wondered, "or was it actually emanating from him?"

"I'm not sure," Dick said. "All I know is that I was sufficiently engaged to tell him straight out that once my time as a law clerk was over, I would like to help in the campaign that was brewing in his offices. No commitment was made. He simply said keep in touch, but my guess was that my name was put into a file of potential staffers when the Kennedy team for a presidential run was assembled."

Perhaps, I later thought, it was from this file that Ted Sorensen picked Dick's name to enter the contest for the post of junior speechwriter.

DECEMBER 1959

"There were no swimming lessons on that job," Dick laughed. "Ted Sorensen handed me folders overflowing with memos, articles, and various background materials on arms control, something I knew next to nothing about. He showed me to a desk in an outer room of the Senate office, and with a brief, 'I'll stop by later, we need the article for tomorrow,' he threw me in the swimming pool to fend for myself and left."

Throughout that first day, Dick pored over position papers, suggestions from a variety of advisers and academics, as well as every public statement Kennedy had made on the topic. Dick had always been a quick study, adept at scanning and cramming, yet somehow also able to distill an immense mass of material into something clear and clean. He told me, however, that as the hours passed and he began to peck out a draft of several thousand words on his typewriter, the work made law school begin to feel like a romp in kindergarten.

By the time Sorensen reappeared to pick up the pages Dick had produced, everyone else had left the office. Sorensen read through the draft while standing. "Not bad" was all Dick remembered as an introductory compliment. Then, Sorensen pulled up a chair, and for the next hour or more, underlined and slashed Dick's pages, his crisp and vigorous mind pointing out the slightest deviations from Kennedy's policy positions while also tightening the syntax to suggest the clipped mannerisms Kennedy favored. No sooner had he finished this intense tutelage session than he rose, slid back the chair, picked up his briefcase, and, turning to Dick, said, "It still needs work and we still need it by tomorrow. Good luck." And then he was gone. So Dick's first day in the office led to his first long night of coffee and cigars, working until dawn.

Sorensen, chief of the speechwriting team, and Dick, the sorcerer's promising apprentice, made for an odd couple. It would be difficult to find two more different characters than Dick and Ted. The mentor, immensely helpful, yet sparing in praise, undemonstrative, guarded, and possessive of his long, exclusive relationship with Kennedy; the student, idealistic and emotional, bright and ambitious. Although Sorensen seemed at least a decade older than Dick, in actuality, only three years separated them. For the prior half dozen years, Sorensen had been Kennedy's sole speechwriter, intellectual and policy sounding-board, adviser, and traveling companion as they had toured every state of the Union.

If conceivable, Sorensen would never have tolerated an assistant speechwriter at all, but the need to generate material for the fledgling campaign had grown to the point where it was no longer possible for him to produce the material that was necessary on his own.

JANUARY 1960

On January 2, 1960, hardly a month into the job—in the immediate aftermath of Kennedy's announcement of his candidacy for the Democratic
presidential nomination—Sorensen gave Dick a chance to collaborate
on an assignment that was different from the usual articles and position
papers. He told Dick that Kennedy wanted to make a speech on the presidency itself. He wanted to draw a line between the complacent, passive
presidential leadership of the Fifties, and the progressive, active conception
of the presidency that he felt certain the new decade of the Sixties required
and that he intended to offer. On that collision between active and passive, old and new, between what he would do in the coming decade and
what had not been done in the previous, Kennedy had decided to wager the
identity of his campaign.

Dick remembered rushing with Sorensen to deliver the speech draft to
Kennedy, in transit from one city to another, at Butler Aviation Terminal
in Washington, D.C. "That presidential draft was the first time I had ever
observed him read a speech I had worked on. Quick marks with his pencil,
nothing encouraging or discouraging, but there was a remarkable intensity of focus. He said he didn't mind "sticking it to old Ike," so long as the
immensely popular president's name was not mentioned.

Rifling through Dick's boxes, we found an advance copy of the speech,
given on January 14, 1960, before the National Press Club in Washington.
As we carefully reread the speech, what surprised me most was that it spoke
of "the challenging, revolutionary sixties," forecasting the future of a decade
then little more than two weeks old!

"What do the times—and the people—demand for the next four years
in the White House?" The speech suggested that they demanded an active
commander in chief, "not merely a bookkeeper." They demanded "more
than ringing manifestoes issued from the rear of the battle." They demanded
that the president "be the head of a responsible party, not rise so far above
politics as to be invisible."

These biting phrases were so transparent that they seemed to me to
clearly cross the line of not directly criticizing Eisenhower. Apparently
at the last minute, Kennedy made a similar assessment. A journalist who
had seen the advance press release recognized that when he delivered the
speech, he "pulled his punches." He dropped the critique of a passive leader

fighting from the rear of the battle. And he eliminated the demeaning "bookkeeper" reference. Nonetheless, the speech was pungent enough to elicit a most unusual round of applause from the press corps.

What I liked most about the speech was that history formed its spine. Quotes from past presidents were sprinkled throughout as they would be in nearly all the work Dick crafted during his speechwriting career. Looking back, I was particularly fascinated to note Kennedy's desire to mold his future presidency in the expansive tradition of Franklin Roosevelt, Theodore Roosevelt, and Abraham Lincoln—"my guys," the presidents with whom I had spent decades of my life. Indeed, Kennedy's speech ended with Lincoln's statement after signing the Emancipation Proclamation: "If my name ever goes into history, it will be for this act, and my whole soul is in it."

After we had finished reviewing this speech, eighty-four-year-old Dick waxed nostalgic: "So there I was," he said, "twenty-nine years old, a history major in college, summoning my passion for the story of America into my first speech for Kennedy in those first days of the Sixties."

"And there I was," I added, "a seventeen-year-old high school senior, dreaming of becoming a high school teacher. You, dreaming of changing history; me, of teaching how those changes were made."

In 1960, the only path to the Democratic nomination for John Kennedy was through the primaries. He was not the darling of the party bosses. Given his age, inexperience, and Catholicism, they had serious doubts about his ability to win the general election.

Kennedy knew there were not enough primary votes to secure his nomination. The primaries did, however, offer a proving ground, an opportunity to audition for the power brokers of the Democratic Party—to demonstrate, in a trial of popular appeal and strength, his viability as a candidate.

From the moment he had announced his intentions on January 2, he had issued the challenge that "any Democratic aspirant to this important nomination should be willing to submit to the voters his views, record, and competence in a series of primary contests."

Hubert Humphrey was the only rival to take up Kennedy's gauntlet, although Stevenson, Missouri senator Stuart Symington, and Lyndon Johnson waited and watched from the wings.

When I asked Dick to tell me about the primary trail with the senator, he said, "Mostly I wasn't there! I was holed up day and night in his Senate office in Washington, an overheated cog in a promise-and-pledge machine."

Dick became adept at Sorensen's tripartite formula of a stump speech, recognizing how a stock opening and closing of every speech would sandwich the meat of what the candidate might promise to persuade that particular audience. It was this formula that enabled him to churn out a variety of stump speeches with great speed, transforming hitherto inscrutable questions concerning wheat markets, coal extraction techniques, and dairy supports into somewhat coherent proposals and pledges that might be accomplished in the future. And of course, there were general patriotic and partisan themes, such as a great America could be even greater.

As Dick and I searched through a sampler of these stump speeches, he estimated that he had written about 40 percent of them. And how dense they were!—he hefted onto the table a stack of stump speeches, fact sheets, position papers, and assorted files. "Wow . . . not so profound maybe," he said, "but I was goddamn prolific."

Afterward, we read a few of them aloud. "Pretty dull," I said to Dick.

"Exactly," Dick nodded, "but designed to show that Kennedy was not a lightweight. He had command of hard facts and issues. He had gravity."

Dick had to assimilate reams of position papers in order to fashion informed statements—about agricultural policy for the South Dakota plowing contest, about timber in the Northwest, about water in California, about hard and soft coal in West Virginia, and about dairy programs for farmers in Wisconsin. After working on a farm speech with the candidate, Dick recalled Kennedy remarking, "Here we are, two farmers from Brookline."

Promises and pledges were the steady drumbeat of Kennedy's stump speeches, variously tailored for a Jewish community center, a grange, a high school auditorium, a luncheon, or a brief after-dinner speech: "We pledge ourselves to passing a water control bill . . . to a program of agricultural research . . . to preserve the fish which inhabit our lakes . . . to assist small businesses to get a larger share of defense contracts . . . promise to strengthen and expand employment services to assist displaced men to find better jobs . . ." His proposals, pledges, and promises to build a dam or dredge a harbor accumulated until, by the campaign's end, Dick compiled a list of more than eighty-one pledges.

While Kennedy was trying to prove himself to the party bosses, he was also learning how to better speak to people crowded before him. It was often difficult to comprehend his accelerated mode of delivery and clipped Boston accent. Dick had kept a copy of a taped interview with Robert Healy, a friend from *The Boston Globe*, who covered Kennedy during the 1960 race. In the early days, Healy recalled, the candidate wasn't a "polished speaker. He spoke so rapidly that nothing really sank in." He raced through his prepared speeches like a young kid giving a report who was eager to get back to his seat. But he excelled during question-and-answer periods, and came across as articulate, informed, and often humorous.

And most impressively, Healy noted, Kennedy actually sought criticism. He would ask reporters all kinds of questions about the crowd's reaction. Did they seem to like him? When and where did their attention drift? Where were they enthusiastic?

"So of all this stuff you and Sorensen helped concoct for the primaries," I asked Dick, "what has stayed with you?"

"Ashland," Dick responded without hesitation, "Ashland, Wisconsin. I remember drafting a pledge for Kennedy's visit there, a promise to clean up the harbor and provide federal aid for this small town on the shores of Lake Superior that was down on its heels. Manufacturing was gone, jobs scarce, a polluted harbor. I'm not sure why," Dick said wistfully, "but over the past half century, I've often wondered about Ashland. I even wanted to go there to see what happened to that harbor, but I never made it."

———•———

Dick's words echoed in my head as I continued sifting through the archive to explore material relevant to the 1960 Wisconsin primary, the first of the competitive primaries (Kennedy had easily won New Hampshire, his neighboring state). I resolved to find the answer to Dick's old question: What *had* happened to Ashland? Had Kennedy's pledges been fulfilled? Or were they only so much political bluster? The answer turned out to be more complicated than I had imagined.

Curious, on a whim, I called the Ashland Historical Society and reached out to longtime residents. I dug up old newspaper clippings spanning the decades from 1960 to the present. I reread Theodore White's *The Making of the President 1960*, which I had first encountered six decades earlier in graduate school.

MARCH 1960

According to White, who shadowed Kennedy during the Wisconsin primary, the candidate had reached Ashland on March 17, 1960, at the close of a long, grueling day that had begun at dawn in the city of Eau Claire. Only eight people showed up for a rally planned at a roadside diner. Driving north through the sparsely populated region, a hatless Kennedy jumped from his car in village centers, walking through the streets, extending his hand to the few passers-by. Unheralded, he slipped into country stores, saloons, and factories, where he was often met with grunts or stares. "I'm John Kennedy," he would say, "candidate for president. I'd like to have your vote in the primary." One worker replied, "Yeah! Happy New Year." This was Humphrey territory. Minnesota was a neighbor, and Humphrey was known and well respected in Wisconsin.

The image of what White described as "a very forlorn and lonesome young man" walking through the streets stuck in my memory. White was impressed by Kennedy's resolution and perseverance. Neither the ten-degree temperature nor the wall of indifference dispirited him. "He had not even once," White reported, "lost his dignity, his calm, his cool, and total composure."

Compared to the grim day of hunting out voters throughout the depressed Ninth and Tenth Districts, the evening event in Ashland was a revelation of warm possibility. Organizers had filled the Dodd Gym with seven hundred people. Before Kennedy spoke, six-year-old Ellen Anich crossed the stage, carrying a bouquet of flowers she had brought to present to the candidate's wife, Jackie Kennedy.

That six-year-old girl was now sixty-eight when I tracked her down for a conversation.

"A bunch of grayheads sitting around the table thought it would be cute to have a little girl deliver the flowers. My uncle, Tom Anich, was active in Democratic politics," Ellen explained, "so I was chosen. We had no money. Everything I wore belonged to a rich girl across the street. That day, I practiced handing things over. . . . But when Kennedy reached down to accept the flowers in his wife's absence, I held back, confused since they were meant for his wife."

Kennedy explained that his wife was pregnant and resting. "My mom's going to have a baby, too," young Ellen announced.

"I promise if you give them to me, I will make sure she gets them," Kennedy assured her—so finally, she surrendered the roses.

The crowd roared with good-natured laughter, sending the night in a positive direction. The high spirits continued as Kennedy spoke of a Democratic bill Eisenhower had vetoed, the Area Redevelopment Bill. He pledged that he would work for its passage so that Ashland and other depressed communities throughout the country would receive the aid they deserved from their government.

On September 24, 1963, Kennedy returned to Ashland, this time as president of the United States. The harbor had not been cleaned up and the grave economic situation had not improved. As president he had passed and signed the Area Redevelopment Bill, but its modest funds had not filtered down to Ashland.

Nonetheless, that presidential visit, the start of an eleven-state conservation tour, would be widely remembered as "the greatest day in Ashland's history." Schools were closed and a holiday mood prevailed.

"It was a big honor for our little town," Ellen's ninety-one-year-old aunt, Beverley Anich, told me.

A radio recording captures the tremendous thunder and screaming of the crowd as Kennedy emerged from a helicopter that had set down at the small airport. "Everyone is most excited," the announcer said, "for the President of the United States to step foot on our land." On his way to the speaker's stand, Kennedy veered suddenly toward the snow fencing, behind which some fifteen thousand people (a crowd larger than the whole of Ashland's population) had gathered.

I could not help but contrast the pandemonium that greeted him that day as he reached across the fence to shake as many outreached hands as he could (much to the dismay of the Secret Service) with the icy reception he had received three years earlier when hunting down votes one by one in the deserted streets of northern Wisconsin.

He issued a clarion call for the preservation of natural resources, for protecting freshwater harbors, lakes, and streams, and once again promising government aid. He spoke of plans for making the nearby Apostle Islands into a national park. His speech lasted only ten minutes. After mixing with the crowd, Kennedy's military helicopter left from the airport that would soon be rededicated in his honor. Yet, even his brief visit, I would discover, had left an impression on the people of Ashland that would continue to inspire them for years to come.

Fifty years to the month after Kennedy's 1963 visit, a reporter interviewed a number of the people the president had encountered that day. Rollie Hicks was a math and physics major at Northland College. He had little interest in politics, but his friends convinced him to go to the airport. When Kennedy was returning to his helicopter following his speech, he made another abrupt turn toward the fence at the very spot where Rollie was standing. "He shook my hand and I gave him a Northland College booster pin." Looking back, sixty-nine-year-old Rollie said he didn't want to overplay it, but something happened on that day that was instrumental in leading him to a life of politics and public service.

And by all accounts, Rollie's experience was not unique. There was an aura surrounding John Kennedy that altered the paths of countless young men and women. One, named Temperance Dede had a similar experience. Kennedy introduced himself and took her hand. "All I could think about is how perfect he looked," the seventy-three-year-old recalled, "his smile, his hair, his suit." Though stunned into silence at first, she summoned the courage to introduce herself, telling him that her friends called her Tempe. "Then I will call you Tempe," he said. He then asked her questions about her life and listened carefully as she told him she lived at the Fond Du Lac reservation. He wanted to know about the reservation. "We need people like you," he told her before taking his leave. That day, she told the reporter, marked a change in her life. "I felt anything was possible." Tempe went on to get an associate degree, a bachelor's and a master's degree in social work. She was a founder of the first preschool program at Fond Du Lac and worked to address mental health issues for Native Americans.

I am not suggesting a causal chain of events, but pointing out an organic narrative that emerged again and again from various witnesses' accounts.

As I talked with seventy-three-year-old lifelong Ashland resident, town historian, and former mayor Edward Monroe, an answer began to surface to Dick's question about what had happened to Ashland's harbor and economy.

"It was a very depressing place in 1963," Monroe said. He explained that an abandoned saw mill had left wood pilings close to shore. It all looked like ruins from a war. The Dupont plant, which had made dynamite and TNT, had shut its doors, but not before an accumulation of discharged chemicals had turned the lake blood red. Waste from the paper mill had left a milky sheen on the bay. The coal power plant had dumped a tarlike substance in the harbor.

"It's been a very long road," Monroe told me, "but I believe it began with the president's visit to our little town. Talk to anyone in Ashland who was there and they will remember every detail. He made us feel good about ourselves. We needed to feel good about ourselves to believe we could make our town better. He had challenged the country to put a man on the moon. Now he was challenging us. Little by little we began to clean up the harbor and the beachfront."

The town was awarded a grant to remove those wood pilings from the shore. A pedestrian tunnel was built to give residents a way of getting from the downtown plaza to the lakeshore without crossing a busy highway. A small community project to paint a few murals on the tunnel walls mushroomed to create 250 murals that now span the entire tunnel. A hospital grew into a medical campus that today houses both cancer and mental health centers that serve seven counties.

And, after decades of legal battles, a federal court finally identified those responsible for the pollutants carpeting the harbor floor. That legal settlement created a multimillion-dollar Superfund to dredge the bottom and clean the harbor.

"The harbor is in good shape," Monroe proudly noted. "The beachfront is restored. Tourists are coming here. You would not recognize Ashland today from the down-and-out place it was six decades ago."

The legislative aid Kennedy had promised in the campaign had not been delivered to Ashland. It had taken more than half a century and a cascade of intervening events to clean up Ashland's harbor and strengthen the town's economic life.

Yet, it seems clear to me that something indefinable had happened when President Kennedy came to Ashland, that his presence had inspired in the townspeople a belief in themselves that had helped set in motion the long journey toward their community's revival. The abandoned industrial plants had left behind a dispiriting gloom as well as an ugly physical residue. Kennedy's visit generated the beginnings of a new mindset.

"We felt after he was here that we were more than we were before,"

Edward Monroe told me. "We began the projects that long needed to be done."

In the long run, the aspirations and inspiration that Kennedy had brought to Ashland may well have proven every bit as vital to leadership as policies and programs. It was a point, I came to understand, that I had never properly realized or conceded to Dick.

APRIL 1960

Kennedy's long days of trudging through Wisconsin paid off on April 5, primary day. He never developed the boisterous and friendly chumminess, the genial touch of Hubert Humphrey. There was always a distance, as if something was withheld, setting him apart and making him less accessible. In the end, that line was perhaps not a liability at all, but a strength.

His victory over Humphrey, however, was not the knockout blow the campaign had anticipated, and the votes, once tallied, revealed a troubling religious split. Kennedy took the predominantly Catholic districts; Humphrey easily won the predominantly Protestant districts.

"What does it mean?" Kennedy was asked. "It means we have to do it all over again. We have to go through every one and win every one of them—West Virginia, and Maryland and Indiana and Oregon, all the way to the Convention."

And so their marathon sprint went on to West Virginia. Day and night, Dick remembered, he tried to make sense of hard coal, soft coal, coal by wire, and burning fuel. Only Catholicism was taboo for the speechwriters. Kennedy decided to address the issue himself in Charleston, West Virginia, when he spontaneously responded to a question about his religion: "The fact that I was born a Catholic, does that mean that I can't be the president of the United States? I'm able to serve in Congress, and my brother was able to give his life, but we can't be President?" The real issues, he repeatedly argued, were poverty, unemployment, and what could be done to make daily life better for the people of the state.

On May 10, West Virginia's primary day, Kennedy beat Humphrey by an overwhelming margin. In the weeks that followed, Kennedy swept the rest of the primaries. In so doing, he demonstrated to the political bosses that a young Catholic could mobilize the support of the American people across the country.

JULY 1960

On the night of Wednesday, July 13, Kennedy secured his party's nomination on the first ballot at the Democratic convention. On Thursday, the convention delegates (not to mention Kennedy's inner circle) were stunned when Kennedy announced that he had chosen Lyndon Johnson as his running mate. Dick had remained in Washington during the convention. I wondered what he and his colleagues in the office had thought when they first heard the news that Lyndon Johnson was suddenly part of their team. Dick said he remembered a general feeling of disappointment and confusion.

"I guess in a sense we'd all profiled him," Dick admitted. "He was from the South, immediately suspect on matters of civil rights. We knew of labor's disapproval. He seemed old, a figure from the past, not a member of the new generation that was at the core of our campaign."

Kennedy had promised that he would seek out new men who would "cast off the old slogans and delusions and suspicion." If Lyndon Johnson seemed to balance the ticket, the perceived conception was that he did so from the right and from the past.

And yet, Dick recalled, in the many months of all-nighters in the Senate office during the primaries, no matter how far past midnight he stayed at the office, he was sure to spy a single light in the darkened Capitol building shining from the office of the Senate majority leader. "It shone like a beacon in a lighthouse. I thought maybe Lyndon had left that light burning to fool people into thinking he was *always* working. The day would come when I learned that my surmise was wrong. He *was* always working."

There are warring narratives as to what really happened in those hours between Kennedy's nomination and his surprise selection of Lyndon Johnson as his running mate. Some observers claim Kennedy's offer was simply a gesture made with the certainty that Johnson would never surrender the power of Senate majority leader for the hapless post of the vice presidency. If so, that calculation failed to understand that throughout his career, Johnson had shown an uncanny ability to turn a sow's ear into a silk purse. As party whip, minority leader, and majority leader, he had taken positions with small bases of power and vastly magnified and multiplied their functions.

Others claim that the offer to Johnson was genuine and made in good faith. Kennedy had carefully weighed the pros and cons, subtracting voters Johnson would likely lose in the North, while adding votes he would gain in the South. In the end, he could not see his way to victory without Johnson. Without Texas, he had an insufficient number of electoral votes.

Lyndon Johnson, an inveterate nose-counter, was doing his own arithmetic. He had even asked his staff to research how many vice presidents had gone on to become president. That number was ten. Seven of them did not have to wage a campaign, inheriting the presidency after the incumbent's death.

Finally, it seems that when Kennedy went to proffer Johnson the post, he did not definitively make the offer, but merely suggested it. Nonetheless, Johnson readily accepted the matter as a done deal. When sufficient displeasure surfaced within the Kennedy ranks and among Democratic activists, however, Kennedy began to have second thoughts.

As John Kennedy's unofficial surrogate, his brother Robert Kennedy was given the unfortunate job of persuading Johnson to rescind his acceptance of the candidate's suggestion regarding the vice presidency. In all likelihood, Johnson identified Bobby as the agent and not the messenger. Bobby warned that if a nasty fight erupted on the convention floor, its fallout could well damage the launch of the entire campaign. Perhaps in compensation for withdrawal, Johnson might consider accepting the chairmanship of the Democratic Committee? Johnson stood his ground. He had been told he would be the nominee. He wanted to be vice president. To withdraw the offer publicly would be calamitous. Kennedy had no recourse but to bring Johnson's name forward.

Robert Kennedy, Dick told me, was disconsolate about Johnson's selection. "Don't worry, Bobby," Kennedy told his brother, a comment Bobby grimly confided to Dick years later, "Nothing's going to happen to me."

The delegates were eventually brought into line. Johnson was nominated by voice vote, but he would forever blame Bobby for the humiliation he experienced during that chaotic afternoon. Mistrust, suspicion, and a scarcely concealed hatred continued between the two men from that day forward.

So, with confusion and turmoil on both sides, the Kennedy-Johnson ticket was born. And in hindsight, without that ticket there would have been no President John Fitzgerald Kennedy in 1961, and no President Lyndon Baines Johnson in 1963.

Several weeks after the convention, Ted Sorensen paused by Dick's desk late one evening as he was about to leave the office. "Beginning in September, you'll be joining me and the senator on the plane for the national campaign."

"I tried to stay composed," Dick told me, "but I felt like I was going to jump out of my skin."

"Maybe get a new dark suit, a few white shirts, and new ties," Sorensen had suggested. "Something conservative."

"I thought the other guys were the conservatives," Dick had said, smiling.

CHAPTER THREE

Aboard the "Caroline"

*During the presidential campaign of 1960, Senator Kennedy
and his aides traveled across the country in the "Caroline,"
the private plane named for his daughter.*

FROM SEPTEMBER 4 TO NOVEMBER 8, 1960, DICK WAS A MEMBER
of the small traveling team that crisscrossed the country with Kennedy on
his private plane for sixty-eight days of nonstop campaigning.

Dick knew from the start he was embarking upon an enormous adventure. It was as if he had been sailing in a small, protected harbor in Washington; now, he suddenly found himself tossed on the open sea where the
waves, wind—everything—was larger and wilder.

For the past ten months, he had tracked the candidate's progress on a
map in the Senate office. Dick had been briefed about the people's reactions to the senator's speeches and provided with stacks of information
that catered to his shifting audiences throughout the primaries. To date,
however, most of his knowledge about the candidate had been gleaned
from impressions and observations of others—newspapers and magazines,
office chatter, conversations with reporters.

Now that he was scheduled to join Kennedy every day, he would be
able to make his own observations. If the earlier pace in Washington had

seemed frantic and burdensome, it was now total immersion. Food and sleep were, of course, necessary, but secondary. There was no outside life.

The "Caroline," christened for Kennedy's daughter, was a Convair 240, the first private plane used by a presidential candidate during a campaign. With meticulous care, it had been modified into a luxurious flying executive office, complete with desk, typewriter, filing cabinet, mimeograph, and small kitchen. There were several plush couches and four chairs that could be converted into small beds for Ted and Dick, the two-man speechwriting team. Dave Powers, Kennedy's longtime friend and companion, and Kenny O'Donnell, master of advance scheduling and logistics, occupied the other two chair/beds. The far corner was the domain of Pierre Salinger and members of the traveling press corps. Kennedy, captain of this crew, had his own suite of bedrooms further aft on the plane.

If Ted and Dick worked like a tag team, writing speeches to order in the field, Robert Kennedy commandeered the entire campaign organization from back in Washington. The whole apparatus was a far cry from the cottage industry Dick had found upon entering the Senate Office Building the year before. The campaign included a research staff, a team of academics, a financial team, and advance men in every state—all sending information both to headquarters in Washington, and to the staff on the "Caroline." Consequently, the plane itself was no more the entire campaign than an orbiting spaceship was independent of Mission Control.

"You were all so young," I marveled to Dick after looking up the ages of the team. "The candidate was forty-three; Bobby Kennedy and Pierre Salinger, thirty-five; Ted Sorensen and brother-in-law Steve Smith, thirty-two; and you—"

"Twenty-eight," he interrupted with a trace of vanity, "youngest of the lot."

Following the campaign's official opening on September 7 at Cadillac Square in Detroit, the "Caroline" headed west to Idaho and Oregon. During rare moments of downtime, some played cards while others worked in silence or napped. Sorensen would often diagram his drafts on yellow legal pads as Dick pecked away on his portable typewriter.

Early on in the campaign, Dick recalled for me a game they would play, a contest to see who could name the most presidential slogans from previous campaigns. "Vote yourself a farm" Dick volunteered from Lincoln's 1860 campaign, and someone said, "Stop showing off, Goodwin!" "Keep

cool with Coolidge," someone else called out. "Stand Pat with McKin-
ley," another offered. On and on they went, rapid-fire: TR's "Square Deal,"
FDR's "New Deal," "Return to Normalcy with Harding," Truman's "Fair
Deal," Stevenson's "New America," "Get on a Raft with Taft."

"That would have been hazardous," I interjected, laughing, "considering
Taft's three hundred pounds!"

"We were in the midst of this game of wits and historical recall," Dick
continued, "when we became aware that the senator himself had paused in
the aisle, leaning forward on the back of a chair, eavesdropping in amusement. All of a sudden, he said, 'You know, there's something to your game.
Republicans are always calling for a return to normalcy, contentment, the
status quo. And we're always pushing forward with our square deals and
new deals and fair Americas. But don't let me interrupt you.' That our game
had set something in motion in Kennedy's mind would become clear several days later."

SEPTEMBER 9, 1960

That occasion was an address Kennedy was to deliver—one on which
Dick had worked with special care—on September 9 at the Shrine Auditorium in Los Angeles. It would be Kennedy's first major speech devoted
to civil rights in the national campaign. Here was an opportunity to imagine what Kennedy might do as president. We found the draft Dick had
prepared along with a transcript of the speech the candidate had actually delivered. Dick's draft reiterated the progressive conception of the
presidency that had been spelled out in the January speech but was now
applied to civil rights.

An overflow crowd of seven thousand people jammed the Shrine Auditorium that evening. Three thousand more were turned away. No longer
was Kennedy searching out an audience as during those solitary days at the
start of the primaries. Clearly, people were now searching out the candidate. "It was by all odds," one reporter noted, "the biggest and most enthusiastic indoor crowd he has drawn on his current political swing."

Dick remembered pacing nervously in the back of the room as Kennedy walked toward the podium. He was eager to gauge the reception to
the speech he had drafted. The crowd was on its feet chanting "We Want
Jack" for three minutes as Kennedy smiled happily from the podium. Their

enthusiasm infected the candidate. This was a more relaxed and animated John Kennedy than Dick had seen before. He opened with a rare personal comment. "First, I would like to have you meet—well, my wife is home having a baby." The crowd burst into laughter and the senator actually seemed to be enjoying himself. Dick said he could feel encouragement well up from the crowd: "Kennedy stoked their zeal with his off-the-cuff riff, building on the game of political slogans our team had played on those long flights."

"You can tell in this country, by contrasting the slogans of the two parties, what the two parties stand for. McKinley, 'Stand Pat with McKinley'; 'Retain normalcy with Warren G. Harding.'" The laughter began to rise and spread. "'Keep cool with Coolidge,'" he added. "Had enough?" he asked the crowd. "The weakest slogans in the history of American politics."

"For the moment, I was so rapt with his remarks," Dick told me, "I almost forgot my draft." One after another, the proud and active slogans of the Democratic Party were recited to a crescendo of applause: "A New Freedom," "A New Deal," "A Fair Deal," all leading to "A New Frontier" for the United States. (The phrase "New Frontier" had first appeared in a draft Sorensen wrote for Kennedy's acceptance speech.)

The spell cast by the candidate's improvisation and utilization of the slogans to illustrate a sharp divide that would help define the coming campaign worked so well that Dick was no longer apprehensive when Kennedy, at long last, retrieved the speech on civil rights from his pocket.

Kennedy promised to fight for civil rights with all the powers of the presidency, "as legislative leader, as Chief Executive, and as the center of moral power of the United States." As legislative leader he would fight for the bills necessary to ensure every American's constitutional rights. As chief executive, he would be prepared to end racial discrimination in every arena of federal activity. He then specifically pledged that he would issue "an Executive Order putting an end to racial discrimination in federally subsidized and supported housing."

Finally, Kennedy promised he would use the bully pulpit to educate the country about "the great moral issues" involved in civil rights.

Dick remembered the singular excitement he felt when he heard the housing pledge and the reference to educating the country on "the great moral issues." But it was not long before Kennedy pocketed Dick's speech, and returned to his extemporaneous performance, which pumped up the energy of the crowd. He never reached Dick's favorite line, "If the President does not himself wage the struggle for equal rights—if he stands above the battle—then the battle will be inevitably lost." Kennedy concluded with the wish that future historians would look back at the present moment and say, "There were the great years of the American life, the 1960s. Give me those years." The crowd erupted in a deafening standing ovation. To Dick, it seemed bizarre that once again Kennedy spoke as if he were looking back on things to come.

Buoyed by the rapture unleashed in the auditorium, the senator shot Dick a smile and a compliment later that evening: "Nice speech, Dick."

"Both of them," Dick acknowledged, knowing full well that the substance of his speech had been drowned out by the virtuoso improvisation that so gratified the Democratic audience.

Reviews the next day spoke of Kennedy's remarkable, rousing ability to improvise, contrasting it to his more restrained and undemonstrative performance when closely adhering to the text. "So much for my speech!" Dick said as we read the reviews. The whole occasion, he admitted, had left him conflicted—entranced and exhilarated, yet somehow disappointed.

Three months later, after the election had been won, President-elect Kennedy asked Dick to compile a list of the specific promises, vows, and pledges he had made during the campaign. We found that complete list in Dick's archive—eighty-one promises in all—including three explicit proposals for medical care for the aged, federal aid for education, and an overhaul of immigration laws.

"Not one of these passed during the Kennedy administration," I reflexively pointed out to Dick. "And every one of them became law under Lyndon Johnson."

Before an argument had time to flare up, however, there it was on the list before us: Promise #52. Kennedy's pledge to put an end to discrimination in federal housing by signing an executive order. And in an added flourish, later in the campaign he had pledged immediate action on the order by "one stroke of the pen."

"Who the hell wrote that," a nettled Kennedy had asked as he went over the list with Ted and Dick. "I didn't," Sorensen readily offered.

Dick told me he never had less desire to take credit for something he had written than at that moment. He stayed quiet. "Well, then," Kennedy said, "I guess nobody wrote it."

——— ·•·• ———

Some couples plan an evening together so they can stream the latest series or watch a major sporting event. When Dick and I reached the box containing materials related to the four 1960 debates between Kennedy and Nixon, we decided to have what Dick called "a debate date." We settled in front of Dick's computer with a bottle of wine, and watched the first debate that had taken place in Chicago more than a half century earlier on September 26, 1960.

To prepare for our "date," I had combed through Dick's debate box. There were pages torn from a yellow pad upon which Kennedy had scrawled requests for clarification or new information. I skimmed reams of material and statistics organized by subject. I knew from Dick's earlier comments and accounts offered by Sorensen and Mike Feldman (the head of research), who had flown in from Washington to assist, what lengths this trio had gone to prepare in the days before the debate. Anticipated questions had been reduced to one hundred. A stack of 5 x 8 index cards summarized, in single sentences, both candidates' positions on every conceivable issue, along with suggested rejoinders to Nixon's likely charges. The candidate committed to memory statistics and numbers to support his arguments concerning every domestic subject. Facts, it was hoped, would give him a mature heft, control, and authority.

I asked Dick to explain how some of these various items found in the box had come into his possession. As the junior member of the team, Dick had been designated the "pack mule," charged wherever they traveled with dragging a heavy nylon suitcase and a Sears footlocker that contained a library of memos, drafts, newspaper clippings, magazine articles, and whatever research materials the team might find necessary. The suitcase was packed with the fabled "Nixopedia," a compilation of every statement Nixon had made on taxes, civil rights, education, domestic policy, and foreign affairs. This assemblage of statements, misstatements, and deceptions had been indexed in an oversized black binder.

"Imagine," Dick said, raising his wineglass to toast the cell phone on the small table beside us, "I could have slipped all the contents of that suitcase and the footlocker into my jacket pocket if I'd had YOU in those days."

"We hardly slept the night before," Dick remarked. "Sorensen was working on an opening statement. Mike Feldman and I had arranged and rearranged the stack of index cards, checked and rechecked the facts."

SEPTEMBER 26, 1960

On the morning of the debate, as the trio approached the candidate's suite at the Ambassador East, Dick was apprehensive—as if the most important exam of his life loomed ahead. Had they done everything they could to prepare Kennedy for what they all knew could well be the hinge of the entire campaign?

"How did Kennedy strike you that morning?" I asked Dick.

"Calm, almost eerily so," Dick said, recalling him propped up in bed in a T-shirt and khakis, barefoot, his breakfast tray still beside him. To conserve his voice, Kennedy spoke as little as possible, writing out questions on a yellow pad, things he wanted checked or confirmed. Sorensen showed him the draft of the opening statement he had prepared, but it was not to Kennedy's liking; he felt it was too ornate for television, and wanted the sentences short, crisp, and straightforward.

Then Kennedy began to review the stack of index cards, stopping every now and then to suggest a shorter answer or ask for clarification. One after another, he would flip through the cards as if playing a game of solitaire. Once each card had been committed to memory, he would flip it away, until the carpet beside the bed was strewn with index cards.

In the early afternoon, when the team had taken a break to gather more supporting data, Dick realized that he'd left his yellow pad full of scrawled questions on the table in the room adjoining Kennedy's bedroom. When he returned to retrieve it, he saw—to his amazement—that on this day of all pressurized days, the candidate had retired for a nap! Unlike the candidate's aides, who had reached the point of near total exhaustion, Kennedy understood the importance of pacing himself, of relaxing and replenishing his energy.

Dick very quietly gathered up the pages and swiftly took his leave to get ready for one final session, after which Kennedy would have a light meal, put on his dark suit, and head to the CBS studio.

Reportedly, Richard Nixon spent most of the day in seclusion at the Pick-Congress Hotel, accompanied only by his wife, Pat. A seeming contrast might be drawn between the two candidates in the degree of preparation, organization, and forethought they invested in an event that would forever alter the course of modern presidential politics. Seventy million people would be watching the debate, two thirds of all the adults in the United States.

———•·•———

"Are you nervous?" Dick asked, smiling and patting the back of my hand as we were about to start watching the debate. "Who do you think will win?"

"I want to hear what you think as we go along," I said.

"Oh, so now you want a running commentary? At the movies you always tell me to keep quiet." Dick's tendency to burst forth with witticisms in the middle of movies invariably embarrassed me. Somehow he had never learned how to whisper.

After CBS anchor Howard K. Smith introduced the candidates, I immediately noticed Kennedy's dark suit, sharply defined against the gray backdrop, in contrast with Nixon's gray suit, indistinct against the gray background. Kennedy's composed posture, hands quietly folded in his lap, one leg crossing the other, similarly contrasted with Nixon's body language, painfully ill at ease, lips pursed, eyes shifting, legs splayed awkwardly beneath his chair.

"It's not fair!" I blurted. "It's a debate, not a beauty contest."

"What does fair have to do with it?" Dick retorted.

Unable to watch with an impartial eye even after five or six decades, Dick relished the contrast: "It's like *Twenty-One* with JFK as glamorous Charlie Van Doren and Nixon as poor Herbie Stempel. A leading man versus a character actor."

John Kennedy's eight-minute opening statement, improved and reshaped from Sorensen's earlier draft that morning, declared his resolve that we must do better at home in order to strengthen our leadership abroad. With statistics absorbed from the campaign and sharpened during the days of rehearsal, he presented a quick survey of steel and power production, education, farming, as well as a comparison between the productivity of scientists and engineers in the Soviet Union and the United States. All suggested that we had become stagnant and were in danger of falling behind. With his staccato delivery punctuating a drumbeat of facts and figures, he unfolded a narrative of dissatisfaction with our domestic policy that, if we did not get moving, boded ill for our stature in the world at large.

For me, the most persuasive moment of the debate occurred when Kennedy deployed statistics to illustrate how the lack of equal opportunity affects the trajectory of Black lives from the moment they are born: "I'm not satisfied until every American enjoys his full constitutional rights. If a Negro baby is born—and this is true also of Puerto Ricans and Mexicans in some of our cities—he has about one-half as much chance to get through high school as a white baby. He has one-third as much chance to get through college as a white student. He has about a third as much chance to be a professional man, about half as much chance to own a house. He has about four times as much chance that he'll be out of work in his life as the white baby. I think we can do better." To this narrative Nixon made no comment.

From the start of his own opening statement, the vice president was on the defensive, eager, as his running mate Henry Cabot Lodge had cautioned him during the one phone call he had taken that afternoon, to avoid "an assassin image." Again and again, he agreed with Kennedy's ultimate goals; their differences, the conciliatory "new Nixon" said, were not in the destination but in the means to get there.

Long before our bottle of wine was gone, I began to feel a slight sympathy for Richard Nixon, his effort to gamely smile while sweat glistened on his chin in the harsh television light.

"Close your eyes," Dick chuckled. "Don't watch. Make believe it's radio. He'll improve."

And it was true—as commentators had noted at the time. If one listened on the radio, the debaters seemed more or less equal. Richard Nixon had counterpunched, making his debating points and arguments capably to answer Kennedy's assertions.

The more striking impression on television, however, belonged to Kennedy. He seemed to ignore Nixon altogether, making his case directly to the people on the other side of the camera. Watching the two men side by side, the contention that Vice President Nixon was the more seasoned and mature candidate, possessed of greater authority and capacity to lead, had vanished before the first debate was over.

Dick loved to tell the story of his ebullience following that first debate. As they settled on the "Caroline" that night, bound for a day of campaigning in northern Ohio, Kennedy relaxed with his favorite meal: a bowl of tomato soup and a beer. He then proceeded to evaluate the entire debate, reviewing where he might improve and what he might amend. To Dick, it all seemed too muted. Unable to restrain his enthusiasm, he exclaimed, "We've got it won now! Not just the debate but the election!" Kennedy smiled, finished his beer, and said, "Next week, Cold War and foreign policy. Better get some sleep and get ready." Dick told me he learned something important that night. Kennedy was a veteran sailor, a professional. Regardless of circumstances, he kept steady and stable, on an even keel.

Yet without question, something decisive and positive had happened for Kennedy during the debate, something that could be seen, felt, and heard in Ohio the next morning. The crowds hadn't merely doubled, they had quadrupled, as had the intensity, excitement, energy, and high-pitched screams. Those millions of television sets that had been tuned in to the debate the night before had given birth to a political celebrity of the first order.

As the YouTube video ended, and our "debate date" was drawing to a close, my mind wandered back to the Lincoln-Douglas debates, each of which had lasted three or four hours, through hot afternoon sun or torch-lit nights, while the debaters fleshed out their positions, explored complexities, and called on history to amuse and entertain the enormous crowds who were not simply spectators but participants, regularly and often loudly voicing their own opinions. "Hit 'em again, harder, harder" was a common chant. When someone in the crowd yelled to Lincoln that he was two-faced, he drew roars of laughter, the story is told, when he responded: "If I had two faces, do you think I'd be wearing this face?"

"Both Kennedy and Nixon were stiff, wary," I said to Dick, "neither had an amusing or reflective moment."

"For good reason," countered Dick. "A TV debate is not exactly a format for levity, complexity, or reflection. Time is short, stakes are enormous. A single, serious mistake could prove fatal to months of campaigning. Style, of necessity, towers over substance."

OCTOBER 1960

After midnight on October 14, 1960, the "Caroline" landed at Willow Run Airport in Ypsilanti, Michigan. Three weeks remained until Election Day. The daily toll of exertions, the level of fatigue, had begun to show. Everyone was bone-tired as the caravan set out for Ann Arbor and the University of Michigan.

The previous evening, the candidates had faced off in a third debate, their faces three thousand miles apart but brought together through the novel magic of the split screen—Nixon in California, Kennedy in New York. Across the continent, they hammered at one another in what many would consider Nixon's best performance of the debates.

As Kennedy headed from New York to Michigan in early morning darkness to arrive at the college campus, there was little to suggest that one of the most memorable and enduring moments of the entire campaign—a signature expression of his future administration—was about to be ignited.

It was nearing 2 a.m. by the time the cars and buses reached the Michigan Union, where Kennedy was scheduled to catch a few hours of sleep before starting on a morning whistle-stop tour of the state. No one with the campaign had expected to find upwards of ten thousand students waiting in the streets to greet the candidate. Neither Ted nor Dick had prepared remarks for the occasion. Flourishing placards and signs of support, the crowd chanted Kennedy's name as he stepped from his car and headed up the stone steps to the Union.

As Kennedy ascended those steps, Dick distinctly remembered making a hasty exit to the cafeteria with Ted Sorensen. "We missed the whole thing. We were famished. At the very moment that Kennedy proposed the Peace Corps, I was eating a piece of lemon meringue pie."

Kennedy began with good-natured flattery, referring to himself as "a graduate of the Michigan of the East, Harvard University." He then fell back on his familiar argument that the 1960 campaign presaged the outcome of the race between communism and the free world. But suddenly, he caught a second wind, and swerved from his stock stump speech that was shot through with pledges and promises of what *he* would deliver as president. Instead, he asked the gathered young people what *they* might be willing to contribute for the country:

How many of you, who are going to be doctors, are willing to spend your days in Ghana? Technicians or engineers, how many of you are willing to work in the Foreign Service and spend your lives traveling around the world? On your willingness to do that, not merely to serve one or two years in the service, but on your willingness to contribute part of your life to this country, I think will depend the answer—whether a free society can compete.

What stirred John Kennedy to these spontaneously formulated questions is not clear. Weariness, intuition, or, most likely I suspect, because it was the last thing in his mind from the debate that had taken place only hours before—whether America's prestige in the world was rising or falling relative to the communist nations. The concept of students volunteering for public service in Africa and Asia might bolster goodwill for America as these third-world countries (as Kennedy had characterized them in the debate) wavered "on the razor edge of decision" between the free world and the communist system.

As he drew "the longest short speech," as he called it, to a close, Kennedy candidly confessed that he had come to the Union that cold and early morning simply to go to bed. This drew raucous laughter and applause that continued to mount when he threw down a final challenge: "Let me say in conclusion, this University is not maintained by its alumni, or by the state, merely to help its graduates have an economic advantage in the life struggle. There is certainly *a greater purpose*, and I'm sure you recognize it."

When prospective students tour the University of Michigan today, there is a bronze plaque at the entrance of the Michigan Union: "Here at 2:00 a.m. on October 14, 1960, John Fitzgerald Kennedy first defined the Peace Corps. He stood at the place marked by the medallion and was cheered by a large and enthusiastic student audience for the Hope and Promise his idea gave the world."

Kennedy's remarks had lasted only three minutes. Yet something extraordinary transpired: The students took up the challenge he posed. They organized, they held meetings, they sent letters and telegrams to the campaign asking Kennedy to develop plans for a volunteer Peace Corps. They signed petitions pledging to give not two but *three* years of their lives to help people in developing countries. There is a direct line between their actions and the altered speech Kennedy would deliver several weeks later in San Francisco, where he formally proposed a Peace Corps.

The Peace Corps "might still be just an idea," Sargent Shriver, the first Peace Corps director, later recalled, "but for the affirmative response of those Michigan students and faculty.... Without a strong popular response [Kennedy] would have concluded the idea was impractical or premature. That probably would have ended it then and there. Instead, it was almost a case of spontaneous combustion."

During the last week of the campaign, Dick met with two Michigan graduate students—a married couple, Alan and Judith Guskin—who had lodged in his memory because they were leaders of both the letter-writing campaign and the petition drive. As I began reflecting on this period of Dick's experience with the Kennedy campaign, these former student activists provided the critical entrance into the Peace Corps story that had been missing for me: the perspective of the students themselves.

Locating the Guskins in California and Florida, now in their eighties (no longer married but still friends), made it possible for me to tell a more intimate story than the standard narrative of "the Great Man" proposing a Peace Corps that was consequently realized. If ever an event illustrates the meaning of the term "grassroots"—how a spark can ignite an enthusiasm that will change hundreds of thousands of lives and literally encircle the world—such an event happened that night.

Both Alan and Judy were in the process of writing memoirs. Both have led lives built on their commitment to help others. And both look on October 14, 1960, as the night that changed their lives. Judy recalls that it transformed her from a graduate student into a citizen armed with a greater purpose than just a degree and a job. I asked them to tell me about the mood of the crowd as they waited for Kennedy's delayed arrival. Alan described a noisy, good-natured gathering, buoyed by intermittent announcements over the loudspeaker, explaining that although bad weather had hindered the candidate he was headed their way.

Judy explained that there was a 10 p.m. curfew for female students at the time, which the dean of women imposed (*in loco parentis*) with an iron fist. If she caught female students out beyond this curfew, or kissing in public, she would call their parents. But on this night, the dean had a problem. Despite the curfew, women made up half the crowd. There was no way for the dean to enforce the despised lock-up rule once the women had assembled there. Consequently, every half hour an announcement was made, extending the women's curfew an additional half hour.

"The campus was alive," Alan recalled. "They called us the Silent Generation, but there were stirrings within us. Many of us had just listened to the third Kennedy-Nixon debate. A spirit of activism had been building for months." The seminal event that had jolted the students' participation, Alan believed, was the burgeoning Civil Rights Movement. He spoke, in particular, of the sit-ins that had spread throughout the South the previous semester after four black college students in Greensboro, North Carolina, refused to leave a Woolworth's lunch counter that had denied them service. That spring, Alan and Judy had marched and demonstrated in front of their local Woolworth's in solidarity with the sit-in movement in the South.

"The energy was there," Judy stressed. "JFK came to the *right* campus at the *right* time."

In the days that followed, students took Kennedy's questions to heart. For Alan and Judy, however, discussion crystallized into action when Connecticut congressman and former ambassador to India Chester Bowles came to UM to speak on Kennedy's behalf. After a student inquired about Kennedy's challenge, Bowles mentioned that his own son and daughter-in-law were currently helping to build a school in Nigeria. "A light bulb went off in my head," Alan said. "This was something concrete, something real. I turned to a fellow student and asked: 'Would you be willing to do something like this?' The emphatic response was YES!"

Alan and Judy went to a late-night restaurant after Bowles's talk. Then and there, they drafted a letter to the campus paper, *The Michigan Daily*, calling for students to write to the Kennedy campaign in support of a program that would allow young people to serve abroad. The *Daily*'s editor at the time was Tom Hayden, already a committed activist, who, two years afterward, would draft the Port Huron Statement—the foundation for Students for a Democratic Society (SDS).

Hayden published Alan and Judy's call for action, and continued to publicize their every initiative in the days and weeks that followed. With the help of the *Daily*, the idea of a petition drive (where each student would pledge to serve overseas for two or three years of their lives) caught fire. A group of faculty members came aboard, allowing the petition to circulate in classrooms. Within a week, a thousand signatures had been gathered.

The next link in the chain was the Michigan director of the Kennedy campaign, Mildred Jeffrey. Millie was "a force of nature," Alan remembered. A leader in the labor movement, she would march with Martin Luther King Jr. and become a founding member of the National Women's Political Caucus. It was this veteran activist who brought the students' efforts to the attention of Ted and Dick. Dick told me that he had no sooner heard from Millie that these students were willing to volunteer a significant portion of their lives for public service, than straightaway he knew that this was no flash in the pan. They were deadly in earnest.

Dick worked with Sorensen to redraft an upcoming speech on foreign

policy to be delivered at the Cow Palace in San Francisco to include a formal proposal for "a peace corps of talented young men and women, willing
and able to serve their country in this fashion for three years." The speech
noted that the nation was "full of young people eager to serve," specifically
mentioning the commitment made by the UM students.

Dick's hand can be readily detected in the closing lines, which used a
favorite quote of his from the Greek philosopher Archimedes. "Give me
a fulcrum," Archimedes said, "and I will move the world." Dick would
later invoke the same line of Archimedes in the historic speech he drafted
for Robert Kennedy to give in South Africa. He used it often in his own
speeches; in fact, he quoted it so often in conversation that I began to imagine Archimedes as one of Dick's friends.

The day Kennedy delivered the Cow Palace speech, Millie Jeffrey
called the Guskins' apartment. When Judy answered, Millie told her that
Kennedy was flying from San Francisco to Toledo, and would like to meet
with them and see their petitions. "Could you repeat that?" Judy asked,
stunned.

The Guskins borrowed a car and drove to Toledo. "We waited on the tarmac for the 'Caroline' to land," Judy recalled. "The senator got off the plane
with Ted Sorensen and Richard Goodwin and they came over to the small
group of us. Millie introduced us. And I had the honor of handing the senator the petitions." A photographer from *The Michigan Daily* captured the
moment when an eager Judy, her shining hair pulled back in a ponytail,
clutched the sheaf of petitions before presenting them to the weary-eyed
candidate, who is holding his outstretched fingers to receive her offering of
proof. That photograph now resides in the Kennedy Library and Museum
in Boston.

"I remember his intensity," Judy recalled. "The way he listened." These
were words I had heard almost verbatim from many people in different
places. With a smile, Kennedy assured Judy that he understood from Millie
he couldn't keep the petitions. They were the originals and the students
needed them for organizing. But Kennedy wanted to hold them, to look
over the ranks of their names. Their earnestness and conviction brought
the reality of the proposal home.

"Are you really serious about the Peace Corps?" Alan asked.

"Until Tuesday [Election Day], we'll worry about this nation," Kennedy
nodded, "after Tuesday, the world."

Once Kennedy had departed the airport to deliver a speech on the American economy in downtown Toledo, Dick and Ted accompanied Judy and Alan for coffee. They talked of the Peace Corps and the upcoming election, then only five days away. Nixon had immediately denounced the idea of a Peace Corps, "a Kiddie Corps," he called it, warning that it would become a haven for draft dodgers.

For both Judy and Alan, as for so many others, the Peace Corps would prove a transformative experience. The Guskins were in the first group to travel to Thailand, where they spent two of "the best years" of their lives. Judy taught English and organized a teacher training program at Chulalong-korn University in Bangkok; Alan set up a new program at the same school in psychology and educational research.

"The values of the Peace Corps stayed with us the rest of our lives," Alan said. "We learned respect for our own ground and respect for the ground of others with different cultures, religions, and languages," Judy added. When they returned home, they served as founders of the VISTA program, LBJ's domestic Peace Corps, and worked with the poverty program before completing their doctoral studies at UM. Alan went on to become a faculty member at the University of Michigan and later a senior administrator at several universities, including the president of Antioch, while Judy became a professor, as well as an educational consultant for school districts on issues relating to racial equality and refugee education.

For Dick, the Peace Corps, more than any other program of the Kennedy years, represented the essence of the New Frontier. After the inauguration, he would join the task force that created the Peace Corps program, using his position on the White House staff to help launch the organization. He was barely older than the typical volunteer. He, too, shared the common desire to find a greater meaning and purpose in life. It was not surprising to me that when Dick's work in the White House later came to an abrupt and dispiriting end, he would find a home working with Sargent Shriver at the Peace Corps.

OCTOBER 1960

Curiously, Dick was able to offer little assistance when I tried to get a sense of what it was like inside the campaign during those final weeks before Election Day. He hardly had any distinct memories at all. "Depleted, nerve-worn, excited," he said. "So exhausted from stress and lack of sleep, the whole thing gave way to a dream state. We were leery of standing still, we wanted to stay aggressive, but we were fearful of making mistakes."

When I found Kennedy's itinerary and speaking schedule for the final weeks of the campaign, I was filled with amazement. No wonder Dick's memory was a blur. In the space of six days (beginning with his impromptu remarks on the steps of the Michigan Union at 2 a.m. on the morning of Friday, October 14, until his remarks at a Democratic dinner in New York the following Thursday, October 20), he delivered forty-three speeches: eleven in Michigan, after four hours of sleep, six in Pennsylvania the next day, three on a zigzag route from New Jersey to Delaware to Maryland on Sunday, six in Ohio on Monday, five in Florida on Tuesday, and twelve more in New York on Wednesday and Thursday.

Of necessity, the candidate relied heavily on repetition, shuffling a handful of speeches that shifted from criticism of the Republican Party to the historic importance of the present election, from economic stagnation at home, to the decline of American prestige abroad. Yet he also managed to deliver new policy addresses on ethics in government, Latin American affairs, and national defense.

The pressure was ratcheted up on the Sorensen-Goodwin speechwriting team as never before. They had spent the past two months in total campaign immersion, living and working beside one another. And what a team they formed!

On the evening of Sunday, October 16, at 6 p.m., after marathon days in Michigan, Pennsylvania, New Jersey, Delaware, and Maryland, Kennedy was scheduled to appear on *Meet the Press*. That afternoon, Dick had worked on preparing the questions for the show, while Ted was drafting the speech on ethics in government to be delivered in Wittenberg, Ohio, the next day. Ted traveled with Kennedy to Wittenberg while Dick stayed in the hotel in Middletown, Ohio, drafting the Latin American speech for Tampa, Florida. That evening, on the plane to Florida, Ted began working on the national defense speech for Miami while Dick went over the Latin American speech with Kennedy. When they arrived in Miami at 2 a.m., the speech on national defense was not yet finished.

The best description of the exertion, skill, and passion this tandem team demonstrated is found in Theodore White's account of their nonstop, pedal-to-the-metal sprint to the finish:

They decided to work in shifts. Goodwin went to bed while Sorensen labored with a secretary until 5 A.M. When Sorensen went to bed at five, his secretary woke Goodwin after his three hours of sleep, to give him the Sorensen draft. Goodwin worked on that draft until eight, when he woke the Senator to present it to him. But now the Senator wanted substantial changes—to include nonmilitary aspects of the cold war as well as the purely military. At 8:30 Goodwin began the last draft, pushing his sheets to the mimeograph machine as he wrote.

. . . So, during the morning, as the candidate barnstormed and spoke at supermarkets and crossroads, the speech writers once more rearranged his words and ideas. Goodwin hailed a taxi when they had finished and sped out to intercept the campaign caravan and present the candidate with a finished text of his ideas on national defense; he intercepted the candidate at a toll gate on the Miami causeway, where he flagged the campaign caravan to a halt, delivering the final version to the candidate forty-five minutes before he was to adopt it as the defense posture of the next President of the United States. Then the two ideologues could take a cat nap; but that afternoon, as Kennedy delivered their Latin America speech at Tampa, they were up again, preparing quips and jokes to be used at the Alfred E. Smith Dinner in New York the following evening.

Out of this punch-drunk cloud, Dick remembered only one episode with any clarity because it was so unpleasant and because he was the cause of what James Reston in *The New York Times* called Kennedy's "worst major blunder of the campaign."

OCTOBER 20, 1960

Late in the evening on October 20, at the staff headquarters of New York's Biltmore Hotel, Dick was hammering away on an anti-Castro statement for Kennedy to release the following morning. At first glance, the statement seemed similar to dozens that Kennedy had made during the campaign. It was a call for collective action against the new communist regime in Cuba.

It was then Dick ran afoul of his own rhetorical fluency. He wrote: "We must attempt to strengthen the anti-Castro forces in exile, and in Cuba

itself, who offer eventual hope of overthrowing Castro. Thus far these fighters for freedom have had virtually no support from our Government."

In the normal chain of campaign protocol, the statement would have
been shown to Kennedy before release. Dick called Kennedy's room at
the Carlyle to read it to him but was told he was already asleep. If ever the
candidate needed sleep, it was that night; the next day was his fourth and
final debate with Nixon, to be focused on foreign policy. If the statement
was going to make the morning papers, it had to be released at once. After
showing it to Sorensen, Dick let it go—the only public statement during
the entire campaign Kennedy had not personally approved. Sorensen later
called the uncleared statement simply "a vague generalization thrown in to
pad out an anti-Castro program." That's not, however, how it was perceived
at the time. It was the phrase *fighters for freedom* that stuck in the craw.

Little did Dick know at the time that the Eisenhower administration
was secretly training a covert force of freedom fighter exiles in a scheme
that would one day become known to the world as the Bay of Pigs. While
Nixon was fully aware of these secret plans, he chose in the course of the
debate to excoriate Kennedy's statement as "shocking," characterizing it as
a dangerous proposal that risked World War III.

The next day, the newspapers echoed Nixon's assault on JFK. "Such a
statement by a man who may become president is reckless and indefen-
sible," observed *The Pittsburgh Press*, arguing that, "It seems another case
of 'shooting from the hip'—an unfortunate quality in a man who aspires
to be president." And *The Arizona Republic* advised the senator to "consult
his college textbooks on international relations before making any more
foreign statements."

Kennedy was forced to issue a clarification. He never intended to dishonor any treaty obligations. He had intended to signal only "moral and
psychological support, not military or political support." Nearing the finish
line of the campaign, with nerves frayed on all sides, it was a bad time for
clarifications.

This period was one of the few times, Dick told me, that he had seen
Kennedy openly peeved. Public outbursts of emotion or anger, yelling or
screaming, were not his style. But Kennedy's only reproach to Sorensen
and Dick came in the form of irony: "If I win this thing, I won it," he told
them, "but if I lose it, you guys lost it."

I often wondered what drove Dick and the core team around Kennedy to such exorbitant efforts and loyalties. Even in his eighties, Dick found no simple answer. "Excitement," he said one day, and after hesitating, "a sense of shared purpose, idealism, and of course personal ambition." Then, after another thoughtful pause, he said, "I realize now I had a young man's hero worship for the man himself . . . I guess it boils down to a kind of love."

NOVEMBER 8, 1960

John Fitzgerald Kennedy was elected president on November 8, 1960, by the smallest margin in the twentieth century. He won the popular vote by only 118,574 votes of the over 68 million cast.

For more than half a century, historians have debated what tipped the balance of the election to give Kennedy his razor-thin victory. In an election this close, any reason sufficed, and reasons abounded. Some, noting the surge that Eisenhower's entry into the race produced toward the close of the campaign, have speculated that Nixon would have won if the president had lent his genial and grandfatherly glow to his vice president's bid earlier on. Others have pointed to the selection of LBJ (bringing aboard Texas and six additional southern states), the impact of the televised debates, the listless economy. Still others credit Kennedy's phone call to assist Martin Luther King Jr.'s release from prison.

Yet when all was said and done, Kennedy had worked longer and harder than Nixon. He had built the superior campaign, powered by a fierce core of believers.

In the weeks following the election, Republicans pressed claims of voting irregularities and provided anecdotal evidence they believed suggested fraud. Recounts were held in a few places, but those efforts were short-lived. The rancor died down and a peaceful transition was initiated.

After the election, Kennedy's first announcement was his selection of Ted Sorensen as special counsel. This was the key post held by Colonel Edward House under Woodrow Wilson, and Harry Hopkins under FDR, and Dick felt that no one was more deserving than Sorensen. Sorensen would be the president's "principal adviser on domestic policy and programs, his source of ideas, his draftsman of speeches, and messages."

But when Sorensen announced that Dick, along with Mike Feldman and campaign adviser Lee White, would come into the White House as his assistants, Dick balked. He wanted to be involved not just in talking about policy, but in making it. He didn't want to continue writing speeches for Ted Sorensen in a job that would be little more than a continuation of the campaign. He did not then foresee that language and policy were often part and parcel of the same action, like two logs that can make a fire.

Dick began to seek out other opportunities within the administration. When his search came to the president-elect's attention, Kennedy called Dick into his office. "I hear you don't want to work in the White House," Kennedy said. Dick explained that he didn't want to work under Ted and that he knew Ted was far more valuable than he was, so he thought he'd try something else. "You know how we do things," Kennedy said in his customary cryptic manner. "I think you better stay on here for a while."

Not by coincidence, from then on Dick received assignments directly from President Kennedy, and the three staffers were given the title assistant special counsel rather than assistant to the special counsel.

That small change signaled a large difference in titles. "It was a question of belief and power to get something done," Dick told me, "proximity to power to make beliefs come true."

Sorensen never forgave Dick. He considered it an ungrateful transgression. Their relationship would never again be as close as it had been. Ted believed he had plucked Dick up and made him who he was. Early in the campaign, he had relayed a conversation to Dick that he'd had with Steve Smith, Kennedy's brother-in law. "I told him how remarkably you had managed to master our way of doing things." What had first seemed a compliment quickly swerved into something else: "I added that any bright man given the same kind of direct, personal instruction would have done the same thing." Dick had searched Ted's face for a glint of humor, but none was to be found.

Four years later, when Dick was comfortably settled in the White House as LBJ's chief speechwriter and policy adviser, he wrote to Sorensen:

> *I have been saddened by reports which have come to me from extraordinary sources [most certainly LBJ himself] of some of the critical comments you have made of me. I made many, almost fatal mistakes when I first came to government. I like to think they sprang more from inexperience,*

*lack of knowledge and naivete, than from opportunism. In any event I have
learned much, and painfully.*

*At the close of the 1960 campaign, I felt very close to you. Admiration is
far too restrained a word to express my feelings. We had worked and traveled
and lived and exchanged confidences together. In an unjustified romanticism—
which I have since given up—I thought this meant something in terms of real
friendship. I remember few things more vividly than trying to call you the
morning after the election, not getting through, and not seeing you for a few
days . . . I know this was pretty callow and innocent stuff, but it was there.*

*As you know, JFK asked me to stay . . . and history took its difficult and
maturing course for me.*

I have always been sorry about what happened.

JANUARY 9, 1961

Kennedy's first speech as president-elect was scheduled for the Boston State
House eleven days before his Washington inauguration. Since Sorensen
was at work on the inaugural, Kennedy tasked Dick to begin drafting the
Boston speech. By this point, having come through the primaries and the
election, Dick had learned, he told me, to decipher Kennedy's manner of
giving directives, however indirect or roundabout:

"I was always fond of Lincoln's goodbye to his fellow townsmen in
Springfield, Illinois," Kennedy had remarked. "It's from his heart, and it's
short. That's important."

"But Dick," he concluded with a nod and a smile, "less God."

Dick set to work reading and rereading Lincoln's adieu until he had com-
mitted it to memory. In the decades that followed, he would often recite
Lincoln's "Farewell Address," along with choice passages from Shakespeare,
Robert Service's "The Cremation of Sam McGee," Emerson's "Concord
Hymn" with its "shot heard round the world," "Casey at the Bat," Edward
Lear's "The Owl and the Pussycat," and countless others. Whenever he
saw fit, Dick would draw from his wide and eclectic repertoire and declaim
in his sonorous voice—whether at the ballpark, on walks with me, at our
favorite bar, or simply waking up in our bedroom to greet the day.

"My friends," Lincoln had begun, speaking from the train platform as he
set forth on his twelve-day journey to Washington,

No one, not in my situation, can appreciate my feeling of sadness at this parting. To this place, and the kindness of these people, I owe everything. Here I have lived a quarter of a century, and have passed from a young to an old man. Here my children have been born, and one is buried. I now leave, not knowing, when, or whether ever, I may return, with a task before me greater than that which rested upon Washington. Without the assistance of that Divine Being, who ever attended him, I cannot succeed. With that assistance I cannot fail.

Arthur Schlesinger had forwarded a memo to Kennedy suggesting an excerpt from John Winthrop's sermon to his shipmates on the flagship *Arbella* as they landed in New England, facing the challenge of creating a new government on a new frontier. "For we must consider that we shall be as a city upon a hill. The eyes of all people are upon us." These words, the "city upon a hill," first delivered more than three centuries before, is how John Kennedy's farewell to Massachusetts would be remembered in history.

It was an emotional speech to write. If it was a nostalgic farewell for Kennedy, it was a trip down memory lane for Dick as well. Massachusetts was Dick's home, the place where he was born, the place he went to college and law school, the place where his mother and brother still lived. It was with his state representative from Brookline, Sumner Kaplan, that Dick had battled for rent control and waged a fight to investigate discriminatory practices in sororities and fraternities on college campuses. Kennedy had often joked with Dick that they were two Brookline boys. Both had deep emotional investments in Massachusetts.

The night before his address to the State House, Kennedy slept in his old apartment on Bowdoin Street, the place Dick had first met him during the spring of 1958 and had prompted him to tell his friend George Cuomo that working with Kennedy "no matter how interesting, is bound to be a sort of dead end for one so young."

"I bet it didn't seem such a dead end that morning of January 9," I remarked.

"Anything but," Dick said. "I had changed a lot in those last two years and so had he."

Despite the bitter cold morning, loud hurrahs and screams of hundreds of people greeted Kennedy as he emerged from his apartment at 10 a.m. before crossing the Charles River to attend a meeting of the Harvard Board of Overseers. There, an equally enthusiastic crowd trailed him through Harvard Yard. "Speech, speech," they cried. Grinning as he climbed the steps to University Hall, Kennedy jested, "I am here to go over your grades with President Nathan Pusey, and I'll protect your interests." That touched off an explosion of applause. After lunch with the overseers, Kennedy spent the afternoon at Arthur Schlesinger's house, where he met with a small group of professors.

He then returned to the great domed Bulfinch building for his address to the joint session of the legislature. Following ancient tradition, two sergeants at arms—in frock coats and top hats, carrying white and gold maces—were granted permission from the presiding officer to admit the president-elect. He had briefly addressed this body only once fifteen years before, as a decorated Navy hero, accompanied by his grandfather and former Boston mayor John Francis Fitzgerald.

The president-elect was in "a nostalgic mood" as he began his speech. "For fourteen years I have placed my confidence in the citizens of Massachusetts. . . . For forty-three years—whether I was in London, Washington, the South Pacific or elsewhere—this has been my home; and God willing, wherever I serve shall remain my home. It was here my grandparents were born—it is here I hope my grandchildren will be born."

On the draft of the speech, Kennedy had made several annotations, crossing out and inserting new words. Those small changes revealed a huge shift in perspective. They delineate an astute distinction between the days before the election and the day after. No longer was he placing his confidence in the *voters*, as the draft had read, but rather in the *citizens*. He was not asking for votes. There were no sides now. We were all working together.

This tribute from a native son produced tumultuous applause in the packed chamber. His delivery barely resembled the clipped voice from the early primaries, and his leisurely pace was no longer that of the candidate who had raced through his talks as if he were a nervous young student speaking before the class. This was the president-elect returning to his home state, channeling Abraham Lincoln, promising that as he created his new administration, he would be guided by John Winthrop's recognition that "we shall be as a city upon a hill—the eyes of all people are upon us."

And then he turned to the future, to the hope that when "the high court of history" came to sit in judgment of his administration, it would note that he had surrounded himself with men of "courage, judgment, integrity, and dedication."

"These are the qualities which, with God's help, this son of Massachusetts hopes will characterize our government's conduct in the four stormy years that lie ahead," Kennedy concluded. "I ask for your help and your prayers, as I embark on this new and solemn journey."

Abraham Lincoln never came back to live in Springfield. Nor would John Fitzgerald Kennedy return to reside in Boston.

CHAPTER FOUR

A Pandora's Box of Cigars

*President Kennedy with Secretary of State Dean Rusk and Dick
in front of the U.S. Army helicopter that landed on the South Lawn
of the White House. February 1, 1962.*

JANUARY 20, 1961

Jackie Kennedy's distinctive handwriting, a large, looping, and decorative cursive, was immediately recognizable on a manila envelope tucked into a box labeled "JFK, Inauguration, 1961." Inside the file were tickets to the inauguration, inaugural guidebooks, inaugural ball tickets, inaugural programs, *Life*'s inaugural special, as well as relevant newspapers clippings and lanyards with picture IDs—Dick had saved every scrap.

Jackie, too, had saved memorabilia, including Dick's talking points for a speech Kennedy had delivered in Anchorage, Alaska, on September 3, 1960, at the very start of the presidential campaign. Five years later, she had sent these notes back to Dick as a fond remembrance.

On a large envelope containing the various talking points, Jackie had written a covering note:

It shows his [JFK's] first use of the phrase that later in his Inaugural
address became "Ask not what your country can do for you; ask what you can
do for your country."

For Dick Goodwin who was there—as he was always—for all the things
that mattered most to President Kennedy and to me.

In that Alaska speech, Kennedy had declared that the New Frontier did
not suggest a geographical boundary line, but rather, a spirit of mind that had
built the country, a people who did not ask for things to be done for them,
but wanted to take action themselves. "This is the call of the New Frontier. It
is not what I promise *I* will do; it is what I ask *you* to join me in doing."

Manila envelope in hand, I raced into Dick's study. If a single line were
to be culled from Kennedy's classic inaugural address, it was the iconic "ask
not" line—this reversal of the typical list of politicians' promises, this call
for public service that presented a core challenge to a new generation that
would crystallize the activist spirit of the Sixties. And here, Jackie was suggesting that its origin could be traced to Dick.

Dick read Jackie's words silently and with obvious emotion, a smile on
his face.

"I wish I could take credit," Dick said, "but Jackie sent this as a shared
memento between close friends, not as a historian. The line, its meaning,
and the challenge it conveyed were already in the air. Something similar
was in Kennedy's acceptance speech at the convention the previous July."

I looked up the acceptance speech. Dick was right. Speaking of the
New Frontier, Kennedy had said: "It sums up not what I intend to offer the
American people, but what I intend to ask of them." By the time of the inaugural, such statements had been refined and recast from prose to a ringing
oratorical poetry.

As I went to return the manila envelope and talking points to the inaugural box, my eye focused again on Jackie's last line: "For Dick Goodwin
who was there—as he was always—for all the things that mattered most to
President Kennedy and to me."

I was well aware that Jackie and Dick had become cherished friends, but
there was something about holding this beautifully handwritten note that
spurred a series of questions in my mind that would only build in the months
ahead as other letters from Jackie would surface in the archive, revealing a
more vulnerable and intellectual confidante than I had previously realized.

After a night of blizzard and frantic snow-clearing, a glittering sky of arctic wind buffeted John Fitzgerald Kennedy as he stood to deliver his inaugural address. "Bone-chilling," Dick remembered, "but, in keeping with the New Frontier heroics of my new president, I wore no hat, had no scarf, no lap blanket. I watched from a few rows behind the podium, frozen solid!"

I had not read the speech in its entirety since I taught the undergraduate American Presidency course at Harvard in the late Sixties and early Seventies. Studying it more than a half a century later, I savored its brevity and rhetorical style, burnished bright as the day of its delivery.

What had inspired me when I was young and had stayed indelibly impressed upon me was the clarion call: "Let the word go forth from this time and place to friend and foe alike, that the torch has been passed to a new generation of Americans," and the ringing "ask not" exhortation to civic duty at the end.

Until this rereading, I had forgotten that the speech had focused almost entirely on the Cold War and foreign affairs, with hardly a mention of domestic issues, and no specific reference to the civil rights struggle at home—the issue that would have a defining impact on the decade to come. For me and for multitudes across the country, the content was obscured by John Kennedy's strikingly dramatic and thrilling mode of delivery.

Once the speech concluded, dignitaries (Dick among them) settled into their seats in the presidential viewing stand in front of the White House to watch the parade.

"You know how I love a parade," Dick said, "but this was different, this was three frigid hours of misery." The procession included 41 floats, 275 horses, 72 marching bands, and 32,000 marchers. While Dick clearly recalled a cowboy in buckskins riding an enormous American bison and President Kennedy's fellow veterans waving from a replica of *PT-109* (the patrol torpedo boat Kennedy had served on in the Pacific during World War II), the stream of various military academies and school bands that proceeded to march along Pennsylvania Avenue seemed to Dick to fuse into a never-ending and indistinguishable train.

When the parade mercifully came to an end, Dick paid his first visit to the small, second-floor office assigned him in the West Wing. Over the years, Dick had told the story of this first eventful visit to the White House many times, and because of what that encounter came to symbolize, it eventually entered dozens of historical accounts of Kennedy's inauguration day.

After surveying his office and walking downstairs to the corridor leading toward the Oval Office, Dick had happened upon the new president inspecting his own quarters.

"Dick." Kennedy gestured him over.

"Mr. President," Dick replied, addressing him as such for the first time.

"Did you see the Coast Guard detachment?"

"The Coast Guard detachment?" Dick repeated, only admitting long afterward, "I didn't know one detachment from another and was so cold I couldn't pay attention even if I had known."

"There wasn't a Black face in the entire group," Kennedy continued without waiting for an answer. "That's not acceptable. Something has to be done about it." Dick understood that this interchange concealed an order.

"Kennedy's response," I said, "seems sudden, surprising. How do you interpret it?"

"It was simply that Kennedy found it intolerable that there wasn't a Black face to be seen. Of course, he was aware of the political statement a snow-white Coast Guard made to the world, but it wasn't just because it looked bad. On a personal level, he found it objectionable."

So this became Dick's first assignment. Like a thunderclap, he understood that the time for promises had passed, and the time for command had begun. But who ran the Coast Guard anyway, he wondered, as he hustled back to his office. The Pentagon? No—it was the Treasury. Picking up his White House phone, he asked the operator to connect him with Secretary of Treasury Douglas Dillon, who promised to get right on it.

Acting swiftly, Dillon ordered Coast Guard officials to analyze the Coast Guard Academy's recruitment policies with an eye toward identifying any discriminatory practices. A memo to Dick on January 25 confirmed that there were currently no Black cadets in the Academy.

Indeed, the statistics revealed that in the entire history of the Coast Guard, not a single Black cadet had ever graduated from the Academy. The lone Black man who had been appointed to the Academy years earlier had withdrawn for health reasons. While Coast Guard officials claimed that there was "no distinction made on the basis of race, creed or color," facts suggested otherwise.

A flurry of memos from the White House "lit a real fire" under the

Coast Guard, setting in motion a search to find and fill the burdensome role of barrier breaker. The following year, an appointment to the Academy was offered to a young black man, Merle Smith Jr.

When Merle Smith died at the age of seventy-six, his classmates posted an open letter acknowledging the weight he carried: "*We* arrived with trepidation and concern, not sure what lay ahead. *You* must have felt the heightened sense of concern, or even fear, as a young African-American male entering a military institution where no one of your race or ethnicity had ever successfully completed the four years to become a commissioned Coast Guard officer."

Hearing this sentiment, I couldn't help but recall Justice Ruth Bader Ginsberg's well-known commentary on the pressures of her experience as a trailblazer. "I did feel in law school," Justice Ginsberg remembered, "that if I flubbed I would be bringing down my entire sex. That you weren't just failing for yourself."

When I had fallen under the spell of Jackie Robinson at six years old, I never considered the immense pressures he was under. I simply thrilled to see his headlong style, sheer energy, and abandon as he tore around the bases—fidgeting off each base, annoying and distracting pitchers, riveting the crowd. And I thanked God he was on my Brooklyn Dodgers. Not until much later did I realize how much withheld fury must have been released on that baseball diamond.

Reflection on the great personal and symbolic weight of trailblazers drew my curiosity to the story of Merle Smith Jr.

Newspaper accounts at the time of Smith's death from Parkinson's disease (linked to Agent Orange exposure in Vietnam) recounted a storied career, an ascending stairway of firsts: the first Black cadet to graduate from the Coast Guard Academy, the first Black commander of patrol boats in combat, the first Black sea officer to receive a Bronze Star, the first Black law professor at the Academy. How had he handled the pressure of his many pioneering roles?

Every account of his career illustrated an unflappable demeanor, quiet strength, and humility. Still, I suspected, bearing the burden of repeatedly being the first person of color in so many professional arenas must have taken its toll.

I reached out to Smith's widow, Dr. Lynda Smith, a family therapist who now lives in New London, Connecticut, home to the Coast Guard

Academy. We talked for hours about her husband's life, his career, their forty-seven-year marriage, their children, and his death.

What soon became evident to me was that Merle Smith's trailblazing journey was not a solitary one. It was decidedly a family affair and a family challenge. "Merle had lived under a microscope his whole life," Lynda explained. "His father had been drafted into the army where he had stayed, rising to the rank of colonel. The family was often the first Black family at various posts—in Germany, Japan, and Maryland. There wasn't much Merle hadn't faced previously."

I could see from the stories I read that it also helped that Merle was a star football player and an outstanding student in high school. He was offered appointments at all four military academies. He chose the Coast Guard because he had personally been recruited by the coach, Otto Graham, a legendary Hall of Fame quarterback who had played for the Cleveland Browns.

When I asked Lynda whether Merle had experienced discrimination at the Academy, she said there had been unpleasant incidents—including a veiled threat of violence—but it was soon understood that the football team had his back. She recalled another occasion when the team bus had stopped at a restaurant, and the waitress had taken orders from every team member except Merle. "I can't take your order," she said. "We don't serve Black people." The entire team stood up and marched out.

Lynda had been an undergraduate at George Washington planning to get her doctorate in clinical psychology when she met Merle at a party for Black law students. After Merle had returned from Vietnam, the Coast Guard sent him to George Washington Law School. This was the late Sixties. Most of the students at the party sported big Afros, she recalled. Merle presented a strikingly different appearance with his navy-blue pea coat, striped pants, and military-style cropped hair. "I was drawn to him," Lynda said. "We started to talk. I knew that night I wanted to marry him and I did."

Merle and Lynda moved to rural Connecticut when he was offered a position teaching law at the Coast Guard Academy. They were the only Black couple in the small town where they first lived. "There was one Black lawyer, Merle, one Black dentist nearby, and one Black psychologist, me. I felt isolated at first. I had loved D.C. and had left behind a host of Black friends. But Merle had found a second home at the Academy and I eventually adjusted."

After the Smiths had grown into a family of four, they settled in Old Saybrook, a small town of less than ten thousand, a picture-postcard New England community not unlike my own Concord. Once again, they were the only Black family. "When our son turned fifteen," Lynda told me, "he announced he wanted to go to boarding school. He didn't want to be the only Black kid in the class. We wanted to keep him in the nest we built. He held his ground, and in the end, we sent both kids to boarding schools known for their diversity. It was through the lives of our children more than ourselves that I became keenly aware that our special status of being the only Blacks in the town was a form of systemic discrimination."

If the family had paid a personal price for Merle's trailblazing role, both Merle and his wife had lived powerfully influential lives. Lynda had forged a distinguished career as a psychologist and Merle had served as a beloved teacher and mentor to hundreds of students. Manson Brown, the first African American to achieve the rank of vice admiral in the Coast Guard, was in Smith's international law class. "I just remember being struck by this image of a Black officer," Brown said, "one of the few I'd ever seen, quite frankly." Smith's example provided Brown with a vision of what his own future might look like—as it did for so many of the Black cadets at the Academy. Lynda remembered a dinner where each of the Black cadets stood up one at a time to say: "Because of you, Commander Smith, we are here."

Today, Smith's story is one of the inspirational stories told at the National Museum of African American History and Culture. "It meant so much to my husband," Lynda explained, "to see his own dress blue jacket on display along with a photograph from graduation day in 1966, when he received his commission from his father, the Army colonel who had been his mentor and role model all his life."

The Coast Guard has surely come a long way since that inaugural day in 1961, when a spontaneous instruction by a newly installed president had set in motion a string of events that would reach far into the future.

Yet even back then, Dick recalled, "an atmospheric change was clear to everyone." There were great expectations surrounding the matters of civil rights, "high apple pie in the sky hopes," as Frank Sinatra had sung during the campaign. And these expectations were set forth in a series of essays written by Martin Luther King Jr. for *The Nation*.

"The new Administration," King wrote during the first weeks of Kennedy's tenure, "has the opportunity to be the first in one hundred years of

American history to adopt a radically new approach to the question of Civil Rights." King proceeded to argue that "a primary goal" should be "an examination of its own operations and the development of a rigorous program to wipe out immediately every vestige of federal support and sponsorship of discrimination."

And beyond the stream of memos regarding the Coast Guard, the new White House ordered an urgent overview of the state of Black employment in all federal agencies. The resulting numbers gleaned from this survey were appalling. Of the 3,674 foreign service officers then serving, only 15 were Black, and of the 950 attorneys in the Justice Department, only 10 were Black.

Consequently, what emerged during these early months was the recognition and acknowledgment of an across-the-board discrimination throughout the federal government as well as a determination to remedy it. By the end of Kennedy's first year, Martin Luther King noted, it had become clear that "vigorous young men have displayed a certain elan in the attention they give to civil rights. Kennedy has appointed more Negroes to key government posts than any previous Administration."

"In those early months," Dick reiterated to me, "it seemed that with a White House telephone, we could change the world!"

––––––·•·––––––

In a stuffed box labeled "JFK 1961 Memos and Speeches," my eye fell upon a folder that read: "Areas of Responsibility of the Counsellors." There, under Dick's name, four primary areas were listed: "Foreign Affairs," "Latin America," "Foreign Aid," and "Civil Rights." The focus on foreign policy seemed odd, since most of Dick's former work had concerned domestic issues.

I knew that Dick had played a central role in creating the Alliance for Progress, a signature initiative of Kennedy's foreign policy—a $20 billion program aimed at promoting democracy and social justice in Latin America. I realized that the Alliance had been patterned on the Marshall Plan, which provided billions of dollars in American aid to rebuild Western European economies after World War II. But how Dick had actually transitioned from domestic concerns and civil rights to this massive Latin America policy initiative continued to mystify me.

It had started by happenstance, Dick explained, beginning the improbable account of his wild rise during the first year of the Kennedy administration.

During the fall campaign, while Sorensen was preoccupied with a speech to a convocation of Houston area ministers regarding the still unsettled tension of Kennedy's Catholicism, Dick had been tasked with drafting a speech on Latin America. The communist takeover in Cuba had sent shock waves of unrest and discontent through Latin American countries. While the propertied, wealthy few and top echelons of the military reaped the benefits of economic growth, the great majority remained in desperate poverty. Kennedy sought to express a fundamental break with America's support for Latin America's dictatorial regimes simply as a matter of anticommunist policy, placing the United States on the side of both social and economic reform.

"We were on a bus rolling through West Texas while I was working on the draft," Dick recollected to me. "I thought we needed a name to dramatize our ideas for a new policy. On the empty seat beside me was a magazine in Spanish with the title *Alianza*. I liked the idea of an Alliance, but an Alliance for what? Alliance for development?—sounded promising, but the Spanish word *desarrollo* was not easy to pronounce, especially for Kennedy, who had a hard time vocalizing foreign languages. So I settled on *Progreso*, and the name Alliance for Progress was born."

I shook my head with amazement. "It still dumbfounds me how a twenty-nine-year-old who had never set foot south of the border, and whose knowledge of Spanish came from a crash Berlitz course, became Kennedy's point man on Latin America."

"Bobby Kennedy was asked a similar question," Dick laughed. He rifled through a stack of letters we had found in his papers, and pulled out Bobby's rejoinder to an irate Robert Kaplan, a large Kennedy campaign contributor. Bobby had suggested that Kaplan seek Dick's counsel on a matter pertaining to Latin America.

"Young Dick Goodwin is less than half my age," Kaplan's response began. "Would it not make sense for him to seek a visit to me?"

"I can believe he is only half your age," came Robert Kennedy's attached reply, "however, I can assure you the President has great confidence and trust in him. Young as he may be, he is the one who happens to have the responsibility at the White House at this time . . . I am sure he would be delighted to see you."

"Great confidence and trust are understandable," I said, "what I have trouble comprehending is how you became the one 'who happens to have the responsibility at the White House at this time.' That can't be simple happenstance."

"Believe me," said Dick, "I nursed that happenstance along as hard as I could. None of this could happen today. The White House staff was so much smaller, less specialized."

During the transition, Dick's primary job had been to help set up a series of task forces on a broad range of issues. Aside from the tensions in Berlin, Latin America was then the new administration's most critical foreign policy issue. With a mixture of calculation, ambition, and an appreciation of the president-elect's foreign policy priorities, Dick had inserted himself into the Latin America task force.

There, he developed a close relationship with the task force chairman, Adolf Berle. Here was a formidable figure, a man who had been a member of Franklin Roosevelt's fabled Brain Trust—and, more importantly, had been involved with FDR's "Good Neighbor" policy, the last progressive attempt to improve U.S. relationships with Latin America and a vague precursor to the Alliance for Progress.

"I liked Berle immediately," Dick recalled. "We were birds of a feather. He was candid, irreverent. We were both mavericks." The other members included economists and public servants with extensive experience in Latin American affairs. While Dick's qualifications were minimal compared to others on the task force, he possessed two compelling credentials: He had a major hand in selecting the other members, and he had a direct channel to the president-elect.

In late January, Kennedy asked Dick if he could prepare a major speech in a month's time that would introduce plans for the Alliance for Progress. "We already have your campaign statements," Dick replied, "and the task force has done a helluva job. It's just a matter of putting it all together. If we can get everyone to agree."

"I don't care if everyone agrees," Kennedy replied sharply. "You know what our thinking is. That's the only agreement you need—with me."

"I was thrilled," Dick told me. "Kennedy had used a similar phrase—you know how we do things—when he made clear that he wanted me to remain in the White House. Now, I felt he had given me a mandate to quash the State Department's entrenched tendency to placate dictators in the name of anticommunism, and instead set forth a genuinely progressive attempt to turn the page and improve U.S. relations with Latin American countries."

In the weeks that followed, Dick convened a series of meetings in the White House Fish Room (so named because it had once housed FDR's aquarium and fishing mementos). Task force members committed to change sat side by side with State Department skeptics and representatives of government agencies with any responsibility for Latin America. The objective now was to distill a one-hundred-page report into a thirty-minute declaration of an Alliance for Progress, the first major foreign policy initiative of the new administration. During this period, Dick recalled, he conversed with Kennedy nearly every day.

The Fish Room meetings intensified as the presidential speech drew near. After all the consultations, meetings, and contributions, drafting the speech was ultimately left to Dick. Arthur Schlesinger Jr., who had joined the White House staff as a special assistant with a wide-ranging portfolio (including Latin American affairs), recalled Dick sitting at his office desk almost completely barricaded by piles of memos, reports, articles, and books as he gamely continued developing the speech despite constant interruptions from White House aides and State Department officials, all pleading for last-minute insertions.

Two days before the speech was scheduled to be delivered, Dick withdrew from the cacophony, retreating to his Georgetown home where he somehow managed to compress weeks of an intensive education into an address that captured essentials of America's past, present, and future policy toward Latin America.

"Good Job!" Kennedy exclaimed after carefully reviewing the draft for several hours, penciling in changes. "But," he added, pointing to a series of Spanish phrases Dick had sprinkled through the text, "do I really have to say these words?" Dick explained that the task force members strongly felt it a sign of respect to the Latin community.

"Do you know any Spanish?" Kennedy asked Dick. "Not much," Dick acknowledged. "Well, I don't know any," Kennedy replied.

So there they were, two Brookline boys who had worked together on a speech to Wisconsin dairy farmers despite having never touched a cow, practicing how to pronounce words in a language with which neither was truly familiar.

MARCH 13, 1961

On the evening of March 13, the speech was unveiled in the East Room of the White House before members of the Latin American diplomatic corps and their wives, along with a bipartisan group of congressional leaders, all seated in gilt chairs arranged in a semicircle flanking the podium. To underscore the importance of the event, the president and first lady had held a reception beforehand in the Red and Blue Rooms, escorting guests on a tour of the White House. Jackie looked dazzling that night, Dick remembered, easily charming diplomats with her perfect Spanish.

The speech opened with revolutionary hero Simón Bolívar's dream that the Americas would one day become "the greatest region in the world," not because of its size or wealth, but because of its freedom.

The president acknowledged that the United States had made grave mistakes in its relationship with Latin America, but insisted that the time had come to move into a future "bright with hope." He summoned all the countries of Latin America to join with the United States in a ten-year social and economic program "of towering dimensions." Kennedy spoke "to the men and women of the Americas—to the *campesino* in the fields, to the *obrero* in the cities, to the *estudiante* in the schools." In closing, he exhorted:

Let us once again transform the American continent into a vast crucible of revolutionary ideas and efforts—a tribute to the power of the creative energies of free men and women—an example to all the world that liberty and progress walk hand in hand.

As I finished reading Dick's speech, I felt a swelling of pride in this not yet thirty-year-old. This clear braiding of history, poetry, policy, and idealism sounded a signature note that marked the best Goodwin speeches in the years that followed. That night, Kennedy's glamour, the rhetorical delivery, and the substance of the striking and hopeful message all combined to mesmerize the 250 members of the audience.

The crowd erupted in applause that did not stop until Kennedy stepped from the dais to mingle with the diplomats. Dick was exhilarated, not simply because the speech had been a triumph, but because he believed America would keep the promises made that night, thereby lessening the suffering of millions of people.

As Kennedy worked his way through the Latin American diplomatic corps, he was told again and again that his speech was *magnífico*, just the leadership statement they needed and wanted. Before he left, he paused by Dick and whispered: "How was my Spanish?"

"Perfect," Dick said.

"I thought you'd say that," Kennedy laughed, placing a hand on Dick's shoulder.

One of the most beguiling aspects of Kennedy's temperament, Dick told me, was his refusal to be swept away by accolades when things went well, and his ability to maintain his balance and wit when things fell apart. Yet that night, Kennedy seemed positively effusive.

The very next morning, however, he told Dick: "All right, that's the easy part. I made a speech. Now let's show we mean it."

So began the complicated planning process for a hemispheric conference to officially launch the Alliance for Progress. As a first step, Dick arranged to go to Rio de Janeiro in early April to work with a group of leading Latin American economists to prepare an agenda for the conference, scheduled to take place sometime that summer. Little could Dick have imagined that plans for the Alliance would hit a massive land mine in the weeks ahead—a land mine of the administration's own making.

APRIL 17, 1961

On the morning of April 17, 1961, an invasion force of 1,400 Cuban exiles, covertly trained by the CIA, landed at the Bay of Pigs. It was presumed that the Cuban people en masse would regard the landing force as liberators, and respond by sparking an insurrection that would lead to Fidel Castro's removal. The invasion was a total disaster. Castro's army quickly overwhelmed the landing force with artillery fire. More than a hundred brigade members were killed, and 1,200 were captured. The invasion was over in just three days. There was no uprising of the Cuban people.

As we sorted through the boxes, there were moments every now and then when I suddenly realized that I was holding the original raw materials from events I had taught long ago in my presidency course. Each year, my syllabus included a lecture on the Bay of Pigs and the Cuban Missile Crisis; I analyzed the lessons Kennedy had learned from the train of gross miscalculations during the Bay of Pigs that had contributed to his successful resolution of the Cuban Missile Crisis.

My interest now was far more personal than academic. I wanted to find out how much Dick knew about the invasion plan before it was launched and whether he witnessed Kennedy's reaction when it was over. Although not a participant in the cabinet meetings where the decision was made (neither was Sorensen or Bobby Kennedy), Dick was aware of the plan and had multiple conversations concerning it with Arthur Schlesinger. Fourteen years older than Dick, a man of broad intelligence and humor, Schlesinger would become a lifelong ally and friend to Dick. Along with a love of good food, wine, and a sense of mischief and wit, they shared a profound devotion to history and literature.

On the very day Dick was scheduled to leave for Rio, he and Schlesinger had shared their misgivings about the invasion during breakfast at the White House. They both questioned the assumption that the Cuban people would rise up in support of the small invading force. Dick was worried that the plan would derail the Alliance and mark as hypocritical Kennedy's claim that he desired a fundamental break with the past. Two days earlier, Schlesinger had written a long memo opposing the plan. He had argued that the "bullying intervention" would undermine the United States' moral authority as well as Kennedy's reputation. But Schlesinger's arguments had gained little traction.

Dick and Arthur decided to make one more attempt to halt the drift toward invasion. They each went to see Secretary of State Dean Rusk to express their doubts. Rusk listened to them and seemed to share their concerns. "You know," Rusk said, "maybe we've been oversold on the fact that we can't say no to this thing." Dick would retain a lifelong contempt for Rusk's bureaucratic ambidexterity, appearing to argue simultaneously for opposite sides of a controversial issue.

By the time Dick returned from Rio, the final decision to proceed with the invasion had been made. "When I went into the Oval Office to report on my meetings with the Latin economists, Kennedy walked me over to the French doors that overlooked the Rose Garden. 'Well, Dick,' he said in a voice that was almost a whisper, 'it looks like we're finally going to put your Cuban policy into action.'

"I understood, of course," Dick explained to me, "that he was needling me for my troublesome 'freedom fighter' statement during the campaign, now supposedly heeded and set in motion!"

I asked Dick to describe the atmosphere in the White House during the days after the failed invasion. Dick remembered a despondent mood. Kennedy kept to his daily schedule, but looked haggard, as if he had scarcely slept.

I knew from reading an interview Jackie gave after her husband's death that in the immediate aftermath of the Bay of Pigs catastrophe, Kennedy had retreated from his office to his bedroom. "He started to cry, just with me," Jackie recalled. "Just put his head in his hands and sort of wept . . . all their hopes high and promises that we'd back them, and there they were, shot down like dogs or going to die in jail."

"How did I ever let it happen," Kennedy repeatedly asked when talking with staff. "How could I have been so stupid? I know better than to listen to experts. They always have their own agenda. All my life I've known it, and yet I still barreled ahead."

Dick remembered the moment he became aware that Kennedy had regained his balance—during an early breakfast meeting on April 21 that was set to prepare the president for his first press conference after the aborted invasion. Dick attended that breakfast, along with Sorensen, Schlesinger, Salinger, and a few others. The papers had been full of speculations, recriminations, accusations. Was it the CIA, the Joint Chiefs, the State Department? Kennedy made it clear from the start of the meeting that there would be no search for scapegoats. He was responsible.

Kennedy understood, he said, that "the happiest people in government today are the ones who can say they didn't know anything about it." He then turned to Schlesinger and said: "Oh sure, Arthur wrote me a memo that will look pretty good when he gets around to writing his book on my administration. And I have a title for the book—*Kennedy: The Only Year*! Only he better not publish that memorandum while I'm still alive."

During the press conference later that morning, Kennedy was ready for the question about conflicting stories of blame. "I'm the responsible officer of the Government," he said with emphasis. "There's an old saying that victory has a hundred fathers and defeat is an orphan."

A president must take responsibility. This was what the American people wanted and this was what Kennedy delivered. His approval rating rose to an astounding 83 percent. "The worse I do," Kennedy shrugged, "the more popular I get."

Equanimity restored, Kennedy turned with even greater resolve to the fledgling Alliance for Progress. "Let's get moving on the Alliance," he directed Dick, "before they think I didn't mean it, that all we care about is Castro."

Dick reported that they were indeed moving ahead, had agreed upon an agenda during the Rio meetings, and had scheduled a conference at the beginning of August in Uruguay for all Latin American countries.

"I wish it could start tomorrow," Kennedy said wistfully.

AUGUST 1961

Three months later, on August 2, 1961, the thirty-three-member U.S. delegation boarded a presidential jet headed for Uruguay's seaside resort city Punta del Este. There, they would be joined by delegations from every Latin American country—including Cuba, which was represented by Castro's right-hand man and minister of finance, Che Guevara, who would attend as an observer rather than a participant.

The night before the conference was set to begin, Dick met with a small group of American delegates in the hotel suite of Treasury Secretary Douglas Dillon, head of the U.S. delegation. The time for rhetoric and abstract goals, Dick argued, had come to an end. No price tag had been attached to Kennedy's speech on March 13. The U.S. had to make a substantial financial commitment to meet their specific pledges for land distribution and tax reform. "We're asking them to make a very difficult effort," Dick said, "and all we're giving them is words."

Dillon listened carefully to the discussion and then summarily announced that he would make an immediate pledge of $1 billion. Veteran State Department official Ed Martin strenuously objected, contending that Dillon did not have the authority, that such a pledge hadn't been cleared with Secretary Rusk. "Of course I have the authority," Dillon countered, "and I'm going to give them a billion dollars." At the opening session the next day, Dillon went even further, pledging that if the Latin American countries truly committed themselves to land and tax reform, the U.S. would provide $20 billion over the next ten years.

Even with Dillon's financial pledge, however, several of the delegations initially resisted making commitments to specific reforms. Dick was ever in motion, like a bee gathering nectar from one delegation to the next—cajoling, explaining, and threatening that without specific pledges of reform there would be no Alliance.

The comprehensive, progressive agreement Dick had envisioned from the start—which combined economic development on the scale of the

Marshall Plan with social and economic reform—was finally hammered out on the last day of the conference. Signed by all twenty countries (except Cuba), the Charter of Punta del Este established the constitution for the Alliance for Progress.

Flush with the accomplishment of this historic charter, Dick could little have imagined that a spontaneous decision to meet with Che Guevara at 2 a.m. that very night would, like a slow-acting poison, prove calamitous to his White House tenure, and perhaps even injurious to the Alliance itself.

While Dick had written about this meeting with Che Guevara over the years, I felt he had hardly confronted his unresolved bitterness over its aftermath. So more than half a century later, after immersing myself in Dick's writings and interviews, I coaxed him to tell me about the emotional toll the incident had taken. Through our conversations, I came to understand the full context of a letter he had written to Sorensen acknowledging "almost fatal mistakes" that sprang from "inexperience, lack of knowledge, and naivety."

Like the fabled tale of Pandora, it all began with the opening of a box— this time, a polished mahogany box filled with cigars: "the best cigars in the entire world," Dick said, with a sorrowful sense of humor.

During the working sessions of the conference, Che Guevara had apparently spotted Dick in a diplomat's dark suit, busily smoking one inferior cigar after another. Only three years older than Dick and dressed in pressed fatigues and a black beret, Guevara had taken measure of Kennedy's young aide. At the same time, Dick had been carefully watching the charismatic revolutionary.

In his hotel room the next day, Dick received the telltale cigar box with a colorful Cuban seal. On the outside was an enigmatic note in Spanish: "Since I have no greeting card, I have to write. Since to write to an enemy is difficult, I limit myself to extending my hand."

"It took great restraint not to open the cigar box and sample one then and there, but I was a trusty aide," Dick jested, "so I decided to surrender it intact to my president."

An intermediary told Dick that Guevara would like to meet with him. Dick checked with Dillon, who initially saw no harm in a casual discussion until Che mustered a parting blast at the Alliance, claiming it was doomed to failure, "for one cannot expect the privileged to make a revolution against themselves." Dillon summarily withdrew his blessing for the prospective meeting.

That was where things stood when the delegation returned to Montevideo to prepare for their flight back to Washington the next day.

"That last night, I was simply going to a late-night dinner party in Montevideo with some of the delegates," Dick told me. "I was hoodwinked. Che had been told I was there, and long after midnight he appeared, flanked by bodyguards. I could have left. In hindsight, I should have left."

"But you didn't," I said.

"What would you have done?" Dick asked.

I momentarily weighed diplomatic protocol against posters of Che, a smoldering icon who had adorned the walls of our graduate school dorm. "I wouldn't have left," I answered at last, "but why did you take the risk?"

"Curiosity, my ambition, his charisma. I never considered the price I'd pay for what turned out to be a four-hour tête-a-tête."

Dick told Che at the start that he had no authority to negotiate anything but that he would report what was said to Kennedy. Che said "good," and the two commenced their marathon conversation.

AUGUST 19, 1961

On August 19, the president welcomed the returning delegation with a ceremony on the White House lawn. He believed, he said, that the conference was "the most important" foreign policy event that had occurred during his administration to date. "You carried with you our best hopes and you have come back with our fondest expectations."

After the ceremony, Dick went into the White House with the president to brief him on the conference. First, he handed over to Kennedy the unopened box of Cohibas that Che had gifted him. Kennedy opened it immediately, put a fistful of cigars in his desk drawer, filled his jacket pocket with others, clipped off the tip of one and carefully lit it up.

"You should have smoked the first one!" he muttered to Dick as he sucked in smoke and examined the colorful Cuban seal on the box's lid. "It's too late now," Dick responded. Kennedy stopped for a moment but then joyfully resumed smoking.

Dick told me they both agreed that the box was not exactly appropriate for the Oval Office desk. So, after taking a handful of the cigars, Kennedy handed Dick the box to keep as a souvenir. And for more than fifty years, the box adorned a shelf in Dick's study.

Kennedy was intrigued by the story of Dick's unplanned meeting with Guevara. "Write up a complete account," he told him. On reading Dick's extensive secret memo, its language seemed to me closer to a novella than an official government memo. It opens with a descriptive portrait of Comandante Ernesto Che Guevara: "Che was wearing green fatigues, and his usual overgrown and scraggly beard. Behind the beard his features are quite soft, almost feminine, and his manner is intense."

Two diplomats were present acting as interpreters. "He has a good sense of humor, and there was considerable joking back and forth during the meeting. He seemed very ill at ease when we began to talk, but soon became relaxed and spoke freely. Although he left no doubt of his personal and intense devotion to communism, his conversation was free of propaganda and bombast."

Guevara began, Dick reported, by stating that the U.S. must understand that the Cuban revolution was irreversible and that it was a mistake to assume that a regime which maintained the strong support of the masses could be overthrown from within. But he then frankly acknowledged that Cuba faced serious economic difficulties.

Though Guevara understood that negotiations between the two countries were not feasible at the time, he felt that perhaps an interim *modus vivendi* around a number of sticking points could be reached: Though the expropriated properties could not be returned, they could be paid for in trade. Cuba would agree not to make any political alliance with the East [Russia]—though they would retain ties based on natural sympathies. They would welcome technicians and visitors from every country to come and work. They might also discuss limiting the activities of the Cuban Revolution in other countries. With these understandings, Guevara hoped, the two countries might be able to live in peace.

Dawn was breaking over Montevideo as the meeting came to an end. Guevara said he would tell no one except Fidel of their conversation. Dick too pledged that he would not publicize it. The meeting ended not with a handshake, but with an embrace between the two men—*un abrazo*.

Within hours of Dick's return to Washington, a steady drip of information about the meeting had begun. Dick and Che had not been alone in the room. The Brazilian and Argentinian delegates/translators had remained with them throughout the discussion. Waiters were coming in and out. A few autograph seekers had interrupted the conversation. Several newsmen were at the party.

Before long, the drip of rumor became a considerable leak. Inaccurate stories proliferated. Soon, their impromptu exchange was termed a formal negotiation. A spontaneous discussion became a planned meeting with the president's prior knowledge. On the floor of the House, New York Republican Steven Derounian denounced Dick as a child "playing with fire," who arranged to meet with "a dangerous communist, an avowed enemy of the American people." For this lack of judgment, Derounian charged, Goodwin should be "summarily dismissed."

As criticism mounted, Oregon Democratic senator Wayne Morse summoned Dick to appear at the end of August before his Latin America subcommittee of the Senate Foreign Relations Committee.

On the day of his appearance, Dick received a telegram, purportedly from Guevara. "Best of luck old comrade. Give my warm personal regards to Comandante Capehart."

"Arthur Schlesinger!" Dick chuckled when I showed him the telegram. "Arthur masquerading as Che to buoy my spirits on that grim day. At tough moments, Arthur was always there with a prank and support."

"Comandante Capehart?" I asked.

"An outspoken conservative Republican senator from Indiana, a member of the Latin American subcommittee, lying in wait for me."

Dick weathered the hearing. In fact, after Dick met with the committee, Morse issued a public statement that Goodwin had neither sought a meeting with Guevara, nor entered into any negotiations with him.

Dick's hopes that Senator Morse's characterization of the incident would be the final word were soon dashed. Long irritated by the freewheeling power Dick wielded from the White House, the State Department bureaucracy struck back at the moment Dick was most vulnerable. Reports multiplied about anarchy in Latin American affairs, lines of authority being confused, along with grumblings about a young upstart in the White House who had the authority to overrule longtime State Department career officials.

NOVEMBER 17, 1961

On the afternoon of November 17, Dick and several White House staff members were standing on the porch outside the Oval Office as the president prepared to depart with his family via helicopter for a weekend retreat at their country estate in Middleburg, Virginia. Catching sight of Dick, Kennedy gestured for him to come over.

"You know, Dick," Kennedy said loudly into Dick's ear so he could be heard over the whirring rotors, "I think you'll be more effective in the State Department." Dick said nothing. "I think I'm going to announce it next week." Then, as Kennedy reached the door of the helicopter, he turned back and shouted, "We'll talk about it when I get back."

That was it. The promised discussion never took place. Kennedy never brought it up again, the downside of his cryptic mode of directive that Dick had previously admired. "The following week," Dick told me, "I was evicted from the White House."

"Evicted!" I exclaimed, "that's a rather harsh term, isn't it?"

"I'm talking about how I felt," he said flatly. "After all, the White House is a house. You certainly know that too."

I smiled. He was right. The White House was indeed a big old house with sofas and cozy nooks, tiny, carpeted offices, small meeting rooms, and the intimate White House Mess, where colleagues meet for breakfast or lunch. Like so many others, I felt a heightened sense of privilege every morning I went to work in that historic building.

Dick was now headed to the State Department—a stone city, a mega complex that had just been extended to cover an area of four square blocks. There were seven floors of office space; the floors were marble, the corridors long and cold.

Newspapers called the transfer a promotion, complete with the title 'deputy assistant of state,' but as Dick packed up his books and pictures in his West Wing office, it felt like anything but an advancement.

"It hurt," he told me. "Everyone watching, the closest thing to being banished that I've ever felt." In the White House, Dick had found ties of friendship and affection with colleagues he saw every day. And of course there would no longer be the informal contact with the president, the sort of chance meetings that had led to conversations and assignments. Missing was the tonic of proximity to power. Although Dick would retain a direct line with Kennedy and accompany him on three trips to Latin America, the camaraderie that had driven the Alliance when the president and his young aide saw each other almost daily was never quite the same.

The transfer was officially announced on November 26. Two days later, Berle wrote a prescient letter—a cloak-and-dagger warning from one who personally cared about Dick and was most familiar with the terrain over which he would now travel. His advice reads like a concise update from Machiavelli's *The Prince* on how to survive and navigate the corridors of power. "The Department has some bad habits," Berle began,

"The assistant designated for you, depending on the man, may be either an assistant or something else. That is, he may be reporting on everything you say, you do and you write to someone else. Your secretary is instructed to listen in and take notes of your telephone conversations. When you find out, it is explained that this is to save time so that you need not make records. Later some of this stuff begins to appear in the Washington gossip columns.

"Also, you are limited by one principle. The close relationship between the President and the Secretary is of first importance. So you have to guard and strengthen that relationship at all points. This may be personally costly to you since it means subordinating your close and fertile relationship with the President to strengthen Rusk's position."

Surprisingly, Dick's first months in the 'belly of the beast,' as he came to view the State Department, were relatively untroubled. He got along well with his boss, Assistant Secretary Robert Woodward, a diplomat who was wholly supportive of the Alliance's progressive goals.

"In truth, Kennedy instigated the troublesome situation at State," Dick explained to me. "He continued to ignore protocol by calling me directly to issue orders or ask advice. But the fault was also mine. I was too proud of my relationship with the president to heed Berle's advice. I had no idea how to serve two masters at once."

In late December 1961, the president and first lady were scheduled to travel to Caracas and Bogotá. Kennedy asked Dick to draft speeches for both him and Jackie, and requested that he accompany them on the trip. The State Department hierarchy strenuously opposed the trip. During a goodwill mission to Venezuela three years earlier, Vice President Richard Nixon's motorcade had been attacked by a crowd shouting anti-American slogans. Before the motorcade made it safely to the embassy, Nixon's car was rocked back and forth, its windows smashed. The prospective trip, the State Department officials and the Secret Service warned, was too dangerous.

Kennedy called Dick to ask his opinion. Dick advised him to go, predicting that the trip would be a magnificent success, illustrating how much the Alliance had changed attitudes toward America. This was most likely what Kennedy wanted to hear. He decided to go. When the plane landed in Caracas, his dry sense of humor was on full display as he turned to his young aide, commenting, "Listen, Dick, if this doesn't work out, you'd better keep on going south."

Hundreds of thousands of enthusiastic Venezuelans lined the streets to greet the first Catholic president and his beautiful wife; "the greatest reception," the UPI reporter noted, "ever accorded a visitor in Venezuela's history." The next day in Bogotá, Colombia, nearly one-third of the capital city's 1.5 million residents, "dressed in their Sunday best," turned out. The trip that Dick had advocated and the State Department had lobbied against turned out to be a historic triumph.

Perhaps not coincidentally, it was around this time that unnamed detractors began to provide bits and pieces of information that, taken together, created an increasingly negative image of Dick. He was regularly referred to as brilliant but brazen, "an enfant terrible," "a mystery man in a gray flannel suit," an "overly ambitious" climber who habitually stepped on toes—with repeated mentions of his "black curly hair" and "swarthy" complexion.

"I guess I wasn't their racial type," Dick said in mock lament as we read such portrayals aloud.

"But something must have set it off," I countered.

"Well, I do remember that tempers flared when I was quoted in an article boasting that, 'only two people were willing for the President to take the trip to Venezuela and Colombia, Kennedy and me.'" Hubris, I thought, an excessive pride and vengefulness spoke loud and clear in that vaunt. "I couldn't help myself," confessed Dick.

If Dick's arrogance and immaturity caused chafing and dissatisfaction, his transgressions were small compared to the weapons the bureaucracy deployed. In March of 1962, Woodward was fired, told that he had failed "to control that boy." He was replaced by Ed Martin, who had a reputation as "a tough crow," and, as Dick would soon discover, had learned and deployed all the techniques Adolf Berle had warned Dick about from the start.

Dick's secretary was asked to keep a record of his phone calls, to listen to his conversations with the president, and report what was said to Ed Martin. Loyal to Dick, his secretary did not comply. Though Dick couldn't be fired because he was still the president's man on Latin America, his authority within the department was undermined at every step. He was not invited to important meetings, and was informed of decisions only after they had been made. He was encouraged to pursue various projects only to have the rug pulled out from under him when the time for implementation came.

He was, for example, given the go-ahead to travel to Wall Street and Ivy League law schools to recruit bright young people to work with the Alliance. He believed the appeal of the Alliance could surpass even that of the Peace Corps, that given the Marshall Plan scale of funding, huge changes could be mobilized. On his first recruitment trip, he met with thirty-five young lawyers and Wall Street analysts in New York. After talking up the Alliance's promise, he asked those interested in coming to Washington to send in their résumés. The Alliance would provide a six-month training program before the new recruits would be deployed to a Latin American country as development officers. An astonishing twenty-two of the thirty-five present forwarded their résumés. Nearly all had superlative records. No follow-up ever happened. Dick's recruitment program was dead on arrival.

"It was unbearable," Dick recalled to me. His days were spent relegated to busywork, while his responsibility for the Alliance was methodically diminished. This was not what he had imagined in that euphoric moment when the charter had been signed and he had made the decision to go to a late-night party.

If only young Dick had been privy to notes I later found in Theodore White's papers of a conversation the journalist had had with President Kennedy in 1962. When White asked the president what new ideas Rusk's State Department had offered, Kennedy scoffed: "The only good idea was Dick Goodwin's—the Alliance for Progress. Dick's over there in the State Department now, driving them crazy, but that's what Dick's over there for."

I wish Kennedy had told Dick how he felt at the time. If his intention had been to send Dick to the State Department in an effort to seed change in the conservative culture of their Latin American section, it was a plan he never shared with Dick. As a result, it mattered little to Dick whether the official ledgers considered the transfer a promotion or a demotion. In his heart, he was marooned.

———•———

The long game of history is filled with surprises and reversals. Four decades later, the meeting with Che Guevara that led to Dick's removal from the White House was transformed into a rollicking story that captivated the members of an international conference in Havana, held to commemorate the fortieth anniversary of the Cuban Missile Crisis.

Dick and I were among the three dozen or so participants attending a unique, three-day meeting hosted by the Cuban government that brought together historians and key players in the Cuban Missile Crisis from America, Russia, and Cuba. All the central figures were now in their seventies and eighties, unlikely to meet together again, lending the gathering an air of nostalgia and intimacy.

Fidel Castro, seventy-six, sat on one side of a long rectangular table, flanked by his Cuban colleagues. No longer smoking his trademark cigars, his black beard turned gray and neatly trimmed, having exchanged his battle fatigues for a business suit and tie, Fidel remained, one reporter noted, "a master entertainer, funny and excitable." Seated on the same side of the long table were half a dozen gray-haired former Soviet military and intelligence officers in khaki uniforms.

Across from Castro, where Dick and I sat, were the former members of the Kennedy administration, "lined up," the same reporter noted, "like a living page from a history book"—although dressed far more casually than in the old White House days. Most of the American delegation, including eighty-six-year-old former secretary of defense Robert McNamara and seventy-four-year-old Ted Sorensen, wore polo shirts. Sorensen had suffered a stroke the year before and was almost blind, but his memory of the Kennedy years burned clear and bright. At eighty-five, Arthur Schlesinger wore a long-sleeved shirt with his signature bow tie. Dick, in a white guayabera shirt, appeared (to my doubtless partial mind) the most splendid of this august lot.

Over the decades, the force fields of global power had drastically shifted. The Berlin Wall had fallen, the Soviet Union had broken apart, the Iron Curtain in Eastern Europe had been largely relegated to the historical past. Reporters noted that it seemed as if old alliances had been turned upside down. While the Cubans and Americans "got along famously," sharing bear hugs as if they were "veterans who'd fought in the same trenches," the

Russians—who had pressured the Cubans to accept the missiles in the first place, suddenly withdrew them as a "bargaining chip" without asking their consent—received a much frostier reception.

That President Kennedy had handled the Cuban Missile Crisis with assurance, wisdom, and skill remained the prevailing opinion of the conferees four decades later. By choosing a quarantine of Soviet ships instead of air strikes to be followed by an invasion, Kennedy had bought time to cut a deal with Premier Nikita Khrushchev, averting a potential nuclear war. The Soviets would remove the missiles which had been installed in the Cuban countryside within striking distance of Florida; the United States would pledge that there would be no invasion of Cuba. If all these conditions were met, Kennedy gave his word that the U.S. would remove nuclear missiles from Turkey, which stood within striking distance of Russia. "There are lessons to be learned," warned Arthur Schlesinger. "This was not only the most dangerous moment of the Cold War. It was the most dangerous moment in human history."

The focus of the conference, everyone agreed, must be on what could be done to ensure that the world would never again come this close to a nuclear confrontation. In that spirit, Dick was asked to talk about his meeting with Che Guevara, which, over the decades, had come to be seen as a lost opportunity to start a dialogue between the two nations. "Goodwin's memo about the meeting with Che," National Security Archive director Peter Kornbluh said, "has become one of the most famous documents in Cuban history."

Dick rose to the occasion with a virtuoso performance. Years seemed to drop away as he described Che's entry to the party, swarmed by adoring women. After a short interval, two delegates from the conference, an Argentinian and a Brazilian, brought Che to Dick. Che told Dick he had things he wanted to say, and suggested they find a separate, peaceful place where they might talk. The party's host led Dick and Che, along with the two delegates acting as interpreters, to a small room with a couch and an upholstered chair—providing seating for only three of the four men.

"Che immediately sat on the floor," Dick told the conferees. "I immediately followed suit. I refused to let him out-proletarianize me. At which point the two interpreters sat down on the floor. So there we were—four of us sitting cross-legged on the floor—until finally Che and I rose, claiming the couch and the chair."

"The 'out-proletarianize' quip was the funniest line in all the conference," Peter Kornbluh recalled. As the curious yarn continued, reporters noted, "the wild-haired and bushy eyebrowed" Goodwin had the conference members in his grip.

While the story Dick told followed the general outlines of the memo, he added embellishments not included in the official document. Guevara opened the conversation, Dick said, by thanking Dick for the Bay of Pigs.

"Our control was incomplete," Che acknowledged. "It rallied the people behind us and allowed us to overcome the middle-class opposition."

"You're welcome," Dick said, adding, "now maybe you'll invade Guantánamo."

"Never," Che said laughing, "we'd never be so foolish as that."

Dick went on to describe the *modus vivendi* Che had proposed. "It wasn't a bad deal," Dick believed. But the mood in America, heightened by the failed invasion, was not one to countenance any such discussions with Castro. After the success of the Cuban Missile Crisis a year later, however, Kennedy, believing that a window had opened, dispatched an emissary to begin talks with Cuba. This could have led, Dick thought, to a rapprochement, but these talks terminated with Kennedy's assassination.

No sooner had Dick finished than Castro followed up with a series of questions. He said he had known about the meeting from Che's perspective, but now, having heard it from Dick's, wanted to hear more. As the first session of the day drew to a close, Castro's aide handed Dick a note: "Fidel invites you and your wife to have lunch with him, after this meeting is over. We'll meet outside the hall."

Lunch was served in Castro's private wing of the conference hall. Castro ate nothing but yogurt. Dick and I were served a full meal. Dick carefully prepared and savored the offered Cohiba while the conversation rambled, beginning with more talk about Che Guevara (Che had been assassinated in Bolivia four years after the Montevideo meeting. He was only thirty-nine). Castro's conversation suddenly swerved to his passion for baseball. Earlier that day, I had spoken to the conference of how I learned to tell a story from the experience of keeping score of Brooklyn Dodgers games for my father. Castro, who had played semiprofessional baseball when he was young, clearly still adored the game. Swerving again, Castro held forth for half an hour with a vivid description of a medical study Cuba was conducting on imprisoned sociopaths to determine if there were anomalies in the structure and function of their brains.

As McNamara departed on the final day of the conference, Castro said he hoped the former defense secretary would come back for the fiftieth reunion. "I won't be here," McNamara said, "I'd have to come down from Hell."

"You've got your geography wrong," Castro countered. "You'll come down from Heaven."

On the final night during an elegant state dinner for which Castro had released a reserve of old rum, I asked our tablemate, President of the Cuban National Assembly Ricardo Alarcón, to explain the source of Castro's extraordinary vigor. Alarcón jumped up from the table, returning a few minutes later with a bottle of blue and green pills. "Take these," he said. "They are protein pills that come from algae, processed by Cubans." Castro maintained that when paired with walking, these pills were the source of his energy. While I was reluctant to sample them, Dick swallowed them as soon as we got home, with indeterminate results.

Only a Gabriel García Márquez might do justice to the bittersweet mixture of memories felt by both the Americans and the Cubans on this occasion. Particularly vivid in my mind is the image of the aging Cuban patriarch, dictator, and godfather Fidel Castro—leaping from one topic to another, spooning yogurt, no longer able to smoke cigars, yet recommending vitality pills, and still avidly devoted to the game of baseball.

The occasion was so pleasant that one might be lulled into forgetting the grim decades of ruthless repression under Castro's dictatorship. And yet, through the nostalgia seeped the sorrows of opportunities not explored, chances not taken, possibilities wasted. It all might have been different.

CHAPTER FIVE

The Supreme Generalist

*Dick escorts First Lady Jacqueline Kennedy to the White House
dinner honoring Nobel Laureates on April 29, 1962.*

"OF COURSE I'M TIRED," DICK SIGHED ONE MORNING, GLANCING
over the unexplored ranks of archival boxes. "Here I am in my eighties and
my thirties at the same time. I'm burning my life candle at both ends!"

It was true that after eighty, he had begun to suffer the typical infirmi-
ties of old age: He needed more sleep, a pacemaker regulated his heart-
beat, his balance was compromised. When he didn't respond to a question
or comment, I realized he was not simply absorbed in his reading, he was
experiencing a loss of hearing. I badgered him until he finally consented
to wear hearing aids that clipped on like earrings. These he regularly mis-
placed, setting off household scavenger hunts. We found them under the
cushion of his reading chair, in the washing machine (clinging to the collar
of his pajamas). One showed up as a lumpy bookmark in a new novel he'd
set aside.

One afternoon, he tripped on the way to feed the koi fish in our backyard pond. Soon afterward, I found him seated on a bench in the garden, a small bruise on his knee. He blamed the fall on a divot in the gravel path, but when I saw his pensive expression I asked him if he was okay.

"I heard time's winged chariot hurrying near," he said, citing Andrew Marvell's "To His Coy Mistress," but then grinned, adding, "maybe it was only the hiss of my hearing aid."

"You once told me Marvell's speeding chariot was a pretext to spur a young woman to make love," I said.

Dick laughed and confessed that if old age sometimes proved a frustrating, trying time, he found a distracting pleasure in our exploration of his flight from the intolerable situation in the State Department during the summer of 1962.

Just as he had fled to the army when claustrophobia set in during Harvard Law School, so now he had simply abandoned his State Department office. He did not serve notice, ask permission, or resign. He simply escaped, walked over to Peace Corps headquarters, and offered his services.

In Dick's memory, the several blocks between the State Department and the Peace Corps building at Lafayette Park (in sight of the White House) seemed to traverse a vast spiritual distance. The staff was younger, less stuffy, and unabashedly romantic. The lights burned all night long.

The Peace Corps was presided over by Sarge Shriver, the husband of Kennedy's sister Eunice. Ever after, Dick appreciated that Sarge had welcomed him with open arms. He provided him an office and gratefully utilized him as his assistant, speechwriter, and adviser on various projects. Shriver never questioned why Dick had come, and the State Department never inquired about why he had left—at least as far as he knew.

There were, of course, loose ends to this story. It was odd that he retained his vacant office and desk at the State Department. And odder still that he remained on the State Department payroll while spending the majority of his time at the Peace Corps.

When Kennedy heard from Bobby that Dick had migrated to the Peace Corps, he called Dick on July 2, 1962, and gave his blessing. "Whatever you feel like doing is okay with me," he said, provided Dick continue to write all speeches pertaining to the Alliance for Progress and remain on call for special projects or any pending presidential trips to Latin America.

What happens in history is often a slippery business and, as ever, depends on *who* is doing the telling, *when* they are telling the tale, and *why*. Recently, I contacted Bill Josephson, an old friend who had been at the Peace Corps from the start, in charge of drafting personnel for the new organization. What Bill told me did not so much conflict with as unexpectedly elaborate upon Dick's version, helping to explain the State Department's laissez-faire attitude toward Dick's departure.

"Rusk called me up," Josephson remembered distinctly, "because a call from the secretary of state was a rare event. His voice was so angry I could feel the heat of his fury through the telephone."

"I know you have control over your personnel system," Rusk said. "I want Goodwin out of State!" The old-timers at State, long supportive of American business interests in Latin America, struggled daily with "that boy," whom they viewed as "the White House's liberal apostle in residence on behalf of Latin America."

The secretary of state was hamstrung: He knew that Dick still had direct ties to the president, and that he had as many friends as enemies in the diplomatic corps. Despite that, the nonconfrontational Rusk wanted peace and quiet in his Latin American Bureau. Transferring Dick would solve his dilemma.

Josephson reported Rusk's scalding request to an amused Shriver. Sarge greeted the transfer idea with palpable excitement. "He loved brilliant people, people who would stimulate him," Josephson explained, "and he couldn't wait for Goodwin's arrival."

How serendipitous this all was. Shortly after Dick's appearance, Sarge called in Bill Moyers, his deputy director, and introduced them. "I liked him instantly," Bill remembered when I spoke to him not long ago. He described his initial encounter with Dick as, "One half black sheep meeting another black sheep. He was *sui generis*, an original mind. It was refreshing to talk about law and Frankfurter, and the quiz show investigation. He was as curious about my world as I was about his. We often jested about the compatibility of Jews and Baptists. And we both loved Cuban cigars. We bonded. From that day. Dick would become my closest friend in Washington."

Shriver immediately gave Dick a wide berth in planning future directions for the Peace Corps and before long, Dick's fertile imagination began to devise expansive new possibilities. Chief among such schemes was his concept of an International Peace Corps. It would stimulate and support other industrialized countries to build their own organizations upon the template of our Peace Corps. With Shriver's endorsement, Dick invented for himself the august and cumbersome title: Secretary General of the International Peace Corps Secretariat.

Space was allocated on the twelfth floor of the Peace Corps building for six professional people and four secretaries. There would be a Secretariat reception hall, providing a setting of sufficient elegance to house Dick's burgeoning conception. The Peace Corps, an elixir distilled from the new generation of American youth, would soon find a powerful global resonance.

"Wow, when you cooked up something," I couldn't help but poke fun at Dick, "it rarely lacked an element of grandeur—or should I say grandiosity?"

But the fact was that within a matter of months, after Dick had traveled from one country to another sparking enthusiasm among students and officials, six industrialized nations had already started the process of setting up their own Peace Corps.

"Before long," Dick told a meeting of the Association of International Students in Washington, D.C., "Americans will be working side by side with young Dutch and Norwegians, Danes, and Germans and many others in a common effort to assist in the great processes of development and progress." In closing, he warned the assembled students, "it will be easy to follow the familiar paths, to seek the satisfaction of personal ambition or financial success, but this is not the road history has marked out for us. For everyone here will ultimately be judged—will ultimately judge himself—on the effort he has contributed to the building of a new world society, and on the extent to which his ideals and goals have shaped that effort."

———————

In a plastic sleeve atop a thick block of memos and miscellaneous papers labeled "Jackie and the Arts (1961–1963)" was a carefully preserved copy of an excerpt from Arthur Schlesinger's *A Thousand Days*:

"It seemed to me that in many ways Dick Goodwin, though younger than the average, was the archetypal New Frontiersman. He was the supreme generalist who could turn from Latin America to saving the Nile monuments at Abu Simbel, from civil rights to planning the White House dinner for the Nobel prize winners, from composing a parody of Norman

Mailer to drafting a piece of legislation, from lunching with a Supreme Court Justice to dining with Jean Seberg—and at the same time retain an unquenchable spirit of sardonic liberalism and an unceasing drive to get things done."

I had first considered this description a good friend's flattering encomium, but the further I ventured into the documents, the more I realized that Schlesinger's eclectic list cast a light on memorable cultural milestones during the Kennedy administration in which Dick played a decisive role.

"God, we did have fun—and did *get things done*," Dick said, leaning back, his head wreathed in cigar smoke as he recollected those crowded days when, barely thirty years old, he was not only traveling from one continent to another to set up global Peace Corps organizations—all the while continuing to write all the president's speeches (and Jackie's) on Latin America—but had also become Jackie's ally in her quest to make the White House a showcase for art, music, literature, and culture. It was during these years that Dick and Jackie became not simply allies, working together on multiple projects, but lifelong friends.

For more than four decades, a photograph of Dick escorting Jackie to the Nobel Prize dinner on April 29, 1962—the largest and perhaps most unique dinner of the Kennedy presidency—adorned Dick's study wall. This was the occasion when Kennedy greeted forty-nine Nobel Laureates in science, medicine, and literature, along with a distinguished assemblage of writers, poets, and scholars—a heady combination of the sciences and humanities—with the memorable line. "This is the most extraordinary collection of talent, of human knowledge, that has ever been gathered together at the White House, with the possible exception of when Thomas Jefferson dined alone."

The photograph in Dick's study captures a beaming Dick, walking arm-in-arm with Jackie toward the State Dining Room, flanked by a line of violinists and the White House military aide. In the margin at the bottom of the photograph, Jackie had handwritten: "Was it a vision or a waking dream—Fled is that music, Do I wake or sleep? To Dick, with appreciation and admiration."

The inscribed photograph, gifted to Dick three years after she had left the White House, cites the final lines of Keats's "Ode to a Nightingale." Jackie's commentary signals far more than a wistful memory of that particular evening. It invokes her emotions on gazing back at that shimmering, evanescent time in their lives, muted now behind a tragic glass, fading into what seems almost a sense of unreality.

When I asked Dick to tell me about the dinner, he seemed amused and bemused. "It was a night I was sure I would never forget; and yet, after all we drank at the reception and the dinner, and then at a party at Schlesinger's that lasted from midnight till dawn, I remember an extraordinary buoyancy and little else."

So I was left to piece together the details of the event from various conversations and written accounts. It all began, Joseph Esposito writes in *Dinner in Camelot* (an entire book dedicated to this single night), with a memo from Dick to Jackie on November 28, 1961: "How about a dinner for the winners of the Nobel Prize?"

Jackie loved the idea, and in the months that followed, she worked with Dick, Arthur Schlesinger, and White House social secretary Letitia Baldrige to plan the event. Schlesinger apprised the president of the evolving guest list as it expanded to include literary figures as well as scientists. In a handwritten response, Kennedy reminded Schlesinger to make sure that Dick was invited.

The black-tie event began with a reception in the grand Cross Hall. "Many were starstruck meeting equally accomplished people from different fields for the first time," Esposito told me. Each personage was formally identified upon entrance: Acclaimed eighty-seven-year-old poet Robert Frost; father of antibiotics Selman Waksman; literature Nobel Prize winner Pearl Buck; astronaut John Glenn; immunologist Thomas Weller, whose virus research enabled the polio vaccine; J. Robert Oppenheimer, Manhattan Project director; celebrated novelists James Baldwin and William Styron—in all, a parade of 127 guests and their spouses.

"A stupendous amount of liquor was flowing around," (martinis, Manhattans, highballs) literary critic Diana Trilling recalled in a long *New Yorker* piece. Smoking had been reintroduced to the Kennedy White House so a number of guests were holding a drink in one hand and a cigarette in the other. "Long before we were put into the receiving line, and the President made his appearance," Trilling wrote, "everybody was saying to everybody else, isn't this a wonderful party."

At the sound of "Hail to the Chief" and the sight of the Color Guard, the guests proceeded in alphabetical order to the East Room to be received by the president and first lady.

Mild apprehension rose when Nobelist Linus Pauling reached the president. Earlier that afternoon, Pauling and his wife, Ava Helen, had joined a group picketing the White House to demand an end to nuclear testing.

"Dr. Pauling, you've been around the White House a couple days already, haven't you," Kennedy said with warm irony. "I hope that you will continue to express your opinions." The potential wrinkle was smoothed over so graciously that Pauling even engaged later in an impromptu dance with his wife. Once the receiving line had finished, Jackie asked Dick to escort her to the dinner, the moment fixed on Dick's study wall.

At the dinner, the president was seated at a center table in the State Dining Room, surrounded by eighteen round tables. The first lady was located in the Blue Room with four surrounding tables. Husbands and wives were separated to facilitate table-wide conversations. Women were identified by their husband's names—as Mrs. Lionel Trilling, for instance, or Mrs. Selman Waksman. Even the place card for Pearl Buck, the sole female Nobel Laureate in attendance, read Mrs. Richard Walsh! Two tables away from the president, Dick hosted his own table.

After dinner, the guests gathered in the East Room where Kennedy praised the guests for their great accomplishments and expressed his hope that their example would "encourage young people to develop the same drive and deep desire" to pursue excellence in science and art. This was more than lip service. This was a celebration of American culture to be seen the world over.

As the evening wound to a close, Dick joined the president, first lady, Bobby and Ethel Kennedy, Sarge Shriver, and a few others for champagne and cigars in the yellow Oval Room on the second floor of the living quarters (where FDR had held his famous cocktail hour).

"One thing I do remember," Dick told me, "is that no one wanted that evening to end."

———

Of all the ingredients mentioned in Arthur Schlesinger's recipe for the "Supreme Generalist," none seemed to me more exotic than "saving the Nile monuments at Abu Simbel." And yet, after an archival stack five inches thick helped substantiate this curious claim, I went to Dick directly for confirmation.

"Did you actually save the monuments at Abu Simbel?"

"Not alone," he said with comic modesty. "I had help."

The documents in that thick folder told the story of the collaboration between Jackie and Dick to save ancient monuments, which were in danger of being submerged by the lake rising behind a dam built across the Nile at Aswan.

From the start, the entire project was entangled in Cold War politics. Angered at the Soviet Union's participation in the Aswan Dam project, the Eisenhower administration had refused to join a UNESCO (United Nations Educational, Scientific and Cultural Organization) international campaign to preserve the colossal temple complex at Abu Simbel, along with dozens of smaller temples and statues. Without American leadership (combined with private philanthropy), it seemed likely that these monuments were to be forever lost beneath the lake.

In 1962, Jackie sent an urgent memo to the president laying out the case for saving Abu Simbel: "It is _the_ major temple of the Nile—thirteenth century B.C. It would be like letting the Parthenon be flooded." Kennedy relayed her memo to Dick "for possible action." To remove these temples would cost tens of millions of dollars, and Kennedy let Dick understand that a successful appropriation of funds was a far-fetched possibility. Kennedy predicted that Brooklyn congressman John Rooney, then in charge of appropriations, would counter such a proposal with the firm opinion that these were "rocks in the middle of the Egyptian desert and there's not one Egyptian voter in the whole country."

Nonetheless, Jackie and Dick worked together to persuade our own government to engage, quite literally, in a monumental quid pro quo. The Egyptian government had promised contributing nations a range of antiquities, including statues, vases, and artifacts—even one of several small temples—all contingent on the size of their contribution. The objective of the whole operation was a rescue from obliteration rather than the cultural appropriation it might seem today. Before long, Dick had assembled a large picture book to illustrate the endangered monuments, accompanied by a description of the "gifts" we might expect in return for our "contribution."

When the picture book of Abu Simbel was ready, Dick brought it to Kennedy in order to convince him that only a direct presidential appeal to Congressman Rooney would loosen the necessary funds. Kennedy leafed through the book. "That's all fine," he responded, "but what do you think Rooney's going to say when I ask him for forty million dollars. . . . He'll say, 'Jack, you must be out of your mind.'" Dick was prepared for this argument. "Napoleon only brought an obelisk back to Paris," Dick said with half-serious flattery. "You can bring an entire temple back to Washington."

Kennedy paused for a moment and then smiled indulgently: "Let's give it a try."

"What a good salesman you were," I said of Dick's photo brochure gambit. I told him that as a young congressman, LBJ had employed much the same technique to corral a busy Franklin Roosevelt. "Don't argue, show," was the advice Lyndon followed when seeking funds to extend electricity into his sparsely populated Hill Country. He came armed with pictures, drawings, and maps of the transmission lines from two recently constructed dams. Unless the guidelines were changed, Johnson maintained, power from the dams would flow only to big shots in cities, stranding poor folk in the dark countryside. FDR intervened. The guidelines were changed.

"Exactly," nodded Dick. "But don't forget, it wasn't me or the voters Kennedy was trying to placate. It was his wife! And believe me, she was dogged."

Meanwhile, Jackie reached out through personal and social channels to private philanthropists—Italian industrialist Giovanni Agnelli among them. Dick followed up at once, promoting the project in detail, and soliciting Agnelli's help.

Jackie and Dick's tag-team efforts were not without shared humor: "Agnelli said he had been trying to reach you for a week, but you were in Africa," Jackie wrote to Dick (Dick was indeed in Africa helping set up a Peace Corps International extension). "You must be dead!!" Jackie added. "Anyway, thank you for everything. Affectionately, Jackie."

Both were aware of the quixotic nature of this quest, and their typewritten notes often contained an air of self-mockery, as when Dick wrote Jackie at the beginning of one memo: "A few assorted notes on your program for the advancement of world culture."

Though Rooney still thought the president was out of his mind to be asking Congress to put up money to save a bunch of rocks, he was a loyal Democrat. "If that's what you want," he told Kennedy, "I'll try it."

Once the money had been appropriated, Jackie and Dick were able to select a temple commensurate to the public and private money they had amassed. They consulted a group of Egyptologists and narrowed the choices. In the end, both wanted the Temple of Dendur, built to honor the Egyptian goddess Isis by the Roman governor of Egypt, Augustus Caesar, around 15 BC. With a walkway that led to the banks of the Nile, the Temple of Dendur seemed perfectly suitable for transplant to the banks of the Potomac.

Preserving the temple complex at Abu Simbel proved more complicated and expensive than originally conceived. The massive figures and temples had to be cut into pieces and reassembled at a higher elevation. That process had not yet begun by the time Kennedy died. It was left to President Johnson to secure the necessary additional funds.

By the fall of 1964, when a decision had to be made, Dick was a member of LBJ's White House. "I have worked on this project for four years at the personal request of Mrs. Kennedy," Dick told Johnson. "Because of Mrs. Kennedy's deep interest, it might be appropriate if you communicated with her before you announce your action."

Once the additional appropriation of $12 million was secured, Dick drafted a statement for President Johnson to deliver. After outlining the contributions that both administrations had made, he said: "These temples were built before western civilization began. But they speak to us across the centuries of man's ability to create that which will endure through conflict and difference and history itself. I am glad that one of our youngest nations can make this contribution to the citizens of one of the oldest civilizations."

Instead of being reassembled on the banks of the Potomac as a memorial tribute to John Kennedy as Jackie would have preferred, the Temple ended up encased in a specially constructed glass wing at the Metropolitan Museum of Art in New York. In a controlled atmosphere to prevent erosion, a sandstone pylon opens onto a small courtyard where, after unimaginable travels of six thousand miles and nearly two thousand years, rises the exquisite Nubian Temple of Dendur.

———•———

The pleasure we took in reviewing Dick's expansive Peace Corps activities and work with Jackie on the arts and humanities was nowhere in evidence when our discussions turned to President Kennedy's retreat on civil rights after his initial flurry of Black appointments.

When I first found a copy of the signed Executive Order #11063—to end discrimination in federal housing—and saw the date of issuance, *November 20, 1962,* I thought it must be in error. Nearly two years into

Kennedy's administration? The promise had been to issue the order immediately upon taking office.

It is a puzzling story of procrastination and political calculation, a story
in which Dick had far more than a passing interest. After all, he had written
the initial pledge to sign the order into the Civil Rights speech Kennedy
had delivered at the Shrine Auditorium back on September 9, 1960.

Of all the pledges made during the campaign, the promise to sign the
housing order was the most prominent. No other aspect of executive leadership mattered more to civil rights leaders than housing. "Here," Martin
Luther King Jr. argued, "the Negro confronts the most tragic expression of
discrimination; he is consigned to ghettoes and overcrowded conditions."

"Two years! Why so long?" I asked Dick.

"You could say," Dick began to explain, "we learned that governing is a
different animal altogether than winning an election."

As Dick began to list the reasons behind the long series of delays, I
could tell his heart was not in his explanations. He felt a lingering personal
responsibility for that speech in Los Angeles, not simply because he had
written the words—but because he *believed* them. Dick had been certain
that Kennedy would follow through on his promise. He expected that
the order would be issued on Day One of his presidency. When it did not
happen, he hoped it would be signed on February 12, 1961—Lincoln's
birthday—but it was not.

Reasons for the delay began to gather from different quarters, and Kennedy's caution grew. Blowback from the real estate community was more
shrill and powerful than expected. They argued that continued prejudice—
whites not wanting to live next door to Blacks—would hamper the housing
market and fuel recession. So Kennedy delayed the signing.

Meanwhile, Kennedy had introduced legislation to create a cabinet-level
department of urban affairs, with an African American, Robert Weaver,
as its leader. Convinced that the contentious executive order would cost
southern votes for the proposed cabinet post, Kennedy decided to delay
the signing until this bill was passed.

His strategy boomeranged. While the housing order languished, the
House Rules Committee refused to issue a rule allowing the bill to come
to the floor, dashing the opportunity to appoint the first Black cabinet
member in history. I couldn't help but remind Dick that it was LBJ who
finally secured the legislation to create what became the Department of

Housing and Urban Development (HUD), and that it was LBJ who actually appointed Weaver, the first Black cabinet officer.

Not once during this period of delay on the housing order did Kennedy use the persuasive power of the bully pulpit to educate the country on the issue, to drive words into realized action. Not once did he speak of Civil Rights as a "great moral issue" as he had promised at the Shrine Auditorium.

The positive review King had given Kennedy during the first year of his administration had become more mixed, and was darkening. "In the election, when I gave my testimony for Kennedy, my impression then was that he had the intelligence and the skill and the moral fervor to give the leadership we've been waiting for and do what no other President has ever done. Now I'm convinced that he has the understanding and the political skill but so far I'm afraid that the moral passion is missing."

In the absence of presidential leadership, civil rights leaders decided to mount pressure from the outside. Since Kennedy had promised to sign the order with "one stroke of a pen," they organized an "Ink for Jack" campaign. Hundreds of pens and bottles of ink pelted down on the White House to jog Kennedy's memory of the pledge he had given.

At last, with a carefully orchestrated minimum of fanfare, at a press conference devoted to foreign policy announcements the weekend before the Thanksgiving holiday of 1962, Kennedy issued the order. It had been softened and pared down from the bold pledge set forth during the campaign. Despite the dilution and the delay, Martin Luther King Jr. called it "a good faith step in the right direction."

Grassroots organizations had made a difference, a preview of the growing power of public sentiment that would become the signature of the decade ahead.

For unlike today, the Sixties were still a time when a candidate's word represented a commitment to a prescribed course of action. What one said mattered. If one reneged on that word, a future time of reckoning would be waiting.

MAY 3, 1963

"Double D-Day" was the name civil rights leaders in Birmingham, Alabama, gave to March 3, 1963—a day when local law enforcement officers, under orders of Commissioner of Public Safety Eugene "Bull" Connor, used high-pressure fire hoses and police dogs to assault Black children who had been peacefully marching to City Hall to protest segregation at lunch counters, department stores, and other public places. Newspaper accounts, photographs, and newsreel images of the savage attack upon this "Children's Crusade" shell-shocked millions of people across the country.

That day changed my conception of the country I lived in. I couldn't believe this was happening in my lifetime in America. In the aftermath of these protests, my Russian professor at Colby College unfolded pages in *Pravda* that featured the brutal violence in Birmingham: images of fire hoses trained like guns on the children, their high-pressure nozzles tumbling bodies against brick walls and down the pavement; a German Shepherd from a K-9 unit, its teeth clamped on a boy's abdomen; paddy wagons transporting scores of children to jail. We all took turns reading aloud in Russian the articles that accompanied these pictures. Of course these articles were filled with Soviet propaganda, contrasting a racist America with the archetype of the Soviet Union's "new man," selflessly dedicated to the interests of the collective. But the photos were authentic, and they were spreading around the world.

The front-page *New York Times* photograph of the police officer forcing the boy toward the attack dog made President Kennedy "sick." It captured a moment, once seen and known, which could not be unseen and unknown. "At Birmingham, as at Concord," Martin Luther King Jr. said, "a shot had been fired that was heard around the world." The federal administration's current stance—that responsibility for dealing with local protests rested with local, not federal, authorities—flew in the face of the fact that people had come to feel that the violent response of local officials was unwarranted, that it was incongruent with our responsibility as Americans.

JUNE 11, 1963

In the weeks after Birmingham, the protests gained momentum. Across Nashville, Greensboro, and Raleigh, as in dozens of other southern cities, thousands of demonstrators gathered in front of segregated restaurants, hotels, and department stores. Pictures captured the mayhem: white bystanders throwing bricks and eggs at peaceful protesters, a Black high school freshman girl lying unconscious on the street after being hit with a policeman's club. The Civil Rights Movement was fast becoming a revolution. Patience with the well-meaning equivocations of the Kennedy administration had worn out.

"President Kennedy hasn't done all he could in the area of civil rights," Martin Luther King Jr. was quoted in newspapers on the morning of June 11. "He has not yet given the leadership the enormity of the problem demands."

Later that same morning, while watching televised coverage of Alabama's governor George Wallace literally standing in the doorway to block two Black students from integrating the University of Alabama, Kennedy surprised his staff by announcing that he wanted to go on television that very night to speak about civil rights. He intended to signal that behind the scenes, lawyers at the Justice Department, under Robert Kennedy's guidance as attorney general, were in the process of drafting a comprehensive bill to protect Blacks from discrimination in schools, restaurants, department stores, hotels, and other public facilities.

All his advisers—except Bobby—disagreed with his decision. The Civil Rights Bill, they argued, was still a work in progress. No speech had been prepared. Bobby countered that his brother could speak from notes or, if necessary, extemporaneously. President Kennedy pressed on. He personally placed calls to the heads of the three networks and reserved eighteen minutes of airtime for 8 p.m. that evening. Then he left for a swim and a nap while Sorensen and others scrambled to put together what would become one of Kennedy's most important speeches. By the time the camera rolled, the text was still not finished.

The speech is one of the strangest and most powerful and rough-edged speeches of Kennedy's presidency. He is serious, somber, and the camera is right in his face. At times, he looks down at notes or improvises. It is jagged, but all the better for being so. Something in the lack of polish conveys conviction:

We are confronted primarily with a moral issue. It is as old as the Scriptures and as clear as the American Constitution. The heart of the question is whether all Americans are to be afforded equal rights and equal opportunities. . . . If an American, because his skin is dark, cannot eat lunch in a restaurant open to the public . . . cannot enjoy the full and free life which all of us want, then who among us would be content to have the color of his skin changed and stand in his place? . . .

Next week I shall ask the Congress of the United States to act, to make a

commitment it has not fully made in this century to the proposition that race has
no place in American life or law.

As Dick and I were listening to the words across a half a century, I noted
that they echoed the speech Dick and Ted had drafted for the National
Press Club, when Kennedy first promised he would be an activist president. There were echoes from the civil rights speech that Dick had drafted
for the candidate at Shrine Auditorium when he'd vowed "to use the bully
pulpit to educate the public about the great moral issues."

Kennedy had also deployed the same statistics he had used to powerful
effect during the first debate with Richard Nixon to illustrate how the lack
of equal opportunity affects the chances for a Black baby versus a white
baby to complete high school, finish college, and enter a profession.

"The words are similar," Dick agreed, "but it's not simply *what* is said,
but *when* it is said, and *how*."

The televised speech we had watched together was not just a campaign
pledge. This was no longer a hopeful candidate speaking in the heat of a
presidential debate. It was a prologue to the announcement that President
John Fitzgerald Kennedy would put the weight of his presidency behind
the most sweeping Civil Rights Bill of the past century.

"It reminds me of something I wrote once about Patrick Henry," Dick
said. "Give Me Liberty or Give Me Death, spoken to a Chamber of Commerce convention in a time of prosperity and serenity would be ludicrous."

The shocking events in Birmingham and the tumultuous growth of the
Civil Rights Movement across the country lent urgency and power to Kennedy's language.

"It wasn't only Kennedy's speech that has stayed in my mind from that
night," Dick said. "It was Medgar Evers's murder in front of his family as
they waited for him to come home to tell them what he thought of that
speech."

AUGUST 28, 1963

The March on Washington for Jobs and Freedom was the first of a half
dozen occasions when Dick and I would be in the same place at the same
time without meeting. That our paths did not cross on that day was not
surprising, of course, for we were among a quarter of a million people who
had gathered for the event.

I had spent that summer before my senior year at Colby as an intern in the European Affairs Bureau at the State Department. Unlike Dick, I loved my experience at State. There were around twenty of us in the program, providing a warm enclave within the massive building. Although interns were assigned to different bureaus, we regularly gathered for lunch and dinner. The march took place during my last week in Washington.

I still remember the nervous excitement I felt that morning as I walked with a group of friends toward the meeting place at the Washington Monument. All government employees had been given that Wednesday off—not, however, to enable our attendance; on the contrary, we were cautioned to stay home, warned that it wasn't safe.

I was twenty years old. We had no intention of staying home. My friends and I had planned to attend the march for weeks. We'd been following the reports of buses, trains, and cars carrying tens of thousands of marchers to Washington from all over the country. To support the Civil Rights Movement promised to be the highlight of our summer.

A state of emergency had been declared. Marchers arriving by bus and train Wednesday morning were ordered to depart the city proper by Wednesday night. Hospitals canceled elective surgery to make space in the event of mass casualties. The Washington Senators baseball game was postponed, and liquor stores and bars were closed for the day. We learned that 2,500 National Guardsmen had been mobilized to bolster the entire D.C. police force. And across the Potomac, 4,000 additional soldiers stood in readiness. My father had called the night before to tell me he had read accounts of the massive preparations in Washington, and wanted to make sure I was out of harm's way.

"In hindsight, don't you think these restrictions and expectations of pandemonium were a bit much?" I asked Dick.

"Kennedy was worried that if things got out of hand, it could unravel not only his civil rights bill, but take his administration with it."

Dick remembered Schlesinger's description of a White House meeting with civil rights leaders earlier that summer, when plans for the Washington march had been discussed. Martin Luther King Jr., A. Philip Randolph, Roy Wilkins, Whitney Young, and a few others had attended that meeting in the Cabinet Room. Kennedy had told the leaders he considered the prospective march a mistake. To flesh out Dick's recollections, I found Schlesinger's contemporary report in his *Journals* especially reliable—given his roles as both top White House aide and first-rate historian.

"We want success in Congress, not just a big show at the Capitol," Kennedy had said. (The original plans called for a march on the Capitol.) "We are in a new phase, the legislative phase, and results are essential. Give Congress a fair chance to work its will."

"The Negroes are already in the streets," countered A. Philip Randolph. "It is very likely impossible to get them off." The momentum of the movement against segregation could not be stopped. "Is it not better that they be led by organizations dedicated to civil rights and disciplined by struggle?"

Reading Randolph's statement called to mind something Lincoln had said about the inexorable approach of Emancipation. "He believed from the first," his friend Leonard Swett recalled, "that the agitation of slavery would bring its overthrow," and that whoever "stands in its way will be run over by it." Timing, Lincoln believed, was everything. The challenge was to be in the right place with the right response when events began moving forward.

According to Schlesinger's account, King acknowledged at the close of the meeting that the march might seem "ill-timed"; but "frankly," he tellingly added, "I have never engaged in any direct action movement which did not seem ill-timed." For his part, King was convinced the timing was right. It would "serve as a means of dramatizing the issue and mobilizing support in parts of the country which don't know the problems at first hand."

Planning proceeded for the August event; as a concession to Kennedy's trepidation that Congress might view a march on the Capitol as a form of intimidation, however, the venue was transferred to the Lincoln Memorial. To me, it seemed just right that a march for freedom would take place under the tutelary gaze of Abraham Lincoln.

"Were you officially forbidden to go to the march?" I asked Dick.

"Not forbidden," he said, "but certainly discouraged."

"So what did you do?"

"I grabbed Bill Moyers and we both headed toward the Lincoln Memorial."

So there we were, unknown to one another, me a college intern at the State Department, and Dick a secretary general at the Peace Corps, both streaming along with what seemed to be all of humanity, from the

Washington Monument toward the Reflecting Pool and the ascending steps of the Lincoln Memorial.

It's no simple task to retrieve accurate memories of what we saw and heard during that landmark day. The grand panorama spread before us has become a defining symbol in our American culture. We have read countless accounts of the march, watched documentaries, and studied photographs. Like a grand painting that has been repeatedly overlaid by the needs and demands of the passing years, it now seems almost impossible to remove all such layers in order to get to the prime image, the original.

So what do I remember most clearly?

Foremost, I remember the powerful atmosphere and my feelings as we gathered near the Washington Memorial at the start of the march, before setting out on parade. I received a round pin—March for Jobs and Freedom—and chose a poster stapled to a stick: *CATHOLICS, PROTESTANTS, AND JEWS UNITE IN THE STRUGGLE FOR CIVIL RIGHTS.* The march slowly began to file along the side of the Reflecting Pool. People were everywhere, watching from tree branches, dangling their feet in the Reflecting Pool to cool off from the oppressive heat. Armed with pin, sign, and song, I felt not simply witness to, but an integral part of, the march. As we moved toward the Lincoln Memorial, a sense that I was connected to something larger than myself took hold—together, we were moving forward to a better place.

It is easy to cast a cynical eye upon this youthful exultation, to look back on such emotions as sentimental idealism. But the feelings were genuine and they were profound. At the outset of the march, I had wondered what proportion of the vast throng was white (it was later estimated at 20 percent). By the time I returned to my rooming house in Foggy Bottom, I had forgotten about calculations and proportions of Black and white. I had seen and been part of a finer world. I had set out to the march apprehensive, yet afterward, was lifted up by the most joyful day of public unity and community that I had ever experienced in my life.

I have already noted that Dick loved to sing and, at the spur of any moment might recite all manner of ballads and narrative poems. When I asked him what he remembered most clearly from King's "I Have a Dream" speech delivered that day, he burst forth with a soaring rendition of the place in the speech where the freedom bell tolls from one shore of our country to the other:

"Let freedom ring from the prodigious hilltops of New Hampshire. Let freedom ring from the mighty mountains of New York. Let freedom ring from the heightening Alleghenies of Pennsylvania. Let freedom ring from the snow-capped Rockies of Colorado. Let freedom ring from the curvaceous slopes of California. But not only that, let freedom ring from Stone Mountain of Georgia. Let freedom ring from Lookout Mountain of Tennessee. Let freedom ring from every hill and molehill of Mississippi. From every mountainside, let freedom ring."

After a long pause, Dick murmured, "King was unrolling a freedom map of the whole country before our eyes. The march had broadened the Civil Rights Movement from south to north, from east to west, enveloping the whole country from coast to coast.

"It was different from a speech," Dick said, "and it was different from a sermon, though the rhythm of the Black Church is in every line. It was a rare instance when vision and purpose become the music of a national movement."

As the march drew to a close, we all clasped hands and raised them to the sky as our voices rose to sing "We Shall Overcome"—the hymn that had long instilled purpose and courage to the foot soldiers of the Civil Rights Movement. It was that moment that made the deepest impression upon both Dick and me.

A year and a half later, memory of that transcendent chorus would return to become the heart of the most important speech Dick would ever write.

SEPTEMBER 1963

As I returned to my senior year in college, I felt my first misgivings about the blueprint for my future. I had applied to graduate school to study international relations and foreign languages. I envisioned, perhaps, a career in the foreign service. My boss at the State Department had nominated me for a Fulbright to study in Brussels and Paris. Never having traveled abroad, such prospects seemed wondrously thrilling. After the march, however, an amorphous feeling began to take hold, a desire to be where important change was taking place in my own country.

The lingering effects of the march and the growing power of the Civil Rights Movement could be felt at Colby that year, as a campus-wide campaign to address discrimination in the Greek system was ignited. A combined student-faculty committee on discrimination had submitted a recommendation to the administration and Board of Trustees: Within two years, all fraternities and sororities must declare their intention to select their members without regard to race, religion, or national origin. This two-year timeline would allow national organizations the opportunity to alter their charters and discriminatory practices. If not, the local chapters would be required to terminate relations with the national organization. The recommendations were endorsed by the full faculty, the administration, and the board.

That fall, the president of Tri Delta, Mrs. J. L. Perry of Nashville, Tennessee, wrote a letter to the president of Colby College, formally severing the national organization's fifty-seven-year relationship with our college. This decision was forced upon them, she stated, because Colby's "criteria for fraternal operations cannot be reconciled with our organization." We hailed the publication of this letter as a local victory in the war against discrimination!

"Oh yes, the Tri Delta affair," Judy Turner Jones said of the controversy sparked by our chapter making her our first Black pledge. Our paths had converged several years before when she and her husband, Vann Jones, a physician who had graduated from Cornell and Howard Medical School, conversed with me about our children, our work, and mutual friends from Colby. Tri Delta never entered our conversation.

When I asked Judy in a later phone call what specifically she recalled about our sorority's exit from the national fold, she remembered that at first she had been saddened and self-conscious when the charter was rescinded: "There was the illusion that attending a New England liberal arts college would be a refuge, safe from racial turmoil. But the tentacles of the national organization reached into our little group. At the time, I confess, I was worried some of the girls might resent my presence as the cause of their loss in status as members of Tri-Delta. But everyone was on board. The spirit of our group never faltered. We built a great new local sorority. When I tell the story, I consider it a badge of honor."

"Badge of honor"—this same concept was the theme of a powerful commencement address delivered to my graduating class by two-time presidential nominee and then ambassador to the United Nations, Adlai Stevenson.

"We older people ignore students at our peril these days," Stevenson began. "I think especially of the participation of American students in the great struggle to advance civil and human rights in America. Indeed, even a jail sentence is no longer a dishonor but a proud achievement." Images of Freedom Riders, sit-ins, attack dogs, assault hoses, and paddy wagons ferrying peaceful demonstrators to jail in Birmingham were summoned to mind.

"Perhaps," he continued, in a phrase that would make headlines in *The New York Times* the next day, "we are destined to see in this law-loving land people running for office not on their stainless records but on their prison records." None of Stevenson's remarks struck me as boilerplate graduation rhetoric. When he spoke of the duty incumbent upon us to shape public affairs, "the duty to speak of the burning issues of our time," I felt he was speaking directly to me.

Was it that moment that impelled me to turn down the Fulbright I had just been awarded so I could go straight to Harvard graduate school and focus upon American history and government? Or had the decision been made during Colby's skirmish with the national Tri-Delta organization? Or, perhaps, was it the enduring inspiration of the March on Washington? All I knew then was that I wanted to be in America, to be part of the "vast social revolution" that Stevenson referenced, "the great struggle to advance civil and human rights."

Wherever Dick traveled in the aftermath of Birmingham and the March on Washington—bouncing from Brazil to Bolivia, the Dominican Republic to Africa, Israel to England to drum up support for the thriving International Peace Corps—he was met with avid curiosity about American politics, the Peace Corps, and especially civil rights. While at Cambridge University in England, he remembered "serious-minded students who seemed to be much more intense and interested in the world than their elders," their eyes fastened on what was happening in the United States. "But this is true," he happily remarked during his travels, "of young people all over the world."

The more Dick spoke with young people abroad, the more he also felt a powerful tug to be back in the United States. The March on Washington had even evoked a desire to be outside government altogether, perhaps working with the Civil Rights Movement, where transformative action was taking place in what he considered the crucial issue of the age. "I wanted to contribute something firsthand," he told me. "I wanted to be home."

The unlikely avenue that would provide such a homecoming came by way of Dick's work with Jackie Kennedy and Arthur Schlesinger on the Nobel Prize dinner and the campaign to preserve the Abu Simbel monuments. Around the same time, a position had opened up at the White House for the president's special consultant on the arts. Jackie asked Dick to help find the right person for the job.

"I would come out for a vigorous young man rather than a big, but doddering name," Dick had responded in a note to her, "an intelligent fellow with real feeling for the arts, the ability to talk with artists and museum directors and who can be effective in government would be far better than a well-known person who likes to make effective speeches and who would be fully frustrated."

"Wow," Jackie exclaimed. "What a perfect description of you!"

When it became clear to both Jackie and Arthur Schlesinger that Dick really did want this position, they approached Kennedy, who was delighted to bring Dick back into the White House fold. By executive order, the president established the National Council on the Arts, to be administered by his special consultant. Members of this council would be chosen from prominent figures in the arts—literature, poetry, painting, architecture, music, theater, dance, movies—all carefully weighed and measured to fit like a jigsaw puzzle. The announcement of the council members would be synchronized with the news of Dick's appointment.

"For the first time," Kennedy proclaimed when he signed the executive order, "the Arts will have some formal government body which will be specifically concerned with all aspects of the Arts."

From the beginning, Kennedy was never unmindful of the larger political resonance of the arts, particularly as a foreign policy tool to promote a better understanding and display of American culture abroad. He was keenly aware of our rivalry with the Soviet Union, which was skillfully exporting ballet groups and symphony orchestras throughout Latin America, while our State Department had cut down on such cultural activities. There was no doubt we were losing the cultural cold war.

Some colleagues were puzzled as to why Dick even wanted the job. The budget accorded the arts council was far smaller than the staff and capacious headquarters he had working with the Peace Corps International.

"Why *did* you want the job?" I asked Dick, wondering myself.

"A job is what you can make of it," Dick quickly answered.

Long ago I had heard nearly identical words when Lyndon Johnson described how he could take a strategically placed small job—like messenger to a college president or secretary to a congressman—and build them into something exponentially greater. One staffer from Lyndon's younger days remembered "his imagination," his ability to think of "new approaches that we could take to stretch the boundaries or the limitations under which we operated."

"Mostly," Dick said, "I wanted to be back in the magic circle, back in the White House. Kennedy prized versatility, the willingness and ability to tackle whatever came up. That unique way of operating informed his whole administration. Anything was possible. Anything could happen. And the election was only a year away."

By October, as the council members were being assembled, a broad conception of the arts had begun to percolate in Dick's mind—a conception far beyond financial support and grants to theaters and museums—one that stretched the boundaries of what was meant by the arts, that included the beauty of our natural environment and even the restoration of our cities.

"Before long," Dick smiled, "the idea of the arts had grown until it seemed a necessary and integral ingredient of a healthy society. It led to basic issues of human dignity and social justice in an increasingly prosperous America."

So November began with a hopeful and positive surge of energy that would lead to his promising return to the White House. After an interval of more than a decade, Dick even picked up his diary again. His busy entries reflect a sense of those happy crowded days in late November of 1963. Great expectations filled the air.

NOVEMBER 20, 1963

On Wednesday, the day before the president and first lady were to leave for an early campaign jaunt to Texas, Dick arrived at the Oval Office to confer with Kennedy on a few additional names for the arts council. Kennedy agreed to the proposals and added the name of another person who had been very helpful to the administration. This brought the council number to forty. Then, in an interchange recorded in his diary, Dick mentioned to the president his preliminary thoughts about the arts "as something far more than a public relations thing, worrying about who came to dinner at the White House, etc." Instead, he explained:

It should concern itself with the entire problems of the aesthetics of our society, the way our cities looked, the beauty of our environment as well as the general encouragement to the arts. I said I thought that this whole business of the aesthetics of our environment could be to him what Conservation was to Teddy Roosevelt.

"It's a good idea," Kennedy responded. "Let's work on it."

Later that day, Dick returned once again to the Oval Office with Arthur Schlesinger and a group of Latin American ambassadors and intellectuals. Both Dick and Arthur had recently sent memos to Kennedy about the need for a more robust and inspirational leadership at the top levels of the Alliance for Progress in order to break through the bureaucratic inertia at the State Department. "The Peace Corps has helped show what an overseas program can be when approached with great imagination and skill," Dick had written. "The *Alianza* is intrinsically more exciting, bigger and more glamorous than the Peace Corps and there is no reason why it should not attract as good or better people." They recommended moving either Sarge Shriver or Bobby Kennedy to head the Alliance.

According to Dick's diary, the Latin ambassadors voiced the same concern about bureaucratic obstacles at the State Department. Kennedy asked for recommendations about what they thought should be done to remedy things. One of the ambassadors spoke up, again emphasizing the importance of appointing someone of real stature like one of his brothers. Dick's diary recounted Kennedy's reply:

I'm running out of brothers. . . . But you're going over to see Bobby, why don't you offer him the job. Later when they did, Bobby took it quite seriously, and said, "I'd like to do something like this . . . It interests me very much."

THURSDAY, NOVEMBER 21

News of Dick's coming appointment had already circulated. The proverbial cat was out of the bag. The *New York Times* cultural reporter called Dick on Thursday night. As Dick noted in his diary,

He told me that he was doing a story for next day's paper saying I was expected to be named Advisor on the Arts and doing a man in the news profile

on me. I told him he might be making a big mistake, that nothing was definite. He ignored this as he obviously had the story pretty cold. He asked some personal questions for the profile and I gave them to him. If he was going to do it anyway I wanted it to be as good as possible.

Dick called the assistant White House press secretary, Malcolm Kilduff, in Texas to tell him what had happened. After speaking with the president, Kilduff reached Dick at a dinner party for Latin American artists and intellectuals. Kilduff told Dick the president wanted him to prepare a statement and send it down for release tomorrow. Dick's diary recounts:

I said I would, went back to the party and returned home about 4 a.m. to bed, thinking I would not go in tomorrow but would stay home, get some sleep (it had been a hectic week, out every night) work on the council and on the statement.

FRIDAY, NOVEMBER 22

Very gradually did Dick groggily arise from the partying of the previous night. First off, he snatched the morning edition of *The New York Times* and searched for the "Man in the News" profile about him.

It was a very favorable story, without the snide cracks which usually accompany such articles about me. The picture was nice and the whole thing had a good tone and ring.

The profile, which Dick had saved, was indeed exceedingly positive. Dick was described as "one of the bright young men on the New Frontier," who had already accomplished more than most men before he had even reached his thirty-second birthday. "He has a quickness of mind, a mind that darts about and picks up things quickly," says one Washington observer. "He moves with a natural instinct wherever new ideas are being developed," and he has "won the respect and gratitude of many Latin American statesmen."

While "controversy" was often yoked to "brilliant" in descriptions of Dick, this profile emphasized that Dick was "someone whom the president turns to naturally and with a sense of intimacy."

Well pleased with the *Times* article, Dick quickly and happily finished the draft of the White House's announcement of his new position early in the afternoon. He wanted to add several additional names to the list of council members. He wanted to be sure they got into the appropriate hands.

He called the White House secretary and said he was prepared to dictate his announcement. At that point, the anguished voice on the line broke:

Oh! Mr. Goodwin, didn't you know, the president is dead. I said, What? She said yes, he was killed in Texas. Somebody shot him. He's dead.

CHAPTER SIX

Kaleidoscope

*Dick is among mourners and members of the Color Guard witnessing
the funeral procession of President John Kennedy from the White House
to the Capitol. November 24, 1963.*

"POLITICAL AFFAIRS ARE KALEIDOSCOPIC," CAUTIONED THEODORE
Roosevelt in a letter to his sister Anna in 1907. The image of the kaleidoscope was never far from Roosevelt's mind when contemplating either his
personal life or his political career. He knew from experience how a turn of
the kaleidoscope could either open an opportunity or block a future path,
brighten prospects or darken the road ahead.

After the sudden death of his twenty-three-year-old wife—on the very
day and in the same house where his mother also died—Roosevelt felt he
would never love again. "For joy or sorrow," he wrote, "my life has now been
lived out." Yet, three years later, he once more fell deeply in love and entered
a fulfilling, lifelong second marriage.

Such sharp changes in fortune in the historical lives I have studied are
scarcely different from the vicissitudes of our own lives, excepting that their
experiences are writ large, dramatized on a stage that can affect multitudes
in their own country and even around the world.

Cases in point—Both Theodore Roosevelt and Lyndon Johnson—

were men of irrepressible energy who chafed within the strictures of the vice presidency. Both men languished in such misery that they considered their circumstances intolerable. "I am not doing any work," Roosevelt confessed, "and do not feel as though I am justifying my existence." Lyndon Johnson likewise feared that "he had come to the end of the political road."

Then, in most violent twists of the kaleidoscope, the cell doors of the vice presidency were blasted open for both men. As President William McKinley was shaking hands on a receiving line at the World's Fair, an anarchist's revolver, concealed in a handkerchief, awaited him; and under a bright Dallas sky, President Kennedy's motorcade turned the corner past the Texas School Book Depository building and into Dealey Plaza.

NOVEMBER 22, 1963

"I didn't know what to do," Dick said. His jumbled thoughts on the day of Kennedy's death were recorded in his diary.

My only instinct was to dress and go to the White House. There would be others there, something would be happening. I would know more. I drove to the White House. I clung to the wheel and watched the road with concentration of energies. The city was quiet. Nothing seemed very different. A maze of thoughts, Jackie, Bobby, Johnson was President, my future. But under it, over it, he was dead.

"But you weren't working yet at the White House; you had no office there," I said to Dick.

"I didn't know where else to go," Dick said. "It wasn't rational. I needed company. I wanted to help."

When Dick first arrived, any awkwardness he felt at intruding was erased because Sarge Shriver was there and in charge of the funeral planning. Shriver knew he could count on Dick to help him in this final and darkest of White House occasions.

Foremost among Shriver's instructions was to fulfill Jackie's wish that Kennedy lie in state in the East Room, and that this largest room in the Mansion be arranged to resemble as closely as possible its appearance when Lincoln lay in state after his assassination one hundred years before. Within minutes, Dick had tracked down Carl Sandburg's biography of Abraham Lincoln from the Cabinet Room and located a description of the catafalque upon which the coffin rested, beneath "a canopy of folds and loops of black silk and crape."

Further details were needed, so Dick called Arthur Schlesinger, who convinced someone to open the closed Library of Congress in order to find contemporary accounts and illustrations of Lincoln's body lying in the East Room. Before the hour was out, *Frank Leslie's Illustrated Newspaper* and the May 6, 1865, issue of *Harper's Weekly* were delivered to the White House. When Dick had laid out the lithographs before Shriver and his small crew, they decided that rather than try to replicate the ornate Victorian tent of black mourning crape that had surrounded Lincoln's coffin, they would instead aim to simplify, yet suggest, that somber and stately atmosphere.

Working with a small team (including Kennedy family friends Bill Walton and Dean Markham), Dick located a catafalque at Fort Myer similar to the one used for Lincoln's casket and made arrangements for its urgent delivery to the White House. Less garish candlesticks were found and Shriver sent for his own crucifix, to be taken from his bedroom for placement upon the coffin. A simple floral arrangement was prepared. The upholsterer who had refurbished furniture for Jackie was brought in. "It was going slowly," Dick noted in his diary.

Meanwhile, the plane carrying Jackie and the late president from Texas, along with Lyndon Johnson and the entire presidential party, was due to arrive at Andrews Air Force Base about 6 p.m. Bobby would meet Jackie there and accompany her to Bethesda Naval Hospital where the president's body would be autopsied and embalmed. When they returned to the White House at some point in the middle of the night, everything had to be ready.

It was getting late. The catafalque had not yet arrived. I called the military office, asked where it was. They put a tracer on it, sent a man out looking for it. It had left the Fort. I was harsh. We need it right away, hurry up. It shortly arrived. We set it up in the middle of the room. Black stand on black base.

The decorating team grew larger as the hour of arrival approached. "We were fearful we would not get it done in time," Dick told me. So everyone joined in—from Shriver and Schlesinger to the White House butlers and the president's dog handler. The volunteer crew raced up and down ladders to drape black crape on the chandeliers. Everyone pitched in—upholstery tacks in pursed lips and hammers in hand—to trim the entrance, the windows, and the doorways in black.

As the room was nearing completion, Shriver walked with Dick and a few others to the Front Portico. A huge crowd had gathered on the streets. This East Room ceremony was for family and friends only. The public would be able to view the coffin at the Capitol Rotunda over the weekend. The people who had waited on the streets would never see the East Room decorated to convey something of the spirit of Abraham Lincoln lying in state there a century before.

"The occasion should be made memorable for them, too," Shriver mused. "I know he isn't really coming home, but I want it to look that way." The grounds were dark. Shriver remembered that during White House parties Jackie had the grounds lit by small flaming pots. After a frantic search, highway flame pots were found, delivered, and placed in a curve to gently illuminate the driveway leading to the North Portico.

The result was stunning, William Manchester wrote in *The Death of a President*, "the flame-lit drive, the deep black against the white columns, the shrouded doorway, the East Room in deep mourning, the catafalque ready to receive the coffin."

Only one problem remained, as Dick noted in his diary.

The troops for outside guard had not come yet. Spoke harshly to [Naval aide Captain] Shepard as did Sarge. He ordered the troops out of marine barracks at 8th and I. They arrived a few minutes before the coffin.

I was amazed that by 4:30 a.m. the team had managed to organize a dignified nocturnal homecoming to an illuminated White House for the reception of the president's coffin—all arranged for an audience of one, the president's widow.

The East Room, the same sparkling chamber where Kennedy had announced the Alliance for Progress and welcomed a throng of Nobel Laureates, had been transformed into a private, dignified space to usher the slain president home.

Dick's eyewitness account of that moment from within the private globe of the East Room draws me into the scene with its simplicity and immediacy.

I stood on the front portico. I wanted to see the car enter. It came in, black, dark, headlights, the guard began its march. I rushed back and through the back entrance to the East Room in the far corner where we had agreed we would stand. Pierre [Salinger] was there and Arthur and Bill [Walton] and Ralph [Dungan] and others who had worked through the night.

The casket slowly came in the door. He was there, in that casket, dead. They placed the casket on the catafalque. Mrs. Kennedy stood there beside Bobby, her face was fixed straight ahead, lovely and painful to see.

She walked over to the coffin, knelt on the base, turned her head away from where we were standing and rested her cheek along the flag which draped the coffin. Her hands went up over it, holding for a moment. She then got up, and, Bobby holding her by the arm, walked out. The rest of us stood there for a moment, weeping.

It was about 5:15 a.m. Drove to Arthur's. I sat and had a drink with him, and we consoled each other with our talk. I then left as the sun was coming up and was in bed around 6:30 to rise the next day at 8:30. I then dressed and returned to the White House.

Dick's journal chronicled episodes of the following morning.

Saturday was the day of preparation for the funeral. Jackie had issued personal instructions that everyone was to walk behind the casket on the way to the funeral.

She also wanted bagpipers to be at the graves and play over the hills—Air Force bagpipers. Arrangements were made to bring the Black Watch bagpipers. The Irish Guard was to come over. Their routine was to be fitted into the ceremony. Word came that many heads of state would attend the funeral. It is said when [Charles] de Gaulle arrived he said that he came because the little people of France demanded it.

We kept drinking coffee that was brought out to us, and then sandwiches. I had gone down to [White House physician] Janet Travell and gotten some Dexamyl. She asked me to lie down for five minutes. I said I couldn't. I took the pills and went.

The planning team was so exhausted and consumed by their tasks that at one point, while compiling the lists of foreign leaders to invite to the church service at St. Matthew's, Shriver suddenly realized they had overlooked the three living former presidents—Hoover, Truman, and Eisenhower.

On Sunday morning, as the flag-draped coffin was being readied to travel by caisson to the Capitol for the public viewing in the Rotunda, Shriver received a call that the president's alleged assassin had just been shot in the basement of the Dallas police station while being transferred to the Dallas County Jail. "Somebody just shot Oswald," Shriver announced. There was no response. "We went on with our business," Dick later told an interviewer. "I wouldn't have cared if I'd been told that [Texas governor John] Connally had been charged with the shooting."

"In hindsight," Dick told me, "while millions watched television, transfixed by the chaos that followed the shooting, I had virtually forgotten the outside world. I had forgotten there was a new president—and Lyndon Johnson is not easily forgotten. The only thing important to me was to figure out how to get the eternal flame Jackie wanted to the gravesite in Arlington in less than twenty-four hours."

While Jackie was accompanying her husband's body to the Rotunda, she had suddenly remembered the eternal flame she had once seen at the Tomb of the Unknown Soldier at the Arc de Triomphe in Paris. At once, she decided she wanted one placed at her husband's grave.

Shriver was taken aback: "Some people might think it's a little ostentatious," he warned.

"*Let* them," Jackie said.

I knew that Manchester had reported that Dick was given the responsibility of getting the flame and that he had interviewed Dick for this section, so I located those pages in *Death of a President* and we read them aloud:

Dick Goodwin was designated flame expediter. Goodwin was as tough as he was smart, brass and braid didn't impress him, and the past three years had taught him that the most common word in the Army bureaucracy was can't.

"We can't do it," an MDW [Military District of Washington] staff duty officer told him.

"Why not?"

"We'd have to fly to Europe. That's the only place they know about them."

"O.K.," Goodwin snapped. "It's six hours to Europe. Go get it."

There was an uneasy silence. Then: "Maybe we can fabricate it."

"Good. Fabricate it."

"We have a request from Mrs. Kennedy," the staff officer told Lieutenant Colonel Bernard Carroll. "She wants an eternal flame at the gravesite."

To Carroll this sounded somewhat vague. He asked, "What's eternal?"

"Before, during, and after the ceremony," the officer said promptly.

That sounded easy, Carroll could use almost any kerosene pot which would burn for an hour or so. On reflection, however, it sounded too easy. He suspected that the widow had something else in mind, and he raised so many questions that the officer said he'd have to call back.

In the West Wing, Goodwin was summoned to a phone. He listened a moment and then said icily, "Eternal means *forever.*"

The staff duty officer hemmed and hawed, but each time he raised
an objection he was cut down with whipsaw orders to stop giving reasons why it couldn't be done and start doing it.

Driven back to his last outpost, the officer raised a final obstacle.

"She can't light it."

"*Why not?*"

"There's too much danger. It might go out."

"Listen," Goodwin said. If you can design an atomic bomb, you can put
a little flame on the side of that hill, and you can make it so she can light it."

Upon finishing our reading of Manchester, I asked Dick, "Is that how
you remember these conversations?"

For the first and only time during our discussion of the funeral procession and burial, Dick smiled. "I was so tired then I could hardly stand up.
But I heartily endorse that picture of me, so I believe every word of it!"

As it turned out, the army engineers assigned to the mission did a first-
rate job of emergency tinkering. Though most electrical supply stores were
closed on Sunday, they finally found a gas-fueled luau lamp made for out-
door parties and built a base for it. They brought several bottles of propane
gas to the cemetery, covered them with evergreens, and ran a copper tube
underground from the tanks to the gravesite, a safe distance away. Midnight
was approaching by the time they were ready for a test run. A lighted torch
sparked, the flame ignited, and the flame burns today.

MONDAY, NOVEMBER 25

Through the television screen in 1956, my mother and I had first been
introduced to John Kennedy; now, again via television, like the rest of the
nation, I would spend days bidding him farewell. I was caught up in the
traumatizing whirlpool surrounding the president's death and the capture
and subsequent murder of his assassin.

The central figure of my attention that day, however, was Jacqueline
Kennedy. I watched intently as she led the funeral procession behind the
casket down Pennsylvania Avenue, two and a half miles on foot from the
Capitol to the Cathedral of St. Matthew. The first lady was followed by

other members of the Kennedy family, then the new president and Lady Bird Johnson, as well as seventy-two heads of state, many in military attire. I remember the caisson carrying the president's flag-draped coffin, the riderless horse with an empty saddle and reversed boots in the stirrups, the image of three-year-old John Kennedy Jr. saluting. Finally, I recall the moment Jackie touched a lighted taper to the gravesite fixture and the eternal flame leapt up. Instinctively, she had wanted her husband's inaugural exhortation—that the torch be passed to a new generation—to be literally remembered in this flame representing both his spirit and his vision.

More than ever, I now realize that the order and decorum Jackie had insisted upon—the historical resemblances to Abraham Lincoln's last rites in Washington—went far deeper than ceremonial trappings. In those four days, she demonstrated to everyone in America and around the world, a noble response to the fatal twist of the kaleidoscope that had afflicted us all, a composed will and a resilient grace, providing continuity and dignity in the midst of the violence, chaos, and pandemonium that had unfolded in Dallas.

The presidency is a Ptolemaic universe; staffers and aides are forever encircling the presidential planet Earth. What would the team of New Frontiersmen circle around now? There was an empty space where their leader had been. These were the questions I examined with Dick as we searched his diaries and boxes of stored materials from the weeks following the assassination.

As we talked, a wave of heaviness seemed to wash over Dick, even after more than half a century. Kennedy remained his hero, although his abrupt transfer from the White House to the State Department had heartbroken the young aide. He had traveled the country with Kennedy for sixty straight days on that small two-engine plane. With pride, he had watched the candidate's steady growth under mounting pressure. He had reveled in Kennedy's victory, had accompanied him on several occasions to Latin America, and had cherished the intimacy of working closely with him in the West Wing where he was on the cusp of returning when the president had been slain.

The two Brookline boys could not have been more different; but after seeing the candidate shave with a badger brush and mug in the bathtub, Dick had ordered a similar brush from London, keeping it in a wire caddy to shave in the tub for the rest of his life. Over the years Dick would respect, revere, and develop close friendships with other political figures, but never again idolize a political leader.

Something had changed for Dick during those frenetic days and sleepless nights as he joined the small team helping to prepare for the return of Kennedy's body, his funeral, and burial. As never before, Dick had been drawn into the inner circle of Kennedy family and friends. This was not a simple political alliance. They had bonded in a common mission and were now united in a post-traumatic haze. During that time an emotional attachment was formed, a fellowship with traces that would last for the remainder of Dick's life.

Bobby and Ethel, Sarge and Eunice, Arthur and Dick, as well as Paul Warnke, Bill Walton, and occasionally Jackie, would often gather together for lunch or dinner, taking regular trips to Boston and New York to begin making detailed plans for a John Fitzgerald Kennedy Library.

During one of the early dinner meetings at Ted Kennedy's house, talk revolved around where the library should be situated and who should sit on its board of incorporators. Dick made two suggestions: *One, we had to give more thought to the theme of the library. More than a repository of books, it should be a living study center. We should think this through. Two, we could probably raise money from some of the Latin American countries.*

The next afternoon Dick was off to New York to talk with Luis Muñoz, governor of Puerto Rico, and Antonio Carrillo Flores, a leading financial figure in Mexico. To avoid any future charges that government pressure had been exerted, Dick went "to great lengths" to assure them this was "a personal request, having nothing to do with the U.S. Government." They promised to secure funding right away. And in the weeks that followed, Dick helped to raise hundreds of thousands of dollars from Latin America for the prospective Kennedy Library.

Ostensibly, the little group's most pressing objective during these nonstop meetings and planning sessions was to ensure and preserve Kennedy's memory, as if the intense focus on a library that would be a living legacy might somehow shelter them from the fatal turn of the kaleidoscope that had struck them all.

Inevitably, however, conversations turned to their individual futures. The career trajectories of some (like Sorensen) were so intertwined with Kennedy's own course that they had no appetite to continue in public service. Others, caught in a welter of depression, anger, and insecurity, tried to figure out where they might best fit if they decided to stay in Washington.

"I hardly knew what my own job was," Dick told me. "It seemed certain that my pending White House appointment as adviser on the arts had also perished in Dallas. Would I stay at the Peace Corps? Would Sarge stay?"

At dinner with Sarge and Eunice one evening, Dick noted in his diary that the morning paper had carried a column suggesting that Sarge, young and handsome, was "the leading prospect for the Vice-Presidential nomination."

Eunice said it was no fun to be a Vice-President's wife. Sarge leaned across the table and earnestly tried to convince her that it would be fun. You could do a lot as a Vice-President's wife, a lot more than Lady Bird did. I said yes, she had to realize that previously the President and Jackie had overshadowed everyone, but this wouldn't be true. She laughed, a little nervously, and said "look what we're talking about" and the conversation shifted.

Dick told me that it was clear that Sarge sincerely wanted to be VP but that his greatest obstacle was Bobby, who also was considering the VP job. In his diary Dick recounted another dinner shortly afterward where he talked with Eunice about Bobby's prospects:

She [Eunice] said the alternatives seemed to be to stay in a government job, perhaps another job, run for vice-President, or go back to Mass, and run for governor or something. I suggested that he might go to NY and build a political base there.

But, she said, that will take so long. I said there was no short-cut—that Lyndon had taken the only short cut.

A few days later, Bobby called Dick.

He said that before I did anything drastic we might have a little chat. I thanked him and asked how about him. He stumbled a little for the first time since I knew him, said he would stay around a little, see how things went, etc. He sounded disturbed and confused. This was an awful blow for Bob. His brother was as McNamara told me that awful weekend his teacher, his idol, friend, the fixed star around which Bob Kennedy's life revolved.

Arthur told me he really took all this stuff about the Kennedys dominating the last half of the 20th century as the Roosevelts had the first half quite seriously and he doesn't really know where to go now that his ambit has been so circumscribed.

As I read this entry, I began to comprehend how terribly raw Robert Kennedy's feelings remained, experiencing a pain that could hardly tolerate seeing another in his brother's chair at cabinet meetings, could not bear to meet his brother's absence in the eyes of his replacement. After attending Johnson's first cabinet meeting Bobby rarely went again. Unable to endure riding on the president's plane without his brother, he turned down Johnson's invitations to fly with him to official functions on Air Force One.

Nonetheless, there were passages in Dick's diary that troubled me greatly. He recounted conversations that revealed a complete lack of empathy and interest in the mammoth problems that beset the new president and the country at large.

One quiet morning at dawn, I tried to sort out my thoughts on these entries—specifically concerning a disturbing record of a long meeting Arthur and Dick had over bourbons with Bobby in the attorney general's office. I read it over and over before Dick prevented any further possibility of concentration by trumpeting his regular morning greeting from the top of the stairs.

As we sat down to work in his study after breakfast, I slowly read each paragraph aloud to Dick. From hindsight, it is easy to discern in these interchanges the deepening fault lines between the Kennedy and Johnson camps that would play out for the better part of the decade—and would prove a recurring irritant in our marriage.

On Friday Arthur and I went to see Bob Kennedy about the Kennedy library. He was standing at the door to his office, no jacket, tie loosened to greet us. I said, here come representatives of the 16%. (A morning Gallup poll had shown that 16% of rank and file demos favored Bobby for the nomination—66% for LBJ).

RFK grinned when I mentioned the 16%. If we could get a little more, we'd take it away from the bastard.

After they went over the material relating to the Kennedy Library, Arthur and Dick turned the conversation to the Alliance for Progress. Earlier that morning, they had heard that LBJ was about to appoint Tom Mann as the new assistant secretary of state for Latin American Affairs. "This indicated a major step backwards," Dick explained to me. "In politics, an appointment can signal which way the wind is blowing. Mann had been at State under Eisenhower. He was a colonialist who believed the main job of the U.S. in Latin America was to make the world safe for big American business. He didn't believe in the demand for land reform and social justice. We were devastated." In his diary Dick recounted Bobby's response:

The Alianza isn't just important to Dick Goodwin or Arthur Schlesinger. It's important to me and Ed Henry and a lot of other people.

I haven't thought through how to go about it but the secret is collective action. There are hundreds of guys around here in positions of influence. We're important to Johnson. I'm the most important because my name happens to be Kennedy. But we're all important if we act together.

(He stood, hands at side, head down, fighting a show of emotion) Sure, I've lost a brother. Other people lose wives, his voice trailed off. I've lost a brother but that's not what's important. What's important is what we were trying to do for this country. We got a good start, we had a committee working on juvenile poverty, juvenile delinquency study, you can't do a lot in three years. We could have done a lot in five more years. There are a lot of people in this town. They didn't come here just to work for John Kennedy, an individual, but for ideas, things they wanted to do. I don't want people running off.

We're very important to Johnson now. After November 5 we'll all be dead. We won't matter a damn. But between now and then he needs us, he needs me most of all. I haven't talked to Johnson yet. I'm not mentally equipped for it, or physically.

The Vice-Presidency may be the key job, but not just because someone wants to be V.P., not just to hold office, but to do something with. When the time comes we'll tell him who we want for Vice-President.

What does he know about people who've got no jobs, or are under-educated. He's got no feeling for people who are hungry. It's up to us. The secret is to act together, collective action.

Remember, after November 5th we're all done. We won't be wanted or needed.

"Who does he think he is?" I said, taken aback. "He wildly overrates his clout over the vice presidential choice!"

"That's easy to say now," Dick argued, "but remember, no one suspected who Lyndon was, much less what he would become."

"It's the arrogance of the '*we'll* tell *him* who *we* want' that sticks in my craw."

"I understand," Dick replied, "but it seemed to us all then that Bobby's public cooperation, as the head of the Kennedy family, was crucial to the transition."

Nonetheless, that notion of *collective action* sounded to me like some sort of subversive insurgency plan. After all, Lyndon Johnson was the constitutional successor of a ticket that had been elected by the people of the United States. By grim default, he was the rightful chief executive of the country.

"What was Bobby thinking?" I asked.

"He wasn't thinking. He was venting, from grief, from the need to ensure that the goals of the New Frontier would be carried forward."

"Even if I can fathom that, what really drives me crazy is Bobby's mean-spirited caricature of LBJ. A man without empathy for the poor? Even then that was simply wrongheaded."

"Don't get so upset," smiled Dick gently. "This was all a long time ago."

———

Bobby's description of Johnson as someone having no empathy for the poor and no feeling for people who are hungry continued to rile me. I spent the rest of the day in my study reviewing some of my own materials on Lyndon Johnson. While doing research for my latest book on leadership, I had come upon a conversation Johnson had held with three of his core aides on the very night of Kennedy's assassination. Seated together long after midnight on Johnson's gigantic bed, watching the nonstop coverage of the events in Dallas, the new president had outlined his plans to pass Kennedy's deadlocked proposals for medical care for the aged, civil rights, voting rights, and federal aid for education. "We're going to get a law," he pledged, "that says every boy and girl in this country, no matter how poor, or the color of their skin, or the region they come from, is going to be able to get all the education they can take."

This was no impromptu wish list that LBJ delivered that nightmare night. The vision that the role of government was to look after those who needed help had been germinating in Johnson's mind for decades. It had taken root in the stories his populist father told and had matured during the New Deal. Now, he was no longer representing the conservative state of Texas; he was president of all the people.

I couldn't wait to review these ruminations with Dick to counter Bobby's patently false caricature. But first I decided to look over my own lengthy conversations with LBJ that I had recounted in my first book, *Lyndon Johnson and the American Dream*. I wanted to refresh in my mind what Johnson was feeling during this same period, memories he had shared with me when I first arrived at the White House.

In those early months, while I worked on unemployment issues in low-income urban areas during the day, my unofficial role was to be available to listen to the president when he wanted to talk. Evenings would often find us in the little sitting room next to the Oval Office. There, Johnson liked to relax with a drink and talk . . . and talk and talk.

Perhaps because I had joined the White House staff shortly after Johnson had withdrawn from the presidential race on March 31, 1968, those first conversations often returned to the very beginning of his presidency, to those most difficult, challenging and ultimately successful hours when he had been thrust into office. "I took the oath. I became President," he told me.

But for millions of Americans I was still illegitimate, a naked man; with no presidential covering, a pretender to the throne, an illegal usurper. And then there was Texas, my home, the home of both the murder and the murder of the murderer. And then there were the bigots and the dividers and the Eastern intellectuals who were waiting to knock me down before I could even begin to stand up. The whole thing was almost unbearable.

We were like a bunch of cattle caught in the swamp, unable to move to either direction, simply circling round and round. I understood that. I knew what had to be done. There is but one way to get the cattle out of the swamp. And that is for the man on the horse to take the lead, to assume command, to provide direction. In the period after the assassination, I was that man.

If Dick's diary registered small concern among the Kennedy team for LBJ's untenable position at that time, LBJ expressed to me a keen awareness of *their* profound unhappiness:

I knew how they felt. The impact of Kennedy's death was evident everywhere— in the looks on their faces and the sound of voices. He was gone and with his going they must have felt that everything had changed. Suddenly they were outsiders just as I had been for almost three years, outsiders on the inside.

So I determined to keep them informed. I determined to keep them busy. I constantly requested their advice and asked for their help.

One by one, Johnson had beseeched Kennedy's White House aides with a nearly identical message: "I just want to say that I need you far more than John Kennedy ever needed you. . . . I'm asking you for my sake and for the sake of the country, to stay with me for at least a year. By that time I hope that I will have earned from you the same confidence and faith which I know you had in John F. Kennedy."

I'm not suggesting that Johnson was more softhearted than the Kennedys.

Far from it. This was no mere demonstration of empathy. His outreach, as can be seen in our conversations, was also driven by a hard-edged calculation.

I needed that White House staff. Without them I would have lost my link to John Kennedy, and without that I would have had absolutely no chance of gaining the support of the media or the Easterners or the intellectuals. And without that support I would have had absolutely no chance of governing the country.

Most importantly, a delicate and complicated task had been handled with sensitivity and strength. There was no public display of abandonment of the new president before the public. Though a few cabinet officials and White House staffers were soon to leave, a majority stayed on, even as Johnson gradually added his own men to the team.

Reviewing these conversations and my reactions to them, remembering the many hours I spent with Lyndon Johnson both in the White House and later at the ranch, I realized I was every bit as emotionally involved with LBJ and his plight as Dick was with the sorrow and anger of the Kennedys. It struck me that at bottom, my debate with Dick was not a question of logic or historical citation. It was about the respective investments of our youth, questions of loyalty and love.

I tried to balance one side of the widening fault line with the other. Although I better understood Bobby's fervent need to delay Johnson's planned address to a joint session of Congress—to allow time and space for the country to pause, to mourn his brother before turning their attention to the new president—I knew that neither time nor space were Lyndon Johnson's to give. The country had different needs and he now represented them. In deference to Bobby, he delayed the speech another day. But no longer. The country sorely needed reassurance that together, we would continue, that if the nation was brokenhearted, it was not broken.

Dick and I watched a recording of Johnson's speech to Congress later that night after dinner. I had last watched that address when I worked on *Leadership* and knew what an extraordinary performance he had delivered that day under appalling pressure. Dick said he had only the vaguest impression of the speech. There was no mention of it in his diary. As we opened my computer to view it, Dick remarked that he felt none of the high spirits we had shared when we settled in with a bottle of wine for our "debate date," and relished John Kennedy's bravura performance.

As I said earlier, Dick was often the worst person in the world to have as a companion during any kind of public performance. His brash, distracting, ongoing commentary at movies would irritate everyone within twenty feet. Even at baseball games, where anything goes, his outbursts drew disapproving glances. Now, however, he simply listened with an intent silence to the sorrowful remarks when Lyndon Johnson presented himself to the American people.

WEDNESDAY, NOVEMBER 27

"All I have I would have given gladly not to be standing here today," Johnson began, setting the tone for an emotional address that would blend a funeral oration with a call to bring new life to Kennedy's stalled legislative agenda. Johnson's words came softly, slowly, in stark contrast to the sharp vigor of his predecessor.

"For 32 years Capitol Hill has been my home," he said. "I am here today to say I need your help." Humbly, he had pleaded with Kennedy's staff to stay with him; now he beseeched the entire Congress for their support, and through them, the country at large. "Our most immediate tasks are here on this Hill."

Johnson spoke of Kennedy's domestic dreams, "the dream of education for all our children, the dream of jobs for all who seek them and need them, the dream of care for elderly, the dream of an all-out attack on mental illness, and above all the dream of equal rights for all Americans, whatever their race or color."

The new president made clear that his primary task was to turn Kennedy's blueprints into actual buildings, to honor the architect so that his work would live on forever. "First," Johnson emphasized, "no memorial oration or eulogy could more eloquently honor President Kennedy's memory than the earliest possible passage of the civil rights bill for which he fought so long. We have talked long enough in this country about equal rights. We have talked for one hundred years or more. It is time now to write the next chapter, and to write it in the books of law."

"Impressive," Dick broke his silence, extracting his well-chewed cigar. "A huge risk at the time," he added. "He knew the path he was taking would cut him off from the southern bloc that was his heritage, isolate him from his oldest friends, and might well not succeed. But he was willing to take that path.

"One hell of an introduction to the American people," Dick concluded.

MARCH 9, 1964

"How splendid to be flies on the wall, to eavesdrop across the decades!" Such was Dick's gleeful response after I read him a transcript of the conversation between President Johnson and Bill Moyers recorded on the evening of March 9, 1964—more than six decades earlier. There Dick and I were, in our eighties and seventies respectively, finally privy to the very conversations that (previously unbeknownst to Dick) had led to his second tour of duty on the White House staff. What had been a period of confusion and drift for Dick in the aftermath of Kennedy's assassination, now gave way to an instant of uproarious entertainment.

The revealing phone call in question began with President Johnson grousing to Moyers about the dreary language of the poverty message that he soon planned to deliver to Congress. Passionately invested in the poverty program, he was dissatisfied by the various drafts he had seen and was now pressing Moyers to find "whoever's the best explainer of this that you can get."

LBJ: Since [Ted] Sorensen left, we've got no one that can be phonetic, and get rhythm.

MOYERS: The only person I know who can—and I'm reluctant to ask him to get involved in this because right now it's our little circle—is [Richard] Goodwin.

LBJ: Why not just ask him if he can't put some sex in it? I'd ask him if he couldn't put some rhyme in it and some beautiful Churchillian phrases and take it and turn it out for us tomorrow.

If he will, then we'll use it. But ask him if he can do it in confidence. Call him tonight and say, I want to bring it to you. Now, I've got it ready to go, but he wants you to work on it if you can do it without getting it into a column.

MOYERS: All right, I'll call him right now.

LBJ: Tell him that I'm pretty impressed with him. He's working on Latin America already; see how he's getting along. But can he put the music to it?

As we reached the end of this conversation in the transcript, Dick swore he could hear Johnson's voice clearly in his mind's ear. So this was the story, Dick marveled, that explained his crossover from the nucleus of the Kennedy camp to the highest circles of the Johnson administration.

"Lyndon's a kind of poet," said Dick seriously. (From the time Dick and I met, we often referred to the president simply as Lyndon when speaking to each other. We both knew him so well; and after all, there are a lot of Johnsons but only one Lyndon.) "Rhyme, sex, music, phonetics, and beautiful Churchillian phrases," Dick said with wonder. "What a recipe for high oratory."

"In private, on the phone, one-on-one—there was no one like him," I added. "Yet when playing the role of a proper public statesman, he was often boring, even dull."

If the Kennedy camp condescendingly called him "Colonel Cornpone" and worse, and somewhere inside he was dogged by a similar voice of mockery, remaining insecure about who and what he was. If only Johnson had trusted himself to speak in public as he did in private, he would be considered one of our grand, historical characters in American folklore.

I told Dick that I understood why Moyers was "reluctant" to bring him into LBJ's "little circle"—despite the close friendship he and Dick had formed in the Peace Corps. The rift cut both ways: the LBJ circle on the one side, the remnant Kennedys on the other. And in Lyndon's mind, if anyone seemed a charter member of the Kennedy corps of loyalists, it would be Dick—barely thirty years old, the quintessential New Frontiersman with his Harvard pedigree and his intimate friendships with Bobby, Jackie, and the Kennedy family. While Lyndon needed Dick, he wondered if he'd be able to trust him.

I asked Dick why LBJ had told Moyers to warn him to avoid getting his name into a column.

"Nothing infuriated Lyndon more than leaks from the inside," Dick explained, "even if they only dimmed his luster a single watt. On the other hand, he never embraced me more lovingly and toasted me more lavishly than when I added to that brightness."

———•———

In the first of the many "LBJ" boxes in Dick's archive, we found a memo from Moyers dated March 10 (the morning after his conversation with LBJ), instructing Dick that "what the President wants is 1800 to 2000 words, a kind of state of the union message on poverty." Over the next few days, five drafts developed, rapid-fire, all of which had been saved in an accordion packet.

The final version, delivered to Congress on March 16, 1964, proposed a "Nationwide War on the Sources of Poverty." It began with a simple state-ment of fact:

We are citizens of the richest and most fortunate nation in the history of the world. . . .

But we have never lost sight of our goal: an America in which every citizen shares all the opportunities of his society, in which every man has a chance to advance his welfare to the limit of his capacities. We have come a long way toward this goal. We still have a long way to go. . . .

To finish that work I have called for a national war on poverty. Our objective: total victory. There are millions of Americans—one fifth of our people—who have not shared in the abundance which has been granted to most of us and on whom the gates of opportunity have been closed.

The next day, St. Patrick's Day, Dick was at a Peace Corps meeting with Sarge Shriver in the Fish Room of the White House. Out of the blue—or so Dick thought for the next fifty years—he "chanced" to encounter President Johnson as he stepped into the West Wing corridor. "Dick, can you come here a minute," Johnson said, ushering him into the Oval Office and shutting the door behind them.

"This was my first experience of 'the treatment,'" Dick told me. "People speak of the treatment humorously but I understood at once why Bobby felt he wasn't mentally or physically equipped to talk with Lyndon in the wake of his brother's assassination."

When I asked Dick to explain, he spoke of Lyndon's height, his close-ness, his violation of the conventions of personal space. But most of all, it was a formidable combination of will, conviction, and energy, all focused on you, his eyes locking down into yours like an unnerving force field of persuasive power.

"Tell me, Dick," the president had asked in a soft whisper, "what do you think we should do about this Panama thing?"

Dick knew that anti-American rioting had erupted in Panama over our continued control of the Panama Canal Zone, and that Panamanian presi-dent Francisco Chiari, nearing a national election, had severed diplomatic ties with the United States. This was Johnson's first foreign crisis and he had reacted swiftly. "I'm not going to be pushed around by a country no bigger than St. Louis," he had publicly stated, flatly rejecting any negotiations until peace was restored. The crisis had deepened.

Dick found it hard to gather his thoughts with the president looming overhead. Finally, he spoke up. "We're a great big, powerful, rich country. Panama is tiny, weak, poor. They know we could just come in and take what we want and they'd be helpless. All they've got is their pride, and if we make threats and demands, they can't give in. They'd lose their dignity."

"So what would you suggest," Johnson asked, "that we give them whatever they want?"

"Tell them they're a great country, our allies in the fight for freedom . . . that we're grateful, glad to have them as friends, anxious to keep a small misunderstanding from damaging such a valuable relationship."

"Can you write me a statement?" Johnson asked.

"Of course," Dick replied.

His objective gained, the president relaxed, slung his long arm over Dick's shoulder and steered him back into the corridor. What had made the deepest impression on Dick from this first engagement was that Johnson had asked what *he* would do before asking him to draft a statement. The conciliatory statement Dick wrote struck a note of humility, softening the bellicose tones and posturing into which both sides had hedged themselves. The statement spoke of the long friendship between our countries and called for a meeting to resolve our differences. A White House messenger picked up his draft and for days Dick heard nothing at all.

MARCH 21, 1964

Then, four days later, Johnson suddenly interrupted George Reedy's press conference on March 21 to read Dick's statement virtually verbatim. Johnson's about-face in tone was immediately reciprocated by President Chiari of Panama. And with that, the acute phase of the Panama problem was diffused.

We found the final piece of the puzzle tracing Dick's path back to the White House in another taped conversation—this time between LBJ and Secretary of State Dean Rusk, recorded at 4:42 p.m. on the same day of the interrupted press conference.

LBJ: I want to get Dick Goodwin delegated to do stuff. I had him to work on poverty for me. And he needs a good deal of supervision and direction, but he's on your payroll delegated to the Peace Corps and I want him delegated here.

RUSK: We can do that.

LBJ: And if you can find a way to give him a $50 raise, I'd like to do it, if I have to steal it from my mother-in-law.

RUSK: Right.

LBJ: Because I want him to feel that I've done a little something for him. And I want to put him in a hideaway over here and try to get him to get some stuff over there.

So if you don't mind, you just call him and tell him Monday or whenever you get a chance that the President has talked to you about this and that he feels very strongly. And most of the men over here make more money than he does, and I just hate to see him working for less than they do. But I imagine he makes as high as you can pay somebody and you may have a serious problem on that, but all my boys that work like he does make 21 thousand.

RUSK: Right. Well, I'll talk to Bill Crockett.

LBJ: I'd just work him day and night. The poverty message, and then the foreign aid stuff and things of that kind and I just don't have anybody else here who can do that. He turns them out.

RUSK: Right.

LBJ: And he's the only one we've got, so you just boost him up a little bit, and tell him the President is crazy about what he's doing on poverty and other things, and that he wants him assigned there. And then we'll put him over here in the EOB [Executive Office Building].

RUSK: All right, sir. Fine.

———•———

Before either private acceptance or public appointment to LBJ's White House staff became official, Dick had promises to keep and explanations to make.

When Dick had first told Bobby that overtures had been made for him to work for the new administration, Bobby responded with a weird riptide of emotions. Dick recounted Bobby's reactions in his diary.

He thought for a while and said, well from the selfish point of view—you can think selfishly once in a while—I wish you wouldn't, but I guess you have to. After all, any of us is in a position to keep him from blowing up Costa Rica or something like that, then we ought to do it. Although anything that makes him look bad, makes Jack look better I suppose.

But I guess you should do it. If you do, you have to do the best job you can, and loyally, there's no other way.

Although I was uncertain about Bobby's tone (grim sarcasm, perhaps?), the assertion that Lyndon's mistakes would improve his brother's legacy seemed repellent. Bobby's concluding sentiment about loyalty, however, was sound, sane, and true. Once again, I felt caught in a crossfire of conflicting feelings toward Bobby.

As with Bobby, Dick felt the need to offer Jackie an explanation regarding his work with the Johnson administration. In a note on March 22, he wrote:

Dear Jackie,
This Sunday the President called and assigned me to work at the White House. This is a very difficult thing for me, but I think President Kennedy would have advised me to do it. He was always proud of the men he brought into public life. We will all always be Kennedy men . . . to drop out of the fight would be a defeat for this whole idea.

Unlike Sorensen, who had been crushed by JFK's death as if his life's purpose and sustenance had vanished—or Schlesinger, who had taken a hiatus from an established academic career to work in government—Dick had found his vocation in public service well before he met JFK.

As attached as he was to the Kennedys, and as conflicted as he was about crossing the bridge to the rival LBJ camp, he recognized that his greatest loyalty lay neither to Kennedy nor to Johnson, but to his country and to his long-held mission to pursue whatever work might help to close the gap between our national ideals and the reality of our daily lives.

Little could Dick have imagined that this new twist of the kaleidoscope would give him the opportunity to participate in a transformation of American society.

"Lyndon Johnson was as good as his word," Dick said to me with a mild look of horror. "He put me in a hideaway in the Executive Office Building. And he worked me day and night!"

APRIL 7, 1964

From the start of Dick's public career, reporters, writers, scholars, and artists of all kinds were his natural after-hours cohorts and companions. Without their information and contacts, he would never have been able to draw information from all over Latin America that eventually contributed to the Alliance for Progress. While he had initially benefited from off-the-record conversations with reporter friends, he had also been scorched by the exposure of his "secret" dialogue with Che Guevara. Accordingly, from the outset of his work for LBJ at the Executive Office Building, Dick was understandably apprehensive about how to handle press inquiries concerning his new fields of responsibility.

A column in *The Washington Post* at the time had speculated that LBJ suffered from a "word gap"—was lacking someone who could use language to communicate with the public in a convincingly Johnsonesque manner. After focusing on the roles Bill Moyers and advertising executive Jack Valenti played in the new administration, the column related that the president had even tapped "talented and controversial" Richard Goodwin, the "enfant terrible" of the New Frontier.

Wishing above all to avoid hitting a perpetual raw nerve with Johnson, Dick called press secretary George Reedy for advice. Reedy, in turn, called the president. Their conversation on April 7 was recorded:

REEDY: Dick Goodwin tells me he's being called by Rowland Evans about what he's doing over here, and he has not answered the call.

LBJ: Just say that he works for the State Department, that he's not over here. He's not in the White House. That he was quite helpful to us on the Panama thing . . . but that's got to be off the record.

REEDY: I would recommend, sir, rather than Panama we say he's made a couple of studies on the poverty program or something like that . . . because on Latin America he's pretty controversial.

LBJ: Just say he's been with the Peace Corps and in that connection he had helped us some on the poverty [bill], in developing the message.

REEDY: The only problem here, of course, is that they know he's over here in the Executive Office Building.

LBJ: I don't know whether they know that or not. I don't know how they know it.

REEDY: That's where they called him. Sir.

Tears of laughter in Dick's eyes led to a brief fit of coughing. It was clear that one of the compensations of exceeding eighty years of age was that matters which may have stoked frustration and anger at thirty now only elicited mirth at the grand absurdity of it all.

———·•·———

Wherever Lyndon Johnson happened to find himself—behind his desk, sprawled over his bed, at a baseball game or a movie, seated on the toilet, cutting across the dance floor, or taking gentle laps in the ranch or White House pool—that location became his "office," his inexhaustible place of business.

So it was not as peculiar as it might appear that, as Dick recounted in a hilarious episode in his memoir, a policy meeting of the highest order took place in the White House pool as the naked president and his two naked aides—Dick and Bill Moyers—paddled together around the pool's perimeter.

As the president propelled himself from one end of the pool to the other, with Dick and Bill trailing in his wake—he held forth about where he hoped to take the country and how he wanted to get there. Finally, he stopped paddling and as the trio held on to the pool's edge, Johnson addressed them with force and urgency:

"Kennedy had some good programs, but they were stalled in Congress. I had to pull them out of the ditch." (LBJ could rightly take credit for rescuing Kennedy's tax bill from the clutches of Senator Robert Byrd's Finance Committee and for outmaneuvering Rules Committee chairman Howard Smith to bring Kennedy's Civil Rights Bill to the House floor where it had passed and moved onto the Senate to face a determined filibuster organized by the southern forces.)

"But it's not enough to just pick up on the Kennedy program. We've got to use the Kennedy program as the springboard to take on Congress, summon the states to new heights, create a Johnson program, different in tone, fighting and aggressive. Hell, we've barely begun to solve our problems.

"Everyone, deep down, wants something a little better for his children, everybody wants to leave a mark, something he can be proud of. And so do I. You, too, Bill and you, Dick. Well now's your chance."

"Before we toweled off at the poolside on that memorable day," Dick told me, "we had our marching orders—to articulate his domestic agenda."

"Now boys," Johnson said, cinching his bathrobe, "you let me finish the Kennedy program. You start to put together a Johnson program and don't worry about whether it's too radical or if Congress is ready for it. That's my job. And I hope you don't think I'm being arrogant to tell you I'm a little better at that than you."

Dick entertained dinner guests for years with that story of this presidential skinny dip. And in the intervening years, it also made its way into dozens of history books and biographies. Indeed, the conversation in the pool that day is widely regarded as the signal event to which we can trace the changing of the guard, the advent of the most progressive legislation of the last three quarters of a century which would soon enter public life as the Great Society.

When I asked Dick if he remembered how and why he had chosen the name "Great Society," he sidetracked: "It's not like naming a baby. I never looked over the crib-side at this massive infant thing and said, 'Great Society.'"

I reminded Dick of the game he and the Kennedy team had played on the "Caroline" as they headed west to California during the presidential campaign—the contest to see who could reel off the most presidential slogans such as the New Freedom, the Square Deal, the New Deal, the Fair Deal, etc.

"These slogans cut deep into communal memory," I said to Dick.

"I know one thing," Dick intoned. "The Great Society didn't have all capitals when I first wrote it. It took time before it marked an administration, characterized a man, and designated an era. I tried it out in lowercase in a number of small speeches in March and April. I can't remember exactly. You're the historian, not me!"

So, I too had my marching orders. Surveying the boxes, the clearest instance I found of the first use of the "great society" was in a speech Dick had drafted for an Eleanor Roosevelt memorial award presentation:

We now have the opportunity to move not only toward the rich society and the powerful society but toward <u>the great society</u>.

In *Time*, reporter Hugh Sidey's book about LBJ, I discovered that he had been present when Dick first typed these words. Late one chilly evening, Sidey had stopped by Dick's office to chat. He found "the rumpled Goodwin, as usual puffing his way through a collection of large cigars." As Dick was finishing up, Sidey watched as the "great society" phrase "simply appeared" on the page in Dick's small Smith-Corona typewriter. That night it meant little to Sidey, but memory of its use returned when it became a touchstone for the entire Johnson agenda.

The president, Jack Valenti recalled, liked "the spacious theme" of the Eleanor Roosevelt speech, but decided to withhold the draft for a later, more significant occasion. In the weeks that followed, Dick experimented with the "great society" phrase in nearly everything he wrote. For the Montana Territory Centennial in the middle of April he intimated the generational span necessary to accomplish this new surge of ambition:

We are trying to build a great society that will make your children and your grandchildren and the people three or four generations from today, proud of what we are doing.

From within the White House, Moyers and Dick lobbied for the phrase against advocates who preferred "The Good Society," "A Better Deal," or "The Glorious Society." But after a dozen more trial balloons to gauge the response to Dick's persistent use of the "great society," the phrase ultimately caught Johnson's fancy and fulfilled journalists' need for a label to employ in their headlines.

"Consequently," Dick told me, "I proudly watched my great society grow and grow until it entered the world as THE GREAT SOCIETY. Great never meant great in size and quantity. Rich and powerful never added up to great. For the first time in history, we had a chance to construct a society more concerned with the quality of our goals than the quantity of our goods."

———·•·———

The time and place Johnson chose to mark the separation of the Kennedy and Johnson administrations—a booster rocket falling away while the rocket pushes higher and further than ever before—was the commencement address at the University of Michigan on May 22. The university setting seemed the proper place for a philosophical talk about the meaning and goals of the new administration. And Johnson recognized that young people leaving college had the greatest investment in shaping the public issues of the day.

That Johnson chose the same location where Kennedy's extemporaneous remarks had inspired the Peace Corps, the most popular program of his administration, reveals a certain confidence and competitiveness, a pluck built on his success in putting an unmistakable stamp on American politics in the space of barely six months.

Johnson's masterful accomplishment in navigating the most extreme and difficult of transitions was chorused by reporters. "Washington is now a little girl settling down with the old boyfriend," James Reston had written in *The New York Times*. "The mad and wonderful infatuation with the handsome young stranger from Boston is over—somehow she always knew it wouldn't last—so she is adjusting to reality. Everything is less romantic and more practical, part regret and part relief, beer instead of champagne, not fancy but plain; and in many ways more natural and hopefully more durable. . . . The lovers of style are not too happy with the new Administration, but the lovers of substance are not complaining."

For the Michigan address Dick and Moyers solicited ideas from government officials, academics, and citizens from all walks of life. They collected editorials, sociological studies, political manifestos, and cultural critiques. In addition, once word got out that a major presidential address was under construction, heaps of memos began to pile up on Dick's desk.

An entire box of Dick's archive was full of memos lobbying for special inclusion in the president's address, pleading for a spotlight for some pet project. Sometimes I only found a line or two forwarded to Dick under the rubric "Ideas for Michigan commencement speech," but, more often than not, entire speeches had landed heavily on his desk. And all this had to be reviewed in the six-week span between the poolside marching orders and the graduation address in Ann Arbor.

The task of pulling all this together—moving beyond the path laid out by John Kennedy, sketching out a philosophic statement to launch Lyndon Johnson's own vision of America, setting in motion the domestic agenda that could serve as a prospective platform for the coming election—seemed overwhelming to me. This was not speechwriting by committee. This was Dick collating and cobbling together these bits and pieces into a coherent philosophy.

"How was that possible?" I asked Dick. "The pressure! The clock was ticking."

"For the Alliance speech," Dick said, "I had to sort through mountains of material. I had a mission to chart a new course for America's relationship with Latin America."

"But this was exponentially larger," I said. "This is the future design and direction of our entire domestic policy. How did you even begin to approach it?"

"Chutzpah," grinned Dick, "and the stamina of youth."

To avoid a laundry list, a catalogue of problems to be addressed, and to make certain he would not be drowned by wave upon wave of data piling upon his desk, Dick whittled down his focus to three interrelated subjects: the rebuilding of the Cities, the preservation of our Countryside, and the expansion of our Classrooms—in part, Dick belatedly confessed, this device was used because Johnson considered alliteration a keystone to the success of JFK's oratory. So three Cs it would be. The real thrust of the speech, however, was the declaration of a new national purpose. The three Cs upon which the speech was constructed are, in reality, not separate categories, but entangled throughout the daily lives of all Americans.

The theme of the cities involved the decay of urban centers, dilapidated housing, a loss of community. The theme of classrooms cast a light on how many children of poverty were dropping out of schools. And in the countryside, farmland and green fields were disappearing, while city parks were overcrowded, and people were breathing foul air and drinking dirty water. The Great Society would be built on the belief that America's affluence must work for all its citizens.

With Moyers as his sounding board and chief support throughout the process, Dick finished the final draft the night before it was to be delivered. He had not slept for the previous day and a half. This was "the Goodwin code," Jack Valenti observed, "to hold onto the speech until the very last minute to prevent some lower form of animal life (me) from fooling around with his prose. To actually withhold the speech until the president mounted the rostrum was really Goodwin's objective." As difficult and abrasive as Dick could be at such times, Valenti acknowledged, he was, "at his best, incandescent and possibly a near-genius in his field."

Early morning on the day of the Michigan commencement, flanked by Moyers and Valenti, Dick presented his completed draft to the president. The three aides watched intently as he silently read the twenty-minute speech, marking it as he went. Without response he rearranged the papers, tapping them together into a neat stack on his desk and even more slowly— still without comment—began again. After an interminable stretch of time, he laid the speech flat and said softly and simply, "It ought to do just fine, boys. Just what I told you."

Too tired to be demonstrably pleased, Dick only wanted to go home and sleep. He declined the President's invitation to join him on the trip to Michigan. Not until the following day did Dick watch a video of the speech in the basement of the White House.

MAY 22, 1964

I have come today from the turmoil of your capital to the tranquility of your campus to speak about the future of your country, Johnson began after some preliminary remarks.

"I remember one thing about the opening," Dick said. "I should have written OUR capital, YOUR campus, OUR country, but before long, the president's conviction took hold. All my memorized words dissolved into Lyndon Johnson's ownership of them."

He presented the aspirational Great Society, "*a place where men are more concerned with the quality of their goals than the quantity of their goods.*"

He sketched the problems of the City, Countryside, and Classrooms; he pledged that he would "*assemble the best thought and the broadest knowledge from all over the world to find those answers for America.*"

His voice then rose to challenge the young graduates who filled the massive arc of the stadium:

For better or worse, your generation has been appointed by history to deal with those problems and to lead America toward a new age. You have the chance never before afforded to any people in any age. You can help build a society where the demands of morality, and the needs of the spirit can be realized in the life of the Nation.

The huge audience rose to its feet with shouts and applause.

As I studied the conclusion of Johnson's Great Society speech, I returned in my mind's eye to the night at that same university when JFK had posed a string of questions to the dogged young students huddled in the cold rain. "How many of you," the weary candidate had asked, "are willing to spend your days in Ghana? How many of you are willing to work in the Foreign Service and spend your lives traveling around the world?"

Dick's speech had employed the same technique of rising questions when on this hot graduation day the president had invited eighty thousand people in the stadium to *"help build a society where the demands of morality and the needs of the spirit can be realized"*:

Will you join in the battle to give every citizen the full equality which God enjoins and the law requires, whatever his belief or race, or the color of his skin?

Will you join in the battle to give every citizen an escape from the crushing weight of poverty?

Once Johnson implored them all to *"join in the battle to build the Great Society"* he hit such a taproot of Baptist fervor that Dick himself was converted. He remembered jumping from his chair in the White House basement and joining the videotaped roar of the masses at University Stadium, cheering and applauding until the palms of his hands burned.

The Lyndon Johnson era, the launch of the Great Society, had begun.

"Try some of this scotch, Dick," said the president, so euphoric from his commencement day triumph at Ann Arbor that he had summoned Dick to his favorite place to relax, the intimate anteroom adjacent to the Oval Office. "Henry Luce called me this morning. Old man Henry himself. He said he'd support me on the basis of the Great Society speech alone. You helped get me *Time*'s support and I want you to know I appreciate everything you've done since you came here."

This was the irresistible side of Johnson's nature. Never, Dick told me, had he experienced such effusiveness from John Kennedy. "You're going to be my voice, my alter ego," Johnson promised Dick, "like Harry Hopkins was to FDR."

In promising Dick a role in policymaking, by likening Dick's position to FDR's chief policy adviser, Harry Hopkins, Johnson had locked upon something fundamental in Dick. Flattery and promises were undeniably enticing, but nothing persuaded Dick more than the absolute conviction with which Johnson spoke of his vision to transform the country, the enormity of his will, and the intensity of his resolve to leave a mark on the country that would rival, even surpass, that of his "political daddy," Franklin Roosevelt.

Soon Moyers and Valenti had joined them in the anteroom. Not three months before, Moyers had been reluctant to get Dick involved "in our little circle." Now, Dick had earned his place in that ebullient circle orbiting the president.

Another drink and with great animation, like the producer, playwright, and lead actor all in one after a triumphant premiere, Johnson began to perform rather than read the packet of reviews in the newspapers and magazines strewn at his feet. He recounted the twenty-nine rounds of applause that were said to have interrupted him in twenty minutes. He impersonated the voices of Walter Lippmann, Arthur Krock, and James Reston, mimicking their high praise of the emerging Great Society. "LBJ has done more in the first six months than even his enemies or even his friends expected on that tragic day," Reston says. "The basic question is: What is the end and purpose of all this political skill? This is the question LBJ answered at the University of Michigan."

And so, improbable as it seemed, yet another twist of the kaleidoscope had landed Dick within this small White House circle, and before him now lay the opportunity to help shape the policy and language of the most significant progressive movement of his lifetime.

CHAPTER SEVEN

Thirteen LBJs

An animated LBJ regales Dick with a story at his Texas ranch
while Jack Valenti looks on. January 17, 1965.

"LYNDON JOHNSON WAS THIRTEEN OF THE MOST COMPLEX people I ever knew," recalled Bill Moyers. "You had to deal with a different persona from day to day or from week to week. And sometimes it was difficult to figure out who he was at that particular time."

Sometimes those changes, as Dick and I discovered, could tear open a peaceful blue sky with a lightning bolt. Sometimes warmth would inexplicably erupt from cold or coldness from warmth. We experienced the man at different times—Dick at the height of the Sixties, me toward the end of the decade and the end of Lyndon Johnson's life. And during that decade of the Sixties, he so changed both our lives that here we were, in our seventies and eighties, still arguing, bantering, and trying to come to terms with his enormous impact on us and on the country.

In the weeks that followed the May 22 Great Society speech, Dick would experience abrupt fluctuations in Lyndon Johnson's emotional weather.

From one day to the next Dick might find himself included, excluded, elevated, or derided—until he hardly knew what ground he stood upon.

Yet like many other members of the White House staff, Dick would discover that Lyndon Johnson's all-consuming pursuit of a better America far surpassed any personal hazards suffered along the way.

In the afterglow of positive responses to the Ann Arbor speech, Dick continued to bask in LBJ's fervent gratitude and appreciation. "You've been working too hard," the president commented, reaching out to Dick in the wee hours of the morning at a New York fundraising party, insisting, "Come with me tonight to Texas and spend the [Memorial Day] weekend at the Ranch."

The day had begun in Washington with a brief memorial service in the State Dining Room for John Kennedy (the next day was JFK's birthday), followed by a quick visit to Arlington Cemetery to lay a wreath at his grave, then a swift change into black tie before a flight to New York to address a fundraising dinner at the Hilton Hotel, then on to the Americana to speak to twelve hundred members of the Young Democrats, before being whisked off to Madison Square Garden for a fundraising gala—attended by scores of celebrities and luminaries, including Gregory Peck, Johnny Carson, Joan Baez, and Mahalia Jackson—where Johnson spoke of the pending challenges of civil rights and the importance of the coming election.

Dick had helped draft and polish the speeches, one after the other, that had been given during that jam-packed day. Not until a private midnight reception at the home of Arthur Krim, the chair of the Democratic fundraising committee, was there finally time to pause. It had been a productive evening with a huge amount of money generated for the campaign war chest. "Come with me tonight," Johnson urged Dick a second time. "I'll call your wife and arrange for her to come down."

While Dick hesitated—he had nothing for the trip except the tuxedo he was wearing—the president offered to take the shirt off his own back, as well as supply pants, shaving gear, and a toothbrush, whatever was necessary. With a smile, I pictured Dick mantled in Lyndon's shirt, the cuffs dangling below his knees. Dick, of course, accepted the invitation and was aboard Air Force One shortly before 2 a.m. when it departed New York for Texas.

MAY 29–31, 1964

As the sun rose over the Texas Hill Country, Dick breakfasted in his tux. At 9 a.m. he was at the door of the general store in the small town of Stonewall—perhaps the first customer to enter the store in formal attire. Before long, now dressed in a short-sleeved shirt, khaki pants, and tennis shoes (his tuxedo folded in a bag along with shirt, dress shoes, and a new bathing suit), Dick was ready to make the acquaintance of the Texas White House.

No sooner had he returned from Stonewall than he was asked to join the president, Jack and Mary Margaret Valenti, and Liz Carpenter (Lady Bird's press secretary) at poolside. He changed into his new bathing suit and donned a bathrobe. There would be no co-ed skinny-dipping at the Texas White House that weekend.

"What was the first thing that struck you about the ranch?" I asked Dick.

"It was that there was no pretension," he said. "Everyone was included in everything, and everything was in perpetual motion night and day and all that motion depended on what Lyndon was doing and what he wanted to eat. The whole place around the ranch, including a working cattle farm, was a real-life theme park. And that theme," Dick concluded, "was Lyndon Johnson. I got a memorably hospitable reception to Lyndonland."

Fortunately, we came across a description of that weekend in the archive that Dick had preserved—an account written by his wife Sandra who had arrived that afternoon with a supply of clothes and much needed cigars.

Sandra related how, on the evening of her arrival, the president had taken her, Dick, and a small group of friends to the Johnson City High School graduation. During this ceremony, the high school was rededicated the Lyndon Baines Johnson High School. When Johnson graduated there were only six students in his class, and now there were thirty. From the small community had come "lots and lots of people, all dressed in cotton dresses and suits. No fancy jewelry or hairdos. Lots of kids." Although this was a "leisurely holiday weekend," Dick had drafted the president's brief remarks for the high school graduation speech in addition to the commencement address to be delivered on the following night at the University of Texas.

For the townspeople, Johnson's words touched a heartfelt chord: "Forty years ago, almost to this very night, I left my high school diploma at home and I headed West to seek the fame and fortune that I knew America offered. About 20 months later I came back, back to Johnson City, with empty hands and empty pockets. I came back because I realized that the place to really begin was the place that I had been all the time."

Particularly vivid was Sandra's description of the dynamic between Lady Bird and the townspeople once the ceremonies had concluded:

"The people in the audience yelled 'Lady Bird, Lady Bird' and clapped and she got up and the applause for her was terrific. She said a few words. She had an extraordinary manner of speaking, which has huge stops and starts and rises, and the words gush out between. . . . Her voice is magnetic, and attractive."

The entire event seemed so genial that once they had all returned to the ranch it was startling to see how the president's mood darkened, how abruptly he grew petulant and glowering. It turned out that the cause of this sudden fury was that "fifty-nine of the press got seats while people from Johnson City were turned away." Johnson had explicitly instructed his advance team to allow only a small press pool. He threatened to sack any-one who had facilitated what he viewed as condescension toward his local friends.

Yet beyond this single outburst, the president was in the best of moods the entire weekend. "We were included in all activities all weekend," Sandra noted. "So were the secretaries. Everything was extremely democratic." Johnson never tired of playing tour guide on visits to the landmarks of his private world. He took Sandra and Dick to see the house where he was born, the grammar school that he attended, the family cemetery on the Pedernales River where his grandparents, parents, and other relatives were buried. Along the way, Sandra noted, Lady Bird "pointed out many flowers and trees everywhere whose names she knew."

Early the next evening the motorcade left the ranch and headed to the Austin Coliseum. Despite a hectic weekend of car rides to inspect cattle, poolside conversations, barbecues, and stag helicopter visits to neighboring farms, Dick had managed to consolidate the series of ques-tions that had launched the Great Society in Michigan into the challenge that would become the backbone of scores of stump speeches during the upcoming presidential campaign. "Will you leave the future a society where lawns are clipped and the countryside cluttered," he challenged the young graduates of the University of Texas, "where store buildings are new and school buildings are old; a society of private satisfaction for some in the midst of public squalor for all? Or will you join to build the Great Society?"

If his weekend at his Texas ranch demonstrated LBJ's ease within his private sphere, the moment he returned to Washington the president found himself immersed in a pressurized chess match of the highest order—the endgame of the longest filibuster in American history. The ancient wall of the filibuster had to be breached. The stakes were nothing less than the viability of his administration, his party's momentum leading into the coming election, and, most importantly, the success of the Civil Rights Bill to end legal apartheid in America.

The qualities Johnson displayed during the ten-week filibuster were consistent, astonishing, and unerring. Where he had often seemed intemperate and impulsive, he now showed great patience; if he had sometimes bullied, he now employed methodical and specific persuasion; where he had appeared to crave the spotlight for himself alone, he now focused on working behind the curtain; and if he had displayed an inclination to grandstand, he now publicly shared credit, appealing to the future legacy of vital actors as the drama of cloture neared its culmination.

To this conflict he gave his masterful best. From the outset, he had promised that there would be no whittling down of Kennedy's original bill. "It would," he stated emphatically, "be a fight for total victory or total defeat, without appeasement or attrition."

Georgia's Democratic senator Richard Russell, the leader of the southern bloc and Johnson's old friend, believed he would have defeated Kennedy, "or at least forced him to make substantial concessions"; but with Johnson's refusal to compromise the integrity of the bill, his absolute lack of flexibility, it would make it "three times harder" for Russell to maneuver. The southern forces must either win by defeating cloture or they would lose. There would be no middle ground.

JUNE 8, 1964

On June 8 as the filibuster reached its seventy-third day (preventing any other legislation from reaching the floor), the bill's supporters determined that the time had come to set a date for the cloture vote. Their hope of wearing down the southern forces had not been realized. Richard Russell's three six-member platoons had sustained the filibuster day after day. Senate Majority Leader Mike Mansfield set the date for the vote on June 10, forty-eight hours away. Though the supporters had not locked down the necessary sixty-seven votes (a two-thirds majority), they hoped to rally their troops at the moment of decision.

Earlier that morning, Johnson was agitated. Tension in the White House was high. Two days later—the same day as the cloture vote—he was scheduled to give the commencement address at the College of the Holy Cross in Massachusetts. Moyers had assigned the speech to White House aide Doug Cater, who specialized in education. Dick recorded that rising stress in his diary.

Cater gave his speech to the President before we saw it and it didn't turn out well. President called Bill and said don't send me a speech that is over 1200 words. I ask you for a Ford and you send me a Cadillac. I ask you for a Cadillac and you send me two Fords, etc. A long speech. If you don't do what I ask, why you can realize your dream to go back to the Peace Corps.

In the months to come, Dick said, Johnson would level this charge at both Bill and him, suspecting they both secretly pined to return to the source of youthful idealism galvanized by JFK. In the meantime, Dick was tasked with rewriting the graduation speech.

JUNE 9, 1964

On the evening before the vote, Johnson called floor manager Hubert Humphrey to check on how things stood. "I think we have enough," Humphrey said.

"I don't want to know what you *think*," Johnson said. "What's the vote going to be? How many do you *have*?" The detailed conversation that followed made it clear that the legendary nose-counter Lyndon Johnson was acutely aware of which way every senator was leaning—Republican and Democrat—and what it would take to bring them to the finish line.

After hearing Humphrey's report on the Democrats, Johnson turned to the Republicans. Johnson had known from the start, given the sectional split in the Democratic Party, that "without Republican support we'd have absolutely no chance of securing the two-thirds vote." And he made clear to me during our conversations that "there was but one man who could acquire us that support"—the minority leader, Everett Dirksen.

"The bill can't pass unless you get Ev Dirksen," he repeatedly instructed Humphrey. "You've got to let him have a piece of the action. He's got to look good all the time. . . . You drink with Dirksen! You talk with Dirksen! You listen to Dirksen!"

In answer to Johnson's query about how many Republicans Dirksen had rounded up, Humphrey reported that "Dirksen tells me he's got 28 votes. But I don't think he has. I think he's got 26." And there was still some uncertainty about several western Democrats who were in favor of the Civil Rights Bill but hesitant to relinquish the muscles their small states could flex thanks to the filibuster. When the phone call ended, Humphrey returned to work, lobbying the last three Democrats whose votes were wavering.

At 1:15 a.m., Humphrey walked onto the deserted House floor and "exchanged good natured quips" with Virginia senator Harry Byrd, who was in the middle of the final speech of the filibuster, a round-the-clock marathon that had begun at 7:38 that morning and was, by agreement, due to conclude before the scheduled 11 a.m. cloture vote. For six hours, Byrd had been reading poetry and philosophy. He dedicated his next poem, "My Neighbor's Roses," to Humphrey.

Despite dire differences on the Civil Rights Bill, the two senators were still friends. The next morning, Humphrey brought a red rose from his garden to put in Byrd's lapel.

JUNE 10, 1964

At 8 a.m., Dick flew with the president, Moyers, and Valenti on a DC-6 to Worcester, Massachusetts, home of the College of the Holy Cross. As usual, last-minute edits to the speech were made in transit.

When the plane landed in the heavily Democratic city of Worcester, the president was met by a cheering crowd of three thousand. Schools had been closed for the day. One hundred fifty thousand cheering people and dozens of school bands lined the six-mile route from the airport to the football stadium.

While the president was about to be introduced at the college, the Senate had convened back in Washington for final statements before the cloture vote was taken. Humphrey recalled the speech Henry V made to his men before the battle at Agincourt, saying they would remember that they "fought with us on St. Crispin's Day," while Dirksen invoked Victor Hugo, "Stronger than all the armies in the world is an idea whose time has come."

Johnson was still seated on the dais when an aide brought the news that the sixty-seventh aye vote had been recorded. The long siege was over at last.

Reporters in attendance noted "a broad grin" lit the president's face. For the first time in history, cloture had been achieved on a Civil Rights Bill. Against Senate rules, spontaneous applause rocked the chamber.

When the president rose to speak, he broke from his prepared remarks to share the stunning news. The graduating class at Holy Cross delivered a long, loud standing ovation—for the president, for the Congress, and for the country.

Neither Dick nor Bill had witnessed the president interrupt the commencement with the historic announcement that the filibuster was broken. As soon as the presidential motorcade had reached Worcester, both men had taken a detour to Cambridge where Dick guided Bill through his old haunts at Harvard Square—pointing out the Gannett House, home of the *Harvard Law Review*, and visiting other favorite stomping grounds.

This side foray entailed far more than nostalgia; later that afternoon they attended a working luncheon that economist Ken Galbraith had set up with a group of professors from Harvard and MIT. This was not only an academic powwow; the group was off and running to actualize the promised task forces from which the Great Society was intended to develop.

Returning to Washington on the shuttle in the early evening, they found a relaxed and ebullient Johnson, not simply willing but eager to share credit with the many fathers of the victorious cloture vote. When Bobby Kennedy, who, as attorney general, had handled many of the day-to-day negotiations with Dirksen, arrived at a White House meeting, Johnson hailed him with a hearty, "Hello, hero!"

Throughout the struggle, Johnson had worked closely with Bobby and the Justice Department to ensure that the administration sanctioned only those amendments that did not in any considerable way dilute the bill. "We won't do anything you don't want to do on the legislation," had been Johnson's refrain during every conversation with Bobby. And that strategy had worked. The final bill that would now proceed to the floor was stronger than President Kennedy's original measure.

Johnson had promised Dirksen that if he helped to pass the bill he would "get credit." And the president kept that promise, heaping accolades on the Republican senator in the days that followed. Such hyperbole filled the air that the president told Dirksen that "two hundred years from now, schoolchildren would remember only two names—Abraham Lincoln and Everett Dirksen." Johnson's praise kept coming—not only for Dirksen, but for Bobby, Humphrey, Mike Mansfield, and especially for the civil rights community.

Illuminated by the shining full moon of Lyndon Johnson's nature that day, Dick found it incomprehensible that in less than twenty-four hours he would, for the first time, come to know the cold, dark side of that same moon.

JUNE 11, 1964

Without a specific chronology it's easy to miss the exact coordinates that chart an emotional graph of Lyndon Johnson's changeable behaviors. Only weeks had passed since the unveiling of the Great Society. The following holiday weekend, Dick was regaled at the ranch; and on June 10 the president had won the grueling battle to stop the filibuster and bring the Civil Rights Bill to the floor for inevitable passage. There was a great rising tailwind of achievement behind the Johnson administration.

That auspicious wind changed direction the moment the press began to seek out stories about what Dick was doing in the "hideaway" Johnson had constructed for him. A handful of newspaper columns mentioned that Goodwin had become a valued member of the White House writing team. One column even noted that "Goodwin cranks out major texts in far less time than Kennedy's Ted Sorensen and Johnson insists that he does it with just as much style."

Hugh Sidey, the journalist friend who had witnessed the "Great Society" label come into being on Dick's typewriter and had honored his agreement with Dick to keep their conversations off the record, soon realized that the cat had escaped the bag. The opportunity had arrived for him to write a major article on Dick Goodwin's return to the White House, the Great Society speech, and his roles as speechwriter and policymaker.

To further research Dick's contributions, Sidey reached out to Horace Busby, a member of the speechwriting team and a longtime confidant of the president. In a straightforward manner, the quiet, gentle Busby described the division of responsibilities on the team and credited Dick with the Great Society speech.

Accordingly, Sidey felt released from his off-the-record understanding with Dick and at 3 p.m. on June 11 called upon press secretary George Reedy to tell him of his plans to write a piece on Goodwin for *Time* magazine. No sooner had Reedy informed Johnson that Sidey was in the press office than the president instructed him to bring the reporter into the Oval Office. Before the reporter was admitted, an irate Johnson placed a call to Busby. When told Busby was unavailable, he cross-examined Dorothy Nichols, Busby's secretary, who tried in vain to defend her boss. I read the transcript of that recorded call aloud to Dick.

LBJ: [Sidey] says he got the story from Buzz about Dick Goodwin writing a lot of speeches and specific ones, and it just guts me. And Joe Kraft says the same thing, and I just can't believe Buzz would do me that way.

NICHOLS: I don't think he ever would do that.

LBJ: Where is Buzz now?

NICHOLS: Oh . . . Buzz is . . . had a luncheon appointment with Tom Wicker.

LBJ: He's telling them things, and I guess he's going to be prominent with them, but it hurts us. I've told him to please be careful and not do this.

NICHOLS: Mr. Johnson; I know they're after him, but I did not know he was—

LBJ: Well, you see, if he's going to lunch with them, honey, he's got to say something, [Liz Carpenter] gave a big story out about Dick Goodwin going to the Ranch in his tuxedo and gave it to Les [Carpenter, her husband], Les wrote it up, and now *Time's* doing a special article on Dick Goodwin, and they got the information from Buzz, according to *Time*.

Tell him I'll buy his lunch if he's got to go to them.

NICHOLS: I think this is the first time he's been to lunch . . . The guy goes through the day without lunch most of the time.

LBJ: I'm going to have to either let him go, or stop it, or lock the door on him or something. I just got to keep my little amateurs away from these newspaper people telling them what's happening.

NICHOLS: Oh, dear.

LBJ: They're going to get him and get Goodwin. They're going to be the first two to go because he's talking, and I think he might be a little hurt that Goodwin's doing some of my speeches. Maybe he's a little jealous.

NICHOLS: I don't think so, Mr. President.

LBJ: 3:10's a hell of a time to be at lunch anyway. If he comes in, though, anytime, tell him to call me.

"What a heroic secretary," I said.

Before Hugh Sidey was ushered into the Oval Office, Johnson's tone had hardened into something uglier, as can be seen in his brief conversation with George Reedy.

REEDY: Hugh Sidey is here and asking me about Goodwin's role.

LBJ: Role in what?

REEDY: As a speechwriter, as an advisor in the White House.

LBJ: Well, tell him he's neither but I'll be glad to talk to him about what he does, if it's any of his business, any of his interest.

REEDY: OK, Sir.

LBJ: Bring him on in.

In response to Sidey's initial question about Goodwin's role as a speech-writer, the president asserted that "Goodwin has not written a single speech for me. As far as I know, he had nothing to do with the Ann Arbor speech. He never is called on as an advisor on policy questions. He makes suggestions that are a result of research."

"I was somewhat at a loss for words," Sidey later recalled. "I looked rather blank. Johnson sensed my confusion. He turned to George Reedy and asked, 'Isn't that so, George?' Reedy made a sound which was neither yes nor no and shook his head, neither up nor down."

Hugh Sidey was befuddled. He had personally witnessed Dick writing speeches and knew he had become Johnson's chief speechwriter. Johnson, however, was just getting started. Petulance began to rise into a rant: "I resent that to hell. People on the outside, on the edge, they want to appear that they know something they don't know."

Johnson's diatribe seemed to indict Dick, Busby, and anyone else talking to the press without his prior consent and directive. The president continued to fume: "They ought to be working, that's not their job to be spending their time telling *Time* about who does what. I'll tell them if they want to know."

Referring to the newspaper stories about Goodwin's long weekend visit to the ranch in his tux and his trip to Stonewall to get clothes, Johnson said "Goodwin spent one day on the [LBJ] ranch," maintaining it was arranged solely to accompany him to a commencement speech at the University of Texas. As if offering proof that would somehow validate his tirade, Johnson removed a felt tip pen from his shirt pocket and angrily dashed off a White House organizational chart for the journalist. Along the bottom edge, under the category "Miscellaneous," appeared someone named "Goodman"—apparently a most marginal figure in the Johnson White House.

"It is a singular experience," Sidey maintained, "to be told by the President of the United States—the most powerful man in the world—that something you know to be true is not so." It was still early in the Johnson presidency but for Sidey "a warning flag" had gone up. "The president's word was suspect"—a "credibility gap" had emerged that would infect Johnson's presidency in later years.

While Johnson's previous denial that Dick had an office in the Executive Office Building had made us both laugh, this bizarre incident was not at all amusing. What was so disturbing was Lyndon's ability to lie with such astonishing force, and the vast canyon that separated his effusive private praise from his withering public condemnation.

It also troubled me that Lyndon felt compelled to erase the days of family hospitality with Dick and Sandra—taking meals together, reading the newspaper, going to barbecues, visiting friends, and tracing the landmarks of his life.

"Such large ammunition, such a small target," Dick said. "He belittled me, but the real damage wasn't done to me. He belittled himself in Sidey's eyes. He emphatically told Sidey what they both knew to be lies. A dangerous thing."

"Did Sidey tell you about his interview with Johnson?" I asked.

"Yes," Dick said. "It made no sense to me. It seemed so petty. Such enormous, important things were happening. After all, later on the day that Lyndon relegated me to the bottom rung of the White House staffing ladder, he told me to begin working on a signing statement for the historic Civil Rights Bill.

"Did he never once bellow and rant at you?" Dick asked me all of a sudden.

"No. If he was angry," I said, "he would simply ignore me. He would direct his conversation to anyone but me. Freeze me out, like I didn't exist."

"No fire, only ice," Dick reflected. "You know, JFK's favorite poet, Robert Frost, said that when it comes to destruction, either fire or ice would suffice."

———•·•———

Washington during the Johnson administration was a city where the president knew everything; the Oval Office was the center of the web, and he was alert to anything that touched a strand of that web. In the midst of the civil rights filibuster, he had learned that retired Supreme Court justice Felix Frankfurter had suffered a series of strokes that left him with slurred speech and difficulty walking. Johnson decided to pay a visit to the ailing justice at his Embassy Row apartment on Massachusetts Avenue. Well aware that Dick had clerked for Frankfurter, the president asked Dick to escort him to the home of the mentor he knew Dick revered.

Kindness, empathy, compassion—these qualities were every bit as marked in Lyndon Johnson as meanness, ruthlessness, and cruelty. In my years of studying this perplexing man, I noted he often went out of his way to show deference to the elderly, especially after the spotlight which had once focused on them had moved on.

On the afternoon when Dick accompanied the president to Frankfurter's house, Johnson made a great show of needing, appreciating, and asking for a continuation of the Justice's advice. For decades the Justice had stood at the intellectual center of the court. Though social engagements had grown difficult for the eighty-one-year-old, Frankfurter relished the president's company and managed to rally for the occasion.

Felix Frankfurter was never shy in sharing his feelings about politicians. He had been initially dismayed when Dick had joined John Kennedy's fledgling presidential bid. In Frankfurter's eyes Kennedy had inherited some of the utter scorn in which the Justice held his father, Ambassador Joseph Kennedy.

Frankfurter greatly admired Lyndon Johnson. They had both worked their way up from difficult circumstances through talent and endurance. They shared a lifelong devotion to and a working relationship with FDR. And they both believed deeply in the value of public service. Over the years,

Frankfurter had trained an eager pack of loyal clerks and students to enter government service—Frankfurter's "happy hot dogs" they were called.

Before the pleasant visit ended, Dick told me, the Justice turned the conversation to Dick, for whom he retained an obvious paternal affection. "That boy has politics in his blood," he said. Johnson smiled and nodded his head in agreement. "That's what I like about him," Johnson said. "He's got feelings for people. And the boy can write."

In the years to come, Dick would give much thought to the Justice's "politics in the blood" comment. Sometimes, he considered it a compliment and sometimes an accurate description of an addiction. But more often, he half seriously wondered if it described a blood disease for which he might need a bone marrow transplant or dialysis.

It would be easy to view Johnson's deference to his elders as a calculated maneuver designed to aid his rise to power in a Senate built upon seniority; but, as Lyndon recounted to me, it was a quality he possessed even as a youngster.

When I was a boy, I would talk for hours with the mothers of my friends, telling them what I had done during the day, asking what they had done, requesting advice. Soon they began to feel as if I, too, was their son, and that meant that whenever we all wanted to do something, it was okay by the parents so long as I was there.

While the confidence and trust he gained was useful, the truth was that Johnson simply felt relaxed with older people and loved to chatter with them. Later, he would direct similar warmth and affection toward the Senate elders who had helped him along in his career. He spent long hours with Richard Russell, a lifelong bachelor. Johnson explained to me that Russell was often lonely.

Richard Russell found in the Senate what was for him a home. With no one to cook for him at home, he would arrive early enough in the morning to eat breakfast at the Capitol and stay late enough at night to eat dinner across the street. And in these early mornings and late evenings, I made sure that there was always one companion, one Senator, who worked as hard and as long as he, and that was me, Lyndon Johnson.

On Sundays the House and Senate were empty, quiet and still, the streets outside were bare. It's a tough day for a politician, especially if, like Russell, he's all alone. I knew how he felt for I, too, counted the hours till Monday would come again, and knowing that, I made sure to invite Russell over for breakfast, lunch, brunch or just to read the Sunday papers. He was my mentor and I wanted to take care of him.

Their relationship went far beyond simple collegiality and mutual respect. They were family. On the most intimate and personal level, the historic civil rights battle over the filibuster became for them also a dire family clash. Only with this understanding does Russell's comment in the wake of the battle come clear. "Now you tell Lyndon," Russell instructed Bill Moyers, "that I've been expecting the rod for a long time, and I'm sorry that it's from his hand the rod must be wielded, but I'd rather it be his hand than anybody else's I know. Tell him to cry a little when he uses it."

Such was Johnson's empathy for older people that if he saw any senator slowing down, he would help with their committee assignments and provide talking points on issues. He knew, he later told me, that they, too, had once been on center stage and that one day he might be in their place: *They feared humiliation, they craved attention. And when they found it, it was like a spring in the desert.*

Toward the end of June 1964, with the passage of the Civil Rights Bill imminent, Dick delivered the latest draft of the signing statement to the president. More than a simple milestone, the Civil Rights Act of 1964 would alter the legal, political, and social landscape of America as radically as any law of the twentieth century.

Because of the surpassing importance of the approaching occasion, a half dozen cooks had helped concoct the brief statement. Dick watched as the president squinted at his pages, then began to read through them a second time. "That'll do just fine, Dick. Maybe you could add something to show I understand that a law doesn't change people's feeling," he said, couching his order in a suggestion.

"I know a lot of people around those Georgetown parties are saying that I wasn't much of a crusader for civil rights when I was in the Senate," Lyndon acknowledged to Dick. "On balance they're right about me. I wasn't a crusader. I represented a southern state, and if I got too far ahead of my voters they'd have sent me right back to Johnson City where I couldn't have done anything for anybody, white or Negro. Now I represent the whole country and I can do what the whole country thinks is right. Or ought to."

Dick never questioned Johnson's absolute conviction in matters of civil rights. In particular, he was struck by the dogged courage he had shown through the long battle. In the end, Johnson would out-liberal the liberals in the North who despised, patronized, and caricatured him and who would always, regardless of his consistent achievements in civil rights, harbor suspicion and contempt for him.

"I'm going to be the best friend the Negro ever had," Johnson told Dick, "and I want you to help me. . . . Get that statement in shape; then let's you and me make a little history."

A little history was an understatement. Once signed, this bill would outlaw the legal system of segregation that had provided the underpinnings of daily life in the South for seventy-five years. "Jim Crow" laws had prohibited Blacks from entering and eating in white-only restaurants, from sharing drinking fountains, bathrooms, and pools, hotels and motels, and from sitting at lunch counters or in movie theaters, sports arenas, and concert halls. Overnight the new law of the land would begin to erase many of the indignities of the deep-seated system of segregation. The provisions of the bill would take effect immediately upon signing.

How, where, and when to stage the signing of the statement became Lyndon Johnson's pressing quandary. "Do you think we ought to quietly sign it or do you think we ought to have a big hullabaloo about it?" the president asked his civil rights adviser Lee White. "It's so monumental," answered White. "It's equivalent to . . . signing an Emancipation Proclamation, and it ought to have all the possible attention you could focus on it."

With final passage expected on the afternoon of Thursday, July 2, some suggested waiting to embrace the July 4 anniversary. Others worried that trouble was more likely to occur by conflating the bill with the raucous fireworks on the celebration of the Declaration of Independence.

"We are going to have a rather difficult weekend, a holiday weekend," Bobby Kennedy said. "If it's possible," he recommended, "postpone it until Monday and sign it so it's in the middle of the week." But Republican leader Charles Halleck cautioned against postponement, concerned that Republicans would be leaving Washington after the weekend for their convention in San Francisco and would be unable to attend the ceremony.

Johnson recognized the absolute importance that the signing be a public demonstration of bipartisanship. Therefore, he resolved to sign the bill as soon as it got to him. "We've got to make this an American bill," he told Humphrey, "and not just a Democratic bill."

JULY 2, 1964

Although hastily scheduled, the dignified ceremony was carefully prepared in the white and gold East Room of the White House before two hundred bipartisan guests, civil rights leaders, and a national television audience. A stolid Robert Kennedy sat in the front row along with Hubert Humphrey, Speaker Mike Mansfield, Everett Dirksen, Charles Halleck, and Lady Bird. Behind them sat Martin Luther King, Whitney Young, and Rev. Walter Fauntroy.

The president spoke quietly and soberly, sheaves of pens arrayed before him to be distributed among the many contributors who had helped make the Civil Rights Bill of 1964 a reality.

After watching a video of LBJ's remarks, I read his statement over and over. What struck me was how, in the starkest terms, the speech's simple architecture juxtaposes the ideals of freedom forged in the American Revolution and the Constitution with the actual circumstances of our daily lives:

We believe that all men are created equal. Yet many are denied equal treatment.

We believe that all men have certain unalienable rights. Yet many Americans do not enjoy those rights.

We believe that all men are entitled to the blessings of liberty. Yet millions are being deprived of those blessings—not because of their own failures but because of the color of their skin.

But it cannot continue. Our Constitution, the foundation of our Republic, forbids it. . . . Morality forbids it. And the law I will sign tonight forbids it.

This language recalled again for me the letter Dick had written to George Cuomo eight years before while awaiting discharge from military service at Fort Dix. Dick had drawn a comparison between the Europe which had enchanted him and the America to which he was then returning. Though riddled with inequities, America was a place, he felt, where people believed they could get somewhere. In other countries, he had found no such belief—not even the hope that genuine equality might one day exist.

I was powerfully moved by the fact that, in the many years since Dick's return from the army, he had, indeed, lent his voice to articulate speeches and legislation that contributed to demolishing the walls that separate our ideals from our life experiences.

In his closing remarks, Johnson said: *"We have come now to a time of testing. We must not fail. Let us close the springs of racial poison."* As his instructions to Dick made clear, no one was more aware than the president that the act of signing into law would not guarantee compliance with that law. The testing time LBJ spoke of was not simply a literal testing that would happen in the courts, but a time that would try communities across the country and take place in the hearts of all Americans.

As the applause sounded, Lady Bird observed Bobby Kennedy's "impassive face and the very measured clapping of his hands, which would not have disturbed a gnat sleeping calmly in his palm." Several other accounts of Bobby's behavior that night also suggest he was sulking or even angry; but from his deeply distracted appearance, I gleaned a wave of grief brought forth by the occasion, his anguish over the absence of a brother he loved more than himself.

As the crowd surged forward, clustering around the president to receive the signing pens and take photographs, Bobby held back, passively awaiting his turn. Finally, he approached the table where Johnson filled his hand with a cluster of pens for him and his assistants in the Justice Department. Bobby later sent one of these pens (framed along with a picture of the signing ceremony) to his assistant attorney general, John Doar. At the bottom he added the following notation: "Pen used to sign President Kennedy's civil rights bill."

When I discussed the brutal dynamics between Robert Kennedy and Lyndon Johnson with Dick, he acknowledged that Bobby was haunted by the fact that his brother had only been given three years in office, that his legacy seemed shrunken by Johnson's accomplishments. "All these things he's doing, poverty, civil rights, they're things we had just begun," Bobby said to Dick. "We just didn't have time."

"Julius Caesar is an immortal, and he was only emperor of Rome for a little more than three years," Dick pointed out in an effort to assuage Bobby's grim state of mind.

At this, a slight grin brightened Bobby's face. "Yes," he agreed, "but it helps if you have Shakespeare to write about you."

"So whose bill was it?" Dick and I asked each other and this time we both agreed that it wouldn't have been possible without the fusion of JFK's inspiration and LBJ's execution. In any case, far and away the most profound force behind the bill belonged to the Civil Rights Movement itself. By touching the conscience of the country, the Civil Rights Movement transformed public sentiment and drove Congress to act.

As for Lyndon Johnson, he was positively ebullient as he signed the bill, calling for more pens when his supply was depleted by the congratulatory throng. Afterward, he met informally with the civil rights leaders in his office. Finally, despite the late hour, he decided that he, Lady Bird, and Bill Moyers should fly to the ranch that very night. We were all "exhilarated with that sense of adventure and youth and release, the perfect beginning for a vacation," Lady Bird recorded in her diary. "This was one of those rare nights, starry in every way, when one does not think about tomorrow, a wonderful sense of euphoria rarely attained."

"But later that very night," Moyers recalled, "I found [Johnson] in a melancholy mood as he lay in bed reading the bulldog edition of the *Washington Post* with headlines celebrating the day. I asked him what was troubling him." In reply, Johnson said, "I think we just delivered the South to the Republican Party for a long time to come."

This quiet, introspective Lyndon Johnson, despondent just when one might expect nothing but elation, was one few people, except Lady Bird, saw.

"I think he felt an extreme sense of loneliness," I said to Dick. "He knew there'd be trouble ahead and that some of his closest friends and oldest allies in the South would feel he had betrayed them. And it was, after all, the exact anniversary of the heart attack that had nearly killed him. Mortality and achievement were much on his mind."

"And he feared there might be mutiny and bloodshed when the bill went into effect," Dick added.

In the short run, the desegregation law was initially implemented more smoothly than anyone could have predicted, though Lyndon Johnson could not have known this at the time. In the long run, however, his forebodings of violence and bloodshed would come to pass.

Suddenly, an expression of sorrow crossed Dick's face. "Who would have thought that the testing time that lay ahead would still be with us more than half a century later, that the springs of racial poison have still not been closed?"

As the season of politics began in earnest in the spring and summer of 1964, Lyndon Johnson was so harassed by what the White House termed "the Bobby problem"—the selection of his running mate for the coming campaign—that it became a full-blown obsession. He was deluged by a spate of articles and reports lobbying for him to choose Bobby. "Every day, as soon as I opened the papers or turned on the television," Johnson confessed to me years later:

there was something about Bobby Kennedy; there was some person or group talking about what a great Vice President he'd make. Somehow it just didn't seem fair. I'd given three years of loyal service to Jack Kennedy. During all that time I'd willingly stayed in the background; I knew that it was his Presidency, not mine. If I disagreed with him, I did it in private, not in public.

And then Kennedy was killed and I became custodian of his will. I became the President. But none of this seemed to register with Bobby Kennedy, who acted like he was the custodian of the Kennedy dream, some kind of rightful heir to the throne.

But no matter what, I simply couldn't let it happen. With Bobby on the ticket, I'd never know if I could be elected on my own.

Like Bobby, Lyndon Johnson had skin as thin as an onion's and a memory—particularly when it came to a grudge—as long as an elephant's. The real "Bobby problem" went far deeper than the question of who was the rightful heir. It had begun well before the assassination when Bobby had not only ignored Vice President Johnson and blocked him from meaningful access to his brother's administration but treated him in a manner Johnson considered derisive and condescending.

In the aftermath of the assassination, as Dick's diary revealed, Bobby had stigmatized LBJ and was possessed of a grief-distorted estimation of his own power: "When the time comes," he had gloated, "we'll tell him who we want as Vice-President." In Bobby's mind, Johnson had taken on more than the aura of a despised potential rival during these weeks. He had taken on the unmistakable aspect of a nemesis.

Dick's March 1964 diary recounts an interchange of indelible ferocity in the White House concerning Paul Corbin, Bobby's close friend, who had organized a vice presidential write-in campaign for Bobby in the New Hampshire primary. When Johnson found out, Bobby, having just returned from a diplomatic mission, had been called into the Oval Office. There was no standing on ceremony. According to Dick's account, LBJ said "I want you to get rid of Paul Corbin."

RFK: "Well, he was appointed by President Kennedy who thought he was good."

LBJ: "President Kennedy isn't president any more. I am."

RFK: "I know you're President, and don't you talk like that to me anymore."

LBJ: "I did you a favor sending you to the Far East."

RFK: "A favor, I don't want you to do any more favors for me, ever." And he stalked out the door.

Adjudicating who was right or wrong in the Corbin incident is pointless. The antagonism here is searing and elemental.

True, they had worked together for the passage of the Civil Rights Bill because it meant more to both than their hostility toward one another. And yet, no sooner was the bill signed into law than Bobby turned sullen, as if LBJ had picked his brother's pocket of the credit JFK deserved.

On July 16, the Republican convention's choice of Barry Goldwater solved Lyndon Johnson's "Bobby problem" for the time being. From the moment of Goldwater's selection as flag-bearer, Johnson had no need for Bobby's credibility in matters of civil rights, trade unions, and the liberal Kennedy political organization in the Northeast. Goldwater's nomination automatically soothed any qualms liberals might have had toward Lyndon Johnson, once their alternative was the ideological apostle of the far right.

JULY 29, 1964

All that remained for Lyndon Johnson was to determine the most effective and least damaging way to eliminate Bobby from all vice presidential consideration. He decided to tell Bobby face-to-face in the Oval Office. There was nothing casual about the meeting which took place on that afternoon of July 29. It was given the care and preparation of an important matter of state. Johnson would read to Bobby from an extensive memo of talking points that explained why he was not going to select him as his running mate. He wanted to leave no loopholes or doubts about the matter, to remove, if possible, all personal contention from the discussion. He was hopeful that in return, Kennedy would publicly withdraw his name from consideration for the position he had sought for months.

All Johnson's reasons to eliminate Bobby rested, ostensibly, upon data-driven political strategy, a geographical analysis of the upcoming election. Goldwater's strength, he told Bobby, referring to the memo, lay in the South, the Southeast, and potentially the Midwest. Just as LBJ had been selected to meet JFK's political requirements—to buttress his position in Texas and the South—so now, Johnson emphasized, he must put forth a ticket appealing to the Midwest and border states—one that would arouse minimal antagonism in the South. Bobby's inclusion on the ticket, in his opinion, did not fit those requirements.

The president sought to soften the blow by offering Bobby the position of campaign manager or any desirable cabinet post or ambassadorship he might want, along with his assurance of support should Bobby choose to run for the presidency in the future.

While this meeting was in process, Moyers telephoned Dick with the news that "Lyndon's telling Bobby that he can't have the nomination."

"I wasn't surprised," Dick told me, "but I was deflated." After hearing from Moyers, Dick left his office and walked over to the White House driveway. He lingered there until a black limousine headed down the drive with Bobby in the back.

Bobby, as Dick described the scene, "told the driver to stop, rolled down his window, and sat there wordlessly."

"It's too bad," Dick said.

"That's okay," Bobby replied. "He looked at me, lips closed tightly in a slightly pained expression."

"I suppose there's nothing to be done about it," Dick commented.

Bobby "shook his head in agreement and drove off."

Much to Johnson's chagrin, Bobby refused to notify the press, insisting that the White House—not he—announce his 'withdrawal' from the race. Not wanting Bobby to be the sole person removed from consideration as his running mate, Johnson hit upon a cunning, if drastic, political solution.

At 6 p.m. the following night he delivered a televised statement: "I have reached the conclusion that it would be inadvisable for me to recommend to the convention any member of the Cabinet or any of those who meet regularly with the Cabinet." So vital was the work they were doing, he maintained, that he wanted them to concentrate exclusively on their jobs.

In one stroke, he had eliminated not only Bobby, but five of the most likely candidates mentioned in the papers: Defense Secretary Robert

McNamara, Secretary of State Dean Rusk, Agriculture Secretary Orville Freeman, Sargent Shriver, director of both the Peace Corps and the new Office of Economic Opportunity, and U.N. ambassador Adlai Stevenson.

Immediately after his announcement, he informed his friend Dick Russell that he had canceled the prospects of his entire cabinet and those who sat regularly with them. An amazed Russell said, "That'll eliminate a whole lot of 'em."

LBJ chuckled gleefully: "I just had to eliminate one."

And that one, Bobby clearly understood, was him. "I'm sorry I took so many nice fellows over the side with me," he stated. But his droll humor hardly concealed his bitter disappointment.

The incident should have ended there. The "damn albatross," Johnson exulted, was off his back. But what had begun as a brilliant "masterstroke" quickly degenerated into a most unsavory episode. The next day, reveling in victory, the president regaled three reporters at lunch, telling them he had carefully watched Kennedy at the meeting, "like a hawk watching chickens." Upon receiving the news that his vice presidential hopes were over, Johnson explained, Bobby's "face changed, and he started to swallow. He looked sick. His Adam's apple bounded up and down like a yo-yo." With his gift for mimicry, Johnson gulped for the reporters, describing Bobby as "a fat fish pulling in a mouthful of air."

Once he had begun, he couldn't stop himself. He mimicked Bobby's funny voice with such caustic zeal that I was put in mind of another incident by another gifted mimic—Abraham Lincoln. Lincoln's friend William Herndon said that on one occasion early in his career, Lincoln had taken umbrage at a Democrat named Jesse Thomas and retaliated by imitating him "in gesture and voice, at times caricaturing his walk and the motion of his body." In a mocking burst of vindictiveness, Lincoln gave way to such "intense and scathing ridicule" that old Thomas broke down into tears. The public incident spread through the town and became known as the "skinning of Thomas."

Lincoln came to his senses later that night. He went to see Thomas and gave him a deeply felt apology, but for the rest of his life, he bore the memory of that night with sorrow and shame. When Johnson's much embellished account of his "skinning" of Bobby became the talk of the town, Kennedy demanded an apology. Denials were forthcoming. Apologies never followed.

As I opened the first of a series of archival boxes devoted to the 1964 convention and campaign, I was filled with amusement. The contents looked more like a kid's toybox than an archive. A collection of campaign buttons of all sizes—"LBJ all the way" on a field of red, white, and blue, "LBJ and HHH," alongside smiling miniature portraits of LBJ and running mate Hubert Humphrey—piled next to matchbooks labeled "LBJ & USA," bumper stickers endorsing Johnson/Humphrey, folded campaign brochures and posters, stacks of old newspapers and magazines, ticket stubs, convention badges, miniature cowboy hats, and all manner of additional memorabilia that Dick had stashed away from half a century before.

"Politics in your blood!" I said to Dick, smiling down on his souvenir trove, "like a ten-year-old baseball-card junkie!"

"Guilty!" said Dick holding up both palms in surrender. "I loved the convention hoopla, the placards, the parades, the packaged extravagance of it all."

As the August Democratic convention in Atlantic City drew near, Dick believed that the campaign against Goldwater answered a politician's prayer, with only the size of Johnson's victory remaining in question. But the president would not tolerate such a cocksure attitude. In fact, as the convention approached, he became fraught with anxiety. So abrupt and crippling was his descent from self-confidence into doubt that he actually drafted a statement withdrawing from the race altogether.

In his memoir, Johnson revealed that he was assailed by fears that the nation would not "unite indefinitely behind any Southerner," given the "deep-seated and far-reaching attitude—a disdain for the South that seems to be woven into the fabric of Northern experience." He mistrusted and stressed over "the Metropolitan press on the Eastern seaboard." And he worried about the physical condition of his overworked heart. In his drafted withdrawal, he stated that he would carry on until the new president was sworn in and then would retire to his ranch in Texas.

"Preposterous!" Dick exclaimed after I had read these lines from Johnson's memoir aloud. "I don't believe a word of it. Everything was going for him. To give up the office that he craved with his entire being? So you believe that Lyndon Johnson, like a bride on the eve of the wedding she'd dreamt of her whole life, got cold feet?"

"Yes," I countered, "I think he *was* serious."

"What was he fleeing from?" asked Dick, "from prosperity, peace, the prospect of a huge victory in November?"

"Maybe a sense of foreboding," I said, "an intuitive feeling about the future."

Lady Bird was familiar with Lyndon's galloping depressions. She had seen him enveloped in them before, often on the verge of either great triumph or great challenge. She referred to such periodic downward slopes as Lyndon's descent into the "Valley of the Black Pig," alluding to a W. B. Yeats poem filled with premonitions of doom and dreams of massive destruction.

Two weeks after the Civil Rights Act was signed, riots had burst out in Harlem when a white police officer shot and killed a fifteen-year-old Black boy. Stores were looted, more than one hundred injured, another one hundred arrested, and one man was killed—an ominous reflection of the combustible conditions of impoverished pockets of northern cities where segregation was decreed by economics rather than by law.

In early August, Johnson's hopes of keeping a lid on the simmering situation in Vietnam until after the election were dashed when North Vietnamese torpedo boats attacked the USS *Maddox*, an American destroyer patrolling international waters in the Gulf of Tonkin off the coast of Vietnam. The United States retaliated. A second incident, wrapped in obscurity or perhaps invention, resulted in the Gulf of Tonkin Resolution—a congressional carte blanche for the president to take any measures he deemed necessary to promote peace and security in Southeast Asia. The day would come when that resolution, along with a penchant for secrecy, would help lead to the fulfillment of the nightmare prophecy of Yeats's ominous poem.

Underlying these portentous incidents at home and abroad were more personal undercurrents that furnished an index to Lyndon Johnson's shifting moods and behaviors. From my own study of LBJ, I knew that in the last days before every election, physical complaints and waves of runaway anxiety would take hold of Lyndon's body.

In the final stretch of his first congressional race, he suffered acute stomach pains, an uncontrollable sweating, and a nausea that lingered for days. Delivering a speech at his biggest rally, he collapsed and was rushed to the hospital where his appendix was removed.

"So you blame his appendicitis on politics?" Dick asked.

Ignoring Dick's gentle mockery, I pressed on, recounting the story of how during Lyndon's run for the Senate, he was racked by fevers, chills, and stomach pains. Finally, he was hospitalized for kidney stones. If he was unable to pass them, the doctors explained, an operation would be required as well as time for recuperation. Once the press discovered his whereabouts, he drafted a statement withdrawing from the race. Lady Bird convinced him to postpone its release until morning. That night he passed the kidney stones and immediately resumed the campaign.

"Political kidney stones," Dick smiled skeptically. "The Senate race threatening his body. Politics threatening his life!"

"Politics *was* his life," I said.

And Lady Bird was his anchor. On August 25, 1964, the day before the Democrats were scheduled to nominate their presidential candidate, Lady Bird once again guided her husband back on track. After reading the draft of his withdrawal that he had planned on releasing later that day, she told him unequivocally that there was no honorable way to turn back. "To step out now would be wrong for your country," she insisted, "and I can see nothing but a lonely wasteland for your future."

Lady Bird's argument struck a chord. Her husband filed the statement away and readied himself for the convention. The decision made, he rebounded from valley bottom to mountaintop. High spirits returned. On a whim, he decided to fly to Atlantic City to personally introduce his running mate at the convention. Johnson asked Dick to accompany him and his yet-to-be announced running mate, Hubert Humphrey. Having already drafted Johnson's introductory remarks about Humphrey, Dick continued to work in transit upon Johnson's acceptance speech.

"I had never seen him in a better mood," Dick recalled as the president filled glasses with whiskey, toasting everyone.

When Johnson arrived at the convention hall, he was greeted by a tumultuous ovation. Flanked by mammoth portraits of himself, he took the gavel and announced that he had selected the popular and effervescent Hubert Humphrey as his running mate. Humphrey was nominated by acclamation, and Johnson made his way to the floor. Much to the Secret Service's chagrin, he plunged into the adoring delegates like a rock star.

"This was his moment, the culmination of a political lifetime," Dick wrote some years later. "The party to which he had devoted three decades of labor, which had rejected him four years earlier, was now at his feet—admiring, obedient, the instrument of his personal will."

Air Force One returned the president's party to Washington at 2 a.m. only to come back to Atlantic City the following afternoon for closing events—the two acceptance speeches, the first by Humphrey (which Dick had edited only minutes before delivery), and then Johnson's, a hodgepodge which read like the committee project that indeed it was. But literary quality was small matter that night; much to the president's delight and gratification, the speech was interrupted by applause more than fifty times.

Once the official events had concluded, the party began. Four thousand guests flooded into the decorated ballroom to celebrate Lyndon Johnson's fifty-sixth birthday. Along with thousands in attendance, comedian Danny Thomas and actress Carol Channing raised their voices to sing "Happy Birthday" to the president. LBJ used a huge knife to carve a three-hundred-pound birthday cake shaped like a map of the United States.

The night was a celebration both for and of Lyndon Johnson. The Democratic Party's ceremonial coronation of LBJ was complete. Even delegates who had spurned him in 1960 in favor of the charismatic young John Kennedy were now ecstatically marching toward a victory that seemed like a fait accompli before the national election campaign had even begun.

When Johnson stepped onto the balcony, he was greeted by cheers from thousands of people on the boardwalk below, along with the music of scores of high school bands—all capped by a spectacular display of fireworks that one witness described as "the loudest birthday bang in the world." On this night, Lyndon Johnson was able to lift his eyes and gaze upon a gigantic portrait of himself in the red, white, and blue fireworks materializing in the night sky above Atlantic City.

SEPTEMBER 7, 1964

At thirty-two, Dick was the youngest of the campaign veterans. Once again he exhibited the versatility of "the supreme generalist" he had proven himself to be as a New Frontiersman. In box after box of archival material we detected traces of Dick's busy hand in his multitasking role of all-purpose strategist. He traveled with LBJ to the convention; he helped develop the party platform and central campaign themes; he not only drafted a lion's share of the president's speeches, but worked over and polished Lady Bird's whistle-stop statements for her solo tour of the South; every morning he met with a small team in the West Wing to plot the campaign and discuss a range of responses to Goldwater; and he worked with Moyers and the advertising firm of Doyle Dane Bernbach to concoct a handful of devastating media spots and print advertising.

We pawed through the boxes of materials from the Johnson campaign which had kicked off on Labor Day, as was tradition in those days when the official presidential race was only three months long. He chose to speak in Cadillac Square, Detroit, Michigan, the same site from which John Kennedy had launched his campaign four years before. For that occasion, Ted Sorensen had written JFK's initial launch statement while Dick, as his deputy speechwriter, was relegated to writing Kennedy's Alaska remarks. Now Dick was LBJ's chief speechwriter.

And that September 7 morning, such were the travel advantages of the presidency that Dick departed with LBJ by helicopter from the South Lawn of the White House at 9:51, set down at Andrews Air Force Base ten minutes later, and immediately sped off on the presidential JetStar, scheduled to arrive in Detroit in less than an hour. On the way, Johnson suggested some changes to the speech, stressing how Kennedy's Nuclear Test Ban Treaty (which Goldwater had voted against) had "slowed down the deadly poisoning of the air we breathe, and the milk that our children drink. We do not want every mother to live in fear."

Dick instantly understood the rationale behind this apparent digression from the general domestic themes of prosperity and justice. Several weeks earlier, Moyers, Dick, and the media team had approved a revolutionary sixty-second spot created by Doyle Dane Bernbach. The ad, scheduled to premiere later that evening, focused upon the threat of nuclear war.

Large crowds greeted the president as his motorcade made its way from the airport into Detroit. Reporters noted that Johnson was traveling "under the greatest security protection the official might of Michigan and the United States could provide," far exceeding Senator Kennedy's security in 1960. As became his habit, Johnson "ignored all precautions to mingle with great crowds and shake hundreds of outstretched hands," forcing Secret Service agents to chase after him as he stepped over the chain.

The President's Daily Diary records that "everyone was most enthusiastic about the trip" on the way home. The presidential party was back in Washington by 3:30 that afternoon. That evening, Dick and his colleagues watched what would become the iconic "Daisy Girl" ad make its national debut during NBC's *Monday Night Movie*:

As the ad opens, we hear birdsong and see a summer field of flowers where a small girl is busily at work plucking petals from a daisy. She counts aloud, 1-2-3, until a harsh male voice intrudes with a countdown, 10-9-8-7 . . . The camera closes in on the child's face in a frozen image, finally narrowing to her eye. The moment the countdown reaches "one," the child's pupil is obliterated by the swirling mushroom cloud of a nuclear explosion. "We must either love each other," says the voice of Lyndon Johnson, "or we must die." A narrator's neutral voice has the all-important last word: "Vote for President Johnson on November 3. The stakes are too high for you to stay home."

Although the "Daisy Girl" ad never mentioned Goldwater's name, people were well aware of the candidate's reckless statements about the bomb. He had argued that generals in the field should have the authority to use tactical nuclear weapons. He had once jokingly recommended that a nuclear bomb be lobbed into the men's room at the Kremlin. More significant was the vote Goldwater had earlier cast against the Nuclear Test Ban Treaty.

The Goldwater camp's outcry over the "Daisy Girl" ad was shrill and immediate. "We knew it would create controversy," Dick told me, "so we saturated the airwaves that first night." As soon as the cry went up that Johnson's campaign had hit below the belt, the president, with theatrical indignation, ordered that the ad (which he had overseen) be pulled at once. The ad had done its work. Goldwater would never recover from that coordinated strike on the first day of the campaign. Fear and anxiety about the rash candidate from Arizona shot from coast to coast.

And, as Dick proudly recalled to me, other clever—if far less brutal—ads followed suit. In response to Goldwater's promise to privatize Social Security, a hand was shown cutting up a Social Security card. When Goldwater facetiously suggested that the Eastern Seaboard be removed from the United States, an ad portrayed the East Coast being sawed off a map of the country and set adrift in the Atlantic Ocean. "This spot," Dick later wrote, "was only shown east of the Appalachians, on the very sound premise that it would bring cheers of approval in every western bar."

Negative campaigning had grown far more sophisticated since the days when Dick was "the pack mule," charged with lugging around the "Nixopedia," White House aide Mike Feldman's big black binder that contained an indexed list of Nixon's statements and misstatements used in Kennedy's debate preparation and rebuttal.

In fact, there were no debates at all during the 1964 campaign, no sleepless nights of preparation for them, no stacks of index cards reducing answers to complex questions into pithy, easily memorized and digestible sound bites. Early on, Dick had argued strongly against debates for Lyndon Johnson. "It would not be to our advantage to debate," Dick had written him in a memo.

"The debates helped Kennedy, not so much that he did well, but that they gave him enormous public exposure. The Republican argument that Kennedy was a young inexperienced playboy who didn't know much—their principal issue—was stripped away. The debate format must always be to the advantage of the lesser known candidate, unless he is absolutely hopeless on television. Thus, even if you are two times as effective as your opponent, he will gain in stature, recognition, and prestige from appearing with you."

Johnson held firm with the advice not to debate despite strident demands from Goldwater and mounting pressure from reporters. In fact, on the basis of similar reasoning, presidential debates were discontinued until 1976 when Gerald Ford, to his great misfortune, agreed to debate Jimmy Carter.

———•—•———

In early September, having decided to run for the Senate seat in New York, Robert Kennedy resigned from Lyndon's cabinet. It promised to be a tough race. Bobby would be seen as a "carpetbagger" rather than a native New Yorker running against Kenneth Keating, a popular Republican incumbent. That Lyndon and Bobby continued to loathe one another is undeniable, but political pragmatism dictated that they work effectively—even amiably—when a reciprocal public show of support would prove beneficial to both. Much as Bobby despised having to solicit Johnson's help, he needed the president's momentum and his political machine in New York. Much as Johnson may have preferred Bobby suffer a loss, his overriding priority was building a liberal Democratic majority for the Great Society.

And Dick, I discovered, was right in the middle of the two men's public rapprochement. It was Dick who drafted a warm letter of support to his friend Bobby from the president who detested him:

"Dear Bob,
    It is with great regret that I have received your resignation. That regret is tempered by satisfaction with the knowledge that you intend to continue your outstanding career in the service of your country."

Later he states that,

"around the world and in our own country—you have been one of the leading exemplars of the idealism, the spirit of adventure, and the strong, moral convictions which are characteristic of America at its best."

In finishing, the letter notes that this is only a temporary farewell, expressing satisfaction that, "You will soon be back in Washington where I can again call upon your judgement and counsel."

"Wasn't it awkward?" I asked Dick, "the antipathy between them was so strong. Here you were, writing as Lyndon to Bobby. You knew that Lyndon was always worried about divided loyalties and you were never far from the top of his list of suspects."

"I was doing my job," Dick replied. "Believe me, if Lyndon had asked me to draft a letter to myself upon my own resignation, I'd have written one beauty of a letter in praise of myself!"

It soon became clear, however, that Lyndon's public alliance with Bobby, which included plans for the two of them to campaign together, did not extend to the president allowing members of his White House staff to take time away from their own work to help Bobby. Arthur Schlesinger wrote Bobby that "Dick Goodwin and Mike Feldman both want very much to help but are somewhat stymied by LBJ." Indeed, Johnson threatened to fire anyone who shirked their duties in order to moonlight for Bobby or even advise him.

Despite the risk, we found in Dick's archive a long memo of advice to Bobby on his prospective debate with Senator Keating. The memo was entitled "Preparation for a Debate (based on the 1960 experience)." "I knew Lyndon would be mad if he found out," Dick told me, "but I supposed we were all on the same team and Bobby was a friend."

The memo included a list of suggestions for Bobby and his team:

"You are not trying to win an argument. You are not trying to score points. You are trying to make people vote for you.

"The basic element is the candidate's own ability and personality.

"Remember you may be on camera while he speaks. Always listen to him attentively. If he says something funny—often directed against you—smile. If he says something ludicrous—smile. And don't forget to smile anyway, once in a while.

"Don't answer immediately, hesitate a moment to think and not appear over eager or impetuous.

"Keep remarks brief and understandable. Don't use a lot of facts. One or two will show you know what you are talking about. Then speak for a minute, affirmatively and simply, giving your position."

After much bickering and combustion the Kennedy-Keating debate never materialized, but I considered how useful Dick's simple suggestions would have been for candidates in the years that followed: for George H. W. Bush, for instance, during his 1992 town hall debate with Bill Clinton, when he was spied checking his watch while an audience member posed a question, a display of frustration and impatience in stark contrast with Clinton's empathetic demeanor. Or for Al Gore in 2000, when, exasperated by George W. Bush's responses, he projected a sophomoric condescension, rolled his eyes, and loudly sighed.

———•·•———

"I had a lot more power in Lyndon's campaign," Dick mused one day, "but not as much fun."

"Fun?" I exclaimed. "Fun is a strange word to describe such a grueling marathon."

"There were so few of us in 1960," he explained. "We were underdogs. We traveled together day and night for sixty odd days on this little plane. The election was so close that any blunder could trigger the failure or success of the entire enterprise. It was the grandest, most quixotic adventure of my life."

"You make it sound so romantic!"

"Day after day, week after week of no sleep, unhealthy food, smoking and drinking, endlessly talking and working, writing under great pressure. Such a life can only be glamorous in hindsight. And only if you win, of course."

"On Lyndon's campaign, the outcome of the election was no cliffhanger. Wasn't there less tension?" I asked.

"Less tension but double the workload and more daily pressure. Don't forget," Dick added, "Lyndon was the president. We had all the work of the presidency doubled upon the work of the campaign. And on the road Lyndon was selling the Great Society across the nation."

In addition to his campaign chores Dick was one of a handful of task force liaison officers. His designated task was to focus on the cities and the preservation of natural beauty. The goal was to produce finished reports that could be easily fleshed out into messages to Congress the moment the campaign was over, done, and won.

"There was not enough time in the day," Dick said. "The most frightening thing of all was that Lyndon demanded every minute of your day and night, and every second of every minute."

A job under Lyndon, as I would also come to understand one day, was tantamount to signing over your entire life. I found an odd confirmation of this in a note folded in one of the campaign boxes. It was typed, but signed "Lyndon" in pencil, a reasonable facsimile of the president's looping autograph we both knew so well. It read:

Dickie Baby:

I came to see you this afternoon and you weren't in—SHAME! I thought I told you when I let you come out into the open that you must never leave your little cubicle.

From now on please contact my personal confidential secretary, Mrs. Juanita Roberts, and request permission to leave. If she isn't available, you may direct your request to my valet.

With fondest regards and admiration,
Your loving friend,
Lyndon
P.S. I wouldn't be too pleased to see the above in Evans & Novak.

"Moyers!" Dick cried out, laughing and coughing so robustly it was hard to tell one from the other. "Moyers the prankster. He knew the stress and pressure of Lyndon more than I ever did. Bill was the principal architect of the campaign and he was in charge of the task forces. This was the way we blew off steam, our kind of fun."

After listening to Dick's recollections about the two campaigns it seemed to me that JFK's campaign was a quest, LBJ's an organized juggernaut. The two campaigns were as different as the two men who led them. Kennedy so cool, Lyndon hot and demonstrative. Kennedy ironic and detached, Lyndon overbearing, kindly, and brutal. Both men worked with punishing energy and both summoned belief and devotion from their core circle. If anything, Lyndon pushed so hard he used those people up. And if John Kennedy was self-contained and unflappable in Dick's depiction of him, Lyndon, the taskmaster, struck me as most flappable, and all-too-human.

As we came across the thick files of Dick's drafts for LBJ's campaign speeches, I asked Dick how he wrote in styles as different as JFK's and LBJ's.

"Like a tailor," Dick replied, "if you don't take the right measure of a man, the clothes won't fit, the clothes won't feel good, they won't look good."

Early on, when Dick was first entering Lyndon's circle, he showed Jack Valenti, who was supervising Johnson's speeches, a sampler of "straightforward, unadorned language." In his diary, Dick recorded that "Valenti said [it] was just the sort of thing" he wanted—a style Valenti described as "simple with a touch of eloquence." Both concurred that LBJ's speech was "a lot closer to Roosevelt than to Kennedy."

Kennedy's style was more formal, employing classic rhetorical constructions of inversion and repetition. His language often had a sharp edge that emphasized a style that was far more arresting, oratorical, and theatrical than anything that would have fit Lyndon Johnson. Kennedy's style lent itself to the inspirational, Lyndon's spoke to more workaday aspirations.

Johnson's cadences were more colloquial. When he trusted himself, as in the final weeks of the campaign, he spoke in shorter sentences, in an elevated conversational tone that made direct connection with a broad swath of middle-class America. He touched that nerve because the stories he told contained the policies and programs he intended to implement: He spoke of the working man who "doesn't ask much . . . a little vacation . . . a little sick leave . . . a little medical care . . . a rug on the floor . . . a picture on the wall and a little music in the house." He repeatedly pointed out that while a minority still says "no," an overwhelming majority "says yes" to the policies he was proposing—minimum wage, the rights of the workingman, better education for our young, hospital care for our aged, a war on poverty, equal rights for all. I have often wished I had witnessed firsthand the tumultuous response Lyndon received during the last laps of the campaign. The crowds Dick described to me were frenzied, overwhelming. Even in his own Northeast, Kennedy never saw the like.

And this Lyndon Johnson was one I was not personally familiar with—an ecstatic figure who absorbed the pandemonium and grew in confidence and power as the surging crowd responded to him. This figure was a far cry from the televised president with the halting voice we would all come to know so well, a character who resembled a slicked-back preacher far older than his fifty-six years.

It was hard for me to imagine this force of nature reaching out to the mass of extended hands that wanted to touch him, clasp his fingers. Afterward, he happily exhibited for Dick his own swollen hands scratched and nicked by fingernails. "Positively exuberant," Dick described him to me, "holding out his hands for inspection, like a red badge of courage."

———•·———

As the campaign drew to a close, it struck me that if Dick had "politics in the blood," Lyndon Johnson was the most ferocious political animal in the jungle. The same man who had proclaimed that he would rather quit than take Bobby Kennedy as his running mate later said, "If I need Robert Kennedy I'll take him. I'll take anybody. I want to get elected. I'm a pragmatic fellow."

The two antagonists campaigned together throughout the state of New York in the middle and at the end of October. This was no case of simple hypocrisy. It was a practical relationship illustrating the heart and soul of politics. They rode through human corridors six feet deep in Harlem. By the time they reached the Waldorf-Astoria, the crowds were so dense that the president instructed the driver to take another tour around the square to let more people see them together.

The New York Times described how the president "threw his arm literally and figuratively around the Democratic candidate for the Senate." And Bobby reciprocated. When queried about reports of the bitter rift between them, Bobby countered that, on the contrary, their relationship was "very warm, very close." At a thunderous rally in Rochester the following day, Kennedy declared Johnson "already one of the great presidents of the United States."

After full-throttled weeks of campaigning that carried the relentless president from New England to the Midwest to the West Coast and back, he returned to New York on Saturday, October 31, for another day of joint campaigning with Bobby Kennedy before the Tuesday election. Such buoyant crowds greeted their bubble-topped car that it already seemed like a victory parade. And later that night the same air of victory filled the jam-packed event at Madison Square Garden where Johnson received an ovation that rolled on for ten minutes followed by the earsplitting chant "We want Lyndon! We want Lyndon!"

When the tumult subsided at last, Johnson told the audience that in this final hour of his campaign he had come to ask for their support to return him to the presidency, and bring Robert Kennedy to the Senate. "I don't have to tell you of Bob Kennedy's talents or his energy or his great patriotism," Johnson said. "He has demonstrated this in ways and actions that are far beyond my inadequate description." The address, broken up by applause fifty-four times (LBJ always wanted to know the exact number) elaborated on his dreams for a Great Society.

———•—•———

Lyndon had given everything he had to the campaign—the full measure of his head-spinning welter of contraries: calculation and impulsivity, discipline and recklessness, kindness and cruelty, depression and manic energy, generosity and mean-spiritedness, confidence and insecurity, secrecy and candor, dishonesty and bravery. For all his willingness to compromise and dissemble, this man who seemed willing to do anything to win had also shown himself a man willing to put it all on the line—as with the Civil Rights Bill—willing to push in all the chips for his beliefs.

Johnson returned to Texas to watch the returns and let the soothing landslide victory-in-the-making wash over him. He had won over Republican and Democratic voters old and young, from cities and suburbs and farms. He attended a boisterous party at the Governor's Mansion and a coffee hour with jubilant campaign workers before settling in to watch the returns on television with family and friends in a suite at the Driskill Hotel.

Back in Washington, Dick gathered in the White House Mess in the West Wing basement for a party with his colleagues. Surrounded by posters and streamers, they spent the evening talking, drinking, exchanging stories, celebrating in a relaxed manner only possible when the outcome had long been assured. They were assembled around the television when the network picked up Bobby Kennedy's victory party. Kennedy had won by a little more than 700,000 votes, his total maximized by Johnson's overwhelming margin of 2.7 million. "If my brother was alive," Kennedy reportedly said, "I wouldn't be here. I'd rather have it that way."

———•—•———

"You have to realize," Lyndon Johnson once said, "that a politician—a good one—is a strange duck. Anyone who periodically has to get down on hands and knees to beg voters to prove they love him by giving him their vote is really sick. . . . Try to think of me as a seriously ill, dear relative or friend who needs all the care, compassion, comfort, and love he can get to get well."

He would be restored and get well now. He had won by more than 15 million votes, 61 percent of all the votes cast. He had earned the mandate he sought to build the Great Society.

And for the first time he had earned something more. By his own reckoning, he had earned something greater even than votes. "It was a night I shall never forget," Johnson later told me. "Millions upon millions of people, each one marking my name on their ballot, each one wanting me as their president. For the first time in all my life, I truly felt loved by the American people."

CHAPTER EIGHT

"And We Shall Overcome"

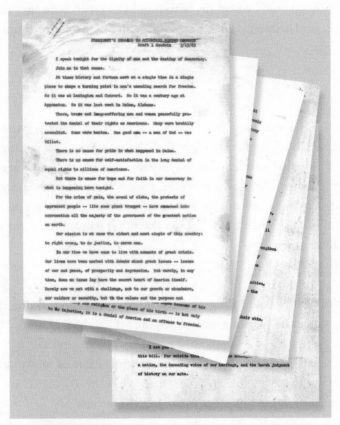

*Pages of Dick's draft of LBJ's "We Shall Overcome" speech
delivered before a joint session of Congress. March 15, 1965.*

DURING THE YEARS OF OUR JOINT VENTURE, DICK AND I, LIKE
two nosy neighbors on a party line, had listened in on conversations
recorded on LBJ's secret taping system. On the whole, the experience was
grand entertainment—making us laugh, bewildering us, clarifying things
we didn't know. Even if particular moments might anger or irritate us, the
audiotapes and published transcripts always furnished a touchstone for further reflection and discussion.

The first phone call Lyndon Johnson made on the morning of November 4, 1964, after a long night of celebration and only a few hours of sleep, was to Special Assistant Bill Moyers.

After joyfully reviewing results of state races from different parts of the country, their conversation turned to potential staff changes at the White House: Who should be kept on, who should be let go, who they might try to recruit. And suddenly, Dick was at the center of the conversation.

NOVEMBER 4, 1964

MOYERS: The one thing that does bother me most, frankly, is the writing end of it, not just from the standpoint of getting it done, but getting it done in such a way that you leave an impression on history. And I argue very strongly, therefore, for doing everything we have to do to keep the fellow who's already made another commitment, and that's Dick Goodwin. I recognize all of Dick's liabilities, but, on the other hand, there's not another man in town who can—
LBJ: What are his liabilities?

"Liabilities!" I could imagine Dick interrupting their phone call, and slapping down the morning newspaper. "What liabilities?"

MOYERS: He is a—he got himself in hot water three or four years ago as an aggressive overly ambitious young man.
LBJ: Well, he's not in hot water to me to a damn certainty.

As I read on, I was filled with delight and pride.

The telephone exchange now transcribed between Johnson's Texas bedroom and the White House became even more intriguing once National Security Adviser McGeorge Bundy chimed in.

BUNDY: Dick is a loner, and he's a—he's ambitious and proud. He's been magnificent—
LBJ: I think he's entitled to the highest job we got, the highest pay, I think that even if he is a loner we just can't afford to have him—
BUNDY: Can't afford to lose him.

MOYERS: Cannot afford to lose him, Mr. President. You could lose me but you can't lose Goodwin.

BUNDY: You couldn't lose either one. I think the fundamental thing about Dick is that it <u>has</u> to be clear . . . where he's supposed to check in.

Moyers notes that he heard from a good friend of Dick's that he would stay if Moyers "put it on a personal basis that he just had to stay."

LBJ: Well, go on and put it on a personal basis and let's get that straightened out.

A loner . . . Overly ambitious . . . Aggressive . . . Proud . . . Magnificent: Over the years I had read dozens of extreme descriptions of Dick's character and behavior, the impressions he made on others. On the one hand, "loveable as a sullen porcupine," stated Jack Valenti. On the other hand, Valenti also acknowledged that he could be "incandescent, a near genius . . . the most skilled living practitioner of an arcane and dying artform, the political speech." Such characterizations rarely occupied a middle ground, and even now—all these years later—these negative opinions make me feel like a defensive mother at a middle school conference.

Other comments over time focused on Dick's eccentric appearance, the billowing smoke from his ever-present cigars, his rumpled suits, untamed eyebrows—the direct, arresting gaze that had captivated me from the moment we met. To those who did not know him well, his irony was thought abrasive, his shyness construed as aloofness or arrogance. And he was always difficult to classify—an intellectual but not an academic, a literary lawyer without a practice, first gregarious, then withdrawn, undeniably brilliant but sometimes socially awkward. Clearly, he never had the makings of a conventional bureaucrat or a company man. He would vanish from the office for days at a time without telling anyone where he was going or when he would return. His gifts, nonetheless, became indispensable to Lyndon Johnson in the year ahead.

When Moyers suggested that Dick had "already made another commitment," I remembered that Wesleyan University had offered him a standing invitation to become a writer-in-residence, and that he had planned to start the fellowship once the election was over. There, in the quiet college town of Middletown, Connecticut, Dick had hoped to return to his original dream of becoming a full-time writer—and, in no small part, to try to repair the damage that absolute immersion in politics inflicts on a person, a marriage, and the very possibility of a conventional family life.

After both Moyers and the president implored him to stay through the new administration's "formative period," Dick finally agreed. The moment he made that commitment, Dick recalled, the White House issued a public announcement that he had been appointed a special assistant to the president. Indeed, I found a copy of the announcement in Dick's archive, preserved by him with special care in a plastic sleeve.

When I showed him the unearthed formal notice, Dick wagged it happily in the air. "No longer hidden away in the Executive Office Building, transferred at last from the State Department payroll to the White House, back in the same office suite I had been evicted from after my date with Che Guevara, even given permission to speak with the press about what I was doing!"

Dick's satisfaction recollecting his return to Room 212 was palpable, as was our anticipation about the next step of our journey. We were about to revisit the wondrous year when the 89th Congress would produce the greatest progressive legislation in our lifetime.

"Let's get to work," Dick said to me, sweeping his hand toward the boxes we had yet to explore. "It's time for us to start building the Great Society," he smiled. "I hope I'm up to it."

———•·•———

The actual planning of the Great Society, Dick recalled, had begun six months before Johnson's reelection. At the University of Michigan the previous May, the president had promised to "set our course toward the Great Society" by corralling "the best thought and the broadest knowledge" from every section of the country to establish working groups that would address major problems facing the country.

As Johnson explained in his memoir, over the years he had watched "the standard method" of developing legislative proposals, which depended on ideas from governmental agencies. He concluded that reliance on internal sources thwarted fresh thinking. By their very nature, government bureaucracies were invariably "dedicated to preserving the status quo."

While Kennedy had also reached out beyond the agencies, Johnson believed his predecessor's task forces had been "overweighted with scholars." Very few practical ideas had emerged from them. By contrast, Johnson directed that his working groups be comprised of "doers" as well as "thinkers"—politicians, philanthropists, business leaders, and community activists as well as scholars and academics. The entire process, which was kept secret until the reports were completed to allow freedom from speculation, was more expansive, accelerated, and imaginative than the traditional "standard method."

As a result, the Johnson task forces were able to find a remedy for a long-standing problem that had stymied Kennedy's legislative agenda. While Kennedy's team failed to resolve the central problem of how to include parochial schools in federal aid to education, Johnson's education task force devised a formula for providing aid to poor districts rather than schools, thus avoiding the old thorny issue of separation of church and state. Similarly, the task force on health managed to unravel the problem of doctors' fees before the Medicare bill was sent to the Hill.

Johnson assigned Moyers the massive job of quilting together and coordinating the various task forces. Looking back after fifty years, Moyers considered his work helping to create and coordinate the 1965 legislative agenda "the most important" and "exhilarating" of his entire time in government service.

Each task force was given a White House aide as a liaison. Dick was charged with the task forces on the cities, conservation, and the arts. He wrote the special messages to Congress that called for legislation suggested by those task forces. Meanwhile, a dozen additional task forces and messages were concurrently underway in the hands of other White House aides.

Taken together, a factory was assembled that was able to investigate and produce landmark legislation on medical care, economic opportunity, education, the environment, the cities, immigration, housing and urban development, the arts, and much more that would come to alter the social, economic, and political landscape of the country.

LBJ instructed the task forces to set goals "too high rather than too low." Final reports were to reach his desk around Election Day. It was imperative that the administration be prepared to move forward on the first day, operating on the assumption that he would win.

Two weeks after Johnson's victory, Dick presented the president with the report from the Task Force on the Cities: "It has new ideas and a fresh approach. It represents the first direct attack by any American President on the biggest single problem of American life. It can be the first step toward really making our cities a decent place to live, thus improving the lives of the great majority of the American people."

The massive problems of the cities were so interrelated, Dick noted, that legislation had to cut across fields of housing, public schools, poverty, jobs, transportation, crime, and delinquency. Existing programs were not reaching the urban poor, incarcerated within "an iron ring of affluence that has led not only to the doom of school integration but to a physical segregation that has condemned many to lives of corrupting despair." These problems had reached such a magnitude that they demanded representation at the highest level—resulting in a call for a new Department of Housing and Urban Development.

In similar fashion, the task force on conservation moved beyond the purview of traditional concerns with national parks and wildlife preserves to knock on the door of a wide range of environmental concerns. The report recommended new legislation to regulate water and air pollution, clean up rivers, control the manufacture of pesticides, and rescue both cities and countryside from the uncontrolled waste products of modern technology.

There was emotion in Dick's voice as he recounted for me these developmental months of the Great Society. "The White House was boiling with excitement and activity," Dick recalled, "I had never felt it to the same degree before. We all felt that way. This is what it was all for. We wanted to—no, not wanted to—we *believed* we were about to make the country far better from top to bottom. It was an awesome, intoxicating time."

JANUARY 4, 1965

After leafing through sheaves of memos and suggestions vying for inclusion in Johnson's 1965 State of the Union message, we found a series of drafts Dick had worked up for the occasion. At last, we discovered the version the president actually delivered:

On this Hill which was my home, I am stirred by old friendships.

Though total agreement between the Executive and Congress is impossible, total respect is important.

I am proud to be among my colleagues of the Congress whose legacy to their trust is their loyalty to their nation.

I am not unaware of inner emotions of the new Members of this body tonight. Twenty-eight years ago I felt as you do now. You will soon learn that you are among men whose first love is their country, men who try each day to do, as best they can, what they believe is right.

"What an unusual opening," I commented to Dick. "Emotional, sentimental, so flagrantly flattering to the assembly."

"Of the many proposals Lyndon made during that speech," Dick replied, a grin lighting his seriousness, "the most important was his marriage proposal to the Congress. He told me he wanted to make love to the Congress just like he made love to Lady Bird."

I laughed. No further elaboration was necessary.

Calls for partnering with Congress to take some form of action marked nearly every paragraph of the speech. LBJ proposed federal aid for education to ensure every child, from preschool to college, achieved the fullest development of his or her skills; a medical care program for the elderly and the underprivileged; a national effort to make the city a better place to live; an environmental program to end the poisoning of rivers and the air we breathe; a national foundation to support the arts; an initiative to eliminate barriers to the right to vote, and major reform of restrictive immigration laws.

Johnson barely mentioned the war in Vietnam, according it only 132 out of over 4,000 words in the address. America, he stressed, was "in the midst of the greatest upward surge of economic well-being in the history of any nation." The challenge before the president and the Congress was how to use that wealth to benefit the everyday lives of the American people.

This full-blown courtship of Congress—an appeal deeper than partisanship, beyond camaraderie, and nostalgia—was propelled by Johnson's profound insight into the political process. It was his golden ticket to board an express train that would become known as the historic 89th Congress.

Everything was set. This was no longer the preliminary vision of the Great Society that LBJ had set forth in Michigan eight months before. Now the trucks and wheelbarrows, the bricks and mortar had been assembled and the work of realization was ready to begin.

Johnson reflected on these beginnings as he and I later worked together on the chapter of his memoirs dealing with Congress. He talked as we walked together around the ranch inspecting his Hereford cattle, talked as he drove his Lincoln Continental convertible on the roads of his beloved Hill Country, talked as we sat over the edge of the pool, talked over barbecue.

He never stopped talking! At the time I hardly realized what a remarkable opportunity this was for me—still in my twenties, fresh from earning a doctorate in government and teaching a course on the presidency—to spend my days as the sole student listening to the real thing, the greatest presidential practitioner of the legislative process in the last half of the twentieth century. After all, he could talk from experience as director of the National Youth Administration, a congressman, senator, majority leader, vice president, and president. Drawing from a service in government almost without parallel, he was without a doubt the most overwhelming teacher of government I had ever had.

There is, he explained to me, underlining his point with an emphatic tap of his finger on the desk, *but one way for a president to deal with the Congress, and that is continuously, incessantly, and without interruption. If it's really going to work, the relationship between the President and the Congress has got to be almost incestuous. He's got to know them even better than they know themselves. And then, on the basis of this knowledge, he's got to build a system that stretches from the cradle to the grave, from the moment a bill is introduced to the moment it is officially enrolled as the law of the land.*

Without this marriage, this full-court press, no Great Society would have been possible. From start to finish he included Congress, even seeking their counsel on which problems the task forces should tackle. Members of Congress contributed to the resulting reports. Their input was solicited on the very messages they themselves would later receive on the Hill.

Was it not, I asked Johnson, the formal prerogative of Congress to decide which bills to take up and when? LBJ agreed with a nod, but explained that a president can shape the legislative calendar by determining the order and the speed with which he sends messages to the Hill.

A measure must be sent to the Hill at exactly the right moment, and that moment depends on three things: first, on momentum; second, on the availability of sponsors in the right place at the right time; and third, on the opportunities for neutralizing the opposition. Timing is essential.

Momentum is not a mysterious mistress. It is a controllable fact of political life that depends on nothing more exotic than preparation.

The machinery must be paced properly, as LBJ explained to staffers: "It's like a bottle of bourbon, if you take it a glass at a time, it's fine. But if you drink the bottle in one evening, you have troubles. I plan to take a sip at a time and enjoy myself."

Johnson decided to space the messages on the production line, delivering one or two a week to avoid pushing the "sensitive animal" of Congress so hard that it would balk or turn on him. He resolved to deliver messages to Congress on Tuesdays and Thursdays, to allow briefing sessions on Monday and Wednesday evenings for key members of Congress. These briefings would take place over dinners in the small dining room in the basement of the West Wing, creating social occasions while simultaneously providing a preview of coming messages, an opportunity for members to ask questions of cabinet officials and White House staff. "It may seem like nothing," he told me, while describing these intimate dinner meetings, "but, in fact, it was everything."

It gave the chosen ones—between the charts and the tables and the answers to their questions—a knowledgeable understanding of what often turned out to be complex legislation. This understanding put them in good shape the next day when reporters and cameramen began pounding the Hill for reactions. The ones who had been at the briefing had their thoughts in order; they made the best statements on the 6 o'clock news. They looked smart before their constituents and that made an enormous difference in their attitude toward the bill.

Shortly after the State of the Union, the president gathered his core team in the Fish Room to lay out the legislative schedule they must implement posthaste. Here Johnson's intuitive sense took over. The first two messages to be sent up were medical care and education, "two monumental measures," White House staffer Eric Goldman noted, "with long accumulated support behind them and an excellent chance of going through without serious trouble." As soon as these bills had begun moving forward, two more messages would be sent up and then several more. Each new law, Dick remembered Johnson saying, would put "meat on the bones of the Great Society."

Laurels, Johnson warned his team, were nothing to rest upon. Though he had been elected by more than fifteen million votes, "the biggest popular margin in the history of the country," by early January he was already feeling the size of his victory and the political capital thereby amassed beginning to dwindle: "Just by the natural way people think and because Barry Goldwater scared hell out of them, I have already lost about two of these fifteen million and am probably getting down to thirteen. If I get in any fight with Congress, I will lose another couple of million and if I have to send any more of our boys into Vietnam I may be down to eight million by the end of the summer."

Such shrinkage, he explained, was "in the nature of what a president does. He uses up his capital."

This exercise in subtraction added up to a single exhortation, a goad to drive his team. "So I want you guys to get off your asses and do everything possible to get everything in my program passed as soon as possible before the aura and the halo that surround me disappear."

JANUARY 15, 1965

"They were in cahoots from the start," Dick exclaimed as we studied the January 15 telephone exchange between LBJ and Martin Luther King Jr.

The president had called King shortly after noon to wish him a happy birthday. "Only thirty-six years old," I said. "And you, just turned thirty-three. Astonishing."

"Yes," Dick said wistfully.

The transcript of the conversation between the politician and the activist that day was revelatory. Each man seemed so astutely aware of the needs and pressures on the other that it occasionally became difficult to distinguish their positions.

Like almost every other conversation LBJ had in his life, he did most of the talking. After accepting King's congratulations on the vision of the Great Society laid out in the State of the Union message, Johnson solicited the Reverend's support for the initial bills that had already been sent to the Hill by illustrating exactly how one hand could help the other:

LBJ: We've got to try with every force at our command—and I mean every force—to get these education bills that go to those people under two thousand dollars a year income. . . . And this poverty [bill] that's a billion and a half, and this health [bill] . . . We've got to get them passed before the vicious forces concentrate and get them a coalition that can block them. . . .

Your people ought to be very, very diligent in looking at those committee members that come from urban areas that are friendly to you to see that those bills get reported right out. Because you have no idea—it's shocking to you—how much benefits they will get.

The assembled members of the Harvard Law Review *of 1957–58. Dick is in the center, holding the baton as president. On the far right is Ruth Bader Ginsburg. On the far left, Nancy Boxley, the only two women among the sixty members.*

This letter from Dick to Ruth Bader Ginsburg hangs on the wall of Gannett House, home of the Harvard Law Review. *In it, Dick is trying to help Ruth balance her work on the* Review *with the needs of her young family. July 11, 1957.*

July 11, 1957

Mrs. Ruth B. Ginsburg
37 Dogwood Lane
Rockville Centre, New York

Dear Ruth,

I am delighted to know that you will be working with us next year. My congratulations to Marty on having assembled a top notch legal team. I fully expect that your baby will be reading advance sheets rather than Mother Goose.

Our schedule after the 19th is pretty full, but I may be able to help you. We generally try to arrange things so that each editor has two and possible three free weekends during the year. These are full three day weekends. I see no reason why you could not take one and possibly two of these weekends during the first few weeks of work. You may take off Friday-Sunday or Saturday-Monday.

Although I can arrange for both weekends in August, I strongly advise against it. We may not be able to give a third weekend and you might really want that free time after a few months work.

There is no need for you to further inform me of your plans before your return on the nineteenth. I hope you enjoy the short remnant of your summer vacation and give my best to Marty.

Sincerely yours,

Richard N. Goodwin

RNG/bmp

For Dick Goodwin, in happy memory of our work and living together during the October Term 1958, with the best wishes of Felix Frankfurter June 30, 1959

Dick spoke of his "elfin good fortune" when he was selected as a law clerk for Supreme Court Justice Felix Frankfurter, a "warm man of wide culture and interests, known for taking a strong personal interest in his clerks." Dated June 30, 1959.

Senator John Kennedy's aides Dick, Ted Sorensen, and Myer "Mike" Feldman in conversation in the junior senator's campaign office on May 3, 1960.

Senator Kennedy speaks before delegates at the 1960 Democratic convention in Los Angeles, where the winning JFK-LBJ ticket was born. July 14, 1960.

Tens of millions of Americans tuned in for the ABC television broadcast of the fourth and final debate between Republican Vice President Richard M. Nixon (left) and Democratic Senator John F. Kennedy (right). October 21, 1960.

University of Michigan graduate students, led by Judith Guskin (center), present Senator Kennedy with a petition signed by hundreds of students pledging to serve their country overseas in what would become the Peace Corps. Alan Guskin, Judith's husband, is standing behind her. November 4, 1960.

Merle Smith Jr. (left), the first African American Coast Guard Academy graduate, is awarded the Bronze Star for his actions in Vietnam. His father, Army Colonel Merle J. Smith Sr., congratulates him. This photo is on display at the National Museum of African American History and Culture in Washington, D.C. June 8, 1966.

Dick stands between Attorney General Robert F. Kennedy and President Kennedy, as all eyes (left to right: Captain Tazewell T. Shepard Jr., VP Lyndon Johnson, Assistant Secretary of Defense for International Security Affairs Paul Nitze; and Special Assistant to the President Arthur Schlesinger Jr.) are focused on the black-and-white television screen watching the first suborbital flight by astronaut Alan Shepard Jr. May 5, 1961.

Dick leans over the desk as President Kennedy works with him on a speech draft.

This cigar box with the colorful Cuban seal, presented to Dick by Che Guevara at the Punta del Este Conference establishing the Alliance for Progress, would lead to a train of events that would prove injurious to Dick's career. August 1961.

President Kennedy and First Lady Jacqueline Kennedy pose with Nobel Prize Laureates at a glittering dinner that later became known as a Dinner in Camelot. April 29, 1962.

I was twenty years old when I joined the March on Washington along with 250,000 other people. I carried a poster stapled to a stick, "Catholics, Protestants, and Jews Unite in the Struggle for Civil Rights." It was the most joyful day of public unity and community that I had experienced in my life. August 28, 1963.

Lyndon Johnson is sworn in as president on Air Force One after the assassination of President Kennedy. Lady Bird is on the left and Jackie Kennedy stands by his side (right). November 22, 1963.

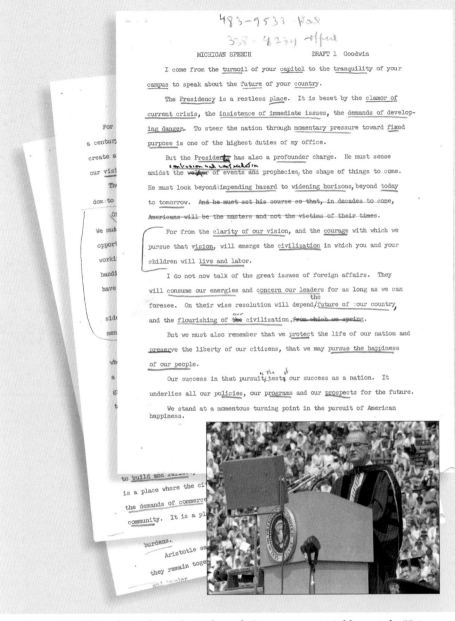

483-9533-Hone
358-8234-office

MICHIGAN SPEECH   DRAFT 1 Goodwin

I come from the turmoil of your capitol to the tranquility of your
campus to speak about the future of your country.

The Presidency is a restless place. It is beset by the clamor of
current crisis, the insistence of immediate issues, the demands of developing danger. To steer the nation through momentary pressure toward fixed
purpose is one of the highest duties of my office.

But the Presidency has also a profounder charge. He must sense
amidst the welter of events and prophecies, the shape of things to come.
He must look beyond impending hazard to widening horizons, beyond today
to tomorrow. And he must set his course so that, in decades to come,
Americans will be the masters and not the victims of their times.

For from the clarity of our vision, and the courage with which we
pursue that vision, will emerge the civilization in which you and your
children will live and labor.

I do not now talk of the great issues of foreign affairs. They
will consume our energies and concern our leaders for as long as we can
foresee. On their wise resolution will depend the future of our country,
and the flourishing of the civilization, from which we spring.

But we must also remember that we protect the life of our nation and
preserve the liberty of our citizens, that we may pursue the happiness
of our people.

Our success in that pursuit tests our success as a nation. It
underlies all our policies, our programs and our prospects for the future.

We stand at a momentous turning point in the pursuit of American
happiness.

...to build and...
is a place where the ci...
the demands of commerce...
community. It is a pl...

burdens.
        Aristotle sa...
they remain toge...

Pages of Dick's Draft #1 of President Johnson's Commencement Address at the University of Michigan which became known as the "Great Society" speech. It challenged the young graduates to "join in the battle to give every citizen the full equality which God enjoins." May 22, 1964.

(Inset): President Johnson delivers the Spring Commencement keynote address to more than 70,000 people at the University of Michigan in the school's first commencement speech to be televised. May 22, 1964.

Alabama police officers approaching civil rights marchers after crossing Edmund Pettus Bridge in Selma. At right front, John Lewis and Hosea Williams lead the group of marchers. March 7, 1965.

President Johnson calls for voting rights in a speech before a joint session of Congress that would later become known as the "We Shall Overcome" speech. March 15, 1965.

Lyndon Johnson interrupted Dick only briefly while he was writing the speech to remind him to reference the young students he taught and cared about at the Welhausen School in Cotulla, Texas, back in 1928.

Dick and White House aide Bill Moyers peering over President Johnson's desk in the Oval Office to see the edits the president is making on a speech draft. In the second picture, Johnson is handing the pages back when the edits were completed, May 4, 1965.

Pages of Dick's Draft #1 of Johnson's pathbreaking commencement speech at Howard University, where LBJ laid out the intellectual framework for the concept of affirmative action. June 4, 1965.

1st Draft   Howard Univ, 2,604 and   6/4/65
Wash. D.C.   Civil Rights

Our earth is the home of revolution.

In almost every corner of every continent men charged with hope contend with ancient ways in pursuit of justice. They reach for the newest of weapons to realize the oldest of dreams: that each may walk in freedom and ~~satisfaxxx~~ pride, ~~xxxxgxkixxfxilxx~~, stretching his talents, enjoying the fruits of the earth.

Occasionally our enemies may seize the day of ~~xxx~~ change. But we are a friend to ~~the xpixitxxf~~ this great revolutionary idea. As well we might be. For it is our idea too.

Our own future is linked to ~~thexpxxxxxxfxxhxbgxxx~~ this process of ~~change~~ in many lands. But ~~none touch~~ us more profoundly, ~~none~~ is more ~~in~~ freighted with meaning for ~~the~~ this ~~Amexix xxx nat)~~ than the revolution of the American Negro.

In many ways, in far too many ways, ~~the~~ American Negroes another have been ~~xxxixxxxxxxixy~~ nation: deprived of freedom, crippled by hatred, the doors of opportunity closed to hope.

But in our time change has come to this nation too. Heroically the American Negro has protested and ~~xxxxhxd~~ marched, entered the courtroom and the seats of government, demanding a justice long denied. The voice of the Negro was the call to action. But is a tribute to our nation that, once aroused, the courts and the Congress, the President and most of the people, have been the allies of progress. They have tried to remedy the wrongs of the past and ~~pxxxidx~~ guard justice for the future.

Thus we have seen the high court of the country provide that any legal barrier based on race was repugnant to the Constitution, and therefore void. We have seen--in 1957, 1960, and

American society. The number of ~~Neg~~... learning has almost doubled in fifteen years. In the past decade employment of nonwhite professinal workers almost doubled--and ...ing force.

A telegram from Martin Luther King Jr. to President Johnson following the Howard Commencement address stated: "Never before has a president articulated the depths and dimensions of the problems of racial injustice more eloquently and profoundly." June 7, 1965.

From Martin Luther King

The White House
Washington

65 JUN 7 PM 12 52

WA058 PD

FAX ATLANTA GA 7 907A EST

THE PRESIDENT

THE WHITE HOUSE

PLEASE ACCEPT MY BELATED THANKS FOR YOUR MAGNIFICENT SPEECH AT THE HOWARD UNIVERSITY COMMENCEMENT. NEVER BEFORE HAS A PRESIDENT ARTICULATED THE DEPTHS AND DIMENSIONS OF THE PROBLEMS OF RACIAL INJUSTICE MORE ELOQUENTLY AND PROFOUNDLY. THE WHOLE SPEECH EVINCED AMAZING SENSITIVITY TO THE DIFFICULT PROBLEMS THAT NEGRO AMERICANS FACE IN THE STRIDE TOWARD FREEDOM. IT IS MY HOPE THAT ALL AMERICAN WILL CAPTURE THE SPIRIT AND CONTENT OF THIS GREAT STATEMENT. I WOULD APPRECIATE VERY MUCH HAVING A COPY OF THE SPEECH

MARTIN LUTHER KING JR.

President Johnson meets in the Oval Office with aides and advisors about Vietnam. Dick's arm is slung over the couch. July 27, 1965.

In a smoke-filled room, Dick, Bill Moyers, and White House aide Joe Califano go over drafts for Johnson's 1966 State of the Union address. January 12, 1966.

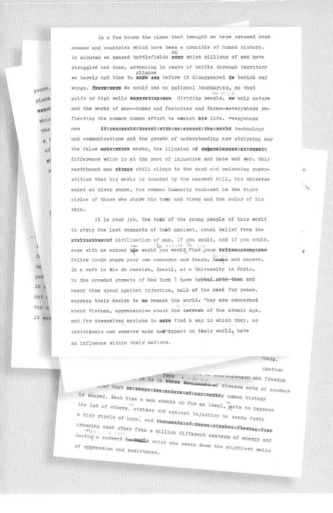

Pages of Dick's draft for Robert Kennedy's "Day of Affirmation" speech in Cape Town, South Africa. On the bottom of the last page the "ripple of hope" section that is on Kennedy's grave can be seen. June 6, 1966.

Senator Robert Kennedy is surrounded by South African students and reporters as he tours Stellenbosch, near Cape Town, on June 7, 1966.

This letter and envelope from Jackie Kennedy to Dick was handwritten on rice paper from the Chinese brush lessons she was taking in Hawaii. Postmarked July 13, 1966.

Dick accompanies Jackie Kennedy and her lawyer, Simon Rifkind (rear), to testify about the publication of William Manchester's The Death of a President. Fall 1966.

Sixteen White House Fellows pose for a photo with President Johnson before entering the White House for dinner and dancing to celebrate our selection. I am to the left of the president in a white dress and gloves. May 1, 1967.

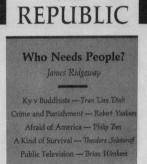

How to Remove LBJ *Kearns & Levinson*

THE NEW

May 13, 1967, 25 cents

REPUBLIC

Who Needs People?

James Ridgeway

Ky v Buddhists — *Tran Van Dinh*
Crime and Punishment — *Robert Yoakum*
Afraid of America — *Philip Ben*
A Kind of Survival — *Theodore Solotaroff*
Public Television — *Brian Wenham*

The New Republic *cover, published shortly after the celebration for the White House Fellows, announces the article "How to Remove LBJ," written by me and Sandy Levinson. Its publication set off a commotion in the White House. May 13, 1967.*

The three female White House Fellows with President Johnson who howls with his dog, Yuki, as we talk and look on in the background. Barbara Currier is to the left, Betsy Levin to the right, and I am in the middle. October 26, 1967.

Senator Eugene McCarthy campaigns in Manchester, New Hampshire, three days before the nation's first Democratic primary, which changed the contours of the election. March 9, 1968.

A portrait of Dick in 1968.

Dr. Martin Luther King Jr. made his last public appearance at the Mason Temple in Memphis on April 3, 1968. He was assassinated the next day while standing on the balcony of the motel where he was staying.

In the aftermath of Martin Luther King Jr.'s assassination, riots broke out in cities across the country. Washington, D.C. was the hardest hit. The fire and billowing smoke in the area of 9th Street and Massachusetts Avenue could be seen from the White House. April 5, 1968.

Weary and dejected, Robert Kennedy sits next to Dick on the plane following his loss in the Oregon primary. May 29, 1968.

RFK is heartened by his victory in Los Angeles following his loss in Oregon, but minutes after celebrating with campaign workers and supporters he was fatally shot in a kitchen hallway at the Ambassador Hotel. June 5, 1968. He died the next day, June 6, 1968.

A few photos of me and LBJ and Lady Bird in 1968. At top, I am in the Oval Office with LBJ after officially joining the White House staff. Left, I'm receiving a certificate from the president at a reception; and at right, I'm talking with Lady Bird, whose kindness to me I shall always remember.

Chicago police attempt to disperse demonstrators outside the Conrad Hilton, the downtown headquarters for the Democratic National Convention. August 29, 1968.

Vice President Hubert H. Humphrey and his wife, Muriel, at the podium of the Democratic National Convention in Chicago, with the crowd of delegates on the convention floor behind them. August 29, 1968.

Doris Kearns next in line to speak following President Johnson's remarks at an event organized by the White House Fellows. October 29, 1968.

Me with LBJ in the Oval Office. November 15, 1968.

Dick and I are married in front of 170 guests—family, friends, and colleagues—on December 14, 1972.

Dick and I four decades later, in front of our Concord home. November 11, 2015.

Dick with his friend, Michael Rothschild. November 11, 2015.

Portrait of Dick, with his trademark colorful socks showing, at the wedding of our son Joe and Veronika in Playa del Carmen, Mexico. December 15, 2016.

(Top) We transformed a three-car garage to make this library to hold our history and biography books. The entire wall on the right is filled with books on Abraham Lincoln. (Above) This room, with the old blue leather couch, a rug I had hauled home from Morocco, and a low chestnut table, was my writing space and is now replicated in my city apartment. (Below) This is the pathway where Dick took his morning strolls through our garden with a view of the tower attached to the library, inspired by Dick's admiration for Galileo.

Here, in what we called the Great Room, we held Dick's "Irish wake," his hospital bed positioned against the window, surrounded by his favorite works of fiction, as scores of friends came from far and wide to say goodbye.

The Goodwin Forum Room in the Concord Free Public Library, where I found a home for the thousands of books I couldn't take with me to Boston when I moved from Concord after Dick died. It is a bustling place, surrounded by shelves holding our books, where lectures and poetry readings are held, where people come to discuss and debate matters of civic discourse.

Johnson confided that he wasn't advertising how tilted these first bills were to Blacks for fear of losing white support, but knew that King understood who the people were who made less than $2,000 a year.

Though King was in Alabama, organizing what was then his top priority—the coordinated drive to register Black voters—he did not bring up voting rights. He knew that the president believed that voting rights should be addressed later so as not to lose southern support for federal aid to education, Medicare, poverty, and the cities. Furthermore, within the administration, there were many who believed that after the process of desegregating public facilities, "some breathing space" was necessary before being plunged into another dramatic battle.

Aware of LBJ's legislative agenda, King therefore opened up with his hope that the president would appoint the first Black cabinet member. Such a trailblazing appointment, King argued, would "give a new sense of dignity and self-respect to millions of . . . Negro youth who feel that they don't have anything to look forward to in life," and "would improve the health of our whole democracy." Johnson wholeheartedly agreed, strongly hinting that if his bill to create a new department of housing and urban affairs (HUD) got through, he would likely make Robert Weaver the cabinet secretary.

Then, to King's surprise and delight, Johnson himself turned the conversation to voting rights.

LBJ: There's not going to be anything, though, Doctor, as effective as all of them voting. That will get you a message that all the eloquence in the world won't bring because the fellow will be coming to you then, instead of you calling him.

Once LBJ had laid out his reasoning on the absolute primacy of the vote, a reversal of roles took place. King insisted that LBJ would gain massive political advantage if Blacks could vote in greater numbers while LBJ followed with strategic advice on how to advance and accelerate the Civil Right Movement itself.

KING: It's very interesting, Mr. President, to notice that the only states that you didn't carry in the South . . . [the five southern states] have less than 40 percent of the Negroes registered to vote. . . .

It's so important to get Negroes registered to vote in large numbers in the South. It would be this coalition of the Negro vote and the moderate white vote that will really make the new South.

The key to their entire interchange was sounded when Johnson suggests to King that they take steps to expose the severity and the bigotry that was still employed to prevent the participation of southern Black voters.

LBJ: I think you can contribute a great deal by getting your leaders and you yourself—taking very simple examples of discrimination where a man's got to memorize Longfellow or whether he's got to quote the first ten amendments, or he's got to tell you what Amendment 15, 16, 17 is. . . .

If you can find the worst conditions that you run into in Alabama, Mississippi, or Louisiana, or South Carolina . . . and if you just take that one illustration and get it on radio and get it on television, and get it in the pulpits, get it in the meetings, get it every place you can, pretty soon, the fellow that didn't do anything but drive a tractor will say, "That's not right. That's not fair." And then that will help us on what we are going to shove through in the end.

KING: Yes you're exactly right about that.

LBJ: And if we do that . . . it will be the greatest breakthrough of anything . . . it'll do things that even the '64 Act couldn't do.

KING: That's right. . . .

LBJ: . . . And let's try to get health, and education, and poverty through the first ninety days.

KING: Yes . . . You can count on our absolute support.

In essence Johnson's advice to King boiled down to this: While the president would work within the federal government, directing the Justice Department to focus on a voting rights bill, King would take the cause directly to the American people.

If not exactly a collaboration, the heart of the conversation between the politician and the activist reveals that their hopes and dreams were linked from the start.

———•·•———

By the time Martin Luther King next visited President Johnson in the White House, on February 9, 1965, he had spent the month busily organizing street marches and demonstrations throughout Alabama. He had settled upon Selma, labeling the city "a symbol of bitter-end resistance to the civil rights movement in the Deep South," the perfect staging ground for mobilizing empathetic public sentiment. "In a democracy," Dick often held, "life on the streets is the horse and the government is the cart."

Better than three fifths of the city's population was Black, yet only 2 percent were registered to vote. Black residents were only able to register on two days a month. And the demeaning bag of tricks and tests to which Black applicants were subjected were not simply formidable, but absurd and contemptible. "How many bubbles in a bar of soap?" applicants were asked. "How many seeds in a watermelon?"

Through relentless organization and demonstrations on the streets, King had resolved "to turn Selma upside down and inside out in order to make it right-side up."

King's meeting with the president that February day was brief. Johnson was preoccupied. The simmering problem of Vietnam was beginning to boil. Three days earlier, Viet Cong guerrillas had raided a barracks in Pleiku where U.S. Army advisers were housed. Eight American soldiers were killed, scores were wounded. After a series of meetings with State, Defense, and military leaders, Johnson decided to retaliate with air strikes against military targets in North Vietnam.

Before the meeting with King concluded, however, Johnson had given his tacit support to the organized marches, though both he and King worried about the thickening atmosphere of retribution and violence that hovered over Alabama.

As the demonstrations continued day after day, tensions mounted. Into this already flammable circumstance was thrown an accelerant in the person of Sheriff Jim Clark, a rabid racist straight out of central casting who would terrorize the demonstrators much as Commissioner of Public Safety Bull Connor did in Birmingham.

On the evening of February 18 in Marion, Alabama, Sheriff Clark and a squad of twenty nightstick-wielding state troopers launched a brutal attack against a peaceful voting rights march, sending the protesters—including young Jimmie Lee Jackson, his mother, and eighty-two-year-old grandfather—fleeing for safety. The troopers chased Jackson and his family into a café where they beat him as he tried to protect his mother, then shot him twice in the stomach and dragged him into the street. He died eight days later. Since turning twenty-one, Jimmie Lee Jackson had tried to register to vote five times. Dead at twenty-six years old, he became a martyr to the cause that believed the right to vote and the right to freedom were one and the same.

Out of such savage but all too commonplace depravity was conceived the idea of a fifty-four-mile march from Selma to the state capital at Montgomery to confront Governor George Wallace and demand an end to brutality and voter suppression. The call went out. Six hundred marchers answered and assembled. On Sunday, March 7, the procession set out for Montgomery from Selma's Brown Chapel across the Edmund Pettus Bridge.

SUNDAY, MARCH 7, 1965

I was twenty-two years old that Sunday, March 7, and had gathered with a group of Harvard school friends to watch *The Sunday Night Movie*, featuring the televised premiere of the Nazi war crimes film *Judgment at Nuremberg*. Shortly after the movie began, ABC made the rare decision to interrupt the broadcast with a special news report that a violent clash had taken place that afternoon at the Edmund Pettus Bridge in Selma, Alabama. The quickly cobbled footage taken of the confrontation and flown to New York ran for nearly fifteen minutes before the station returned, with grim irony, to "Nuremberg."

Along with tens of millions of Americans, we watched the peaceful parade of marchers, led by John Lewis and Hosea Williams, civil rights leaders and associates of Martin Luther King, reach the crest of the bridge. Ahead, a wall of helmeted state troopers blocked their way. The footage glimpsed troopers with protective gas masks in readiness and behind them ranks of men on horseback.

As I had discovered while trying to retrieve something of my experience at the March on Washington, iconic events make it difficult to separate out actual memories from what we later learned from newspapers, television, and multiple historical accounts absorbed over the years. What I do remember, unfiltered, was a stunned sorrow at witnessing the wrenching events that followed on what was to become known as "Bloody Sunday."

What I know now is that police whistles shrieked and a megaphoned voice commanded: "You are ordered to disperse. This march will not continue."

"May we have a word," Hosea Williams asked of the major in charge of the troops. "There is no word to be had," the major replied. The marchers were told they had two minutes to disperse. They stood in silence.

Then suddenly an order came: "Troopers Advance," and the blue uniformed line tore into the marchers' orderly columns. Troopers bludgeoned the marchers with clubs, nightsticks, and whips, felling the unarmed activists to the ground. Then, as tear gas bombs were set off, the mounted men spurred their horses forward, trampling fallen bodies and lashing the retreating crowds with nightsticks. Over the screams and cries of the marchers could be heard the crazed whoops and cheers of white spectators waving Confederate flags.

Few public events in my lifetime have caused the ground to shift, as if the ocean had pulled the sand out from underfoot, leaving you unbalanced. We learned that dozens had been hospitalized with fractured skulls, arms, and legs and scores more were receiving emergency treatment on-site. Long into the night we talked about what we had witnessed on the black-and-white television screen and what we might do.

Two days later we heard the news of the brutal beating of a white Boston minister, James Reeb. He had answered King's call, issued immediately after Bloody Sunday, asking for clergymen of all denominations to come to Selma and join the demonstrators. As Reeb and two colleagues were walking on the street the night of their arrival in Selma, four white men shouting "Nigger lovers" attacked them with clubs. One assailant swung a three-foot club at the side of Reeb's head. The other assailants kicked and bloodied Reeb's colleagues before vanishing down a nearby alley. The three ministers stumbled into Brown Chapel, where Reeb fell unconscious. He soon developed a large blood clot on the side of his head and was transported to a Birmingham hospital for emergency brain surgery.

The story of the ambush made national news, far surpassing the notices of the pursuit and murder of the young black activist Jimmie Lee Jackson. President Johnson called the minister's wife, Marie, and provided a plane to take her to Birmingham. As she and the nation sat vigil in the days that followed, we learned that the thirty-eight-year-old Reverend Reeb, a father of four, had moved his family to an impoverished, predominantly Black neighborhood in Dorchester where he had launched a public campaign to improve housing for the urban poor. He wanted his family to live in the same community where he served, to have his children attend the same public schools.

When Reverend Reeb died two days later on Thursday, March 11, he was hailed a civil rights martyr. Throughout the country newspapers carried stories of this exemplary young minister and prayer rallies were held in churches and synagogues across the country.

I joined with three thousand others who marched to the Boston Common the following Saturday afternoon. A large contingent of us walked from Harvard Square, merging with others from the surrounding suburbs. There was no cheering, no singing of freedom songs. We listened in silent grief and reflection, many in black armbands, as colleagues spoke of the Reverend Reeb's life and work.

Toward the end of the memorial service, however, the assembly began to shake off the pall of despondency, and before long the mourning transformed into a rally. We cheered in response to the call for federal troops to be sent to protect the Selma marchers, who were determined to try again to reach Montgomery. And we cheered even louder when the demand was made to expedite legislation to ensure voting rights for all. Such calls for action renewed our spirits. Anger and determination transcended grief, and we began to focus on the urgent work that lay ahead.

———

Coming and going from the West Wing during this turbulent period, Dick encountered an atmospheric change both surrounding and inside the White House. The days of prayer and protest held across the country had come home to roost in the nation's capital. Hundreds, then thousands of protesters began to picket in front of the White House, demanding that Johnson send federal troops to intervene directly in Selma. Vigils were held day and night in Lafayette Park, protesters blocked rush-hour traffic, and crowds chanted the warning: "LBJ just you wait, see what happens in '68." Inside the White House, a dozen young Black and white demonstrators refused to leave following a regular White House tour, commencing a sit-in for immediate federal action in Selma.

Dick sensed the mounting tension, and saw that it had begun to take its toll on both the White House staff and LBJ. At a staff meeting, Johnson clearly laid out his quandary: "If I just send federal troops with their big black boots and rifles, it'll look like Reconstruction all over again. I'll lose every moderate, not just in Alabama, but all over the South. If it looks like Civil War all over again that'll force them into the hands of extremists and make a martyr out of Wallace."

Desiring "a real victory for the black people, not a psychological victory for the North," Johnson ordered Attorney General Nicholas Katzenbach "to work night and day" to settle the complex legal and constitutional questions involved in designing a federal law that would strike down the restrictions being used to deny southern Blacks the right to vote. But the immediate action that committed civil rights activists demanded—sending federal troops to Selma—was precisely the action Johnson feared would destroy all chances for securing such a comprehensive Voting Rights Bill.

In her diary, Lady Bird, ever a keen reader of her husband's emotional thermometer, noted that a "fog of depression" had settled upon him. Caught in a whipsaw between doing nothing and overreaching, he seemed paralyzed by a "gloom" that Lady Bird described as "thick enough to cut by a knife."

A shaft of light was cast into that gloom when news arrived that George Wallace had requested an immediate meeting with the president. Johnson understood Wallace's dilemma: He knew that continued brutality would destroy the governor's dreams of national leadership. If Johnson could find a way to persuade Wallace to carry out his gubernatorial duty to send state troops to protect peaceful marchers without losing his hard-core base, the problem for both men might be solved. The bond between the Civil Rights Movement and the federal administration would hinge upon the outcome of that encounter—a bond that was needed against their segregationist adversary, Wallace, masquerading as a champion of states' rights.

Dick had a peculiar vantage of this historic three-hour meeting with the Alabama governor and the president. He pieced together—from his own view, from what Moyers related to him afterward, and especially from Johnson's elaborate rendition (recounted later with theatrical gusto during which the president played both himself and the beleaguered governor)—such a compelling story that it has since taken its place in scores of history books.

Despite the enormous stakes and strain, Johnson, like an Oval Office set designer, saw to every detail. He led Wallace to a low, deep-cushioned sofa beside the fireplace, where Wallace sank down. Then Johnson pulled up his own rocking chair so close that he hung above the little governor like a six-foot-four-inch hammer over Wallace's five-foot-seven-inch nail.

For the first fifteen minutes as Wallace recited a prepared speech defending states' rights against federal intervention, Johnson never took his eyes off Wallace's face. Finally, the president began to speak:

LBJ: Now Governor, I know you're like me, not approving of brutality.

WALLACE: Of course Mr. President, but they were just doing their duty.

Johnson raised his hand and was delivered the evidence, a newspaper with photos showing the onslaught on the bridge in Selma, troopers kicking a Black man in the fetal position.

LBJ: Now that's what I call brutality. Don't you agree?

WALLACE: Yes, but they were just trying . . .

LBJ: Now, Governor, you're a student of the Constitution. I've read your speeches and there aren't many who use the text like you do.

WALLACE: Thank you Mr. President. It's a great document, the only protection the states have.

LBJ: And somewhere in there it says that Nigras have the right to vote, doesn't it Governor?

WALLACE: They can vote.

LBJ: If they're registered.

WALLACE: White men have to register too.

LBJ: That's the problem, George; somehow your folks down in Alabama don't want to register them Negroes. Why, I had a fellow in here the other day, and he not only had a college degree, but one of them Ph.Ds, and your man said he couldn't registra because he didn't know how to read and write well enough to vote in Alabama. Now, do all your white folks in Alabama have Ph.D.s?

WALLACE: Those decisions are made by the county registrars, not by me.

LBJ: Well then, George, why don't you just tell them county registrars to registra those Nigras?

WALLACE: I don't have that power, Mr. President, under Alabama law . . .

LBJ: Don't be modest with me, George, you had the power to keep the president of the United States off the ballot. [Johnson had been omitted from the 1964 presidential ballot as the Democratic candidate.] Surely you have the power to tell a few poor county registrars what to do.

WALLACE: I don't. Under Alabama law, they're independent.

LBJ: Well, then, George, why don't you just persuade them?

WALLACE: I don't think that that would be easy.

LBJ: Don't shit me about your persuasive power, George. Just this morning I was watching you on television . . . and you was attacking me. And you know what, you were so damn persuasive I had to turn off the set."

"I'd seen the president's nose-to-nose, space-violating, physical treatment," Dick said, shaking his head at me of the memory of it, "but this was a masterpiece of persuasion. He knew Wallace in his bones, and before the meeting was over, Wallace was simply ground down."

Before he was done with Wallace, Johnson reached a level that transcended simple political arm wrestling. He began to talk about the decades to come, of future legacy:

> "You and me we'll be dead and gone then, George. Now you've got a lot of poor people down there in Alabama, a lot of ignorant people. You can do a lot for them, George. Your president will help you. What do you want left after you when you die? Do you want a Great . . . Big . . . Marble monument that reads, 'George Wallace—He built'? . . . Or do you want a little piece of scrawny pine board lying across that harsh, caliche soil, that reads, 'George Wallace—He Hated'?"

The meeting over, they came to a tenuous pact. The president maneuvered the governor into a press conference where he announced that "the Governor told me the problems he had in Alabama, the fears that he entertained, and he expressed the hope that I do something to help bring the demonstrations to an end. I told him that our problem . . . was to remove the cause of those demonstrations."

The governor had agreed that "if local authorities are unable to function [because of the enormous costs of needed protection] the federal government will completely meet its responsibilities." In short, federal force was not going to invade Alabama. Rather, the governor was asking for federal help; Alabama was inviting the federal government to maintain peace and law and order. "That," Johnson later said, "made all the difference in the world."

"Hell, if I'd stayed in there much longer," Wallace later groused to the press, "he'd have had me coming out for civil rights."

"I knew what it was like," Dick remembered, shaking his head, "to be on the receiving end of the 'Johnson Treatment.' It was almost enough to feel a bit of sympathy for little George Wallace." Dick met my eyes with a sardonic smile, "But not quite."

Lyndon Johnson's swift recovery from depression was stunning and authentic. When Lady Bird Johnson next laid eyes on her resilient husband, the "Black Pig" of depression had lifted and all of a sudden he was "composed, in charge, in command of the situation." Now that the troop dilemma had been resolved in Alabama, he could focus on the Voting Rights Bill and the accompanying message to the Hill that he aimed to send to Congress two days later—on Monday, March 15.

Late Sunday afternoon, Johnson convened a bipartisan meeting in the Cabinet Room with Vice President Hubert Humphrey and the leaders of the House and Senate. Ostensibly, he wanted their advice on how best to approach Congress, whether in writing as tradition dictated, or in person—a rarity; nearly twenty years earlier, President Harry Truman had been the last president to go to the Hill in support of a bill.

While Johnson had already decided he wanted to speak at a joint session, he let the conversation flow, hoping by the conclusion of the meeting he would gain their consensus and the desired invitation.

The conversation did not begin well, according to Jack Valenti's notes. Republican Minority Leader Everett Dirksen forcefully argued for sending the traditional written message. "Don't panic now," Dirksen advised Johnson. "This is a deliberative government. Don't let these people say: 'we scared him into it.'"

Democratic House Speaker John McCormack disagreed. He strongly recommended that the president go before a joint session to describe the reasons behind a bill. Humphrey supported the idea of a public appeal. (LBJ had gone to church with the vice president that morning and had lunch with him afterward.) "Logic is what you are saying," Humphrey addressed Mansfield and Dirksen, "but emotions are running high. A message of what the government is doing—simply—is what is needed."

Eventually everyone came around to what Johnson had wanted all along, a televised speech delivered before an extraordinary convening of a joint session of Congress that would allow him simultaneously to address the Congress and the nation at large. Despite his awareness that a push for voting rights might disrupt his carefully designed production line for the Great Society, it was a risk he was willing to take.

Just as the conclusion of Johnson's meeting with Wallace had hinged upon whether federal troops intervened or were invited into the state of Alabama, so now the president would not be circumventing Congress by appealing to the public directly on television. Instead, he would be accepting a formal invitation to the Hill. At the conclusion of this Cabinet Room meeting, the following statement was issued:

> The Leadership of Congress this afternoon invited the President to address a joint session of the Congress on Monday evening to present the President's views and outline of a voting rights bill and any other matters that the President desires to discuss.
>
> The President has accepted the invitation and will address a joint session at 9 p.m., Monday evening, March 15th, in the House of Representatives.

Johnson phoned civil rights leaders Whitney Young, Roy Wilkins, and Martin Luther King to invite them to attend the joint session as his special guests. After spontaneously accepting, King discovered that by the time he finished his scheduled eulogy for Rev. James Reeb in Selma on Monday afternoon, there were no flights that could get him to Washington in time. "Please know that I regret this very deeply," he telegraphed the president. "I had looked forward to being there with all of you. I will be listening to your message with great interest and appreciation."

Now the clock was ticking. In about twenty-four hours, 535 members of the House and Senate, along with the nation, would be focused on the president and no speech had yet been drafted. It was like "deciding to climb Mt. Everest," said Lady Bird, "while you are sitting around a cozy family picnic."

Dick spent that Sunday evening at a dinner party at historian Arthur Schlesinger's home. As the party neared its end, the guests learned that the president was going to address a Joint Session of Congress the following night. Having heard nothing about these plans, Dick called the White House to see if any special messages had been left for him. No messages had been left.

"I was perplexed and disappointed," Dick told me. "Someone else, I thought, must be writing the speech. We had several more drinks and decided to call it a night."

MONDAY, MARCH 15, 1965

The moment Dick stepped into the West Wing on the morning of March 15, there was an unusual hubbub and tension. And there, pacing back and forth in a dither outside Dick's second floor office, was Jack Valenti. Normally full of glossy good cheer, Valenti pounced on Dick before he could even open his office door. "He needs the speech from you, right away."

"From me! Why didn't you tell me yesterday? I've lost the entire night," Dick responded.

"It was a mistake, my mistake," Valenti acknowledged.

"Poor Valenti was distraught," Dick told me. "Apparently, the first words out of the president's mouth that morning were, 'how's Dick coming with the speech?' When Valenti confessed that he had assigned the speech to Horace Busby, who was in the office the night before, Johnson exploded: "The Hell you did. Don't you know that a liberal Jew has his hand on the pulse of America? Get Dick to do it and now!"

The overwrought Valenti handed Dick a folder of notes from his conversations with the president the prior night as well as draft notes for a written message that would accompany the bill. The speech had to be finished before 6 p.m., Valenti told Dick, in order to be loaded on the teleprompter in advance of the president's televised address. Valenti asked Dick if there was anything—anything at all—he could get for him.

Dick told me he remembered giving Valenti a one word response, "Serenity."

"Serenity?" inquired the puzzled Valenti.

"A globe of serenity," Dick replied. "I can't be disturbed. If you want to know how it's coming, ask my secretary."

Dick looked at his watch. Nine hours away!

"I didn't want to think about time passing," Dick recalled to me. "I lit a cigar, looked at my watch, took the watch off my wrist and put it on the desk beside my typewriter. Another puff of my cigar and I took the watch and put it away in my desk drawer."

"The pressure would have short-circuited me," I said. "I never had the makings of a good speechwriter or journalist. History is more patient."

"Well," Dick laughed, "miss the speech deadline and those pages are only scraps of paper."

Dick examined Valenti's notes. Johnson wanted no uncertainty about where he stood. He wanted no argument about states' rights versus federal rights, no blaming oppositions between South and North. To deny fellow Americans the right to vote was simply and unequivocally wrong. He wanted the speech to be affirmative and hopeful. He would be sending a bill to Congress to protect the fundamental right to vote for all Americans, and he wanted this speech to drive and speed public sentiment.

In the year since Dick had started to work at the White House, he had listened to Johnson talk for hundreds of hours—on planes and in cars, during meals in the Executive Mansion and at the ranch, in the swimming pool and over late-night drinks. He understood Johnson's deeply held convictions about civil rights. He knew the cadences of his speech. The speechwriter's job, Dick explained, was to clarify, heighten, and polish the speaker's convictions in the speaker's own language and natural rhythms. If the words did not sound authentic to the speaker, the emotional current of the speech would not hit home.

I knew that Dick often searched for an arresting short sentence to begin every speech or article he wrote. On this day, he surely found it.

I speak tonight for the dignity of man and the destiny of democracy.

He then sought to situate this pivotal moment in the sweep of our nation's history.

At times, history and fate meet at a single time in a single place to shape a turning point in man's unending search for freedom. So it was at Lexington and Concord. So it was a century ago at Appomattox. So it was last week in Selma, Alabama.

"The basic concept underlying the entire speech," Dick explained to me, "is that our government has been summoned, pushed by the people, and to that force and pressure, we will respond."

There is no cause for pride in what has happened in Selma. . . . But there is cause for hope and for faith in our democracy in what is happening here tonight. For the cries of pain, and the hymns and protests of oppressed people—like some great trumpet—have summoned into convocation all the majesty of this government of the greatest nation on the earth.

No sooner would Dick pull a page out of his typewriter and hand it to his secretary than Valenti would somehow materialize, a nerve-worn courier, eager to personally express pages from Dick's secretary into the president's anxious hands. Johnson's edits and penciled notations were incorporated into the text while he awaited the next installment, lashing out at everyone within range—everyone except Dick.

It soon became clear that the speech was no lawyer's brief debating the merits of the bill soon to be sent to Congress. Rather, it was a credo of what we are as a nation, and who we are as a people—a redefining moment in our history brought forth by the foot soldiers of the Civil Rights Movement.

The real hero of this struggle is the American Negro. His actions and protests, his courage to risk safety and even to risk his life, have awakened the conscience of this nation.

He has called upon us to make good the promise of America. And who among us can say that we would have made the same progress were it not for his persistent bravery, and his faith in American democracy.

By mid-afternoon of that day, as the pages were beginning to flow from Dick to the president and back again, the Reverend King mounted the pulpit of Brown Chapel in Selma to eulogize the Reverend James Reeb: "<u>Who</u> killed James Reeb?" asked King, only to replace that question with the far darker one:

"<u>What</u> killed James Reeb?" *When we move from the who to the what, the blame is wide and responsibility grows.*

James Reeb was murdered by the irrelevancy of a church that will stand amid social evil and serve as a taillight rather than a headlight, an echo rather than a voice. He was murdered by the irresponsibility of every politician who has moved down the path of demagoguery, who has fed his constituents the stale bread of hatred and the spoiled meat of racism.

Yet, out of this darkness and evil, King believed, goodness would emerge.

One day the history of this great period of social change will be written in all of its completeness. On that bright day, our nation will recognize its real heroes. They will be thousands of dedicated men and women with a noble sense of purpose.

When this glorious story is written, the name of James Reeb will stand as a shining example of manhood at its best.

Reading these words, I realized that at nearly the same moment Dick was extolling the heroism of the Black foot soldiers from the South, King was eulogizing the bravery and courage of the young white minister from the North who had answered the call and given his life for Black voting rights and freedom.

As the light shifted across the room, Dick became aware that the day suddenly seemed to be rushing by. He opened the desk drawer, peered at the face of his watch, took a deep breath, and quickly slammed the drawer shut. For the first time that day he walked outside to get air and refresh his mind.

In the distance Dick heard the muffled voices of chanters, singers, and demonstrators. Mindful of the vanishing afternoon, Dick hustled back to his office. There had seemed something forlorn about the sound of their receding voices—such a great contrast to the March on Washington only a year and a half earlier when he heard the joyous chorus of "We Shall Overcome," the anthem that had instilled courage, purpose, and hope to the Civil Rights Movement. That spirited resolve was what he was after now. Loud and clear, the words "We Shall Overcome" sounded in his head.

Already, the sun was beginning to set that chilly March evening when the phone in Dick's office rang for the first time that day. It was after six o'clock, past the deadline to feed all the finished pages of the speech into the teleprompter. The voice at the other end was "so calm, sweet, and sedate" that Dick hardly recognized it as the voice of the president of the United States.

"Far and away," Dick told me, "the gentlest tones I ever heard from Lyndon."

"You remember, Dick," Johnson said in a whisper, "that one of my first jobs after college was teaching young Mexican Americans in Cotulla. I told you about that down at the Ranch. I thought you might want to put in a reference to that," Dick recalled Johnson telling him.

What Johnson impressed on him, Dick told me, was that those kids in Cotulla had nothing. They had a hard, hard life. "Hell," he told Dick, "I spent half my pay to buy sports equipment for the school."

Not twenty minutes had passed when the phone range a second time. In that second call, Dick told me, Johnson was still musing about his time in Cotulla. "It was a long time ago," he said, "but those kids have their own kids. And now we do something about it."

Hardly four minutes passed and the phone rang a third time. "I almost forgot, Dick, I'd like you to ride up to the Hill with me tonight."

"When I finished," Dick recalled, "I felt perfectly blank. It was done. It was beyond revision. It was dark outside and I checked my wrist to see what time it was, remembered I had hidden my watch away from my sight, retrieved it from the drawer and put it back on."

There was nothing left to do but shave, grab a sandwich, and stroll over to the Executive Mansion. There, greeted by an exorbitantly grateful

Valenti, Dick hardly had the energy to talk. Before he knew it, he was sitting in the presidential limousine with Valenti and Busby. There was a flurry of Secret Service activity around the limousine and, without a word of hello, Johnson was ushered into the backseat.

As they exited the White House gate, they passed picketers demonstrating against government inaction. Motorcycles with police and Secret Service glided by outside their windows, flanking the limousine as it proceeded along the emptied streets to the Capitol.

Inside, a reading light was shining onto the president's lap illuminating the black-leather loose-leaf notebook that contained his speech. Dick told me that he remembered the silence in the limousine, the eerie, trancelike focus with which the president fastened on the pages before him.

"Amazing concentration," said Dick. "No distraction. No small talk. No talk at all." Johnson's somber concentration was totally narrowed upon the words and feelings of that long day, all squeezed into the notebook on his lap.

When they arrived at the Capitol, the president met with the welcoming committee in the Speaker's office. Dick and his companions were escorted to the well of the House, the small area in front of the rostrum where there was room to stand in the chamber filled beyond capacity. On the floor was arrayed the full panoply of the United States government—members of Congress, the cabinet, the Supreme Court, the diplomatic corps; and from the galleries families and invited guests peered down.

A hush filled the chamber as the president began to speak. "From the moment the speech began," Dick remembered, "it was not a matter of oratory or rhetorical display, but intensity, conviction, and heart." The president placed the events in Selma alongside pivotal moments in history—the battles in Lexington and Concord that signaled the start of the Revolutionary War, the armistice signed at Appomattox that brought the Civil War to an end, and the savagery that had rocked Selma and the entire country eight days earlier and had gathered the audience together in this chamber on this night.

"Once the speech started," I asked, "were you able to relax?"

"It was eerie. At first there was no applause. A weird silence, an acute listening greeted his opening words. I was too tense, too tired standing there. The whole place seemed transfixed, as if holding its collective breath." The atmosphere in the historic chamber seemed to intensify, Dick remembered, filled with the soft, slow deliberate voice of the president:

Rarely in any time does an issue lay bare the secret heart of America itself. Rarely are we met with a challenge, not to our growth or abundance, or our welfare or our security, but rather to the values, and the purposes, and the meaning of our beloved nation. The issue of equal rights for American Negroes is such an issue.

A single person in the galleries began to clap. Others followed and soon a mounting round of applause swept the entire chamber, the first of thirty-six interruptions over the course of the thirty-minute speech. The president paused for only a moment.

As he watched from the well, Dick marveled at Johnson's emotional gravity. They had worked together on the speech only a single day. Yet, the president's somber, urgent, relentlessly driving delivery gave the occasion something that transcended a virtuoso performance. He demonstrated a conviction and exposed a vulnerability that surpassed anything Dick had experienced from him before.

There is no Negro problem. There is no southern problem. There is no northern problem. There is only an American problem. And we are met here to meet that problem—not as Democrats or Republicans. . . . We are met here as Americans to solve that problem.

The applause began to roll again, wave after rising wave.

Many of the issues of civil rights are very complex and most difficult. But about this there can be and should be no argument. Every American citizen must have an equal right to vote. . . .

Wednesday I will send to Congress a law designed to eliminate illegal barriers to the right to vote. . . .

There is no constitutional issue here. The command of the Constitution is plain. There is no moral issue. It is wrong—deadly wrong—to deny any of your fellow Americans the right to vote in this country. There is no issue of states' rights or national rights. There is only the struggle for human rights. . . .

This time on this issue there must be no delay, no hesitation, no compromise with our purpose. . . .

But even if we pass this bill, the battle will not be over. What happened in Selma is part of a far larger movement which reaches in every section and state of America. It is the effort of American Negroes to secure for themselves the full blessings of American life. Their cause must be our cause too. Because it's not just Negroes, but really it's all of us, who must overcome the crippling legacy of bigotry and injustice. . . .

AND ... WE ... SHALL ... OVERCOME.

The words came staccato, each hammered and sharply distinct from the others. Then Johnson paused. "There was an instant of silence," as Dick later described the moment, "the gradually apprehended realization that the president had proclaimed, adopted as his own rallying cry, the anthem of black protest, the hymn of a hundred embattled black marches." Senators and representatives, generals and diplomats, leapt to their feet, delivering a shouting, stomping ovation that Johnson later said he would "never forget as long as I live."

In Montgomery, Alabama, Martin Luther King had gathered with friends and colleagues to watch the president's speech. At this climactic moment, John Lewis witnessed tears rolling down King's cheeks, a sight he had never seen before. Lewis saw something different in King at that moment, and something different in the president as well. For the first time he saw Lyndon Johnson not simply as a politician, but "a man who spoke from the heart, a statesman, a poet."

"The Voting Rights Act," King murmured with certainty, "WILL be passed!" King had instantly understood what had just been accomplished with Johnson's speech. A current had been generated from outside the government and the president had directed that force to the Congress, and the country beyond.

My circle of graduate school friends had been transfixed by the unfolding civil rights drama of the past week. Many had accompanied me on the solemn march to the Boston Common to honor the slain Minister James Reeb. We had come together again to watch this nighttime address to the joint session. A chill ran through me when Lyndon Johnson uttered the words "And we shall overcome" leaving me in tears of joy and pride in my president, my government, and my country. I was not alone. Side by side, we stood and circled the television. I felt a connectedness I had not felt since the March on Washington. And to this day, after hundreds of readings and listenings, these lines retain their potency.

Johnson was keenly aware of how these words would wrench his southern colleagues, many of whom had remained in their seats. The finger of blame should not only point to the South, but to every point of America's compass. To that end he began the process of stitching the country together.

Now let none of us in any section look with prideful righteousness on the troubles in another section, or the problems of our neighbors. There is really no part of America where the promise of equality has been fully kept. In Buffalo, as well as in Birmingham, in Philadelphia as well as Selma, Americans are struggling for the fruits of freedom.

The time had come to draw on his own experience, to tell the formative story he had related to Dick only hours before.

My first job after college was as a teacher in Cotulla, Texas, in a small Mexican-American school. Few of them could speak English, and I couldn't speak much Spanish. My students were poor and they often came to class without breakfast, hungry. And they knew, even in their youth, the pain of prejudice. They never seemed to know why people disliked them. But they knew it was so, because I saw it in their eyes. I often walked home late in the afternoon, after the classes were finished, wishing there was more that I could do....

Somehow you never forget what poverty and hatred can do when you see its scars on the hopeful face of a young child. I never thought then, in 1928, that I would be standing here in 1965. It never even occurred to me in my fondest dreams that I might have the chance to help the sons and daughters of those students and to help people like them all over this country.

But now I do have that chance—and I'll let you in on a secret. I—mean—to—use it.

And I hope that you will use it with me.

After Lyndon Johnson laid bare the depth of his personal commitment to the cause of civil rights, reaching back to his days as a young teacher, the audience stood to deliver perhaps the largest ovation of the night. He had transformed the lectern into a bully pulpit from which, as never before, he inspired, roused, and consolidated public sentiment across the nation. A witness recounting the response in Selma's Brown Chapel said, "everyone in the room where we stood throughout, was crying. Men and women, old and young, black and white."

Even as the president exited the chamber, surrounded by jubilant colleagues reaching out to touch his shoulder or shake his hand, he remained acutely sensitive to the power of momentum. He called out to the chairman of the Judiciary Committee, Emanuel Celler, "Manny, I want you to start hearings tonight."

As for Dick, he told me he was so exultant after the speech that he barely remembered the ride back to the White House with the president. "I only remember that the protesters whose voices and placards had harried Johnson for what seemed to be weeks had vanished."

A very small group gathered in the sitting room of the White House. Hour after hour, calls of congratulations flooded the small room. Dick called it "one of the happiest nights the president and I ever spent together." It was almost midnight by the time they sat down for dinner. They began to decompress. Finally, after much drinking and storytelling, Johnson rose to retire from a night that no one wanted to end.

Back on November 4, when Moyers had urgently championed Dick to the president, he had insisted that Dick's contribution as a speech-writer would leave "an impression on history." Lyndon Johnson's "We Shall Overcome" speech had done just that. "Your speech," Martin Luther King telegraphed Johnson the next day, "was the most moving, eloquent, unequivocal, and passionate plea for human rights ever made by any president of this nation."

"Of course, the praise was gratifying," Dick said to me. "But most important was not the music of the speech, but what it helped set in motion." A huge impetus was given to the Voting Rights Bill. The president had infused the bill with a massive jolt of emotion.

I told Dick that I had read an account that when Johnson was later asked who had written the speech, he pulled out a photo of his twenty-year-old self surrounded by a cluster of Mexican American kids, his former students at Cotulla, Texas. "*They* did."

"You know," Dick smiled, "in the deepest sense, that might just be the truth."

"Cotulla," exclaimed Dick fondly, "there aren't too many things left on my bucket list, but Cotulla, Texas, is one of them. Let's go there someday." Patting his knee, I promised, "We'll do just that."

———————

"God, how I loved Lyndon Johnson that night," Dick remembered. "Unimaginable it would have been to think that in two years' time I would, like many others who listened that night, go into the streets against him."

Nor, as I talked excitedly with my school friends late into that night, certain that a new tide was rising in our country, could I have imagined that only a few years later I would work directly for the president who delivered that speech. Or that ten years later I would marry the man who drafted that speech.

CHAPTER NINE

The Never-Ending Resignation

President Johnson presents a signing pen from the
Voting Rights Act to Dick. August 6, 1965.

"THE STORY OF MY ATTEMPT TO LEAVE THE WHITE HOUSE IN THE fall of 1965 and the strategies Lyndon used to prevent my departure make for a very dark and very comic tale," Dick told me. "Like a fly stuck on a sticky spiral of flypaper, it was not so easy to wriggle free."

In the late spring of 1965, Dick wrote a letter to the president, letting him know that he was planning to commence his postponed fellowship at Wesleyan in September. The promise he had made after the election to stay until the legislative programs were moving along had been kept. Indeed, the entire Great Society agenda was proceeding at lightning speed through Congress. Far from clogging the production line of Johnson's Great Society agenda, as many had feared, Selma and its aftermath had proved an accelerant, releasing a floodtide of legislation that would mark the first session of the 89th Congress as arguably the most transformative in our history. Dick figured his timing for departure could not have been better.

It was one thing for Dick to decide to leave government, quite another to actually extricate himself from the clutches of Lyndon Johnson. That the leave-taking process would be problematic had become immediately clear when the president completely ignored the letter Dick had written serving notice of his plans. Johnson gave no indication that he had even received the letter. It seemed to have vanished from the face of the earth. On several occasions, when Dick hoped to raise the issue with the president, pressing matters intervened or there were others in the room.

Finally, one morning in late May, the president called Dick to a meeting in the intimate sitting room beside the Oval Office. Dick steeled himself for an uncomfortable conversation. In his mind, he had prepared a litany of reasons to argue his case on why he needed to leave. Johnson's summons that morning, however, had nothing to do with Dick's future plans.

"Now voting rights are important," Johnson burst out the moment Dick entered the office. "But it's only the tail on the pig when we ought to be going for the whole hog."

"We've got the biggest pulpit in the world up here," he continued, "and we ought to use it to do a little preaching. Why don't you see what you can do?"

"Tails, whole hogs," I said to Dick as I considered this perplexing directive, "how did you even know what he was talking about? The barnyard stuff might be colorful, but—"

"No," Dick cut me off. "It's straightforward Lyndonese. He saw the 1964 Civil Rights Act as the backbone of the pig. Voting Rights as the tail, heart, and head. He wanted me to address the whole hog—the economic and social dimensions of racial prejudice."

"Hell, what good are rights," Johnson had asked Dick, "if you don't have a decent home or someone to take care of you when you're sick? Now we've got to find a way to let Negroes get what most white folks already have. At least the chance to get it."

"So you can see, it wasn't barnyard stuff. I understood exactly what he meant," Dick said. "But speaking of barnyard stuff, you should know that more than once Lyndon introduced your future husband in the Oval Office as his 'Stud Duck.'"

"Was that a compliment or an insult?" I inquired, suppressing my amusement.

"Seems you know less about ducks than you do about pigs," Dick said with mock indignation.

In the days that followed that Oval Office meeting, Dick shelved talk of his planned departure to discuss a prospective speech on racial justice with Bill Moyers, Jack Valenti, and Daniel Patrick Moynihan, the assistant secretary of labor. Moynihan had recently completed a report showing that on every statistical measure of achievement—from level of education to ownership of a house—Black Americans fell far behind whites.

Dick joined Johnson several times over meals to explore the substance of the speech. Without dramatic events such as Birmingham or Selma, Johnson knew it would be more difficult to fire the conscience of the country. But, he felt, the time had come not simply to react or respond. The time had come to lead. The president wanted to use his platform to speak about the devastating impact of racial prejudice, to argue the need for additional economic and educational boosts—beyond the Great Society programs— to pry open the gates of opportunity for all Black Americans.

"I left these sessions amazed," Dick told me. "Amazed by Lyndon's willingness to gaze straight into the eye of racial prejudice—the taproot of the intertwined difficulties Black people face."

Johnson's identification of the problem offered Dick no easy answers, only a series of questions. How could economic justice be realized for a people who had been denied from birth a fair chance in the race of life? If, from the beginning, history had skewed the playing field against Black people, what might be put in place to compensate? Should a thumb be put on the scale to speed that long-awaited justice?

Meanwhile, discussions were held as to where and when the speech-in-progress might be delivered. The University of Michigan had proved the right place to sketch out the basic philosophical stance of the Great Society. Accordingly, another commencement seemed the appropriate venue for a meditation upon a new and expansive agenda that would mark the next stage in the battle for civil rights.

Amongst the memos on this subject in Dick's files, one from Valenti to LBJ on May 25 inquired, "Do you want to go ahead with Howard [University] on Friday, June 4th? If you do, we need to move forward immediately." A box was provided for a yes or no answer at the bottom. Johnson checked the "yes" box.

Although Johnson had courteously declined an invitation in early March from Howard University president James Nabrit Jr. to speak at their commencement, Valenti had reached out to Nabrit to say that LBJ would be able to speak at the Historically Black College after all.

JUNE 4, 1965

At 6:30 a.m. on June 4, Dick sent his finished draft to the president. "This is a pathbreaking speech," Dick asserted in his covering memo. "It clearly will put us ahead of the trends—not responding to developments." Dick mentioned that Valenti and Moynihan had gone over the draft and that he had also reached Moyers in Texas and read it to him in its entirety.

As soon as Johnson received the draft, he called Dick into his bedroom, which often doubled as his office. Dick stood at the foot of the bed while Johnson penciled his edits. When Dick asked if he should alert civil rights leaders of its contents, Johnson replied: "If you'd like to," but it was clear that this was what he wanted to say.

Dick returned to his office, spending the next several hours reading key passages to Martin Luther King Jr., Roy Wilkins, Whitney Young, and A. Philip Randolph. All excitedly approved the speech. That afternoon, Dick accompanied Johnson to Howard's campus in the Northwest section of Washington where an audience of five thousand awaited.

Fittingly, Johnson spoke in front of a building named in honor of Frederick Douglass overlooking the crowded university quadrangle. Here, it is widely agreed, the intellectual framework for the concept of affirmative action was first given voice.

Years later, as I revisited the Howard speech with Johnson for his memoir, he told me he was especially proud of it. He failed to credit my future husband's collaboration. Nor, for that matter, had he ever mentioned Dick when we discussed the origin and composition of the "We Shall Overcome" address to Congress. At the time, I was unaware of Dick's contribution to two of the greatest moments in both their public lives and in the country's progress. It was as if Dick had been erased from Johnson's memory.

In my mind's eye, I can still see this Lyndon, silver hair curled down the back of his neck, thick sideburns, sunburned face. I had asked him what he remembered best from the Howard speech. In the stack of papers on his desk he found a copy of the speech, leafed through it quickly and lit another forbidden cigarette. Then he put on his glasses, settled back in his chair—cowboy boots up on the desk—and in his slow, mellow voice read the following passage, which followed shortly after the speech's opening assertion that the barriers to freedom would come tumbling down upon the imminent passage of the Voting Rights Bill.

But Freedom is not enough. You do not wipe away the scars of centuries by saying: Now you are free to go where you want, and do as you desire, and choose the leaders you please.

You do not take a person who for years, has been hobbled by chains and liberate him, bring him up to the starting line of a race and then say, "you are free to compete with all the others," and then still justly believe that you have been completely fair.

Thus it is not enough to open the gates of opportunity. All our citizens must have the ability to walk through those gates.

This is the next and the more profound stage of the battle for civil rights.

Dick was in his early eighties when I asked him the same question I had put to LBJ four decades earlier. What passage still stayed in his mind today? While Dick considered his answer, he prepared a cigar, rolling it and fondly puffing to evenly light it with a wooden match. Not surprisingly, he first selected the identical passage depicting the starting line of a race. Then, he read a second passage, his voice still a deep, crackling baritone:

Men and women of all races are born with the same range of abilities. But ability is not just the product of birth. Ability is stretched or stunted by the family that you live with, and the neighborhood you live in—by the school you go to and the poverty or the richness of your surroundings. It is the product of a hundred unseen forces playing upon the little infant, the child, and finally, the man.

As we continued to talk about the commencement speech, I detected a certain cheerfulness in his voice.

"Why so upbeat, when the core of the speech reveals an ever-widening gulf between the races?" I asked.

"Because then we still had a conviction that sweeping change was possible," Dick replied. "If we could describe the problem, we could do something about it. We felt that the world ahead not only *could be* but *would be* different and better than the society in which we lived."

As Dick and I finished our work for the day, tucking piles of material back into his boxes, I turned up an envelope containing the telegram President Johnson had received from Martin Luther King after that speech. There is something wondrous about holding an original piece of history that sparks an emotional current. "Never before," King stated, "has a President articulated the depths and dimensions of racial injustice more eloquently and more profoundly." The reaction in the press echoed King's response. *The New York Times*'s Tom Wicker deemed Johnson's speech "remarkable in the history of the presidency, as well as of the Civil Rights Movement."

But shot through the overwhelmingly positive reactions were warning signs of a backlash that would reverberate far, far into the future. In a letter, a woman from Boston excoriated Johnson for blaming the white race "for just about all the shortcomings of the Negro people over the past two hundred years." C. Harrison Mann, a member of the Virginia House of Delegates found the "preaching of hatred and racism" inexcusable. "You keep this kind of thing up and it's just a matter of time before everyone questions your judgment on every matter," he wrote.

Dick always found a bedrock wisdom in the warning of Eugene O'Neill's Mary Tyrone in *Long Day's Journey into Night*: "The past is the present, isn't it? It's the future, too. We all try to lie out of that, but life won't let us."

JUNE 14, 1965

Any confusion about whether Johnson had received and considered Dick's letter of intended departure was dispelled at midnight on June 14 when an agitated Bill Moyers stepped into Dick's West Wing office. Moyers had just left the Oval Office, where he had endured two hours of tense conversation with the president about Dick's plans to resign as well as his own hopes to leave the White House later in the year and return to the Peace Corps.

In Johnson's irritated mind, both Moyers (a fellow Texan for whom he often professed a fatherly affection) and Dick (a Harvard/Kennedy holdover for whom he harbored a stepfatherly distance, combined with admiration) were threatening to abandon him in his greatest time of need.

Dick's diary recounts Moyers's description of the heated exchange. At times, the fuming president seemed to fuse them together as if Moyers and Dick were planning to be roommates at Wesleyan.

I plucked both of you up from obscurity. I made you, he railed at Moyers, *and now you want to leave me, to walk out in a crisis when I need you.*

I like that boy [Dick] I've done a lot for him, and he's done a lot for me. I've made him my alter ego, my voice, and my mind. And now he wants to leave me and suck around some Conn college.

[Said to Bill] You are my number one man but I have been dissatisfied with our relationship these past three months. It has been cold, distant, removed. You don't answer my invitations—always seem to have baby sitter troubles. I expect my number one man to be outside the door when I come out. But you are never there. You act like maybe you'd prefer to be no 4 or even no man.

Then, switching back to Dick, he said: *What will he do up there . . . you and Dick will write a book about me.*

JUNE 15, 1965

The next day Dick no longer needed to rely upon Moyers's hearsay. LBJ invited both Dick and Moyers to lunch with him at the Mansion. The ensuing disentangling, which would go on for months, commenced with such force that it was difficult to discern menace from humor. As related in Dick's diary, it began with a bang.

Walking over from the office he said to me, either you stay here or go over to the Pentagon and get your black boots.

This was an allusion to the fact that he might draft me into the army. He intimated there was a statute—McNamara and [Cyrus] Vance laid it on my desk—whereby you could keep or induct specialists vital to the national interest. That is the way they were keeping Harold Brown [a nuclear physicist in Defense who wanted to return to private life].

I said, will you make me a general?

You don't want to be a general. They'll be the first ones to lose their heads, you want to be a private. When he referred to this later in the conversation, I said I used to be a corporal.

You'll be demoted, he said.

"He wasn't serious about all this, was he?" I asked, interrupting our reading of the diary. "At first, I thought he was just joking," Dick said, "but his eyes narrowed with such ferocity I called McNamara later that day to ask if this was possible. McNamara was somewhat evasive so I began to think, my God, this might really happen!"

After lunch, Dick and Bill accompanied the president to his bedroom. Never for a moment did Johnson stop talking. Slowly, he took off all his clothes and put on his pajamas. It was his habit to take a forty-five-minute nap in the afternoon whenever his schedule permitted. "The only way to relax is to peel off all your clothes," Johnson said, "and make believe you are going to bed for the evening."

Before closing his eyes and dismissing his two aides, he pointedly told Dick he had "serious business" to discuss with him. His tone had softened now into a weary and sad negotiation. Without rancor, as Dick described in his diary, he declared simply:

*You can't go. I can't get along without you—the President of the United
States can't get along without you. I need you here, and you're not going.*

I said you can—you got along without me before. He said that's not true.

When are you supposed to get up there?

I said the term starts in the fall.

*He said well you better call them up and give them plenty of notice because
you can't go and you're not going. It's your duty and I need you.*

I was really sweating at this point. Said I could still work on major speeches.

*If you want to live there and come down and work a forty hour week, that's OK.
If you want to commute. Asked me do you want to live in the country (I thought he
was going to offer me a house in the country). Not making enough money?*

I said [money] was no problem.

That wasn't really true. Money was a problem, a fact which Johnson
probably suspected. As a White House special assistant, Dick was earning
$28,500 a year. At Wesleyan (where he would follow his dream of being
a writer) he would be paid $15,000 for the academic year though the fel-
lowship included a rent-free house, an office, and secretarial assistance.
Nonetheless, his salary would be cut almost in half. As a further incentive,
Johnson later told Dick that in addition to his White House base salary,
he would arrange an extra payment from the Johnson Foundation. Such
enticements failed to hit the mark, however. All his life, Dick never worried
about money—even when he probably should have. When bribery failed,
it was replaced by a call to duty, to him and to the country.

*Well, he said, you have got to help pull me through this crisis, can't walk out
on me in a crisis [the deteriorating situation in Vietnam]. He said Bill and you
are the only two I can count on.*

When nothing seemed to work, Johnson continued to search out any
incentive that might persuade Dick to stay. One tactic we discovered in a
taped conversation between the president and McNamara that took place
on June 17. After a discussion on Vietnam was winding down, McNamara
disclosed that he was planning to have dinner with Jackie Kennedy in New
York—unless the president saw "some reason not to." Johnson voiced no
reservation about the dinner. On the contrary, he figured, it might help
with Goodwin. "Confidentially," Johnson began: "After your second drink,
when you think that you can have some influence, I would urge her to keep
Dick Goodwin down here to help us. I think [he's] getting some encouragement to move away."

"I don't like that phrase 'getting some encouragement to move away,'" Dick said to me, obviously still peeved after all these years. "I had no encouragement from anyone on the outside. I think Lyndon assumed Bobby was putting pressure on me to leave. He was always spooked by Bobby."

"Well, what seems strange to me," I said to Dick, "is that McNamara felt he needed LBJ's permission just to have dinner with Jackie. How did Johnson know that you and Jackie had remained good friends after she left Washington for New York anyway?"

"You're forgetting that Johnson knew everything," Dick reminded me, "either through his own network of sources or through the exhaustive dossiers on all of us that FBI director J. Edgar Hoover was only too happy to supply."

The various stages of Dick's prolonged extrication from LBJ's orbit would display the full scope of Johnson's range of persuasions. On some days, Dick would leave a private meeting with the president's new ties around his neck, his pockets jangling with cuff links and Zippo lighters embossed with the presidential seal and Lyndon's engraved signature. Within a day, however, such expansiveness would shrivel into an icy rage or pouting self-pity. Then, for no discernible reason, the rancor would be forgotten, the ice would thaw.

"Sometimes it seemed that no matter what, I had made no headway in all my efforts to leave the administration," Dick said. "Lyndon appeared to have forgotten about the whole matter."

———•———

When Dick persisted in his determination to leave, LBJ's hostility began to harden. "It's just as well that Goodwin is leaving," Johnson told Moyers. "He's in with that other crowd." He'd be fine without Dick, he said, declaring, astoundingly, "I just won't give any more national speeches."

As Johnson's animosity grew, Dick was excluded from vital White House meetings. Stories reached Dick that Johnson was telling staffers that Dick's impending departure was "an act of disloyalty," that he had determined that his "future was with those Kennedys."

Such insinuations of disloyalty reached a troubling extreme when Dick overheard that Johnson himself had spread a story that Dick had conferred with Russian ambassador Anatoly Dobrynin on the preparation of a speech he was drafting for the president's late June trip to San Francisco to commemorate the twentieth anniversary of the United Nations.

This purported consultation had taken place at Ambassador Averell Harriman's home.

"How can something so preposterous as the 'Dobrynin episode' continue to rankle me after half a century?" Dick wondered aloud. "At the time I was beside myself."

"Well, some wounds leave scars as reminders," I said. "Look what your one-night stand with Che Guevara cost you. It launched a whole right-wing critique of your youth, your character, and your loyalty."

"That's what infuriates me the most about the Dobrynin thing. It all started with a joke that Lyndon jumped on and wove into the nightmarish side of the resignation melodrama."

In one of the boxes, we found an angry memo Dick had written to the president refuting the gossip he was spreading:

Harriman asked me to come by his house for a swim at 5pm, Sunday. Since I had worked till 3am the night before on the speech, and all day Sunday, I thought I could use the break.

Present were the Harrimans, my wife and myself, Arthur and Mrs. Schlesinger . . . and four or five other people. About a half hour after I got there the Soviet Ambassador and his wife arrived.

Five or six of us sat around one of the poolside tables. Harriman said, in an entirely joking tone, well Mr. Ambassador now you have the chance to advise the US Government (Harriman knew I was or would be working on the speech although I had said nothing about it).

Dobrynin and I laughed, and I said that would be certainly an historic event. Dobrynin said maybe you could send me a draft for clearance. I said how about a copy of [Russian U.N. envoy Nicolay] Federenko's speech?

The conversation moved to other subjects—everything from synthetic caviar, and Black Sea resorts, to some political topics. The point is I did not disclose a single idea that might be in your speech.

It is absolutely incredible that I would think of discussing the contents of your speech with the Soviet Ambassador.

If anyone has implied the contrary to you, they are guilty of either the most reckless negligence, springing from ignorance, or an outright and shameless lie.

I would be delighted to confront anyone who implied such a thing—in your presence—and say to them exactly what this memo says.

At the bottom of this typed memo Dick had attached a handwritten postscript—*On re-reading this memo, it is not one half as strong as I feel.*

Averell Harriman verified Dick's account in his own memo sent to the president. He acknowledged that he was the one who mentioned to Dobrynin that Dick was working on the U.N. speech. Harriman also admitted that he had suggested—in jest—that this might be "a great chance to advise Dick what he wanted it to say." Harriman significantly added that Dick of course ducked this."

Unfortunately, the story of the U.N. speech did not end there. In preparing that speech, Dick had been given approval, through consultation with the president and his foreign policy team, to use the anniversary occasion to float serious proposals for nuclear arms control. Johnson was initially "delighted" with the draft and instructed that "it be prepared for delivery" on June 25. Two days before the president was scheduled to leave for San Francisco, however, Robert Kennedy delivered his maiden speech on the Senate floor. Kennedy's theme was the vital need to control nuclear weapons.

Johnson urgently called Dick to the Oval Office. "I want you to take out anything about the atom in that speech," he directed. "I don't want one word in there that looks like I'm copying Bobby Kennedy." Dick tried in vain to persuade Johnson that the two speeches were not comparable. Bobby's statement was an opinion issued by a freshman senator. On the other hand, an address from the president of the United States offering specific proposals regarding the nuclear threat would doubtless rivet world attention. But Johnson was adamant. A speech that had held the promise to stir negotiations to potentially reduce nuclear weapons was reduced to a banal birthday wish to the United Nations.

Worried and frustrated, Dick believed that Johnson was doing this to damage him. Fearing that the president's personal pique had reached the point where it had begun to alter policy, Dick grew more anxious than ever to leave.

———•·•———

Then, just when Dick had become certain the relationship could not be salvaged, that neither man trusted the other, Johnson suddenly reversed course. He reached out with warmth and affection and reeled Dick back into his palm like a yo-yo. For the time being, once again, the matter of resignation hung fire.

On July 9, shortly after the House of Representatives passed the Voting

Rights Act, a high-spirited Johnson called Dick to compose a congratulatory message to the House members. Having already passed the Senate, the bill was headed to a Joint House/Senate Conference Committee to iron out differences. The buoyant president told Dick he was about to leave for Andrews AFB where Air Force One would take him to the ranch for the weekend. "Maybe by the time I get to the plane you'll have something or call me on the plane."

When Dick called Air Force One with the finished draft, the president was halfway to Texas. Such was Johnson's euphoria, given the success of the day's legislation—Medicare had passed the Senate and was also on its way to a Joint Conference Committee—that out of the blue, he invited Dick to the ranch for the weekend. The presidential Learjet was fueling up at Andrews, he told Dick, and would be ready at 4 a.m. to whisk him and a small group of guests to relax, swim, and eat barbecue down in Texas.

After hustling to pack, Dick joined Jack and Mary Margaret Valenti and Joe and Hilary Califano on board the Learjet. A young lawyer from Brooklyn, Califano had recently agreed to leave McNamara at Defense and join the White House staff.

They arrived in time for a breakfast of scrambled eggs and spicy deer sausage, followed by a swim in the pool. Over the course of that weekend, Dick recalled, he witnessed the same initiation, almost a rite of passage, for Califano that he had experienced during his own first trip to the ranch. This time, the new aide was given the honor of sitting in the front seat of the president's white Lincoln convertible as they jounced around the ranch; likewise, now the president's stories were directed toward Califano. There followed a tour of Johnson's birthplace and boyhood home, a cruise on the lake, and the obligatory visit to his favorite cousin, Oriole Bailey.

"I felt like a veteran watching a young recruit," Dick said, "happy for him, yet knowing the complications that lay ahead. Lyndon couldn't have been kinder to me. He praised and flattered me at every turn. His mood toward me had changed so dramatically and so swiftly that the whole Dobrynin incident seemed a passing nightmare."

Johnson had brought charts with him, updated daily, illustrating where each of his Great Society bills stood—in subcommittee or committee, ready for markup, debate on the floor, or scheduled, at last, for a vote. While his landmark federal aid to elementary and secondary education had been signed into law earlier that spring, most of the bills were still in transit along the production track—including the cities, conservation, the arts, immigration reform.

"Those charts," Dick told me, "struck an emotional chord," as Johnson surely knew they would.

"You've had your hand in these things right from the beginning," Johnson said to Dick, praising his way back to the contested issue of resignation. "You were there at the start of the Great Society. You were with me during the whole election. The task forces, the messages to the Hill. Now, passing these bills into law is what it was all for. You can't leave until you finish the job," he pressured. "Someday, you'll be proud to tell your children and grandchildren that you were there from start to finish."

"I was shaken," Dick acknowledged. "No appeal to stay could have mattered more."

After they had returned to Washington, Dick was once again invited to meetings. At an overall staff gathering a few days later, Johnson leaned across the table, engaging Dick with an air of special confidentiality. Everywhere he went, Johnson said, he told people what "a hell of a job" Dick Goodwin was doing.

Then, suddenly the president's mood darkened. "Vietnam's like being in a plane with four engines, all of which have failed, and being without a parachute," he said. "If you jump out you'll get crushed and if you stay in you'll crash and probably burn. That's what it is." The intrusion of an unwelcome thought could change the entire aura of the man.

———

It is now evident that Lyndon Johnson's entire presidency had reached a fork in the road by the middle of that July 1965. "Vietnam is getting worse by the day," he confided to Lady Bird. "I have the choice to go in with great casualty lists or to get out with great disgrace." Despite Operation Rolling Thunder and the presence of 75,000 American troops, the Viet Cong forces had taken the initiative with large attacks on the South Vietnamese Army. The civilian government in South Vietnam had collapsed, its economy was in free fall. The time had come for a major decision about America's commitment to South Vietnam.

"I knew from the start," Johnson told me in 1970, "that I was bound to be crucified either way I moved.

If I left the woman I really loved—the Great Society—in order to get

involved with that bitch of a war on the other side of the world, then I would lose
everything at home. All my programs. All my hopes . . . All my dreams . . . But if I
left that war, and let the Communists take over South Vietnam, then I would be
seen as a coward and my nation would be seen as an appeaser.

Dick remembered how distraught, seemingly overwrought, Johnson
sometimes appeared during those early summer months of 1965. "I was
accustomed to the fluctuations of Lyndon's temperament, how ebullience
could suddenly give way to brooding anger. But that summer, the fire
burned hotter and the gloom was more leaden than I had ever seen before."
Moyers, too, recalled that Johnson had fallen into a profound depression.
"He would just go within himself, just disappear—morose, self-pitying,
angry . . . He was a tormented man." When he reappeared, he was full of
fury and suspicion at his critics—the liberals, the intellectuals, the columnists, the Kennedy loyalists in the State Department. They are "trying
to get me," he told Moyers. He said this in "an intense, low-keyed way—
characteristic of his most irrational moments."

Tensions in Vietnam reached a boiling point on July 20 when Secretary of
Defense McNamara, in what would become a historic memo, told Johnson
that "to stave off defeat," the U.S. had to substantially expand its military presence in the South to 375,000 troops. Along with the majority of Johnson's
military advisers, McNamara recommended the issuance of an emergency
declaration, the mobilization of 235,000 Reservists, an increase in draft calls,
and the passage of a war tax to defray the escalating costs of the war.

Johnson accepted McNamara's argument that serious and immediate
measures had to be taken "to stave off defeat." In doing so, he expanded
America's commitment to a level that indelibly stamped the war as an
American war. But he refused to issue a dramatic emergency declaration,
was unwilling to call up the Reserves, and would not ask Congress for a
war tax. Instead, he decided to increase draft calls and extend enlistments,
and, with a sleight-of-hand he determined to manipulate the budget to find
the money he needed. He disclosed only what he deemed essential for the
public to know. He chose to announce his decision to bolster the army's
fighting strength during a crowded press conference in the middle of the
day. He stressed in his remarks that even as he responded to the command-
ing generals' needs, he stood ready at any moment "to move from the battlefield to the conference table."

Five years later, as Johnson looked back at this inflection point with me during his retirement at the ranch, he invoked the Great Society in an attempt to justify his decision to conceal the full extent of the war from the American people. All his work of the previous year was about to come to a head late that summer and early fall. Dozens of bills had been carefully nursed along at every stage of the legislative process, scheduled to roll off the assembly line, get passed by Congress and be signed into law.

I could see and almost touch [my] youthful dream of improving life for more people and in more ways than any other political leader, including FDR, he told me, explaining:

I was determined to keep the war from shattering that dream, which meant I simply had no choice but to keep my foreign policy in the wings. I knew the Congress as well as I know Lady Bird, and I knew that the day it exploded into a major debate on the war, that day would be the beginning of the end of the Great Society.

I understand now far more than I did then. The passing of time has revealed the tragic consequences of the president's failure to level with the American people at that pivotal time. It would lead to a loss of trust in his leadership, in the presidency, and in government itself—a mistrust that has permeated attitudes toward the federal government to the present day.

In the short run, however, Johnson's political gambit worked. *The New York Times* front-page story reported his decision not to call up the Reserves as evidence that he "would meet the manpower requirements put forward" in the "least provocative way possible," leaving the door open to diplomatic negotiations. His decision, commented one relieved senator, was "an indication of the president's desire for peace."

Once that July 28 decision had been made, it was as if a massive electrical storm had bypassed Lyndon Johnson and the charged air finally cleared. He had feared that taking the road of expanding the war would lead to the demise of the Great Society. He had devised a temporary solution, at least for the short term. He would take *both paths* at the same time—the one toward the Great Society would be overt; the other, toward an expanding ground war in Vietnam, would be covert.

JULY 30, 1965

Nothing better illustrates Lyndon Johnson's rise from the abyss of fitful, sleepless nights and daylong depressions that Lady Bird called the "Black

Pig" than his elated response to Medicare's passage through both houses of Congress. Just two days after his agonizing decision on Vietnam, it was as if a gravely sick man was suddenly restored to the picture of health.

Although plans were already set to stage Medicare's signing in the White House Rose Garden before a large contingent of congressmen and senators, LBJ impulsively struck upon a far more dramatic and personal scenario. He would transport the guest list (in its entirety) to Independence, Missouri, so that the bill signing might be graced by the presence of former president Harry Truman himself. He wanted to remind the country that the battle for national health insurance had really begun with the thirty-third U.S. president.

Congressional leaders and cabinet officials, including undersecretary of health, education and welfare Wilbur Cohen, balked at the difficulties of this homage to the ailing Truman. There would be chaos trying to drag half the government across the country at the last minute.

"Why, Wilbur, don't you understand? I'm doing this for Harry Truman," Johnson explained. "He's old and he's tired and he's been left all alone down there. I want him to know that his country has not forgotten him. . . . I wonder if anyone will do the same for me."

The first call Johnson made on the morning of July 30 was to Dick. "He wanted me to look over and smooth out the Medicare signing statement," Dick said. "I was astonished when I saw Lyndon a little later in the day. The haunted look in his eyes was gone. He was invigorated, like he'd escaped, been reprieved."

"The next day I was leaving for my vacation on Martha's Vineyard," Dick recalled, "myself badly in need of an escape, a change of scene. He put his hand on my shoulder and gave it a friendly pat. As we parted, there was not a trace of my proposed resignation."

"As the President boarded the plane," a White House secretary reported, "he went through the passenger compartment greeting each Congressman and Senator—smiling and shaking hands with them—thanking individual ones . . . and joking with old friends from the Hill days." Crowds had gathered to greet the president and first lady on their drive from Kansas City to Independence. "The day was warm and sunny," the diarist recounted. "Everyone was in a good mood."

The president spoke in the packed auditorium of the Truman Library. "I am so proud that this has come to pass in the Johnson Administration," he said. "But it was really Harry Truman of Missouri who planted the seeds of compassion and duty which have today flowered into care for the sick and serenity for the fearful. . . . And so, it is fitting that we have come back here to his home to complete what he began." Far more than a sentimental gesture, Johnson awarded the well-deserved Medicare card #1 to eighty-one-year-old Harry Truman and card #2 to his wife, Bess.

"You have done me a great honor in coming here today, and you have made me a very, very happy man," Truman said, his voice filled with emotion. "It is an honor I haven't had for, well, quite awhile."

AUGUST 6, 1965

Early in the morning of August 6, 1965, Dick navigated his small sailboat off the waters of Martha's Vineyard, carefree at last in those tranquil days before cell phones, far beyond the tentacles of the president. His month-long vacation had just begun, though he had spent the previous day at work on a draft for the signing of the Voting Rights Bill, later dictated to his secretary back in Washington.

He relished being out in the wind on the water and savored the camaraderie of the island's literary community—Lillian Hellman, Philip Roth, Jules Feiffer, John Updike, William Styron—a writers' enclave that represented for him a long-held interest and a future direction. Once he began to unwind, he felt his desire to leave Washington stronger than ever.

On this morning sailing off the Vineyard, Dick felt expansive and relaxed—until he spied an enormous boat growing on the horizon. Soon, a Coast Guard cutter, some sixty feet in length, hailed his tiny Sailfish. Upon interception, Dick was told that the president of the United States requested his immediate presence at the White House.

How Dick loved to tell this story. "I knew the president would stop at nothing to get in touch with someone if he wanted to," Dick said, "but this was rather heavy-handed, even for Lyndon. It was the talk of islanders for years afterwards."

Dick rushed back to his rented cottage on Vineyard Haven, deciding on the spur of the moment to invite his neighbor, novelist William Styron, to accompany him to D.C. "They sent up the Vice-President's Jet Star for the two of us," Styron wrote fellow novelist James Jones, "and it took us back to Washington in 50 minutes."

A limousine brought them from Andrews Air Force Base to the White House where Dick made final edits to the speech before returning with Styron to the limo to join the presidential motorcade to the Capitol. At the last minute, the president invited Dick to ride with him in the presidential limousine to the signing ceremony, leaving Styron alone in their original limo. "I became half scared out of my wits," he recounted to Jones, "for without Dick to vouch for me, I was the only person in that motorcade [which included Vice President Humphrey, the entire Cabinet and the Joint Chiefs of Staff] who was totally unknown to the Secret Service and indeed I really did almost get arrested at the Capitol when the motorcade stopped and I tried to worm my way into the procession to the Rotunda. I was saved by the new Secretary of Health, Education, and Welfare, Mr. [John] Gardner, to whom Dick had fortunately introduced me a half-hour before."

Dick joined the excited party in the presidential limousine, which included the president's daughter Luci and White House aides Joe Califano and Marvin Watson. Califano later mentioned that he had "rarely seen [the president] happier." Johnson spoke of the "new day" that would come when Black Americans were finally able to register and vote as freely as white Americans.

In choosing the Capitol Rotunda rather than the customary White House for the final stage of the voting rights struggle, Johnson demonstrated the same scrupulous attention he gave to every step of the legislative process. To reward "this good Congress," as he repeatedly termed the bipartisan 89th Congress, he had decided to revive an older custom whereby presidents from Abraham Lincoln to Herbert Hoover had gone to the Capitol to sign bills. This gesture signaled both a profound gratitude to Congress and also a recognition of the special gravity of this occasion.

Standing under the great dome of the Capitol flanked by a statue of Abraham Lincoln and John Trumbull's painting of Lord Cornwallis's surrender to George Washington at Yorktown, Johnson delivered a short, lyrical statement—which bears the same linguistic watermark that imbues the "We Shall Overcome" speech and Howard University address and provides them all with a coherence of style, of image, and of substance:

Today is a triumph for freedom as huge as any victory that has ever been won on any battlefield.

Yet to seize the meaning of this day, we must recall darker times.

Three and a half centuries ago the first Negroes arrived at Jamestown.
They did not arrive in brave ships in search of a home for freedom. . . .
They came in darkness and they came in chains. . . .
Today the Negro story and the American story fuse and blend.
And let us remember that it was not always so.
The stories of our Nation and of the American Negro are like two great riv-
ers. Welling up from that tiny Jamestown spring they flow through the centuries
along divided channels. . . .
It was only at Appomattox, a century ago, that an American victory was also
a Negro victory. And the two rivers—one shining with promise, the other dark-
stained with oppression—began to move toward one another.
Yet, for almost a century the promise of that day was not fulfilled.
Today is a towering and certain mark that in this generation, that promise
will be kept.
In our time the two currents will finally mingle and rush as one great stream
across the uncertain and marvelous years of the America that is yet to come. . . .

Johnson, Califano recalled, was "almost carried by the crowd to the President's Room" just off the Senate chamber. There, one hundred invited guests had gathered to witness the signing of the bill into law. Just as the Rotunda address had been a concise unrolling of our history, so every detail of the signing was symbolically staged to evoke that history.

The exquisitely ornate President's Room on the Senate side of the Capitol was where presidents had once settled in to sign bills at the close of legislative sessions. Johnson had directed his aides to find a special table "so people can say, 'This is the table on which LBJ signed the Voting Rights Bill.'" The table they had secured was the same green felted table on which, exactly 104 years earlier, Abraham Lincoln had signed a bill that allowed the federal government to seize property, including slaves, pressed into the Confederate army. Once in Union hands, the slave was a free man.

"There was such jostling for pens," Califano recalled, "that the President used a different one not just for each letter of his name, but even for parts of letters." He gave the first one to Humphrey, the next to Dirksen, and then he reached for Martin Luther King, John Lewis, and Roy Wilkins. "Several times," the White House diarist recorded, "the President sat down at the desk and signed his name again because of the tremendous demand for signing pens." At one point in the midst of this joyous turmoil, Johnson asked for Dick Goodwin. Upon Dick's arrival he handed him a pen as

Speaker John McCormack, Whitney Young, Hubert Humphrey, and the other guests looked on.

A photograph of this moment captures Dick and President Johnson beneath the gilded chandelier, both genuinely engaged in the moment, right hands clasped. The attention of each man is focused on the other with such intensity it almost seems they are alone in the room. With his left hand Lyndon holds out the translucent signing pen that would be inset beneath the photograph, proudly displayed on the wall wherever Dick worked for the rest of his life.

On the day of the signing, I was a twenty-two-year-old intern on Capitol Hill. The Voting Rights Act seemed the crown jewel of civil rights advances during that summer of 1965. We celebrated the occasion in the office of my boss, Congressman Herbert Tenzer, a liberal Democrat representing my home district in Long Island. A philanthropic businessman, Tenzer had been swept into office with Johnson's landslide victory. Week after week, we celebrated the passage of yet another concrete achievement. By the time the first session of the 89th Congress ended, eighty-four major administration bills had become law, a number that after more than half a century still staggers the mind.

Yet, it was not simply the quantity of bills that excited us. It was the fact that President Johnson's domestic agenda spoke directly to our daily lives. Head Start programs would provide preschool children from low-income families with healthy meals and offered them greater likelihood to graduate from high school. Government loans, scholarships, and the Work-Study Program would allow millions of first-generation students to attend college. Pollution would be reduced from the air we breathe and the water we drink.

Life expectancy would be increased and infant mortality reduced through Medicare and Medicaid. Segregated hospitals would vanish from the South once the government made clear that hospitals requesting Medicare funds would have to comply with the nondiscrimination provisions of the 1964 Civil Rights Act. And the diversity of our country would be dramatically expanded by a landmark immigration reform ending a discriminatory quota system that favored European whites, opening immigration access to people from Latin America, Asia, and Africa.

Concerning foreign policy in general—and Vietnam in particular—we paid little heed. Our attention was completely swept up by the feeling that we were part of an innovative legislative factory working to revolutionize domestic policy from top to bottom. We were at work trying to make lives better.

Was it naïve to feel this way? Perhaps, but that was how I experienced that season of wonder following my first year of graduate school. It seemed an enchanted time to be young and working in government.

AUGUST 11, 1965

Only five days after the signing of the Voting Rights Act, which Johnson had rightly termed "a triumph for freedom as huge as any victory that has ever been won on any battlefield," Watts erupted—"Watts," a name that for decades to come would connote racial riot and mayhem rather than denote a predominantly African American neighborhood of Los Angeles.

White policemen had arrested a young black man on suspicion of driving under the influence. The incident triggered a nuclear rage. Before the six days of chaos in Watts had subsided, the statistics of destruction were crushing: thirty-four dead, a thousand injured, many hundreds of buildings looted, set on fire, and burned to the ground.

Lyndon Johnson was so beleaguered by the news he received at the ranch that he withdrew, for days incommunicado. "How is it possible?" a bewildered president pondered. "After all we've accomplished, how could it be?" From the White House, Joe Califano was hardly able to reach him.

Like Johnson, Martin Luther King was stricken by the news and personally shaken by the rage and destruction so counter to his core belief of nonviolent protest. Watts darkened the hopefulness and optimism of both men's progressive dreams.

"Watts was heartbreaking," Dick told me, "but it wasn't incomprehensible. It was all too comprehensible. It was the point of the Howard speech and the substance of the message on the cities I'd written earlier that year laying out the interrelated problems of housing, education, and chronic unemployment that plagued American inner cities."

When Johnson finally emerged from his mental bunker, his initial self-pity had given way to the need for urgent confrontation with the scope of the dilemma posed by a contagion of urban violence. "We are on a powder keg in a dozen places," he told former CIA director John McCone:

"You have no idea of the depth of feeling of these people. . . . They have absolutely nothing to live for, 40 percent of them are unemployed. These youngsters live with rats and have no place to sleep . . . We have just got to find a way to wipe out these ghettoes and find some housing and put them to work."

As the images of rioters setting fire to whole neighborhoods were viewed night after night on television, voices of reaction began to directly assail Johnson and his policies. The Los Angeles police chief bluntly stated that such appalling violence resulted from "you telling people they are unfairly treated and teach[ing] them disrespect for the law"—a hardly veiled reference to the core of Johnson's legislative initiatives for civil rights.

The same member of the Virginia House of Delegates, C. Horace Mann, who had first sounded a warning after the Howard speech now fired off an I told you so letter, telling Johnson that "the dangers of his demagogic address" had indeed come "home to roost."

Dick was back on vacation on Martha's Vineyard when the president sought to locate him again—this time to write a statement on Watts. When Johnson's efforts were not immediately successful, the president, nerves worn thin, vented to Califano: "We ought to blow up that Goddamned island!"

The statement Johnson issued from Austin attempted to balance both sides of the issues raised by Watts. On the one hand, the "resort to terror and violence . . . shatters the essential right of every citizen to be secure in his home, his shop and in the streets of his town." On the other hand, "we must also strike at the unjust conditions from which disorder largely flows"—young men "coming of age in the poverty of the slums."

With her distinctive insight, Lady Bird Johnson recognized the difficulty of finding the elusive fulcrum between law and order and social justice. "I hope a lot of people heard him, because he's going to get the blame for letting [Blacks] go too far too fast. I think he's tough enough to stand up to both sides, but he sure is the one in the middle."

"I was incredibly sad watching Watts incinerate itself day after day," Dick said to me, "and I knew Lyndon would be devastated. It struck right at the heart of everything he wanted most to accomplish."

"Did you change your mind about leaving in September?" I wondered.

"No," Dick recalled, "I knew that my time to think about politics, policy, and speeches day and night had fast approached its end. In Johnson's White

House, you had to be all in, every moment, day and night, ready to respond to crisis. And for Lyndon, crisis was perpetual."

Returning to the White House following his vacation, Dick discovered that Johnson had enlisted Moyers for a renewed effort to convince him to stay. Moyers had postponed his own desired departure, capitulating to Johnson's intense pressure that he take over the job of press secretary—perhaps the most challenging post in LBJ's White House staff.

"He knew how close you were to Moyers," I said. "If anyone could have convinced you to stay on, it was Bill."

"Bill tried hard to persuade me," Dick admitted. "But I knew his heart wasn't in it. Still, I was so rattled I sat down and wrote Bill a long memo listing all the reasons why I had no choice but to leave."

In a blue folder in the archive we located that memo. I was struck at once by its odd, capitalized title: "WHY DICK GOODWIN PERSEVERES IN HIS PLAN TO LEAVE."

At key moments in his life, Dick resorted to this third person, seeking to emotionally distance himself from inner turmoil as if he were sketching out talking points for a debate:

All the personal reasons which seemed so compelling a month or two ago are just as compelling today. The only thing that has changed is the degree of pressure which it would be unworthy to yield to.

I have talents and abilities which I want to use and if I don't use them soon it will be too late. All my inclinations—in fact most ardent desires—are for a life where I can express and develop myself beyond anything I can gain from staying where I am.

It will be impossible for me to go through all this again. When I again resign he will be even more disgusted at me for raising it, than he is now.

The only reason for staying is that I hate to leave you almost alone. But I will stay close from the outside.

In a way difficult to explain, even to myself, my personal integrity—in the sense of personal wholeness—is on the line.

I know it may be bad for my career. I know it may make Johnson an enemy. Hope these things don't happen. But anyways I have to do it.

At the bottom of Dick's memo, Moyers had scrawled an effusive response in hasty cursive:

My personal integrity, what is left of it, is also on the line. Also something more important, my friendship with you, closer than a brother. So—I simply have to say I agree with you!!

"All this might seem excessive to you," Dick told me. "But those were such fraught times in our personal lives, our ambitions and our own relationship—me with terrible misgivings about leaving, Bill with terrible misgivings about staying."

In the middle of September, Dick tendered his formal resignation. Before Johnson accepted, however, he extracted a promise that Dick would return to help write the 1966 State of the Union—a promise Dick would greatly come to regret.

Upon finding the extravagantly gracious, if obligatory, exchange of letters between Dick and the president that followed, I handed Dick his own fifty-year-old letter to read. Dick skimmed it silently, shaking his head with a frown.

No man I have ever known has been kinder or warmer to me. . . . It is a relationship that will always be the most prized of my life. . . . I hope I have communicated how agonizing it is for me to leave a man I admire so greatly.

"So ingratiating, this young Goodwin!" he protested, turning to me to hand back the letter. "Don't make me read it all!"

I answered Dick's abridged reading with Johnson's response:

Dear Dick: Few letters I have ever received have touched me so profoundly as yours . . . I know that the unique opportunity to serve your country during these years has been a blessing to you, for it has given you the means of applying your brilliant talents to the problems that beset your fellow men. It has also been a blessing for the country—for within the high councils of government you have articulated with great force and persuasion man's hunger for justice and his hopes for a better life.

"Not a bad job," Dick said, moved despite himself.

"Do you think Moyers wrote it?" I asked.

"Probably," Dick said. "But if I'd still been there, Lyndon would have asked me to write this last tribute to myself!"

"You're impossible!" I exclaimed.

"No, I'm serious. Sometimes I wrote dozens a day—his condolences to a late senator's widow, a fond note to Justice Frankfurter after our visit, congratulations to a mayor upon a new litter of beagles. Why not write a real beauty to commemorate my own passing?"

A few days later, the White House Press Office under Moyers's auspices released the president's tribute letter to Dick. Excerpts appeared in the *Baltimore Sun*.

Johnson was left fuming. He had considered his letter a private and confidential communication. "I've learned my lesson," he grumbled in typically overblown fashion. "I'm never going to write a letter to anyone again."

Over the years I have read scores of descriptions of Dick's time in public service, some glowing, others raining hellfire. Dick had saved a stack of such commentaries, good and bad, including one that especially delighted and amused him from *Time* magazine reporter Hugh Sidey, which I shared aloud with him.

"Goodwin more than almost anyone else in the White House was responsible for taking the raw emotion of Lyndon Johnson and sculpting it into the graceful and promising lines of the Great Society. Goodwin almost single-handedly provided the most inspiring moments of Johnson's first two years.

"Goodwin was one of those comets which come through the national government from decade to decade. They are rare. They sometimes produce more of a spectacle than a lasting impact, but while they burn they light the dark corners. His was certainly the most facile and remarkable mind in government under both Kennedy and Johnson."

To me, what hits harder than LBJ's eloquent parting tribute or even Sidey's comet (Better to *see* one than *be* one, muttered Dick sardonically) were the words Dick never heard, captured in a recently available transcript of a taped conversation between the president and NAACP head Roy Wilkins on November 1, 1965, two months after Dick's departure.

"There's one boy that—I don't know how well you know him," Johnson said. "He's the best civil rights man I've really had, this boy, Goodwin."

CHAPTER TEN

Friendship, Loyalty, and Duty

*Robert Kennedy delivers his "Ripple of Hope" speech to
South African students at the University of Cape Town,
among them Margaret H. Marshall. June 6, 1966.*

ONE SPRING MORNING IN 2016 I FOUND DICK MUMBLING AND
grumbling as he worked his way along the two-tiered row of cardboard
boxes in his collection. "Look how many boxes we have left," he exclaimed,
pulling an unlit, well-chewed cigar from his lips and waving it over the boxes.
"See, Jackie and Bobby here, more Lyndon, riots and protests, McCarthy,
antiwar marches, assassinations. Look at them! Boxes of treasure and Pandora's boxes."

"I guess we'd better pick up our pace," I offered.

"You're a lot younger than me," Dick said. "Shovel more coal into our
old train and let's go!"

This determination to steam ahead had only increased with the approach
of his mid-eighties. Dick scoffed at his wheezing and coughing, insisting
once again that it was only allergies and spring pollen. Nevertheless, shortness of breath made for long pauses when climbing stairs. Recently, he had
taken another fall on the gravel path while inspecting the forsythia, telling

me as he scrambled to his feet that it was not a fall, but a slip, like a boxer trying to convince the referee it wasn't a knockdown.

"Who would you bet on?" he asked me one night at bedtime, nothing particularly morbid in his tone. "Who will be finished first: me or the boxes?"

During visits to our cardiologist, Dick was surprisingly low-key, letting me steer questions about his shortness of breath, unsteadiness, troubling test results concerning the state of his heart. Knowledge and research were my shield against anxiety and fear. I took notes on every medical visit and kept daily observations in a notebook, hoping I'd record some detail that might prove useful to the doctors.

For Dick, the opposite was true. His lack of specific curiosity about his health allowed him to sustain an upbeat and cavalier attitude. He didn't want to know details as long as I heard them. Our cardiologist later told me that when Dick was alone with him, he cut detailed conversations short. "I trust Doris," Dick had explained to the doctor. "She trusts you. So I trust you. It's simple—a transfer of trust."

He only wanted to get better. He recoiled from the words "congestive heart failure" but was reassured when the doctor told us that with proper medication, this diagnosis was far less menacing than it sounded. And with a powerful regime of digoxin and an array of other medicines, the pumping of his heart markedly improved.

He did not want to know what pills he was prescribed or why. When I sat before the kitchen table filling his weekly pill organizer he would peer over the newspaper to provoke and pester me with questions: "Do you know what you are doing?" he teased me. "Can you keep the pills straight?" Yet he took his medication like an obedient child. He followed our doctor's orders on exercise and diet, only drawing the line at relinquishing cigars or giving up a nightly gin with dry vermouth and a pickled onion.

We complemented each other perfectly.

So with the promise of quickened purpose and renewed effort, we plunged back into the autumn of 1965, the months following Dick's departure from the White House—in particular, his deepening friendships with Jackie and Bobby Kennedy.

Lyndon Johnson had been mistaken to suspect Dick of disloyalty while he was in the White House, of being "in bed with the Kennedys." All the chatter about Dick leaving to go to "the other side" wasn't accurate. Both his diary and his correspondence with Bill Moyers make clear that his exit had nothing to do with the Kennedys or his own future political ambitions. In Johnson's mind, however, Dick had not only been with John Kennedy from the very beginning but had remained friendly with Jackie ever since. For Johnson, these were sufficient grounds to prevent him from ever completely trusting an original young New Frontiersman.

The development of a friendship with Bobby after Dick resigned confirmed for Johnson that Dick had been disloyal all along—as if future events might prove past presumptions. Dick had been found guilty well before the crime of his real friendship with Bobby had even begun.

In actuality, Dick's relationship with Jackie had long preceded his friendship with Bobby. The picture Dick painted of Jackie for me through his description of their work together on various White House projects was very different from the one generally portrayed to the public. She worked ferociously hard, advocating for the things she cared about with a sweetness that had a powerful edge. The breathy voice and saccharine manner that is so often depicted barely coincided with the disarmingly honest, funny, sarcastic, bookish, chain-smoking buddy who sought peace within the safety of her apartment from the pandemonium her celebrity stirred outside.

Perhaps Dick's favorite story in a series of personal recollections about Robert Kennedy took place on a fall evening in 1965 when he was visiting Jackie's Fifth Avenue apartment.

The doorman recognized me and nodded as he passed me through the entrance fronting 1040 Fifth Avenue to the elevator whose operator smiled in greeting, and without asking my destination, took me straight to the fourteenth floor to the entrance of Jacqueline's apartment. A few minutes after I had pressed the small ivory button, the door opened.

We sat in the sitting room of her apartment, side by side on an upholstered couch—preferred in friendly evenings to the adjacent library . . . the books now arranged by color—all the red bound volumes in shelves facing the couch.

Going to the kitchen, she returned with a bottle of champagne, her favorite evening drink, and a bucket of ice. She poured the champagne and then placed some ice cubes in the glass to keep the wine chilled.

An intermittent ritual developed during these relaxed evenings. She would offer me a cigar from a supply she kept in an antique table drawer, a Por Larranaga. One evening as she crushed out a cigarette and prepared to light another, she asked me. "Why do you like those things?"

"Try it," I responded, handing her the lit cigar, which she took, held gingerly between forefinger and thumb, and began to puff. "Don't inhale," I cautioned.

"They have a real taste," she remarked, handing it back to me.

"Well, that's why we like them," I responded.

She would take a few puffs from my cigar, and then relinquish it to continue her chain smoking. I would estimate that over a period of years, beginning with Lyndon Johnson's presidency, she consumed the equivalent of an entire cigar. I never pointed out to her the obvious—that her Cuban cigars must have been illegally obtained.

On the night of my "ice capade fiasco," I heard the apartment door open and close. In a moment he was at the entrance to the library wearing a brown leather flight jacket, half zipped.

"Oh, it's only Bobby," she remarked.

"I thought we were going skating," said Bobby, a pause. "Let's go."

"I don't know how to skate," I confessed.

"Well," Bobby replied, "let's all go anyway."

We rose.

They were both carrying their own skates, and as we approached the rink, Bobby said to me: "You can rent skates here." In a minute or two they had put on their skates and glided together across the ice. I went to the cubicle where skates were rented, and sat, somewhat nervously, as the attendant sized my foot, and brought me the skates.

I had no idea even how to begin. But I put them on and walked haltingly to the rink, gratefully grasped the wooden railing which encircled the ice, and moved totteringly along the rail, using it for support. Every once in a while I would let go, and try to move, only managing to keep from failing by re-grabbing the rail. I was, to myself, a comic figure, stumbling, ankles beginning to hurt.

Mercifully, I heard him call across the ice: "We're going now." The three of us walked off in the direction of the Plaza hotel. Entering the relieving warmth of a bar on the Central Park side of the Plaza, I rubbed the cold from my hands as we ordered drinks.

Bobby began to discourse on his newly discovered knowledge in astronomy, as if new wonders had suddenly been revealed to him. He had since his brother's death begun to read far more widely than before, when it had seemed that he was confined to politics, public affairs and his catechism. I listened politely as he told us of the vast numbers of stars and of galaxies—billions of each. He sounded like *a kid who had made his first visit to a planetarium. "Do you know," he asked, "that some stars are moving away from us faster than the speed of light."*

"Aha," I thought with delight, "I have him."

"No, they don't," I said.

"What do you mean?" he said, somewhat annoyed by this interruption of his monologue.

"They don't move faster than the speed of light, nothing does."

"Of course, they do," he insisted.

"Impossible," I rejoined, "at that speed the mass would become infinite. It would mean a violation of the theory of relativity." I didn't know much about the subject, but I knew more than he did.

"Let's bet a case of champagne," I said.

Jacqueline sat across from me, next to her brother-in-law, watching the men joust.

The next day I called JFK's presidential science advisor Jerome Wiesner and set up a conference call with Bobby. I posed the question to Wiesner, who, obviously uncomfortable at being caught between the truth and Robert Kennedy, hesitatingly confirmed the accuracy of my position.

"I never got the promised spoils of that jousting," Dick said, ending his story, "but I got something better than a mere case of champagne. Before the week was out I received an invitation from Bobby: "Would I like to accompany him, some family and friends on a trip to South America, all expenses paid, and 'you won't be expected to do any work, just come along?'"

"Improbably, that trip was the beginning of a bond that changed the rest of the decade for me," Dick said. "Actually," he added after a thoughtful hesitation, "it would change the rest of my life."

NOVEMBER 10–30, 1965

"Didn't you suspect there might be more to that invitation than camaraderie?" I asked. "A stint as a traveling speechwriter, perhaps? He knew you had traveled extensively through Latin America with President Kennedy, writing speeches along the way."

"I never wrote a word for Bobby on that trip," Dick maintained. "Nor was I ever asked to."

Dick was simply along for the adventure, together with a traveling party that included Bobby's wife Ethel Kennedy, Senate staff members Adam

Walinsky and Tom Johnston, several friends, as well as a small contingent of chosen reporters. When asked about his role, Dick insisted that he was neither working nor writing for Bobby. It was bad enough he had abandoned Lyndon Johnson to go to Wesleyan; if he had gone to work for Bobby only weeks after leaving the White House, it would have been a genuine betrayal.

Neither did Bobby want the trip to signal any distancing from or challenge to the president. Before the plane departed from Miami to Peru, Bobby told reporters: "I am not thinking of running for the presidency. I have a high feeling for President Johnson. He has been very kind to me. I would support his bid for reelection in 1968, and I strongly wish to campaign for him."

Despite these precautions, the privately funded trip had all the energy of a campaign from the moment the plane landed in Lima. Everywhere Bobby went—from Peru to Chile, Argentina, Brazil, and Venezuela— massive crowds greeted him with shouts of "Viva Kennedy, Viva Kennedy." The aura of John Kennedy, who was perhaps even more popular in death than he had been in life, surrounded his brother. Dick remembered being "brought to a halt" upon hearing the thunderous response of the crowd, "as if some nerve had been severed. How many times in how many places had I heard that same rising shout?"

They would be accompanied on this three-week journey not only by the ghost of John Kennedy and the fervor that the Kennedy name evoked, but also by the surveilling ghost of Lyndon Johnson who was monitoring the entire trip. Unbeknownst to either Bobby or Dick, a mysterious source (most likely someone working for conservative Assistant Secretary of State Thomas Mann) was sending biased impressions of the trip to the Oval Office. This informant insinuated that Kennedy was engaged in a full-blown presidential campaign, "obviously well-tutored by Richard Goodwin, his new South American advisor," a misleading title Lyndon Johnson would neither forgive nor forget.

That same informant told the president that during a press conference, Bobby "took time out to introduce Goodwin as the author of the Alliance for Progress. Goodwin stood in the back of the room with his arms folded and a wise smile on his face. He badly needed a haircut and, of course, so did Bobby."

Columnists Rowland Evans and Robert Novak reported that State Department conservatives were "apprehensive" about the trip, worried that "the romantically inclined Latin mind will view RFK as a sort of government-in-exile who will give them what Tom Mann won't." Adding to their fears, the columnists noted, is "the presence of Richard Goodwin," whose more radical views about the need for economic reform and social justice were "anathema" to the State Department's old guard, which was partial to private enterprise and the status quo.

Dick later learned that Johnson had parsed wire reports of Kennedy's speeches, and singled out various sentences that "could only have been written by Goodwin"—including one in particular, where Bobby warned a group of young Peruvian students that "the responsibility of our time is nothing less than a revolution—a revolution that would be peaceful if we are wise enough, humane if we care enough, successful if we are fortunate enough. But a revolution will come whether we will it or not."

"That surely sounds like you," I said.

"It's a great line," Dick said. "I wish it were mine. It was his young speechwriter Adam Walinsky."

From Day One of their South America trip, Dick told me, it became clear this was not to be the jaunt down memory lane he had expected. A different style emanated from Bobby than from his older, more aloof and regal brother—something hotter, more demonstrative and more accessible. He delivered intensity when nothing was to be gained beyond the moment. When Bobby played soccer with the kids in the barriadas, the slums of Lima, it was not for a photo op. It was his impetuous warmth, his affability toward the kids, that caught Dick's attention. As they departed from the hovels and open sewage of the Lima slums, Bobby turned to Dick and asked, "What happened to all our AID money? Where is it going? Wouldn't you be a communist if you had to live there?" concluding the outburst with a straightforward, "I think I would."

As the trip went on, the memory of John Kennedy's ironic, self-contained demeanor began to recede and the demonstrative figure of his younger brother began to take shape before Dick's eyes. The self-righteousness and combativeness Dick had witnessed in Bobby in the past seemed diminished, replaced by a deepening empathy and compassion, an emerging fatalism.

Dick recalled one evening at the University of Concepción in Chile when Kennedy's intrepid nature and openness particularly revealed itself. Alerted that an organized group of Marxist students planned to disrupt his speech that evening, Bobby spent several hours in the afternoon patiently listening to their arguments about capitalism and communism. He sought to appease discord and open a dialogue with them. By the end of the session the communist student leader conceded, "We do not condemn you personally, but we oppose you as a representative of a government whose hands are stained with blood." And as such, they remained determined to prevent him from speaking.

Among an audience of three thousand, more than a hundred of their group awaited Kennedy's entrance to the gym. "They were in the balcony directly over the podium," Dick recalled, "and eggs, tomatoes, and even stones began to rain down on us."

Bobby was somehow untouched by the pelting debris. "If these kids are going to be young revolutionaries," he softly remarked to one of his traveling partners, "they're going to have to improve their aim."

Bobby's speech was drowned out by the student protesters. Nevertheless, he plowed ahead at the top of his lungs. After he finished speaking, he approached the section of the overhanging balcony where the communists were clustered, mounted a chair, and shook the hand of the student leader he had met earlier that afternoon. Another student standing beside the leader spat in Kennedy's face and was immediately dragged away by his comrades. A wild burst of applause sounded as the resolute Kennedy exited the gym.

With each passing day of Kennedy's South America travels, the crowds came out in greater numbers and excitement. When the small Kennedy troupe reached the seaport city of Natal in eastern Brazil, more than 100,000 people filled the streets to meet him. Standing atop the roof of a truck, Bobby shouted with newfound confidence and stridency, "Every child an education! Every family adequate housing! Every man a job!"

"Sounds like Lyndon's talking points." I remarked, "Education . . . housing . . . jobs—the nucleus of his Great Society."

"Fair enough," Dick said. "It always baffled me that the Alliance for Progress never grabbed Lyndon. Maybe because the Alliance was Kennedy's, not his. South of the border, Lyndon let the reactionary State Department make decisions."

On November 22, two days after celebrating his fortieth birthday, Bobby attended mass in Salvador on the second anniversary of his brother's assassination. He had wanted to be absent from the formal ceremonies back in the United States. The schedule he had kept in South America had run everyone ragged but the incessant activity still wasn't enough to drown his grief. Dick witnessed several occasions where Kennedy's defensive reaction seemed almost engraved in his nervous system; once when a string of firecrackers exploded below their vehicle, and another time when a car backfired close by, he flinched, instinctively covering his face. "Sooner or later," he said quietly, "sooner or later."

At Dick's suggestion and subsequent arrangement, the group decided upon a recreational detour from their grueling schedule. Through a Brazilian friend of Dick's from his Alliance days, a charter was arranged to carry the party to Manaus, the port city in the midst of the Amazon Rainforest. There they all boarded a paddle-wheeled steamer to carry them further up the river.

The most memorable day of the entire journey lay ahead. Dick convinced Bobby and a few others to board an ancient single-engine seaplane to take them deeper into the jungle. "I must be crazy to get on this thing," said Bobby as he kissed Ethel goodbye.

The flight was unsettling, even alarming. Reminded of the frightful turbulence he had once experienced on the twin-engine "Caroline," Dick told me he turned to Bobby and said, "Whenever I traveled with your brother I never worried. One look at him and I felt protected."

"And now?" grinned Bobby as our seaplane bucked over the green sea of trees. "Feel protected?"

"I think we'll be fine," I told him hopefully, "I'm with you."

"Well, don't bet on it," he laughed. "But regarding your protection theory with Jack and me I think you're wrong twice."

Finally, the seaplane skidded down without incident on the Nhamundá River, a tributary to the Amazon located near a small native village of several hundred thatched-roofed huts. With the translation of a missionary couple, Bobby asked if he and Dick might join two native fishermen he had spotted in a dugout canoe downriver.

"On that day we had a great Amazon adventure," Dick fondly remembered. "I saw a whole new facet of Bobby. As we paddled over the water, Bobby shouted, 'You know, I bet there are piranha in there. Want to go swimming?'"

Without delay, Dick cannonballed into the water. Kennedy immediately followed. Then, treading to keep afloat, Bobby—in an unmistakable imitation of celebrated TV anchorman Walter Cronkite—comically proclaimed: "It was impossible to pinpoint the exact time and place when he decided to run for president. But the idea seemed to take hold as he was swimming in the Amazonian river of Nhamundá, keeping a sharp eye for man-eating piranhas.

"Piranhas," he added, "have never been known to bite a U.S. senator."

"Well, I'm not a senator," Dick had replied, "and I'm getting out of here."

"This is going to be one of those things," Bobby said, laughing as they reached the side of the canoe, "that's going to be a hell of a lot more fun to talk about *afterwards.*"

And so it was. Finding a homemade scrapbook of their Amazon adventure put together by a member of the traveling party proved a delightful entertainment for Dick and me. It contained snapshots of Kennedy meeting with the villagers and playing with children, of Dick in a basket-brigade unloading supplies from a canoe, and of Dick and Bobby spearfishing on a stretch of rapids. The entire jungle foray was presented as a spoof, a parody of a preposterous campaign for votes since nothing could have been further from a political canvass. The villagers here had never heard of Bobby or, for that matter, of his slain brother. It was fun, pure and simple.

Shortly after returning to the United States and his fellowship at Wesleyan, Dick wrote of Robert Kennedy to his old college chum, George Cuomo.

He's a remarkable guy with a reasonable chance of being president someday; and a large chance, if he does make it, of becoming an outstanding president.

About those observations, Dick never changed his mind. The trip to the Amazon and the adventures they shared had strengthened his friendship with Robert Kennedy, a friendship that would last, Dick said, "for as much time as we had left."

JANUARY 12, 1966

In the aftermath of his well-publicized South American jaunt with Robert Kennedy, Dick feared he would not be warmly welcomed back to the White House by Lyndon Johnson. Regardless, he would keep the promise made upon leaving—to return and draft the State of the Union speech, scheduled for January 12, 1966.

Unknown to Dick at the time, Jack Valenti and Joe Califano (working under Moyers's supervision) had originally sought permission from the president for Dick to commence drafting the speech in early December. LBJ's response: an emphatic "NO."

On December 7, Dick's thirty-fourth birthday, Valenti informed Califano, by now the president's top domestic adviser, of Johnson's obstinate rancor: "[The president] specifically objected to the man you and I had discussed doing any work on it. I intend to press the suggestion real soon—but he flatly refused to let him work on the draft now."

"Well, a Happy Birthday from Lyndon to me," Dick caustically remarked to me after reading of the president's directive so many years later.

But before that December was over, if Lyndon didn't have a change of heart, he had a change of mind. None of the preliminary drafts that had been sent to him met his approval. At last, quietly, he let Valenti and Califano know he would allow them to summon Dick to Washington.

When Dick arrived at the White House on January 4, he was given an empty office in the West Wing. There was no affectionate greeting from the president; indeed, there was no reception of any kind, not even a phone call. Nor did the president reach out to contact Dick in the days that followed. Barely sleeping for days, only briefly retiring from his office to the Hay-Adams hotel for naps, Dick worked on draft after revised draft with Valenti, Califano, and Moyers acting as middlemen. The president steadfastly refused to see Dick, who felt he had been grudgingly invited to a party he was not allowed to attend.

"No way to draft a major speech," Dick told me.

Prior to this experience, whenever Dick prepared any of Johnson's major speeches, they had spent many hours together thrashing out what the president wanted to say. Over lunches, dinners, and late-night drinks, Dick had become privy to Johnson's thoughts and sentiments. Even under the enormous pressure of drafting the "We Shall Overcome" speech in only nine or ten hours, Dick had been able to draw on his knowledge of the president's deep emotional engagement with civil rights and his familiarity with the stories Johnson wanted to tell. Over time, the Texan and the New Frontiersman had developed a rare collaboration of feelings, thoughts, and language.

The atmosphere of trust that had made such collaboration possible was now gone, destroyed by Johnson's notion that Dick had defected to the rival camp in order to write speeches for his political nemesis Bobby Kennedy.

The problems that beset this State of the Union, however, went far deeper than Johnson's mistrust of his former chief speechwriter. There was already discord and bickering within the White House about the purpose of the speech—how to create a synthesis between the sustained but costly momentum of the Great Society, and its antithesis: the brutal, expanding war in Vietnam. Proponents of each side squabbled for more space and emphasis. At stake was the future direction of the country.

During the summer of 1965, Johnson had sought to resolve the problem of this fork in the road by attempting to take both paths at once. Now, in the State of the Union, he aimed to convince the entire nation to do much the same. This wishful synthesis would come to be known as the "Guns and Butter" speech.

The writing of a State of the Union is "always as full of tension as an opening night," Lady Bird wrote in her diary. Recalling "the exhilaration" of the 1965 address, she contrasted that shining moment to the dreary tensions of the present. Then, "we were on the crest of the great victory of the November election, bolstered, assured the people were behind us, a sort of peak in our lives and here, in 1966, we are in a trough of a wave: erosion and frustrations have set in."

Dick's draft attempted to address that standoff of the Great Society and the Vietnam War with a confident and tone-setting opening: "This Nation is mighty enough, its society is healthy enough, its people are strong enough, to pursue our goals in the rest of the world while still building a Great Society at home." This hopeful frame would be followed by an appeal to members of Congress to ask themselves whether they, "the representatives of the richest Nation on earth, elected servants of a people who live in abundance unmatched on this globe," were "going to sacrifice the children who need the learning or the sick who need medical care or the families who dwell in squalor."

Repeatedly, Dick drafted the sections of the speech that focused upon the revitalization of domestic concerns. Time and again these would be returned with notes suggesting shortening and revision. He had worked nearly thirty-six hours straight and still had not finished when, an hour past midnight on the day the president was scheduled to deliver the speech before the joint session, he realized that he had hit the wall. He was empty.

In desperation, he phoned the White House doctor. "I only need a few more hours," he entreated. Soon, the White House physician appeared, drew a hypodermic partially filled with fuchsia liquid from his bag, and injected it into Dick's shoulder. Whatever it was, Dick told me, it enabled him to finish the speech, which concluded, of necessity, with "the troubling awareness of American men at war tonight." Though Vietnam was different from other wars, "finally, war is always the same. It is young men dying in the fullness of their promise. It is trying to kill a man you do not even know well enough to hate. Therefore, to know war is to know there is still madness in this world.

"Many of you share the burden of this knowledge tonight with me. But there is a difference. For finally I must be the one to order our guns to fire, against all the most inward pulls of my desire. For we have children to teach, and we have sick to be cured, and we have men to be freed. There are poor to be lifted up, and there are cities to be built, and there is a world to be helped."

"At about 4 a.m., on the morning of the day the speech was to be given," Califano recalled, "as the President slept, we slipped under his bedroom door what we thought was the final version. I went to sleep on the couch in my office and Goodwin went to his hotel, utterly drained."

When Johnson awakened, he immediately read the draft and summoned Valenti, Califano, and Moyers—pointedly omitting Dick—to his bedroom. He told the three of them "it was getting there," but was much too long and "he wanted it cut by a third." He told Valenti and Califano to make the revisions, later calling in two old friends—Supreme Court Justice Abe Fortas and chairman of the Defense Intelligence Advisory Board Clark Clifford—to help speed the editing process.

The remainder of the morning and into the afternoon, knives and cleavers were taken to the draft to carve off the required third of its length. For the first time since Dick had written Johnson's "Great Society" speech, he had lost control of the final editing and overall shaping of his work. The majority of the cuts pared down the domestic side of the equation. Aspects of Dick's draft remained, but the design of the speech was shattered, replaced by the hodgepodge of committee production.

The White House Diary records that there were brief calls from the president to Dick in the West Wing that morning and afternoon. When I asked him if he had any memory of the calls he shrugged. "Nothing stands out except his vague desire to clarify something or other."

Later that afternoon, Dick staggered back to his room at the Hay-Adams at about five o'clock that afternoon. Suit jacket and pants still on, he flopped on his bed and slept at last. When the ring of the phone on the nightstand wrenched him awake, it seemed like a bizarre dream. It was the White House calling. Lyndon Johnson's secretary informed him that the president—whom Dick had not laid eyes on during the whole bitter week-long sojourn—would like Dick to ride up to the Hill with him on his way to deliver the State of the Union.

Befuddled by the request, Dick mumbled that he would call back. He remembered the excitement and promise of previous rides to the Capitol; but then all the disappointment and anger at Johnson's refusal to work face-to-face with him, all the endless revisions of his drafts, flooded over him. "It was just too much," he later told Califano, "I couldn't go through with it. I was exhausted and disgusted with the way I was treated." He called the hotel desk, told the operator to hold all calls, threw his jacket and pants on a chair, and crawled back into bed.

Later that night after the ceremonials and speech were long over, Lady Bird Johnson wrote in her diary, with characteristic forthrightness: "The audience was cold and lethargic." In the Speaker's office following the speech, she likewise observed that while everyone shook hands, "the pervasively friendly atmosphere seemed missing from that normal, social interchange."

Reviews of the speech noted a disquietude, a doubleness, a sense that something was out of joint. While liberal papers applauded the promise to sustain and even expand the Great Society, they were disconcerted by Johnson's emphatic pledge "to give our fighting men what they must have; every gun, every dollar and every decision—whatever the cost or whatever the challenge."

In the end, it had been worked over by too many hands, Califano acknowledged, leaving a "dull message, primarily concerned with foreign policy."

The real problem with the speech, Dick later came to believe, was the flawed supposition at its "Guns and Butter" heart. Dick told me he couldn't bring himself to read the final speech then and he refused to have me read it to him now. The whole thing had all been too infuriating and humiliating. He had been ignored, disrespected, and punished for a betrayal that had never happened.

When he returned to Connecticut the next day, a letter had arrived which Dick had preserved in his archive.

Dear Dick,

You left Washington so swiftly I had no opportunity to talk with you. I am told that exhaustion conquered you, finally, last evening, and you were unable to be with me.

I am not unaware of the long hours and sleepless nights that were your companions this week. But your gifts of skill and eloquence were gratefully received by me.

Sincerely,

Lyndon

"Cosmetic bullshit!" said Dick. "Once again, I sense the hand of my friend Moyers, upset by how things had turned out."

As I mulled over this entire episode, I felt a lingering sadness, remembering what Dick and LBJ had accomplished together. They had never been friends, perhaps, but they had been awesome allies. This wounding sequence would mark the last time they would work together. Dick would never see Lyndon Johnson again.

———————

I'm afraid I can no longer awe the letter carriers of my friends with White House stationery and envelopes, Dick wrote George Cuomo in early February 1966 under the letterhead of Wesleyan's Center for Advanced Study.

I'm slowly disentangling myself from seven years of politics. It's taken quite a time to get used to this life. I don't miss the decisions or being at the center of power at all. What is hard is the absence of all external discipline—no office to go to, no hours, no deadlines, no pressure—it all has to come from inside. This is an old story to you, but not to me.

I've been sleeping a lot, reading a lot, building up a record collection, running to parties in New York, and not getting much work done. But that is now changing, my metabolism seems to be quieting down, and I am full of hopes for the future.

I am writing—I am still playing around with ideas.

"How does one get one's sea legs," I asked Dick, "after being on the ship of state for so long?" He had, after all, been a Washington denizen since leaving law school. Suddenly, he had to organize his own time. He would no longer spend his days honing a justice's opinions, decisions, or dissents;

elucidating documents for a congressional committee; or designing policy and drafting speeches for the very different cadences and characters of JFK and LBJ. He would have to find his own voice.

The experience of the State of the Union, Dick declared to George, had "cured" him forever from speechwriting and politics. But as Justice Frankfurter's observation about Dick having "politics in his blood" suggests, it was a malaise not easily remedied.

Dick's escape from politics and Washington proved short-lived. After writing until 3 a.m. one mid-February morning, Dick was awakened before seven o'clock by the persistent ringing of his home phone. He ignored it, but moments later the phone sounded again. The third time he picked up. It was Bobby Kennedy: "Have you been following the Fulbright hearings?" he asked.

"That's how it all began, again," acknowledged Dick.

"So much for your forever cure from politics," I laughed. "A speedy relapse!"

"You know," said Dick earnestly, "there are times when private lives are drawn into public debate. This was the very beginning of such a time."

Dick had of course been following the televised hearings launched in early February by Chairman of the Senate Foreign Relations Committee William Fulbright on the conduct and wisdom of the Vietnam War. Coming on the heels of the administration's resumption of bombing after a six-week halt, the hearings had a huge national audience. Up to this point, Bobby Kennedy had been leery of publicly expressing his private misgivings about Vietnam. His motives would immediately be attacked, and any statement construed as opportunism fueled by ambition and personal animosity toward President Johnson. But now, Kennedy felt compelled to enter the debate.

"Do you think there's anything constructive I can add?" Bobby asked Dick.

Later than morning, Dick called Bobby back with a suggestion.

"Everyone, even the administration, claims that the only solution is a negotiated settlement," Dick said, "but nobody's been willing to spell out what it would look like, what terms would be acceptable."

That same day, Dick phoned Bobby again and read him a rough draft of a potential statement. Kennedy suggested additions and alterations and asked Dick to send it down to Washington posthaste.

FEBRUARY 19, 1966

"Ho Chi Kennedy," headlined the *Chicago Tribune*:

"He is not the junior senator from New York, he is the senior senator from Communist North Vietnam—Ho Chi Minh's Trojan horse in the United States Senate. . . . Out of his ignorance and political ambition, he [Kennedy] has compromised his loyalty to the United States."

"Of all the gratuitous advice Pres. Johnson is getting on what to do in Vietnam," charged the *Buffalo Evening News*, "it would be hard to conceive any more ill-conceived counsel."

I could hardly believe my eyes when I scanned the savage headlines and editorials that greeted Dick's first significant collaboration with Robert Kennedy. Strangely, Dick had preserved a packet of them, like a poisonous batch of book reviews.

Kennedy had delivered his statement at a press conference with all the fanfare and "trappings of a presidential news session," according to *The Los Angeles Times*, complete with "more than 30 reporters, glaring lights, TV cameras, a dozen microphones."

Dick had warned Kennedy when he sent the draft that it approached "the edge of political danger," recognizing that any variance from the Johnson administration would be construed as self-serving. Consequently, the statement began with a preemptive declaration: "We are all Americans. To attack the motives of those who express concern about our present course—to challenge their very right to speak freely—is to strike at the foundations of the democratic process which our fellow citizens even today, are dying to protect."

Reiterating Johnson's own statements about the desire for a negotiated settlement, Kennedy then veered from the administration's boilerplate by proposing that the Viet Cong be admitted "to a share of power and responsibility" at the conference table. "Each side must concede matters that are important in order to preserve positions that are essential." Acknowledging that such deliberations may yield "a compromise government fully acceptable to neither side," he maintained that "if negotiation is our aim," an unwillingness to compromise will only lead to the "hazards of widening conflict and devastation."

Kennedy left that press conference for a ski trip with his family. But an avalanche of organized scorn and ridicule trailed him. As Dick later wrote, "the roof fell in." Although Johnson kept his silence, he delegated his team to close ranks and, knives out, attack Bobby. Vice President Humphrey led the charge, claiming the proposal for a coalition government "would be like putting a fox in the chicken coop, or an arsonist in the fire department." McGeorge Bundy assailed Bobby's naïveté, condescendingly reminding him that his brother had once warned that "forming a coalition with the Communists was like trying to ride a tiger."

Kennedy hustled back to Washington to control the damage and "clarify" his position. While not abandoning his original proposal, he sought to introduce qualifications that only confused the matter. This appearance of waffling and vacillation made matters worse.

"It sure got me down," Dick said, recalling that "my first bid to write something for Bobby seemed to have damaged—if not destroyed—his career. I was caught in a snarl of friendship, loyalty, and duty, trying to do what I felt was right."

I was curious about Bobby's response to this whole matter—in particular, his reaction to Dick. I remembered Dick's "freedom fighter" statement that some deemed such a reckless and incendiary mistake that it threatened to capsize JFK's 1960 campaign in its final days. John Kennedy's coolly ironic reproach telling Dick and Sorensen—"If I win this thing, I won it. But if I lose it, you guys lost it"—had only enhanced Dick's adulation.

From the start, Dick's relationship with Bobby differed from such hero worship. They were closer in age (only six years apart as opposed to the fourteen-year gap with JFK). They were becoming fast friends. Dick told me Bobby assured him not to worry. "I went over every word of that with you," Bobby said, "made changes, additions. I delivered it. The real mistake was not the statement, but how I handled it afterward."

That Dick continued to be deeply troubled by the episode is clear from the long letter he wrote to Bobby after the dust had begun to settle.

It's hard for me to talk about whether it was "all worthwhile," since I have to share responsibility for getting you into it, and I don't want to sound self-justifying.

However, I have tried, as best I can, to purge myself of that, and look at the whole thing clearly and with some detachment.

Vietnam is the central issue of today. It not only involves a present war in which many will be killed, but the serious possibility, even probability, of far greater war. It seems to be right that someone of your insight and standing should stand up and talk about it.

It is a mistake to think that the American people delight in the idea of fighting wars in Asia or anywhere else. They don't want it. That's why they elected Ike, and underneath the reluctance is even stronger today because people are doing well, and they don't want to give it up. And remember that half the country is under 25. As the war grows those that cry for more of it are going to be in great difficulty.

There are many who will tell you, and write, that you have hurt yourself . . . I am miserable at the thought I might have contributed to damaging you. But you spoke truly, in the interests of the nation. And there is nothing else to be done— except to deceive or stand silent at a moment of great crisis. I believe history and politics will reward that courage.

Justice Frankfurter told me, when I had been attacked in an editorial, there were two kinds of pain in public life. One was the deep continuing pain of serious emotional blows. The other, the pain of immediate controversy, was like a toothache. It was terrible, but once fixed, you forgot it ever existed. You have already known the first kind. This is the second.

JUNE 6, 1966

If the "roof had fallen in" after Dick's first collaboration with Bobby, his next effort proved so durable that its words have inspired generations around the world and would one day be inscribed on Robert Kennedy's untimely grave.

The iconic speech had a difficult birth. Kennedy had been invited by Ian Robertson, a young student and president of the nonracial National Union of South African Students (NUSAS) to be the keynote speaker on its Day of Affirmation, an annual occasion students had organized to proclaim their opposition to apartheid—the country's system of racial segregation that kept the majority-Black population under the brutal rule of the white minority.

For five months, the South African government procrastinated in issuing Kennedy a visa. An earlier invitation by NUSAS to Martin Luther King Jr. had been rejected by the government out of hand. Finally, the apartheid government determined that as much as it disliked the idea of letting a civil rights champion into the country, Kennedy was the brother of a president and might someday be president himself. Reluctantly, a limited visa was granted for four people only for a four-day visit in June. No U.S. journalists were allowed to accompany Kennedy.

The first draft of Kennedy's speech was penned by Adam Walinsky, the talented speechwriter who had worked for Kennedy in the Justice Department and written all his speeches and statements during the South America trip. Dick had befriended Walinsky during that adventure, admired his work, and eventually became something of a mentor to him.

The writing of the speech was "very, very tough," Adam recalled in an oral history. Kennedy's advance man, Thomas Johnston, had warned that the senator would be "going into a terribly explosive and delicate situation where the government was completely against him. . . . The whole trip had the makings of one of the major disasters in his life." As Walinsky worked up the first draft, he felt compelled to address the racial situation cautiously, without "totally antagonizing" the staunchly anticommunist regime that had the full support of an overwhelming majority of the voters, not surprising since no Blacks were allowed to vote.

Two days before their departure, political activist Allard Lowenstein, recently returned from South Africa, paid a visit to Kennedy's office to talk about what he had seen and learned. Walinsky showed him the draft he had prepared. Lowenstein reared up. "Terrible," he pronounced, "all wrong!" If Kennedy were to deliver such a tepid speech, Lowenstein implied, there was no point in going. Immediately, Kennedy and Walinsky decided to recast the speech. Walinsky remembered that he was relieved that his "delicately phrased non-revolutionary" draft had now "happily passed into oblivion."

At this juncture, only a day before Kennedy's small party was set to embark for Africa, Bobby called Dick, seeking his help on the speech. Somehow, Walinsky recalled, Dick managed to produce a dazzling improvement overnight. "It was brilliant, the best stuff he [Dick] ever did." Walinsky stitched together the final draft; but in his oral history for the JFK Library, he graciously acknowledged that all the "really brilliant rhetoric"—the language suggesting the impact young people can make when they stand up for justice—"came from Dick."

When I asked Dick to explain how he had done it with such speed and polish he only said, "It's funny. I worked one night and there it was. It's like a song. You can work on something for weeks and months. Nothing happens. Then one morning you take a shower and it all comes together before you can dry off."

En route to South Africa, Kennedy stopped in London where he saw his good friend, the Pulitzer Prize–winning *New York Times* reporter Anthony Lewis, who had covered the Justice Department when Kennedy was attorney general and then headed the *Times*'s London bureau. Because his bureau reported on South Africa, Lewis was able to brief Kennedy about the complexities of the situation he was about to encounter.

I had known Tony Lewis even before I met Dick. We had traveled together as part of a delegation to Russia in 1973 when I was in graduate school. Later, when Tony married South African native Margaret Marshall, Dick and I saw them together a number of times at dinner parties and events. All those years, neither Dick nor I ever made the connection between Robert Kennedy and Margaret Marshall, who, I only discovered a short time ago, had played a central role in Kennedy's visit.

It would have heartened Dick to learn—as I did through a long conversation I recently had with Margaret, now the retired chief justice of the Massachusetts Supreme Judicial Court (the first naturalized American citizen to serve on that historic court), that Dick's words had left a permanent impact on both Margaret and her late husband, Tony Lewis.

Back in 1966, Margaret was the twenty-year-old vice president of the National Union of South African Students. Just prior to Kennedy's arrival, the government retaliated against the student organization by "banning" its president, Ian Robertson, confining him to his house for a period of five years and prohibiting him from engaging in politics—even from talking to more than one person at a time. As Robertson's surrogate, Marshall greeted Kennedy at the airport and accompanied him throughout his visit.

"Robertson's banning terrified me," Marshall admitted. It also seemed to unnerve Kennedy. "He kept asking, 'Is this going to hurt anyone? I can do this, but is anyone going to pay the price for me?'" He worried that even his presence might put Marshall and other NUSAS leaders at risk. Although she sought to put Kennedy at ease, she had good reason to fear a knock on the door in the middle of the night. She was well aware that if the government banned or arrested her, no court of law would protect her from losing her freedom, her place in college, her passport.

More than fifteen hundred people of all races had gathered at the airport for Kennedy's arrival. Cries of "Yankee go home" and "Chuck him out" shrieked from a few hecklers until cheers and enthusiastic screams drowned out any abuse. Over a thousand students packed the auditorium at the University of Cape Town. Hundreds more milled around outside enduring the cold winter night to listen to the speech through loudspeakers. Even after South African security forces cut the wires to silence the transmission, the students remained huddled together outside the auditorium for the next three hours, waiting for their fellow students and Robert Kennedy to emerge.

Inside, anticipation and anxiety filled the room as Kennedy stepped to the podium. Dozens of uniformed and nonuniformed South African security police were present to intimidate the students, take photographs and record what they said to use against them later. Despite the threatening atmosphere, Kennedy began his speech with a passage that seemed to refer directly to South Africa's troubled history.

I come here this evening because of my deep interest and affection for a land settled by the Dutch in the mid-seventeenth century, then taken over by the British, and at last independent; a land in which the native inhabitants were at first subdued, but relations with whom remain a problem to this day; . . . a land which has tamed rich natural resources through the energetic application of modern technology; a land which was once the importer of slaves, and now must struggle to wipe out the last traces of that former bondage.

Marshall was seated on the stage behind the podium. An empty chair symbolized the absence of Ian Robertson. "There was great tension in the room at that point," she told me. "People were on edge." And then Kennedy said:

I refer, of course, to the United States of America.

"As soon as the audience realized what he said," Marshall recalled, "there was laughter and a sense of total relief. It was simply fabulous."

Kennedy's voice gained in strength as he reached the core of the speech, his challenge to the young people to battle the "danger of futility, the belief there is nothing one man or woman can do against the enormous array of the world's ills."

To refute this sense of despair, Dick cited his old philosopher muse, Archimedes, "Give me a place to stand, and I will move the world":

Few will have the greatness to bend history, but each of us can work to change a small portion of the events, and in the total of all these acts will be written the history of this generation. Thousands of Peace Corps volunteers are making a difference in the isolated villages and the city slums of dozens of countries. Thousands of unknown men and women in Europe resisted the occupation of the Nazis and many died, but all added to the ultimate strength and freedom of their countries. It is from numberless diverse acts of courage such as these that human history is thus shaped.

Each time a man stands up for an ideal, or acts to improve the lot of others, or strikes out against injustice, he sends forth a tiny ripple of hope, and crossing each other from a million different centers of energy and daring, those ripples build a current which can sweep down the mightiest walls of oppression and resistance. . . .

So we part, I to my country and you to remain. We are—if a man of forty can claim the privilege—fellow members of the world's largest younger generation. Each of us have our own work to do. I know at times you must feel very alone with your problems and your difficulties. But I want to say how impressed I am with what you stand for and for the effort you are making; and I say this not just for myself, but for men and women all over the world.

There was an unnerving moment of silence after the speech was done. Marshall remembered how Kennedy glanced back to those sitting on the platform, "as if to say, was the speech okay?" But then a rushing sound of overwhelming applause rose from the audience, followed by a lengthy standing ovation. The words had hit a communal nerve.

During the previous months, Marshall and her fellow students had wondered if all their marches and demonstrations against the apartheid government were in vain. The oppressive power of the government had reached a frightening stage. Civil rights had been decimated, there was no protection against arrest, torture, and jail. Once imprisoned, there was no access to lawyers. Leading opponents of apartheid, including Nelson Mandela, had been convicted of treason and sentenced to prison for life. Opposition parties were outlawed. Books were banned. Television was forbidden. "It was as if a heavy boot had come down and smashed everything," Marshall told me.

Robert Kennedy's words, Marshall said, had suddenly "reminded us— me—that we were not alone. That we were part of a great noble tradition, the reaffirmation of nobility in every human person. . . . He put us back into the great sweep of history. Even if it's just a tiny thing, it will add up. He reset the moral compass, not so much by attacking apartheid, but simply by talking about justice and freedom and dignity—words that none of us had heard, it seemed, in an eternity."

The South African novelist Alan Paton, author of *Cry, the Beloved Country*, which had been banned in his native land, remarked that Kennedy's visit was no ordinary moment, it was momentous: "Kennedy was like a fresh wind from the outer world," reassuring us that "independence of thought is not a curse, that to work for change is not a species of treachery.... It was to feel part of the world again."

As Kennedy traveled around the country in the days that followed, something extraordinary happened. While initially students had comprised the large majority of his crowds, now thousands of others flooded the streets—cheering him, shouting encouragement, reaching out to touch him.

A speech in the right place and at the right time, in this instance beginning with the reflecting mirrors of American and South African histories, had resulted in an explosive demonstration that words, like individuals, can make a difference. Words are flammable.

For Margaret Marshall, the fire that started that winter night in South Africa has continued to burn throughout her life. When she came to America to get a master's degree in education and a law degree at Yale, she became involved in the antiwar movement, the women's movement, and the fight to impose sanctions against South Africa until apartheid was lifted.

Once she became a United States citizen, the apartheid government denied Marshall a visa to return home to South Africa. In America, her adopted country, she would become Harvard's general counsel and vice president before being selected as the first woman to be named chief justice of the Massachusetts Supreme Judicial Court.

In 1984, when she married Anthony Lewis, she told me that they had incorporated the entire "ripples of hope" passage into their wedding ceremony. In 1996, Marshall was able to hear Kennedy's voice actually delivering the Cape Town speech—for the first time since she was twenty: "I did not even know there had been a recording," she said to me. "Someone, an admirer of Kennedy's, had sent it to me. I listened to it on my way to work. It had such an impact on me that I had to pull over to the side of Memorial Drive. There were tears coming down my face."

As chief justice in 2003, Judge Margaret Marshall authored the ruling (*Goodridge v. Department of Public Health*) that made Massachusetts the first state in the country to legalize gay marriage. When asked how growing up in South Africa had affected her groundbreaking decision, she told me, "At the time I was not at all conscious of any connection between my decision and my South African roots. Later, when asked about it, I thought: If you grow up like I did under a government, which I had fought against, saying with no evidence that Black South Africans cannot be educated or become engineers or doctors or—fill-in-the-blank—while in *Goodridge* the state is arguing without evidence that gay couples cannot be good parents, will harm children or whatever, in retrospect I did not think that would survive scrutiny, especially where my court had previously authorized gay couples to adopt children."

As I read over and over this South Africa speech and a half dozen others Dick had helped to craft that had also become historical markers, it became freshly evident that for Dick, words *were* actions. He often downplayed the importance of the words he had written. After all, he would repeatedly say, the impact of any speech depends on the right place and the time in which it is delivered. If this were the case, he seems to have been in that right place and time with uncommon frequency. And he delivered something different and deeper than mere skillful rhetoric. Kennedy's words on South Africa's Day of Affirmation speech were drafted by a young man who himself stood up for ideals and struck out against injustice, sending forth ripples of hope that would change lives in future times and places.

SEPTEMBER 17, 1966

"I felt like I was walking the plank from Lyndon's ship of state," Dick said to me as he remembered preparing his first public statement against the war to be delivered before the board of the Americans for Democratic Action (ADA) in September. He knew that once he spoke out against Vietnam there was no return.

All summer long, as every conversation centered on Vietnam, Dick had wrestled with exactly what to say about a war that seemed increasingly out of control. The number of American troops had increased from 23,000 at the end of 1963 to 350,000 by July of 1966.

Dick now deemed an earlier piece on Vietnam he had written for *The New Yorker* far too timid. Then, he had not doubted "Lyndon Johnson's desire to end the war" with some kind of political settlement. Now, both he and Arthur Schlesinger had become convinced that Johnson had "turned a corner toward the systematic enlargement of the war." The two good friends feared that the president had embraced Secretary of State Dean Rusk's domino theory, namely that "if we don't hold the line in Vietnam, we are condemned to 'wars of national liberation' all through the underdeveloped world."

Things had now reached such a dire impasse that summer leisure seemed untenable. "It would be terrible," Dick said to Schlesinger with hyperbolical flair, "if when the nuclear bombs begin dropping on Peking or Washington, we had to reflect that all we did in the summer of 1966 was to rest comfortably on one or another beach."

At dinner with Bobby Kennedy in late July, Dick and Arthur aired their decision to speak out against the escalation—Dick at the ADA, Arthur in a long piece for *The New York Times Magazine*.

"What's your plan of action?" Bobby inquired of Dick.

"The only thing likely to reach Johnson," Dick replied, "is vigorous political opposition." He described their plan to bring together a national coalition of prominent citizens opposed to the continued escalation. He proposed using LBJ's 1964 campaign slogan, "No Wider War," as a common ground of agreement. They hoped to line up former generals, university presidents, scientists, and former cabinet officials known to have questioned the conduct of the war. They were intending to reach former Generals James Gavin and Matthew Ridgway, along with former treasury secretary Douglas Dillon, though Dick told Bobby he feared Dillon, given his hope of becoming secretary of state, might be hesitant to speak publicly.

"That's wrong," Bobby pushed back at once. "Dillon will do what he thinks is right. He's my friend." Dick immediately understood, as he confided in his diary, that with Bobby, "the integrity of friends, especially those who served John Kennedy, was not to be doubted."

"Well, Senator, what are *you* going to do about it?" Dick asked his friend, hoping to find some solid ground. "What's *your* plan of action?"

Bobby grinned and with a self-mocking jab said, "Why, I'm going to make speeches. That's what a Senator does. I might even write a book. That'll show them."

Responding to the suggestion of a coalition against escalation, Bobby argued that a successful movement had to be tied to a leader, not simply a concept. There he stopped short. He was not ready to consider a presidential bid in 1968, despite the fact that recent polls showed that he was "running well ahead of LBJ both in voter preference among Democrats and as matched against various Republican possibilities."

Dick and Bobby continued to talk and drink at Bobby's New York apartment until 2:30 a.m. "We discussed all the great opportunities that were going down the drain," Dick recorded in his diary, "the hunger of the people for leadership, that this was a critical moment in the life of the country."

The task of pulling together an influential group, a consensus in search of a committed leader, was the context within which Dick prepared to address the Americans for Democratic Action on September 17.

Recalling his nervous tension, Dick told me: "I had always had a persona, a mask. I was accustomed to speaking for or through someone. This time it was me, my own skin in the game. Not that my own skin in the grand scheme of things was so important, but I had been at the core of Lyndon Johnson's administration and now I was trying to stake out a place against his administration's increasing militancy in Vietnam."

We each read the ADA speech separately and Dick surprised me with a critical shake of the head.

"Not much of a speech," he muttered with dissatisfaction. "Pretty restrained."

"Even though the ADA endorsed your proposal for a national coalition against widening the war and offered resources to help?" I asked.

"All and all, a pretty modest proposal," he insisted.

"From hindsight," I told Dick after leafing through a sheaf of newspaper articles, it sure made an impact at the time. *The New York Times* headlined "Ex-Johnson Aide Assails Vietnam War Policies." A widely syndicated columnist called the speech "the most sweeping and explicit critique of the present role in Vietnam by a former member of both the Kennedy and Johnson White House teams."

"A former ghostwriter has come back to haunt President Johnson," *Washington Post* columnist Mary McGrory wrote. "Goodwin, who put thousands of words into Mr. Johnson's mouth, has now turned his rhetoric against his former boss." He has made, she observed, "a devastating case against the effectiveness of bombing the North." Most tellingly, he had charged the administration with "deliberate lies and distortions" in describing the progress of the war. As an example, he presented a caustic bit of arithmetic. "If we take the numbers of enemy we are supposed to be killing, add to that the defectors, along with the number of wounded . . . we find we are wiping out the entire Vietnamese force every year. This truly makes their continued resistance one of the marvels of the world. Unless the numbers are wrong, which of course they are."

In closing, he said:

Some have called upon us to mute or stifle dissent in the name of patriotism and the national interest. It is an argument which monstrously misconceives the nature and process and the greatest strength of American democracy. . . . It is not our privilege but our duty as patriots, to write, to speak, to organize, to oppose any President and any party and any policy at any time which we believe threatens the grandeur of this nation and the well-being of its people. This is such a time.

If Dick's assessment that it was not a particularly distinguished speech was accurate, it was nonetheless a gigantic stride in his personal dissent. No immediate response was forthcoming from the White House, but Dick knew his bridges to the administration had been burned.

"I did not feel elated," Dick later wrote. "Liberated perhaps, but sad—at the loss of a relationship that had meant so much, at the knowledge that what I thought an act of integrity would, for a very long time, cause others to suspect that my convictions were shaped by personal expediency. But it was done. And rightly done." Dick only regretted he had not called for more extreme measures.

"Of course, that was unforgivable to Johnson," I said to Dick after reading newspaper accounts and interviews. "You were the first from the inside to speak out on Vietnam. He felt betrayed."

When a reporter asked the president directly about Dick's address to the ADA, Johnson evaded the question with acerbic humor: "It's like being bitten by your own dog."

———•———

During a halcyon moment between them only a year earlier, Dick had sent Johnson a memo suggesting a writing project to document the Great Society's achievements:

"Mr. President," Dick had written: "I think it would be a good idea to publish a book containing your speeches and messages since assuming the presidency." An initial book, Dick suggested, would cover the first two years, after that they could put out a book every year.

"We could get someone to edit the book, and perhaps a distinguished historian to do an introduction. I have talked to the people from McGraw-Hill who are doing your mother's book. They would be delighted to do this.

"Shall I go ahead?"

Johnson boldly checked "YES" and directed Dick to contact Abe Fortas to assign royalties to the LBJ Foundation.

Dick had not only arranged the contract for publication and selected the public statements to best represent the Great Society's scope and impact, but, at Johnson's bidding, had written the introduction and subsequently reviewed the galleys for the entire book project.

Now, in the aftermath of Dick's public break on Vietnam, the publisher quietly received a request from the White House to remove Dick's name not only from the introduction but from the book as a whole. It was no longer tenable for the president, after what he considered an act of disloyalty, to allow Dick's name to be associated with the achievements of the Great Society.

Because Dick had edited the book and written both the introduction and commentary, the publishers felt they had no choice but to refuse the White House request. Johnson thereby withdrew the book, repaying all advances and costs.

The whole episode saddened me. I understood why Johnson was so upset with Dick. His former White House aide had, after all, accused the administration of deliberate lies and deceptions. But to whom did Dick owe loyalty? Behind the charge of disloyalty, Dick later wrote in an essay, "The Duty of Loyalty," was "the assumption that a man who has worked for a president owes continuing loyalty to his policies; that once having served a president, a man is barred from expressing his views on public issues unless he happens to agree with the administration." The loyalty that was paramount to Dick was of a different kind. It was not to Johnson or his administration but to America and what he felt was in the best interest of the country. And the war was casting a long shadow over the growth of the domestic agenda that both he and the president had cherished most of all.

One Saturday morning while I continued sorting through the files containing letters and documents from 1966, Dick sat engrossed reading Cicero's treatise on friendship. It was his habit to launch into off-the-wall explanations on philosophy, botany, physics, or whatever caught the fancy of this perpetual and eclectic reader. "How would you describe the taste of this?" he'd ask me at dinner, "the smell of that? Is the language of taste better or worse than the language of smell?"

The dialogue in his mind on this morning was Cicero's comparison of various types of friends: useful friends with whom we have transactional relations, amusing friends with whom we share pleasure and games, and those rare friends that Cicero calls "another self" with whom we share soul secrets and deepest feelings. After describing these categories of friendship, Dick put Cicero's dog-eared treatise in his lap and said, "You know, I bet twenty times I heard President Kennedy use the aphorism 'in politics there are no friends, only allies.'" Suddenly he began to grunt softly, as if some thought was troubling him before pronouncing, "He was wrong about that."

He followed this pronouncement with a reminiscence of his shared friendship with Bill Moyers, a brotherly bond formed during their long days and nights in the White House when their teamwork provided inspiration, humor, and counsel during the formation of the Great Society. If Dick's devotion to John Kennedy verged on hero worship, they shared neither leisure nor social time. With Lyndon there were many occasions of celebration and liquor, but sustained leisure or recreation was hardly to be found anywhere in Lyndon's life. Nonetheless, if not friends, they were historically effective allies and shared the deepest of convictions. Never before or after had Dick met such a fearsome force who inspired such awe and wonder. By contrast, once Dick was out of government, he had developed friendships with Bobby and Jackie Kennedy that provided advice, companionship, emotional support, and reciprocated trust.

Our rambling dialogue about friendship quickened when, carefully preserved in Dick's archive, we found a striking, oversized letter from Jackie Kennedy that suggested the nature of the friendship between them. I gently unfolded the sheet of rice paper, its left hand border displaying a hand-painted stalk of bamboo in black ink, postmarked July 13, 1966, from Hawaii.

Dear Dick,

I am writing you on rice paper from my Chinese brush lessons – as you can see I am not doing too well on bamboo leaves –

I'm glad you wrote – I have had so many thoughts out here – like Chinese painting – it's better not to put them all in words –

It took a long time to unwind – & then in the mindless beautiful days you find you can enjoy just simple things – I read about so many people who found peace out here – they were all rather complicated souls – Robert Louis Stevenson – Jack London – Mark Twain – & Gauguin – I've read all their memoirs and stumbled upon Alan Moorehead's book –

The hardest thing for civilized people to do I guess is just be peaceful & fill

their days with so little – though you think so much – Once you get that way –
you don't want to go back to the other –

There have been 3 places in the last year I thought I'd like to stay –
Argentina, Spain & here – and it's because each offered a new life & new
thoughts – a new civilization to learn about – & nature to lose yourself
in – Now I know that that's what I must do – & I hope I will figure out how
eventually – as I'm just not strong enough to go back into the old world –
with memories that drag you down into a life that can never be the same – &
you struggle against the despair – & lose the battle bit by bit – & then you
go away and recoup and start again – I've given up smoking here – which
means you give up drinking too – as it makes you want to smoke – I go to bed
so early – I want to stay like that – Maybe it's cowardly to decide what I've
decided –

I read the Greek way here to counteract all the Eastern bit – & Greeks
would face life – & Orientals when life is unbearable – just avoid it – which
isn't a bad idea – You are the only person I even want to tell that to – as you are
kind of a lost soul too & I know what you mean about Vietnam & everything –
I think you must do what you are going to do – & thank God there is Bobby.

What struck me most powerfully about Jackie's letter was the candor
and emotional vulnerability of the phrase: "you are the only person I even
want to tell that to – as you are kind of a lost soul too." It was no coincidence
that at the same time Jackie spoke of her enervating struggle against despair
and her efforts to rebound, Dick felt he was losing ground in his own search
to find balance in a time of transition, to establish his own voice as a writer.

Though he had a writing fellowship at Wesleyan during the year and
spent his summers among other writers on Martha's Vineyard, he still had
not found the internal discipline or the personal tranquility to make progress on the ambitious work he had in mind. In addition to procrastination,
he was drinking far too much as he confided to his oldest friend, George
Cuomo, that same summer of 1966.

I am in the middle of a literary colony here. On my right is Lillian Hellman.
Philip Rahv is in the adjoining house to the left and Bill Styron is three houses
down. Philip Roth lives down the road along with Robert Brustein. And other
writers keep floating through. The effect is opposite of what you can expect. Writ-
ing is discouraged. There is so much 4 a.m. drinking that it is almost impossible
to get anything done at all.

A diary entry after a sailing trip with friends revealed that he struggled with a far deeper sense of despondency and dread.

It is funny you think about the possibility of drowning, or the boat sinking and look out at the lovely sunny day—quiet and green in beauty—and think there are no auguries of disaster. No way to tell if in a day or two all will be different and you will be struggling in the ocean. There is no real warning of disaster anywhere, anytime. It just comes out of sunlight to darkness. But I am recurrently stricken with morbid thoughts.

In the fall of 1966, Dick's friendship with both Jackie and Bobby led to a prolonged and scathing episode wherein all three were drawn into a public controversy that erupted over the impending publication of biographer William Manchester's book on John Kennedy's assassination—a book the Kennedys themselves had authorized him to write.

The contract Manchester had signed four months after President Kennedy's death stipulated that "the final text shall not be published unless and until approved" by Jacqueline and Robert Kennedy. Jackie allowed Manchester two five-hour interviews. Bobby also sat down with the author and asked dozens of Kennedy family members and colleagues to make themselves available. Two years later, when Manchester submitted his manuscript to Bobby and Jackie, neither were able to bring themselves to read it. They knew the book would trigger gruesome memories. In their stead, the task of approval was relegated to two longtime Kennedy aides, Ed Guthman and John Seigenthaler.

Dick had also looked over the manuscript that spring, not as a surrogate for the Kennedys, but as an acquaintance and colleague of Manchester's at Wesleyan. A "masterful achievement," Dick blithely told his neighbor, suggesting he change the title from *The Death of Lancer* (JFK's Secret Service code name) to *The Death of a President*. Manchester was delighted with Dick's opinion and the new title for the book.

Guthman and Seigenthaler recommended more than a hundred changes, mostly to soften the relentlessly demeaning portrait of LBJ and to delete some of the intimate details Jackie had revealed in confidence to the author. Manchester accepted most of these changes, and in July received a telegram from Robert Kennedy that while he had not read the book, "the members of the Kennedy family will place no obstacle in the way of publication of his work." If serial rights were sold, he importantly added, he "would expect that the incidents would not be taken out of context or summarized in any way which might distort the facts or the events."

Manchester's publisher, Harper & Row, then felt free to send out copies of the manuscript to magazines for serialization. A bidding war resulted in *Look*'s offer at $665,000 (equivalent to over $6 million today) for seven installments—the largest amount ever paid at that time for serial rights. When Bobby delivered this news to Jackie, who had just returned from Hawaii, she was sent reeling in panic. "I thought that it would be bound in black and put away on dark library shelves," she later said. The frenzy surrounding the serial rights horrified her; she realized that each installment would provide fodder for major news stories, forcing her to confront anew, day after day, the assassination she was desperately trying to survive.

She wanted it all to vanish: the magazine rights, even the book itself. That wish could not be granted unless she sued to stop publication. Bobby initially agreed, although he realized that a lawsuit would bring on a public circus. Far better, he eventually decided, would be the removal of the most troublesome passages; if unsuccessful, they could "issue a statement vigorously disclaiming the book."

It was at this impasse in the story that Dick officially entered the morass. The Kennedys appointed him their "literary broker" to negotiate further changes with Manchester. "It made sense," Manchester later wrote. "His Middletown home and mine were a short walk from one another. Jackie trusted him. His dedication to Bobby's ambitions for national office was absolute."

"At the outset of his fracas with Jacqueline Kennedy," Garry Wills would later write, "William Manchester could not decide whether Goodwin was on his side or hers."

"I wish I had never gotten involved," Dick admitted to me. "My friendship with Jackie, her acute distress, impaired my judgment." As a neighbor and fellow writer, he wanted to be fair to Manchester. He fully understood that the removal of a string of words here, a sentence there, could jeopardize the whole thing. "Like that game with hardwood blocks where you remove one block at a time," he said emphatically, "the unstable tower trembles and can tumble down." But Jackie was his major concern.

Look reluctantly agreed to reduce the seven installments to four and to delay the publication date until January to allow sufficient time for Dick and Manchester to make revisions. "However," Dick acknowledged in his diary, "we are trapped." The contract Manchester had signed with *Look* gave him no rights to make additional changes unless the magazine agreed, and they were "refusing to budge" on many of the attempted revisions.

The same two issues Seigenthaler and Guthman had dealt with in the lengthy manuscript—the mean-spirited comments concerning LBJ and the private revelations Jackie had let slip—were magnified in the short installments, where every offending sentence stuck out more clearly, a danger Bobby's original telegram had foreseen in the matter of serial rights when an excerpt in isolation could change the proportion and substance of the whole. Dick described the dilemma in his diary.

We would like to remove those things which are enormously intimate about Jackie and are in bad taste. She talked to Manchester at great length after the assassination in that period when talking was a great form of therapy, telling everything, including intimate details of their life together—the Modern Screen stuff.

The other things we would have liked to get out are the many episodes, comments, quotes etc. which reflect on Johnson. I don't think anyone will be helped by these, for it also creates the impression that the Kennedy people were down on LBJ from the very beginning, never giving him a chance to assume the Presidency properly without their instant enmity.

We have given up on the political things—they will come out and be damaging—but will try everything to get the stuff harmful to Jackie, a violation of her privacy, out of the manuscript.

By early December, Dick had succeeded in securing the agreement of both Manchester and *Look* to delete a significant number of passages containing indiscreet details Jackie had provided. Manchester believed he had done all he could without shredding his manuscript. The publishers of both Harper & Row and *Look* sent letters to Jackie informing her that they realized she might not be "entirely happy with all the particulars" but they had "gone the limit to try to be fair and thoughtful of everyone's feelings and yet consistent with accuracy." They had therefore determined to proceed with publication.

When Jackie read these letters, she phoned her longtime lawyer, Sy Rifkin, and instructed him to sue. Bobby refused to join the suit, believing it "a terrible mistake." In public, however, he would support Jackie without reservation.

I asked Dick if he had tried to change her mind. "No," he said, "her mind was made up. She was in terrible shape. With Bobby pulling away, she felt abandoned. For her sake, I had no choice but to support her suit."

The suit, as Bobby had predicted, became the talk of the country. Most editorials roundly criticized Jackie's decision to sue. "History belongs to everyone, not just to the participants," *The New York Times* editorialized; "having made her original decision she cannot now escape its consequences." Television crews camped out on the sidewalk in front of Manchester's house. Stress landed the beleaguered Manchester in the hospital with a serious case of pneumonia.

Public opinion turned against both Bobby and Jackie. A Harris poll found that one person in five "thought less" of Bobby as a result of the controversy, while one in three "thought less" of Jackie. The whole tawdry business had delivered the first public bruise on Jackie's reputation.

If anyone acted well in the wake of this debacle, it was Lyndon Johnson, the recipient of a consistently obtuse and boorish portrayal in Manchester's book. Much of that scorn was attributed to comments from Jackie. At Lady Bird's sage prompting, Lyndon personally hand wrote Jackie a preemptive note. "Lady Bird and I have been distressed to read the press accounts of your unhappiness about the Manchester book. Some of these accounts attribute your concern to passages in the book which are critical or defamatory of us. If this is so, I want you to know while we deeply appreciate your characteristic kindness and sensitivity, we hope you will not subject yourself to any discomfort or distress on our account. One never becomes inured to slander but we have learned to live with it. In any event, your own tranquility is important to us, and we would not want you to endure any unpleasantness on our account."

Settlement talks commenced shortly after the suit was announced. *Look* agreed to delete an additional 1,600 words from the installments, consisting of seven pages from the book. All the taped interviews Manchester had made with Jackie would be locked under seal in the Kennedy Library until 2067. The suit was dropped. "JACKIE WINNER IN BOOK BATTLE," *Newsday* announced in bold letters. "Magazine Agrees to Changes Say Book Publisher." An editorial in the London *Daily Express* suggested: "We are not now dealing with the whispering baby-voiced mincing shy wife devoting herself to culture but to a steel-minded woman willing to risk exposing herself to a fabulous court battle in order to preserve her domestic secrets."

In actuality, it seemed like anything but victory to Jackie. During the magazine bidding war, copies of the original July manuscript had been circulated. Passages that Dick and Manchester had worked hard together to redact had inevitably trickled their way into the press, magnifying the attention paid them.

"I am sick at the unhappiness this whole terrible thing has caused everyone," Jackie responded to President Johnson's tender letter. "Whatever I did could only cause pain," she wrote, "I am so dazed now I feel I will never be able to feel anything again."

Even in Antigua, where Jackie had gone to escape after Christmas, the scandal pursued her, giving rise to a second letter to Johnson. She had read in an article that the Manchester book claimed she objected to the president calling her "honey."

"All the rage that I have been trying to suppress and forget down here boiled up again." She noted that only a good friend would call her "honey" and that she hoped he would call her that again. She was writing simply to express "the fondness I will always feel for you—no matter what happens, no matter how your feelings may change towards me. Once I decide I care about someone—nothing can ever make me change."

The whole episode left Dick with such unpleasant memories he cringed to recall them. Friendship and loyalty had aligned him with Jackie, but he had failed to protect her by not pushing back on her decision to sue. And he would always regret the role he had played as "literary broker," pressuring Manchester, on behalf of the Kennedys to delete words, sentences, and entire passages from his manuscript. He had allowed himself to be caught in a crossfire, a figure who, as Garry Wills had noted, endeavored to serve both sides at once.

Despite, or perhaps because of, this controversy, the book was a sensation. The first installment sold more than four thousand copies in Times Square alone in a matter of hours. In hardcover, *The Death of a President* sold more than a million copies within the first twelve months. Manchester's royalties after the first printing were contractually obligated to the Kennedy Library. When the publisher's check for $750,000 was received after that first year, Manchester became, ironically, donor-in-chief to the JFK Library.

JANUARY 1967

Where to stand? What to do? By the start of 1967, debate and discord over Vietnam rumbled through families and generations, town halls, schools and colleges, churches and synagogues. The issue of deciding what to do and where to stand on a war that had become firmly and forever an American war had reached a critical point.

We were no longer simply supporting South Vietnam. The United States was waging an escalating war against North Vietnam. American troops deployed to Vietnam now numbered 435,000. America had dropped more bombs on North Vietnam than it had dropped on Japan during World War II or during the entire Korean War. In spite of this, there was no evidence that the bombing had diminished North Vietnam's capacity to carry on the war.

At home, the war continued to drain momentum from the Great Society. In the November midterms, the Democrats had lost forty-seven seats in the House, more than they had gained from Johnson's 1964 landslide. Johnson's drive to pass a third major civil rights law—to outlaw discrimination in the rental and sale of housing—had been thwarted by a Senate filibuster. The vote was not even close. Efforts to expand funding for his war on poverty had been defeated. People's attention and inclination had turned away from the progressive accomplishments of the past two years.

Since burning bridges with the administration at the ADA meeting the previous September, Dick had sharpened his criticisms of the war, which he then considered "the single most costly error in the history of American foreign policy." In a combination of speeches and articles, he began to hammer away at "a government which feels little obligation to tell the truth to our country, always ready to change the facts in order to suit the needs and politics of the moment," a government which has let loose an "outpouring of deception so torrential it has almost numbed our capacity to separate truth from falsehood, reality from wishful thinking."

In his "The Duty of Loyalty" essay, he acknowledged that "one does not lightly attack the policies of a president, who, as in my own case, offered a magnificent chance for significant public service. To do so is not only damaging, raising the question of the dissenter's trustworthiness in the minds of other men, but personally difficult and disturbing. It is, however, President Johnson's misfortune and ours that the Vietnamese war is precisely the kind of issue which compels such a choice."

While Dick refrained from publicly narrowing his attack against Johnson himself, his anger at the president mounted, fueled by his sorrow over the withering Great Society program that he had helped to launch. In private conversations, he attacked Johnson's character with increasing ferocity, at times reducing the president to a caricature. In Dick's estimation, the immensely complicated man he had worked with day after day receded as the war raged on. Dick worried in his diary during the fall of 1966 that "the country is now in the most dangerous hands of its history."

Dick began to visualize the necessity of a political future without Lyndon Johnson. In that same diary entry, he had already predicted that LBJ could be defeated in 1968. "The greatest issue against him is not the war or inflation—but simply that people no longer trust him, nor do they like him. He can never come back from this. I have briefly mentioned 1968 to Bob [RFK]. He is reluctant to mention it, but we agreed, he silently, that there was nothing he could do about it now except what he was doing—so best sit tight and wait. It means a real party revolt, and the seeds are there."

The content of the boxes of articles and speeches on Vietnam from 1967 reflected the ascending tension and acrimony that pervaded the atmosphere that year. One exception was an interview with Dick that made us both burst out laughing. Citing an article in the London *Observer*, the interviewer suggested that Dick was a central figure in a secret conspiracy to discredit Johnson's policies in Vietnam. The London paper had identified his co-conspirators as Arthur Schlesinger and John Kenneth Galbraith. His evidence: All three "full-fledged members" of a "government in exile," were seen having lunch together in a quiet restaurant in Manhattan. Arthur denied the conspiracy in a letter to the editor, suggesting that sometimes a lunch is simply a lunch. "I don't think we'd be very good at plotting," Dick told the interviewer, "we all talk too much." And if they were part of a government in exile, Dick added, "it must be one of the most unobtrusive in history. It never makes any decisions and it has no power. If you mean that there are a lot of people who aren't running things that wish they were, I think that's true. But that's always been true."

Such buoyant sarcasm was hardly in evidence at a dinner party at Robert Kennedy's house, Hickory Hill. In normal times, rules of decorum and civility generally prevail at such occasions, but these times were hardly normal. Now the social gloves were off. In public and in private, members of the administration began to attack the motives, loyalty, and patriotism of those who dissented from their standard line.

"I was floored," Dick told me, "when Averell Harriman confronted me at Bobby's house."

"'You and Schlesinger are murderers,' he flatly accused me, 'you're killing American boys.'

"I tried to calmly explain to him that exactly the opposite was true. We were trying to stop the killing."

"You're just encouraging Hanoi," Harriman charged, his voice growing shrill. "All this protest just makes them think we're going to give up."

"In an earlier time," Dick told me with more seriousness than I am comfortable with, "I would have challenged him to a duel."

Dick was further enraged when Dean Rusk assailed "pseudo-intellectuals who had served under JFK and LBJ and are now in dissent over Vietnam." Words such as "traitor," "unpatriotic," and "disloyal" were bandied about. Dick had prepared his essay on loyalty to counter such charges. "Where to stand" had ceased to be an issue for Dick; exactly what to do and how to do it was now all that mattered:

"The government of the United States is not a private club or college fraternity. Its policies are not private oaths or company secrets. Presumably a man enters public life to serve the nation. The oath taken by every high officer of the nation, elected or appointed, is to support and defend the Constitution of the United States, not an Administration, a political party or a man.

"Dissenters are sometimes accused of demeaning the presidency. That office should demand respect. Its dignity, however, flows not from private right or title or the man who occupies it, but solely from the fact that its occupant is chosen by the people of the United States. It is their office, and if they, or any among them, feel that it is wrongly used, then it is their obligation to speak."

MARCH 2, 1967

For Senator Robert Kennedy, the answer to the question of where to stand on Vietnam was fraught with complications. "If another speech would do any good," he had told his friend *Village Voice* columnist Jack Newfield in

December 1966, "I would make it tomorrow. But the last time I spoke," referring here to the speech Dick had helped draft the previous February, "I didn't have any influence on policy, and I was hurt politically. I'm afraid by speaking out I just make Lyndon do the opposite."

As the bombing intensified and the discord on the home front deepened, however, Kennedy felt that America had reached "a critical turning point." He determined he had no choice but to take a risk and speak out. Several of his closest relatives and friends pleaded with him to remain silent, including his brother Senator Ted Kennedy, Ted Sorensen, and Bill vanden Heuvel. Their counsel was counterbalanced by young aides and allies Adam Walinsky and Jeff Greenfield, Al Lowenstein, Arthur Schlesinger, and Dick—who urged him to make a clear and decisive stand against the war.

Kennedy's announcement that he would make a major speech on the Senate floor on March 2 spurred a wave of anticipation across the country. While other senators had spoken out against the war, Kennedy was not only the second most powerful figure in the Democratic Party but was, without question, the figure who most bedeviled President Johnson. With assistance from Dick, Schlesinger, and Walinsky, the speech gradually took shape over several weeks in February. Kennedy would call for a bombing halt, followed by an announcement that America stood ready to start peace negotiations within the week—as well as an agreement with the communists that neither side would increase the scale of the war so long as negotiations were underway.

Bobby continued working on the speech with Dick and Adam until 3:30 a.m. on the day it was to be delivered. A Gallup poll had suggested that only 24 percent of the country favored a bombing halt. Bobby understood that very well and when he came down to breakfast, he told his tablemates that Teddy Kennedy had called to "make sure they announce it's the Kennedy from New York."

Before a packed chamber, the junior senator from New York rose to the floor and spoke, Newfield recalled "in a quiet, tense voice" from his allotted desk at the rear of the room. To head off accusations that Lyndon Johnson was the real target of his address, Kennedy pointed a finger in many directions, careful to shoulder his own share of responsibility. He acknowledged that three American presidents—Eisenhower, Kennedy, and Johnson— had taken action in Vietnam. "If fault is to be found or responsibility assessed, there is enough to go around for all, including myself," Kennedy said. At that time, this acknowledgment made him, according to *The Facts on File* almanac, "the only major official in either Democratic administration who admitted publicly to being wrong about Vietnam."

He then spoke to the "horror" of war, the night air saturated with bombs, "destroying yesterday's promise of family and land and home." The responsibility for this horror belongs to all of us, he said. "It is we who live in abundance and send our young men out to die. It is our chemicals that scorch the children and our bombs that level the villages. We are all participants."

Counterattacks in the press were immediate. As Kennedy had feared, the speech was largely construed within the context of his personal and political clash with Johnson. No sooner had he finished than a coordinated retaliation commenced: Senator Henry Jackson read a letter from the president, insisting that "the bombing had been effective and would continue." General William Westmoreland followed up, stressing that the bombing was "vital to the U.S. war effort and meant fewer American casualties." The commander of U.S. forces in Vietnam was unwilling, he said, to pay "one drop of blood" for any proposed bombing halt. Senator Everett Dirksen charged that Kennedy's peace proposal was already "undermining" our efforts to win the war. And from resurgent Republican candidate Richard Nixon came the cut-and-dried judgment that "Johnson is right and Kennedy is wrong." The speech, Nixon stated, "had the effect of prolonging the war by encouraging the enemy."

While the speech may have hurt Kennedy politically in the short run, it was a "watershed" moment, Jack Newfield said. "It emancipated Kennedy psychologically and intellectually about Vietnam."

"He had now become the leading voice in the antiwar movement," Dick recalled. "There was no turning back."

APRIL 15, 1967

The tidal pull of the great public questions that beset Dick and Bobby Kennedy about what to do about Vietnam had invaded the private lives of all of us at Harvard that spring. As a twenty-four-year-old graduate student working on my PhD thesis, I was a teaching fellow for courses on the American government and the American presidency. But in a real sense, the core curriculum for everyone during that time was the war.

I was learning from my students who were busy signing petitions, passing out leaflets, planning marches and demonstrations, analyzing "the System." If Dick had gone further than Bobby in expressing his convictions against both the war and LBJ, I was lagging behind them both. I was clearly against the war but not with the passion and conviction I had for the Civil Rights Movement or the domestic agenda of the Great Society. I still believed and hoped—as Dick and Kennedy no longer did—that Johnson was angling for a way to bring North Vietnam to the table and that outside pressure might hasten that goal.

Across the country, protests and demonstrations were beginning to converge into a full-blown antiwar movement. Teach-ins on the history and conduct of the war had spread from the University of Michigan to scores of college campuses, including Harvard. Fierce debates resounded on the morality of the war, the fairness of student deferments, enlistment, or resistance to the draft. Pressing choices lay ahead for my own students. One third of Harvard's graduating class, a poll revealed, would refuse to fight in Vietnam.

Dunster House, where I was a tutor, was alive with arguments and debates about the war, sometimes led by students, faculty members, or guest lecturers. One memorable night that spring, the liberal activist Al Lowenstein delivered a ringing antiwar speech, conversing with students for hours afterward. At the time I was only dimly aware that Lowenstein was organizing a "Dump Johnson" movement on college campuses and searching for someone to challenge Lyndon Johnson in the primaries. I can still see Lowenstein with his thick glasses and wrinkled suit sitting cross-legged on a carpet amidst a large gathering of graduate and undergraduate students at Dunster House, urging us to go to New York on April 15 to join the "Spring Mobilization March to End the War," which, he predicted, would be the largest antiwar march to date.

Afterward, I talked long into the night with my fellow graduate student and friend, Sanford "Sandy" Levinson, and we decided to travel down to the march together. Two years older than me, Sandy had been involved in the Civil Rights Movement from his early days at Duke, then an all-white institution. One of the founding members of the school's NAACP, Sandy had been a member of the student union committee that brought to Duke Morehouse College president Dr. Benjamin Mays, the first African American to speak at the university. In the summer of 1964 Sandy had joined Black and white activists who drove to Montgomery, Alabama, the day

President Johnson signed the civil rights law to be the first diners to integrate the Holiday Inn. He had been a staunch partisan of Lyndon Johnson's leadership on civil rights, but by 1967 had come to believe that the administration had turned a deaf ear to antiwar voices. The sheer number of protesters expected in New York, he hoped, would compel attention.

Early in the morning of April 15, we drove to New York together with Sandy's wife, Cynthia, a senior at Wellesley, and our friend Simeon Wade, a doctoral student in history. We had greatly anticipated hearing from the scheduled keynote speaker, Martin Luther King Jr., but his participation was now in doubt. Several days earlier, King had made his first major public statement against the war at New York's Riverside Church. All his senior advisers had counseled against it, considering any detour into foreign policy a disastrous mistake. But King insisted that the time had come to speak up: "My conscience leaves me no other choice," he declared at the opening of a searing indictment against the "madness" of a dishonorable war that was poisoning "the soul of America."

The speech had sparked "a firestorm of criticism" within the civil rights community. The NAACP Board of Directors passed a resolution denouncing King's "serious tactical mistake." *The Washington Post* noted "the irony that the Government which has labored the hardest to right these ancient wrongs, is the object of the most savage denunciation." Lyndon Johnson was reportedly "crushed."

Conversation on the way down to New York City was intense and nonstop. We discussed the war and politics, the collision of the Civil Rights Movement and the Antiwar Movement—the two great movements of the decade—friendship and loyalty and the meaning and direction of our lives.

As Lowenstein had predicted, this march was, indeed, the largest antiwar march on record. Upon reaching our destination near Central Park, I saw a vast mosaic of American life in the crowd of 125,000—mothers toting babies, girls with daffodils painted on their foreheads, boys wearing headbands and beads, Black Power advocates, a contingent of Native Americans from South Dakota, college students from the East Coast and Midwest with knapsacks and bedrolls, professors and graduate students, anarchists with black flags, Peace Corps volunteers.

Pete Seeger, along with Peter, Paul and Mary led us in a medley of folk songs. Banners implored us to "Make Love not War," others insisted "Don't Give a Damn for Uncle Sam." There was a raucous and unruly aspect that seemed like it might get out of hand. Seventy Cornell students burned their draft cards and released signed pledges to resist conscription. An American flag was burned. Construction workers hurled nails at marchers as they passed their site. Flour, eggs, and red paint were spilled from windows.

We were too far back to hear the speeches clearly but the next day we saw photographs and read accounts in the papers of King, Harry Belafonte, Stokely Carmichael, and Dr. Benjamin Spock marching arm-in-arm from Central Park to the speaker's platform at the United Nations Plaza. Speaking first, King's tone was no longer as strident as it had been a few days before in the speech that had put his position here in jeopardy. He had come, today, he said, to speak in sorrow, not in anger. He was wistful when he mentioned the Great Society and did not take direct aim at President Johnson. His softened rhetoric on this day called simply for a stop to the bombing. But the Riverside speech had already done its damage. The break between the two most powerful leaders of the decade was permanent. They would never see each other again.

Leaving New York, we were badly vexed by the increasing level of raw anger and violence we had witnessed throughout the day. "A few minutes of us on television," one antiwar protester lamented at an earlier march, "the rest of the country has redoubled its fervor to win with LBJ."

It was on the ride back to Cambridge that Sandy and I decided to collaborate on a statement suggesting some way "to convert into a meaningful political voice the wide base of support that was demonstrated at the march." We proposed the organization of a third party comprised of people not truly represented by the two major parties—students disaffected by the war, the urban poor, the marginal farmer, the unskilled laborer.

We argued that "it need not be posited that a third-party candidate would win." After all, the traditional role of third parties had been "to demonstrate a bloc of voters for whose support a major party must bid." How, we asked ourselves, could marches and protests impact policy? What is the most productive relationship between outside movements and the channels of inside power?

If the article was somewhat politically naïve, as Dick pointed out when we read it together four decades later, it was propelled by the same aspiration that Dick had expressed in his ADA speech—the longing to prod the political establishment to rein in the war. With Al Lowenstein's connections, we forwarded our piece to *The New Republic*. Then we waited.

During this waiting period, I learned I had been selected as a finalist for a fellowship program I had applied for the previous January. A nonpartisan program, the White House Fellows was designed to allow young people to work for a year as special assistants to the president and members of his cabinet. Each prospective fellow could identify two or three preferred departments, and matches would be made after the winners were chosen. If selected, I wished to be assigned to the Labor Department or the Department of Health, Education, and Welfare, some place I might play a role in the domestic agenda.

With great fanfare, thirty finalists were assembled for a weekend at a Virginia conference house where we would be interviewed by a commission of government officials, judges, and journalists. Finally, we returned together to an office in Washington where thirty envelopes were placed on a round table. About half of us, we were told, could be selected. I have no recollection at all of the moment I opened my envelope to discover that I was one of the sixteen chosen.

The following evening, we were invited to a festive White House reception to honor our selection. First off, we gathered in the Rose Garden for a photograph with the president, my first time in the presence of a president. We walked with Johnson into the East Room where he delivered remarks and introduced each of us to the crowd of invited guests. Cocktails and dinner followed. Music began to play and dancing commenced.

When it was my turn to dance with the president—he danced with all three women in our class of fellows—what I remember most clearly as he whirled me with surprising grace around the floor was that he hardly resembled the stilted figure I had glimpsed on television in recent months, eyes squinting, speaking solemnly about the war. This was not the face I had seen on incriminating posters in Harvard Yard and at antiwar demonstrations. His presence dominated the entire room filled with senators, representatives, cabinet members, White House staffers, and reporters.

"Do your men ever dance at Harvard?" he bantered. He never stopped talking the entire time we danced.

"Of course they do," I said.

"Bull," he said. "I know what goes on up there." If I, like so many of my generation, harbored the makings of a simplified caricature of him, he had similarly made one of me—as a "Harvard."

As my turn to dance with the voluble president ended, he said in a loud whisper that I would work directly for him in the White House.

Hardly a week passed before my first published article appeared in *The New Republic.* Suddenly, my excitement gave way to dread when I saw, atop the magazine cover, our article's title—selected by the magazine's editors:
"HOW TO REMOVE LBJ IN 1968."

Panic set in. I felt I had let down everyone on our newly chosen team of White House Fellows. Not only would I lose my place, I anxiously speculated, but I had cast a shadow on the entire program, jeopardizing it, perhaps destroying it.

I was not merely catastrophizing. Years later I learned of the trouble *The New Republic* article had stirred up among White House staffers. On May 8, a week after the White House ceremony, the president was flying back to Washington from Texas on Air Force One when an advance copy of the article was transmitted on the secure communications system used to relay time-sensitive documents. A young air force officer retrieved it from the printer, handing it off to assistant press secretary and former White House fellow Tom Johnson (a member of the program's original class). "You better be the one to give him this one," the young officer said.

"It was with great trepidation that I handed LBJ the printed copy of the article," Tom Johnson told me as we recently reviewed the whole incident together. "I thought this could be the demise of the Fellows program. Surprisingly, he read it quietly and said nothing."

According to the White House diarist, that night at 8:33 p.m., the president called Civil Service commissioner John Macy concerning "White House Fellow (just appointed) Doris Kearns whose article is coming out in the May 13 issue of *The New Republic.*" He wanted to see my FBI report.

Meanwhile, I received calls from several White House aides requesting that I elaborate on my version of events. I acquitted myself less than nobly. I stressed that the title chosen by the magazine—"How to Remove LBJ in 1968"—had given the piece an unintended sensational thrust. That was accurate. But I also tried to distance myself from the passages dealing with the 1968 election, claiming my contribution focused mainly on the need for a third party to represent disaffected voters. In truth, there was no division of responsibility in the writing of the article. Sandy and I had collaborated on the entire piece.

When giving talks on college campuses in recent years, I am often asked what advice my older self would give to my younger self. "Some things travel well over time," I would tell them, but if applied to this tempest and my disappointing response, I might add that I would warn my youthful self that shame and regret can sting, even after five decades.

In the course of writing about this episode I called Sandy, who is a professor of law at the University of Texas. I reached him at Harvard where he was spending the fall semester teaching a seminar on constitutional law. We went to dinner, and after catching up on our lives, I asked him how he had felt about my reaction a half century ago. He said his major worry as my friend was that I might lose the fellowship. When I told him of the guilt I had felt all these years, he said: "I am not authorized to grant absolution, but if I were, I would do so!"

While reading the White House diarist's notes during this period I further discovered that the situation was treated with urgent gravity, discussed by the president and the first lady, explored with close advisers, researched by investigative agencies and vetting interviews.

Four days after the president had first read the article, I was, embarrassingly, once again, under the microscope. At 10:20 p.m. on May 12, the presidential daily diarist recounts, the president was in the small lounge beside the Oval Office with Lady Bird, Senator Russell, and White House speechwriter Harry McPherson:

"He [LBJ] and Sen Russell were discussing Doris Kearns, and the President asked Mrs. Johnson to read her FBI [file]. After the President told Sen Russell the story of how she was selected etc., Mrs. Johnson returned the file to the President and the President said, 'I think she's been framed.' At this point the President was handed an item from tonight's reading from [special assistant] Douglass Cater giving Miss Kearns' accounting of how the matter came about. The President read this quietly and then handed it to Harry McPherson asking him to study both her explanation and the file."

Russell remained for dinner where the talk swerved to the grim topic of the expansion of bombing in Vietnam, politics, and finally a tirade against the press that flared and threatened to last past midnight when Senator Russell arose and announced, "Mr. President, it's midnight, and I have to go to bed because I'm an old man, and you have to go to bed because you're President of the United States."

After his full review of the files, Johnson determined that I should keep the fellowship and join my classmates in September. The White House then coordinated a simple and positive story. Tom Johnson told reporters that "Miss Kearns was selected on the basis of her ability and not on the basis of her political views." Even Alex Campbell, the managing editor of *The New Republic*, weighed in on the side of putting the episode to rest, commenting, "I certainly don't see what the story would have to do with her work in the White House."

Newspapers had a field day with the president's decision, with mocking headlines that read: "She Panned LBJ, Still Has a Job"; "LBJ Chooses Aide, She Maps His Defeat"; "Swinging Blonde LBJ Critic Wins Post."

In the end, however, the only word that mattered was LBJ's and he told his White House staff: "Bring her down here for a year, and if I can't win her over, no one can."

There was no more talk of my working directly for Johnson. Indeed, I was uncertain if any cabinet member would select me; but soon after the commotion died down, Secretary of Labor Willard Wirtz called me to Washington for an interview. Despite my melodramatic initiation to public service, I now had a chance to land at the Labor Department, the place I had most wanted to work from the beginning.

Beforehand, I read all I could find about Wirtz and his enormous career in labor history, which reached from World War II to the present. An outspoken liberal, he had been a key adviser, law partner, and chief speechwriter to Adlai Stevenson during both his presidential runs. As labor secretary under both JFK and LBJ, he was considered an unquestioned champion of the poor and the unemployed.

Walking into his office, I hardly knew what to expect, but within moments the tall, gentle, and droll figure with a graying crew cut escorted me into a small sitting area. He asked me why I wanted to work in government service, took his pipe from his pocket, and listened thoughtfully as I spoke of the March on Washington and Adlai Stevenson's speech on civil rights at my Colby College graduation. Referring to the civil rights freedom fighters, Stevenson had predicted that someday they might run for office on their prison records. Before the hour had passed, this man—steeped in law and in public oratory, a scholar of labor history and fighter for the workingman—took his pipe from his mouth. "Welcome," he smiled, "I would like you to be my White House fellow."

FALL 1967

When Dick and I had first met, he had questioned why I wanted to work in the Labor Department or anywhere else inside LBJ's administration. So fierce and sweeping was Dick's indignation toward LBJ that he believed the Great Society had simply vanished, that the war had assumed center stage in every bureau of every department. He was wrong, of course. Live currents of the Great Society clearly remained in the Labor Department and throughout the government, even as the funding for domestic programs had shrunk in the wake of increased military expenditures abroad.

And Secretary Wirtz turned out to be a powerful advocate for the Great Society and the best mentor a twenty-four-year-old could have. He gave me a series of challenging assignments and was always ready to answer my questions or offer advice.

No sooner had I begun the fellowship in September of 1967 than Wirtz put me to work overseeing skills training and remedial reading programs for young at-risk Black students. He sent me to the U.S. employment office in Cleveland to pose as an unemployed worker to see how the personnel treated those seeking jobs. Under his auspices, I played a significant role in setting up a government-funded halfway house for drug addicts in the capital's Cardozo neighborhood that included employment opportunities right within the house and incorporated the newest theories about addiction. Occasionally he asked for my help on speeches he was writing, though he needed little assistance; he was widely considered the best writer in the cabinet.

Furthermore, he was fun to work with, leavening serious situations with verbal silliness by using one of the many malapropisms he had collected over the years. Before I caught on, I tried to correct him when he once told me, "a word to the wise is deficient."

"You mean 'sufficient'?" I blurted.

"If you'd prefer," he said, chuckling.

Once accustomed to the secretary's wordplay, I simply shook my head and smiled in amusement.

I often recalled Wirtz's wordplay when Dick would endlessly quote from one or another of Yogi Berra's famous quips—"It ain't over till it's over," or "The future ain't what it used to be." And Dick had his own collection of playful word combinations. He could almost always bring any small argument we had to an end by saying: "Just remember, I a-window- you" (rather than I a-door-you), and I always will." I couldn't be mad at him anymore. It was infuriating.

If work on urban poverty provided a temporary sanctuary from events overseas, there was no real escape from the war. Vietnam had infiltrated everything, including the relationship between the president and his secretary of labor. "For two or three years, I was very close to Lyndon Johnson," Wirtz told reporters years later. "And then in about 1966 or 1967, I began to have a feeling that his Vietnam program did not make sense and should be stopped and wrote him to that effect. That was the end of the close relationship."

In the fall the fellows were invited to the White House several times to meet with the president or attend receptions. On one occasion, seated together around an oval-shaped table, Johnson spoke to us about the importance of the war effort in Vietnam. After finishing, he said he had only time to take a question or two. He then pointed at me and said, "You." Startled, I simply spoke aloud what I had been thinking while he had been speaking. I asked him if he understood the depth of young people's opposition to the war.

I hardly remember more of what I said, but my fellows classmate Tim Wirth recalls that awkward moment more clearly. "You gave an impassioned statement about the war. LBJ was this enormous man. It seemed as if he half rose from his seat toward you. It was terrifying. But then, in a low voice, he simply looked at you and said: 'AND THEREFORE?'" In other words, What do you propose? What next? Where do we go from here? The president's question made such an indelible impression on Tim Wirth that from then on, he explained, during his long career as a congressman and senator from Colorado, when someone issued an impassioned challenge, Lyndon Johnson's words would drum in his head: "And therefore?"

CHAPTER ELEVEN

Crosswinds of Fate

*Doris Kearns whispers to President Johnson during an event
organized by the White House Fellows. October 29, 1968.*

DICK KNEW FULL WELL WHAT LAY AHEAD. WITH RISING apprehension we began to look over the boxes that held files from the end of 1967 through the cataclysms of 1968.

He seemed reluctant to venture back to that time, a reluctance so extreme that one evening he opened Herman Melville's *The Piazza Tales* and began to read to me in his baritone voice the opening of "Benito Cereno." I thought at first his performance was an effort to distract us from where he didn't want to go. It was anything but that. With slow gravity, he read the description of the unsettled time before the arrival of a terrible storm:

"Flights of troubled grey fowl, kith and kin with flights of troubled grey vapors among which they were mixed, skimmed low and fitfully over the waters, as swallows over meadows before storms. Shadows present, foreshadowing deeper shadows to come."

"What a grand portentous opening to introduce the hellish year of

1968," Dick said, slumping into the chair and into silence. "Just how violent the storm to come, I had no idea."

Dick's strongest memory from the autumn months of '67 (when his Wesleyan fellowship had ended and he had accepted MIT's offer to be a visiting professor) was his acute frustration over the interminable back-and-forth as to whether Bobby Kennedy should or shouldn't run against Lyndon Johnson in 1968.

Only a year earlier, Bobby had self-deprecatingly responded to Dick's query about his plan to end the war with a quip about making speeches, "That's what a senator does." But now that another year had passed, it was clear that speeches, articles, and widespread protests in major city centers and on college campuses had made no discernible impact on Lyndon Johnson. An additional 50,000 American troops had been deployed to Vietnam, bringing the total to more than 475,000. And the war had continued to expand and grind on with no end in sight.

Reporters and students repeatedly asked Robert Kennedy why he continued to support Lyndon Johnson for the presidency in 1968 if he was so unwavering in his opposition to the war. Why was he unwilling to challenge the man most responsible for the war? It was the question Bobby was most uncomfortable addressing in public, but it was a question that persisted.

From the start, Dick was in favor of Bobby's entering the nomination battle against LBJ in '68—not as a profile in courage or a symbolic gesture for peace, but to win. It was a risk worth taking, Dick was convinced, a risk with the potential of victory. If, in my *New Republic* article, I had argued for combining unrepresented factions into a third party capable of pushing LBJ to moderate his war policy, Dick wanted to unseat him altogether, convinced that Robert Kennedy was the magnet able to draw together disparate fragments from across the nation and successfully defeat the incumbent president. Months before the election year began, one recounting of the '68 campaign noted that "Richard Goodwin had been telling anyone who would listen—and some, like RFK, who wouldn't—that Lyndon Johnson was the easiest President to beat since Herbert Hoover."

But the consensus resulting from a series of meetings with Kennedy's veteran advisers (with the exceptions of Dick and Arthur Schlesinger) was that it would be "political suicide" for Kennedy to run. Conventional wisdom said that an incumbent president could not be beaten. Kennedy's run would only result in fracturing the Democratic Party, thereby enabling a Republican victory. A private poll commissioned in New Hampshire showed Johnson at 57 percent, Kennedy at 27 percent. Dick made no headway with his argument that if Bobby entered the primaries and fared as well as he believed he would, all bets were off.

While Kennedy was treading water, Al Lowenstein pursued his quest to find an alternative candidate to lead his "Dump Johnson" movement, which was gaining momentum on college campuses and in liberal enclaves. Having failed to recruit Robert Kennedy, his friend and first choice, Lowenstein turned to Senators George McGovern and Eugene McCarthy, both staunch war critics. McGovern, facing reelection in 1968, turned him down. McCarthy hesitated at first. "I think Bobby should do it," he told Lowenstein. But after Bobby showed no indication of movement, McCarthy agreed to take the risk.

Announcing his candidacy on November 30, McCarthy acknowledged that if Kennedy had come forward, "there would have been no need for me to do anything." Asked by a reporter if Kennedy might enter the race later if McCarthy "made a significant showing," McCarthy said there was "nothing illegal or contrary to American politics if he or someone else were to take advantage of whatever I might do." Indeed, he expressed the desire that his challenge would be supported by other senators and politicians, hoping that it might "restore to many people a belief in the processes of American politics and of American government," potentially helping to alleviate the growing sense of alienation from politics, especially felt on college campuses.

Dick recalled spending a great deal of time with Bobby during this period of indecision, which stretched into a colossal and destructive hemming and hawing. "We would have lunch or dinner almost every week," Dick told me, "and I would often stay with him at his New York apartment or at Hickory Hill." Bobby's good friend and close adviser Fred Dutton vividly recalled the sight of Bobby and Dick "walking on the wide expanse of lawn at the edge of Hickory Hill deep in conversation. They were remarkably similar men," Dutton observed, "the same hostilities, the same awkwardnesses, the same introversions. I remember them walking there for an hour or two and no one felt they could interrupt them."

"Did you ever think," I asked Dick, "that you and Bobby were 'similar men'?"

Dick avoided my question, instead drolly replying: "Well, he was richer than me. Though it was more my choice that I was poor than it was Bobby's that he was rich."

"Be serious. Were you talking the whole time, ad nauseam, about THE QUESTION?" I asked, "whether or not he should run?"

"Of course not," scowled Dick, rolling his eyes. "Food, fate, women, history. We talked about our lives, about poetry and literature. He was asking questions, reading in a more urgent and expansive way than ever before—Camus, Aeschylus, Euripides, Shakespeare." It seemed to Dick that Bobby was breaking out from the confines of a guarded and wounded nature.

Shortly after McCarthy's announcement, Dick drove with Bobby to Hyannis Port on Cape Cod, where they spent several days alone, talking about personal ambition and the timing of events. During a walk along the beach Dick remembered citing a passage from *Julius Caesar*, hoping to spur Bobby to act—and act at once.

"There is a tide in the affairs of men, which, taken at the flood leads on to fortune. Omitted, all the voyage of their life is bound in shallows and in miseries."

"There's nothing like poetry to drag you back to your fate and your future," Bobby had rejoined with a melancholy smile.

Before they departed from the Cape, Kennedy asked Dick to prepare a memo making the case for him to run, an outline Dick could present at a gathering of Kennedy's advisers on December 10. He had asked Schlesinger to do the same. Ted Sorensen and Ted Kennedy would take the lead in making the argument against Bobby entering the race.

The December "debate" took place at Bill vanden Heuvel's Central Park West apartment. That insiders' meeting included Fred Dutton, press secretary Pierre Salinger, and Kennedy's administrative assistant Joe Dolan. Kennedy's staffers on the Hill—Adam Walinsky, Jeff Greenfield, and Peter Edelman—were not invited. This younger cohort was strongly in favor of his running, but for such a consequential political decision, Kennedy turned to his veteran advisers whose pedigree reached back to JFK, and whose awe of presidential power weighed heavily.

In his journal, Schlesinger recorded that he led off with the argument that "if McCarthy did moderately well in the primaries, he might expose Johnson without establishing himself; that state leaders would understand that their own tickets would go down if LBJ were at the head of the ticket;

and that Bobby should then emerge as a candidate, rescue the party and end the war in Vietnam."

Bobby questioned Schlesinger's assumption that McCarthy would quietly leave the race if he entered later. "If Gene had any success he wouldn't get out," Bobby predicted, "no matter what he might be saying at this point." The antiwar vote would thereby be split, ensuring Johnson's nomination.

Dick took a different tack, arguing that the senator should enter the primaries at once and battle for victory in every state. He began by quoting the same lines from *Julius Caesar* about the tide in men's affairs that he had recited on the beach in Hyannis Port, just a week prior.

"If you were to come out in open opposition for the nomination, it might well strike a real chord," Dick said, reading from the memo he had prepared for Bobby. "These things change very fast and if done right, you might really soar in political appeal. If you represent what the American people want—and I think you do—then they'll go for you. And if I am right, you can win the primaries." And if he won the primaries, Dick concluded, then political leaders in states without primaries "may very well make the move."

Ted Sorensen, the chief spokesman for making the case for waiting until 1972, opened with the categorical statement that, given the power of the presidency, "it would be futile for Bobby to enter the primaries hoping to win." Why should he "run against his brother's designated successor in a divisive campaign" that could not be won, when he "would have a much clearer path to both the nomination and the presidency in 1972?"

Ted Kennedy, Schlesinger recounted, echoed Sorensen, stating that "LBJ is sure of reelection and that Bobby is sure of nomination in 1972." Dick interrupted to say that if LBJ were reelected, "he would do everything in his power to prevent RFK's nomination in '72." Bobby agreed, "suggesting that LBJ would die and make Hubert [Humphrey] President rather than let me get it." Ted Kennedy held his ground. "To do anything now, would be to jeopardize, if not destroy Bobby's future."

Dick felt a surge of hope for his own argument when Bobby interrupted the repetitious back-and-forth to make a statement. Schlesinger recalled Bobby saying that "the talk up to this point had revolved around himself and his party. He did think another factor should be weighed—i.e., the country. He was not sure whether the country or the world could survive four more years of Lyndon Johnson. Whether or not he was sure of winning, was there not a case for trying in 1968?"

The conversation soon returned to practical considerations, however, and began to wind down. A survey of political leaders in bellwether states had produced almost unanimous agreement that Bobby should not run. The dozen or more antiwar senators who privately supported Kennedy's position did not feel they could go public without jeopardizing their own political futures.

The meeting ended where it began. Dick and Schlesinger remained the only two urging Kennedy to enter the race. The long debate had produced no break in the stalemate. Demoralized and frustrated, Dick left the meeting, feeling like a dog chasing its own tail.

JANUARY 30, 1968

On the morning of January 30, Kennedy had long been scheduled for a breakfast meeting with a group of journalists at the National Press Club. In anticipation of being asked about his plans for the '68 election, Kennedy decided "to clear the air" by giving out a short statement to put the matter to rest: "I have told friends and supporters who are urging me to run that I would not oppose Lyndon Johnson under any foreseeable circumstances."

From a personal and political point of view, Kennedy's timing was disastrous. The very next day, "shattering expectation and belief," Dick later wrote, the Tet Offensive began: "Explosions ripped through the streets of every major city in South Vietnam. A Vietcong squad blasted its way into the 'invulnerable' American Embassy in Saigon, and then retreated leaving death, damage and recrimination." This, after we had been told from "the highest sources" that the enemy was "half-defeated, exhausted," and "that the war was finally going well."

Dick had hoped that Tet would change Bobby's mind about running. And, for a short period, it seemed to have done just that. Bobby asked Dick to have dinner with his brother Ted in Boston to see if his brother had softened his opposition. On February 13, they met at a restaurant at the foot of Beacon Hill (where I would have my first date with Dick four years later).

At first, in notes Dick made of their conversation which he then sent to

Bobby, it seemed that Ted was coming around: In the end, however, Ted returned to the old saw of the invincible power of the presidency, the formidable problem of challenging an incumbent. "If Bobby doesn't do this," Ted said, "he'll be elected president in 1972." At the end of the evening, Dick asked Ted what he thought his brother Jack would have advised. "I know what Dad would have said," Ted replied quickly, "he would have said, don't do it. And Jack would probably have advised against it." Here he paused a long moment. "But he might have done it himself."

Dick concluded his report for Bobby on the conversation with a humorous rendition of historical facts.

No one has successfully challenged an incumbent President in this century.

No President's brother has been elected President.

No New York senator has ever been elected President.

No man with ten children has ever been nominated or elected.

No candidate has ever been Robert Kennedy in 1968, with Lyndon B. Johnson as President.

Five days later Dick was invited to a brief, conclusive meeting at Hickory Hill. During a reception in the main house, a select group—including Dick, Bobby, Ted, and Bill vanden Heuvel—withdrew to the bathhouse that adjoined the swimming pool. Standing in the corner, staring at the floor, Bobby said: "The support just isn't there. I guess I'm not going to do it." There was nothing left to say.

Bobby asked Dick to drive with him to the airport. He was on his way to attend Senate hearings on issues Native American people were facing in Oklahoma. There was little conversation. But, as Dick recounted in his oral history, when they reached the airport, he said to Bobby, "Well, if you're not going to run, I guess I'll go up and work for McCarthy. He's the only one fighting Johnson and I guess that's the best place to be . . . the only place to be."

"I guess that'll be helpful," murmured Bobby, and left for the plane.

After Dick and I had reviewed his files covering this period of Bobby's painful hesitation, he said to me, "Doing nothing is also an action." He judged Bobby's decision not to run early on "the biggest political blunder he ever made." Had he entered around the same time as McCarthy, the thousands of antiwar students who flocked to New Hampshire might well have considered Kennedy their leader. Dick slumped forward sadly and said: "Bobby was the right person at the right time. That time would never return in quite the same way. To this day I think that if he had taken the risk, it all might have been different."

FEBRUARY 23, 1968

Dick took a leave of absence from MIT and traveled to New Hampshire on February 23. Earlier that winter, McCarthy had invited him to dinner and asked him to join his campaign. Dick had told him he could do nothing until Bobby made a decision. Now, he called McCarthy headquarters, learned the candidate was in the small city of Berlin campaigning, and asked them to tell the senator he was coming. "Maybe it was hopeless," he said to me, "but it was something, better than sitting on my ass in Boston."

At midnight, Dick arrived at the Perkins Motel where the McCarthy staff was staying. At the desk, he requested the room number for Seymour "Sy" Hersh, McCarthy's press secretary.

For years afterward, both Sy and Dick never tired of the tale of their first meeting. "We were still floundering," Sy recalled. "We got a huge boost one night in remote Berlin, New Hampshire, after a long day, when I answered the door of my motel room and found Richard Goodwin standing in the cold. There had been rumors in the press that Goodwin, a veteran of the Kennedy and Johnson administrations who was famed for speeches on civil rights he had written for both presidents, had been disappointed by Bobby Kennedy's refusal to run for president and was thinking about joining our campaign. And here he was, at a run-down motel at a pretty much useless campaign stop.

"He walked into my room, carrying an electric typewriter, dramatically dropped it on a bed and said, 'You and me and this typewriter, kid, are going to overthrow a president.'"

The recollection of Dick's arrival in frozen New Hampshire that February cast a welcome, if fleeting, glow over our work in Dick's study fifty years later as we pieced together—from Dick's earlier writings, lengthy oral histories, press clippings, articles, pamphlets, and books—the story of those transformative weeks, perhaps the happiest of his political campaigning life.

Listening to his reminiscences, I was enchanted by the real-life tale of democracy-in-action, as if an elixir compounded of New Frontier idealism,

Peace Corps zeal, and the grandest days of the Civil Rights Movement and the Great Society had been discovered at winter's end on the hawkish and largely conservative terrain of New Hampshire.

Dick's first impression of the campaign had proven less than hopeful. The turnout at McCarthy's various campaign stops in Berlin was respectful but small. There were no reporters following the candidate, no radio or television coverage. Polls predicted that McCarthy might garner only 10 or 12 percent of the vote. There was hardly an acknowledgment that a viable presidential campaign was underway. They were, it seemed, operating in a vacuum.

Prospects scarcely improved as Dick traveled with McCarthy from Berlin down to campaign headquarters in Manchester. "I remember walking with McCarthy into the Sheraton-Wayfarer Hotel," Dick said in his oral history, "the biggest dining room in the state of New Hampshire. Not a single head looked up. Nobody recognized him." While the fact that no one came over to wish McCarthy luck or chat for a moment worried Dick, the candidate himself remained unperturbed at the lack of attention. As they left, McCarthy put his arm across Dick's shoulder: "Dick, as St. Augustine said, 'When one person goes across the fence to steal a pear, he is filled with weakness and fear. But when two people go across the fence to steal a pear, they feel assured of success!'"

"It was such an unexpected comment," Dick remarked to me, "so eccentric and original, that I felt a glimmer of hope when we left that dining room. I liked him."

That glimmer of hope expanded as Dick entered the corridor leading to the suite he shared with Sy Hersh. The entire hallway was crowded with young student volunteers, hard at work typing statements, making lists of voters, talking animatedly. "It was like a massing hive of bees," Dick told me, "humming and busy, different from anything I had ever seen on a campaign before."

"You're Dick Goodwin!" shrilled a voice that silenced the hubbub of all the voices in the corridor. This exclamation had issued from Marylouise Oates, Sy's comrade-in-arms and assistant press secretary. "Come on in," she beckoned to Dick, "and meet the teeny-boppers." In a large room Dick saw a small sample of what would become many thousands of young men and women flooding into New Hampshire during the days ahead. They greeted him enthusiastically. "It was extraordinary what Dick's arrival meant," Mary Lou, now eighty, recently explained to me. "He was so major, a huge deal. Maybe now, we began to think, we have a real shot."

"It was Mary Lou who dubbed me 'the Che Guevara of the teeny-boppers,'" Dick laughed fondly as he said to me, "a title I proudly carried but did not deserve. The volunteers had their own young leaders [Sam Brown, Curtis Gans]. I was like the Ancient Mariner. I stayed up late that night and many subsequent nights, telling stories about the White House, about John Kennedy and Lyndon Johnson. Their appetite to hear actual tales from someone who had been there before was bottomless. Every time I tried to call it a night, they asked for more, eyes filled with eagerness and excitement."

Dick's regard and admiration for these intelligent, motivated, and inde-fatigable young workers would grow until he "felt more closely bonded in friendship and in love" with the kids in New Hampshire than he had ever felt in any campaign. What was forming before his eyes was a genuine movement, the gathering of foot soldiers in an army. "Not a Kennedyesque band of brothers," he would remember, "but a congregation of brothers and sisters willing to work any hours, undertake any task, give any effort to win an election that might end the war."

The remarkable, unique circumstance was that these young volunteers had not gathered because of the candidate; he had materialized because of them. The next day, Dick toured the headquarters of the field organization in Concord, New Hampshire, twenty minutes away. "It was the biggest and best field organization ever assembled for any political campaign," Dick concluded. "Every day of every week they came—from as far away as Mich-igan to the west and Virginia to the south; in buses and cars, by prearranged transportation, or by hitchhiking. Some stayed a few days at a time, others had dropped out of school for full time service."

The field organization found the students accommodations in base-ments of supporters' homes, churches, and gyms. All that was required was a sleeping bag and a willingness to make a few adjustments in their appear-ance. Male volunteers had to cut their hair and beards ("Clean for Gene"), while women were required to exchange miniskirts for longer garments. When they knocked on doors, the campaign wanted them to be "the boy or girl next door come to call." They were told to listen, to see how people felt about the country, to explain why they believed in McCarthy, and to suggest that if he were president, divided generations "could talk again, just as we're talking now."

Jeremy Larner, a writer Dick recruited for McCarthy's speechwriting team, shared Dick's conception of the New Hampshire primary as a kind of romance and a crusade. "The McCarthy kids loved McCarthy, they loved each other, they loved New Hampshire," Larner later wrote, noting that the volunteers were not the young protesters who engaged in violence at the Pentagon or carried the flag of the Viet Cong. "Though they hated the war and the draft, they still believed that America could be beautiful—if it would live up to its own principles."

"You would have fit in perfectly with the whole spirit of the enterprise," Dick exclaimed to me. "Why weren't you there?"

"You know perfectly well why. I was in my own bubble, busily engaged in domestic affairs at the Labor Department."

"Oh yeah," he needled, "I forgot. Anyway, I can easily visualize you in New Hampshire. You belonged there!"

When Dick left the field organization headquarters to return to Manchester, he realized that this volunteer aspect of the campaign was running brilliantly on its own. They had no need for his professional experience.

Instead, he put his expertise to work at McCarthy's main headquarters in Manchester—where it was sorely needed. In that makeshift main office, which Theodore White described as a "grisly, paper-cluttered two-room suite made bedlam by amateurs all engaged in their first campaign," Goodwin was the "one man who made sense . . . a veteran of the Presidential campaigns of 1960 and 1964." Even McCarthy's wife, Abigail, who never trusted Dick because of his friendship with Bobby, conceded that Dick, with "his ugly, compelling face, his direct, black eyes, and his cheerful permanent half-grin brought a lift to the campaign. To Gene it meant that a man of real talent and reputation was willing to certify the validity of Gene's effort by his presence and help." (I must confess the mere fact of Abigail's use of the word "ugly" to describe my husband so pissed me off that I consigned her to a place of eternal contempt.)

Dick's real contribution was based upon the central paradox that although it was the war that had brought him and the growing youth movement to New Hampshire, it was not solely the war that was going to make McCarthy a bona fide candidate for the presidency. Beyond this single issue, the people of New Hampshire would have to view McCarthy as a genuine alternative to Lyndon Johnson as president.

The first person Dick had to convince of this shift was McCarthy himself.

In those early days, McCarthy "wasn't even saying he was a candidate for president. He was saying he was conducting a referendum on Vietnam." In the end, McCarthy was persuaded by Dick's argument. The five-term congressman and two-term senator had, after all, enjoyed a long and successful career as a vote-seeking politician. He simply had to cross the threshold to see himself as a candidate capable of challenging an incumbent president. And with the arrival of more and more volunteers each passing day, that belief began to take hold. Time was short. McCarthy agreed to shift his focus to the broader theme of leadership, the direction of the country, and whether people were satisfied or dissatisfied with where it was going.

As Jeremy Larner observed, Dick "was always doing things and was much better than anyone else at getting the candidate to do things, too. He even got McCarthy to say he was running for President."

As Dick spent more and more time with this aloof, yet engaging, candidate, he was taken by his thoughtful precision of language and charmed by his sense of humor. McCarthy was the furthest thing imaginable from the effusive, flesh-pressing, crowd-embracing figure of the stereotypical Irish politician. He was on the opposite end of the spectrum from Bobby Kennedy's palpable empathy.

"Overstatement and sentimentality were certainly not his mode," said Dick, trying to sketch for me a sense of this unorthodox man and politician. He told me of McCarthy's lack of interest in rousing the crowd. He was often more keen to chat with Dick about a new poem by friend and fellow-poet Robert Lowell than to plot campaign strategies. And sometimes Dick was intrigued, drawn in, and felt the same way.

"We connected," Dick told me, "but I often had the feeling he was more interested in ideas and words than in people. All in all, however, we worked well together. He had his own dark charisma. The most original mind I had ever known in politics."

———•———

In the midst of our conversations about this happy political adventure, I came upon a handbill in Dick's papers that he had composed as a print advertisement to be included in a kit of written materials readied for door-to-door delivery by the McCarthy youth army. Under a rare picture of McCarthy and President John F. Kennedy walking side by side, both smiling, my eye was drawn to a quote from McCarthy:

"There is only one issue in this contest. It is not Vietnam. It is not the cities. It is the state of this nation and the quality of its leaders."

What followed was a binary division of the good times that began with John Kennedy in 1960, and ended with his death in 1963 juxtaposed to the bad times of 1968.

In 1963 the economy was booming. Taxes were being lowered. Today our prosperity is slowing down.

In 1963 our great cities were relatively tranquil. Today we look upon a period of almost civil war—of violence, discontent, fear and lawlessness.

In 1963 our children in colleges and universities were primarily concerned with the Peace Corps and Civil Rights. Today it is marijuana and draft protests.

In 1963 we were at peace. Today we are at war.

When he took office, President Johnson said "Let us continue." Now on every front there is decline, decay, and deterioration—mounting danger and destruction.

That handbill instigated such an immediate flash of anger in me that I set it down before Dick on his lapboard. "What happened to the Great Society?" I asked. "What happened to 1964 and 1965?"

Dick set his glasses on the end of his nose and peered down to find the excluded middle of the decade—civil rights, voting rights, Medicare, all the historic achievements of the Great Society.

"The tax cuts you talk about weren't even passed in 1963," I pointed out with obvious frustration. "LBJ passed the tax bill in '64."

When I had simmered down somewhat, Dick countered that he "wasn't a historian and he wasn't writing history. This wasn't a debate; it was an election. I was making a contrast, drawing a cartoon. I was trying to drive home points. To win."

"But look what it erased," I grumbled. "It erased the heart of Lyndon Johnson's vision and accomplishments, as well as your own."

I reminded Dick that he had once lamented how Lyndon had erased his own legacy as well as Dick's when he canceled that book of the messages and speeches of the Great Society. "You've returned the favor with a vengeance!"

Dick listened thoughtfully. "I was in the midst of a political battle," he said, "and as we've well established, I had politics in the blood."

Print ads, pamphlets, and handbills, however, could only accomplish so much. With three weeks until the March 12 primary, the only way to switch the master conception of the campaign to *leadership* was by way of radio and television. So Dick took charge of McCarthy's media campaign. "I didn't really get appointed to do media," Dick recalled. "I just took it over."

A New York ad agency had prepared a series of campaign ads for radio and television, featuring images of burned children, bombs falling from planes, buildings destroyed. "I threw them out," Dick told an interviewer, "and most of their literature, too. People who really felt terribly strongly against the war were already for McCarthy. They were going to come out and vote."

The media campaign was not complicated. Television, in particular, was perfect for McCarthy's cool and stately demeanor. He sat behind a desk and spoke directly about the state of the country and the need for leadership. After going over a prepared list of topics (pollution, civil rights, the cities, etc.), McCarthy was able to perform without script.

"He was the first and last candidate I had ever worked with," Dick later wrote, "who could speak coherently, even eloquently, for thirty or sixty seconds and, with only the help of cue cards, end his presentation on a perfectly rounded paragraph." And, Dick recalled in his oral history, "when people saw that midwestern face and the manner of speaking, it was absolutely clear that here was no radical, they were looking at a man, who whatever his position on the issues, in his heart was a conservative."

Since there were no limits on individual campaign contributions in 1968, a small circle of wealthy contributors could theoretically supply the money needed to keep the campaign afloat. But it was a constant struggle, Dick noted, "since men of means are little inclined to throw their money away on a hopeless cause," which the campaign of a little-known candidate against an incumbent president seemed at first to be. Therefore, Dick said, "we had to depend upon that scarcest of all breeds—the romantic rich"— men like "the Gold Dust Twins" as Oates nicknamed the duo of Arnold Hiatt, CEO of Stride Rite shoes, and Howard Stein, chairman of the Dreyfus Corporation. Both men were so passionate in their opposition to the war that they had taken an extended furlough from their successful businesses to go to New Hampshire and drive the fundraising effort.

Both Hiatt and Stein proved indispensable to the campaign and later became lifelong friends of Dick and our family. Dick particularly remembered one episode when the campaign was so financially squeezed that an emergency meeting was called the Saturday before the election. Hiatt told Dick their campaign chest was empty. Radio stations were demanding cash to keep spots on the air. Twenty thousand dollars was required immediately for their final push, Dick waited for a tense and silent moment, took his checkbook from his jacket pocket, and asked whether to make the check out to the advertising agency or the campaign. Whether driven by compassion or the humor of Dick's audacious bluff (suspecting Dick had $500 at most in his bank account), Hiatt plucked the pen from Dick's grip: "Don't worry about it, Dick. We'll take care of it."

In the last two days of the campaign, Dick took down all the radio spots on a full range and variety of domestic issues and ran a single thirty-second ad over and over on every radio station in the state:

Think how you would feel to wake up Wednesday morning to find out that Gene McCarthy had won the New Hampshire primary—to find that New Hampshire had changed the course of American politics.

"This brilliant ad was created by Richard Goodwin," Jack Newfield wrote, "who understood that, in hawkish New Hampshire, the winning issue was an inchoate desire for change, and a desire to participate as individuals in the act of change."

MARCH 12, 1968

On election night, the big dining room of the Sheraton-Wayfarer—the same dining room where McCarthy and Dick had slipped in unnoticed just three weeks earlier—was overflowing with people, print reporters, television correspondents, staff members. "In every vacant space," Dick recalled, "sitting against the walls, standing in crowded rooms, were the young volunteers—having made their way along snow-flanked roads from every part of the state to share in the moment."

Exuberance filled the room. Week after week the polls had risen like a thermometer, charting the rising heat of McCarthy's ascent, from 10 percent to 12 to 18 to 25 percent. But far more important and more accurate than the pollsters' "scientific samples" were the reports of volunteers who had canvassed the homes of nearly every registered Democrat in the entire state. Yet, even the campaign's most optimistic accounting did not foresee the extent of the stunning "victory." By night's end, McCarthy had won 42.4 percent of the vote. Lyndon Johnson, who had not been on the ballot, had been denied a majority, drawing only 49.5 percent. And when the write-in votes were tallied, only several hundred votes separated the Minnesota senator from the president of the United States.

Several of my own good friends were there that night. They had gone up to New Hampshire for the last ten days of the campaign. When I called to congratulate them, they said they wished I'd been with them. I would have loved the door-to-door conversations with the people. And what a feeling it was to know that they had made a difference.

With hundreds cheering, crying, and chanting McCarthy's name, the man who approached the rostrum at midnight was so buoyed by his jubilant supporters or so radiantly reflected their jubilation that he seemed a different man altogether from the gray eminence Dick had dined with less than a month before. "He waved happily to the crowd," Dick remembered, "letting the cheers and applause wash over him, exulting in the moment before beginning to speak."

"People have remarked that this campaign has brought young people back into the system," McCarthy said. "But it's the other way around. The young people have brought the country back into the system."

When Dick and I had finished the story of that triumphant moment, I brought two glasses of port to the study and we toasted to the memory of youth and that night half a century before. "And what a night of celebration it was, what great fun we had," Dick recalled, leaning back in his chair, and with a deep breath, he carefully lit a Cuban Robusto, savoring it as after an excellent meal with old friends.

MARCH 13, 1968

The campaign's ecstasy over Gene McCarthy's astonishing "victory" was brought to an abrupt halt the next morning when Robert Kennedy, asked by reporters to comment on the New Hampshire results, delivered an impromptu statement: "I am reassessing the possibility of whether I will run against President Johnson" in the battle for the nomination.

McCarthy heard the unwelcome news the moment his plane landed in Washington, where he was bound for a celebration as well as meetings to plot campaign strategy with an assembling national staff. On the flight down from New Hampshire, he had been in a rare, euphoric mood, chatting amiably with reporters, even enjoying an early martini. "We'll be able to pay our hotel bills," smiled McCarthy. As Dick had predicted, McCarthy's strong showing in New Hampshire had primed the pump of contributors. Upon hearing of Bobby's reconsideration, however, McCarthy's demeanor altered drastically. One reporter witnessed how "the happy man was put away somewhere and the black Irishman was very dominant."

Back in New Hampshire, Kennedy's "reassessing" reached hundreds of McCarthy volunteers in the lobby of the Sheraton-Wayfarer, where they had gathered, ready to travel to the next campaign stop in Wisconsin. They had been singing "Happy Days Are Here Again," the theme song of their parents' generation. "Bobby didn't even give us 24 hours to enjoy the results of last night," one young college woman lamented to a reporter. "We woke up after the New Hampshire primary, like it was Christmas day," another student chimed in, "and when we went down to the tree we found Bobby Kennedy had stolen our Christmas presents."

Fifty years later, I could not help but agree with them. "Of course, the kids resented him," I complained to Dick. "His timing was beyond insensitive. It's not surprising people called him ruthless. He brought it on himself. And that bitterness would last."

"Remember, I was with those kids then," Dick exclaimed, "on the other side of the fence from Bobby, and for the moment, loving where I was and what we'd accomplished together."

That moment was to be short-lived. Dick had told McCarthy from the beginning that problems of commitment and loyalty would only surface in the event of a direct contest with Bobby. "If that ever comes to pass," Dick had informed McCarthy soon after arriving in New Hampshire, "I won't be able to work to defeat my good friend."

While the arrangement was clear between Dick and McCarthy, the specter of loyalty and friendship was to muddle things between Dick and Bobby. Five days before the March 12 primary, Bobby had asked his brother Ted to inform McCarthy that he was planning to run. Ted declined, not wanting to cast a shadow on the last days of McCarthy's campaign. Ted tried to reach Dick in the room he shared with Sy Hersh to see if he could convince Dick to deliver the message. Sy and Dick had become fast friends. Sy's energy and passion, Dick told me, had been indispensable to McCarthy's campaign. Nonetheless, Hersh recalled, he "quickly grew tired of picking up the private telephone we both used and hearing Teddy Kennedy ask to speak to Dick. Kennedy called so often," Hersh remembered, "he eventually began calling me Sy."

Ted Kennedy's request put Dick in a bind. He told Ted that he had no choice but to decline. Shortly afterward, Bobby himself called. He was considering running, he said to Dick, and would like McCarthy to know his intention before the voters went to the polls in New Hampshire. "I don't want him to think that if he does well next week I just suddenly began to consider running," Bobby persisted. "I want you to transmit this before the results."

"I can't do that, Bobby," Dick told him. "I'm working for McCarthy now. I can't act as *your* agent." There was silence on Bobby's end. And then Dick considered the difficulty of his friend's position and agreed to relay a message to McCarthy, not as Bobby's confidant, but as any staffer would do. Bobby thanked him and the call was over.

McCarthy received the message calmly. "Why don't you tell him that I only want one term anyway," he replied to Dick tersely. "Let him support me now, and after that he can have it."

MARCH 16, 1968

Robert F. Kennedy officially announced his decision to run in the same Senate Caucus Room where his brother JFK had announced his 1960 presidential bid. "I do not run for the Presidency merely to oppose any man but to propose new policies. In private talks and in public, I have tried in vain to alter our course in Vietnam. I cannot stand aside from the contest that will decide our nation's future," Bobby declared.

He could no longer delay, he explained, especially after word had leaked out that the generals had made a formal request for more than 200,000 additional troops. Clearly, there was no end in sight to the war. Moreover, the decision to run had been made easier now that McCarthy was already in the field. Kennedy could not be accused of being the instrument tearing the party apart. "His fear of being called ruthless for running," Jack Newfield concluded, "was at last overcome by his fear of being called a coward for not running."

Immediately after his announcement, Bobby contacted Dick, who was on his way to Wisconsin with McCarthy to prepare for the April 2 primary.

"I'd like you to be with me," Bobby told him straight out, without any small talk. And then, Dick told me, he added, "I need you to be with me."

Dick tried to explain to me how raw and torn he felt at that moment. Much of the past decade of his life, ever since law school, was entwined with the Kennedys. "But I couldn't leave the McCarthy campaign in the middle of the Wisconsin primary," he said to me. "I didn't want my departure to damage McCarthy. Even more, I didn't want to abandon those kids. I felt pulled every which way."

"Look," Dick recalled saying to Bobby. "You're not on the ballot in Wisconsin. A defeat for Johnson is as important for you as to McCarthy."

"If that's your decision," Bobby said, his voice tense, angry, profoundly disappointed.

"That's it," Dick said, equally upset.

———·———

By Wisconsin, McCarthy's campaign was growing in leaps and bounds in the short time since the New Hampshire primary. McCarthy headquarters in Milwaukee at the Sheraton-Schroeder Hotel was alive with activity.

Volunteers were everywhere—stuffing envelopes, rolling posters and bumper stickers, boxing McCarthy pins, sleeping wherever they could find space, carrying in stacks of pizza boxes. Using techniques developed in New Hampshire, the army of young people was able to canvass 1.3 million homes. The numbers they gleaned were increasingly confirmed by pollsters, who were beginning to predict a looming landslide for McCarthy.

Despite the McCarthy campaign's great momentum, there were episodes that rankled Dick. On the advice of pollsters, McCarthy had canceled rallies scheduled for Black neighborhoods and had declined to issue a civil rights statement. The rationale behind such maneuvers was that he would lose votes in the white German and Polish wards. Hersh was "frantic" upon learning this. He felt it imperative to verify the information at once, directly with McCarthy. "I raced to his hotel suite. I asked him if this were so. He told me very coldly," Hersh recalled, "that it was none of my business." Profoundly disappointed, he and Oates resigned from the campaign that afternoon.

Even as Dick kept his pledge to remain through Wisconsin, old friends and members of the Kennedy family, including Jackie Kennedy, repeatedly called Dick, urging him to support and protect Bobby. Even though Jackie had wholeheartedly supported Bobby in public, she privately expressed grave reservations: "Do you know what I think will happen to Bobby," she said to Arthur Schlesinger. "The same that happened to Jack . . . there is so much hatred in this country and more people hate Bobby than hated Jack."

Wherever he went Bobby created a frenzy few politicians were able to generate. Dick could hardly avoid the coverage of Bobby's frenetic campaign on television and in the newspapers. Here was Bobby, a counterpoint to McCarthy, walking through the poorest Black neighborhoods of Sacramento and Los Angeles, meeting with Mexican American farmworkers. "In California, he finished his first day with reddened scratched hands and fingernail marks on his cheek," columnist Jimmy Breslin wrote of Kennedy. "They screamed and pushed and clawed at him. They reached for his hair."

While Kennedy lacked the cool reserve that made McCarthy so effective on television, he was far more at ease in contact with people. When encircled by the swirling energy of a crowd, Breslin observed of Bobby, when he is "smiling, emphasizing, fighting, his voice gets loud and much more powerful. He is not the brother. He is rough and emotional. But strong. Very strong."

"Our strategy," said Adam Walinsky on the first day of campaigning for Bobby, "is to change the rules of nominating a President. We're going to do it in a new way, in the streets."

"I had seen it dozens of times before, standing right next to him amidst the throngs in South America and in the streets of America," Dick told me. "It was like a chemical phenomenon, a force of nature." I laughed at Dick's turn of phrase. I told him of the British visitor who said that "he had seen two tremendous works of nature in America—Niagara Falls and Mr. [Theodore] Roosevelt." A critic conceded that when Roosevelt "is in the neighborhood, the public can no more look the other way than the small boy can turn his head away from a circus parade."

"Well," said Dick, "that's how I felt about Bobby's campaign even while I was up to my eyeballs doing everything I could for McCarthy."

MARCH 31, 1968

Every passing day it seemed more apparent from the raw data the volunteers collected throughout the state that Lyndon Johnson was headed for an overwhelming loss. He was trapped in a war that was killing thousands of American soldiers each week, and tearing the country apart. Desperate and depleted, he was searching for some silver lining in the national black cloud, some way to end the war he loathed—some way, even in defeat, to salvage his legacy.

On Sunday morning, the last day of March, with the Wisconsin primary looming on Tuesday, the White House announced that the president would make a televised address on the war in Vietnam that same night. Rumors spread throughout McCarthy headquarters that a bombing halt and reversal of administration policy was imminent. Dick had worried about the extremes LBJ might take to control the political weather and enhance his political standing. A pause in the bombing? A major escalation? A new offer of negotiation? Or anything else that might alter the president's grim and likely fate in the primary two days hence.

So while McCarthy was scheduled to speak at a college in nearby Waukesha on Sunday evening, Dick decided to stay behind to monitor the president's speech and prepare a response. Theodore White, at work on his next volume on presidential campaigns, had joined Dick and several staffers in a hotel suite at campaign headquarters just as the broadcast was about to begin.

The announcement of the president's speech had generated anticipation, even suspense. White was particularly eager, he later wrote, to observe Goodwin's reaction on this night. "Of all those engaged emotionally by McCarthy," White believed, "none was more so than Goodwin, and none with greater complications." White surmised that Goodwin was conflicted, torn in a love/hate relationship with Lyndon Johnson. No aide had worked harder to help Johnson create the language of the Great Society; no former aide had worked with greater diligence to throttle the administration's war machine.

Five days earlier White had interviewed the president and was stunned by his weary, listless demeanor—in glaring contrast to their previous conversation during the 1964 campaign when "Lyndon Johnson had bestrode the nation's politics like a bronco-buster." The reporter was shocked by Johnson's appearance. "His eyes, behind the gold-rimmed eyeglasses, were not only nestled in lines and wrinkles, but pouched in sockets blue with a permanent weariness." His voice so soft it could hardly be heard. The very contours of his body reflected lethargy and depression as he "slouched in a large rocking chair."

Few leaders in history had craved attention more than Lyndon Johnson and few had been, for months on end, more savagely jeered and derided. By the end of March, the president's approval rating had dropped to 36 percent, the lowest of his career. The percentage of those who supported his handling of the war had fallen to 26 percent. He had lost the people's trust.

The administration's optimistic projections about the progress of the war collided with the reality reported in newspapers and magazines. In the weeks after the Tet Offensive, seven major newspapers, including *The Wall Street Journal*, the *New York Post*, and the *St. Louis Post-Dispatch* had turned against the war.

"I felt that I was being chased on all sides by a giant stampede coming at me from all directions," Johnson later told me, speaking of that late winter and early spring of 1968.

On one side, the American people were stampeding me to do something about Vietnam. On another side the inflationary economy [the result of Johnson's earlier refusal to call for a war tax] was booming out of control. Up ahead were dozens of danger signs pointing to another summer of riots in the cities. I was being forced over the edge by rioting blacks, demonstrating students.

The man who had basked in the affection of crowds could no longer venture into major cities without encountering protesters chanting: "Hey, Hey, LBJ, how many kids did you kill today." No longer finding pleasure in daily activities, he dreaded the nights of insomnia even more. When able to fitfully sleep, he was beset by a recurring anxiety dream. As he recounted it to me later, *he saw himself swimming in a river. He was swimming from the center toward one shore. He swam and swam but he never seemed to get any closer. He turned around to swim to the other shore, but again he got nowhere. He was simply going round and round in circles.*

During the third week of March, LBJ's senior advisory group on Vietnam (until the Tet Offensive, his strongest supporters) told him they had now concluded that the present policy could not achieve its goal of victory without a major escalation and unlimited resources. Even if he sent the additional 200,000 troops the generals were requesting, the North Vietnamese government would simply match the numbers. The most that could be expected, he was informed, was a perpetual stalemate. Widening the war to achieve an elusive victory was no longer feasible. He finally acknowledged that the time had come to reassess his Vietnam policy.

———•◦•———

From the moment Lyndon Johnson appeared on camera to address the nation, Theodore White noticed a marked change: "The weariness of his mien was gone, he was poised, smooth and collected."

"Something's up," Dick remembered thinking.

But neither man could have foreseen the president's abrupt reversal of policy. Johnson had resolved to make "a roll of the dice," he told his speechwriter Horace Busby. "I'm shoving in all my stack on this one," he had said, making use of the same poker game metaphor he had used when he made passage of JFK's stalled civil rights bill his first priority. "I want out of this cage."

"Tonight I want to speak to you of peace in Vietnam," Johnson began. He immediately followed up with an offer "to stop the bombardment of North Vietnam unilaterally," without any assurances from North Vietnam. A limited bombing would continue north of the Demilitarized Zone where it was necessary to protect the lives of American and Allied soldiers. If Hanoi responded to the offer, he would be prepared "to withdraw our forces from South Vietnam as the other side withdraws its forces to the North . . . and the level of violence thus subsides." He stood ready, he said, to send American representatives "to any forum, at any time, to discuss the means of bringing this ugly war to an end."

The fuse lit by his opening remarks continued to spark for thirty-five minutes as he delineated a promise to do what his critics had been urging him to do all along. Then, almost before anyone had time to react, the fuse triggered the explosion at the end of the speech, dumbfounding the gathering in the suite and stunning the entire country:

With America's sons in the fields far away, with America's future under challenge right here at home, with our hopes and the world's hopes for peace in the balance every day, I do not believe that I should devote an hour or a day of my time to any personal partisan causes or to any duties other than the awesome duties of this office—the Presidency of your country.

Accordingly, I shall not seek, and I will not accept, the nomination of my party for another term as your president.

"With this, as though touched by an electric prod," White witnessed, "everyone in the room came erect, babbling so the last few words on television were lost. And Goodwin in glee striding about, 'It took only six weeks,' he was saying, pointing directly at Johnson's image on the television screen, 'six weeks earlier than I thought.'"

In the corridors of the hotel headquarters McCarthy's army of young volunteers shouted: "The war is over. The war is over. We did it, we did it." There were cheers and crying. They hugged Dick, they hugged each other.

"Thunderstruck," Dick said to me, trying to recall his feelings that night. "More than thunderstruck, Lyndon's abdication hit me like a lightning bolt. For more than a year I'd dreamed of the moment, worked for it. And along the way I'd come to feel that Lyndon Johnson and the war in Vietnam were one and the same thing. For those kids it was a clear-cut morality play between war and peace and, in an instant, right had triumphed over wrong, peace over war. My feelings weren't much different from all those volunteers shouting and whooping through McCarthy headquarters. Finally, it seemed, the war would be brought to an end. And we had all helped make that happen!"

I understood Dick's jubilation about the prospects of ending the war. I felt that same joy when I listened to the president that night, but I also believed Johnson had done something extraordinary by putting the country above his own ambitions. "Did you not feel any of this," I asked Dick. "What Teddy White witnessed—you dancing around the television screen and pointing a taunting finger at Johnson's image—strikes me as a spiteful, personal vendetta against Johnson."

"It had elements of all that," said Dick, "spite and brazen joy at his abdication. But there was something else that followed some years after the gloating—a sadness that has dogged me for the better part of my life."

"Sadness for Lyndon?" I asked.

"And for me, and for the country," Dick continued.

"We had gone so far so fast in those first years of the Great Society. The greatest moments of my public life were bound up with Lyndon Johnson. I wholeheartedly believed in the Great Society. I believed it was drawing the entire country closer than at any other time of my life to the ideals I had believed in since I was in college. And then the man who had driven the Great Society drove the war that eclipsed it.

"So, yes, I blamed him. And yes," he said, his voice trailing off, "I was heartbroken."

Dick and I talked many hours that night, way beyond our normal bedtime. He had often spoken about his experiences with LBJ, but on this night, it was as though our discussion of Lyndon's decision to withdraw from public life (which for Lyndon, Dick thought, was tantamount to *ending* his life) had triggered "a kind of summing up." We spoke of our long sessions of reminiscences, of plodding through his boxes, listening to Lyndon's voice on tapes, reading transcripts—all leading to a reevaluation of his brief, powerful time with Lyndon Johnson. Memories flooded back of the days when he and Johnson worked in tandem, when he listened to the president's declaration of the Great Society from the basement of the White House, when, from the well of the House, he witnessed the "We Shall Overcome" speech that accelerated the passage of the Voting Rights Act. As Dick traveled this stream of memory late into the night, he felt able at last, he said, to begin to measure the full size of Lyndon's achievements.

Historians had begun a similar reevaluation. As the cluster of fifty-year anniversaries took place commemorating Johnson's landmark legislation on Medicare, civil rights, voting rights, Head Start, NPR, PBS, immigration reform, and so much more, reporters and documentarians had begun to seek Dick out, not simply to talk about the long-ago past, but to explore the countless ways the Great Society agenda still permeated our daily lives.

The odd thing, he said to me with a laugh in the dark, was that our exploration of the papers in all these boxes, our work on this project, had changed his life, softening the bitterness toward Johnson that had festered within him for so many years, allowing him to remember Lyndon with admiration and even, he murmured, "God help me," with affection. As he slipped into sleep, he said he felt better not only about Lyndon but about his eighty-five-year-old self and what they had both contributed to the country they so loved.

The month of April 1968 brought furious atmospheric crosswinds, lifting our hopes for peace, before suddenly plunging us down. Following his March 31 speech, Lyndon Johnson rode an updraft of such tremendous force that the lame duck rose like a phoenix from the ashes of his leadership. By relinquishing power, Johnson now had the chance of retrieving it. "It all would have seemed staged," reflected Dick, "an April Fool's trick, if not for his withdrawal. That stamped a seal of authenticity on his quest to end the war."

Immediate and overwhelming acclaim followed Johnson's peace initiative coupled with his willingness to withdraw from the presidential race. Overnight, the national political landscape was turned upside-down. A Harris poll the day after the president's speech registered this reversal, flipping from 57 percent disapproval to 57 percent approval. That afternoon, the stock market reached a record high in response to the possibility of peace.

One editorial after another applauded the president's renunciation, interpreting it as "a magnificent display of patriotism" . . . "putting principle above personal ambition" . . . "a stirring, galvanic example of answering JFK's question: ask not what your country can do for you, ask what you can do for your country" . . . "his most stunning move in a 37-year career in politics." *The Washington Post* pronounced that LBJ "has made a personal sacrifice in the name of national unity that entitles him to a very special place in the annals of American history."

The same wind that boosted Lyndon Johnson's spirits also stirred Martin Luther King Jr. Like Johnson, King had been burdened by a dreary stretch over the winter months of 1968. Coretta King later described her husband as "terribly distressed" during these months, noting, "I had not seen him like this before."

Against the counsel of his closest advisers, King had embarked on a "Poor People's Campaign" to bring a caravan of thousands of people who had been struggling economically to the nation's capital where they planned to build an encampment and "stay until America responded, even if this meant forcible repression." He hoped their daily presence, "a new kind of Selma or Birmingham," would jolt Congress into hearing their plea for jobs, housing, and a massive rehabilitation of economically depressed city neighborhoods. But recruitment for the campaign had proven to be slow, money hard to raise, and leading members of the civil rights community considered the entire project a grave miscalculation.

King's "first reaction" upon hearing of the president's peace overtures to North Vietnam, according to biographer Nick Kotz, "was renewed hope— for an end to the Vietnam War, and for the prospects that America would face its responsibilities to the country's minorities and to its poor." If the president's peace initiative was realized and monies began to flow back into domestic programs, then the controversial Poor People's Campaign might no longer be necessary. Without the wedge created by the war, there was a flicker of hope that the old alliance between King and Johnson, which had accomplished so much, might be revived.

Johnson's withdrawal also completely rearranged the contours of the race for the Democratic nomination. It rendered McCarthy's lopsided

April 2 win in Wisconsin (56 percent to 35 percent) anticlimactic. Abruptly deprived of their chief target (an unpopular president) and their central theme (an unpopular war), McCarthy and Kennedy now found themselves on a collision course. Always partial to odd and arresting imagery, McCarthy observed that prior to Johnson's self-removal, the race was "three-cushioned billiards. Bobby could only hit me if he flanked the shot off Lyndon. It was a case of who could hurt Lyndon the most, and he seemed to be winning. Now he will have to hit me directly."

Likewise, McCarthy would now have to take a similar approach to Kennedy. For that eventuality, McCarthy seemed confidently prepared. When asked about the wild and overheated crowds Bobby was drawing he said, "You know the difference between a grass fire and a fire in a peat bog? A grass fire just burns off overnight. Peat bog fire holds on for six months." McCarthy was committed for the duration against Kennedy.

This was precisely the scenario that Dick had foreseen and long dreaded. From the start, he had told McCarthy that if Bobby entered the race he would not be party to a direct effort to defeat his longtime friend. Later, after the New Hampshire victory and Bobby's entry, Dick made good on his promise that he would stay until the completion of the Wisconsin primary, where Kennedy was not on the ballot. He had wanted to lay the groundwork for his departure—to train the three young speechwriters he had brought on board and put together a team that could handle television and radio. On the morning after McCarthy's Wisconsin victory, Dick returned home to Boston, then headed to Washington to wrap up his work with McCarthy, before joining the ranks in Robert Kennedy's campaign.

APRIL 3, 1968

Speechwriter Horace Busby's notion that Johnson "had begun the happiest week of his presidency and possibly of his public career" was set in motion when, at 10 a.m. on April 3, White House aide Tom Johnson brought him a bulletin from Reuters: *Hanoi is ready to talk.*

Lyndon Johnson had waited for years to receive this simple message. "Perhaps," he thought, "a real breakthrough has arrived at last." As he had done so often in domestic affairs, Johnson sought to capitalize at once on this opening. He called a press conference to announce that in reply to

Hanoi's welcome response he would depart the following night for a strategy session in Honolulu with General Westmoreland and other American
officers stationed in South Vietnam. If the war could be brought to a close,
he would be able once more to focus on the unfinished business of his
domestic agenda. He did not want to waste a moment.

APRIL 4, 1968

Lyndon Johnson awakened on Thursday morning with an optimism and
buoyancy that had been strangers to him for a very long time.

Reporters who trailed his activities throughout the day spoke of his
"ebullient mood," cheered both by Hanoi's offer and by the praise for his
March 31st speech. Shortly after noon he flew to New York to attend the
investiture of the new Catholic Archbishop of New York. As the presidential limousine neared St. Patrick's Cathedral, hundreds of well-wishers
lined the streets, encouraging him with a warmth and enthusiasm he had
not received for many months. As he entered the church, the entire congregation began to applaud, continuing until he reached his front row pew.
In the history of the cathedral only one other person—His Holiness, Pope
Paul VI—had received such a spontaneous ovation.

Next, the president stopped at the United Nations to confer with U.N.
Ambassador Arthur Goldberg and Secretary-General U Thant. "Hanoi's
agreement had given all of us a great lift," Johnson observed. On the plane
ride back to Washington, the press was surprised to receive an invitation to
the president's stateroom, an offer that had become increasingly rare. He
held forth in a jovial manner, while acknowledging the stack of congratulatory letters and telegrams that had been handed to him.

When Johnson returned to his office early that evening, the West Wing
seemed unnaturally quiet. Members of the White House staff had already
left for Andrews Air Force Base to board Air Force One for the flight to
Hawaii. The importance of the Hawaii trip, the *Honolulu Star-Bulletin* had
observed, was signaled by the number of attending press and television
correspondents on their way to Honolulu. "The three networks alone
are sending more than 100 correspondents and technicians for coverage."
Johnson was expected to board Air Force One around midnight, immediately following a long-planned congressional dinner. For that occasion, he
was told, an exceptionally thunderous reception was in the offing.

"The world that day seemed to me a pretty good place," Johnson recalled in his memoir.

Then at 7:30 p.m. Tom Johnson handed the president a second message, this one from Memphis, Tennessee, bearing a one-sentence bulletin: *Martin Luther King has been shot.*

———————

"Thirty-nine, only thirty-nine years old," exhaled Dick, and it was clear that the distant night of King's murder in Memphis cast a pall on both our mood and discussion. "Far and away the grandest figure in an age of titanic figures—Lyndon, JFK, and perhaps Bobby."

Bit by bit, gruesome scraps of the narrative filtered back to the White House: a single shot from some sixty yards away, a "gaping hole" through King's jaw, neck, and spine.

King had traveled to Memphis at the behest of an old civil rights comrade to support Black sanitation workers fighting for decent pay, better working conditions, and the right to establish a union. Relaxing at the Lorraine Motel with his core circle of Andrew Young, Ralph Abernathy, and Jesse Jackson, King had strolled onto the balcony overlooking the parking lot. Leaning over the railing, he chatted with friends who had gathered below. He asked a trumpet player to play his favorite song, "Precious Lord, Take My Hand," at the rally later that night in honor of the striking workers. From a room across the parking lot, a sniper had fired the shot. An hour later, Martin Luther King Jr. was pronounced dead.

The report from the rifle resounded across the nation, spreading grief, foreboding, and fear. Lyndon Johnson's initial task was to console that grief and attempt to steady and calm the nation. At nine o'clock he stood at the West Wing podium where only the day before he had told the nation that Hanoi had agreed to commence peace talks. He summoned prayers for King's family and asked everyone "to reject the blind violence that has struck Dr. King, who lived by nonviolence." He canceled his plans to go to the congressional dinner and postponed his trip to Hawaii intended to forward the peace initiative.

Lyndon feared that in one fell swoop, "everything we've gained in the last few days we're going to lose tonight." When Horace Busby saw him in the Oval Office later that day, "the exuberance of the week seemed to be draining from his long face." Momentum gone, sadness, confusion, and despondency took hold: "We had been pummeled by such an avalanche of emotions the last four days," Lady Bird wrote in her diary, "that we couldn't feel any more, and here we were, poised on the edge of another abyss, the bottom of which we could in no way see."

Indeed, Johnson seemed despondent, even unusually taciturn, during what Lady Bird described as a "strange, quiet meal" after eleven o'clock that night. If her husband seemed subdued on the outside, he was already keenly attuned to the possibility of serious trouble ahead. He was anything but passive. Through the night, calls were made to mayors and governors, urging them to be proactive, to reach out to the poor Black neighborhoods in their cities. "For God's sake, go see the people," was his directive, "let them see you, let them know you care, that we all care." He feared, he told Busby, that he was "not getting through. They're all holing up like generals in a dugout getting ready to watch a war."

But the unrest he had foreseen and tried to prevent had already started. Crowds gathered in the Black retail section of 14th and U, Columbia Heights, only blocks from the White House. A brick shattered the glass of Peoples Drug Store. Dozens of teenagers poured in, smashing display cases, carting out merchandise. "Within minutes, as if a switch had been flipped, everyone was looting," a *New York Times* reporter wrote. They were breaking into appliance stores, stealing televisions and radios, raiding clothing stores and jewelry stores. Fires were set, ribbons of smoke rose in the sky. Dozens of buildings burned to the ground. Flames could be seen from the windows of the White House.

Black districts in Memphis (where King's body lay) exploded in violence. Soon, Chicago, Baltimore, Kansas City, and more than a hundred other cities followed suit. But none of the outbreaks of that night surpassed the fire and turmoil raging in the nation's capital.

Johnson requested that a dozen civil rights leaders with whom he had worked closely over the years meet with him at the White House the next morning. He had resolved to focus his attention on something concrete that had eluded him for the last two years, passing legislation to prohibit racial discrimination in the sale and rental of housing. He figured that now might just be the time to ram it through. If anyone knew how to rake through the ruins of tragedy to salvage something beneficial during a time of chaos, it was Lyndon Johnson. He had harnessed John Kennedy's murder to propel

the stalled Civil Rights Bill. He would now try to push for fair housing legislation to honor Martin Luther King.

————•—•————

When Robert Kennedy learned of King's death, he was in Indiana to launch
his campaign for the May 7 primary, his first direct contest with McCarthy.
That cold, drizzling evening he was on his way to a rally planned in a poor
Black section of Indianapolis. Despite the weather, a crowd of a thousand
people was in a festive mood. Word of King's murder had not reached them.
Against his advisers' recommendation that he cancel the event, he had jotted
down a few notes, climbed onto the back of a flatbed truck, pushed his hair
back from his forehead, and announced directly: *I have some bad news for you
and for all our fellow citizens, and people who love peace all over the world, and
that is that Martin Luther King was shot and killed tonight.*

There were screams and gasps of horror, collective pain made audible.

*In this difficult day, in this difficult time for the United States, it is perhaps
well to ask what kind of a nation we are and what direction we want to move in.
For those of you who are black—considering the evidence there evidently is that
there were white people who were responsible—you can be filled with bitterness,
with hatred and a desire for revenge. . . .*

*Or we can make an effort, as Martin Luther King did, to understand and
to comprehend, and to replace that violence, that stain of bloodshed that has
spread across our land, with an effort to understand with compassion and love.*

He then raised a subject he had never spoken of in public before—the
pain of his own brother's death.

*For those of you who are black, and are tempted to be filled with hatred
and distrust at the injustice of such an act, against all white people, I can only
say that I feel in my own heart the same kind of feeling. I had a member of my
family killed, but he was killed by a white man. But we have to make an effort to
understand . . . to go beyond these rather difficult times.*

*My favorite poet was Aeschylus. He wrote: In our sleep, pain which cannot
forget falls drop by drop upon the heart until, in our own despair, against our
will, comes wisdom, through the awful grace of God.*

*Let us dedicate ourselves to what the Greeks wrote so many years ago: to
tame the savageness of man and to make gentle the life of this world. . . .*

*Let us dedicate ourselves to that, and say a prayer for our country and for
our people.*

Before he left, he ordered all the rally bunting torn down. He had no more appetite for the signs of political festivity.

Dick told me that when he first read an account of Bobby's remarks the next morning, he found himself in tears. He had heard Bobby cite those same lines from Aeschylus when they were alone. He knew what they meant to him and that they came from the depth of his heart. "On that terrible night," Dick said, "he was able to share his own throttled rage and grief over his brother's murder. He was able to share his vulnerability, to meet emotion with emotion."

On a night when riots broke out in cities all across the country, Indianapolis managed to stay calm, one of the few major cities to be spared.

APRIL 5, 1968

Upon entering the Cabinet Room shortly after 11 a.m., Lyndon Johnson was relieved to see familiar faces—Clarence Mitchell, Whitney Young, Bayard Rustin, Roy Wilkins, and other civil rights leaders—with whom he had teamed to secure two historic civil rights acts. Also seated around the long table were Vice President Humphrey, Chief Justice Earl Warren, Associate Justice Thurgood Marshall, as well as cabinet officials, White House aides, and congressional leaders from both parties.

Sorrow and anxiety permeated the room. All were in mourning for King and all were filled with dread at the expectation of violence in the coming days. "If I were a kid in Harlem," Johnson admitted to the group, "I know what I'd be thinking right now; I'd be thinking that the whites have declared open season on my people, and they're going to pick us off one by one unless I get a gun and pick them off first."

The civil rights leaders were in agreement that the vast majority of Black Americans did not favor violence, but they maintained that something immediate and positive was needed to ameliorate the situation. Johnson wholeheartedly concurred, proceeding to put forward his plan to "seize the opportunity" and push at once for an open housing law.

Most of the leaders, both Black and white, disagreed with the president's proposal. They knew that at the grassroots level, opposition to the regulation of private housing ran deep. Even congressmen who were "normally civil rights supporters," Califano noted, "were besieged by middle-class white constituents who wanted to keep blacks out of their neighborhoods."

Johnson's efforts had failed two years in a row and were likely to fail again. Instead, they argued for a new, strong executive order.

But Johnson had learned from the failure of JFK's 1962 executive order that "without the moral force of congressional approval behind us, the struggle would be lost before it had even begun." So, without fanfare, he set in motion a campaign to do what he did best. He launched a behind-the-scenes press to pass fair housing legislation, spending hours on the phone with individual congressmen, determining which projects or programs would be most persuasive to rally their votes.

Following his discussion of fair housing, Johnson opened the floor for suggestions from the assembled leaders as to what they wanted him to do now. With near unanimity, they called for a massive expansion of the war on poverty, along with multilayered programs to attack the deplorable conditions in poor Black neighborhoods. Johnson decided to keep both options—the open housing bill and the widespread initiative to renovate the cities—on the table, at least for now.

After the meeting, Johnson went before the press, with civil rights leaders by his side, to ask the Speaker of the House for permission to address a joint session of Congress early the following week. He intended to present a comprehensive legislative agenda to address the crisis in the cities. This speech, he told Busby, "can make or break us." The withdrawal speech the previous Sunday, he said, "was good and accomplished what we wanted, but King's death has erased all that, and we have to start again."

———•·•———

That afternoon, word circulated that the president had asked Secretary Wirtz, my boss at the Labor Department, to contribute to the joint session speech. Later that day, Wirtz called me into his office, explaining that he had been directed to gather ideas and recommend programs that might dramatically improve the lives of poor Black people in the cities. He wanted me to be part of his small working team.

As we brainstormed into the evening, I was filled with nervous energy. All around us Washington was in turmoil. The rioting was even more severe and extensive than the night before. More store windows were smashed, hundreds of fires were burning, whole blocks were aflame. Two teenagers trapped in a clothing store had been burned to death. The mayor of Washington, we learned, had officially requested the president to bring in the

National Guard. And by 9:30 that April 5 evening, thousands of troops were patrolling the streets. An official curfew had been set. Martial law had been proclaimed.

That entire weekend we worked through the day and late into the night. Special passes allowed us to drive home through a city that had become a fortress. Men in fatigues were piling sandbags around the White House, while soldiers with machine guns and bayonets manned checkpoints. My coworkers and I drove through otherwise deserted streets, often well past midnight. Soldiers would periodically halt us at barricades to check our passes and peer into our car.

I was tasked with sorting through the recommendations of the National Advisory Commission on Civil Disorders (the Kerner Report), which Johnson had established the year before to investigate the causes of the riots that had bedeviled inner cities every summer since 1964. The president had been upset by the stark conclusion that we were "moving toward two societies, one black, one white, separate and unequal." He resented the report's findings, which seemed to dismiss the strides of his Great Society programs. But we hoped the Kerner report might offer a roadmap to remedy the inequities that fanned the fires all around us.

For several days our small Labor Department troop hashed out what we considered a historic effort to improve lives in poor city neighborhoods. We suggested a series of interrelated programs of sufficient size and breadth to be paid for by transferring money from the defense budget and the Highway Trust Fund and by raising taxes on the affluent. We had convinced ourselves that King's martyrdom had created an opportunity equal to the shock and urgency of the violence that took place at the Edmund Pettus Bridge in Selma, Alabama. The president could speak now as he had spoken then. We believed, with an idealistic naïveté that matched our intensity, that Congress would respond to the denial of economic justice, just as it had responded to the denial of voting rights in 1965.

———•———

So many things were happening so fast that perilous April weekend in 1968 that as Dick and I compared notes almost fifty years later, we had to put together our respective movements like a jigsaw puzzle. Although Dick and I would not actually meet until four years later, he liked to imagine that we had crossed paths on the deserted streets of Washington.

He had arrived in Washington on Sunday, April 7, resolved to visit with McCarthy that afternoon at his Cleveland Park home, thank him in person for his courage and grace, wish him luck, and say goodbye.

He found McCarthy sitting outside in the sun. His home was three miles away from the center of the riots, the barricades, and the soldiers.

"Was it awkward?" I wondered.

"Not at all," Dick said. "The meeting had a peculiar warmth. I reiterated what I had said when we first talked back in New Hampshire—that if things changed and Bobby entered the race, I couldn't stay and be part of a campaign to end the career of one of my best friends."

"Well," said McCarthy matter-of-factly, "that's the kind of campaign it has to be."

"What a tough moment," I said. "Not a trace of petulance?"

"Perfectly stoic," Dick answered. "I thanked him, he thanked me in return, and we shook hands. "Good luck," he smiled wryly, "but only up to a point."

Before Dick turned to leave, McCarthy said, "Maybe we'll meet again." Those last words lingered in Dick's mind because it all came to pass.

Leaving the McCarthy campaign had been more difficult than Dick imagined. Were it not for his friendship with Bobby, he would have liked to stay, he explained to an interviewer shortly afterward. He found great joy working with the kids. He relished "the whole atmosphere, open, free-wheeling, relatively free of the usual infighting, maneuvering for position."

"In the McCarthy campaign," a *Boston Globe* reporter observed, Goodwin "was a major figure. He had squads of writers and students working for him. They looked up to him and admired his political work. He has an excellent political network and worked smoothly with media people. He works well with television advertising people and played a big role in this part of the McCarthy campaign."

In the Kennedy organization many of these slots had already been filled. He would be surrounded by a group of veteran professionals in a far more hierarchical structure. It would be less fun, but Dick felt he had no choice.

That same evening Dick drove to Hickory Hill to join Robert Kennedy's campaign. Kennedy had provided Dick with a pass, allowing him to cross over the bridge spanning the Potomac to reach his home in McLean. There was a sharp line of demarcation between the debris-strewn streets of Washington and the well-protected country estates in Virginia.

"Bobby came to the door alone when I arrived," Dick told me. "'Well, it's about time,' he needled me, shaking my hand and briefly throwing his left arm around my neck. He was happy and relieved and so was I.

"'If you'd listened to me from the start,' I whispered, 'you'd already be the nominee.'

"'Believe me, I know,' Bobby said. 'Don't rub it in.'"

He led Dick inside to see all his old professional teammates in "the Kennedy political firm," men who had vigorously opposed Bobby's entry into the race but now had all jumped on the campaign wagon.

APRIL 10, 1968

Unlikely as it had seemed, only six days after King was killed Lyndon Johnson's strenuous efforts to pass the Fair Housing Bill succeeded. "Cheers rang from the House floor and the packed galleries," *The Los Angeles Times* reported, "as Speaker John McCormack announced the vote." Although weakened during the legislative process, the bill nonetheless outlawed discrimination in the sale and rental of 80 percent of America's homes.

When he signed the bill the next day, Johnson dedicated it to Martin Luther King, pronouncing it the third great civil rights law of his administration, after the 1964 Civil Rights Act and the 1965 Voting Rights Act. "The proudest moments of my Presidency," he said, "have been the times such as this when I have signed into law the promises of a century."

That afternoon shortly after we had celebrated the bill's signing in the Labor Department, we learned that the president had decided not to give his joint session speech. A canvass of congressional opinion had made clear that the riots had turned compassion for Martin Luther King's death into bitterness and fear. The public was in no mood to hear about massive programs for the inner cities.

Johnson's decision to cancel the address saddened me; yet, as it turned out, in a curious turn of events, it would lead to the beginning of my close working relationship with Lyndon Johnson.

MAY 6, 1968

My disappointment over the cancellation of the speech lingered. A few weeks later, I encountered the president at a White House Fellows reception held to honor the new class of fellows who would replace us the following September. After his welcoming remarks, the president greeted all of us, shaking hands down the line. When he reached me, he paused, stooped down, and asked how I was doing.

I couldn't help myself; I launched into a speech of my own about the speech he should have given. He sighed, started to reply but, mercifully, was swept away by the White House photographer.

The next day at the Labor Department, Secretary Wirtz summoned me to his office, explaining that the president had called him to arrange for me to be transferred to the White House staff. I was perplexed. The sudden prospect of leaving Wirtz and the Labor Department left me in tears. "Do I really have to go?" I asked. Wirtz smiled as he tamped tobacco down into his pipe with the ball of his thumb. Then, watching me intently as he lit the pipe and pulled the stem from his mouth, he said, "Believe me, you'd regret it your whole life if you didn't take the chance to go there and work with him."

I was hardly settled in my new West Wing office when the White House appointments secretary called to say that the president wanted to see me in the Oval Office. He was signing documents as I entered. After a moment, he swiveled in his chair and without so much as a greeting, began.

First you say I should be dumped from the ticket. Then you criticize me for not making a speech. I've got nine months left in office without another election. I want to use those months to do and say all the things that should be done and said simply because they're right. And you can help me.

I've always liked teaching. I should have been a teacher, and I want to practice on you. I want to do everything I can to make the young people of America, especially you Harvards, understand what this political system is all about.

He pointed to a couch for me to sit down and for the next twenty minutes he paced around the Oval Office while he recounted his recent visit to former president Harry Truman's home in Independence, Missouri. He said he like to talk periodically with Truman. He valued his wisdom and advice.

The great thing about Truman is that once he makes up his mind about something—anything, including the A bomb—he never looks back and asks, "Should I have done it? Oh! should I have done it?" No, he just knows he made up his mind as best he could and that's that. There's no going back.

Then he sat on the padded rocker opposite me and added:

I wish I had some of that quality. There's nothing worse than going back over a decision made, retracing the steps that led to it, and imagining what it'd be like if you took another turn. It can drive you crazy.

Truman, LBJ told me, had given him much solace during his hardest days, reminding Johnson that he, too, had been under brutal, nonstop criticism and had somehow managed to ride it out. It was refreshing to talk to someone who had sat in the same office, to hear his thoughts, to explore, as he had during his recent visit, Truman's opinions of Paris as the site for the upcoming peace talks on Vietnam.

Johnson's storytelling was such that it seemed as if a book of contemporary history had come to life before my eyes and ears. I was spellbound.

Most of my work in the weeks and months that followed revolved around the same work training and jobs programs for poor youths that had been my focus in the Labor Department. I worked on these projects daily with Joe Califano and deputy special counsel Larry Levinson rather than with the president.

In the early evenings, I was often summoned to meet the president in the small sitting room beside the Oval Office. There, he recounted his activities of the day or, more and more often, began to unfold tales of his life as a young New Deal congressman in Texas. He would entertain me with stories of the time when he was director of the National Youth Administration in Texas where he had created projects to put tens of thousands of unemployed youths to work building roadside parks, schools, libraries, and recreational facilities. He relaxed as his thoughts returned to those times. His presidential demeanor vanished.

It clearly made him happy to tell these stories and it was a delight for me to hear them. As the months passed, he began thinking about the memoir he intended to write. He told me he wanted me to work with him on it after he returned to live on the ranch.

MAY 7, 1968

While I slowly got used to working in the West Wing, Dick was with Kennedy in Indiana, where Bobby's first direct primary contest against Eugene McCarthy would take place on May 7.

Over the years, Dick had played multiple roles in both primaries and presidential campaigns: general strategist, speechwriter, debate coach, radio and television advertising consultant. Dick's boxes contained copies of bound books of speeches written for the campaigns of both John Kennedy and Lyndon Johnson, volumes several inches thick. His experience in these various battles helped him develop the facility of being able to produce whatever was needed under immense pressure and at warp speed.

Bobby himself had told friends that he believed that Dick had added at least 10 percentage points to McCarthy's showing in New Hampshire by reconstructing his campaign strategy from a one-dimensional antiwar crusade to one of overall leadership and purpose. And Dick had helped McCarthy spell out a new direction for the country in simple and effective television and radio ads.

McCarthy's campaign had been a cottage industry compared to the size and scope of the Kennedy enterprise. Dick decided early on that he could best contribute to Bobby's campaign by focusing on the media. In short order, he cobbled together his own production company, hired a crew, and enlisted the help of legendary film director John Frankenheimer (*The Manchurian Candidate, Seven Days in May*), who had volunteered his services for the duration of the campaign.

Journalist Ward Just observed that it was often "extremely difficult" to determine exactly what Goodwin was doing, "or why he is so good at whatever he does." A member of the media team tried to explain: "Well, look, you've got five or six guys sitting around a table trying to work out an ad, Goodwin would come in late and sit down, listen a minute, and begin to write. He would be able to put into words what we wanted said."

"Exactly what was it you wanted those ads in Indiana to say?" I asked him.

"It was more how Kennedy spoke than what he said," Dick explained. "I wanted to cool him down."

The image of Kennedy projected in the campaign ads that ran in Indiana was not Bobby the firebrand, capable of igniting crowds to near hysteria, half-pulling him from his open car so they could shake his hand, grab his sleeve, or touch his hair. This was former attorney general and senator Robert Kennedy speaking in a mellow voice about policies he would enact for a better America, walking a tightrope between offering justice for Black people living in pockets of urban poverty on one side and promising law and order, safety and security for white working-class districts on the other.

Bobby became the common denominator connecting divergent groups. Both Blacks and low-income blue-collar workers, he stressed, were discriminated against by the affluent white establishment who not only didn't care about either of these groups but often harbored an active disdain for both. By hammering at the broader issue of class rather than race as his central theme, Bobby was able to articulate something no other candidate could convey—the prospect of reconciliation and healing.

Bobby worked eighteen-hour days. He reached for every hand that reached for his. Even at midnight, with crowds awaiting him for blocks ahead, he insisted that his depleted team press on. "If they're waiting for me, we'll go see them." Having found his voice, he was able to banter with the crowd, poke fun at himself, and engage them in dialogue. "Who do you want for your President?" he would ask. "You," they roared back. "We want Kennedy, We Want Kennedy," they chanted. "Will you help me?" he asked. And the crowd shouted "YES."

When the votes were tallied, Kennedy had scored a huge victory. He won 42 percent of the overall vote, carrying 85 percent of the Black vote, and seven white counties that had voted for George Wallace in 1964. Indiana's popular Governor Robert Branigin (a stand-in for Vice President Humphrey, who had entered the race on April 27, but was not competing directly in the primaries) secured 31 percent of the vote. McCarthy came in a distant third at 27 percent.

Both industrial blue-collar workers and economically oppressed Black people felt that Robert Kennedy had listened to them and recognized their problems. "This was not political chicanery," Dick said. "They both felt he was on their side. I felt it, too. And it was true."

That same night, Kennedy scored an overwhelming victory in the District of Columbia. And in Nebraska one week later, the formula he had hit upon in Indiana produced another resounding victory, leading to the increasing possibility that Kennedy would become the standard-bearer for a reformulated Democratic Party.

MAY 28, 1968

But then came Oregon, a relatively well-educated, mainly middle-class state, only one percent black, nine percent Catholic—what Dick called a great, sprawling suburb. Oregon's May 28 primary day found Bobby Kennedy campaigning in California. Only a week remained before the crucial June 4 California primary. Dick was already stationed in Los Angeles orchestrating the California TV and radio ads with Frankenheimer and the media team.

In the early evening, Dick flew with Bobby to Portland, Oregon, on the campaign's jet to be there with supporters as the returns came in. While they were in flight, early results came in over the cockpit radio. A crewman came down the aisle to deliver the gloomy forecast: McCarthy was projected to win with 44 percent to Bobby's 38 percent.

While this outcome was not wholly unexpected, Bobby's response to the information was surprising. After taking a moment to silently digest the news, he rose and, according to one reporter, "smiled as he made his way down the crowded aisle. He squeezed an arm, spoke briefly and warmly to those on the plane."

At McCarthy's Portland headquarters, more than three thousand jubilant supporters jammed a ballroom awaiting McCarthy's entrance. Once the final winning results were in, McCarthy, a radiant victorious smile on his face, said, "We knew we had the right issues and the right candidate. It was just a question of finding our constituency." This win, the candidate added, "should silence people who question my credentials as a real contender for the nomination."

Kennedy immediately wired a congratulatory telegram to McCarthy though he had never received a similar gesture from McCarthy following his string of victories. Then Bobby went straight to the seventh floor of the Benson Hotel where thousands of his supporters were waiting in a state of dreary disbelief.

"The people of Oregon were very fair," he told his deflated workers. "They gave me a complete and full opportunity to present my views and then they made a judgment—as they must." He sought out the chairman of his young volunteers to say: "I'm sorry, I let you down."

Later that night, Dick sat with Kennedy on the plane as they returned to Los Angeles. They huddled together weighing how to respond to the press the next morning when he would inevitably have to field questions like, "Since Kennedys have won the last twenty-eight popular elections they have entered, how does it feel to be the first one to lose? Are Kennedys no longer invincible?" A photo taken on the flight reveals both Bobby and Dick looking bedraggled and weary as they sit under a handmade poster that reads, "All the Way with RFK."

The first decision they made was that Bobby now had no choice but to debate McCarthy, a challenge he had mistakenly refused before this first loss. Conventional wisdom held that the better-known candidate should not provide free exposure to the lesser-known rival. Oregon had flipped such calculations. "I'm not in much of a position now to say he's [McCarthy's] not a serious candidate," Kennedy told Dick. "Hell, if he's not a serious candidate after tonight, then I'm not a candidate at all."

"I saw something different about Bobby when the press questioned him the next day," Dick said to me. "I think that loss in Oregon made him a better candidate." All his life Bobby had been told that "nothing was worse than to finish second," but now he had suffered defeat and was still marching forward. "More vulnerable perhaps," Dick told me, "but more sympathetic, more appealing."

There was something disarming about his frankness. Asked if the Oregon loss had wounded his chances he admitted, "It certainly wasn't the most helpful development of the day." When reporters asked what changed his mind about the debate, he candidly responded, "I'm not the same candidate I was before Oregon and I can't claim that I am."

In Los Angeles, fifty thousand people gave Kennedy "a wild welcome," showering him with confetti as he began his last week of campaigning. Los Angeles County, reporters noted, "held more Democratic voters than all of Indiana, Nebraska and Oregon combined." Kennedy was "obviously heartened by the tumultuous reception," reporters noted. "If I died in Oregon," he jokingly said, "I hope Los Angeles is Resurrection City."

MAY 29–JUNE 3, 1968

During the exhausting, exhilarating, and anxious final days of the California campaign, I was far removed from the bustle of Robert Kennedy's campaign. I was in Washington, D.C., having made plans with friends for the Memorial Day weekend, when at noon on May 29, I received my first invitation to accompany the president, his family, and friends to the ranch on Air Force One.

Departure would be that same afternoon. I hurried home to pack. I was advised to bring comfortable clothes, a nice dress or two, and a bathing suit. Wheels up was from Andrews Air Force Base at 4:45. After stopping at Texas Christian University in Fort Worth, where the president delivered a commencement address calling for a constitutional amendment to grant eighteen year olds the right to vote, we reached the ranch around 10 p.m.

I hardly had time to unpack before the president invited me to join him and a few others for a swim in the pool at 10:15 p.m. The next day we returned for an early morning swim at 8:15 followed by a second swim in the evening at 5:30 and a third at a little past midnight. This pattern of early morning and evening swims continued though it is an exaggeration to call these swims "exercise." While we sometimes sidestroked slowly up and down the length of the small pool, most of the time we just stood in the shallow end or sat on the edge with our feet dangling in the water as he talked and talked and talked. It seemed to me he never stopped talking and I never stopped listening.

Half a century afterward, just as I thought Dick had been lulled to sleep by my recitation of the President's Daily Diary (which described what everyone, including me, was doing every minute of the day), he interrupted with a burst of amusement, recalling his legendary swim session with Lyndon and Bill Moyers in the White House pool and his own first visit to the ranch when he appeared in his tuxedo at the Stonewall general store to purchase a bathing suit.

"Just think," he exclaimed, "both of us began with Lyndon in the water of swimming pools!"

"At least I wore a bathing suit," I added.

We both recalled how the ranch pool was strangely equipped with special rafts for a telephone, a notepad, and a pencil; if the president thought of someone he wanted to call or something important he wanted to record, he could float over to the various rafts that held the necessary equipment.

Such was the swirl of activities that awaited me during that first visit to the ranch that I could never have reconstructed it without the benefit of the President's Daily Diary.

Altogether, it seemed to me the most extravagant country fair imaginable, complete with sheep auctions, golf carts, rides to inspect herds of Hereford beef cattle, cowboy hats and boots, madcap drives with the president in his Lincoln convertible, helicopter trips to neighboring ranches, a boat ride on a lake called LBJ, cocktails and meals with a boggling array of dignitaries and celebrity guests, movie nights at a home theater, and early morning, noon, and midnight swims in the pool.

The guests for that Memorial Day weekend included actor Gregory Peck, Hollywood's dominant talent agency head Lew Wasserman, chairman of United Artists Arthur Krim, Henry Ford II, and their spouses. Activities included horseback riding and a visit to Johnson City. Late one afternoon a chopper ride landed us at the Haywood Ranch, the president's recently purchased hideaway retreat for hunting, boating, and water-skiing. While at the Haywood Ranch, Johnson took me for a ride in a small blue convertible. We drove to the top of a hill overlooking the lake. As we started down, a Secret Service man cautioned him to drive slowly; apparently, the brakes needed to be checked. Lyndon sped down the hill like a defiant teen, steering the car straight into the water which exploded around us. "We're going under!" he shouted. Then the blue convertible revealed itself to be an amphibious craft that began to bob as it floated in the lake.

I hadn't screamed or even been frightened. After all, I was with the president of the United States. We were surrounded by Secret Service agents. I figured that was sufficient security. As the disappointed president putted the Amphicar around the lake, he turned to me: "What is the matter with you Harvard people anyway?" he asked. "Don't you even know enough to be afraid?" I learned later that this was a prank he played on unsuspecting passengers with the same scripted warnings from the Secret Service.

One evening after dinner, we all watched the generational satire *The Graduate*. The president sat in a comfortable recliner. I'd been warned that he would often fall asleep as soon as the lights went down. But this night, with all his guests present, he stayed wide awake. And the next day he asked me, "How in the hell can that creepy guy be a hero to you?" referring to the recent college graduate played by Dustin Hoffman. He continued:

"All I needed was to see ten minutes of that guy, floating like a big lump in a pool, moving like an elephant in that woman's bed, riding up and down the California coast polluting the atmosphere, to know that I wouldn't trust him for one minute with anything that really mattered to me. If that's an example of what love seems like to your generation, then we're all in big trouble. All they did was to scream and yell at each other before getting to the altar. Then after it was over, they sat on the bus like dumb mutes with absolutely nothing to say to one another."

"Exactly the point," I managed to squeeze in while he caught his breath. "They didn't have a clue. They only knew they didn't want to be their parents."

If I didn't think much of the president as a movie critic, he proved to be a wizard analyst of political debates when we all gathered in the main house living room on the night of June 1 to watch the highly anticipated televised debate between Robert Kennedy and Eugene McCarthy.

Much later I learned that Dick was a coach on Bobby's team. Despite intense fatigue, Bobby spared nothing and crammed for the contest with all the energy he could muster. That Saturday they held two briefing sessions. For hours the team assailed the candidate with the expected questions, working to produce succinct answers they then recorded on index cards for Kennedy to study and rehearse. "Bobby was in surprisingly good spirits as we hurled our questions at him," Dick recalled. "He was thoroughly familiar with the issues."

An overconfident McCarthy had spent the evening before the debate at a Dodgers baseball game. Most expected the Minnesota senator to win the debate. He had a studied command of language, and was widely considered to be the more intellectual of the two candidates. After briefly perusing the materials his aides had prepared, he had chatted with his poet friend Robert Lowell and joined in singing a round of Irish folk songs and ditties.

It was important for Bobby not to appear harsh, aggressive, or unduly argumentative. He needed to show command of facts. Most importantly, the team stressed that he emphasize his experience—his years as attorney general, being a member of the president's cabinet and the National Security Council—to counter the ten-year age gap with McCarthy. At forty-three, JFK was the youngest elected president in history. If Bobby were to win, he would undercut that record by a year.

When I asked the president about the outcome of the debate the following day, he grinned. "You are looking at the debate coach at Cotulla Elementary and at Sam Houston High School," he informed me. When I laughed at the unexpected bit of history, he declared, "And I turned them into state champions. So, drawing on all my long debate experience, I can tell you that there wasn't much blood drawn last night."

"So you think it was a draw?" I asked.

"No. Without question, Bobby won. With passion, force, and humor he won. But it sure wasn't much of a debate."

Before I left that first visit to Texas, I walked alone down the road in front of the ranch house. I remember watching the peaceful Pedernales River that seemed more like a stream winding below the road. The road itself narrated LBJ's life's story. If a giant compass was spread with one point at the ranch house, while the other arm inscribed a large circle, that circle would contain all the various sites of Lyndon's childhood. Only then did I sense something about the place that was different from the showmanship and spectacle and constant activity I had shared throughout the holiday weekend of eating and movies and conversation and swimming.

The ranch was Lyndon's playground of course, but it was also his sanctuary. It was a place where he felt relaxed and protected. At the time, I did not know that I would return and work there many times in the future. And one day the property would even become a national park, displaying his beginnings, his life, and in the family cemetery, his end.

Before my departure I had learned something I hadn't recognized before my visit. I came to understand Lyndon Johnson's abiding love for the people of the Hill Country, for the history of the place, for his land, for the importance of this site to the roots of his character and finally, to his legacy.

JUNE 4, 1968

"By the end of the California campaign, like the last round of a heavyweight fight, it wasn't a matter of simple fatigue," Dick said, "we were bone-weary. Desire and stamina mattered more than strategy."

On the last day of the campaign, Bobby had traveled 1,200 miles. He shuttled from Chinatown in San Francisco to Long Beach; he walked through Watts; then zigzagged down to San Diego; and finally, back to Los Angeles.

Dick recollected being surrounded by auspicious signs and symbols. "It was not simply the polls and editorials," he maintained, "you could sense it in the crowds, you breathed it in the air. I felt uplifted by a growing sense of great expectations. All that remained now was the waiting."

On the morning of the primary, Bobby called Dick after breakfast, asking him to spend the day with him at John Frankenheimer's beach house in Malibu. In addition to his family—Ethel and six of their children, the dog and the monkey—only journalist Theodore White and political adviser Fred Dutton would be there.

Upon arrival in Malibu, Dick's first glimpse of Bobby (as he described afterward in an article in *McCall's* magazine, "A Day in June") was poolside, "stretched out across two chairs in the sunlight, head hanging limply over the chair frame." Before long, however, he was roused from his weariness by the early exit-based returns. CBS was predicting that Kennedy would likely win by a margin of 49 percent to 41 percent. Dick excitedly calculated that "if the 49 percent in California could be pushed up to 50 percent, a clean majority, it would be total breakthrough." In an instant, White observed, "Kennedy became crisp executive again," figuring how their field team might be mobilized to persuade an extra two voters in each of the twenty thousand precincts to go to the polls, allowing them to reach the magic majority number. Bobby wondered if any news had come in from South Dakota, whose primary was the same day. Early indications were more than hopeful that he would win that rural state as well as urban California.

Later that afternoon, White noted, "as the warmth and the taste of victory came over him," Bobby began to relax. He asked Dick to draft a victory statement, something strong and also generous toward McCarthy.

Early that evening Dick returned to the Ambassador Hotel on Wilshire Boulevard where Kennedy had taken a six-room suite to await results with his family, friends, and reporters. By 9 p.m. CBS altered its projections to favor Kennedy even further, forecasting a 52 to 38 advantage. In addition, the first returns from South Dakota now looked overwhelmingly positive, sending a wave of elation through the crowded suite. In those moments, in those rooms, the momentum toward the nomination seemed unstoppable. White observed that Kennedy's "glee was absolutely uncontained."

"Bobby signaled to me and Sorensen," Dick recalled. They maneuvered through the crowd, room to room, to find someplace free of the deafening din in the suite. Finally, the three entered a bathroom and locked the door. Twice Bobby scanned the victory statement, wrote down a list of names of people he wanted to be sure to thank, and looking up, said with urgency, "I've got to get free of McCarthy. While we're fighting each other, Humphrey's running around the country, picking up delegates. Talk to McCarthy. Tell him if he withdraws I'll make him Secretary of State."

It was nearing midnight when Dick rose to accompany Kennedy and a small group of family and staff down to the hotel's Embassy Ballroom where nearly two thousand supporters awaited his arrival and victory statement. Just as they were leaving, Dick received a call from an important McCarthy supporter. Dick never looked up as Bobby touched him on the shoulder and said, "I'll go downstairs and do this, then we can talk some more over at the Factory," a local club where the campaign had reservations for a private party.

————◆————

Dick was still working the phone in a preliminary search for new allegiances and delegates when shouts and shrieks sounded up and down the corridors outside, shrieks multiplied on every television set in the bedrooms and sitting rooms of the nearly deserted suite as the news came that Robert Kennedy had been shot. Dick joined Ted Sorensen, who was sitting alone at the end of a bed, his arms hanging limply between his knees, his eyes frozen on the television screen. There was nothing to say. Familiar strangers, bonded by triumph and anguish, they sat in silence.

Two years earlier Dick had written in his diary: *There is no real warning of disaster anywhere, anytime. It just comes out of sunlight to darkness.* Now it had come again. "But this wasn't the same," Dick remarked to me, as he reflected on that moment so many years later. "This time it was not my youthful hero and president. This time it was my friend, someone I loved. I grieved for our stolen future."

For the next twenty-five hours Dick paced the hospital corridors, drinking coffee, eating sandwiches, conferring anxiously with colleagues. Early on the morning of June 6, one of Bobby's oldest friends approached him. If Dick wanted to say goodbye, he said, "you better go in now." It was almost over. When Dick entered the hospital room, the family was gathered around his bed. The only sound was the rhythm of the machines. Ethel lay on the bed beside him, clasping his body. His brother Ted knelt at the bedside, praying. Jackie murmured something to the doctor. In the midst of this tableau, only the life support machines lent Bobby Kennedy the facsimile of life.

————◆————

At 5:01 a.m. on June 6, 1968, National Security Adviser Walt Rostow called Lyndon Johnson. "Mr. President, it has just been announced that Senator Kennedy is dead."

When I spoke with the president two days later, I had never seen him so withdrawn, downcast, overtly emotional. He explained that he had just heard that Bill Moyers had said that with Bobby's death, the Blacks had lost the best friend they ever had. "Nothing has hurt me so much," Johnson said to me.

———•—•——

Dick and I reflected a long while on the brutal twists of fate that had so powerfully shaped our own lives and those of our countrymen that year. We decided to watch Bobby's last victory speech together. Dick had never seen or heard Bobby deliver that speech, written on the last day of Bobby's life.

Dick had often said that for him, the Sixties came to an end that day. But over the previous years of sorting through his papers, we had come to understand that the idealistic fervor, energy, humor, violence, and transforming progress that defined that decade had not truly ceased at the Good Samaritan Hospital on June 6, 1968.

So, for the first time, Dick began to watch Bobby's victory speech delivered in the ballroom of the Ambassador Hotel fifty years before.

After many thank-yous and jests and pauses to allow for abounding high spirits, Bobby declared, *I think we can end the divisions in the United States . . . the violence, the disenchantment with our society; the division, whether it's between blacks and whites, between the poor and the more affluent, between age groups, or the war in Vietnam.*

Suddenly Dick rose from our couch. "I can't watch this anymore," he said. And with that, he quickly left the room. I stayed on to listen to a voice that did indeed seem capable of bringing us together.

We are a great country, an unselfish country and a compassionate country. And I intend to make that my basis for running . . .

CHAPTER TWELVE

Endings and Beginnings

Former President Johnson at the
LBJ Ranch, September 18, 1972.

"IT WAS A SAD TIME, A DISMAL TIME," DICK RECALLED AS WE
sorted through a box overflowing with materials saved from the 1968
Democratic convention in Chicago: delegate guides, memos, newspaper
clippings, memorabilia, voter surveys, a draft for a platform plank on Vietnam, and, most curiously, a splintered police club. From Theodore White's
reporting, I knew that Dick had come into possession of the splintered club
that served as a gruesome symbol of the violent encounters between police
and antiwar protesters that would doom the Chicago convention, but it
startled me to discover the actual club still in a box nearly half a century
later.

After Bobby Kennedy died, Dick had officially rejoined McCarthy's
campaign. "The whole country seemed to be suffering from paralysis, a

post-traumatic stress after the deaths of King and Kennedy. I felt I had to do something," Dick said, "be with people where something might happen."

Commenting upon Goodwin's return, McCarthy speechwriter Jeremy Larner noted that Dick was "more manic than before, as if constant activity were the only remedy for the stunning loss he had suffered the second time over. Passing up speechwriting, he spent most of his time phoning and planning to see politicians, working up new statements for the press and trying to get McCarthy to do something effective on TV. . . . He seemed always to have ten schemes, plans, plots, and press releases at the same time. But he worked well with McCarthy." While the candidate himself seemed to be suffering from a sense of disorientation and uncertainty about how to proceed after Kennedy's death, "Goodwin was undaunted; he would wake up in the morning ready to wheel and deal, phone and fly."

The campaign was not the same crusade it had been in the snows of New Hampshire. It lacked the innocence and the devotion of those early days. But it was the war that had brought Dick to New Hampshire, and it was the ongoing war that returned him to McCarthy.

The Vietnam peace talks had never regained momentum after the initial boost following Johnson's withdrawal from the presidential race. Weeks and eventually months were spent arguing over where the talks should take place—and then, when Paris was finally agreed upon, what the shape of the negotiating table should be. North Vietnam wanted a round table so all parties, including the National Liberation Front representatives, would be "equal"; South Vietnam demanded a rectangular table reflecting their conception of the two clear-cut sides to the dispute. And the North was now demanding an unconditional end to all bombing (even sorties designed to protect American and allied troops) before any negotiations could begin in earnest.

Dick wanted to be wherever he might best exert pressure to end the war—back with McCarthy, preparing for the Democratic convention in late August in Chicago. No sooner had he returned to McCarthy, however, than a series of mocking articles highlighting his vacillation between candidates began to appear. Cartoonist David Levine depicted him as a butterfly, first collecting pollen from one flower, then fluttering to another, suggesting the zigzagging path of a moral waffler. Other unflattering caricatures followed. He was likened to a moth flitting out of the darkness into the light of one ascendant leader after another, drawn toward the voltage of power.

"Such personal antagonism," I remarked to Dick at breakfast. He looked up from the sports pages, blinked his thick eyelashes, and said, "I was too smart, too sexy," and with a raucous laugh, "too swarthy."

"Gore Vidal even said of me," Dick added, "'Goodwin is forever an Iago in pursuit of Othello.' What a pedigree! Sometimes I ignored such things, sometimes I shrugged, but Iago? Later Rasputin and Machiavelli! I never switched sides at all. I was with JFK from the start and left when he was suddenly gone. Then I served Lyndon with everything I had until I left for Wesleyan. When the war heated up and I failed to get Bobby to run against Johnson, I went with McCarthy. When Bobby changed his mind, I went with my close friend and stayed until he was gone. I went back to McCarthy because his campaign was the only place I had any chance to take actions that might help bring an end to the war."

If anyone understood Dick's moral clarity, the code that he adhered to and was driven by, it was McCarthy himself. While others questioned Dick's loyalty, McCarthy was never among them. "Goodwin is like a professional ballplayer," he reflected. "You could trade him from the Braves to the Cardinals, and he wouldn't miss his pitching turn and he wouldn't give away your signals to the other team."

AUGUST 25–30, 1968

"If I'm not mistaken," Dick maintained, "I spotted you on the sidewalk across Michigan Avenue when I arrived at Chicago's Hilton Hotel at the start of the Democratic convention. You were surrounded by a group of young men on the margin of Grant Park."

Dick always enjoyed adding episodes to the ongoing improvisational story he loved to tell of the two of us having been in the same place at the same time over the years before we met. It made me happy to imagine that, as he often said, he had been looking for me all those years. And it was true that I was in Chicago for the convention. Unlike Dick, however, who had credentials to travel freely as a member of McCarthy's staff, I had no official role. The convention happened to correspond to my week of vacation, and I had been invited to Chicago with a friend who was a congressman's chief of staff. Like the majority of young people in attendance, I hoped the convention would result in actions that would help hasten the end of the war.

We were among the tens of thousands of people who had descended upon Chicago during that last week of August. There were the usual convention insiders—the six thousand or so delegates and alternates, governors, senators, congressmen, staffs, contingents of press and media, party donors, and hangers-on. But beyond these participants in the normal functioning of the convention, a large, unruly, and growing mass of antiwar militants had congregated. Gathered in nearby parks and streets with and without permits, this patchwork of American youth had come to protest the war, deride the expected nomination of Hubert Humphrey, and ridicule the proceedings of an establishment they no longer respected or trusted.

There was widespread fear—even expectation—of violence. More than eleven thousand police officers were deployed on twelve-hours shifts. Members of the National Guard and army troops were on alert. McCarthy had appealed to his own followers to stay away and avoid ramping up the discord, warning that "the presence of large numbers of visitors amidst the summer tensions of Chicago may well add to the possibility of unintended violence or disorder. This would be a tragedy—for any hurt or arrested, and a tragedy for those of us who wish to give the political process a fair and peaceful trust."

Nonetheless, many hundreds of McCarthy volunteers ignored his warning. They had come to Chicago, "not to march or protest, but to work," Dick later wrote in unpublished recollections we found in his files, "preparing press releases, keeping delegate counts, scheduling the candidate. Serious, intent, laboring far into the night, they undertook the myriad tasks of McCarthy's candidacy, some moved, as perhaps I was, by the felt need to complete the long journey from New Hampshire; many still hopeful that some miraculous turn of events might avert the inevitable defeat. More hardened to realities, I did not share that hope," he wrote.

On the day after the convention opened, it became clear that the cards had already been dealt, and with remarkable and dispiriting frankness, McCarthy acknowledged that Humphrey "had the presidential nomination wrapped up."

The real fight, Dick became convinced, was no longer between McCarthy and Humphrey, but what kind of Vietnam plank would emerge from the convention to establish the platform upon which the nominated candidate was pledged to run. McCarthy had put Dick in charge of working with like-minded delegates to draft a "peace plank" for the party platform.

A strong plank emerged from the negotiations, calling for "an unconditional cessation of all bombings," and the "mutual withdrawal of United States forces and North Vietnamese forces from South Vietnam." The U.S. would "encourage South Vietnam to negotiate a political reconciliation with the National Liberation Front looking toward a government broadly representative."

The establishment plank, a continuation of the present negotiation policy in Paris that had produced no meaningful results, stipulated that bombing sorties to protect our troops must continue despite North Vietnam's refusal to engage in serious talks until all bombing had halted. This plank "had been drafted at the White House," Dick told reporters, "and flown out to Chicago." For a brief time, it had seemed that Humphrey might break with Johnson on this issue and establish an independent stance. But when the southern bloc warned that it would turn against him if he separated from Johnson, thereby denying him a first-ballot victory, Humphrey went along with the establishment plank.

"The issue was clear," Theodore White concluded. "On the one side: a forthright renunciation of America's commitment to a nearly hopeless war, withdrawal, a diversion of America's resources to its home problems." Then, "on the other side: an open-end commitment to go on with the war until the enemy should also tire and then meet us to discuss a real peace at whatever cost." That cost had been horrific. In the five months since Hanoi had signaled a readiness to begin peace talks, more than seven thousand American troops had been killed.

At this juncture, on the second day of the convention, more votes were likely for the peace plank than for the nomination of Eugene McCarthy. It was Dick's hope that when the vote was taken, a powerful show of force in favor of the peace initiative might impact the Paris negotiations and change the direction of the country.

———————

The hotel suite I shared with my friends was several miles from the headquarters for both McCarthy and Humphrey at the Hilton. During the days, we made forays into Chicago's downtown, returning to our hotel with eyewitness accounts of face-offs between demonstrators and police. One of my friends had gone to the old Coliseum, where, I was dismayed to hear, a large and contemptuous crowd had thrown an anti-birthday party for LBJ, a mocking affair arranged by the National Mobilization Committee to End the War in Vietnam. At the Hilton, the windows looked down on Michigan Avenue and across to Grant Park where thousands of demonstrators and protesters had gathered. Hour by hour, the sounds of their belligerent chants—"Dump the Hump! Join us, Dump the Hump!"—filled the air around the old hotel. And with each passing day, the response of the police grew increasingly violent.

At night, we remained in our hotel, completely engrossed in television coverage of the proceedings from the International Amphitheatre where the convention was held. Just as the peace plank was scheduled to be voted on, our telephone rang. A wide-eyed friend, her hand cupped over the receiver, called my name, mouthing, "It's the president of the United States." At first, I thought and hoped she was just joking, but when—with extreme self-consciousness—she handed me the receiver, the operator told me the president was coming on the line.

After I said hello, Johnson said in a soft voice, "I have a favor to ask." What followed was the last thing I could ever have imagined. "When you were last down here at the ranch, you borrowed my flashlight. Do you know where it is? I've looked everywhere."

After telling him where he might look for it, I asked him simply, "How are you?"

"How do you think I am? I never felt lower in my life. I can't go up to Chicago in front of my own people, my own party, on my own birthday. And you never even wished me a Happy Birthday!"

Johnson had hoped to attend the convention to celebrate his sixtieth birthday. Plans had been made for his helicopter to land on the Amphitheatre's rooftop platform. A five-foot-high cake had been baked and the Imperial Suite in the Hilton had been reserved for him. But these hopes had been dashed by the contentious atmosphere within the convention hall and the clashes in the city's streets and parks. Friends had warned him that "a personal appearance would throw the convention into turmoil." And platform chair Congressman Hale Boggs had told him flatly that "no one can control the delegates," who were likely to greet him with jeers and boos.

I remember how confused and upset I was in the aftermath of that call with the president. I felt a deep personal sadness for the man who, on his fifty-sixth birthday four years earlier at the Democratic convention, had been feted by thousands of cheering supporters and had been thrilled to see his portrait emblazoned in fireworks over the Atlantic City night sky. Now, he was denied even an appearance at his party's convention without risking widespread uproar from the enraged masses outside, and the contempt of nearly half the people inside. If Johnson blamed North Vietnam for the continuing stalemate, the antiwar movement blamed him.

Having been delayed by a tumultuous fight over credentials that lasted past midnight, the vote on the Vietnam plank finally took place on Wednesday afternoon. Although the peace plank was defeated by a vote of 1,568 to 1,042, the number of Democrats willing to reject the majority plank dictated by their president and the leader of their party was remarkable. When McCarthy was asked "whether he had sent Goodwin to the convention floor to lead the platform fight," he replied with a smile. "Oh, I haven't really sent Dick Goodwin anywhere. He's gone a lot of places for me, but I haven't sent him. He's rather a free operator, but I don't fault him for that."

During the voting on the Vietnam plank, demonstrators in Grant Park, numbering around ten thousand, announced their intention to march to the convention hall. They had no permit to do so. When three protesters climbed the flagpole and started to take down the American flag, the police charged into the crowd surrounding the flagpole. Chaos ensued. The police threw tear-gas bombs; the demonstrators responded with rocks and bottles. As people spilled into the street, the *Chicago Tribune* reported, "Michigan Avenue was turned into a bloodied battleground. Scores were injured and thousands affected by tear gas; scores were thrown into police vans and arrested; glass windows on the Michigan Avenue side of the Hilton were shattered." Blue lights flashed from a lengthening line of police cars, and barricades thickened to shield the hotel.

The city was in a state of siege. Enraged by the protesters, the police wielded clubs with such abandon that bystanders, reporters, and demonstrators were indiscriminately thrown to the ground and bludgeoned. A police car crashed into the barricades, pushing people through the windows and into the hotel restaurant. McCarthy, peering down from the twenty-third floor of the hotel, saw his worst fears—those he had warned his followers of in imploring them to stay home—realized on the streets below. When his volunteers asked if a first-aid station could be set up in their fifteenth-floor suites at the Hilton, he readily agreed.

Dick had returned to the Hilton during the break between the peace plank vote and the late-night balloting for the nomination. Standing in the lobby, Jack Newfield reported, "Richard Goodwin, the ashen nub of a cigar sticking out of his fatigued face, mumbled, 'This is just the beginning. There'll be four more years of this.'"

Before going back to the convention hall, Dick and Al Lowenstein secured a thousand candles from a Chicago synagogue which would allow the peace delegates to protest Humphrey's nomination even if Mayor Richard Daley cut the lights. Recognizing the risk of crossing the embattled streets to the Amphitheatre, Dick somehow managed to commandeer a Secret Service limousine to take him back to the heavily guarded convention hall, now so armored it was being called the "Fortress."

The roll call did not begin until after 11 p.m. As the delegates' names were called, the American public viewed a split screen. On one side, the uproar at the convention, with cheers and jeers in equal order; on the other, edited footage from the bloodbath earlier that night, the sight of bodies cowering under police clubs, the sounds of shrieks and sobbing. Humphrey captured the nomination on the first ballot, but on this night, Theodore White's notes read: "The Democrats are finished."

To mark the sorrow of the moment, show solidarity with the victims of the carnage, and repurpose the tapers they had brought, Dick and Lowenstein suggested a peaceful candlelight procession from the convention to Grant Park, where the bloodied demonstrators were still gathered. More than six hundred delegates joined in, mostly McCarthy and Kennedy supporters, including Paul Newman, Julian Bond, New York congressman William Ryan, and George Brown Jr. of California.

It was after 2 a.m. when the candlelit procession, stately, sad, and silent, reached Grant Park. A Bennington College student described the sight: "We hadn't dared believe reports of delegates marching from the Amphitheatre. But they were there," she recalled. "The grown-ups had come and no one was going to hurt us anymore. . . . There was a cheer; it didn't just shout, but welled up, grew and grew as realization came. . . . Whatever happened before or will happen ever, nothing will shake my faith in those few hours. The candlelit delegates filed into the crowd on pathways cleared for them, winding through, they were hugged and blessed and loved at every footstep."

A reporter asked Dick if he had a statement to make. Gesturing to the many hundreds of candlelights moving like fireflies through the clustered field of young people huddled together, he said, "*This* is a statement."

———·•·———

Throughout the Sixties, Dick had participated in an inordinate number of pivotal, defining moments of the decade. He was there with JFK on the "Caroline," a member of the small team that traveled with the candidate through the 1960 presidential campaign; he was in the room to help JFK for his first debate with Richard Nixon; he was in the White House in the middle of the night when the president's coffin returned from Dallas; he was at Lyndon Johnson's side during the summit of his historic achievements with the Great Society and civil rights; he was in New Hampshire with Eugene McCarthy's crusade, and with Robert Kennedy when he died in a Los Angeles hospital. Now, in Chicago, he was a central figure in the convention's debate over the Vietnam peace plank.

What were the odds of being struck by lightning once, much less twice? And yet, Dick seemed to be in places where lightning struck with unusual frequency. And now, just when everything seemed to be over, he was about to be struck by lightning once more!

Dick returned to the Hilton after the convention had finally adjourned around midnight on Thursday. Recalling that moment, I asked him if he had any premonition that he was walking into pandemonium. "Absolutely not," he said. He had stayed in the Amphitheatre to listen to Humphrey's acceptance speech, "a decent speech by a decent man," he said, but drowned out by the turbulent days that preceded it. By this final night of the convention, the violence on the streets had largely been spent. Dick had joined friends at a bar before heading back to his room. "On my way up," he recalled, "I stopped in at the 15th floor. I wanted to look in on the McCarthy kids. I knew many of them would still be there. I loved those kids. I wanted to thank them and say goodbye."

No sooner had he stepped off the elevator, heading toward the sounds of conversation and muffled singing, than another elevator door opened and a squadron of police streamed down the corridor in the same direction. Within seconds another wave burst forth. Boots shattered the doors; the McCarthy kids, some half asleep, were pushed, pummeled, and dragged like cattle back to the elevator doors. The enraged police attacked a group of people playing cards, an assault so furious that one student, using the card table as a shield, was smashed on his shoulder with enough force to break the policeman's billy club. Dick was herded along with the kids into an elevator to be taken down to the lobby so they could be hauled off to jail.

I asked Dick what had set things off. Had he any idea what was happening at the time? "Not then," Dick said. "It just seemed like an explosion of madness. It was an assault, bent on revenge for the accumulated events of the entire week."

Later, there were allegations that the police had been provoked by the beer cans, ashtrays, cocktail glasses, Bibles, and toilet paper rolls that had rained down on them from the fifteenth floor on them as they were guarding the hotel. Apparently, several objects had been hurled from somewhere above but there was "no evidence whatsoever," Theodore White concluded after an investigation, "that the McCarthy students had been throwing anything."

Dick soon found himself in a nightmarish scene in the hotel lobby where frightened students, some with deep scalp wounds, were being rounded up. Every time I've read Theodore White's vivid account of what transpired next, I'm filled with a special pride in my husband—which he has always tried to minimize, insisting he escaped being bludgeoned simply because he was wearing a business suit and tie and was older than the kids. White's account belies Dick's modesty:

> Help us, Mr. Goodwin, help us! was the first cry that came to him as he reached the lobby—and there he saw the little knot of students, surrounded by police, the girls crying and hysterical, several boys bleeding. They were teen-agers who had first ventured into politics eight months before and only now were tasting its raw and underlying violence. Goodwin, assuming authority, told them to squat on the floor. The police ringed the sitters. Goodwin told the police that both Senator McCarthy and the Vice-President himself were on the way down to the lobby to take command. [This was not true.]
>
>   This stilled the police momentarily. Loudly, Goodwin gave directions to the youngsters, dispatched one or two to telephone the press and television, made known to the police that television was coming to witness this; and several of the police began to drift away. Surreptitiously, Goodwin told another student to telephone immediately to the McCarthy and Humphrey suites and ask both men to come

at once—the candidates, with their Secret Service guards, might quench the violence and save the youngsters.

"I knew how fragile my authority was," Dick later wrote. "The police were already doubtful, restless. Should the scales tip toward disbelief—we would all be swept away into the police wagons already stationed, engines running, just outside the hotel entrance."

Humphrey's press secretary had refused to awaken his boss, but like a deus ex machina, the elevator doors opened, and Senator McCarthy emerged. He was "calm, assured, authority in his carriage," Dick continued. "Taking my place, he looked over the seated students toward the police. 'Who's in charge here?' he asked. No one answered. 'Just as I thought, no one's in charge here.' Then turning from the police with an indifference transcending mere contempt, he began talking to his volunteers; there was nothing to be afraid of; a nurse would be available for anyone who had been hurt; just get up now and return to your rooms; you've all worked hard and need a good night's sleep; I'll see all of you tomorrow. As McCarthy talked the police began silently to file toward the hotel entrance. By the time he had finished they were gone. The students then rose, re-entered the elevators, and went back to their rooms."

Dick, too, returned to his room. By then it was nearly 5 a.m., and he needed to pack before flying out that morning to return to Boston. On his way down to the lobby, he stopped on the fifteenth floor to survey the sad postscript of the 1968 convention. Walking past broken doors and a shattered floor lamp, he spotted the broken police club. He opened his suitcase and slipped it among his peace plank notes, identification lanyard, and memorabilia.

What stayed with Dick the rest of his life was his certainty that the McCarthy students had not provoked the police; they had broken no laws. The police had become a mob—an armed mob, a mob that wore badges. That night gave him the smallest taste of what it must have been like to be on the receiving end of the enduring violence—the nightsticks, the fire hoses, the dogs, the gas and guns—wielded against the foot soldiers of the Civil Rights Movement as they conducted the peaceful sit-ins, marches, and Freedom Rides that had marked the earlier part of the decade.

Throughout the many clashes during the convention, more than 300 people were injured; more than 650 were arrested. The entire week of bedlam displayed a lawless disorder for all the country to see, a mayhem that would christen the "Law and Order" campaign of Richard Nixon.

———·•·———

A Gallup poll taken in September 1968 registered the devastating impact of the Democratic convention on Humphrey's fortunes: Nixon stood at 43 percent; Humphrey, far behind, at 28 percent. Segregationist George Wallace, running as an independent, had 21 percent. Humphrey was widely viewed as a satellite caught in the gravity of Lyndon Johnson's fall. To Dick's mind, a continuation of the administration's war policy—with no progress on the peace negotiations, and hundreds of troops dying week after week— guaranteed certain failure in the coming election. An abrupt break from the status quo was essential.

There was no leader left for Dick to endorse. He would vote for Humphrey of course, but as he explained in a long letter to Lawrence O'Brien, an old colleague from both the Kennedy and Johnson administrations and now Humphrey's campaign manager, he was "unable to endorse the Vice President (for what little that's worth) despite my personal affection for him. To me an endorsement is more than a preference or a vote, but also implies a fundamental identification on at least the great issues."

In a nationally televised speech from Salt Lake City on September 30, Humphrey finally declared his independence from the president. He pledged that as president, he would stop all bombing unconditionally, believing the move "an acceptable risk" that could break the stalemate in negotiations and shorten the war. The speech proved a turning point. "The most important things about the speech," O'Brien said, "was the effect on Humphrey himself. He felt good about it, he was his own man." Antiwar activists stopped heckling him; McCarthy supporters returned to the Democratic fold; his poll numbers began to rise, swiftly and steadily.

But Dick did not believe that Humphrey had gone far enough to set a new direction for the country. Just as he had urged McCarthy to broaden and deepen his campaign beyond the war, so now he advised Humphrey, through O'Brien, to turn the page to the unfinished business of the Great Society with fresh ideas: jobs, not welfare; a Marshall Plan for the cities; the decentralization of federal programs allowing people who receive support to participate in setting priorities; government-sponsored day care centers so "college educated women who feel some discontent at their inability to use their abilities" could enter the job market. "Male politicians tend to laugh at this," Dick urged O'Brien, "but it's a potential gold mine."

First and foremost, however, was to end the war. Dick proceeded to advise: "Stop playing around with the bombing issue, etc. You can't be subtle with this one. You have to say that whatever its original merits, the war is too costly in terms of life, resources, effect on our society. You will do whatever is necessary to bring about an honorable end—short of unilateral withdrawal. . . . If talking to the Viet Cong will bring peace, you will talk to them. If a settlement involves all the elements of South Vietnam participating in the government, you will agree to that—the key thing is you are going to end it and not let [South Vietnamese president Nguyen Van] Thieu or anyone else stand in the way of a negotiated settlement." Nothing would dramatize this better, Dick suggested, than allowing McCarthy and Ted Kennedy to conduct the negotiations.

By mid-October, as Dick was writing this memo to O'Brien, Lyndon Johnson made his own move to break the frozen negotiations. After much back-and-forth, Johnson wrote in his memoir, he believed that "the ice was beginning to melt," that "Hanoi was ready to shift from the battlefield to the conference table." The North agreed that if America stopped bombing altogether and if South Vietnam agreed to come to the table with the Viet Cong, "serious talks" could start within twenty-four hours. Everything seemed set for a major announcement on October 31.

Then, at the last minute, South Vietnamese president Thieu suddenly backed away from the agreement, refusing to join the peace talks if the Viet Cong participated. Johnson decided to go ahead on his own. He had given his word to the North that he would stop all bombing. He announced the decision in a televised speech, but any momentum toward peace it might have provided was crushed by the intransigence of South Vietnam.

An intercepted cable Johnson received explained President Thieu's unexpected shift. People claiming to speak for Nixon were telling Thieu it would be advantageous for him to procrastinate: "Nixon is going to win; a Nixon administration will be more friendly to Saigon than the Democrats will be; stick with us and we will stick with you." Johnson was furious, but he had no direct evidence that Nixon himself was involved, and without that, did not feel he could publicly charge him with what he considered to be treason.

Only much later did hard evidence of Nixon's direct involvement emerge, both from an interview with the intermediary (Anna Chennault, Nixon's representative to South Vietnam's government) and in contemporaneous notes from telephone conversations between Nixon and his aide H. R. Haldeman, on October 22, 1968, where Nixon instructed Haldeman to "Keep Anna Chennault working on South Vietnam."

Nixon won the election with 43.4 percent of the vote; Humphrey received 42.7 percent, Wallace 13.5 percent. With such a narrow margin, "the outcome would have been different," Johnson was convinced, "if the Paris peace talks had been in progress on Election Day."

"It's all or nothing" was the gist of Lyndon Johnson's job offer to me in the waning months of his administration—a mantra he repeated a half dozen times. By "all," he meant his invitation for me to return to Texas with him after his presidency to work with a small team on his memoir. He also wanted my assistance with plans for his presidential library and the LBJ School of Public Affairs at the University of Texas at Austin. I could live with the family at the ranch on weekends, he suggested, but keep an apartment in Austin during the week to access his presidential papers, temporarily stored in a federal office building until the presidential library was built.

He categorically rejected my suggestion that I come to work for him part-time. I told him I wanted to return to Harvard and begin my teaching career, but promised to come to Texas during long weekends, academic breaks, and summer vacations. His rejoinder was emphatic: "Either you come full-time, or you don't come at all."

The comic array of incentives he offered to sway me have added a note of levity to my lectures over the years, but the situation was complicated. To be sure, there was comedy in the manner with which he countered each of my arguments. When I spoke of my desire to teach, he said: "Done. I'll get you a position at the University of Texas. You can teach all you want. Hell, you teach about the Presidency, don't you? Well, I *am* a President. . . . Now what could be better than that."

When I tried to explain that I had made plans to volunteer at a job training program in Roxbury, the predominantly Black section of Boston, he cut me off. "I can get you all the poor people you want. I can get them from Austin and San Antonio. If you go to Roxbury with no money and lots of goodwill, you'll accomplish absolutely nothing. If you really want to help poor people you better come to Texas."

When I told him I wanted to write, he told me I could have a peaceful cabin on Lake LBJ. "I'll get you a blue sky and some rippling water and some old trees, all the things you thinkers need to produce big thoughts. And you can go there whenever you want, except when you're working for me."

I had heard many tales of Johnson's bullying "treatment" when pressuring someone to give way to what he wanted. In the many decades since then, I have collected a small library of books by those who worked under him, including accounts from White House aides and assistants that variously portrayed a man capable of scorched-earth hostility. Dick had told me firsthand episodes illustrating both Johnson's brutality and his warmth—the crushing rage and lavish generosity that created such confusion, one moment leaving you feeling beaten down and abused, the next lifting you with flattery and encouragement. And most of the time, he tightened the vise sufficiently to get his way.

Never once, however, did he direct his fabled aggressiveness—that could verge on savagery—toward me. He never humiliated me. But I, too, felt caught in an emotional vise. I had come to understand and care about him; I knew I would miss sitting with him on the edge of the pool, listening to his inexhaustible store of tales, driving with him on early morning inspections of the ranch as he gave instructions to his field workers. I realized the opportunity he had offered would not come again. It was one thing to teach presidential history, quite another to listen hour after hour to the perspective of a president who had helped make that very history.

I had been invited to spend the 1968 Christmas holidays at the ranch with the Johnson family—their last Christmas there as sitting president and first lady. It was initially a festive time—helicoptering to parties at neighboring ranches, lunches and dinners with friends of the family, dancing at the Mermaid Club, attending a New Year's Eve party. However, as the date of our return to Washington approached, Johnson initiated a new round of talks intended to persuade me to join him and his team of writers in Texas on January 20, to begin the process of sorting through his papers. Again, I suggested that I could split my time between teaching and working on the memoir. Absolutely not, he repeated, turning his back and walking away.

Over the next few days, he ignored me, refusing to look at me, directing his warmth and attention to everyone else—completely freezing me out. Lady Bird noticed what he was doing. She had seen such behavior before. She took me aside and told me not to be upset, his mood would pass. And she was right. The next morning, I heard over the intercom—"Would Doris Kearns please join the president and first lady in the pool in five minutes?" By the time I arrived, he was already in the water. He smiled warmly, as if nothing had happened the days before. I suspected Lady Bird had coached him. I knew then that I was no match for him. I had made the right decision. I wanted to go back to Harvard to start the next chapter of my career.

------·•·------

On the morning of Lyndon Johnson's final day in office, the White House called me to say that the president wanted to see me in the Oval Office that afternoon—before the farewell dinner that had been planned for the White House staff that evening. As I entered the White House gate, I felt apprehensive, fearing a renewal of our "All or Nothing" wrangling that had dragged on for weeks. I tried to devise in my mind a final rebuttal, but felt my resolve begin to waver. I became unsure what to do at this late moment.

The White House was in a state of upheaval as a result of the transition—Packing boxes lined the hallways, vacuum cleaners and floor buffers were noisily at work, ladders were set on drop cloths so painters could touch up walls. When I peered into my own former office in the West Wing, I felt an unpleasant sensation upon seeing the rug rolled on the desk, pictures stacked against the wall. It felt empty—both the end and the beginning of something—which is exactly what it was.

This dismantling was unsettling, and I was happy to find that it had not yet extended to the Oval Office when I entered. Nothing inside had been changed, boxed, or crated. On that final day, this was the last shrunken refuge of LBJ's tenure.

The president was seated at his desk, quiet, and as I approached him, the first words that he said were barely audible: "All right, *part-time.*"

I could hardly believe what I heard.

"I need help," he continued. "As soon as I get settled at home, I'm going to write my memoirs. I've got to do it right . . . Will you help me?"

There were no exorbitant promises this time. There was no deal-making and no bargaining.

"Of course, I will," I said, nodding.

A brief conversation followed in which we determined that I would come down to the ranch for a long weekend as soon as possible. "Now you take care of yourself up there at Harvard," he cautioned me with a grim smile. "Don't let them get at you, for God's sake, don't let their hatred for Lyndon Johnson poison your feelings about me."

When I turned to go, he called me back. "It's not easy to get the help you need when you're no longer on top of the world. I know that and I won't forget what you are doing for me."

The farewell dinner was held on the second floor of the living quarters. Music filled the hallways as people gathered for cocktails before the buffet dinner. The guests were the president's and first lady's top assistants. Many had been with the Johnsons since his Senate days. I had only been on the White House staff nine months and felt honored to be included.

Tender nostalgia suffused the evening. "The atmosphere was charged with emotion," Lady Bird wrote in her diary, "overflowing feelings, of keen awareness that this was the last goodbye."

Toasts were made, the president delivered short, emotional remarks, and we all held hands in a circle in the hallway and sang "Auld Lang Syne." Joe Califano expressed the feelings of many of Johnson's longtime aides. "All of us knew we'd been part of a monumental social revolution. For many of us these would be our most productive years, when more was accomplished than would be the case for the rest of our lives."

But for me, this pervasive note of nostalgia was eclipsed by my relief at the resolution of my own dilemma and my excitement for the future. I could work with Lyndon Johnson in Texas, and maintain my own independent space in Cambridge. That evening, it was not the poignancy and joyful sadness of looking backward that captivated me, but the enormous thrill of all that lay ahead.

———•———

So for the next two years I lived what I considered a charmed life in two very different places—the Boston and Harvard of John Kennedy and the Austin and Hill Country of Lyndon Johnson.

A quick walk from Harvard Square along the icy Charles River during the short days of February brought me to Harvard's Dunster House where

I would live as a resident tutor and assistant professor. Each day, I walked across the Yard to the reading room at Widener Library where I began preparing for my first big course on the American Presidency, to begin that fall. I was taking over this storied course from my mentor, Richard Neustadt, who was engaged in designing the curriculum for the new JFK School of Government. In the evenings, I joined my friends for dinners, movies, poetry readings and lectures, and jaunts into Boston for plays and concerts.

The first of my monthly trips to Texas began in late February. That no insulated boots, scarves, gloves, or hooded down jackets were needed proved a welcome relief. Weekdays, I stayed at Austin's historic Driskill Hotel, within walking distance of the federal office building where the writing team, led by two former White House aides, Harry Middleton and William Jorden, held daily meetings to divide up the work, sort through LBJ's papers, and prepare interview questions for the former president.

It was my great good fortune that the chapters on civil rights and Congress were assigned to me. No two subjects evoked happier memories in Johnson. He was delighted to talk about the passage of the Civil Rights Act ending segregation in the South or the Voting Rights Act. His voice would grow animated, his enthusiasm contagious, as he recounted—or rather acted out—both serious and hilarious anecdotes. By contrast, when others called upon him to talk about Vietnam or foreign policy, he would purse his lips, tightening up as he shuffled through documents with barely disguised discomfort and throttled impatience.

As the months passed, he began to shed his presidential armor. He let his hair grow. With his tanned face, white hair curling over his collar, dressed in khaki pants, he looked more like an aging counterculture leader than a former president. If only he had trusted his own marvelous range of conversation and humor we later savored in his tapes, instead of insisting on the 'dignified' presidential image he felt he must project, he might have written a unique and extraordinary memoir.

The first drafts of my chapters of the memoir included all the colorful stories I had heard him tell in his own expansive and uncensored voice. He was not pleased. Pointing to my inclusion of his barbed comment about the powerful House chairman of the Ways and Means Committee, Wilbur Mills, that he was so concerned with saving face that someday he would lose his ass, Johnson said, "I can't say this. Get it out right now, why he may be Speaker of the House someday. And for Christ's sake, get that vulgar language of mine out of there. It's a presidential memoir, damn it, and I've got to come out looking like a statesman, not some backwoods politician."

Weekends at the ranch were always fun and I eagerly joined in the rhythm and routines of that life. A city girl, I found peace and relaxation in the endless projects of ranch operations—the inspection of fields and fencing, the laying of pipes for new irrigation systems, the planting of seedlings and grass, the collection of hundreds of eggs each day. In the mornings, I jounced around the ranch's pastures with the former president as he looked over his fieldhands' work.

Meals were set to begin the moment he returned from these excursions. Like a camel, he could go for hours without food or drink. He was served first and kept up a running critique of everything he loved, what he hated, what he found tolerable. He would banter with all of us. But other times, he would sit morosely at the end of the table, petulant. His silence would become oppressive until Lady Bird managed to draw him back into conversation. If the conversation failed to hold his interest, he would bolt from the room to make phone calls.

He could not bear to be alone. During his daily nap after lunch, he asked me to sit in a chair in his walk-in closet so I would be there if he needed something—or, more importantly, if something happened to him—someone would be there. So much did he dread solitary moments that it seemed as if he felt the wings of death brush his forehead. But his request surely made for a most curious picture: me sitting in the middle of his closet, reading a book, formal dress suits hanging above polished oxfords on one side, casual clothes over cowboy boots on the other, waiting for the former president to arise from his nap.

When a suggestive piece appeared in a magazine during this period archly questioning my frequent trips to the ranch, I received a reassuring call from Johnson in Cambridge, telling me not to give such chattering nonsense a second thought. Still, such insinuations troubled me and on my next visit to Texas, I felt self-conscious. I was scheduled to meet Johnson at a luncheon reception in Austin before going to the ranch. When I arrived at the venue for the lunch, I glanced around, trying to spot Johnson. Suddenly, I felt a hand on my shoulder. It was Lady Bird, gentle, gracious, and—as always—knowing. She took my arm and threaded us through the room toward her husband. "Don't worry about these silly newspaper reports," she whispered. "You give comfort to my husband and that is all that matters."

In the late afternoon, Johnson and I would often take slow walks along the banks of the Pedernales River. Before long, these walks became strolls down memory lane—not an imaginary path, but actual sites that evoked scenes from Lyndon's childhood. We passed the house where he had been born (restored now and converted into a museum), the fields where he had played as a child, his grandfather's porch where, as a small boy, he had been mesmerized by the old man's tales of the great cattle drives from Texas to Kansas, and the Junction School where his mother had convinced his teacher to allow him to sit on her lap during reading lessons. Many times, we would pause to sit on the old stone wall in the shade of the towering, massive live oaks that shelter the peaceful Johnson family cemetery. As we sat on the stone wall, he would point out the graves of his grandparents, his mother and father, and then, finally, direct attention to the plot where he would one day be buried.

Increasingly, the stories he told me when we were together at the ranch were no longer preparation work for the memoirs, or even the future volumes that were planned to chronicle his rise to power. Sometimes, our conversations would go on and on as we unrolled his life in reverse, traveling from the presidency back to the days when he had mastered the Senate, then to his years as a young congressman idolizing Franklin Roosevelt, followed by his work enlisting young people in the National Youth Administration, leading to the lifelong impact of his early days teaching in Cotulla, and finally, to revelations of the harsh, troubled dynamics of his early family life, his childhood dreams, fears, and sorrows.

I always carried a small notebook where I would scrawl down Johnson's reminiscences in my own mode of shorthand. Every now and then he would pause suddenly and tell me to shut the book. "I don't want you to tell this to anyone in the world, not even to your great-grandchildren." Then, later that same day he would burst out, "Hey, why aren't you writing all this down? Someday someone may want to read it!"

As time went on, the vulnerability he showed during the unrolling of his life reflected the trust we had established. Little did I know that these conversations were a gift he was giving to me, one that was quickened by his conviction that he didn't have long to live. Our talks and walks together along his real-life memory lane would become the foundation of my first book and mark the beginning of my career as a presidential historian.

Late Thursday night on March 12, 1970, I was flown to the Brooke Army Medical Center at Fort Sam Houston in San Antonio, Texas. Lyndon Johnson had been rushed to the hospital with severe chest pains. When I entered the room at 11 p.m., I was shocked to see how small this enormous figure looked in the hospital bed. He looked half asleep as a masseur worked on his neck and shoulder.

"Don't worry," he said, upon seeing me, "it's only angina, not a heart attack."

He seemed in serious pain. In the past, he had often rambled on about his "legacy," about the importance of the memoir, about the School of Public Affairs, the eventual transformation of his ranch into a national historic site, the creation of his library that would document his place in history. But on this night, for the better part of several hours, until early the following morning, he wanted a glimpse of how he would be represented in the history books. With a calm introspection, he brushed aside my positive efforts for a more optimistic outlook about his posthumous standing. The laws on the books, he maintained, were only the starting point of the things he dreamed of getting done. He had wanted to do so much more.

"You're the professor," he said quietly, "how do you think I'll be remembered?"

"I think you have a lot more living to do," I insisted, "before we have to remember you."

And after he returned to the ranch, he resolved to begin a healthier regime. He lost weight, tried to walk regularly, and stopped smoking and drinking. For a brief time, he even became a calorie counter.

Little by little, however, efforts to organize a healthy and disciplined life began to backslide and not many months passed before he began gaining weight, surrendering to the barbecued ribs, fried catfish, and desserts he relished. He returned to his favorite Cutty Sark scotch and relapsed into smoking, only a few a day and then more. "I'm an old man, so what's the difference," he said, although he was still in his early sixties. "I don't want to linger the way Eisenhower did."

Before two years were out, while visiting his daughter Lynda's Virginia home, he suffered the massive heart attack he had considered his destiny. Against doctors' orders, who wanted him to remain at some length in the Charlottesville hospital, he returned to Texas, "the place where," as his father had told him, "people know when you're sick and care when you die." While his mornings usually began fairly well, by afternoon, there often came what he described as "a series of sharp, jolting pains in the chest that left him scared and breathless." Dizzy and listless, he would tend to lie down by late afternoon, seeking relief provided by the oxygen tanks that were kept by his bedside.

———•·•———

Nine months later, on December 11, 1972, Lyndon Johnson was scheduled to deliver the keynote address at a major civil rights symposium at the LBJ Library. "Lyndon had been quite sick the night before and up most of the night," Lady Bird would later remember. "The doctor insisted that he absolutely, positively, could not go." Furthermore, such a treacherous ice storm had fallen on Austin that it was unclear whether the event would proceed. "So cold and icy was it," remembered library director Harry Middleton, "that we got word that the plane carrying many of the participants from Washington could not land at the Austin airport and they would have to come here by bus." Weather notwithstanding, LBJ headed out from the ranch on the seventy-mile trip to Austin. Though he had given up driving months earlier, he became so overwrought by the driver's cautious pace on the icy roads that he demanded the driver pull over so he could take the wheel himself.

He was determined at any cost to deliver this keynote address. The symposium offered him an emotional reprise of a time during his presidency that had meant the most to him. His furious determination that day also represented his hope that history would remember the time when he had been willing to risk everything for civil rights and voting rights, to push in all the chips, risking the entire capital of his presidency. Now he was willing to use whatever bodily energy he could muster to speak to the living members of the civil rights community who had worked with him to make it possible. "He knew what he was spending," Lady Bird said, "and had a right to decide how to spend it."

Upon his arrival, a convocation of civil rights leaders of the previous two decades watched Lyndon Johnson pause before the two steps to the dais, slip a nitroglycerin tablet into his mouth, and approach the rostrum. The strain was obvious. There was an emotional quality to his voice as he looked over an audience that included Chief Justice Earl Warren, Associate Justice Thurgood Marshall, Hubert Humphrey, Roy Wilkins, and Clarence Mitchell—as well as the new generation of activists, including Barbara Jordan, Vernon Jordan, and Julian Bond. At the Democratic convention two years earlier, Bond had demonstrated against President Johnson. Now he would praise him before this library audience. "For once," Bond said, "an activist human-hearted man had his hands on the levers of power and a vision beyond the next election. He was there when we and the nation needed him, and, oh, my God, do I wish he was there now."

Johnson began hesitantly, acknowledging that he rarely spoke in public anymore, but emphasizing that on this night there were things that he wanted to say. Something in his earnest and slow delivery reached out to his audience, caressing them with intense gratitude and affection.

"Of all the records that are housed in this library, 31 million papers over a 40-year period of public life," he began, the record relating to civil rights "holds the most of myself within it, and holds for me the most intimate meanings." While admitting that civil rights had not always been his priority, he had come to believe that "the essence of government" lay in ensuring "the dignity and innate integrity of life for every individual . . . regardless of color, creed, ancestry, sex, or age. . . .

"I don't want this symposium to come here and spend two days talking about what we have done," he continued, "the progress had been much too small. We haven't done nearly enough. I'm kind of ashamed of myself that I had six years and couldn't do more than I did."

The difficulty of being "Black in a White society," he argued, remained the chief unaddressed problem of our nation. "Until we overcome unequal history, we cannot overcome unequal opportunity." Until Black people "stand on level and equal ground," we cannot rest. It must be our goal "to assure that all Americans play by the same rules and all Americans play against the same odds. . . .

"And if our efforts continue," he concluded, "and if our will is strong, and if our hearts are right, and if courage remains our constant companion, then, my fellow Americans, I am confident we shall overcome."

———•———

Six weeks later, in his bedroom at the ranch, Lyndon Johnson had a fatal heart attack. He had been taking a nap and was alone. He was sixty-four, the age he had long predicted he would die.

CHAPTER THIRTEEN

Our Talisman

Dick and Doris. November 11, 2015.

JANUARY 2017

With the coming of the New Year in 2017, Dick and I decided to celebrate passage through all his Sixties boxes with a bottle of champagne. At last, after two years of work, we had sifted through all the documents and all manner of memorabilia that Dick had saved from the 1960s. Nearly every weekend we had relived events of that tumultuous decade during which Dick seemed to have crammed three or four lifetimes into his thirty-eight years.

But our exploration of his boxes was not over. Roughly one hundred unopened boxes lay ahead, documenting the mass of Dick's accumulated work after he left public life. Following Robert Kennedy's assassination, the debacle at the Democratic convention, and the improbable resurrection of

Richard Nixon, Dick had retreated to the remote hill country of western Maine. It was a defiant, not a defeated soul, however, who had moved to the mountainous lake district.

His belief in the necessity for fundamental change was greater than ever, but the time of waiting for the advent of heroes—the great man or woman who would set things right—was over. Real change, he felt, would only come when an aroused public sentiment made it happen. He wanted time to think and write, to follow the path of critic, social analyst, and, very infrequently, political adviser and even speechwriter. After all, the addiction to politics would never be fully flushed from his blood.

On this New Year's night, we were not concerned with the boxes that lay ahead but with celebrating those people with whom we had traversed the jagged terrain of the Sixties. All the major figures were now gone—John Kennedy, Martin Luther King, Robert Kennedy, Lyndon Johnson, Jackie Kennedy, Eugene McCarthy, Lady Bird Johnson. Yet, as we looked back, we had spent so much time in the presence of these figures, sharing our memories and stories of them, that they had remained vivid and compelling in our minds.

Dick handed me a glass of champagne. Extending his glass to mine, he said, "to you, who have helped bring all these people back to life for me."

And for the next hour or more, we recollected and toasted our departed friends and colleagues. When Dick began to speak of Jackie Kennedy, he dropped ice cubes in both our champagne glasses in tribute to Jackie's preference for drinking champagne with ice. Dick's friendship with Jackie had lasted long after his exit from politics. He remembered lunching with her in New York at P. J. Clarke's soon after her diagnosis of cancer in 1994. She told him she was hopeful that her chemotherapy would prove successful. They had reminisced about their teamwork to save the Egyptian monuments, their selection of the Temple of Dendur as the gift from the Egyptian government, and their camaraderie planning the Nobel Prize dinner that would come to be known as "A Dinner in Camelot." Only four months after their luncheon meeting, at the age of sixty-four, she was gone.

I toasted Lady Bird Johnson, the ballast of Lyndon's life. How often had I seen her douse his flaring temper, draw him out of morose silence, or smooth ruffled feelings with her gentle touch. In the years before her death at ninety-four, Lady Bird suffered a series of strokes that left her unable to speak.

Although macular degeneration prevented her from reading, audio books continued to bring joy to this woman who had loved reading all her life.

One day, a year before Lady Bird died in 2007, her daughter Luci called me from Texas. She told me her mother had just finished listening to my book on Abraham Lincoln. Lady Bird wanted me to know how much she loved it. Luci asked me to wait and listen, and, after a pause, I heard the clapping of Lady Bird's hands—beginning softly, then rising in intensity and volume. I was greatly moved by Lady Bird's graceful gesture.

Much later, I wrote Luci to ask her what she recalled from that phone call. "I remember a crescendo in Mother's applause," she wrote, "as she wanted to make sure you heard her respect, her pride in your work. She wanted you to feel a part of our family again."

One of the unexpected benefits of our explorations back through the Sixties had happened very gradually. For years, we had taken opposite sides in our prolonged, obstinate personal battle over the merits and demerits of JFK and LBJ. Now our arguments had by and large—though not completely— vanished. Not only had Dick's acrimony toward LBJ mellowed as we reviewed his courage on matters of civil rights and mastery of the 89th Congress, but at the same time, my appreciation for JFK had grown. With Dick as my guide to revisit the thrilling days of the New Frontier and experience the birth of the Peace Corps, I had come to a far deeper, heartfelt understanding of Kennedy's role in personifying the spirit of change and citizen activism that would become the hallmark of the Sixties. And, after hearing the voices of the people of Ashland, Wisconsin, it was apparent that Kennedy's charismatic visits had roused the community and left a mark on the small town that would continue for decades into the future.

Sometimes Dick and I played the maddening, irresistible, and of course unanswerable, historical "what if" guessing game: Would Kennedy have been able to get Congress to pass the Civil Rights Bill in 1964? Would JFK have escalated the Vietnam War into an American war? Would LBJ have addressed flaws in various Great Society programs if his attention had not been diverted by the war? Would RFK have won the nomination had he lived?

In conversations that winter of 2017, we reviewed the terrain we had passed through, in particular matters of civil rights, where Dick had crucial and consequential involvement with both John Kennedy and Lyndon Johnson. Once more we recounted Dick's first directive from President Kennedy on the very day of his inauguration to find out why there was not a single Black face in the Coast Guard's detachment in the parade.

"Was Kennedy truly ready to force the Coast Guard to end discrimination as a matter of justice," I asked Dick, wondering if the president's sensitivity stemmed from the embarrassment that a snow-white Coast Guard might be handing the Russians a propaganda stick to beat his administration on its first day. "Was he more interested in symbolic gestures than integration?"

"You talk as if you think symbolic gestures are always superficial," Dick said. "Sometimes, symbolic gestures are the language of political actions."

Dick conceded Kennedy had been slow in recognizing a revolutionary Civil Rights Movement rising to the surface during the first years of his administration. But the events in Birmingham—the leadership of Martin Luther King, the bravery of the civil rights marchers, and the brutality of the southern opposition—had kindled the conscience of the people and brought Kennedy to an urgent awareness of the impatience, anger, and frustration of the growing Black movement. When Dick and I listened together to Kennedy's televised speech to the nation after the savage attacks on peaceful demonstrators seeking equal access to public places in Birmingham, we had heard a new, authentic conviction in his voice as he labeled civil rights a "moral issue" and presented to Congress the most far-reaching Civil Rights Bill of the twentieth century.

One indisputable fact remained. In the fall of 1963, the Civil Rights Bill had been locked in legislative paralysis along with every major initiative of Kennedy's administration, including Medicare and federal aid to education. This Congress, a *Life* editorial charged, had sat longer than any previous body "while accomplishing practically nothing."

It took Lyndon Johnson, a master legislative mechanic, to drive this same Congress to function as never before, passing not only the Civil Rights Bill, but a historic tax cut, a food stamp act, and a series of poverty programs to provide early education and vocational training for low-income families, as well as a volunteer service program at home, designed to be a domestic counterpart to the Peace Corps. And from the moment of Kennedy's murder, Lyndon Johnson would suffer no equivocating talk of diluting or compromising the Civil Rights Bill. From his first sessions with LBJ, Dick, who had initially been leery about the new president's commitment to civil rights, never again doubted the strength of his convictions.

Kennedy and Johnson had different temperaments, different modes of operating, vastly different styles. JFK was focused primarily on foreign policy, Johnson on domestic affairs. "Domestic policy can only defeat us," Kennedy said, "foreign policy can kill us." JFK was worldly, cool, restrained; LBJ, combative and effusive. In the end, Dick and I had come to believe that the two men had left legacies forever intertwined, more powerfully influential than either had left alone.

For us, the concept of their braided legacies was best illustrated by a photo from May 5, 1961, which we found in one of the boxes and had framed for Dick's study wall. In this photo a small group of men—JFK, LBJ, RFK, Dick, Arthur Schlesinger Jr., and Admiral Arleigh Burke—are gathered in the office of Evelyn Lincoln, President Kennedy's secretary. The tension in the room is evident. JFK's bearing, his hand nervously stroking his chin and lip, reflects the strain everyone was feeling. Dick, his arms locked on his chest, stands between the president and his brother Bobby, with the intent vice president standing next to him.

All eyes are focused on the black-and-white television screen as they watch the broadcast from Cape Canaveral, Florida, where the countdown has begun for the liftoff of navy pilot Alan Shepard's flight, hoping to become the second man—after Russia's Yuri Gagarin—to fly beyond the earth's atmosphere. The rocket, Freedom 7, rises to more than one hundred miles above the earth before beginning its descent, becoming the first manned flight of Project Mercury. Shepard's parachute opens and he splashes down safely in the Atlantic Ocean. The dramatic fifteen-minute flight put America back in the Space Race.

Lyndon Johnson's presence in this small group witnessing the flight was fitting. As Senate majority leader in 1958, he had been instrumental in creating the National Aeronautics and Space Administration (NASA). As vice president, he had been given major responsibility for the administration's space program. "You know, Lyndon," Kennedy had quipped with relief in the aftermath of Shepard's successful flight, "nobody knows that the Vice President is the Chairman of the Space Council, but if that flight had been a flop, I guarantee that everybody would have known that you were the Chairman."

Joking aside, Kennedy understood the signal role Johnson had played in leading the effort to catch up to the Russians. In response to the tremendous public excitement generated by Shepard's flight, Johnson had prodded Kennedy to put all necessary resources behind a far more breathtaking goal: a manned trip to the moon. Nevertheless, it was Kennedy who stood before a joint session of Congress three weeks later, taking the risk of pledging to land a man on the moon before the decade was out. And it was Kennedy's inspiring words a year later that came to symbolize the soaring ambition of the moonshot as a literal extension of the New Frontier.

We choose to go to the moon in this decade and do the other things, not because they are easy, but because they are hard, because that goal will serve to organize and measure the best of our energies and skills, because that challenge is one that we are willing to accept, one we are unwilling to postpone.... And, therefore, as we set sail we ask God's blessing on the most hazardous and dangerous and greatest adventure on which man has ever gone.

Kennedy's words inspired those who first heard them and have continued to enthrall subsequent generations. After Kennedy's death, Johnson never wavered in his support for the moonshot—despite the mounting pressures of providing funding for both the Great Society programs and the war. Without Johnson's hard work during the years before and after Kennedy made his pledge to go to the moon, the Apollo project might never have launched. Indeed, one historian argues, "no one did more than L.B.J. to commit the U.S. to landing men on the moon and returning them safely to earth."

I happened to be at the Johnson ranch on Sunday, July 20, 1969, the day that Neil Armstrong stepped from the last rung of the space module's ladder, leaving man's first footprint in moon dust. Johnson was as animated as a small boy. We watched the coverage throughout the day, even eating dinner in the living room in front of the television. By late evening, his mood of excitement had tapered and sadness engulfed him as he listened to reporters credit Kennedy for having begun the moon-quest and Richard Nixon for having fulfilled it. It was as if Lyndon Johnson, the excluded middle, had been erased from history.

The next morning, CBS aired a Walter Cronkite interview with Johnson that had been filmed five days earlier. Well aware of Johnson's substantial leadership role on the moonshot program throughout the preceding decade, Cronkite referred to Johnson as the "Father of the Program," while

Johnson tossed the compliment back to Kennedy by acknowledging that he was the one who "set our goal . . . and he succeeded." By lunchtime, LBJ had shaken off his gloom and high spirits filled the ranch.

Here was a small emblem of the interlocking legacies of JFK and LBJ. Yet today, what is remembered most clearly and simply is the iconic moment in the torrid heat of the Cold War contest between the Soviet Union and the United States, when John Kennedy set a stirring deadline that galvanized purpose and direction within the government, and engaged the American people in a dramatic contest between freedom and tyranny that would play out before the eyes of the world.

SPRING 2017

Dick was eighty-five years old in the spring of 2017. As we approached the boxes containing his work after he had left public service, it was immediately apparent that what remained was different in kind from the long train of memos, diary entries, and speech drafts encircling and defining well-known events in our nation's history. These boxes contained notes of a working writer who was reading widely in history, philosophy, and literature. Here was the raw material for long *New Yorker* pieces, a philosophical book about America, newspaper columns, a memoir, a manifesto calling for a new American revolution, and draft upon draft of a play that was eventually produced with great success in England and Boston, depicting the savage machinations behind the warring worldviews of Galileo and Pope Urban VIII, drawing on Dick's own political experience.

Even from my brief look into these boxes, it was clear that they were anything but the papers of a placid spirit. In the words of his old sidekick, Bill Moyers, Dick remained "an unrepentant idealist and an unrelenting patriot"—or, as he was dubbed by former California governor Jerry Brown, "the Tom Paine of our generation."

Although Dick still voiced an eagerness to explore these boxes, there were disturbing signs that he was slowing down. I worried about his shortness of breath as he walked around our backyard gardens, his pauses and fatigue when climbing the stairs. One morning I found him sitting a third of the way up the stairs reading the newspaper. When I asked him why he was perched up there, he said he had started an interesting article on black holes and wanted to finish it.

At the next appointment with our cardiologist shortly afterward, we checked out his pacemaker. It was functioning fine. All his medicines still seemed to be working. After carefully listening to his heart and lungs, the doctor asked, "How many cigars are you smoking a day?" Mentally counting the multiple times when he settled into his favorite chair and lit one of his cigars, he said, "Five, maybe six, but I smoke less of each of them."

"Well, my advice, categorically," the cardiologist said, "is to give up cigars."

Once we were in our car, Dick drew the line. "There's no problem with my heart," he declared. "Feel it." He slipped my palm inside his shirt and onto his chest. "See!" he said. As if to hammer home his point, he insisted that we stop at his favorite tobacco store on our way back from the doctor's to buy a new box of cigars.

"I won't quit," he said to me in a huff when we got home. "I'm left-handed. I have aggressive eyebrows. I smoke cigars. That's who I am." Yet, after he calmed down, he promised to limit himself to two a day. One after breakfast, the other after dinner. Meanwhile, he had a plan: "You know," he said, taking a cigar from the humidor, "there are a lot of things you can do with a cigar beside smoke it. You can chew it, suck the nicotine out of it, lick it, twirl it, play with it. Not as good as smoking it, maybe, but not bad." He placed the unlit cigar tenderly in the ashtray beside him, "Not bad at all."

So we continued our daily rituals. We would eat breakfast together while reading the newspapers, go to our separate studies for the morning, come together for a small lunch—after which Dick, like LBJ, would put on his pajamas to take a full-scale nap—followed by a brief working session in the afternoon, then most nights we would have dinner out with the same cluster of friends in the same bars and restaurants in our small town of Concord. And so things quietly continued into the spring. What comfort such daily regimens bestow upon a long marriage.

More ominous than Dick nodding off now and then over a book on his lapboard were the mysterious nosebleeds which began that spring of 2017. At first, I thought they were a consequence of his prolonged, violent bouts of sneezing. He once counted thirty-six sneezes in a row. When his coughing and wheezing worried me, he reminded me it was merely the spring asthma that had plagued him all his life. I was not placated.

Dick finally agreed to see a specialist in diseases of the nose and sinuses. He took an immediate liking to the doctor, who was direct, smart, young, gentle, and attractive. She cleaned crusted sores inside his nose that were hindering his breathing and took a precautionary biopsy.

When the doctor called with the biopsy result, I had my notebook ready. My mind froze at the words I carefully wrote down:

May 18. Aggressive squamous cell cancer in nose . . . CT scan needed to see if spread to neck, lymph nodes.

May 22. Scan shows no indication cancer has spread. Great Relief. But operation necessary to remove tumor not easy. Could result in disfiguring, flattening of nose, compromise of breathing. All complicated by age.

Dick had no second thoughts about the surgery. He said we had too much left to do. He wanted the operation as soon as possible.

That night, I felt panic rise as I lay beside him in bed. He sensed it and said, "Well, all these years you've worried about my heart. I told you there was no problem." Once again, he placed my hand over his heart. "Strong!" he boasted. "No problem. It's just cancer. It's all in one place. We'll be fine."

The weekend before the operation Dick's closest friend, Michael Rothschild, arrived in Concord. Michael and Dick had met in Maine at the end of the Sixties, and for the next fifty years had spoken almost daily on the phone when they weren't together. They would talk about literature, art, politics, the Red Sox, what they were reading—sometimes sharing sections of their own works in progress. Dick took a boundless interest in Michael's fiction, sculpture, and printmaking as well as the seasonal activities on his hill farm—the pruning of apple trees and birthing of lambs in late winter, grafting new trees in spring, gardening vegetables all summer.

Most summers we would visit this farm on Tory Hill, and both our families would gather there for Thanksgiving. I will never forget the hot summer day when I was tasked with turning a young piglet on a spit above applewood coals for six hours. When Michael visited us in Concord, he would bring us the lamb, beef, poultry, and other produce raised on the farm. Dick was particularly fond of the apple cider they pressed and the maple syrup they boiled in the evaporator house. Late one winter, Michael came down and hung galvanized buckets on several of the rock maple trees in our yard on Monument Street. Dick would gather the sap and boil it down carefully to make his own small batch of maple syrup.

Beginning the weekend of Dick's operation, Michael made monthly trips to Concord so we could all be together for whatever lay ahead. My anxiety grew as the day of the operation approached. I remember watching the clock in the waiting room with Michael and my sons as we all sat huddled at Brigham and Women's Hospital. When we saw the smiling young surgeon approach us with her arms uplifted, thumbs pointing straight up in the air, I felt I could exhale at last. The operation had been a success. The tumor had been removed. The bridge of his nose had not collapsed.

Despite having bandages on his bruised face days after returning home, Dick insisted on joining our regular gang in the cozy bar at Concord's Colonial Inn where he was buoyed by their toasts and cheers. It was a Thursday night and every Thursday local folk singer John Fitzsimmons led us all in song. That night he played Dick's favorites: "If I Had a Hammer," "This Land Is Your Land," ending, as usual, with "America the Beautiful." No matter what his condition, Dick was one for a parade, fireworks, or a patriotic songfest.

Our celebration was premature. A CT scan a few days later revealed that the cancer had penetrated the space around a nerve, increasing the risk that it could return. With radiation, however, the prognosis was good.

Dick asked if the radiation might be delayed until early fall. It was important that we continue our routine of summers on the Cape with friends and family, which now included two grandchildren. There he could rest from the ordeal, and we could continue to press forward on our book project. A short summer hiatus, the doctors agreed, would do no harm so long as radiation commenced in September.

SUMMER 2017

Once we had settled in the big red house in Falmouth that we rented for several summers, Dick seemed surprisingly content. He spent the early hours of each day on the porch, watching the swells of the ocean, perusing the newspapers, and reading the various novels and poetry we had carted down to the shore. Once a day we would take a short walk to the ocean, where he liked to wade in the shallows and track the peculiar meanderings of horseshoe crabs.

Yet, when I was alone, I found myself sliding down the harrowing rabbit hole of the internet, reading about the side effects of radiation on the nose which reportedly felt like the worst sunburn imaginable. I read medical papers on septums and facial nerves, stumbling across scenarios that kept me awake at night.

We worked on the book project at a far more leisurely pace, only an hour or so a day. I had cherry-picked clippings and documents I knew would give him pleasure to revisit. In the Eighties, he had written a prescient series of columns for *The Los Angeles Times*, warning that democracy was teetering on the edge of the middle-class squeeze as a consequence of the growing income gap, globalization, and the loss of the manufacturing base. In the Nineties, he had called for major changes in the political structure—an overhaul of campaign finance laws, an end to gerrymandering, and a return to free and equal time on television for all office seekers qualified for election under state law.

Despite Dick's firm resolve to write no more speeches after he moved to Maine, I found a handful of speech drafts. One for Maine senator Edmund Muskie was delivered before all three networks the night before the 1970 midterms. The speech was designed to counter a central accusation in Nixon's "law and order" campaign that the Democrats were soft on crime, that they "actually favor violence and champion the wrongdoer. That is a lie," Dick had written for Muskie. "And the American people know it is a lie."

More important and far-reaching was Dick's work with Vice President Al Gore's on his 2000 concession speech to George W. Bush, delivered thirty-five days after Election Day had ended in national acrimony and uncertainty. While the recount to determine which candidate had won Florida—and therefore, would win the election—was underway, Gore had contacted Dick to ask him to help with both a victory and concession speech. Dick focused his efforts on the concession speech, knowing that, if needed, it would have lasting consequences.

As soon as I read the draft that November of 2000, I felt it had struck exactly the necessary personal and historical tone. I urged Dick to send it to Gore at once. Dick balked, explaining that Gore wouldn't want to look at it until he knew the race had been lost. And, he added, he wanted to wait to send it as late as possible so that Gore could see his draft before others began working on it.

So Dick kept the draft until Gore asked him to send it—the day the Supreme Court stopped the recount, awarding Florida's twenty-five electoral votes, and the election, to Texas governor George W. Bush. The next evening, Gore delivered his concession with the grace and dignity the occasion demanded.

When I handed Dick the final speech I had found in a file, he handed it back. He asked me to read it, closed his eyes, and listened to the description of the peaceful transition of power, the hallmark of our democratic system, dating back to George Washington.

Almost a century and a half ago, Senator Stephen Douglas told Abraham Lincoln, who had just defeated him for the presidency, "Partisan feeling must yield to patriotism. I'm with you, Mr. President, and God bless you."

Well, in that same spirit, I say to President-elect Bush that what remains of partisan rancor must now be put aside, and may God bless his stewardship of this country. . . .

Over the library of one of our great law schools is inscribed the motto, "Not under man but under God and law." That's the ruling principle of American freedom. . . .

Now the U.S. Supreme Court has spoken. Let there be no doubt, while I strongly disagree with the court's decision, I accept it. . . . And tonight, for the sake of our unity as a people and the strength of our democracy, I offer my concession.

Our work on the files that summer was not the sustained, systematic approach we had taken to the papers of the Sixties, but for both of us, our book project provided solace. These sessions kept Dick anchored and entertained. It was during this time that I came to realize that the concept of the book that we would do together had taken on a far greater meaning. It was as if we were both in the grip of a fantasy—maintaining the enchanted thought that so long as we had more boxes to unpack, more work to do, his life, my life, our lives together, would not be finished.

We had both written books, but this one was different. In a strange manner, marching through the boxes together had become a way Dick would not die. He would tell me, as he would later tell his doctors, "I want to live long enough to finish the book." This determination had much more to do with living than with writing. And it was more than a matter of legacy. So long as we were working together, so long as we were opening boxes—learning, laughing, discussing the contents—we were alive. If a talisman is an object thought to have magical powers and to bring luck, this book was our talisman.

FALL 2017

During our marriage, there were often times when a splinter in Dick's finger caused whining as I tried to remove it; a sore throat drove him to bed waiting for soup; or a high fever brought the worry that his father's leukemia had visited itself upon him. What a revelation now was the emergence of this character, under the greatest of duress, into someone whose patience, tenderness, tolerance, and serenity surprised everyone—most of all me.

Who was this man, we all asked ourselves, this iconoclast who had bucked authority all his life and now acquiesced to his medical team? Shortly after we returned home from the Cape, a protective mask was cast from Dick's face upon which were mapped the coordinates to direct the radiation he would receive six days a week for the next seven weeks. The first time he donned the mask, he beckoned me, his palm outstretched like in *The Phantom of the Opera*, to "listen to the music of the night."

For the next forty-two days, we took turns bringing Dick to Boston— our sons, Deb Colby, Michael Rothschild, and me. Dick was the oldest of the patients who gathered in a special waiting room around the same time every afternoon. He instilled a confidence in his younger mates. If he, at his advanced age, could tolerate radiation, so could they. He brought his daily stack of newspapers, and, at their request, would read aloud an article or two. The room was filled with relaxed banter, rather than simply a group of patients waiting silently to be called by the technicians. And every day he would sport a different pair of colorful socks from his vast collection— some with stripes or polka dots, others featuring illustrious figures, like George Washington or Abraham Lincoln.

By October, the radiation was taking its toll on Dick. He was losing weight and muscle mass. The ascent of the steep stairs to our bedroom proved problematic. Despite his exhaustion and unsteady gait, Dick initially refused to consider a stair lift. I reminded him that he had once told me that long ago, he had organized his fellow Supreme Court clerks to chip in together for the purchase of a similar device for Justice Frankfurter. This memory helped my case. Dick finally agreed that we could order the automatic lift, but on the day of its installation he stayed in his study on the other side of the house, refusing to lay eyes on it. Before evening, his petulance gave way to grudging acceptance, and then, after careful perusal of the instruction manual, to delight. The chair carried him backward up the stairs and then, when a button was pressed, it revolved so he was facing the right direction to exit at the top of the stairs. Ever a lover and collector of gadgets, he went from refusing to consider it, to riding it up and down a dozen times to display the excellence of the apparatus to our granddaughters, as if it were a carnival ride at the fairground.

The course of radiation ended in the third week of November, but Dick was not in shape to travel to the Rothschild farmhouse in Maine where we had celebrated Thanksgiving every year for nearly forty years. Our children and grandchildren had grown up together with Rothschild's children and grandchildren.

Only the year before, we had been part of the usual gathering around the twenty-foot cherrywood table, surrounding a forty-pound turkey and a wide range of side dishes that had all been grown on the farm. Dick had stood up and asked for silence. He held up his wine glass, and in his crackling, theatrical voice read Abraham Lincoln's 1863 proclamation that established the last Thursday of November as a Day of Thanksgiving. His recitation began: "The year that is drawing toward its close has been filled with blessings of fruitful fields and healthful skies," continuing on to voice Lincoln's prayer "to heal the wounds of the nation, and to restore it, as soon as may be consistent with the Divine purposes, to the full enjoyment of peace, harmony, tranquility and union." Even the smallest of grandchildren listened quietly, mesmerized by Dick's performance, even if they hadn't understood a word of what he was saying. "So let us toast Abraham Lincoln," Dick said, "for our Union and, for proclaiming this day, Thanksgiving, our national holiday."

WINTER 2017/2018

Dick's precipitous weight loss initially fed his vanity. He liked the way his newly "chiseled" face looked. He reminded me, I told him, of FDR, who had shed so much weight after his diagnosis of congestive heart disease that he would slap his stomach with glee and crow: "I'm a young man again. Look how flat my stomach is." But when swallowing became difficult for Dick and he continued to lose weight, the doctors told him a temporary feeding tube was necessary. Most reluctantly, he agreed, but immediately began to drink so much Ensure that his weight loss stopped, and the hated feeding tube was removed. He had won a small battle.

And through it all, he continued to accompany me to our regular dinners with our group of friends. Night after night, as we drove down Monument Street, he'd begin the same half-serious refrain. "There's the old North Bridge. That's where it all began, Doris. There's the Old Manse—Hi Hawthorne." He would talk about how much he loved our town and our street, "the most beautiful street in the country," he would say. He would join our friends in conversation, and even in drink, though when liquor began to sting and finally burn going down his throat, he substituted water for gin while retaining his signature onions.

By December, his sense of smell and taste were gone. One evening as we were returning from a dinner he had insisted we attend, watching his friends eat food that he couldn't eat and drink what he couldn't drink, he began to drift away and I gripped his hand in the car. "So much has peeled away," he said. "I love cigars but can no longer smoke. I love to drink but liquor has become a blowtorch in my throat. I love good food but my taste is gone. On the positive side," he chuckled softly, "I can still read, I can listen, and, more or less, I can think."

The lengthening days after the winter solstice renewed the ancient wish that more light and sun signaled a turning point—in this case, our hope that the radiation had worked, that perhaps a healing process had begun. And for a moment, the tests seemed to reveal an absence of cancer. When Michael Rothschild visited us in March, he brought with him a quart of golden, first-run maple syrup. Dick poured it over his oatmeal, tasted, and stopped. Another spoonful and he tilted back his head and slapped his hand down on the top of the breakfast table. He could detect, he thought, a faint taste of vanilla. We held our collective breath.

Before the day was out, we were planning a fantastical eating and drinking tour of the great capitals of the world that would reprise the happiest meals we had ever shared—mushroom week at the Ritz in Madrid, poularde de bresse at Le Bristol in Paris, wine in the courtyard of Enoteca Pinchiorri in the hills above Florence, where a special stool had been brought out to keep my pocketbook from the floor, prawns and crab roe at T'Ang Court in Hong Kong. We searched out menus on the internet and debated what we would have for appetizers, entrees, and dessert.

SPRING 2018

The fantasy eating tour would take place only in our hopes and dreams. Tests in March revealed that Dick's cancer had returned in an aggressive form. An experimental course of immunotherapy was begun but by the second infusion it was clear that the treatment was not effective. Before we left the office of the medical oncologist, Dick uncharacteristically and directly asked how much time he had left. I froze when I heard the doctor's reply. I distinctly remembered him saying, "In all likelihood, weeks, not months." All along, Dick and I had avoided straightforward talk of his dying, each of us wanting to shield the other from the thought of no longer being together.

That night, quietly reviewing the conversation at bedtime, Dick reversed what the doctor had said. "Well, I've got months, not weeks," Dick stated almost matter-of-factly. "We'll be able to get something done." The strength of his desire to live gave me something to cling to, the hope that passion and purpose would somehow defy medical expectations.

As Dick increasingly found it difficult to read, he would hand me a book or article and ask me to read aloud to him. Sometimes he would doze off in the middle of a story and then abruptly wake up wanting to know what had happened while he was gone. We had lived surrounded by books all our married lives. They were our element. We had written them, read for pleasure, amassed mini-libraries for particular projects, collected them, organized them into ever-shifting categories, and in the end, dwelled inside what we joyfully called our house of books.

One afternoon Dick asked me to slowly recite one of his favorite poems, Wordsworth's "Intimations of Immortality." When I had nearly finished, he was breathing very deeply, and I thought for certain he had fallen asleep. I went on reading until the end. When I finished, he turned toward me, and from memory repeated:

> *Though nothing can bring back the hour*
> *Of splendor in the grass, of glory in the flower*
> *We will grieve not, rather find*
> *Strength in what remains behind*

"I wish I'd paid more attention to that, taking it to heart," he said. "Not anger over what was lost, but the power of what was left behind." Later that evening, he interjected a non sequitur that would long linger in my mind. "Don't think I've forgotten our book project. I've not been much help lately, just promise to get it done." I nodded in agreement.

In the jumbled space of time that remained, the lines are so blurred, days moving so slowly, then so quickly, that I recall things in glimpses, pieces, phrases. Yet it is not the medical chronology of the rapid descent that began at the start of May that has stayed with me: Dick's trouble breathing, then pneumonia, then doctors telling me there was nothing more the hospital could do, that it was time for home and hospice. Rather, what remains is the mellow, springtime atmosphere that prevailed once we brought Dick home and settled him into a big hospital-style bed, positioned against a window in the Great Room with its stone fireplace and floor-to-ceiling bookcases.

Day after day, as scores of friends began to come from far and wide to see Dick and say goodbye, the most extraordinary thing happened. An occasion that promised to be awkward, grim, and uncomfortable was transformed into one of relaxed affection. It seemed a kind of Irish wake, people milling around Dick, in the kitchen, the dining room, eating and drinking and recounting tales of Dick at various stages of their lives and ours. An Irish wake it was indeed, except for the fact that Dick was not deceased but alive, kept from pain by low doses of morphine.

Dick seemed to be comforted by simple affection, by friends holding his hand, by one of our sons moistening his tongue with cooling swabs, another playing the guitar, by grandchildren scampering from one room to another. Sometimes he lapsed into a deep slumber; sometimes his speech seemed disoriented, but then he would wake and be perfectly alert. All day long, old friends came to his bedside, recalling moments that meant something special to them, after which Dick mustered enough strength to say something clear, kind, and sometimes irreverent to each of them. With gratitude, he thanked his team of doctors who had come to see him and bid him an emotional farewell.

As the end drew near, Dick seemed very tired. He sweetly grasped my hand in his and put it on his heart. "You're a wonder," he rasped, his eyes shining with an uncanny light. It was the last thing he said to me. He squeezed my hand, then passed into a luminous state that seemed to straddle this world and the next. And that was all.

Epilogue

"BLACK CARE RARELY SITS BEHIND A RIDER WHOSE PACE IS FAST enough," a depressed Theodore Roosevelt wrote following the sudden deaths of his wife and mother as he headed for a ranch in the Dakotas where daily life would be filled with unrelenting physical activity. I, too, tried to outrun grief in the months following Dick's death. I threw myself into an extended lecture tour for my book on leadership, traveling at breakneck speed from one city to another. Days of nonstop activity left little space for grief, rendering me so exhausted that I was finally able to sleep.

When my mother died during my sophomore year of high school, I had reacted in a similar fashion, plunging into schoolwork and after-school activities with a vengeance. I rarely spoke about my feelings. I didn't want anyone to pity me. My attempt to distract myself from pain didn't work when I was fifteen. Nor did it work when I was seventy-five.

After returning to Concord from my tour, I was submerged in loneliness. No matter where I found myself, I felt Dick's absence: waking up in our bed, walking to the end of the driveway to pick up the newspapers to lay out on the kitchen table, driving into Concord center for dinner.

My routine of starting my day at 5:30 a.m. no longer worked. My early morning workplace—the cozy nook I had created in the reading room we shared with my blue couch, table, rug, and fireplace—did not offer the same refuge when I could no longer anticipate Dick's appearance at the top of the stairs, signaling sunrise and breakfast time like a zany rooster.

Memories of Dick overwhelmed me as I walked down the book-lined hallway into a room that had once been a three-car garage before we relegated automobiles to the driveway and transformed the space into a formal library with entire walls of bookshelves and an attached tower inspired by Dick's adulation for Galileo, about whom he had written his play. Even the dining room, the bedrooms, and the gym were lined with bookshelves that we had built and filled over the years. And then there were the pictures of Dick during his days at the White House with Kennedy and Johnson, amid family celebrations and on trips we had taken with our kids.

An old friend from Concord tried to comfort me one night by reminding me that Dick had lived a long, rich life in his eighty-six years. I knew there was nothing unusual about dying at eighty-six, but his comment provided little solace. Whether eighty-six, sixty-six, or one hundred six, it made no difference. Dick was no longer here.

My children and grandchildren encircled me, filling the rooms with happy squabbles and activity. It was good to be together. Nonetheless, remaining in the house without Dick was unbearable. I decided to put our home on the market and move to an apartment in the heart of Boston.

When my father had made a similar decision to move after my mother died, I was heartbroken. I had never lived anywhere else. My identity, almost every memory I had of my mother, was rooted in our home, on our street, in our neighborhood. I feared that when we moved, memories of my mother would fade away. My father tried to explain why he felt compelled to move. He could not eat in the breakfast room where their days had begun; he could not sleep in the bedroom where her heart had stopped. I did not understand then. I understand now.

Almost as soon as our Concord house went on the market, a buyer was found, and the painful process of downsizing began. Deciding which books to take presented the most immediate challenge. Even after squeezing bookshelves into every available wall of my three-bedroom city apartment, I could accommodate only several thousand volumes. What to do with the remainder was a problem miraculously solved when the Concord Free Public Library came to me with a proposal to take the thousands of volumes I couldn't bring with me.

A construction project was already underway at the library to move the children's books to a new location. The old space, they proposed, would now be transformed into a large, new area dedicated to Dick and me. Custom-built shelves would line the walls, providing permanent public access for our donated collection of books. It filled me with joy to imagine our house of books transported to the same library where, as a young mother, I had found a hideaway to write.

If only Dick could have seen this room become the *Goodwin Forum*, a bustling community space, where people from our town and beyond could assemble, discuss, and debate matters of civic discourse—where high school students gather for projects in the afternoons, and lectures and poetry readings are held at night. And inscribed in raised capital letters across the front wall, high above a small stage, appear the words Dick had written for Lyndon Johnson's "We Shall Overcome" speech.

AT TIMES, HISTORY AND FATE MEET AT A SINGLE TIME IN A SINGLE PLACE TO SHAPE A TURNING POINT IN MAN'S UNENDING SEARCH FOR FREEDOM. SO IT WAS AT LEXINGTON AND CONCORD. SO IT WAS A CENTURY AGO AT APPOMATTOX. SO IT WAS LAST WEEK IN SELMA, ALABAMA.

Yet, as I prepared to move to Boston, there remained an unfinished matter that weighed heavily on me: the long train of the boxes that he and I had explored during the last years of our life together. I brought the boxes down from Dick's big upstairs study to the library where they bordered the entire room. There was no way to avoid their powerful presence. Our project, fraught with emotion, presented a dilemma that I wasn't yet ready to resolve. I had no choice but to leave our unfinished work in limbo. So for the time being, I arranged for the boxes to be stored in a safe, humidity-controlled facility in Boston, aptly named "The Fortress."

The decision to move to the city proved to be just right. Concord was not far off and historic Boston was the city of my young dreams. From the large floor-to-ceiling windows of my high-rise apartment I can catch the glow of night games at Fenway Park. Directly below stretch the Boston Common and the Public Garden, the golden dome of the State House, and Beacon Hill. In the distance I'm able to glimpse the Charles River and beyond, Cambridge, where I went to graduate school and later taught.

Inside, I arranged my new study, a miniature version of my old Concord nook, with the same blue couch, table, lamp, and rug. Little by little, the memories of my life in Concord began to comfort rather than sadden me. Before long the walls became a mosaic of favorite pictures of Dick: LBJ handing him one of the pens he used during the signing of the Voting Rights Act, Dick leaning over JFK's shoulder while he worked over a draft, Dick escorting Jackie to the Nobel Prize dinner. The kitchen and even bathroom walls soon featured photos of kids and grandkids, of family trips to the Galápagos, Europe, and Africa.

Yet I felt the weight of the unfinished project that had given the last years of Dick's life purpose and fulfillment. I knew that to write a book about our exploration of the boxes would require years of reading and research. It would mean retracing the days we had shared working on this project. It would mean dealing all over again with Dick's illness and death.

Despite these concerns, I found myself edging toward a commitment to finish the project, influenced by headlines announcing divisions between Black and white, old and young, rich and poor—divisions that made it increasingly evident that the momentous issues emanating from the Sixties remain the unresolved stuff of our everyday lives. Dick thought of his boxes as a time capsule of the decade, containing messages from the past to be delivered at some appropriate time in the future. Perhaps, I began to think, that future is now.

When Lyndon Johnson signed the 1964 Civil Rights Act, knowing well the massive upheavals its implementation would bring, he spoke of a great "testing time" to come. We are clearly in the midst of a profound "testing time" today, and at such times, I have long argued, the study of history is crucial to provide perspective, warning, counsel, and even comfort. At a moment when the guidance of history is most needed, however, history itself is under attack, its relevance in school curriculums questioned.

When Abraham Lincoln was twenty-eight years old, he delivered a powerful argument for telling the stories of our revolutionary days as he was addressing the Young Men's Lyceum of Springfield. He was troubled by the mood of the country, a tendency to substitute passion for judgment, to engage in mob action in disregard of laws. In such an unsettled time, he cautioned, a dictator might arise. He worried that with the passage of some sixty years since the American Revolution and ratification of the Constitution, the "living history" of that time, the vivid and visceral experiences once found in every family, was fading, along with the founding generation itself. To restore that state of communal feeling so essential to democracy, he argued, the stories of the Revolution and the founding of our nation must be told and retold, "read of and recounted."

Lincoln's words took on a powerful resonance in my mind as I realized that in a similar way, some sixty years after memories of the changes and upheavals of the Sixties have begun to fade, been half-forgotten or become misunderstood, my project with Dick might add our voices—along with a chorus of firsthand participants and witnesses—to the task of restoring a "living history" of that decade, allowing us to see what opportunities were seized, what mistakes were made, what chances were lost, and what light might be cast on our own fractured time. Too often, memories of assassination, violence, and social turmoil have obscured the greatest illumination of the Sixties, the spark of communal idealism and belief that kindled social justice and love for a more inclusive vision of America.

I began to read over notes from our years of conversation, pages of Dick's diary, and letters he had written to his college friend, George Cuomo, and to his parents after he escaped from law school and joined the army. My head was aswirl with thoughts of the unfinished promises of the New Frontier and the Great Society, and our own unfinished love story. At last, I found myself not only ready but excited to embrace the book I had promised Dick I would write. Through the years to come I would have the chance to dwell in the healing afterglow of Dick's memory and our final work together.

I arose at 5:30 a.m. and settled on my blue couch. I decided to begin on the first day I laid eyes on Dick when I was teaching courses on American history and government while writing a book on Lyndon Johnson. My life was moving sensibly and smoothly. I was not yet thirty years old. I had hardly opened the door to the yellow house on Mt. Auburn Street where I had my faculty office, when I learned that Richard Goodwin had taken an office on the third floor . . .

Concord, Massachusetts
Boston, Massachusetts

Acknowledgments

As I begin these acknowledgments, I realize how many of the people I am thanking today I have thanked many times in past decades. Yet, the team that I have worked with for so long remains fresh and invigorating.

I must start with Linda Vandegrift, my research assistant, our lives braided in work and friendship for forty-five years. Her passion for history, striking intelligence, and deep research skills have made her a wondrous teammate.

Simon & Schuster has been my publishing home for more than forty years. At every stage of this book's journey, there are colleagues who have worked with me on three or four of my previous books. I am especially grateful to Irene Kheradi, Lisa Healy, Maria Mendez, and Amanda Mulholland for their grace under pressure as we managed to get the book to the finishing line in these last frenzied months. I thank Jackie Seow for her splendid book jacket, the fourth cover she has designed for me, and Paul Dippolito for the classy design of the book itself. Somehow, Fred Chase, copy editor extraordinaire, made what could have been a tedious process easy, and even fun. And once again, the matchless talents of Julia Prosser and Stephen Bedford are combining to bring the book into the hands of readers. How lucky I was to find Bryan Eaton to enliven the book jacket with his artful colorization of the black-and-white photos.

What a special joy it has been to work so closely with Jonathan Karp, my publisher and editor. It was his inspiration that the story I wanted to tell should weave together history, biography, and memoir. Through our tonic early morning conversations, he provided insight, commentary, and creative ideas on how to propel the narrative forward while switching back and forth in time. His presence was vital throughout.

Amanda Urban, my literary agent for nearly thirty years, has supported and encouraged my writing career from start to finish, but her judgment on this, the most personal of the books I have written, was essential.

And I thank Ida Rothschild, my first reader, who read draft chapters before anyone else, reviewed every word of this book, tightening paragraph after paragraph, page after page, correcting and clarifying with an intensity and skill that amount to a rare gift indeed.

As this book grew, I searched out voices from my generation. Many of the people I interviewed, now in their seventies and eighties, had vivid memories of the Sixties, which they graciously shared with me. Some were old friends, others individuals whose stories I learned and wanted to tell. Talking with them created a new community in my mind and was one of the great delights of this project.

For helping me summon memories from college, graduate school, and my early years with Dick, I am grateful to my beloved sister, Jeanne Kearns, my Colby friends Marcia Phillips Sheldon, Barbara Gordon Schoeneweis, Judy Turner Jones, and Betsy Stevens Palmer; my Harvard friends Sanford Levinson and Peter Gourevitch; and my old friend and wedding organizer, Tommy Clark. I am grateful to Nancy Boxley Tepper for sharing her experiences on the *Harvard Law Review* with me, and to Lynda Smith, who helped me tell the story of the integration of the Coast Guard. Numerous conversations and emails with Al Guskin, Judith Guskin, and Bill Josephson allowed me to capture the heady days when the Peace Corps was born. To enlarge on Dick's experiences in the White House, I drew upon conversations with Bill Moyers, Peter Kornbluh, and Gillian Sorensen. For Robert Kennedy's trip to Cape Town, Margaret Marshall's memories were invaluable as were recollections of Mary Lou Oates and Geoffrey Cowan of the McCarthy campaign and the 1968 Democratic convention. And for my own days in the White House, I am grateful for talks with Tim Wirth, Larry Temple, Tom Johnson, Jim Jones, Ervin Duggan, and Luci Johnson.

For understanding the complexities of Dick's heart disease and cancer, I owe special thanks to conversations with his doctors: Dr. Burton Rabinowitz, Dr. Alice Maxwell, Dr. Danielle Margalit, and Dr. Glenn Hanna. I will always be grateful for the loving support during that time from Deb Colby, Andy Blankstein, Kathy and Drew Meyer, Jeri Asher and Craig Shepard. And for sharing memories of Dick's days in hospice, I thank Mike Barnicle and Anne Finucane, Edward Hall, Issy van Randwyck, and Samantha Power.

On this book, as on all others, I am indebted to dedicated staff members at libraries. At the LBJ Library, I owe special thanks to Jay Godwin, whose encyclopedic knowledge of the photo archive was of tremendous help, and to Chris Banks and the entire AV staff, as well as Mark Updegrove, who heads the LBJ Foundation. I am grateful to Marc Selverstone at the Miller Center's Presidential Recordings Program at the University of Virginia, James Merrick at Colby College, Stephen Plotkin and the staff at the JFK Library, and Virginia Hunt and Martha Whitehead at Harvard Library.

At the Dolph Briscoe Center at the University of Texas in Austin, we found the perfect home for both Dick's archive and mine. There, under the leadership of Chancellor James B. Milliken and President Jay Hartzell, the boxes that are the foundation for this book join a deep collection of archives about the Sixties, the Civil Rights Movement, cultural history, and the news media. I owe deep thanks to Don Carleton, Erin Purdy, Lisa Avra, Sarah Sonner, Stephanie Malmros, and Carol Mead, and the entire team at the Briscoe Center for their friendship as well as the continued access they provided to the files I needed to complete the book after Dick's papers had been shipped to Texas.

I am grateful to the Concord Free Public Library for providing the answer for what to do with the thousands of books Dick and I had accumulated over the years when I moved from our house in Concord to an apartment in Boston after Dick died. I especially want to thank John Boynton, Sherry Litwack, Anke Voss, and Sophia Ghannam for providing the necessary materials to write about the creation of the spectacular room named after Dick and me where our books now reside.

A special camaraderie has developed with the six women of our weekly gathering at a place in Boston called The 'Quin—Heather Campion, Jill Abramson, Kate Walsh, Micho Spring, and Beth Myers. Our lively talks over dinner and drinks cover events in our lives, issues of the day, and for the past two years, the slow, but steady, progress of this book. The first question usually posed is "What chapter are we up to? Are we still on Five or have we started Six?" For weeks we engaged in a debate over what the title would be. Our Tuesday nights will always be warmly associated in my mind with the writing of this memoir.

As for Beth Laski, it is impossible to imagine my life without her. She is usually the first person I call in the morning and the last person I speak to at night. She is my cherished friend and my partner—creatively, emotionally, and substantively in everything I do: books, lectures, television, and film. Her imprint is all over this book, in ways big and small. She can do more things at the same time better than anyone I have ever known. Her energy, intellect, and work ethic make everything possible. She's the steady presence in my life, my cabinet of one.

And to my family—Richard, Michael and Madelyn, Joe and Veronika—it was your encompassing love that helped me slowly gain my bearings after Dick died; and to my grandchildren, Willa and Lena, Alexander "Sasha" and Lucas, you have given me renewed hope and confidence in our future.

Last, and most important, is Michael Rothschild to whom this book is dedicated. Michael and Wendy Slaughter Fleming were with Dick and me during scores of working sessions on the book. Michael had known Dick longer than I had. He could prompt Dick's memory better than anyone else. Some of my fondest memories of this period are of festive meals of scallop stew, lobsters, and wine, shared after long days of work. After Dick died, Michael continued to work with me on the book. Without Michael, this book would not have been possible.

Bibliography

Beschloss, Michael. *Reaching for Glory: Lyndon Johnson's Secret White House Tapes, 1964–1965*. New York: Simon & Schuster, 2001.

Branch, Taylor. *At Canaan's Edge: America in the King Years, 1965–68*. New York: Simon & Schuster, 2006.

———. *Pillar of Fire: America in the King Years, 1963–65*. New York: Simon & Schuster, 1999.

Bryant, Nick. *The Bystander: John F. Kennedy and the Struggle for Black Equality*. New York: Basic Books, 2006.

Busby, Horace. *The Thirty-first of March: An Intimate Portrait of Lyndon Johnson's Final Days in Office*. New York: Farrar, Straus & Giroux, 2005.

Califano, Joseph. *The Triumph and Tragedy of Lyndon Johnson*. New York: Simon & Schuster, 1991.

Caro, Robert. *The Years of Lyndon Johnson: The Passage of Power*. New York: Vintage, 2013.

Carson, Clayborne, ed. *The Autobiography of Martin Luther King, Jr.* New York: Hachette, 1998.

Carter, David C. *The Music Has Gone Out of the Movement: Civil Rights and the Johnson Administration, 1965–1968*. Chapel Hill: University of North Carolina Press, 2009.

Chester, Lewis, Godfrey Hodgson, and Bruce Page. *An American Melodrama: The Presidential Campaign of 1968*. New York: Viking, 1969.

Cowger, Thomas W., and Sherman J. Markman, eds. *Lyndon Johnson Remembered: An Intimate Portrait of a Presidency*. Lanham, MD: Rowman & Littlefield, 2003.

Dallek, Robert. *Flawed Giant: Lyndon Johnson and His Times, 1961–1973*. New York: Oxford University Press, 1998.

Eig, Jonathan. *King: A Life*. New York: Farrar, Straus & Giroux, 2022.

Esposito, Joseph. *Dinner in Camelot: The Night America's Greatest Scientists, Writers and Scholars Partied at the Kennedy White House*. Lebanon, NH: ForeEdge/University Press of New England, 2018.

Evans, Rowland, and Robert Novak. *Lyndon B. Johnson: The Exercise of Power*. New York: Signet, 1968.

Gardner, Lloyd C. *Pay Any Price: Lyndon Johnson and the Wars for Vietnam*. Chicago: Ivan R. Dee, 1997.

Geyelin, Philip. *Lyndon Baines Johnson and the World*. New York: F. A. Praeger, 1966.

Goldman, Eric F. *The Crucial Decade—and After, America: 1945–60*. New York: Random House, 1961.

———. *The Tragedy of Lyndon Johnson*. New York: Knopf, 1969.

Goodwin, Doris Kearns. *The Fitzgeralds and the Kennedys*. New York: St. Martin's, 1987.

———. *Leadership: In Turbulent Times*. New York: Simon & Schuster, 2018.

———. *Lyndon Johnson and the American Dream*. New York: Harper & Row, 1976.

———. *Team of Rivals: The Political Genuis of Abraham Lincoln*. New York: Simon & Schuster, 2005.

Goodwin, Richard N. *Remembering America: A Voice from the Sixties.* New York: Little, Brown, 1988.

Guthman, Edwin, and C. Richard Allen, eds. *RFK: His Words for Our Time.* New York: William Morrow, 2018.

Hersh, Seymour. *Reporter: A Memoir.* New York: Vintage, 2018.

Johnson, Lady Bird. *A White House Diary.* Austin: University of Texas Press, 1970.

Johnson, Lyndon Baines. *The Presidential Recordings: Lyndon Baines Johnson.* 7 vols. New York: W. W. Norton, 2005.

———. *Public Papers of the Presidents of the United States.* Washington, D.C.: Government Printing Office, 1963–1970.

———. *The Vantage Point.* New York: Holt, Rinehart & Winston, 1971.

Kennedy, Jacqueline. *Jacqueline Kennedy: Historic Conversations on Life with John F. Kennedy.* New York: Hyperion, 2011.

Kennedy, Robert. *His Words for Our Times.* New York: Harper Collins, 2008.

King, Martin Luther, Jr. *Witnessing for the Truth.* Boston: Beacon Press, 2014.

Kotz, Nick. *Judgment Days: Lyndon Baines Johnson, Martin Luther King, Jr., and the Laws That Changed America.* New York: Houghton Mifflin, 2005.

Larner, Jeremy. *Nobody Knows: Reflections on the McCarthy Campaign of 1968.* New York: Macmillan, 1970.

Leaming, Barbara. *Jacqueline Bouvier Kennedy Onassis.* New York: St. Martin's, 2014.

Leonard, Richard D. *Call to Selma: Eighteen Days of Witness.* Boston: Skinner House Books, 2002.

Mailer, Norman. *Some Honorable Men.* Boston: Little, Brown, 1976.

Manchester, William. *Controversy: And Other Essays in Journalism, 1950–1975.* Boston: Little, Brown, 1976.

———. *The Death of a President.* New York: Little, Brown, 1967.

Mann, Robert. *The Walls of Jericho: Lyndon Johnson, Hubert Humphrey, Richard Russell, and the Struggle for Civil Rights.* New York: Harcourt Brace, 1996.

McCarthy, Abigail. *Private Places, Public Places.* New York: Doubleday, 1972.

Miller, Merle. *Lyndon: An Oral Autobiography.* New York: Putnam, 1980.

Newfield, Jack. *Robert Kennedy: A Memoir.* New York: E. P. Dutton, 1969.

O'Donnell, Lawrence. *Playing with Fire: The 1968 Election and the Transformation of American Politics.* New York: Penguin, 2018.

Oliphant, Thomas, and Curtis Wilkie. *The Road to Camelot: Inside JFK's Five-Year Campaign.* New York: Simon & Schuster, 2017.

Risen, Clay. *A Nation on Fire: America in the Wake of the King Assassination.* New York: Wiley, 2009.

Sandburg, Carl. *Abraham Lincoln: The War Years,* Vol. 6. New York: Charles Scribner's Sons, 1943.

Schlesinger, Arthur M., Jr. *Journals, 1952–2000.* New York: Penguin, 2008.

———. *Robert Kennedy and His Times.* New York: Houghton Mifflin, 1978.

———. *A Thousand Days: John F. Kennedy in the White House.* Boston: Houghton Mifflin, 1965.

Shesol, Jeff. *Mutual Contempt: Lyndon Johnson, Robert Kennedy, and the Feud That Defined a Decade.* New York: W. W. Norton, 1997.

Sidey, Hugh. *A Very Personal Presidency*. New York: Atheneum, 1968.

Snyder, Brad. *Democratic Justice*. New York: W. W. Norton, 2022.

Sorensen, Theodore M. *Counselor: A Life at the Edge of History*. New York: HarperCollins e-book, 2008.

———. *Kennedy*. New York: HarperCollins e-book, 1965.

Stossel, Scott. *Sarge: The Life and Times of Sargent Shriver*. Washington, D.C.: Smithsonian Books, 2004.

Styron, Rose, ed. *Selected Letters of William Styron*. New York: Random House, 2012.

Sweig, Julia. *Lady Bird Johnson: Hiding in Plain Sight*. New York: Random House, 2021.

Thomas, Evan. *Robert Kennedy: His Life*. New York: Simon & Schuster, 2000.

Updegrove, Mark K. *Incomparable Grace: JFK in the Presidency*. New York: Dutton, 2022.

———. *Indomitable Will: LBJ in the Presidency*. New York: Crown, 2012.

Valenti, Jack. *A Very Human President*. New York: W. W. Norton, 1975.

vanden Heuvel, William, and Milton Gwirtzman. *On His Own: RFK 1964–68*. New York: Doubleday, 1970.

White, Theodore H. *The Making of the President 1960*. New York: Harper Perennial, 1961.

———. *The Making of the President 1964*. New York: Harper Perennial Political Classics, 2010.

———. *The Making of the President 1968*. New York: HarperCollins e-book, 2010.

Wills, Garry. *Nixon Agonistes*. New York: New American Library, 1969.

Wilson, Douglas L., and Rodney O. Davis, eds. *Herndon's Informants: Letters, Interviews, and Statements About Abraham Lincoln*. Urbana and Chicago: University of Illinois Press, 1998.

Witcover, Jules. *85 Days: The Last Campaign of Robert Kennedy*. New York: Putnam, 1969.

Wofford, Harris. *Of Kennedys and Kings: Making Sense of the Sixties*. Pittsburgh: University of Pittsburgh Press, 1980.

Abbreviations Used in Notes

DKG Doris Kearns Goodwin

DKG/LBJ *Lyndon Johnson and the American Dream* (*LJAD*)

JBK Jacqueline Bouvier Kennedy

JFK John Fitzgerald Kennedy

JFKL John F. Kennedy Library

LBJ Lyndon Baines Johnson

LBJL Lyndon Baines Johnson Library

LBJOH LBJ Library Oral History

LBJ, VP Lyndon Baines Johnson, *The Vantage Point*. New York: Holt, Rinehart & Winston, 1971.

LJAD Doris Kearns Goodwin, *Lyndon Johnson and the American Dream*. New York: Harper & Row, 1976.

LTT Doris Kearns Goodwin, *Leadership: In Turbulent Times*. New York: Simon & Schuster, 2018.

PDD Presidential Daily Diary, LBJL

PPP Lyndon Baines Johnson, *Public Papers of the President of the United States*. Washington, D.C.: Government Printing Office, 1963–1970.

PRLBJ *The Presidential Recordings: Lyndon Baines Johnson*. 7 vols. New York: W. W. Norton, 2005.

RFK Robert Francis Kennedy

RNG Richard N. Goodwin

RNG Papers, DBC, UT Richard N. Goodwin Papers, Dolph Briscoe Center for American History, University of Texas at Austin

RNG, RA Richard N. Goodwin, *Remembering America: A Voice from the Sixties*. New York: Little, Brown, 1988.

Notes

A NOTE ON SOURCES

The story of my expedition with Dick through the hundreds of boxes he had saved for more than half a century could not have been told without the research and writings of both of us that had preceded this joint venture.

Our own books and articles provided an initial foundation. Most helpful to us were Dick's *Remembering America* and my *Lyndon Johnson and the American Dream* and *Leadership: In Turbulent Times*. We often read sections of them together to refresh our memories.

New scholarship enlarged and deepend our understanding of the materials we found in the boxes. The ability to watch key speeches on video and listen to LBJ's taped phone conversations altered our original perceptions of people and events. Later, my interviews with witnesses and participants in key moments of the decade provided telling details, amplifications, and new perspectives.

INTRODUCTION

4 *"New Yorkian style...fun and friends"*: *Boston Globe*, December 25, 1975.

CHAPTER ONE: COMING OF AGE

12 *"like some amazing stag"*: Doris Kearns Goodwin, *Leadership: In Turbulent Times* (New York Simon & Schuster, 2018), p. 160.

12 *"September 20, 1952. Starting a journal... lot of rest"*: RNG Papers, DBC, UT.

13 *"June, 1953. You are... in the atmosphere"*: All letters from RNG to George Cuomo are in RNG Papers, Don Briscoe Center for American History, University of Texas, Austin, hereafter DBC, UT.

18 *"Good morning... on the move"*: All letters from RNG to his parents in possession of author.

19 *"practically waiting in line ... legal supermen"*: Jim Anderson, "GIs Flock to Pfc 'Law Firm,'" clipping in possession of author.

22 *"for the good of the sorority as a whole"*: Quoted in Phil Primack, "Opening Doors," *Tufts Magazine*, Spring 2006.

23 *"We accept that responsibility ... to be heard"*: Quoted in Conrad Clark, *Baltimore Afro-American*, October 2, 1956.

23 *"engaged in discriminatory... example to us all"*: Primack, "Opening Doors."

23 *"college students ... take the lead"*: For the year *1956* quoted in *100 Years of Tufts Yearbooks*, https/sites.edu.tufts yearbooks.

24 Manners for Milady: Pamphlet, in box sent by Marcia Phillips Sheldon.

24 *first Jewish pledge:* Author interview with Barbara Gordon Schoneweis.

24 *two women from Tri Delta:* Author interview with Marcia Phillips Sheldon.

27 *"Why are you . . . by a man":* Gregory Wallance, "Justice Ginsburg's Life Was Based on Character," *The Hill*, September 20, 2020.

27 *Harvard provided no housing for women:* Nancy Boxley Tepper, "The Education of a Harvard Lawyer," *Harvard Magazine*, January–February 2021.

27 *"It helped me fulfill . . . Jewish surgeon":* Author interview with Nancy Boxley Tepper.

27 *"Not that we are embarrassed . . . client might be":* Ibid.

28 *"'Young man . . . are inexorable'":* RNG, *Remembering America* (Boston: Little Brown, 1998), p. 26.

30 *Every Wednesday night:* Information about the quiz show scandal from RNG, "Quiz Show Scrapbook," RNG Papers, DBC, UT.

31 *nine-page memo:* RNG to Robert Lishman, July 24, 1959, RNG Papers, DBC, UT.

32 *"I am torn . . . forced to bring him in":* Notes written by RNG, RNG Papers, DBC, UT.

33 *"We don't need" . . . "him guiltless":* RNG, *RA*, pp. 26, 56.

33 *"What an extraordinary . . . possible that you would":* Ibid., pp. 57–58.

34 *"I would give almost . . . in a deception":* Van Doren testimony, November 2, 1959, "History Matters," http://historymatters.gmu.edu/d/6566/.

34 *a "fat fee":* Ray Tucker, "Secrecy for Personal Profit," *Hamilton Daily News Journal* (Ohio), November 24, 1959.

34 *"any information . . . The Public":* RNG, "Quiz Show Scrapbook," RNG Papers, DBC, UT.

34 A Washington Post *editorial:* Ibid.

35 *"'Some pains are . . . like the toothache'":* RNG, *RA*, p. 64.

35 *"We are so proud . . . blessed":* Letter from Belle to RNG, in possession of author.

36 *"astounded" and "almost dismayed":* Eisenhower quoted in Eric F. Goldman, *The Crucial Decade—and After, America: 1945–60* (New York: Random House, 1961), p. 326.

36 *the formula:* RNG, *RA*, p. 63.

36 *"On the wreckage of . . . strength of our land":* RNG Maiden Speech, RNG Papers, DBC, UT.

37 *"A human being lives . . . his contemporaries":* Quoted in DKG, *Team of Rivals: The Political Genius of Abraham Lincoln* (New York: Simon & Schuster, 2005), p. 159.

CHAPTER TWO: "A SORT OF DEAD END"

40 *Midway through the second ballot:* Des Moines Register, August 18, 1956; New York Daily News, August 18, 1956.

40 *What happened next:* New York Times, August 18, 1956.

41 *"good judgment":* William Edwards, "Accounting of VP Nomination," *Chicago Daily Tribune*, August 18, 1956.

41 *"the goddamndest . . . a politician could make":* DKG/LBJ, in Doris Kearns Goodwin, *The Fitzgeralds and the Kennedys* (New York: St. Martin's, 1987), p. 783.

42 *"young whippersnapper . . . never did a thing":* Ibid., p. 780.

42 *"looked . . . television screen":* Ibid., p. 780.

42 *Bowdoin Street:* http://nypost.com/2021/09/01.

42 *"I understand you're . . . greatest fan"*: RNG, *RA*, p. 25.

43 *Theodore Roosevelt's rapid-fire: LTT*, p. 155.

46 *"sticking it to old Ike"*: RNG, *RA*, p. 72.

46 *advance copy of the speech*: RNG, RNG Papers, DBC, UT.

46 *"the challenging . . . to be invisible"*: Ibid.

46 *"pulled his punches" . . . "bookkeeper"*: David Kraslow, *Fort Worth Star Telegram*, January 15, 1960.

47 *"If my name . . . whole soul is in it"*: January 14, 1960, JFK, The Presidency in 1960, National Press Club, Washington, D.C. Online by Peters and Woolley, The American Presidency Project, http//www.Presidency.ucsb/edu/node /274560.

47 *"any Democratic aspirant . . . primary contests"*: January 2, 1960, Remarks of Sen. Kennedy announcing: Ibid.

48 *"We pledge ourselves"*: Memo to Senator JFK from RNG, list of promises, no date, RNG Papers, DBC, UT.

49 *taped interview with Robert Healy: Boston Globe*, April 26, 1983, describes JFK's speaking style; in author's possession.

49 *"polished speaker . . . sank in"*: Ibid.

50 *According to White . . . stares*: Theodore H. White, *The Making of the President 1960* (New York: Harper Perennial, 1961), pp. 83–86.

50 *"I'm John Kennedy . . . in the primary"*: Robert Healy, *Boston Globe*, March 20, 1960.

50 *"Yeah! Happy New Year!"*: Ibid.

50 *"a very forlorn . . . total composure"*: White, *The Making of the President 1960*, pp. 83–84.

50 *"bunch of grayheads . . . meant for his wife"*: Author interview with Ellen Anich Simon.

50 *"My mom's going to have" . . . "make sure she gets them"*: *Ashland Daily Press*, June 2, 2016.

51 *"the greatest day in Ashland's history"*: Julie Buckles, "When JFK Came to Town," *Lake Superior Magazine*, September 18, 2013.

51 *"It was a big honor . . . little town"*: Author interview with Beverley Anich.

51 *"Everyone is . . . foot on our land"*: Transcript provided by Edward Monroe.

51 *clarion call for the preservation: Oshkosh Northwestern* (Wisconsin), September 25, 1963.

52 *"He shook my hand . . . booster pin"*: Buckles, *Lake Superior Magazine*, September 18, 2013.

52 *"All I could think about . . . was possible"*: Ibid.

52 *"It was a very depressing . . . the beachfront"*: Author interview with Edward Monroe.

53 *Superfund: Milwaukee Journal Sentinel*, May 26, 2017.

53 *"The harbor is in good . . . six decades ago"*: Author interview with Edward Monroe.

53 *"We felt after . . . needed to be done"*: Ibid.

54 *"What does it mean" . . . "to the Convention"*: White, *The Making of the President 1960*, p. 94.

54 *"The fact that I was born . . . can't be President?"*: Thomas Oliphant and Curtis Wilkie, *The Road to Camelot: Inside JFK's Five-Year Campaign* (New York: Simon & Schuster, 2017), p. 201.

55 *"cast off the old slogans . . . suspicion"*: July 15, 1960, John F. Kennedy, Address Accepting the Democratic Nomination for President at the Memorial Coliseum in Los Angeles, California. Online by Peters and Woolley, The American Presidency Project.

55 *There are warring narratives:* Oliphant and Wilkie, *The Road to Camelot,* pp. 264–78.

56 *asked his staff to research:* Robert Caro, *The Years of Lyndon Johnson: The Passage of Power* (New York: Vintage, 2012), pp. 113–14.

CHAPTER THREE: ABOARD THE "CAROLINE"

58 *map in the Senate office: Boston Globe,* March 6, 1960.

59 *the "Caroline":* Mark Henderson, "The Caroline," http/www. Pinkpillbox.com/index .php/2-uncategorised/153-caroline-the-airplane.

60 *Dick's draft reiterated:* Draft of Shrine Auditorium speech, RNG Papers, DBC, UT.

60 *An overflow crowd:* Walter Ridder, "Kennedy Takes off Wraps on Nixon," *Press Telegram* (Long Beach, California), September 10, 1960.

60 *"It was by all odds...political swing":* Jack Bell, "Huge Crowd Cheers Jack in LA Speech," *Sheboygan Press* (Wisconsin), September 10, 1960.

60 *"We Want Jack":* Ibid.

61 *"First, I would like ... American politics":* September 9, 1960, John F. Kennedy, Shrine Auditorium, Los Angeles, CA. Online by Peters and Woolley, The American Presidency Project.

61 *"A New Frontier":* Theodore Sorensen, *Counselor: A Life at the Edge of History* (New York: HarperCollins e-book, 2008), pp. 218–19.

61 *"as legislative leader... Give me those years":* September 9, 1960, John F. Kennedy, Shrine Auditorium, Los Angeles, CA.

62 *"Nice Speech, Dick" ... "Both of them":* RNG, *RA,* p. 104.

62 *Reviews the next day:* Roscoe Drummond, "Finds Kennedy Has Effective, Forceful Style of Campaigning," *Racine Journal Times* (Wisconsin), September 10, 1960.

62 *eighty-one promises in all:* Memo to Senator JFK from RNG, no date, RNG Papers, DBC, UT.

62 *"one stroke of the pen":* "New York Coliseum, New York City, 5 November 1960," Papers of John F. Kennedy, Pre-Presidential Papers, Senate Files, Box 914a, JFKL.

62 *"Who the hell wrote ... nobody wrote it":* RNG, *RA,* p. 133.

63 *to prepare in the days before the debate:* Sorensen, *Counselor,* pp. 189–90; Theodore M. Sorensen, *Kennedy* (New York: HarperCollins e-book, 1965), p. 198; Myer Feldman, Interview 2, February 27, 1966, John F. Kennedy Oral History Collection, JFKL; RNG, *RA,* pp. 112–15.

63 *"Nixopedia":* Myer Feldman, Interview 2, February 27, 1966, OH, JFKL; RNG, *RA,* p. 112.

64 *To conserve his voice:* RNG, "Debate Tips from JFK," *New York Times,* September 30, 2000.

64 *yellow pad full of scrawled questions:* RNG, *RA,* p. 114.

64 *Nixon spent most of the day in seclusion:* White, *The Making of the President 1960,* p. 285.

65 *eight-minute opening statement:* "Kennedy vs. Nixon: Sept. 26, 1960," *Philadelphia Inquirer,* September 27, 1960.

66 *Kennedy deployed statistics:* Harris Wofford, *Of Kennedys and Kings: Making Sense of the Sixties* (Pittsburgh: University of Pittsburgh Press, 1980), p. 62.

66   *"I'm not satisfied . . . I think we can do better"*: "Kennedy vs. Nixon: Sept. 26, 1960," PBS Newshour, https://www.youtube.com/watch?v=AYP8-oxq8ig.

66   *"an assassin image"*: White, *The Making of the President 1960*, p. 285.

66   *people on the other side of the camera*: Sorensen, *Counselor*, p. 190.

67   *crowds hadn't merely doubled*: *Democrat and Chronicle* (Rochester, New York), September 24, 1960; *Mansfield News Journal* (Ohio), September 28, 1960.

67   *After midnight on October 14, 1960*: James Tobin, "JFK at the Union: The Unknown Story of the Peace Corps," http://peacecorps.umich.edu/Tobin. html.

68   *"a graduate of the Michigan . . . free society can compete"*: "President John F. Kennedy's University of Michigan Speech," October 14, 1960, https://www.youtube.com /watch?v=ydTaoZ9JSGk.

69   *"on the razor edge of decision"*: Television debates: Transcript: Third Debate, JFK-Nixon, October 13, 1960, JFKL.

69   *"the longest short speech . . . recognize it"*: Ibid.

69   *students took up the challenge*: Tobin, "JFK at the Union: The Unknown Story of the Peace Corps."

69   *"might still be just an idea . . . spontaneous combustion"*: Peace Corps Worldwide, "The Birth of the Peace Corps," November 9, 2019, https://peacecorpsworldwide.org/the -birth-of-the-peace-corps/.

70   *the night that changed their lives . . . additional half hour*: Author interviews with Alan and Judy Guskin.

70   *"The campus was alive . . . building for months"*: Author interview with Alan Guskin.

71   *"The energy was there . . . right campus at the right time"*: Author interview with Judy Guskin.

71   *"A light bulb went off . . . response was YES"*: Author interview with Alan Guskin.

71   *Hayden published . . . call for action*: Letter to the Editor, *Michigan Daily*, quoted in Noreen Ferris Wolcott, "Without the U of M Students the Peace Corps Might Never Have Been," *Michigan Alumnus* Magazine, March 1981.

71   *"a force of nature"*: Author interview with Alan Guskin.

72   *"a peace corps . . . move the world"*: November 2, 1960, John F. Kennedy, Speech of Senator John F. Kennedy, Cow Palace, San Francisco, CA. Online by Peters and Woolley, The American Presidency Project.

72   *Millie Jeffrey called the Guskins'*: Sharon Morioka, "A Challenge to Serve," *Michigan Alumnus Magazine*, Fall 2010.

72   *"We waited on the tarmac . . . the petitions"*: Author interview with Judy Guskin.

72   *"I remember his intensity . . . The way he listened"*: Ibid.

72   *"Are you really serious" . . . "after Tuesday, the world"*: Tobin, "JFK at the Union: The Unknown Story of the Peace Corps."

73   *"a Kiddie Corps"*: Lester Graham, *Kennedy and the Peace Corps: Idealism on the Ground*, https://www.michiganradio.org/politics-government/2020-10-13/kennedy-and -the-peace-corps-idealism-on-the-ground. Transcript of documentary originally aired October 13, 2010.

73   *"the best years"*: Author interview with Judy Guskin.

73   *"The values of the Peace Corps . . . religions, and languages"*: Author interview with Judy and Alan Guskin.

74 *Kennedy's itinerary:* Presidential Campaigns, The John F. Kennedy 1960 Campaign, Part II: Speeches, Press Conferences, and Debates, microfilm ed., JFKL.

75 *"They decided to work ... the following evening":* White, *The Making of the President 1960,* pp. 325–26.

75 *"worst major blunder of the campaign":* James Reston, "There's a Kennedy Feeling in the Air," *Tampa Bay Times,* October 23, 1960.

75 *"We must attempt ... from our Government":* October 20, 1960, John F. Kennedy, Statement on Cuba by Senator John F. Kennedy. Online by Peters and Woolley, The American Presidency Project.

76 *"a vague generalization ... anti-Castro program":* Sorensen, *Kennedy,* p. 205.

76 *"shocking":* Television debates: Transcript: Fourth debate, JFK-Nixon, October 21, 1960, JFKL.

76 *"Such a statement ... aspires to be president":* "Senator Kennedy and Cuba," *Pittsburgh Press,* October 26, 1960.

76 *"consult his ... foreign statements":* "Kennedy Plays with Fire," *Arizona Republic,* October 26, 1960.

76 *"moral and psychological ... political support":* Arthur M. Schlesinger, Jr., *Journals, 1952–2000* (New York: Penguin, 2008), p. 91.

76 *"If I win this thing ... you guys lost it":* RNG, *RA,* p. 126.

77 *won the popular vote:* jfklibrary.org/learn/about-jfk/jfk-in-history/campaign-of-1960.

77 *"principal adviser ... and messages":* Sorensen, *Counselor,* p. 198; RNG, *RA,* p. 139.

78 *"I hear ... for a while":* RNG, *RA,* p. 139.

78 *"I told him how ... done the same thing":* RNG, *RA,* p. 71.

78 *"I have been saddened ... about what happened":* RNG to Sorensen, 1964, RNG Papers, DBC, UT.

79 *"My friends ... I cannot fail":* Abraham Lincoln, "Farewell Address at Springfield," February 11, 1861, *Collected Works,* Vol. 4, p. 190.

80 *"For we must consider . . . are upon us":* Schlesinger memo to RNG, RNG Papers, DBC, UT.

81 *Despite the bitter cold morning:* "Kennedy," *Biddeford Journal* (Maine), January 9, 1961; John Fenton, "Harvard Crowd Cheers Kennedy," *New York Times,* January 10, 1961.

81 *"a nostalgic mood":* W. H. Lawrence, "Kennedy Pledges Rule of Integrity," *New York Times,* January 9, 1961.

81 *"For fourteen years ... will be born":* JFK, "The City on a Hill," transcript of radio speech, WBZ Radio, JFKL.

81 *On the draft of the speech:* Speech draft, RNG Papers, DBC, UT.

81 *"we shall be ... solemn journey":* "The City on a Hill," transcript.

CHAPTER FOUR: A PANDORA'S BOX OF CIGARS

84 *"It shows his ... and to me":* JBK to RNG, RNG Papers, DBC, UT.

84 *"This is the call ... join me in doing":* September 3, 1960, John F. Kennedy, Speech of Senator John F. Kennedy, the Edgewater, Anchorage, AK. Online by Peters and Woolley, The American Presidency Project.

84 *"It sums up not ... to ask of them":* July 15, 1960, John F. Kennedy, Address Accepting

the Democratic Nomination for President at the Memorial Coliseum in Los Angeles, California. Ibid.

85	*"Let the word go forth . . . of Americans":* January 20, 1961, John F. Kennedy, Inaugural Address. Online by Gerhard Peters and John T. Woolley, The American Presidency Project, https://www.presidency.ucsb.edu/node/234470.

85	*The procession included:* St. Louis Post-Dispatch, January 21, 1961.

86	*"Dick . . . done about it":* RNG, RA, p. 5.

86	*"no distinction . . . creed or color":* Memo to RNG from Theodore L. Elliot, Jr., Special Assistant to the Secretary, January 25, 1961, RNG Papers, DBC, UT.

86	*"lit a real fire":* Fred Dutton to Robert Wallace, October 2, 1961, RNG Papers, DBC, UT.

87	*"We arrived with trepidation . . . officer":* Erica Moser, The Day, October 1, 2021.

87	*"I did feel in law school . . . for yourself":* Daliah Lithwick, Slate, July 21, 2020.

87	*Newspaper accounts:* Erica Moser, The Day, June 22, 2021.

88	*"Merle had lived . . . discrimination":* Author interview with Dr. Lynda Smith.

89	*"I just remember being struck . . . quite frankly":* Erica Moser, The Day, June 22, 2021.

89	*"Because of you . . . all his life":* Author interview with Dr. Lynda Smith.

89	*"The new Administration . . . of discrimination":* Martin Luther King, Jr., The Nation, February 4, 1961.

90	*the resulting numbers:* Chester Bowles to JFK, January 1, 1960, RNG Papers, DBC, UT; *15 of 3,674 foreign service officers:* Nick Bryant, The Bystander: John F. Kennedy and the Struggle for Black Equality (New York: Basic Books, 2006), p. 213; *10 of 950 Justice Department attorneys:* Wofford, Of Kennedys and Kings, p. 141.

90	*"vigorous young men . . . any previous Administration":* Martin Luther King, Jr., The Nation, March 3, 1962.

90	*"Areas of Responsibility of the Counsellors":* RNG Papers, DBC, UT.

91	*"Young Dick Goodwin" . . . "to see you":* Robert Kaplan to RFK, September 14, 1961, RNG Papers, DBC, UT.

92	*"We already have" . . . "with me":* RNG, RA, p. 147.

93	*Arthur Schlesinger Jr. . . . recalled:* Arthur M. Schlesinger, Jr., A Thousand Days: John F. Kennedy in the White House (Boston: Houghton Mifflin, 1965), p. 203.

93	*"Good job! . . . don't know any":* RNG, RA, p. 153.

93	*the evening of March 13:* New York Times, March 14, 1961.

94	*"the greatest region . . . walk hand in hand":* March 13, 1961, John F. Kennedy, Address at a White House Reception for Members of Congress and for the Diplomatic Corps of the Latin American Republics. Online by Peters and Woolley, The American Presidency Project.

94	*"How was my Spanish . . . show we mean it":* RNG, RA, p. 159.

95	*an invasion force:* "JFK in History: The Bay of Pigs," https://www.jfklibrary.org/learn /about-jfk/jfk-in-history/the-bay-of-pigs.

96	*breakfast at the White House:* April 7, 1961, Schlesinger, Journals, p. 109.

96	*"bullying intervention":* Schlesinger, A Thousand Days, p. 257.

96	*"You know . . . no to this thing":* RNG, RA, p. 177.

96	*"'Well, Dick . . . into action'":* Ibid., p. 179.

97	*"He started to cry . . . die in jail":* Jacqueline Kennedy, Jacqueline Kennedy: Historic Conversations on Life with John F. Kennedy (New York: Hyperion, 2011), pp. 185–86.

97　*"How did I ever . . . still barreled ahead":* Sorensen, *Counselor*, p. 317.

97　*"the happiest people . . . anything about it":* RNG notes on press conference, April 22, 1961, RNG Papers, DBC, UT.

97　*"Oh sure . . . while I'm still alive":* Schlesinger, *A Thousand Days*, pp. 289–90.

97　*"I'm the responsible officer . . . defeat is an orphan":* April 21, 1961, John F. Kennedy, The President's News Conference. Online by Peters and Woolley, The American Presidency Project.

97　*"The worse I do . . . popular I get":* Mark Updegrove, *Incomparable Grace: JFK in the Presidency* (New York: Dutton, 2022), p. 76.

97　*"Let's get moving . . . could start tomorrow":* RNG, *RA*, p. 190.

98　*The night before the conference:* Ibid., pp. 191, 192.

98　*"We're asking them . . . giving them is words":* Ibid., p. 192.

98　*"Of course I have the authority . . . billion dollars":* Ibid.

99　*"almost fatal mistakes . . . and naivety":* RNG to Sorensen, RNG Papers, DBC, UT.

99　*"Since I have . . . my hand":* Note with cigar box, RNG Papers, DBC, UT.

99　*"for one cannot . . . against themselves":* RNG, *RA*, p. 196.

100　*Che said "good":* RNG memo for the president, conversations with Commandant Ernesto Guevara, August 22, 1961, RNG Papers, DBC, UT.

100　*"the most important . . . expectations":* August 19, 1961, John F. Kennedy, Remarks of Welcome to Secretary Dillon on His Return from the Punta del Este Conference. Online by Peters and Woolley, The American Presidency Project.

100　*"You should have smoked the first one!":* RNG, *RA*, p. 202.

101　*"Write up a complete account":* Ibid.

101　*"Che was wearing green fatigues" . . . would not publicize it:* RNG memo, August 22, 1961, RNG Papers, DBC, UT.

102　*"playing with fire" . . . "summarily dismissed":* Extension of the Remarks of Steve Derounian, August 30, 1961, U.S. Congress, *Congressional Record*, Vol. 107, p. A6834.

102　*"Best of luck old comrade . . . Comandante Capehart":* August 31, 1961, RNG Papers, DBC, UT.

102　*freewheeling power:* June 28, 1961, John F. Kennedy, The President's News Conference. Online by Peters and Woolley, The American Presidency Project.

103　*"You know, Dick . . . when I get back":* RNG, *RA*, pp. 210–11.

104　*"The Department has some bad habits . . . Rusk's position":* Adolf A. Berle to RNG, November 28, 1961, RNG Papers, DBC, UT.

105　*"Listen, Dick . . . keep on going south":* RNG, *RA*, p. 214.

105　*"the greatest reception . . . in Venezuela's history":* Merriman Smith, "JFK Good-Will Visit to Venezuela," *Desert Sun* (Palm Springs, California), December 16, 1961.

105　*"dressed in their Sunday best":* http://thecitypaperbogota.com/bogota/jfks-legacy-in-Bogota-lives-on-55-years later/.

105　*"an enfant terrible" . . . "a tough crow":* Dom Bonafede, "Kennedy's Eager Latin Aide Stirs Controversy," *Miami Herald*, April 8, 1962.

106　*given the go-ahead to travel to Wall Street:* RNG to JFK, September 16, 1963, RNG Papers, DBC, UT.

106　*"The only good idea . . . over there for":* Papers of T. H. White, HUM 1.10, Harvard University Archives, https://id.lib.harvard.edu/ead/hua16004/catalog.

107 *"a master entertainer . . . a living page from a history book"*: Kevin Sullivan, *Washington Post*, October 13, 2002.

107 *"got along famously . . . trenches"*: Marcella Bombardieri, "Brothers in Arms," *Boston Globe*, October 20, 2022.

108 *"There are lessons . . . human history"*: Marion Lloyd, "Soviet Close to Using A-Bomb in 1962 Crisis, Forum Is Told," *Boston Globe*, October 13, 2002.

108 *"Goodwin's memo . . . in Cuban history"*: Author conversation with Peter Kornbluh.

108 *"The 'out-proletarianize' quip . . . all the conference"*: Ibid.

109 *"the wild-haired . . . eyebrowed"*: Marcella Bombardieri, "Former Defense Sec. McNamara and Fidel Castro in Havana," *Boston Globe*, October 20, 2002.

109 *"Fidel invites you . . . the hall"*: Note attached to picture of Castro with the Goodwins. In possession of the author.

110 *"I won't be here" . . . "down from Heaven"*: Bombardieri, "Former Defense Sec. McNamara and Fidel Castro in Havana."

CHAPTER FIVE: THE SUPREME GENERALIST

112 *"Whatever you feel . . . okay with me"*: RNG memo of talk with JFK, RNG Papers, DBC, UT.

113 *"Rusk called me up . . . wait for Goodwin's arrival"*: Author interview with Bill Josephson.

113 *"I liked him instantly . . . friend in Washington"*: Author interview with Bill Moyers.

114 *"Before long . . . that effort"*: Speech by RNG at fifteenth annual conference of the Association of International Students, April 9, 1962, RNG Papers, DBC, UT.

114 *"It seemed to me . . . drive to get things done"*: Schlesinger, *A Thousand Days*, p. 213.

115 *"This is the most extraordinary . . . Jefferson dined alone"*: April 29, 1962, John F. Kennedy, Remarks at a Dinner Honoring Nobel Prize Winners of the Western Hemisphere. Online by Peters and Woolley, The American Presidency Project.

116 *"How about a dinner . . . winners of the Nobel Prize"*: Joseph Esposito, *Dinner in Camelot* (Lebanon, NH: University Press of New England, 2018), p. 44.

116 *make sure that Dick was invited*: Ibid., p. 46.

116 *"Many were starstruck . . . for the first time"*: Author interview with Joseph Esposito.

116 *"A stupendous amount . . . wonderful party"*: Diana Trilling, "A Visit to Camelot," *The New Yorker*, June 7, 1997.

117 *"Dr. Pauling . . . your opinions"*: Esposito, *Dinner in Camelot*, p. 10.

117 *"encourage young people . . . deep desire"*: April 29, 1962, John F. Kennedy, Remarks at a Dinner Honoring Nobel Prize Winners of the Western Hemisphere, Online by Peters and Woolley, The American Presidency Project.

118 *"It is the major temple . . . be flooded"*: http://albertis-window.com/2016/04/abu-simbel-and-jackie-kennedy/.

118 *"for possible action" . . . "Let's give it a try"*: RNG, RA, pp. 222–23.

119 *"Don't argue, show" . . . when seeking funds*: LTT, pp. 91–92.

119 *"Agnelli said . . . Affectionately, Jackie"*: JBK to RNG, April 10, 1963, RNG Papers, DBC, UT.

119 *"A few assorted . . . world culture"*: Memo, RNG to JBK, February 11, 1963, RNG Papers, DBC, UT.

119 *"If that's what . . . I'll try it"*: RNG, RA, p. 223.

120 *"I have worked . . . announce your action"*: RNG to LBJ, September 11, 1964, RNG Papers, DBC, UT.

120 *"These temples . . . oldest civilizations"*: RNG draft, RNG Papers, DBC, UT.

121 *"Here . . . overcrowded conditions"*: Martin Luther King, Jr., *The Nation*, February 4, 1961.

121 *Reasons for the delay*: Wofford, *Of Kennedys and Kings*, pp. 128–29, 140; Bryant, *The Bystander*, pp. 299–302.

122 *"In the election . . . passion is missing"*: Wofford, *Of Kennedys and Kings*, pp. 128–29.

122 *"Ink for Jack"*: Updegrove, *Incomparable Grace*, p. 82.

122 *"a good faith . . . right direction"*: Martin Luther King, Jr., *The Nation*, March 30, 1963.

122 *"Double D-Day" . . . "Children's Crusade"*: Foster Hailey, *New York Times*, March 4, 1963.

123 *The front-page . . . made President Kennedy "sick"*: Updegrove, *Incomparable Grace*, p. 221.

123 *"At Birmingham . . . around the world"*: Martin Luther King, Jr., *The Nation*, March 15, 1965.

124 *"President Kennedy hasn't done . . . problem demands"*: Bryant, *The Bystander*, p. 421.

124 *wanted to go on television*: Updegrove, *Incomparable Grace*, pp. 224–25; *Daily Eagle* (Jasper, Alabama), June 12, 1963.

124 *"We are confronted . . . American life or law"*: June 11, 1963, John F. Kennedy, Radio and Television Report to the American People on Civil Rights. Online by Peters and Woolley, The American Presidency Project.

126 *state of emergency had been declared*: *Kansas City Star* (Kansas), August 25, 1963; *Minneapolis Sunday Tribune*, August 25, 1963.

127 *"We want success . . . work its will"*: Schlesinger, *Journals*, June 22, 1963, p. 196.

127 *"The Negroes are already . . . disciplined by struggle"*: Ibid.

127 *"He believed . . . run over by it"*: Douglas L. Wilson and Rodney O. Davis, eds., *Herndon's Informants: Letters, Interviews, and Statements About Abraham Lincoln* (Urbana and Chicago: University of Illinois Press, 1998), pp. 316–18.

127 *"ill-timed . . . at first hand"*: Schlesinger, *Journals*, pp. 196–98.

129 *"Let freedom ring . . . let freedom ring"*: Martin Luther King, Jr., "I Have a Dream," March on Washington for Jobs and Freedom, August 28, 1963, Lincoln Memorial, Washington, D.C., www.avalon.law.yale.edu/20th_century/mlk01.asp. Transcript.

129 *campus-wide campaign*: *Colby Echo*, April 17, 1964; May 1, 1964.

130 *"criteria for fraternal . . . with our organization"*: Mrs. J. L. Perry, "Colby Sorority Ousted," *Colby Echo*, September 18, 1964.

130 *"Oh yes, the Tri Delta . . . badge of honor"*: Author interview with Judy Turner Jones.

131 *"We older people ignore . . . advance civil and human rights"*: Adlai Stevenson speech, *Colby Alumnus*, Vol. 53, No. 4, Summer 1964; *New York Times*, June 8, 1964.

131 *"serious-minded students . . . over the world"*: RNG Diary, November 2, 1963, RNG Papers, DBC, UT.

132 *"I would come out . . . fully frustrated"*: RNG to JBK, February 11, 1963, RNG Papers, DBC, UT.

132 *"For the first time . . . aspects of the Arts"*: June 12, 1963, John F. Kennedy, Statement by the President Upon Establishing the Advisory Council on the Arts. Online by Peters and Woolley, The American Presidency Project.

132 *signed the executive order*: Executive Order 1102, June 12, 1963, https://www.white house.gov/briefing-room/presidential-actions/2022/09/30/executive-order-on-promoting-the-arts-the-humanities-and-museum-and-library-services/.

132 *Soviet Union . . . exporting ballet groups:* Henry Raymont, *New York Times*, August 3, 1963.

133 *"his imagination . . . which we operated":* LTT, p. 386.

134 *"It should concern . . . Conservation was to Teddy Roosevelt":* November 29, 1963, RNG Diary, RNG Papers, DBC, UT.

134 *"The Peace Corps . . . good or better people":* Memo, RNG to JFK, September 10, 1963, RNG Papers, DBC, UT.

134 *"I'm running out of brothers . . . very much":* RNG Diary, November 29, 1963, RNG Papers, DBC, UT.

134 *"He told me that . . . on the statement":* RNG Diary, November 21, 1963, RNG Papers, DBC, UT.

135 *"It was a very favorable . . . tone and ring":* RNG Diary, November 22, 1963, RNG Papers, DBC, UT.

135 *"one of the bright . . . Latin American statesmen":* "Man in the News Profile," *New York Times*, November 22, 1963.

136 *"Oh! Mr. Goodwin . . . He's dead":* RNG Diary, November 29, 1960, RNG Papers, DBC, UT. On November 29, Dick began his long recounting of the events of the previous "week of horror."

CHAPTER SIX: KALEIDOSCOPE

137 *"Political affairs are kaleidoscopic":* Theodore Roosevelt to Anna Cowles, Feb. 2, 1900, https://www.theodorerooseveltcenter.org/Research/DigitalLibrary/Record?li bID=o28586.

137 *"For joy or sorrow . . . lived out":* LTT, p. 125.

138 *"I am not . . . my existence":* Ibid., p. 158.

138 *"he had come . . . political road":* Ibid., p. 207.

138 *"My only instinct . . . he was dead":* RNG Diary, November 29, 1963, RNG Papers, DBC, UT.

138 *"a canopy of . . . black silk and crape":* Carl Sandburg, *Abraham Lincoln: The War Years*, Vol. 6 (New York: Charles Scribner's Sons, 1943), p. 388.

139 *Further details were needed:* Scott Stossel, *Sarge: The Life and Times of Sargent Shriver* (Washington, D.C.: Smithsonian Books, 2004), pp. 304–5; RNG, *RA*, pp. 336–37.

139 *"It was getting . . . black base":* RNG Diary, November 29, 1963, RNG Papers, DBC, UT.

139 *Everyone pitched in:* Stossel, *Sarge*, p. 306.

140 *"The occasion . . . for them, too":* William Manchester, *The Death of a President* (New York: Little, Brown, 1967), p. 438.

140 *"I know he isn't . . . look that way":* Stossel, *Sarge*, p. 308.

140 *"the flame-lit drive . . . the coffin":* Manchester, *The Death of a President*, p. 438.

140 *"The troops . . . the coffin":* RNG Diary, November 29, 1963, RNG Papers, DBC, UT.

140 *"I stood on the front . . . returned to the White House":* RNG Diary, Ibid.

141 *"Saturday was the day . . . pills and went":* RNG Diary, November 24–25, December 2, 1963, RNG Papers, DBC, UT

141 *"Somebody just shot Oswald":* Manchester, *The Death of a President*, p. 525.

141 *"We went on . . . charged with the shooting":* Ibid.

142 *"Some people" . . . "Let them":* Ibid., p. 550.

142 *Dick Goodwin was designated . . . "she can light it"*: Ibid., pp. 551–52, based on Manchester interview with Dick.

145 *"One, we had to give . . . Latin American countries"*: RNG Diary, December 2, 1963, RNG Papers, DBC, UT.

145 *"to great lengths . . . U.S. Government"*: RNG Diary, December 4, 1963, RNG Papers, DBC, UT.

146 *"the leading prospect . . . nomination"*: Rowland Evans and Robert Novak, "Inside Report: Shriver for VP?," *Boston Globe*, December 3, 1963.

146 *"Eunice said it was no fun . . . conversation shifted"*: RNG Diary, December 2, 1963, RNG Papers, DBC, UT.

146 *"She [Eunice] said the alternatives . . . the only short cut"*: RNG Diary, December 4, 1963, RNG Papers, DBC, UT.

146 *"He said that before . . . has been so circumscribed"*: RNG Diary, December 6, 1963, RNG Papers, DBC, UT.

147 *"On Friday . . . We won't be wanted or needed"*: RNG Diary, December 13, 1963, RNG Papers, DBC, UT.

149 *"We're going to get . . . can take"*: LTT, pp. 308–9.

150 *"I took the oath . . . I was that man"*: DKG/LBJ, *Lyndon Johnson and the American Dream* (New York: Harper & Row, 1976), pp. 170, 172.

150 *"I knew how they felt . . . asked for their help"*: Ibid., p. 175.

150 *"I just want to say . . . you had in John F. Kennedy"*: Schlesinger, *Journals*, p. 209.

151 *"I needed that White House staff . . . governing the country"*: DKG/LBJ, *LJAD*, pp. 177–78.

152 *"All I have . . . the books of law"*: November 27, 1963, Lyndon B. Johnson, Address Before a Joint Session of Congress. Online by Peters and Woolley, The American Presidency Project.

153 *"LBJ: Since [Ted] Sorensen left . . . music to it?"*: PRLBJ, Vol. 5, pp. 63–64.

154 *"what the . . . poverty"*: Moyers to RNG, March 10, RNG Papers, DBC, UT.

155 *"We are citizens . . . have been closed"*: March 16, 1964, Lyndon B. Johnson, Special Message to the Congress Proposing a Nationwide War on the Sources of Poverty. Online by Peters and Woolley, The American Presidency Project.

155 *"Dick, can you come here" . . . "Of course"*: LBJ and RNG quotes from RNG, *RA*, pp. 249–51.

156 *"LBJ: I want to get Dick Goodwin" . . . "All right, sir. Fine"*: PRLBJ, Vol. 5, pp. 386–87.

157 *"He thought . . . no other way"*: RNG Diary, March 4, 1964, RNG Papers, DBC, UT.

158 *"Dear Jackie . . . this whole idea"*: RNG to JBK, March 10, 1964, RNG Papers, DBC, UT.

159 *"word gap . . . enfant terrible"*: Rowland Evans and Robert Novak, "Inside Report," *Washington Post*, March 26, 1964.

159 *"REEDY: Dick Goodwin . . . where they called him. Sir"*: PRLBJ, Vol. 5, pp. 759–60.

160 *"Kennedy had some good programs . . . better at that than you"*: LBJ quotes from RNG, *RA*, pp. 269–71.

161 *"We now have the opportunity . . . the great society"*: Theodore White, *The Making of the President 1964* (New York: Harper Perennial Political Classics, 2010), p. 410.

161 *"the rumpled Goodwin . . . simply appeared"*: Hugh Sidey, *A Very Personal Presidency* (New York: Atheneum, 1968), p. 49.

162 *"the spacious theme"*: Jack Valenti, *A Very Human President* (New York: W. W. Norton, 1975), p. 85.

162 *"We are trying ... we are doing"*: April 17, 1964, Lyndon B. Johnson, Remarks to a Group in Connection with the Montana Territorial Centennial. Online by Peters and Woolley, The American Presidency Project.

163 *"Washington is now a little girl ... not complaining"*: James Reston, *New York Times*, in *LJAD*, p. 190.

164 *"the Goodwin code ... in his field"*: Valenti, *A Very Human President*, p. 65.

165 *It ought to be ... what I told you*: RNG, *RA*, p. 278.

165 *"I have come ... to build the Great Society"*: May 22, 1964, Lyndon B. Johnson, Remarks at the University of Michigan. Online by Peters and Woolley, The American Presidency Project.

166 *"Try some of this ... came here"*: RNG, *RA*, p. 282.

167 *"LBJ has done more ... University of Michigan"*: James Reston, "Period of Reconciliation," *New York Times*, May 24, 1964.

CHAPTER SEVEN: THIRTEEN LBJS

168 *"Lyndon Johnson was thirteen ... particular time"*: Bill Moyers, *Fresh Air*, NPR, August 3, 2017, https://www.npr.org/2017/08/03/541436949/bill-moyers.

169 *"You've been ... at the Ranch"*: Leslie Carpenter, "LBJ: The Little Things Count," *Charlotte Observer*, June 7, 1964.

169 *The day had begun ... coming election:* For events during the weekend: PDD, May 28, 1964.

169 *"Come with me ... down"*: Carpenter, "LBJ: The Little Things Count."

170 *at the door of the general store:* Ibid.

170 *"Everyone was ... Lots of kids"*: Sandra Goodwin, "The Weekend at the Ranch," RNG Papers, DBC, UT.

170 *"Forty years ago ... all the time"*: May 29, 1964, Lyndon B. Johnson, Remarks in Texas to the Graduating Class of the Johnson City High School. Online by Peters and Woolley, The American Presidency Project.

171 *"The people ... whose names she knew"*: Sandra Goodwin, "The Weekend at the Ranch."

171 *"Will you leave ... build the Great Society?"*: *Austin American*, May 31, 1964.

172 *"It would ... appeasement or attrition"*: LBJ, *The Vantage Point* (New York: Holt, Rinehart and Winston, 1971), p. 168.

172 *"or at least forced him ... three times harder"*: Ibid., p. 157.

172 *the bill's supporters determined:* *The Journal* (Meriden, Connecticut), May 28, 1964.

173 *"Cater gave his speech ... Peace Corps"*: RNG Diary, June 8, 1966, RNG Papers, DBC, UT.

173 *"I think we have enough" ... "do you have?"*: Robert Dallek, *Flawed Giant: Lyndon Johnson and His Times, 1961–1973* (New York: Oxford University Press, 1998), p. 119.

173 *"without Republican support ... acquire us that support"*: DKG/LBJ, *LJAD*, p. 192.

174 *"The bill can't pass ... You listen to Dirksen!"*: Nick Kotz, *Judgment Days: Lyndon Baines Johnson, Martin Luther King, Jr., and the Laws That Changed America* (New York: Houghton Mifflin, 2005), p. 115.

174 *"Dirksen tells me ... think he's got 26"*: PRLBJ, Vol. 11, p. 200.

174 *"exchanged good natured quips" ... "My Neighbor's Roses"*: Ronald Shafer, "How Democrats Managed to Beat the Filibuster—58 Years Ago," *Washington Post*, January 12, 2022.

174 *brought a red rose:* Ibid.

174 *cheering crowd: Boston Globe,* June 11, 1964.

175 *"fought with us ... time has come": New York Times,* June 11, 1964; *Philadelphia Inquirer,* June 11, 1964.

175 *"a broad grin":* "Johnson Tells Holy Cross; End of Racial Injustice in Sight," *Boston Globe,* June 10, 1964.

175 *"Hello, hero!": PRLBJ,* Vol. 7, p. 210.

175 *"We won't do ... the legislation":* Arthur M. Schlesinger, Jr., *Robert Kennedy and His Times* (New York: Houghton Mifflin, 1978), p. 644.

176 *"get credit": PRLBJ,* Vol. 6, p. 662.

176 *"two hundred years from now ... Lincoln and Everett Dirksen":* RNG, *RA* (New York: Open Road ed., 2014), p. 7.

176 *Goodwin had become:* "The New Team," *Time,* May 29, 1964, p. 18; Jeanne S. Perry, "Latin America News Notes," *Palm Beach Post,* June 7, 1964.

176 *"Goodwin cranks out ... just as much style":* "The New Team," *Time.*

177 *Sidey felt released ... George Reedy:* Sidey, *A Very Personal Presidency,* p. 156.

177 *"LBJ: [Sidey] says he got ... Bring him on in": PRLBJ,* Vol. 7, pp. 246–47.

178 *"Goodwin has not written ... result of research":* Sidey, *A Very Personal Presidency,* p. 157.

178 *"I was somewhat ... up nor down":* Ibid.

178 *"I resent that to hell ... if they want to know": PRLBJ,* Vol. 7, pp. 246–47.

179 *"Goodwin spent one day on the [LBJ] ranch":* RNG Diary, June 14, 1965, RNG Papers, DBC, UT.

179 *someone named "Goodman":* Sidey, *A Very Personal Presidency,* p.158.

179 *"It is a singular experience ... credibility gap":* Ibid., pp. 159–60.

180 *Johnson decided to pay a visit:* Brad Snyder, *Democratic Justice* (New York: W. W. Norton, 2022), p. 704.

181 *"That boy has politics in his blood":* RNG, *RA,* p. 72.

181 *"When I was ... as I was there": LJAD,* p. 121.

181 *"Richard Russell ... wanted to take care of him": LJAD,* p. 105.

182 *"Now you tell Lyndon ... he uses it":* Dallek, *Flawed Giant,* p. 118.

182 *"They feared humiliation ... spring in the desert": LJAD,* pp. 120–21.

182 *"That'll do just fine ... and me make a little history":* RNG, *RA,* pp. 316–17.

183 *"Do you think" ... "you could focus on it": PRLBJ,* Vol. 7, pp. 374–75.

183 *"We are going to have ... middle of the week": PRLBJ,* Vol. 8, p. 350.

183 *Halleck cautioned:* Ibid., p. 351.

183 *"We've got to make this ... and not just a Democratic bill":* Dallek, *Flawed Giant,* p. 120.

184 *"We believe ... forbids it":* July 2, 1964, Lyndon B. Johnson, Radio and Television Remarks upon Signing the Civil Rights Bill. Online by Peters and Woolley, The American Presidency Project.

184 *"We have come now ... racial poison":* Ibid.

185 *"impassive face ... in his palm":* Julia Sweig, *Lady Bird Johnson: Hiding in Plain Sight* (New York: Random House, 2021), p. 91.

185 *"Pen used to sign President Kennedy's civil rights bill":* Jeff Shesol, *Mutual Contempt: Lyndon Johnson, Robert Kennedy, and the Feud that Defined a Decade* (New York: W. W. Norton, 1997), p. 166.

185 *"All these things . . . about you"*: RNG, *RA*, p. 451.

186 *"exhilarated . . . rarely attained"*: Lady Bird Johnson, *A White House Diary* (Austin: University of Texas Press, 1970), p. 175.

186 *"But later that . . . for a long time to come"*: Todd Gottinger and Allen Fisher, "LBJ Champions Civil Rights Act 1964," *Prologue Magazine*, Summer 2004.

187 *"Every day . . . elected on my own"*: LJAD, pp. 199–200.

187 *"When the time comes . . . who we want as Vice-President"*: RNG Diary, December 14, 1964, RNG Papers, DBC, UT.

187 *"I want you to get rid of . . . favors for me, ever"*: RNG Diary, March 1, 1964, DBC, UT.

188 *He decided to tell Bobby*: Schlesinger, *Robert Kennedy and His Times*, pp. 659–61; LBJ, *VP*, p. 100.

189 *"Lyndon's telling . . ."*: RNG, *RA*, p. 298.

189 *"told . . . drove off"*: Ibid.

189 *"I have reached . . . with the Cabinet"*: July 30, 1964, Lyndon B. Johnson, Statement by the President Relating to the Selection of a Vice Presidential Candidate. Online by Peters and Woolley, The American Presidency Project.

190 *"That'll eliminate" . . . "to eliminate one"*: Michael Beschloss, *Reaching for Glory: Lyndon Johnson's Secret White House Tapes, 1964–1965* (New York: Simon & Schuster, 2001), p. 486.

190 *"I'm sorry . . over the side with me"*: White, *The Making of the President 1964*, p. 279.

190 *"damn albatross . . . masterstroke"*: Shesol, *Mutual Contempt*, p. 209.

190 *"like a hawk watching chickens"*: Schlesinger, *Robert Kennedy and His Times*, p. 662.

190 *"face changed . . . like a yo-yo"*: Shesol, *Mutual Contempt*, p. 210.

190 *"a fat fish pulling in a mouthful of air"*: Schlesinger, *Robert Kennedy and His Times*, p. 662.

190 *Lincoln had taken umbrage . . . "skinning of Thomas"*: LTT, pp. 16–17.

191 *"unite . . . Eastern seaboard"*: LBJ, *VP*, p. 95.

192 *"Valley of the Black Pig"*: Sweig, *Lady Bird Johnson*, p. 94.

192 *riots had burst out in Harlem*: *The Recorder* (Greenfield, Massachusetts), July 20, 1964; *Daily Press* (Newport News, Virginia), July 22, 1964.

192 *In the final stretch of his first congressional race*: LJAD, pp. 88, 101.

193 *"To step out now . . . for your future"*: LBJ, *VP*, p. 98.

193 *"I had never seen him in a better mood"*: RNG, *RA*, p. 301.

193 *"This was his moment . . . personal will"*: Ibid.

194 *the party began*: *Buffalo Evening News*, August 28, 1964; White, *The Making of the President 1964*, pp. 307–8.

194 *"loudest birthday bang in the world"*: Ibid., p. 307.

195 *And that September 7 morning*: PDD, September 7, 1964.

195 *"slowed down . . . live in fear"*: September 7, 1964, Lyndon B. Johnson, Remarks in Cadillac Square, Detroit. Online by Peters and Woolley, The American Presidency Project.

195 *"under the greatest . . . outstretched hands"*: *Detroit Free Press*, September 8, 1964.

195 *"everyone was most enthusiastic about the trip"*: PDD, September 7, 1964.

195 *"Daisy Girl" ad*: https://www.youtube.com/watch?v=U4QVXcPDgjI.

196 *The ad had done its work*: Robert Mann, "How the Daisy Ad Changed Everything About Political Advertising," *Smithsonian Magazine*, April 13, 2016.

196 *"This spot ... in every western bar"*: RNG, *RA*, p. 307.

197 *"It would not ... appearing with you"*: RNG memo to LBJ, April 2, 1964, RNG Papers, DBC, UT.

197 *"Dear Bob ... judgement and counsel"*: Draft, RNG Papers, DBC, UT. For actual letter sent, which is less effusive, see Shesol, *Mutual Contempt*, p. 222.

198 *"Dick Goodwin and Mike Feldman ... stymied by LBJ"*: Shesol, *Mutual Contempt*, p. 224.

198 *"You are not trying ... giving your position"*: Memo, "Preparation for a Debate," October 13, 1964, RNG Papers, DBC, UT.

200 *"Dickie Baby ... to see the above in Evans & Novak"*: RNG Papers, no date, DBC, UT.

201 *"Valenti said ... than to Kennedy"*: RNG Diary, March 4, 1964, RNG Papers, DBC, UT.

201 *"doesn't ask much ... music in the house"*: White, *The Making of the President 1964*, p. 378.

201 says *"no"* ... *"says yes"* ... *equal rights for all*: September 10, 1964, Lyndon B. Johnson, Remarks in Harrisburg at a Dinner Sponsored by the Pennsylvania State Democratic Committee. Online by Peters and Woolley, The American Presidency Project.

202 *"If I need Robert Kennedy ... pragmatic fellow"*: Shesol, *Mutual Contempt*, pp. 182–83.

202 *"threw his arm"* ... *"warm, very close"*: New York Times, October 15, 1964.

202 *"already one ... United States"*: New York Times, October 16, 1964.

202 *"We want Lyndon"*: New York Times, November 1, 1964.

202 *"I don't have to tell you ... inadequate description"*: October 31, 1964, Lyndon B. Johnson, Remarks in Madison Square Garden. Online by Peters and Woolley, The American Presidency Project.

203 *Johnson returned to Texas*: PDD, November 3, 1964.

203 *Dick gathered in the White House Mess*: RNG, *RA*, p. 309.

203 *"If my brother ... rather have it that way"*: Schlesinger, *Robert Kennedy and His Times*, pp. 675–76.

203 *"You have to realize ... get to get well"*: Quoted in *LTT*, pp. 191–92.

204 *"It was a night ... loved by the American people"*: LJAD, p. 209.

CHAPTER EIGHT: "AND WE SHALL OVERCOME"

206 *"MOYERS: He is a"* ... *"straightened out"*: Draft transcript of taped conversation between LBJ and Bill Moyers, November 4, 1964, Presidential Recordings Program, Miller Center, University of Virginia.

207 *"loveable as a sullen porcupine ... the political speech"*: Valenti, *A Very Human President*, pp. 84–85.

208 *"set our course ... the broadest knowledge"*: May 22, 1964, Lyndon B. Johnson, Remarks at the University of Michigan. Online by Peters and Woolley, The American Presidency Project.

208 *"the standard method ... the status quo"*: LBJ, *VP*, p. 326.

208 *"overweighted with scholars ... thinkers"*: Ibid., p. 327.

209 *"the most important ... exhilarating"*: Author interview with Bill Moyers.

209 *"too high rather than too low"*: LBJ, *VP*, p. 327.

209 *"It has new ideas ... American people"*: RNG memo to LBJ, November 17, 1964, RNG Papers, DBC, UT.

210 *"an iron ring ... corrupting despair"*: Ibid.

210 *"On this Hill . . . the history of any nation"*: January 4, 1965, Lyndon B. Johnson, Annual Message to the Congress on the State of the Union. Online by Peters and Woolley, The American Presidency Project.

212 *"There is . . . the law of the land"*: DKG/LBJ, *LJAD*, p. 226.

212 *"A measure must . . . more exotic than preparation"*: DKG/LBJ, *LJAD*, p. 226.

212 *"It's like a bottle . . . enjoy myself"*: Eric F. Goldman, *The Tragedy of Lyndon Johnson* (New York: Knopf, 1969), p. 259.

213 *"sensitive animal"*: LBJ, *VP*, p. 451.

213 *"It may seem like nothing . . . toward the bill"*: *LJAD*, p. 224.

213 *"two monumental . . . serious trouble"*: Goldman, *The Tragedy of Lyndon Johnson*, p. 284.

213 *"the biggest popular . . . surround me disappear"*: Rowland Evans and Robert Novak, *Lyndon B. Johnson: The Exercise of Power* (New York: Signet, 1968), pp. 514–15; *LTT*, pp. 328–29.

214 *"LBJ: We've got to try . . . will get"*: Beschloss, *Reaching for Glory*, pp. 159–60.

215 *"some breathing space"*: LBJ, *VP*, p. 160.

215 *"give a new sense of dignity . . . absolute support"*: Beschloss, *Reaching for Glory*, pp. 160–66.

217 *"a symbol of bitter-end . . . Deep South"*: Kotz, *Judgment Days*, p. 254.

217 *"How many bubbles" . . . "in a watermelon"*: Legacy Museum, Montgomery, Alabama.

217 *"to turn . . . make it right-side up"*: Kotz, *Judgment Days*, p. 264.

217 *Eight American soldiers*: Ibid., p. 279.

217 *Jimmie Lee Jackson*: Ibid., pp. 275–76.

218 *"You are ordered . . . no word to be had . . . Troopers Advance"*: Ibid., p. 283.

219 *James Reeb*: *Boston Globe*, March 10, 1965.

220 *marched to the Boston Common*: *Boston Globe*, March 15, 1965.

220 *protesters began to picket*: RNG, *RA*, p. 319.

220 *"LBJ just you wait . . . in '68"*: LBJ, *VP*, p. 162.

220 *Inside the White House . . . federal action in Selma*: *Alabama Journal*, March 10, 1965.

220 *"If I just send . . . martyr out of Wallace"*: RNG, *RA*, pp. 319–20.

221 *"a real victory . . . for the North"*: LBJ, *VP*, p. 162.

221 *sending federal troops to Selma . . . Voting Rights Bill*: Ibid.

221 *"fog of depression . . . cut by a knife"*: Sweig, *Lady Bird Johnson*, p. 150.

221 *Dick had a peculiar vantage . . . three-hour meeting*: RNG extended description of the meeting in RNG, *RA*, pp. 320–24.

223 *"You and me . . . 'He Hated'?"*: RNG, *RA*, p. 327.

223 *"the Governor told me . . . meet its responsibilities"*: Lyndon B. Johnson, March 13, 1965, Press Conference at the White House, University of Virginia, Miller Center, https://millercenter.org/the-presidency/presidential-speeches/march-13-1965-press-conference-white-house.

223 *"That . . . in the world"*: LBJ, *VP*, p. 163.

223 *"Hell, if I'd stayed . . . for civil rights"*: RNG, *RA*, p. 323.

224 *"composed, in charge, in command of the situation"*: Lady Bird Johnson, *A White House Diary*, p. 150.

224 *a bipartisan meeting*: Mr. Valenti's notes, March 14, 1965, LBJL.

224 *"Don't panic now . . . 'scared him into it'"*: Robert Mann, *The Walls of Jericho: Lyndon Johnson, Hubert Humphrey, Richard Russell, and the Struggle for Civil Rights* (New York: Harcourt Brace, 1996), p. 460.

224 *"Logic is what you are saying ... what is needed"*: Ibid.

225 *"The Leadership of Congress ... House of Representatives"*: Rutland Daily Hearld (Vermont), March 15, 1965.

225 *"Please know ... appreciation"*: MLK telegram to LBJ, March 15, 1965, LBJL.

225 *"deciding to climb ... family picnic"*: Sweig, *Lady Bird Johnson*, p. 151.

226 *"He needs the speech" ... "and now!"*: RNG, *RA*, pp. 326–27.

227 *"I speak tonight . . . American democracy"*: RNG Draft, March 15, 1965, RNG Papers, DBC, UT.

228 *"Who killed . . . manhood at its best"*: Martin Luther King, Jr., *Witnessing for the Truth* (Boston: Beacon Press, 2014), pp. 12, 15.

229 *"You remember, Dick"*: RNG, *RA*, p. 329.

231 *"Rarely in any ... OVERCOME"*: March 15, 1965, Lyndon B. Johnson, Special Message to the Congress: The American Promise. Online by Peters and Woolley, The American Presidency Project.

232 *"There was an instant of silence ... black marches"*: RNG, *RA*, p. 334.

232 *"never forget ... as I live"*: LBJ, *VP*, p. 166.

232 *"a man who ... a poet"*: John Lewis on MLK: Kotz, *Judgment Days*, p. 312.

232 *"The Voting Rights ... be passed!"*: MLK, *Time*, December 25, 2014.

232 *"Now let none ... use it with me"*: March 15, 1965, Lyndon B. Johnson, Special Message to the Congress: The American Promise.

233 *"everyone in the room . . . black and white"*: Richard D. Leonard, *Call to Selma: Eighteen Days of Witness* (Boston: Skinner House Books, 2002), Kindle edition.

233 *"Manny, I want you ... tonight"*: Taylor Branch, *At Canaan's Edge: America in the King Years, 1965–68* (New York: Simon & Schuster, 2006), p. 115.

234 *"Your speech ... any president of this nation"*: Kotz, *Judgment Days*, p. 323.

234 *"They did"*: Evans and Novak, *Lyndon B. Johnson*, p. 522.

234 *"God, how I loved ... streets against him"*: RNG, *RA*, p. 334.

CHAPTER NINE: THE NEVER-ENDING RESIGNATION

236 *"Now voting rights ... you can do?"*: RNG, *RA*, p. 343.

236 *"Hell, what good ... the chance to get it"*: Ibid., p. 344.

237 *"Do you want to go ahead ... forward immediately"*: Memo, Valenti to LBJ, May 25, 1965, RNG Papers, DBC, UT.

238 *"This is a pathbreaking . . . responding to developments"*: Memo, RNG to LBJ, June 4, 1965, RNG Papers, DBC, UT.

238 *"If you'd like to"*: RNG Diary, June 22, 1965, RNG Papers, DBC, UT.

238 *the intellectual framework . . . of affirmative action*: Dallek, *Flawed Giant*, p. 222; Kotz, *Judgment Days*, p. 335.

239 *"But Freedom is . . . the man"*: June 4, 1965, Lyndon B. Johnson, Commencement Address at Howard University: "To Fulfill These Rights." Online by Peters and Woolley, The American Presidency Project.

239 *"Never before ... more profoundly"*: King to LBJ, RNG Papers, DBC, UT.

239 *"remarkable in the history ... Civil Rights Movement"*: Tom Wicker, "Johnson Pledges to Help Negroes," *New York Times*, June 5, 1965.

240 *"for just about . . . two hundred years"*: Charlotte Webb to LBJ, June 24, 1965, LBJL.

240 *"preaching of hatred and racism . . . on every matter"*: C. Harrison Mann to LBJ, June 8, 1965, LBJL.

240 *"I plucked both of you . . . book about me"*: RNG Diary, June 14, 1965, RNG Papers, DBC, UT.

241 *"Walking over . . . he said"*: RNG Diary, June 15, 1965, RNG Papers, DBC, UT.

241 *"The only way to relax . . . for the evening"*: Joseph Califano, *The Triumph and Tragedy of Lyndon Johnson* (New York: Simon & Schuster, 1991), p. 28.

241 *"serious business"*: RNG Diary, June 15, 1965, RNG Papers, DBC, UT.

242 *"You can't go . . . was no problem"*: RNG Diary, ibid.

242 *As a White House special assistant*: John Pomfret, "Two Key Aides Quit Johnson's Staff," *New York Times*, September 16, 1965.

242 *"Well, he said . . . count on"*: RNG Diary, June 15, 1965, RNG Papers, DBC, UT.

242 *"some reason not to . . . to move away"*: Beschloss, *Reaching for Glory*, p. 359.

243 *"It's just as well . . . that other crowd"*: RNG Diary, June 22, 1965, RNG Papers, DBC, UT.

243 *"I just won't give . . . national speeches"*: RNG, *RA*, p. 422.

243 *"an act of disloyalty . . . with those Kennedys"*: Ibid., p. 421.

244 *"Harriman asked . . . strong as I feel"*: RNG to LBJ, June 23, 1965, RNG Papers, DBC, UT.

245 *"a great chance . . . ducked this"*: Harriman to LBJ, June 20, 1965, RNG Papers, DBC, UT.

245 *"delighted . . . for delivery"*: RNG, *RA*, p. 397.

245 *"I want you to take out . . . copying Bobby Kennedy"*: Ibid.

246 *"Maybe by the time . . . call me on the plane"*: July 9, 1965, Draft Transcript, Presidential Recordings Program, Miller Center, UVA.

246 *They arrived in time for a breakfast*: Califano, *The Triumph and Tragedy*, p. 15; PPD, July 9–11, 1965.

247 *"a hell of a job"*: RNG Diary, July 14, 1965, DNG Papers, DBC, UT.

247 *"Vietnam's like being . . . what it is"*: Ibid.

247 *"Vietnam is getting . . . with great disgrace"*: Sweig, *Lady Bird Johnson*, p. 172.

247 *"I knew from the start . . . seen as an appeaser"*: LJAD, p. 251.

248 *"He would just go . . . tormented man"*: Dallek, *Flawed Giant*, p. 282.

248 *"trying to get me . . . irrational moments"*: RNG Diary, June 14, 1965, RNG Papers, DBC, UT.

248 *"to stave off defeat"*: LBJ, *VP*, pp. 145–46.

248 *"to move from . . . conference table"*: July 28, 1965, Lyndon B. Johnson, The President's News Conference. Online by Peters and Woolley, The American Presidency Project.

249 *"I could see . . . end of the Great Society"*: LJAD, pp. 282–83.

249 *"would meet . . . provocative way possible"*: *New York Times*, July 29, 1965.

249 *"an indication . . . for peace"*: RNG, *RA*, p. 383.

250 *"Why, Wilbur . . . do the same for me"*: Quoted in *LJAD*, p. 383.

250 *first call*: White House Diary, July 30, 1965, LBJL.

250 *"As the President . . . in a good mood"*: Ibid.

250 *"I am so proud . . . to complete what he began"*: July 30, 1965, Lyndon B. Johnson, Remarks with President Truman at the Signing in Independence of the Medicare Bill. Online by Peters and Woolley, The American Presidency Project.

251 *"You have done me . . . quite awhile"*: Ibid.

251 *"They sent up … a half-hour before"*: Letter to James and Gloria Jones, August 12, 1965, Rose Styron, ed., *Selected Letters of William Styron* (New York: Random House, 2010), p. 375.

252 *"rarely seen … new day"*: Califano, *The Triumph and Tragedy*, p. 57.

252 *"Today is a triumph … yet to come"*: August 6, 1965, Lyndon B. Johnson, Remarks in the Capitol Rotunda at the Signing of the Voting Rights Act. Online by Peters and Woolley, The American Presidency Project.

253 *"almost carried … to the President's Room"*: Califano, *The Triumph and Tragedy*, p. 57.

253 *"so people can say … 'Voting Rights Bill'"*: Ibid., pp. 56–57.

253 *"There was such jostling … even for parts of letters"*: Ibid., p. 57.

253 *"Several times … for signing pens"*: PPD, August 6, 1965.

255 *"How is it possible … how could it be?"*: Kotz, *Judgment Days*, p. 340.

255 *Califano was hardly able*: Califano, *The Triumph and Tragedy*, p. 59.

255 *"We are on a powder keg … put them to work"*: Kotz, *Judgment Days*, p. 341.

256 *"you telling people … disrespect for the law"*: David C. Carter, *The Music Has Gone Out of the Movement: Civil Rights and the Johnson Administration, 1965–1968* (Chapel Hill: University of North Carolina Press, 2009), p. 62.

256 *"the dangers of his demagogic address … home to roost"*: C. Harrison Mann Jr. to Bill Moyers, August 17, 1965, LBJL.

256 *"We ought … Goddamned island"*: Califano, *The Triumph and Tragedy*, p. 62.

256 *"resort to terror … of the slums"*: August 15, 1965, Lyndon B. Johnson, Statement by the President Following the Restoration of Order in Los Angeles. Online by Peters and Woolley, The American Presidency Project.

256 *"I hope a lot of people … in the middle"*: Beschloss, *Reaching for Glory*, p. 421.

257 *"All the personal reasons" … "I agree with you!!"*: "WHY DICK GOODWIN PERSE-VERES IN HIS PLAN TO LEAVE," DNG memo to Moyers, copy in RNG diary, RNG Papers, DBC, UT.

258 *"No man … I admire so greatly"*: RNG to LBJ, September 15, 1965, RNG Papers, DBC, UT.

258 *"Dear Dick . . . for a better life"*: JBK to RNG, September 15, 1965, RNG Papers, DBC, UT.

259 *"I've learned my lesson … anyone again"*: RNG, *RA*, p. 423.

259 *"Goodwin more than almost anyone else"*: Hugh Sidey, *Time*, copy in RNG Papers, DBC, UT.

259 *"There's one boy that . . . this boy, Goodwin"*: Draft Transcript, LBJ to Roy Wilkins, November 1, 1965, Presidential Recordings Program, Miller Center, UVA.

CHAPTER TEN: FRIENDSHIP, LOYALTY, AND DUTY

262 *"The doorman . . . wine chilled"*: The skating story is from a series of personal recollections about RFK in author's possession.

262 *"An intermittent ritual . . . must have been illegally obtained"*: *Cigar Aficionado*, August 1996.

263 *"ice capade fiasco … accuracy of my position"*: Skating story in possession of author.

264 *"Would I like … come along?"*: RNG, *RA*, p. 433.

265 *"I am not thinking … to campaign for him"*: Sheshol, *Mutual Contempt*, p. 279.

265 *"brought to a halt ... same rising shout?"*: RNG, *RA*, p. 435.

265 *a mysterious source ... "so did Bobby"*: "Impressions of RFK on South American Trip," WHFN-RFK, Box 6, LBJL.

265 *"apprehensive ... anathema"*: Evans and Novak, "Commentary: Bob Kennedy's Career Forces Tested on Junket," *Indianapolis Star*, November 11, 1965.

266 *"could only have been written by Goodwin"*: RNG, *RA*, p. 434.

266 *"the responsibility ... will it or not"*: "Robert Kennedy Ends Peru Trip," *New York Times*, November 14, 1965.

266 *"What happened ... I think I would"*: RNG, *RA*, p. 438.

267 *"We do not condemn you ... stained with blood"*: William vanden Heuvel and Milton Gwirtzman, *On His Own: RFK 1964–68* (New York: Doubleday, 1970), p. 167.

267 *"If these kids ... improve their aim"*: Schlesinger, *Robert Kennedy and His Times*, p. 696.

267 *Bobby's speech*: RNG Notes, South America trip, RNG Papers, DBC, UT.

267 *"Every child ... Every man a job!"*: Schlesinger, *Robert Kennedy and His Times*, p. 697.

268 *Kennedy's defensive reaction ... "Sooner or later"*: Ibid., p. 698.

268 *Through a Brazilian friend*: RNG Notes, South America trip, RNG Papers, DBC, UT.

268 *"I must be crazy ... this thing"*: Schlesinger, *Robert Kennedy and His Times*, p. 698.

268 *"there are piranha in there ... afterwards"*: RNG, *RA*, p. 442.

269 *homemade scrapbook*: RNG Papers, DBC, UT.

269 *"He's a remarkable ... an outstanding president"*: Letter to George Cuomo, n.d., RNG Papers, DBC, UT.

270 *"[The president] specifically ... work on the draft now"*: Califano, *The Triumph and Tragedy*, p. 117.

271 *"always as full of tension ... have set in"*: Lady Bird Johnson, *A White House Diary*, pp. 350–51.

271 *"This Nation is mighty ... who dwell in squalor"*: January 12, 1966, Lyndon B. Johnson, Annual Message to the Congress on the State of the Union. Online by Peters and Woolley, The American Presidency Project.

271 *"I only need a few more hours"*: RNG, *RA*, p. 423.

271 *"the troubling awareness ... world to be helped"*: January 12, 1966, Lyndon B. Johnson, Annual Message to the Congress on the State of the Union.

272 *"At about 4 a.m. ... cut by a third"*: Califano, *The Triumph and Tragedy*, p. 117.

273 *informed him that the president*: RNG, *RA*, p. 423.

273 *"It was just too much ... I was treated"*: Califano, *The Triumph and Tragedy*, p. 118.

273 *"The audience ... social interchange"*: Lady Bird Johnson, *A White House Diary*, p. 352.

273 *"to give our fighting men ... whatever the challenge"*: January 12, 1966, Lyndon B. Johnson, Annual Message to the Congress on the State of the Union.

273 *"dull message ... with foreign policy"*: Dallek, *Flawed Giant*, p. 302.

274 *"Dear Dick ... Lyndon"*: LBJ to RNG, January 13, 1966, RNG Papers, DBC, UT.

274 *"I'm afraid ... playing around with ideas"*: Letter to George Cuomo, February 1966, RNG Papers, DBC, UT.

275 *"Have you been" ... "would be acceptable"*: RNG, *RA*, p. 454.

276 *"Ho Chi Kennedy ... to the United States"*: *Pittsburgh Press*, quoting *Chicago Tribune*, February 21, 1966.

276 *"Of all the gratuitous ... ill-conceived counsel"*: *Buffalo Evening News*, February 23, 1966.

276 *"trappings of a presidential . . . a dozen microphones"*: "Kennedy Urges Share for Reds in Saigon Regime," *Los Angeles Times*, February 20, 1966.

276 *"the edge of political danger"*: RNG, *RA*, p. 455.

276 *"We are all Americans . . . conflict and devastation"*: Press Release from RFK, Statement by Senator RFK, February 19, 1966, RNG Papers, DBC, UT.

277 *"the roof fell in"*: RNG, *RA*, p. 455.

277 *"would be like putting a fox . . . in the fire department"*: *Dayton Daily News*, February 21, 1966.

277 *"forming a coalition . . . to ride a tiger"*: *Philadelphia Inquirer*, February 21, 1966.

277 *"It's hard for me . . . This is the second"*: RNG to RFK, no date, RNG Papers, DBC, UT.

279 *"very, very tough . . . came from Dick"*: Adam Walinsky, Oral History Project, JFKL, March 22, 1992, pp. 185–215.

280 *"Robertson's banning terrified . . . 'the price for me?'"*: Evan Thomas, *Robert Kennedy: His Life* (New York: Simon & Schuster, 2000), p. 321.

280 *"Yankee go home" and "Chuck him out"*: Schlesinger, *Robert Kennedy and His Times*, p. 744.

280 *Over a thousand*: *New York Times*, June 7, 1966.

281 *"I come here . . . former bondage"*: Edwin Guthman and C. Richard Allen, eds., *RFK: His Words for Our Time* (New York: William Morrow, 2018), p. 262.

281 *"There was great tension . . . People were on edge"*: Author interview with Margaret Marshall.

281 *"I refer, of course . . . United States of America"*: Guthman & Allen eds., *RFK*, p. 262.

281 *"As soon as . . . simply fabulous"*: Author interview with Margaret Marshall.

281 *"Few will have . . . over the world"*: "Cape Town, Cape Town, South Africa," Papers of Robert F. Kennedy, Senate Papers, Speeches and Press Releases, Box 2, "Freedom & Democracy," JFKL.

282 *"as if to say . . . the speech okay"*: Thomas, *Robert Kennedy*, p. 322.

282 *"It was as if a heavy . . . smashed everything"*: Author interview with Margaret Marshall.

282 *"reminded us . . . in an eternity"*: Quoted in Thomas, *Robert Kennedy*, p. 323–24.

282 *"Kennedy was like . . . the world again"*: vanden Heuvel and Gwirtzman, *On His Own*, p. 161.

283 *"I did not even know . . . down my face"*: Author interview with Margaret Marshall.

283 *"At the time . . . to adopt children"*: Ibid.

284 *"Lyndon Johnson's desire . . . end the war"*: RNG, "Triumph or Tragedy, Reflections on Vietnam," *The New Yorker*, April 1966, pp. 36, 64.

284 *"turned a corner . . . underdeveloped world"*: Schlesinger, *Journals*, July 28, 1966, p. 247.

285 *"It would be terrible . . . another beach"*: Schlesinger, *Robert Kennedy and His Times*, p. 739.

285 *"What's your plan of action?"*: RNG Diary, July 25, 1966, RNG Papers, DBC, UT.

285 *"The only thing likely . . . political opposition"*: Schlesinger, *Journals*, July 28, 1966, p. 244.

285 *"That's wrong . . . That'll show them"*: RNG, *RA*, pp. 462, 464.

285 *"running well ahead of LBJ . . . Republican possibilities"*: Schlesinger, *Journals*, August 1, 1966, p. 252.

285 *"We discussed . . . life of the country"*: RNG Diary, July 25, 1966, RNG Papers, DBC, UT.

286 *"Ex-Johnson Aide . . . War Policies"*: Max Frankel, *New York Times*, September 18, 1966.

286 *"the most sweeping... White House teams"*: Lawrence Stern, *Courier Journal* (Louisville, Kentucky), September 18, 1966.

286 *"A former ghostwriter... bombing the North"*: Mary McGrory, *Star-Tribune* (Minneapolis), September 26, 1966.

286 *"deliberate lies... This is such a time"*: Speech by RNG at the National Board meeting of Americans for Democratic Action, September 17–18, 1966, Washington, D.C., RNG Papers, DBC, UT.

287 *"I did not feel... rightly done"*: RNG, *RA*, p. 467.

287 *"It's like being bitten by your own dog"*: Charles Bartlett, *Express and News* (San Antonio, Texas), September 24, 1966.

287 *"Mr. President... I go ahead?"*: RNG to LBJ, June 2, 1965, RNG Papers, DBC, UT.

288 *"the assumption that a man... with the administration"*: RNG, "The Duty of Loyalty," RNG Papers, DBC, UT.

289 *"Dear Dick... there is Bobby"*: JBK to RNG, July 13, 1966, RNG Papers DBC, UT.

290 *"I am in the middle ... done at all"*: RNG to Cuomo, Summer 1966, RNG Papers, DBC, UT.

291 *"It is funny... with morbid thoughts"*: RNG Diary, May 25, 1967, RNG Papers, DBC, UT.

291 *"the final text... until approved"*: Sam Kashner, "A Clash of Camelots," *Vanity Fair*, October 2009, p. 10.

291 *"masterful achievement"*: William Manchester, *Controversy: And Other Essays in Journalism, 1950–1975* (Boston: Little, Brown, 1976), p. 17.

291 *Guthman and Seigenthaler recommended:* Ibid., p. 19.

291 *"the members of... or the events"*: Manchester, *Controversy*, p. 25.

292 *"I thought that... dark library shelves"*: Kashner, "A Clash of Camelots," p. 1.

292 *She wanted it all to vanish:* Barbara Leaming, *Jacqueline Bouvier Kennedy Onassis* (New York: St. Martin's, 2014), pp. 204–5.

292 *"issue a statement... disclaiming the book"*: RNG Diary, October 16, 1966, RNG Papers, DBC, UT.

292 *"literary broker... was absolute"*: Manchester, *Controversy*, p. 35.

292 *"At the outset ... on his side or hers"*: Garry Wills, *Nixon Agonistes* (New York: New American Library, 1969), p. 457.

293 *"However... refusing to budge"*: RNG Diary, October 16, 1966, RNG Papers, DBC, UT.

293 *"We would like to remove... out of the manuscript"*: Ibid.

293 *"entirely happy with all... with accuracy"*: Manchester, *Controversy*, p. 59.

293 *"a terrible mistake"*: Schlesinger, *Robert Kennedy in His Times*, p. 762.

294 *"History belongs to everyone... escape its consequences"*: *New York Times*, December 16, 1966.

294 *Harris poll:* Kashner, "A Clash of Camelots," p. 34.

294 *"Lady Bird and I... unpleasantness on our account"*: LBJ to JBK, December 16, 1966, quoted in Leaming, *Jacqueline Bouvier Kennedy Onassis*, pp. 214–15.

294 *"JACKIE WINNER IN BOOK BATTLE"*: Kashner, "A Clash of Camelots," p. 27.

294 *"We are not... domestic secrets"*: *Baltimore Evening Sun*, December 21, 1966.

295 *"I am sick... feel anything again"*: Leaming, *Jacqueline Bouvier Kennedy Onassis*, p. 215.

295 *"All the rage... make me change"*: Ibid., p. 220.

295 *royalties:* Manchester, *Controversy*, pp. 75–76.

296 *dropped more bombs:* www.global security.org/military/ops/VNZ/escalation.htm.

296 *Democrats had lost forty-seven seats:* CQ Almanac, 1966, https://library.cqpress.com /cqalmanac/document.php?id=cqal66-1299950.

296 *"the single most ... reality from wishful thinking":* Remarks, RNG, Boston, November 9, 1967, RNG Papers, DBC, UT.

296 *"The Duty of Loyalty":* RNG, RNG Papers, DBC, UT.

297 *"the country is now ... hands of its history":* RNG Diary, October 16, 1966, RNG Papers, DBC, UT.

297 *"The greatest issue ... seeds are there":* Ibid.

297 *"full-fledged members" ... "always been true":* Richard Neuweiler, "President's Advisor: An Interview with RNG," *Status,* February 1967.

298 *"'You and Schlesinger are ... we're going to give up'":* RNG, *RA,* p. 458.

298 *"pseudo-intellectuals" ... "obligation to speak":* RNG, "The Duty of Loyalty," RNG Papers, DBC, UT.

298 *"If another speech ... do the opposite":* Newfield quoting RFK, in Schlesinger, *Robert Kennedy in His Times,* p. 764.

299 *"a critical turning point":* Excerpts from RFK speech, *New York Times,* March 3, 1967.

299 *Several of his closest ... stand against the war:* Jack Newfield, *Robert Kennedy: A Memoir* (New York: E. P. Dutton, 1969), p. 213.

299 *"make sure ... Kennedy from New York":* Schlesinger, *Robert Kennedy in His Times,* p. 771.

299 *"in a quiet, tense voice":* Newfield, *Robert Kennedy,* p. 150.

299 *"If fault is to be found ... including myself":* Excerpts from RFK speech, *New York Times,* March 3, 1967.

300 *"the only major ... wrong about Vietnam":* Schlesinger, *Robert Kennedy in His Times,* p. 773.

300 *"horror ... We are all participants":* Ibid., p. 773.

300 *"the bombing ... and would continue":* The News Manager, March 4, 1967.

300 *"vital to the U.S. war ... drop of blood":* Miami Herald, March 4, 1967.

300 *"Johnson is right ... the enemy":* Schlesinger, *Robert Kennedy in his Times,* p. 774.

300 *"watershed ... about Vietnam":* Newfield, *Robert Kennedy,* p. 152.

301 *I talked long into the night:* Author interview with Sanford "Sandy" Levinson.

302 *advisers had counseled against it:* Branch, *At Canaan's Edge,* p. 584.

302 *"My conscience leaves me ... soul of America":* Martin Luther King, Jr., "Beyond Vietnam, Time to Break Silence," American Rhetoric, https://www.americanrhetoric.com /speeches/mlkatimetobreaksilence.htm.

302 *"firestorm of criticism":* Kotz, *Judgment Days,* pp. 375–76.

302 *"serious tactical mistake":* Darius S. Jhabvala, "Bunche, King Resolve Spat," *Boston Globe,* April 14, 1967.

302 *"the irony that ... savage denunciation":* Kotz, *Judgment Days,* p. 383.

302 *"crushed":* Ibid.

302 *Banners implored us ... spilled from windows:* The Times (Shreveport, Louisiana), April 16, 1967; *Time,* April 21, 1967; *Star-Tribune* (Minneapolis), April 16, 1967; Branch, *At Canaan's Edge,* pp. 599–60.

303 *He had come:* Address by Martin Luther King, Jr., "Mobilization Against the War in Vietnam," April 15, 1967. *Philadelphia Inquirer,* April 16, 1967.

303 *"A few minutes ... to win with LBJ":* Anderson Sunday Herald (Indiana), March 27, 1966.

303 *"to convert into a meaningful ... party must bid"*: Doris Kearns and Sanford Levinson, "How to Remove LBJ in 1968," *The New Republic*, May 13, 1968.

304 *selected as a finalist*: Selection process author interview with White House Fellows colleague Tim Wirth, former senator from Colorado.

304 *"Do your men ever dance ... what goes on up there"*: LJAD, p. 2.

305 *"You better be the one ... and said nothing"*: Author interview with Tom Johnson.

305 *"White House Fellow ... The New Republic"*: PDD, May 8, 1967.

306 *"I am not authorized ... I would do so"*: Author interview with Sandy Levinson.

306 *"He [LBJ] and Sen Russell ... President of the United States"*: PDD, May 12, 1967.

307 *"Miss Kearns ... political views"*: *Boston Globe*, May 12, 1967.

307 *"I certainly don't see ... the White House"*: Ibid.

307 *"She Panned LBJ ... Has a Job"*: *Miami Herald*, May 13, 1967.

307 *"LBJ Chooses Aide ... Maps His Defeat"*: *Boston Globe*, May 12, 1967.

307 *"Swinging Blonde ... Wins Post"*: *Philadelphia Inquirer*, September 14, 1968.

307 *"Bring her down ... no one can"*: This was the word I received from members of the White House staff.

309 *"For two or three ... close relationship"*: Transcript, Scott Simon, *Weekend Edition*, NPR, December 20, 2008.

309 *"You gave ... 'AND THEREFORE?'"*: Author interview with Tim Wirth.

CHAPTER ELEVEN: CROSSWINDS OF FATE

311 *Reporters and students repeatedly asked*: vanden Heuvel and Gwirtzman, *On His Own*, p. 282.

311 *"Richard Goodwin had been telling ... Herbert Hoover"*: Lewis Chester, Godfrey Hodgson, and Bruce Page, *An American Melodrama: The Presidential Campaign of 1968* (New York: Viking, 1969), p. 78.

311 *"political suicide"*: Thomas, *Robert Kennedy*, p. 354.

312 *A private poll*: Jules Witcover, *85 Days: The Last Campaign of Robert Kennedy* (New York: Putnam, 1969), p. 18.

312 *"Dump Johnson"*: Lawrence O'Donnell, *Playing with Fire: The 1968 Election and the Transformation of American Politics* (New York: Penguin, 2018), pp. 53, 87, 88.

312 *McGovern, facing reelection*: vanden Heuvel and Gwirtzman, *On His Own*, p. 276.

312 *"I think Bobby should do it"*: Witcover, *85 Days*, p. 13.

312 *"there would have ... to do anything"*: Ibid., p. 19.

312 *"nothing illegal ... government"*: O'Donnell, *Playing with Fire*, p. 101.

312 *"walking on the wide ... interrupt them"*: RNG, RA, p. 433.

313 *The December "debate"*: Theodore H. White, *The Making of the President 1968* (New York: HarperCollins e-book, 2010), p. 184; *Boston Globe*, April 5, 1968.

313 *"if McCarthy did moderately well ... war in Vietnam"*: Schlesinger, *Journals*, December 10, 1967, p. 268.

314 *"If Gene had any success ... at this point"*: Ibid., p. 269.

314 *"If you were ... very well make the move"*: RNG to RFK, December 10, 1967, RNG Papers, DBC, UT.

314 *"it would be futile ... in 1972?"*: Sorensen, *Counselor*, pp. 453–54.

314 *"LBJ is sure of reelection" . . . "destroy Bobby's future"*: Schlesinger, *Journals*, December 10, 1967, p. 267.

314 *"the talk up to this point . . . trying in 1968?"*: Ibid., p. 268.

315 *survey of political leaders*: Witcover, *85 Days*, p. 53.

315 *"to clear the air"*: Ibid., p. 24.

315 *"I have told friends . . . circumstances"*: Newfield, *Robert Kennedy*, p. 223.

315 *"shattering expectation and belief . . . going well"*: RNG, *RA*, pp. 484–85.

316 *"If Bobby doesn't do this" . . . "with Lyndon B. Johnson as President"*: Notes of conversation with Ted Kennedy on February 13, 1968, RNG Files, RFK Papers, JFKL.

316 *"The support just isn't there . . . not going to do it"*: RNG, OH, RFK Papers, JFKL; Witcover, *85 Days*, p. 34.

316 *"Well, if you're not going to run" . . . "I guess that'll be helpful"*: RNG, OH, RFK Papers, JFKL.

317 *"We were still floundering . . . 'overthrow a president'"*: Seymour Hersh, *Reporter: A Memoir* (New York: Vintage, 2018), pp. 80–81.

318 *"I remember walking . . . 'of success!'"*: RNG, OH, McCarthy, RNG Papers, DBC, UT.

318 *"You're Dick Goodwin! . . . teeny-boppers"*: RNG, *RA*, pp. 493–94.

318 *"It was extraordinary . . . a real shot"*: Author interview with Mary Lou Oates.

319 *"felt more closely bonded . . . in love"*: RNG, *RA*, p. 495.

319 *"Not a Kennedyesque band of brothers . . . full time service"*: Ibid.

319 *"the boy or girl . . . come to call"*: Ibid., p. 496.

319 *"could talk again . . . talking now"*: Jeremy Larner, *Nobody Knows: Reflections on the McCarthy Campaign of 1968* (New York: Macmillan, 1970), p. 38.

320 *"The McCarthy kids loved McCarthy . . . its own principles"*: Ibid.

320 *"grisly, paper-cluttered . . . 1960 and 1964"*: White, *The Making of the President 1968*, p. 95.

320 *"his ugly, compelling face . . . and help"*: Abigail McCarthy, *Private Places, Public Places* (New York: Doubleday, 1972), p. 38.

321 *"wasn't even saying . . . referendum on Vietnam"*: RNG, OH, McCarthy, RNG Papers, DBC, UT.

321 *"was always doing things . . . running for President"*: Larner, *Nobody Knows*, p. 39.

322 *"There is only one issue . . . danger and destruction"*: RNG Files, RFK Papers, JFKL.

323 *"I threw them out . . . and vote"*: RNG, OH, McCarthy, RNG Papers, DBC, UT.

323 *"He was the first and last . . . rounded paragraph"*: RNG, *RA*, p. 504.

323 *"when people saw . . . a conservative"*: RNG, OH, McCarthy, RNG Papers, DBC, UT.

323 *"men of means . . . the romantic rich"*: RNG, *RA*, p. 501.

324 *"Don't worry . . . take care of it"*: Ibid., p. 510.

324 *"Think how you would feel . . . politics"*: Newfield, *Robert Kennedy*, p. 236

324 *"This brilliant ad . . . act of change"*: Ibid.

324 *"In every vacant space . . . share in the moment"*: RNG, *RA*, p. 511.

325 *"He waved happily . . . beginning to speak"*: Ibid., p. 512.

325 *"People have remarked . . . into the system"*: Chester, Hodgson, and Page, *An American Melodrama*, p. 100.

325 *"I am reassessing" . . . nomination*: Witcover, *85 Days*, pp. 48–49.

325 *"We'll be able to pay our hotel bills"*: White, *The Making of the President 1968*, p. 102.

326 *"the happy man . . . very dominant"*: Ibid., p. 103.

326 *"Bobby didn't . . . of last night"*: *Boston Globe*, March 14, 1968.

326 *"We woke up . . . Christmas presents"*: White, *The Making of the President 1968*, p. 103.

326 *"If that ever comes to pass . . . defeat my good friend"*: RNG, OH, McCarthy, RNG Papers, DBC, UT.

326 *Bobby had asked his brother Ted*: Witcover, *85 Days*, p. 89.

326 *"quickly grew tired . . . calling me Sy"*: Hersh, *Reporter*, p. 81.

327 *"I don't want him to think" . . . "as your agent"*: RNG, OH, McCarthy, RNG Papers, DBC, UT.

327 *"Why don't you tell . . . he can have it"*: RNG, *RA*, p. 508.

327 *"I do not run . . . nation's future"*: White, *The Making of the President 1968*, p. 194.

327 *"His fear of being called . . . for not running"*: Newfield, *Robert Kennedy*, p. 231.

327 *"I'd like you to be with me"*: RNG, *RA*, p. 518.

328 *"Look . . . That's it"*: Ibid., p. 520.

328 *"frantic . . . none of my business"*: Hersh, *Reporter*, pp. 87–88.

328 *"Do you know . . . than hated Jack"*: Schlesinger, *Journals*, April 3, 1968, p. 286.

329 *"In California . . . Very strong"*: Jimmy Breslin, "The Inheritance," *Los Angeles Times*, April 14, 1968.

329 *"Our strategy . . . in the streets"*: Newfield, *Robert Kennedy*, p. 253.

329 *"he had seen . . . Roosevelt"*: DKG, *The Bully Pulpit: Theodore Roosevelt, William Howard Taft, and the Golden Age of Journalism* (New York: Simon & Schuster, 2013), p. 5.

329 *Roosevelt "is in . . . circus parade"*: Ibid., p. 204.

330 *"Of all those engaged . . . greater complications"*: White, *The Making of the President 1968*, p. 142.

330 *"Lyndon Johnson . . . rocking chair"*: Ibid.

331 *seven major newspapers*: LJAD, p. 336.

331 *"I felt that I was being chased . . . demonstrating students"*: DKG/LBJ, *LJAD*, p. 343.

331 *"he saw himself . . . round in circles"*: Ibid., p. 344.

331 *senior advisory group*: Ibid., p. 345.

331 *"The weariness of his mien . . . collected"*: White, *The Making of the President 1968*, pp. 142, 143.

332 *"a roll of the dice . . . stack on this one"*: Horace Busby, *The Thirty-first of March: An Intimate Portrait of Lyndon Johnson's Final Days in Office* (New York: Farrar, Straus & Giroux, 2005), p. 7.

332 *"I want out of this cage"*: Ibid., p. 194.

332 *"Tonight I want to speak . . . as your president"*: March 31, 1968, Lyndon B. Johnson, The President's Address to the Nation upon Announcing His Decision to Halt the Bombing of North Vietnam. Online by Peters and Woolley, The American Presidency Project.

332 *"With this, as though touched . . . 'earlier than I thought'"*: White, *The Making of the President 1968*, p. 143.

332 *"The war is over . . . we did it"*: *Green Bay Press Gazette* (Wisconsin), April 1, 1968.

334 *Harris poll*: *Pasadena Independent* (California), April 9, 1968.

335 *"a magnificent display of patriotism"*: *Columbia Record* (North Carolina), April 4, 1968.

335 *"putting principle above personal ambition"*: Ron Elvin, "Remembering 1968: LBJ Sur-

prises Nation with Announcement He Wouldn't Seek Re-Election," March 25, 2018, WBUR, https://www.wbur.org/npr/596805375/president-johnson-made-a-bomb shell-announcement-50-years-ago.

335 *"a stirring, galvanic . . . for your country"*: Tampa Tribune, April 2, 1968.

335 *"his most stunning move . . . in politics"*: Gazette Reader (Cedar Rapids, Iowa), April 1, 1968.

335 *"has made . . . annals of American history"*: Califano, The Triumph and Tragedy, p. 270.

335 *"terribly distressed . . . like this before"*: Jonathan Eig, *King: A Life* (New York: Farrar, Straus & Giroux, 2022), p. 538.

335 *"stay until America responded . . . new kind of Selma or Birmingham"*: Clayborne Carson, ed., *The Autobiography of Martin Luther King, Jr.* (New York: Hachette, 1998), p. 347.

335 *"first reaction . . . to its poor"*: Kotz, Judgment Days, p. 411.

336 *"three-cushioned billiards . . . hit me directly"*: Capital Times (Madison, Wisconsin), April 3, 1968.

336 *"You know the difference . . . holds on for six months"*: Ibid.

336 *Dick made good on his promise*: Boston Globe, March 28, 1968; RNG notes for talk with McCarthy, RNG Papers, DBC, UT.

336 *"had begun the . . . public career"*: Busby, The Thirty-first of March, p. 207.

336 *"Hanoi is ready to talk"*: PDD, April 3, 1968.

336 *"a real breakthrough . . . at last"*: LBJ, VP, p. 173.

337 *"ebullient mood"*: "Death Saddens LBJ," Spokesman Review (Spokane, Washington), April 5, 1968.

337 *St. Patrick's*: PDD, April 4, 1968.

337 *"Hanoi's agreement . . . great lift"*: Ibid.

337 *"The three networks . . . coverage"*: Honolulu Star-Bulletin, April 4, 1968.

338 *"The world that day . . . good place"*: LBJ, VP, p. 174.

338 *"Martin Luther King has been shot"*: PDD, April 4, 1968.

338 *"gaping hole"*: Urbana Daily Citizen (Ohio), April 5, 1968.

338 *Relaxing at the Lorraine Motel*: Kotz, Judgment Days, p. 414.

338 *"to reject . . . by nonviolence"*: "Text of Johnson Statement," Lewiston Daily Sun (Maine), April 5, 1968.

338 *"everything we've gained . . . lose tonight"*: Califano, The Triumph and Tragedy, p. 274.

338 *"the exuberance of . . . his long face"*: Busby, The Thirty-first of March, p. 35.

339 *"We had been pummeled . . . in no way see"*: Lady Bird Johnson, *A White House Diary*, p. 648.

339 *"strange, quiet meal"*: Ibid.

339 *"For God's sake . . . to watch a war"*: Busby, The Thirty-first of March, pp. 235–36.

339 *Crowds gathered . . . merchandise*: Clay Risen, *A Nation on Fire: America in the Wake of the King Assassination* (New York: Wiley, 2009), pp. 55–58, 63–67.

339 *"Within minutes . . . everyone was looting"*: Ibid., p. 67; New York Times, April 15, 1968.

339 *Johnson requested . . . civil rights leaders*: LBJ, VP, p. 175.

340 *he was in Indiana to launch his campaign*: Risen, A Nation on Fire, p. 50.

340 *"I have some bad news . . . our people"*: Statement by RFK on Assassination of Martin Luther King, April 4, 1968, JFKL.

341 *ordered all the rally bunting torn down*: Risen, A Nation on Fire, p. 51.

341 *Cabinet Room:* LBJ, *VP*, p. 175.

341 *"If I were a kid ... off first":* Busby, *The Thirty-first of March*, p. 238.

341 *"seize the opportunity":* LBJ, *VP*, p. 176.

341 *"normally civil rights supporters ... their neighborhoods":* Califano, *The Triumph and Tragedy*, p. 276.

342 *"without the moral force ... had even begun":* LBJ, *VP*, p. 177.

342 *suggestions from the assembled leaders:* Risen, *A Nation on Fire*, pp. 89–90.

342 *Johnson went before the press:* "Address to the Nation upon Proclaiming a Day of Mourning," April 5, 1968, Lyndon B. Johnson, Statement by the President on the Assassination of Dr. Martin Luther King, Jr. Online by Peters and Woolley, The American Presidency Project.

342 *"can make or break us ... we have to start again":* Califano, *The Triumph and Tragedy*, pp. 278–79.

342 *Washington was in turmoil:* Risen, *Nation on Fire*, pp. 117, 127.

343 *"moving toward two societies ... separate and unequal":* Clyde Haberman, "The Kerner Commission Report Still Echoes, Across America," *New York Times*, June 23, 2020.

343 *He resented the report's findings:* Justin Driver, "The Report on Race That Shook America," *The Atlantic*, May 2018.

343 *transferring money:* LJAD, p. 4.

344 *He found McCarthy:* RNG, OH, McCarthy, RNG Papers, DBC, UT.

344 *"the whole atmosphere ... for position":* RNG, *RA*, p. 527.

344 *"In the McCarthy campaign ... campaign":* *Boston Globe*, April 12, 1968.

345 *"Cheers rang from ... the vote":* *Los Angeles Times*, April 11, 1968.

345 *80 percent of America's homes:* *Boston Globe*, April 11, 1968.

345 *"The proudest moments ... promises of a century":* Kotz, *Judgment Days*, p. 429.

345 *White House Fellows reception:* PDD, May 6, 1968.

346 *president wanted to see me:* PDD, May 15, 1968.

346 *He was signing documents:* PDD, May 15, 1968.

346 *"First you say ... is all about":* DKG/LBJ, LJAD, p. 5.

346 *visit to former president Harry Truman's home:* *Springfield News Leader* (Missouri), May 4, 1968.

346 *"The great thing ... can drive you crazy":* LJAD, p. 349.

348 *Bobby himself had told friends:* RNG, *RA*, p. 520.

348 *"extremely difficult" ... "what we wanted said":* Ward Just, *Tampa Bay Tribune*, July 1, 1968.

349 *"If they're waiting ... go see them":* Witcover, *85 Days*, p. 145.

349 *"Who do you want ... Will you help me?":* White, *The Making of the President 1968*, p. 199.

349 *huge victory:* Newfield, *Robert Kennedy*, p. 290.

350 *"smiled as he made his way ... on the plane":* *Capital Journal* (Salem, Oregon), May 29, 1968.

350 *"We knew we had ... for the nomination":* Ibid.

350 *"The people of Oregon ... as they must":* *The World* (Casco Bay, Oregon), May 29, 1968.

350 *"I'm sorry, I let you down":* Newfield, *Robert Kennedy*, p. 299.

351 *"I'm not in much of a position ... I'm not a candidate at all":* RNG, *RA*, p. 533.

351 *"It certainly wasn't ... of the day":* Newfield, *Robert Kennedy*, p. 298.

351 *"I'm not the same ... can't claim that I am"*: Los Angeles Times, May 30, 1968.

351 *"a wild welcome"*: Capitol Journal (Salem, Oregon), May 30, 1968.

351 *"held more Democratic voters ... combined"*: Progress Bulletin (Pomona, California), May 31, 1968.

351 *"obviously heartened ... reception"*: LA Evening Citizens News, May 30, 1968.

351 *"If I died ... Resurrection City"*: Capital Journal (Salem, Oregon), May 30, 1968.

351 *Memorial Day weekend*: PDD, May 29–June 3, 1968.

353 *"How in the hell" ... "their parents"*: LJAD, p. 332.

354 *briefing sessions*: Witcover, 85 Days, p. 200.

354 *overconfident McCarthy*: Ibid.; Schlesinger, Robert Kennedy and His Times, p. 911.

354 *"You are looking at ... wasn't much of a debate"*: DKG/LBJ notes, "Last Nine Months," in author's possession.

355 *last day of the campaign*: Newfield, Robert Kennedy, pp. 315–16.

355 *beach house in Malibu*: RNG, "A Day in June," McCall's Magazine, June 1970.

356 *"if the 49 percent" ... "crisp executive again"*: White, The Making of the President 1968, p. 211.

356 *"as the warmth and the taste of victory ... over him"*: Ibid., pp. 211–12.

356 *CBS altered its projections*: Los Angeles Times, June 5, 1968; White, The Making of the President 1968, p. 212.

356 *"glee was absolutely uncontained"*: White, The Making of the President 1968, p. 212.

356 *"I've got to get free ... Secretary of State"*: RNG, RA, p. 537.

356 *"I'll go downstairs ... at the Factory"*: Ibid., p. 538.

357 *"There is no real warning ... sunlight to darkness"*: RNG Diary, May 25, 1967, RNG Papers, DBC, UT.

357 *"you better go in now"*: RNG, RA, p. 539.

357 *"Mr. President ... Senator Kennedy is dead"*: PDD, June 6, 1968.

358 *"Nothing has hurt me so much"*: DKG, "Last Nine Months," notes in author's possession.

358 *"I think we can ... my basis for running"*: Chester, Hodgson, and Page, An American Melodrama, p. 353.

CHAPTER 12: ENDINGS AND BEGINNINGS

359 *From Theodore White's reporting*: White, The Making of the President 1968, p. 361.

360 *"more manic than before ... phone and fly"*: Larner, Nobody Knows, p. 159.

360 *peace talks had never regained*: Dr. Jeffrey Michaels, "Stuck in Endless Preliminaries: Vietnam and the Battle of the Paris Peace Table," November 1968–January 1969.

360 *series of mocking articles*: Daniel Yergin, "How Dick Goodwin Got Away," New York, July 22, 1968.

361 *"'Goodwin is forever ... Othello'"*: Garry Wills, Nixon Agonistes (New York: New American Library, 1969), p. 458.

361 *"Goodwin is like ... the other team"*: Yergin, "How Dick Goodwin Got Away."

362 *"the presence of ... peaceful trust"*: Boston Globe, August 13, 1968.

362 *"not to march or protest ... share that hope"*: RNG, Unpublished Recollections of the Convention, RNG Papers, DBC, UT.

362 *"had the ... wrapped up"*: Boston Globe, August 29, 1968.

363 *"an unconditional . . . broadly representative"*: Boston Globe, August 28, 1968.

363 *"had been drafted . . . to Chicago"*: Tom Wicker, "Democrats Delay Fight on the Vietnam Plank; "Kennedy Rejects Draft," *New York Times*, August 29, 1968.

363 *"The issue was clear . . . at whatever cost"*: White, *The Making of the President 1968*, p. 323.

364 *Plans had been made:* Michael Kilian, "LBJ Birthday Party Ready Just in Case," *Chicago Tribune*, August 27, 1968; Bob Considine, "Guarded Birthday," *San Francisco Examiner*, August 27, 1968.

364 *"a personal appearance" . . . "can control the delegates"*: RNG, *RA*, p. 6.

365 *peace plank was defeated:* CBS Evening News for Wednesday, August 28, 1968, Convention / Vietnam Plank.

365 *"whether he had . . . fault him for that"*: Richard Harwood, "McCarthy Workers Raided in Hotel," *Washington Post*, quoted in *Boston Globe*, August 31, 1968.

365 *When three protesters:* Norman Mailer, *Miami and the Siege of Chicago* (New York: Random House, 2016), Kindle edition.

365 *"Michigan Avenue was turned . . . were shattered"*: Chicago Tribune, August 30, 1968.

365 *A police car crashed:* O'Donnell, *Playing with Fire*, pp. 362–63, 365.

365 *first-aid station:* Ibid.; Chicago Tribune, August 29, 1968.

366 *"Richard Goodwin, the ashen nub . . . four more years of this"*: Jack Newfield, *Village Voice*, September 5, 1968.

366 *secured a thousand candles:* Ibid., p. 373; Norman Mailer, *Some Honorable Men* (Boston: Little, Brown, 1976), pp. 269–70.

366 *commandeer a Secret Service limousine:* Larner, *Nobody Knows*, p. 181.

366 *"The Democrats are finished"*: White, *The Making of the President 1968*, p. 348.

366 *More than six hundred delegates joined in:* The Dispatch (Moline, Illinois), August 29, 1968.

366 *"We hadn't dared . . . at every footstep"*: Wofford, *Of Kennedys and Kings*, p. 434.

367 *"This is a statement"*: Meriden Journal (Connecticut), August 29, 1968.

367 *"On my way up"*: Description of police action on the fifteenth floor: RNG, Unpublished Recollections of the Convention, RNG Papers, DBC, UT; *Boston Globe*, August 31, 1968.

368 *"no evidence whatsoever . . . throwing anything"*: White, *The Making of the President 1968*, p. 360.

368 *"Help us . . . and save the youngsters"*: Ibid., pp. 361–62.

369 *"I knew how fragile . . . back to their rooms"*: RNG, Unpublished Recollections of the Convention, RNG Papers, DBC, UT.

369 *300 people were injured . . . 650 were arrested:* Lee Hudson, "Looking Back at the 1968 Demo. Nat. Convention," *Politico*, April 11, 2023; James R. Peipert, "AP Was There: Protesters Fight Chicago Police, Guardsmen," August 27, 2018.

370 *Gallup poll: Jefferson City Post-Tribune,* (MO), September 16, 1968.

370 *"unable to endorse . . . the great issues"*: RNG to Larry O'Brien, October 15, 1968, RNG Papers, DBC, UT.

370 *"an acceptable risk"*: Daily Herald (Provo, Utah), October 1, 1968.

370 *"The most important . . . his own man"*: White, *The Making of the President 1968*, p. 415.

371 *"college educated . . . negotiated settlement"*: RNG to Larry O'Brien, October 15, 1968, RNG Papers, DBC, UT.

371 *"the ice was . . . serious talks"*: LBJ, *VP*, p. 515.

371 *"Nixon is going to win . . . stick with you"*: LBJ, *VP*, p. 551.

372 *interview with the intermediary:* Mark Updegrove, *Indomitable Will: LBJ in the Presidency* (New York: Crown, 2012), p. 308.

372 *"Keep Anna . . . South Vietnam"*: Peter Baker, *New York Times*, January 2, 2017.

372 *"the outcome would . . . on Election Day"*: LBJ, *VP*, pp. 548–49.

372 *"Done. I'll get you a position . . . working for me"*: LJAD, p. xii.

373 *Christmas holidays at the ranch:* PDD, December 27, 1968, to January 3, 1969.

374 *White House was in a state of upheaval:* *Arizona Republic* (Phoenix), January 13, 1969.

374 *"I need help . . . won't forget what you are doing for me"*: LJAD, p. 13.

375 *farewell dinner:* Interviews with Ervin Duggan, Jim Jones, PDD, January 19, 1969.

375 *"The atmosphere . . . the last goodbye"*: Lady Bird Johnson, *A White House Diary*, p. 774.

375 *"All of us knew . . . the rest of our lives"*: Califano, *The Triumph and Tragedy*, p. 335.

376 *"I can't say this . . . backwoods politician"*: DKG/LBJ, LJAD, p. 355.

377 *"Don't worry . . . all that matters"*: DKG/LBJ, LJAD, Foreword to 1991 edition (New York: St. Martins, 1991), p. xx.

378 *"I don't want you to tell . . . to read it!"*: DKG/LJAD, p. 18.

379 *When I entered the room:* Unprocessed Post-Presidential Daily Diary (Box 2, March 12–15, 1970). Courtesy of Ian-Frederick Rothwell and Jenna De Graffenried.

379 *"I'm an old man . . . Eisenhower did"*: Leo Janos, "The Last Days of the President: LBJ in Retirement," *The Atlantic* (July 1973).

380 *"the place where . . . when you die"*: LJAD, p. 352.

380 *"a series of sharp . . . and breathless"*: Janos, "The Last Days of the President: LBJ in Retirement."

380 *"Lyndon had been . . . could not go"*: Merle Miller, *Lyndon: An Oral Autobiography* (New York: Putnam, 1980), p. 600.

380 *"So cold and icy . . . here by bus"*: Ibid., p. 599.

380 *"He knew what . . . how to spend it"*: Hugh Sidey, "The Presidency," *Life*, December 29, 1972, p. 16.

381 *convocation of civil rights leaders:* Harry Middleton, "The Lion in Winter: Johnson in Retirement," in Thomas W. Cowger and Sherman J. Markman, eds., *Lyndon Johnson Remembered: An Intimate Portrait of a Presidency* (Lanham, MD: Rowman & Littlefield, 2003), p. 155.

381 *"For once . . . he was there now"*: Ibid., p. 156.

381 *"Of all the records . . . we shall overcome"*: "Lyndon Baines Johnson Civil Rights Symposium Address," December 12, 1972, "American Rhetoric," Online Speech Bank, Lyndon Baines Johnson Library, Austin, TX.

382 *a fatal heart attack:* LJAD, p. 366; *New York Times*, January 23, 1973.

CHAPTER THIRTEEN: OUR TALISMAN

386 *"while accomplishing practically nothing"*: LTT, p. 310.

387 *"Domestic policy . . . can kill us"*: Updegrove, *Incomparable Grace*, p. 83.

387 *"You know, Lyndon . . . you were the Chairman"*: Dallek, *Flawed Giant*, p. 21.

388 *"We choose to go to the moon ... man has ever gone"*: September 12, 1962, John F. Kennedy, Address at Rice University.

388 *"no one did more ... safely to earth"*: Jeff Shesol, "Lyndon Johnson's Unsung Role in Sending America to the Moon," *The New Yorker*, July 20, 2019.

388 *"Father of the Program ... he succeeded"*: Ibid.

389 *"an unrepentant" ... "Tom Paine of our generation"*: Review statements on back cover of RNG, *Promises to Keep* (New York: Times Books, 1992).

393 *In the Eighties, he had written ... democracy was teetering*: *Los Angeles Times*, October 24, 1985.

393 *In the Nineties, he had called for major changes*: RNG, *Promises to Keep*, pp. 15, 37, 43, 44.

393 *"actually favor violence ... it is a lie"*: Edmund Muskie, "Election Eve speech, November 2, 1970," https/scarab/ bates.edu/msp/2s.

394 *"Almost a century ... I offer my concession"*: RNG, RNG Papers, DBC, UT.

396 *"The year that is drawing ... national holiday"*: Transcript of Abraham Lincoln's Thanksgiving Proclamation, October 3, 1863.

396 *"I'm a young ... my stomach is"*: LTT, p. 358.

398 *"Though nothing ... what remains behind"*: William Wordsworth, "Ode: Intimations of Immortality," https/www poetryfoundation.org.

EPILOGUE

401 *"Black Care ... fast enough"*: Quoted in *LTT*, p. 128.

402 *decision to move*: DKG, *Wait Till Next Year: A Memoir* (New York: Simon & Schuster, 1997), p. 246.

404 *"living history ... read of and recounted"*: Abraham Lincoln Address Before the Young Man's Lyceum, January 23, 1837, Online by Peters and Woolley, The American Presidency Project.

Photo Credits

Photo Credits

453

PAGE 23
TOP: Photo by Richard Pasley / ©Richard Pasley; MIDDLE: Photo by Richard Pasley / ©Richard Pasley; BOTTOM: Photo by Richard Pasley / ©Richard Pasley

PAGE 24
TOP: Photo by Richard Pasley / ©Richard Pasley; BOTTOM: Courtesy of Concord Free Public Library Corporation

JACKET

Colorization by Bryan Eaton
@ 2023 Copyright Doris Kearns Goodwin, all rights reserved

Front (left to right): President John F. Kennedy and Richard N. Goodwin by Jacques Lowe / courtesy of the Jacques Lowe Estate; Richard N. Goodwin and First Lady Jacqueline Kennedy by Art Rickerby / Shutterstock; Richard N. Goodwin and President Lyndon B. Johnson, John W. McCormack center, by Yoichi Okamoto / courtesy of LBJ Library; Robert F. Kennedy and Richard N. Goodwin by Bill Eppridge / Shutterstock; Doris Kearns and President Lyndon B. Johnson by Yoichi Okamoto / courtesy of LBJ Library

Spine: Doris Kearns and Richard N. Goodwin by Marc Peloquin / courtesy of the author

Back (left to right): Doris Kearns and President Lyndon B. Johnson by Yoichi Okamoto / courtesy of LBJ Library; Doris Kearns and President Lyndon B. Johnson by Yoichi Okamoto / courtesy of LBJ Library; L to R: Vice President Lyndon B. Johnson, Robert F. Kennedy, Richard N. Goodwin, Arthur Schlesinger, President John F. Kennedy by Cecil W. Stoughton / US Army, courtesy of LBJ Library

Framed photo: Doris Kearns Goodwin and Richard N. Goodwin by Annie Leibovitz / @ Annie Leibovitz; frame by Adobe Stock

Index

Page numbers in *italics* refer to photographs.

ABC, 218

Abernathy, Ralph, 338

Abraham Lincoln (Sandburg), 138

Abu Simbel, monuments at, 117–20

Acheson, Dean, 25

Aeschylus, 340

affirmative action, 238

Agnelli, Giovanni, 119

Alabama, University of, 124

Alarcón, Ricardo, 110

Alliance for Progress, 90–99, 103–6, 112, 134, 147–48, 159, 265, 267, 268

Americans for Democratic Action, 284–87, 296, 303

Anich, Beverley, 51

Anich, Ellen, *38*, 50–51

Anich, Tom, 50

anti-Semitism, 32, 44

apartheid, 278–84

Archimedes, 72, 281

Area Redevelopment Bill, 51

Arizona Republic, 76

Arlington National Cemetery, 142–43, 169

Armstrong, Neil, 388

arts, support for, 120, 132–34, 146, 209, 211, 246–47

Ashland, Wis., *38*, 49–54

Aswan Dam, 118

Augustine, Saint, 318

Baez, Joan, 169

Bailey, Oriole, 246

Baldridge, Letitia, 116

Baldwin, James, 116

Baltimore Sun, 259

Bay of Pigs invasion, 76, 95–98, 109

Belafonte, Harry, 303

"Benito Cereno" (Melville), 310–11

Berle, Adolf, 92, 104, 105

Berra, Yoga, 308–9

Bibring, Grete, 3–4

Black, Hugo, 29

Boggs, Hale, 364

Bolívar, Simon, 94

Bond, Julian, 366, 380–81

Boston Globe, 4, 49, 344

Boston Red Sox, 1, 3, 7, 19, 391

Bowles, Chester, 71

Boxley, Nancy, 27

Bradshaw, John, 4

Branca, Ralph, 5

Brandeis, Louis, 29

Branigin, Robert, 349

Breslin, Jimmy, 329

Brooklyn Dodgers, 2, 3, 5, 7, 41, 87, 109, 354

Brown, George, Jr., 366

Brown, Harold, 241

Brown, Jerry, 389

Brown, Manson, 89

Brown, Sam, 319

Brown v. Board of Education, 22, 28

Brustein, Robert, 290

Buck, Pearl, 116, 117

Buddenbrooks (Mann), 17, 19

Buffalo Evening News, 176

Bulganin, Nikolai, 20

Bundy, McGeorge, 1–2, 206–7, 277

Burke, Arleigh, 387

Busby, Horace, 176–78, 226, 230, 332, 336, 338, 339

Bush, George H. W., 199
Bush, George W., 393–94
Byrd, Harry, 174
Byrd, Robert, 160

Califano, Hilary, 246
Califano, Joe, 246, 252, 253, 255, 256,
    269–70, 272–73, 341, 347, 375
Campbell, Alex, 307
capitalism, 266–67
Carmichael, Stokely, 303
Carpenter, Les, 177
Carpenter, Liz, 170, 177
Carrillo Flores, Antonio, 145
Carroll, Bernard, 142–43
Carson, Johnny, 169
Carter, Jimmy, 197
"Casey at the Bat" (Thayer), 79
Castro, Fidel, 75–76, 95, 97, 107–10
Cater, Douglass, 173, 306
Catholicism, 47, 54, 90–91, 267
CBS, 30, 65, 355
Celler, Emmanuel, 233
Central Intelligence Agency (CIA), 95
Channing, Carol, 194
Charter of Punta del Este, 99
Chennault, Anna, 371–72
Chiari, Francisco, 155–56
Chicago Tribune, 276, 365
Cicero, 288–89
cigars:
    from Guevara, 99, 100
    from Jackie Kennedy, 262–63
civil rights:
    Coast Guard discrimination, 86–90, 386
    college campuses, discrimination on,
        22–25
    housing discrimination, 61–62, 120–22,
        296, 339, 341–42
    inner city riots and, 192, 255–56, 331,
        341–45
    JFK and, 60–63, 66, 89–90, 120–27
    LBJ and, 214–34, 236–40, 255–56, 296,
        339
    LBJ's speech at LBJ Library on, 380–82

    McCarthy and, 328
    RFK and, 175–76, 183, 184, 348
    segregation/desegregation, 28–29,
        123–24, 127, 183, 186, 192, 215, 254,
        301–2
    urban problems, 164, 209–10, 215, 219,
        255, 348
    voting rights, 149, 211, 215–34, 236,
        251–55, 334, 345
    Watts riots, 255–56
Civil Rights Act:
    Congress and, 127, 172–76, 185
    JFK and, 124–25, 152, 160, 172, 175,
        185–86, 188
    LBJ and, 152, 160, 172–76, 185–86, 188,
        203, 236, 254, 345, 376
    RFK and, 175–76, 183, 184, 348
    signing of, 179, 182–86, 192, 404
Civil Rights Movement, 22–25, 70–71,
    123–29, 185, 214–19, 240
    March on Washington, 125–29, 307
    Selma marches, 218–20, 222, 243
Clark, Jim, 217
Clifford, Clark, 272
Clinton, Bill, 199
cloture, 172–75
Coast Guard, discrimination in, 86–90,
    386
Cohen, Wilbur, 250
Colby, Deb, 9–10, 395
Colby College, 24–25, 123, 126, 129–30,
    307
Cold War, 67, 75, 85, 108, 118, 132, 389
college campuses, discrimination on, 22–25
Colombia, 104–5
communism, 91, 92, 266–67, 277
Concord, Mass., 4–5, 7, 8, 391–92, 396–97,
    401–3
Concord Free Public Library, Goodwin
    Forum at, 402–3
"Concord Hymn" (Emerson), 79
Congress, U.S., 335
    Civil Rights Bill and, 127, 172–76, 185
    89th, 208–9, 211, 235, 254
    Fair Housing Bill passed by, 345

LBJ and, 152, 154–55, 211–13, 247, 342, 345

Medicare passed by, 249–50

quiz show scandal and, 35

Subcomittee on Legislative Oversight, 30–31

Voting Rights Bill and, 224–34

see also House of Representatives, U.S.; Senate, U.S.

Connally, John, 141

Connor, Eugene "Bull," 122–23, 217

conservation, 134, 209, 210, 246–47

Constitution, U.S., 29, 124, 184, 222, 298, 404

Cooper v. Aaron, 28

Corbin, Paul, 187–88

Covington and Burling, 25

"Cremation of Sam McGee, The" (Service), 79

Crockett, Bill, 157

Cronkite, Walter, 268–69, 388–89

Cry, the Beloved Country (Paton), 282–83

Cuba, 75–76, 91, 95–98, 107–10

Cuban Missile Crisis, 107–10

Cuomo, George, 11, 13, 14, 15, 25, 43, 80, 184, 269, 274–75, 290, 405

Daily Express, 294

"Daisy Girl" ad, 195–96

Daley, Richard, 366

"Day in June, A" (R. Goodwin), 355

Death of a President, The (Manchester), 140, 142, 143

Dede, Temperance, 52

de Gaulle, Charles, 141

Democratic Party, 173–74, 183, 296, 312, 349, 393

National Convention (1956), 39–41

National Convention (1964), 192–96

National Convention (1968), 360–70, 381

Derounian, Steven, 102

desegregation, see segregation/desegregation

Dillon, Douglas, 86, 98–99, 285

Dinner in Camelot (Esposito), 116

Dirksen, Everett, 173–76, 184, 224, 253, 300

discrimination:

on college campuses, 22–25

in housing, 61–62, 120–22, 296, 339, 341–42

see also segregation/desegregation

Doar, John, 185

Dobrynin, Anatoly, 243–45, 246

Dolan, Joe, 313

Douglas, Stephen, 394

Doyle Dane Bernbach, 195–96

Duke University, 302

Dungan, Ralph, 140

DuPont, 53

Dutton, Fred, 312, 355

"Duty of Loyalty, The" (R. Goodwin), 288, 296, 298

Edelman, Peter, 313

Edmund Pettus Bridge, 218–20, 343

education, 22, 62, 63, 65, 73, 149, 152, 201, 209, 211, 213–16, 237, 246–47, 254, 255, 267, 286

Egyptian monuments, at Abu Simbel, 117–20

Eisenhower, Dwight, 20, 25, 36, 76, 380

JFK and, 46, 51, 141

Emancipation Proclamation, 47, 183

Emerson, Ralph Waldo, 5, 79

environment, polices on, 53, 219–21, 254

Esposito, Joseph, 116

Evans, Rowland, 159, 265–66

Evers, Medgar, 125

Facts on File almanac, 299–301

Fair Housing Bill, 345

Fauntroy, Walter, 184

Federal Communications Commission, 29

Federenko, Nicolay, 244

Feiffer, Jules, 251

Feldman, Mike, 63–64, 77–78, 197, 198

filibusters, 172–75

Fitzgerald, John Francis, 81

Fitzgeralds and the Kennedys, The (D. K. Goodwin), 6
Fitzsimmons, John, 392
Ford, Gerald, 197
Ford, Henry, II, 353
Fortas, Abe, 272, 287
Frankenheimer, John, 348, 349–50, 355
Frankfurter, Felix, 26, 28–29, 33, 35, 42–43, 44, 113, 275, 278, 395
　　JFK and, 42, 44, 180
　　LBJ and, 180–81
Frank Leslie's Illustrated Newspaper, 139
Freeman, Orville, 190
Frost, Robert, 116, 180
Fulbright, William, 275

Gagarin, Yuri, 387
Galbraith, John Kenneth, 175, 297
Galileo Galilei, 389, 401
Gallup polls, 147, 299, 370
Gans, Curtis, 319
Gardner, John, 252
Gavin, James, 285
gay marriage, 283–84
Ginsburg, Ruth Bader, 26, 27, 87
Glenn, John, 116
Goldberg, Arthur, 337
Goldman, Eric, 213
Goldwater, Barry, 188–89, 191, 195–96, 213
Goodridge v. Department of Public Health, 283–84
Goodwin, Doris Kearns (DKG), *310*, 383
　　Castro's meeting with, 107–10
　　Concord, Mass. and, 4–5, 7, 8, 391–92, 396–97, 401–3
　　and integration of Tri Delta sorority, 129–31
　　JFK and, 40–42
　　at Labor Dept., 304, 307, 308, 320, 343, 345–47
　　LBJ and, 38–42, 180, 211–12, *310*, 331, 345–47, 351–55, 364–65, 372–80
　　at March on Washington (1967), 300–303

　　at Reeb memorial service, 218–20
　　thoughts on LBJ vs. JFK, 38–39, 62, 151, 385–89
　　as White House Fellow, 304–7, *310*, 345
Goodwin, Joe, 5, 6
Goodwin, Michael, 5, 6
Goodwin, Richard "Dick," *11, 83, 111, 137, 168, 235, 383*
　　as Advisor on the Arts, 132–36, 146
　　in Alliance for Progress creation, 90–99, 265, 268
　　army service of, 16–22
　　Ashland, Wis. and, 49–54
　　Castro's meeting with, 107–10
　　Concord, Mass. and, 4–5, 7, 8, 391–92, 396–97, 401–3
　　Death of a President and, 291–95
　　"Dobrynin incident" and, 243–45, 246
　　finances of, 13–14, 25–26, 242
　　Frankfurter and, *see* Frankfurter, Felix
　　Guevara's meeting with, 98–102, 107–9, 208, 244
　　at Harvard, 13–16, 22
　　health problems of, 260–61, 390–92, 394–99
　　"ice capade fiasco" and, 262–64
　　Jackie Kennedy and, 83–84, 115–17, 132, 158, 261–64, 289–95, 328, 384
　　Los Angeles Times columns of, 393
　　as McCarthy's campaign advisor, 316–30, 332–33, 335–36, 343–44, 359–63
　　Moyers's friendship with, 113, 200, 257–59, 261–62, 273–74, 289, 389
　　"Nixopedia" and, 63, 196
　　Panama crisis and, 155–56
　　Peace Corps, work for, 112–15, 119, 131–34, 146
　　"politics in the blood" of, 181, 191, 202, 275, 322, 384
　　quiz show scandal and, 30–36
　　Sorensen and, 77–79, 99
　　at State Dept., 102–6, 112, 113
　　Temple of Dendur monuments and, 117–20, 384

Thanksgiving ritual of, 396

thoughts on LBJ vs. JFK, 38–39, 62, 151, 385–89

at Tufts College, 2, *11*, 12, 22

Vietnam War speeches and writings by, 284–88, 296–98

at Voting Rights Act signing, 235, 251–54

work on rent control in Brookline, 14–15

Goodwin, Richard "Dick," JFK and, 42–44, 77–79, 199, 277, 289

and "Dinner in Camelot" for Nobel Prize Laureates, *111*, 115–17, 384

Goodwin transferred to State Dept. by, 102–6, 112, 113

JFK's funeral and, 138–43

on Latin American trip, 104–5

in 1960 presidential campaign, 58–82

as speechwriter for, 36–37, 44–49, 59–63, 77–82, 83–84, 92–95, 104–5, 112, 115, 125, 200–201, 259, 261–62, 277, 289

Goodwin, Richard "Dick," LBJ and, 155–60, 176–80, 195, 199–200, 205–7, 265–66, 286

and aborted book project, 287–88

"Great Society" coined by, 161, 176

as LBJ's "stud duck," 236

resignation tendered by, 235–43, 257–59

as speechwriter for, 153–58, 162–66, 171, 174, 176–80, 193, 195, 200–201, 210–11, 224–34, 237–40, 251, 257–59, 269–74

at Texas White House, 170–71, 179

in White House skinny dip, 160–61

Goodwin, Richard "Dick," RFK and, 91, 189–90, 261–69, 277–78, 289, 311–15, 320

as campaign advisor, 344–45, 347–51, 353–56

on South American trip, 264–69

as speechwriter for, 275–76, 277–84, 299–300

Goodwin, Richard "Dick," speeches worked on by:

Gore's concession speech, 393–94

JFK's speech on city on a hill, 79–82

JFK's speech on civil rights, 60–62

JFK's speech on Latin America, 92–95

LBJ's Civil Rights Bill signing statement, 179, 184–85

LBJ's Great Society speech, 162–66, 176

LBJ's message on poverty, 153, 155–56

LBJ's speech at Howard University, 237–40, 252, 255

LBJ's statement on Panama, 155–56

LBJ's State of the Union address 1965, 210–11

LBJ's State of the Union address 1966 ("Guns and Butter" speech), 258, 269–74

LBJ's Voting Rights Act signing statement, 235, 251–55

LBJ's "We Shall Overcome" speech, *205*, 224–34, 252, 270, 333–34, 403

Muskie campaign speech, 393

RFK's "Ripple of Hope" speech on apartheid, 72, *260*, 278–84

Goodwin, Richard, Jr., 2–4

Goodwin, Sandra, 2, 3, 170–71, 179

Goodwin Forum, at Concord Free Public Library, 402–3

Gordon, Barbara, 24–25

Gore, Al, 199, 393–94

Gore, Albert, Sr., 40–41

Graduate, The (film), 353

Graham, Otto, 88

Great Society, 161–67, 171, 175, 197, 199, 202, 204, 208–14, 235, 237, 246, 247–49, 259, 267, 270–71, 273, 287–88, 296–97, 303, 308, 322, 330, 333–34, 343, 370

Greenfield, Jeff, 299, 313

Guevara, Che, 98–102, 107–9, 208, 244

Gulf of Tonkin Resolution, 192

Guskin, Alan and Judith, 69–73

Guthman, Ed, 291–93

Haldeman, H. R., 371–72

Halleck, Charles, 183, 184

Harlan, John Marshall, 29
Harper & Row, 292–93
Harper's Weekly, 139
Harriman, Averell, 2, 244–45, 298
Harris, Oren, 31
Harris polls, 294, 334
Harvard Law Review, 15–16, 22, 25–27, 175
Harvard Law School, 13, 14, 25–28, 175
Harvard University, 1, 6, 81–82, 300–302, 304, 346, 372, 374–76
Hawthorne, Nathaniel, 5, 396
Hayden, Tom, 71
Head Start programs, 254, 334
Healy, Robert, 49
Hellman, Lillian, 251, 290
Henry, Ed, 148
Henry, Patrick, 125
Henry V (Shakespeare), 174–75
Herndon, William, 190
Hersh, Seymour "Sy," 317–18, 326, 328
Hiatt, Arnold, 323–24
Hicks, Rollie, 52
History of the Decline and Fall of the Roman Empire, The (Gibbon), 17
Hoffman, Dustin, 353
Holmes, Oliver Wendell, 29
Holy Cross College, 174–75
Honolulu Star-Bulletin, 337
Hoover, Herbert, 141
Hoover, J. Edgar, 243
Hopkins, Harry, 77, 166
House, Edward, 77
House of Representatives, U.S.:
  Rules Committee, 121–22, 224
  Subcommittee on Legislative Oversight, 29
  Voting Rights Act passed by, 246–47
  see also Congress, U.S.
housing, discrimination in, 61–62, 120–22, 296, 339, 341–42
Housing and Urban Development Department (HUD), 121–22, 210, 215, 247
Howard University, 237–40, 252
Hugo, Victor, 174–75

Humphrey, Hubert, 40, 47, 54, 173–76, 183, 184, 191, 193, 224, 252–54, 277, 341, 349, 356, 362–63, 380–81
  at Democratic National Convention (1968), 362–63, 366–67, 369, 370

immigration, 62, 209, 211, 246–47, 254, 334
inner city riots, 192, 255–56, 331, 341–45
  see also urban problems
integration, *see* segregation/desegregation
"Intimations of Mortality" (Wordsworth), 398

Jackson, Henry, 300
Jackson, Jesse, 338
Jackson, Jimmie Lee, 217–18, 219
Jackson, Mahalia, 169
Jackson College, 22–23
Jeffers, Katherine, 23
Jeffrey, Mildred, 71
Jim Crow laws, 183
John F. Kennedy Presidential Library, 72, 145, 147, 279, 294–95
Johnson, Lady Bird, 143–44, 146, 171, 184–85, 186, 192, 193, 195, 211, 221, 225, 247, 256, 271, 273, 294, 306, 338, 374, 375, 377, 380–81, 384–85
Johnson, Luci Baines, 252, 395
Johnson, Lyndon, 12, 47, 119, 120, 133, 137–38, 139, 142–44, 168–204, *168*, 205–34, 235–59, *235*, 267, 270, *310*, *359*, 385–89
  affirmative action and, 238
  campaign for presidency, 188–204
  chosen as JFK's running mate, 55–56, 77
  civil rights and, 214–34, 236–40, 255–56, 296, 339
  Congress and, 152, 154–55, 211–13, 247, 342, 345
  "Daisy Girl" ad and, 195–96
  Death of a President and, 291–95
  in decision not to seek reelection, 329–36
  at Democratic National Convention (1956), 40–42

at Democratic National Convention
  (1964), 192–96
depression bouts of, 192, 203, 221, 224,
  248, 249–50
DKG and, 38–42, 180, 211–12, 301,
  303–7, *310*, 331, 345–47, 351–55,
  364–65, 372–80
educational policies of, 209, 213, 214,
  216, 246–47, 254
environmental policies of, 210, 219–21,
  254
Fair Housing Bill and, 339, 341–42, 345
Frankfurter and, 180–81
Great Society speech of, 162–66, 176
health care policies of, 214, 216, 249–51,
  254
health problems of, 186, 192, 378–82
Howard University speech of, 237–40,
  252, 255
HUD created by, 121–22
Jackie Kennedy and, 291–95
JFK's policies and, 160–61, 163
MLK and, 214–19, 225, 232, 234, 235,
  239, 253, 302, 303, 338–39
moon landing and, 387–89
Panama statement of, 155–56
poverty and, 155–57, 166, 201, 210,
  214–16, 233, 256, 296, 342, 386
in poverty speech to Congress, 153,
  155–56
RFK and, 56, 59, 146–49, 155, 157–58,
  185, 187–90, 197–98, 201–3, 245,
  265–66, 269–70, 276–77, 285,
  311–16
R. Goodwin and, *see* Goodwin, Richard
  "Dick," LBJ and
Russell and, 181–82
as schoolteacher in Cotulla, Tex., 12, 229,
  233, 234, 378
speech at LBJ Library, 380–82
State of the Union address 1965, 210–11
State of the Union address 1966 ("Guns
  and Butter" speech), 258, 269–74
task forces of, 209–10
Texas White House (ranch) of, 38–39,

41–42, 151–60, *168*, 170–72, 176,
  177, 179, 186, 211, 212, 227, 246,
  351–55, *359*, 373, 377–80, 388–89
transition to White House, 147–67
Vietnam War and, 192, 211, 213–14,
  242, 247–49, 254–55, 270–73, 276,
  284–87, 296–303, 309, 311–15,
  329–34, 336–37, 371
Voting Rights Act signing speech of, 235,
  251–55
voting rights and, 215–34, 251, 345
Wallace, meeting with, 221–23
Watts riots and, 255–56
"We Shall Overcome" speech of, *205*,
  224–34, 252, 270, 333–34, 403
Johnson, Tom, 305, 307, 336
Johnson Foundation, 242
Johnson Robb, Lynda Bird, 380
Johnston, Tom, 265, 279
Jones, James, 251–52
Jones, Judy Turner, 130
Jones, Vann, 130
Jordan, Barbara, 380–81
Jordan, Vernon, 380–81
Jorden, William, 376
Josephson, Bill, 113
Journals (Schlesinger), 127
Julius Caesar (Shakespeare), 313, 314
Just, Ward, 348
Justice Department, U.S., 124, 175, 216,
  279, 280

Kaplan, Robert, 91
Kaplan, Sumner, 22–23, 42–43, 80
Katzenbach, Nicholas, 221
Keating, Kenneth, 197–98
Kefauver, Estes, 40–42
Kellam, Lawrence, 19
Kennedy, Edward, 4
Kennedy, Ethel, 117, 145, 264–65, 268,
  355, 357
Kennedy, Eunice, 112, 145, 146
Kennedy, Jackie, 94, 97, 104, *111*, 145, 195,
  242–43, 357
  and *Death of a President*, 291–95

Kennedy, Jackie (*cont.*)
  and JFK's funeral and burial, 138–44
  LBJ and, 291–95
  R. Goodwin and, 83–84, 115–17, 132,
    158, 261–64, 289–95, 328, 384
  Temple of Dendur monuments and,
    117–20, 384
Kennedy, John F., 38, 58, 83, 164, 189, 194,
    195, 196, 208–9, 265, 266, 285, 316,
    322, 335, 354, 385–89
  Ashland, Wis. and, 49–54
  assassination of, 136, 138
  Bay of Pigs and, 76, 95–98, 109
  "Caroline" (private plane) of, 58, 59,
    66–67, 72, 161, 268, 367
  Catholic faith of, 47, 54, 91, 105
  civil rights and, 60–63, 66, 89–90,
    120–27
  Civil Rights Bill and, 124–25, 152, 160,
    172, 175
  and Coast Guard's lack of diversity,
    86–90, 386
  Cuban Missile Crisis and, 108–9
  at Democratic National Convention
    (1956), 39–41
  Dendur monuments and, 118
  "Dinner in Camelot" for Nobel Prize
    Laureates hosted by, 111, 115–17, 384
  Eisenhower and, 46, 51, 141
  Executive Order #11063 on housing
    discrimination signed by, 120–21
  Frankfurter and, 42, 44, 180
  funeral of, 137, 138–44
  inauguration of, 83–86
  Latin American visit by, 104–5
  Latin America policy of, 90–99, 115
  Latin America speech of, 92–95
  MLK and, 77, 89–90, 122, 124
  moon landing deadline set by, 387–89
  National Council on the Arts established
    by, 132
  in 1960 campaign for president, 58–82
  in 1960 Democratic primary, 46–57
  Nixon in debates with, 63–68
  Peace Corps initiated by, 68–73

R. Goodwin and, *see* Goodwin, Richard
    "Dick," JFK and
Kennedy, John F., Jr., 144
Kennedy, Joseph, 44, 180
Kennedy Library and Museum, *see* John F.
    Kennedy Presidential Library
Kennedy, Robert "Bobby," 112, 117, 124,
    134, 145, 243, 245, 260, 297–98, 358,
    387
  assassination of, 357
  Civil Rights Act and, 175–76, 183, 184,
    348
  Death of a President and, 291–94
  Goodwin and, *see* Goodwin, Richard
    "Dick," RFK and
  at JFK's funeral, 139–41
  LBJ and, 56, 59, 146–49, 155, 157–58,
    185, 187–90, 197–98, 201–3, 245,
    265–66, 269–70, 276–77, 285,
    311–16
  MLK's assassination, reaction to,
    339–41
  presidential campaign of, 311–16,
    325–29, 335–36, 348–51, 353–56
  "Ripple of Hope" speech of, 72, 260,
    278–84
  Vietnam War and, 275–78, 298–301,
    327
Kennedy, Ted, 145, 299, 313, 315–16,
    326–27, 357, 371
Kerner Report (National Advisory
    Commission on Civil Disorders), 343
Khrushchev, Nikita, 20, 108
Kilduff, Malcolm, 135
King, Coretta, 335
King, Martin Luther, Jr., 22, 123, 184, 238,
    255, 278, 345
  assassination of, 338–41, 343
  discrimination in federal housing
    protested by, 121–22
  eulogy for Reeb given by, 228
  "I Have a Dream" speech of, 128–29
  JFK and, 77, 89–90, 122, 124
  LBJ and, 214–19, 225, 232, 234, 235,
    239, 253, 302, 303, 338–39

March on Washington and, 126–29
Poor People's Campaign of, 335
Vietnam War opposed by, 302–3, 335
Kornbluh, Peter, 108
Kotz, Nick, 335
Kraft, Joe, 177
Krim, Arthur, 169, 353
Krock, Arthur, 167

Labor Department, U.S., 304, 307, 308,
    320, 343, 345–47
Larner, Jeremy, 320, 321, 360
LBJ Foundation, 288–89
LBJ Presidential Library, 372
LBJ School of Public Affairs, 372, 379
Leadership (D. K. Goodwin), 151
Lear, Edward, 79
Levine, David, 360
Levinson, Cynthia, 302
Levinson, Larry, 347
Levinson, Sandy, 301–3, 305–6
Lewis, Anthony, 279–80, 283
Lewis, John, 218, 232, 253
Library of Congress, 139
Life, 34–35, 386
Lincoln, Abraham, 12, 22, 47, 67, 127, 176,
    190, 253, 385, 394, 404–5
    "Farewell Address" of, 79–82
    lying in state, 138–41, 144
    Thanksgiving established by, 396
Lincoln, Evelyn, 387
Lincoln-Douglas debates, 67
Lincoln Memorial, 127–29
Lippmann, Walter, 167
Lishman, Robert, 31
Lodge, Henry Cabot, 66
Long Day's Journey into Night (O'Neill),
    240
Look, 292–93
Los Angeles Times, 276, 345
    R. Goodwin's columns in, 393
Lowell, Robert, 321, 354
Lowenstein, Allard, 279, 299, 301, 302, 303,
    312, 366
Luce, Henry, 166

Lyndon Baines Johnson High School, 170
Lyndon Johnson and the American Dream
    (D. K. Goodwin), 5, 149

Macy, John, 305
Maddox, USS, 192
Magic Mountain, The (Mann), 37
Mailer, Norman, 4, 114–15
Maine Woods, The (Thoreau), 5
Making of the President 1960, The (White),
    49–50
Manchester, William, 140, 142, 143,
    291–95
Mandela, Nelson, 282
Mann, C. Harrison, 240
Mann, Thomas, 37, 147, 265–66
Mansfield, Mike, 173, 176, 184, 224
March on Washington for Jobs and
    Freedom, 125–29
Markham, Dean, 139
Marshall, Margaret, 260, 280–84
Marshall, Thurgood, 341, 380–81
Marshall Plan, 90, 98–99
Martin, Ed, 98, 105
Massachusetts, University of, 23
Massachusetts Institute of Technology
    (MIT), 175, 311, 317
Massachusetts Supreme Judicial Court, 280,
    283–84
Mays, Benjamin, 301–2
McCall's, 355–56
McCarthy, Abigail, 320
McCarthy, Eugene, 312, 314, 340, 347–50,
    353–54, 356, 371
    civil rights and, 328
    at Democratic Convention (1968),
        359–63, 365, 369
    R. Goodwin as campaign adviser to,
        316–30, 332–33, 335–36, 343–44,
        359–63
McCone, John, 254–55
McCormack, John, 224, 253–54, 345
McGovern, George, 312
McGraw-Hill, 286–87
McGrory, Mary, 286

McKinley, William, 138
McNamara, Robert, 107, 110, 146, 190, 241, 242, 243, 248
McPherson, Harry, 306
Medicaid, 254
Medicare, 209, 246, 249–51, 254
Meet the Press (TV show), 74
Melville, Herman, 310–11
Metropolitan Museum of Art, 120
Michigan, University of:
  JFK's Peace Corps speech at, 68–71, 162–63
  LBJ's Great Society speech at, 162–66, 208, 237
Michigan Daily, 71, 72
Middleton, Harry, 376, 380
Mills, Wilbur, 377
Mitchell, Clarence, 341, 380–81
Monday Night Movie (TV show), 195–96
Monroe, Edward, 52–54
Morrissey, Frank, 42–43
Morse, Wayne, 102
Moyers, Bill, 127–28, 153–54, 159, 160–67, 173, 174, 182, 186, 189, 195, 206–9, 221, 234, 236–37, 238, 240–41, 243, 248, 269–70, 272, 357
  on LBJ, 168
  R. Goodwin's friendship with, 113, 200, 257–59, 261–62, 273–74, 289, 389
Moynihan, Daniel Patrick, 236–37, 238
Muñoz, Luis, 145
Muskie, Edmund, 393

Nabrit, James, Jr., 237
Nation, The, 89
National Advisory Commission on Civil Disorders (Kerner Report), 343
National Aeronautics and Space Administration (NASA), 387–88
National Association for the Advancement of Colored People (NAACP), 259, 301, 302
National Council on the Arts, 132
National Guard, U.S., 342–43, 362

National Mobilization Committee to End the War, 363–64
National Museum of African American History and Culture, 89
National Union of South African Students (NUSAS), *260*, 278–84
National Youth Administration, 212, 347, 378
NBC, 30, 33, 34, 195–96
Neustadt, Richard, 376
Newfield, Jack, 298–300, 324, 327, 366
Newman, Paul, 366
New Republic, 303, 305, 307, 311
Newsday, 294
New Yorker, 116, 284, 389
New York Post, 331
New York Times, 23–24, 75, 123, 131, 134–36, 163, 202, 240, 249, 279–80, 286, 294, 339
New York Times Magazine, 285
Nichols, Dorothy, 177–78
Nile monuments, at Abu Simbel, 117–20
Nixon, Pat, 64
Nixon, Richard, 76, 77, 104, 300, 370, 371, 388, 393
  in debates with JFK, 63–68
  on the Peace Corps, 73
  Vietnam War and, 371–72
"Nixopedia," 63, 196
Nobel Prize Laureates, as "Dinner in Camelot" guests, *111*, 115–17, 384
Novak, Robert, 265–66
Nuclear Test Ban Treaty, 195–96
nuclear war, nuclear weapons, 195–96, 245

Oates, Marylouise, 318–19, 323, 328
O'Brien, Lawrence, 370–71
Observer, 297
"Ode to a Nightingale" (Keats), 115–16
O'Donnell, Kenny, 59
O'Neill, Eugene, 240
Oppenheimer, J. Robert, 116
Oswald, Lee Harvey, 141
"Owl and the Pussycat, The" (Lear), 79

Paine, Thomas, 389

Panama Canal Zone, 155–56

Parks, Rosa, 22

Paton, Alan, 282–83

Pauling, Ava Helen, 117

Pauling, Linus, 117

Peace Corps, 68–73, 240
   International, R. Goodwin's work for,
      112–15, 119, 131–32, 134, 146
   Nixon on, 73

Peck, Gregory, 169, 353

Perry, J. L., 130

Peter, Paul, and Mary, 302

Phillips, Marcia, 24

Piazza Tales, The (Melville), 310–11

Pittsburgh Press, 76

Poor People's Campaign, 335

Port Huron Statement, 71

poverty, LBJ's war on, 153, 155–57, 166,
   201, 210, 214–16, 233, 256, 296, 342,
   386

Powers, Dave, 59

Pravda, 123

Project Mercury, 387

Pusey, Nathan, 81

Quiz Show (film), 30–31, 35

racism, *see* civil rights

Rahv, Philip, 290

Randolph, A. Philip, 126–27, 238

Redford, Robert, 30–31, 35

Reeb, James, 219–20, 225, 228, 232

Reeb, Marie, 219

Reedy, George, 156, 159, 177, 178

Republican Party, 173–74, 183, 312

Reston, James, 75, 163, 167

Reuters, 336

Ridgway, Matthew, 285

Rifkin, Sy, 293

Riverside Church, 302, 303

Robertson, Ian, 278, 280–81

Robinson, Jackie, 87

Rolling Stone, 4

Rooney, John, 118–19

Roosevelt, Anna, 137

Roosevelt, Franklin, 12, 29, 47, 77, 92, 119,
   166, 180, 201, 378, 396

Roosevelt, Theodore, 11–12, 43, 47,
   137–38, 329, 401

Rostow, Walt, 357

Roth, Philip, 251, 290

Rothschild, Michael, 4, 391, 397

Rusk, Dean, 83, 96, 98, 104, 106, 113,
   156–57, 190, 284, 298

Russell, Richard, 172–73, 181–82, 190, 306

Russia, *see* Soviet Union

Rustin, Bayard, 341

Ryan, William, 366

Salinger, Pierre, 59, 97, 140, 313

Sandburg, Carl, 138

Schlesinger, Arthur, Jr., 4, 80, 81, 93, 95–98,
   102, 107, 114–17, 126–27, 132, 134,
   145, 147, 148, 158, 198, 225, 244,
   284–85, 297, 298, 299, 311, 313–15,
   328, 387
   JFK's funeral and, 139–41

Seberg, Jean, 115

Seeger, Pete, 302

segregation/desegregation, 28–29, 123–24,
   127, 183, 186, 192, 215, 254, 301–2

Seigenthaler, John, 291–93

Senate, U.S.:
   Civil Rights Bill passed by, 172–76
   Foreign Relations Committee, 102
   Medicare passed by, 246
   See also Congress, U.S.

Service, Robert, 79

sexism, 26–27, 370–71

Shakespeare, William, 79

Shepard, Alan, 387

"Shot Heard Round the World" (Emerson),
   5

Shriver, Sargent, 69, 73, 112–14, 117, 134,
   145, 146, 155, 190
   JFK's funeral and, 138–41

Sidey, Hugh, 161–62, 176–79, 259

Sigma Kappa sorority, 22–23, 25

Sinatra, Frank, 89

$64,000 Question, The (TV show), 30
slavery, 9, 127, 253, 281
Smith, Howard, 160
Smith, Howard K., 65
Smith, Lynda, 87–89
Smith, Merle, Jr., 87–89
Smith, Steve, 78
Social Security, 196
Sorensen, Theodore "Ted," 36, 44–46, 49,
　　57, 59, 62–65, 68, 71–79, 90–91, 97,
　　107, 124, 125, 145, 153, 158, 176, 195,
　　277, 299, 313–14, 356, 357
　　R. Goodwin and, 77–79, 99
South Africa, 260, 278–84
Soviet Union, 20, 107–8, 118, 123, 132,
　　280, 386, 387, 388, 389
Spock, Benjamin, 303
Sputnik, 36
State Department, U.S., 92–93, 126, 129,
　　134, 266, 267
　　R. Goodwin transferred to, 102–6, 112,
　　113
Stein, Howard, 323
Stempel, Herbert, 32–34
Stevenson, Adlai, 39–41, 47, 130–31, 190,
　　307
St. Louis Post-Dispatch, 331
Students for a Democratic Society (SDS),
　　71
Styron, William, 116, 251–52, 290
Supreme Court, U.S., 22, 28–29, 393–94
Swett, Leonard, 127
symbolic gestures, 386
Symington, Stuart, 47

television, effect on politics of, 42, 65–66
Temple of Dendur, 117–20, 384
Tenzer, Herbert, 254
Tet Offensive, 315, 331
Thant, U, 337
Thieu, Nguyen Van, 371
Thomas, Danny, 194
Thomas, Jesse, 190
Thompson, Hunter, 4
Thomson, Bobby, 5

Thoreau, Henry David, 5
Thousand Days, A (Schlesinger), 114–15
Time, 166, 177, 178–79, 259
Today (TV show), 30, 33
"To His Coy Mistress" (Marvell), 112
Travell, Janet, 141
Tri Delta sorority, 24–25, 130
Trilling, Diana, 116
Truman, Bess, 251
Truman, Harry, 141, 224, 250–51, 346
Tufts College, 2, *11*, 12, 22
Turner, Judy, 24–25
Twenty-One (TV show), 30–32

United Nations, 337
United Nations Educational, Scientific and
　　Cultural Organization (UNESCO),
　　118
Updike, John, 251
UPI, 105
urban problems, 164, 209–10, 215, 219,
　　255, 348
　　see also inner city riots
Urban VIII, Pope, 389

Valenti, Jack, 159, 162, 164, 166, *168*, 170,
　　174, 201, 207, 224, 226, 229–30,
　　236–37, 238, 246, 269–70, 272
Valenti, Mary Margaret, 170, 246
"Valley of the Black Pig, The" (Yeats), 192
Vance, Cyrus, 241
vanden Heuvel, William, 4, 299, 313, 316
Van Doren, Carl, 30
Van Doren, Charles, 30–34
Van Doren, Dorothy, 30
Van Doren, Irita, 30
Van Doren, Mark, 30, 33
Venezuela, 104–5
Vidal, Gore, 361
Viet Cong, 217, 247, 276–77, 320, 371
Vietnam War, 192, 211, 213–14, 217,
　　242, 247–49, 254–55, 270–73, 309,
　　313–14, 321, 360, 362–63, 371
　　debated at Democratic Convention
　　(1968), 360, 362–63, 367

Fulbright hearings and, 275–76
LBJ and, 192, 211, 213–14, 242, 247–49,
    254–55, 270–73, 276, 284–87,
    296–303, 309, 311–15, 329–34,
    336–37, 371
    MLK's opposition to, 302–3, 335
    Nixon and, 371–72
    RFK and, 275–78, 285, 297–301, 327
    R. Goodwin's speeches and writings on,
    284–87, 296–98
    Spring Mobilization March to End the
    War, 301–3
    Tet Offensive, 315, 331
Village Voice, 298–99
VISTA program, 73
voting rights, 149, 211, 215–34, 236,
    251–55, 334, 345
Voting Rights Act, 216, 221, 224–34, 235,
    238, 251, 253

Wade, Simeon, 302
Waksman, Selman, 116
Walinsky, Adam, 264–65, 266, 279, 299,
    313, 329
Wallace, George, 124, 218, 220, 349,
    370
    LBJ's meeting with, 221–23
Wall Street Journal, 331
Walsh, Richard, 117
Walton, Bill, 139, 140, 145
Warnke, Bill, 145
Warren, Earl, 29, 341, 380–81
war tax, 248, 331

Washington Post, 34–35, 159, 186, 286, 302,
    335
Wasserman, Lou, 353
Watson, Marvin, 252
Watts riots, 255–56
Weaver, Robert, 121–22, 215
Weller, Thomas, 116
Wesleyan University, 207, 235, 265, 269,
    274, 290, 291, 311
Westmoreland, William, 300, 336–37
White, Kevin, 4
White, Lee, 77–78, 183
White, Theodore, 50, 74–75, 106, 320, 330,
    331–33, 355, 356, 359, 363, 366, 368
White House Fellows program, 304–7, 310
Wicker, Tom, 177, 240
Wiesner, Jerome, 264
Wilkins, Roy, 126–27, 225, 238, 253, 259,
    341, 380–81
Williams, Hosea, 218–19
Wills, Gary, 292, 295
Wilson, Woodrow, 77
Winthrop, John, 80–81
Wintour, Anna, 4
Wirth, Tim, 309
Wirtz, Willard, 307, 308–9, 342, 346
Woodward, Robert, 104, 105
Wordsworth, William, 398

Yeats, W. B., 192
Young, Andrew, 338
Young, Whitney, 126–27, 184, 225, 238,
    253–54, 341

About the Author

DORIS KEARNS GOODWIN's work for President Johnson inspired her career as a presidential historian. Her first book was *Lyndon Johnson and the American Dream*. She followed up with the Pulitzer Prize–winning *No Ordinary Time: Franklin and Eleanor Roosevelt: The Homefront in World War II*. She earned the Lincoln Prize for *Team of Rivals*, in part the basis for Steven Spielberg's film *Lincoln*, and the Carnegie Medal for *The Bully Pulpit*, about the friendship between Theodore Roosevelt and William Howard Taft. Her last book, *Leadership: In Turbulent Times*, was the inspiration for the History Channel docuseries on Abraham Lincoln, Theodore Roosevelt, and Franklin Roosevelt, which she executive produced.